D0546102

Advanced Subsidiary

Psychology

Approaches and Methods

Christine Brain

First published 2000 by
Nelson Thornes
Delta Place
27 Bath Road
Cheltenham
GL53 7TH
United Kingdom

ISBN 0-17-490057-0

01 02 03 04 / 10 9 8 7 6 5 4 3 2

Illustrations by Oxford Designers and Illustrators

Typeset by Northern Phototypesetting Company Ltd, Bolton
Printed and bound in Great Britain

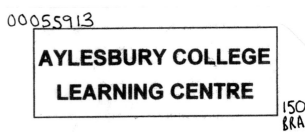

Contents

Acknowledgements   v

Introduction and study guide   vii

1 The cognitive approach   1

2 The social approach   35

3 The cognitive-developmental approach   66

4 The learning approach   107

5 The psychodynamic approach   142

6 The physiological approach   176

7 Methods in psychology   209

8 Ethics and coursework in psychological
   research   249

Appendix A Useful Web sites   265

Appendix B Suggestions, questions and
   exam advice   266

Glossary of terms   271

References   283

Index   294

In loving memory of Kevin Brain

Acknowledgements

I would like to thank everyone who has helped me with this book – for encouragement from some and practical help from Sarah Sterry, David Putwain and others. Steve and Francine at Nelson have been a great help, as has Diana at Edexcel. Rick and Louise at Nelson Thornes have done a great job too. Alex and Doug have been supportive as usual, and Paul has as always not let me down. Kev was here at the start, gave all the encouragement he could, but did not make it to the end. Some things we can't change.

Introduction and study guide

Introduction

This introduction gives you:

- some background on this textbook, its aims and objectives
- plans of how to study the course
- a brief outline of what is in the Edexcel specifications
- some background psychology as an introduction to the subject.

About the book

This book is:

- **Written with the Edexcel Advanced Subsidiary (AS) GCE in Psychology in mind.** Edexcel (formerly the London Board) is offering AS and Advanced Psychology for the first time, starting in September 2000, and a new specification has been written. There is an AS examination, usually taken in the first year of the course, and an A2 part, which you add to the AS to make the full Advanced GCE.
- **Written to help the student of psychology get a good grade in the Edexcel AS.** The main approaches are covered, as are methodology, coursework and ethics. I have deliberately used the words in the specification. The main purpose of the book is to help you to get a good grade. Hopefully, however, you will enjoy reading the material, and it will encourage you to continue your studies in psychology.
- **Also useful as a general textbook.** If you have bought this textbook to learn more about psychology, then you should find what you are looking for. I have tried to use all the interesting examples that my students have enjoyed over the years. You may not need the coursework suggestions, the activities or the links to Key Skills. However, the material itself should suit any student as they start to study psychology. The book focuses on key applications and contemporary issues, so you will be able to relate what you learn to some real-life examples, which should make the study of psychology come alive for you.
- **Pitched at a reasonable academic level.** Well, I hope the book achieves a high academic level, but this is not the primary purpose. The material is gathered from textbooks and journal articles, and these are largely secondary sources. What you need as a student is a collection of all the necessary studies and theories, rather than a thorough investigation of specific areas.
- **Filled with more depth than you might like at first.** Again, an AS textbook could well have less depth. You need to be able to answer short-answer questions, and you don't need everything that I have included. However, I feel that, although there is a place for revision guides, bullet points and spidergrams, you need to produce these for yourself. Hopefully you can read this book and appreciate a flow of words. If you have only lists of points, although these are much better for actually learning the material, you will find you have less understanding of what is being said.
- **Intended to give you more than psychological information.** I have included example test questions and lists of coursework ideas. You can get examples of coursework, and sample papers, from Edexcel.
- **Giving a choice of studies.** The Edexcel specification asks you to learn about studies in detail and gives you a choice of study (for each approach, you need to know two studies in detail). The choices in the specification are only examples, and you and your teacher are free to choose any studies in the area. Studies are outlined that are in some cases different from the ones given in the specification. Those given here are hopefully interesting and relevant, but be aware that you can choose different ones.
- **Giving a choice of contemporary issues.** The Edexcel specification suggests contemporary issues for you to study for the examination. Contemporary issues are also useful in relating the material you study to real-life examples. You are free to choose your own example of a contemporary issue if you are asked about one in the examination. The ones chosen for this book are there because they are topical, interesting and relate to the material presented. However, you and your teacher can choose different ones.
- **Written to help you gather evidence for your Key Skills portfolio.** At the end of each activity there are suggestions as to how you could use it to generate evidence for your Key Skills portfolio. The activities are mainly to help you learn and enjoy the psychology, but they can also generate such evidence. I have only made suggestions, and you will quickly learn how to use your work to show where you have achieved Key Skills. You can find out more about Key Skills and more suggestions as to how these can be achieved in psychology from the Edexcel specification.
- **Full of ideas for learning in the form of activities and study aids.** Some of the activities in the textbook need you to be working in a group, and so might not

be possible. However, they should give you ideas of how the theory is applied to real-life examples. Study aids are included to help you to structure your note taking and plan your learning.

- **Written with the open/distance learner also in mind.** Although many of the activities are planned for those working in a group, the textbook is written with all students in mind, including the open or distance learner. This book is intended to be a complete course of study, and you will find all you need. You should use the questions at the end of the book as assignment questions. You can also get past papers and exemplar coursework from Edexcel.

The Edexcel specification

It might be useful to briefly outline the content of the AS examination. You should have a copy of the specification. You might get this from your teacher, or you can obtain your own copy from Edexcel (www.edexcel.org.uk). Don't rely on the outline below, although it is sufficient. I want you to use the complete specification, so that you know exactly what you need to learn.

The AS is made up of three units, and the A2 has a further three units. You need all six units to achieve the full Advanced GCE ('A' level).

Edexcel Advanced Subsidiary GCE in Psychology (AS level + A2)

A Level Psychology – Edexcel Specification 2000 onwards: course outline

Unit	Topics to be studied				
AS					
Unit 1 – Three approaches	**Cognitive:** assumptions, methods, memory/forgetting, studies, key application, contemporary issue	**Social:** assumptions, methods, obedience/prejudice, studies, key application, contemporary issue	**Cognitive–developmental:** assumptions, methods, Piaget etc., studies, key application, contemporary issue		
Unit 2 – Three approaches	**Learning:** assumptions, methods, conditioning etc., studies, key application, contemporary issue	**Psychodynamic:** assumptions, methods, Freud etc., studies, key application, contemporary issue	**Physiological:** assumptions, methods, sleep/biorhythms, studies, key application, contemporary issue		
Unit 3 – Coursework	**Methodology and ethics**				
A2					
Unit 4 – Choose two applications	**Clinical:** classification, therapies, mental disorders	**Criminal:** eyewitnesses, offender profiling, juries, media influence, treatments	**Education:** Learning theories, teacher and student variables, assessment, special needs	**Work:** personnel, leaders and groups, managing change	**Sports:** trait approaches, socialisation, motivation, social influences, arousal and anxiety
Unit 5a – Choose one application	**Child:** attachment, deprivation, play, friendships	**Environmental:** personal space, territory, architecture, stress, crowds, recycling	**Health:** substance abuse, stress, health promotion		
Unit 5b – Methodology	**Methodology:** Unit 3 + inferential statistics and analysis				
Unit 6 – Issues and debates	Approaches and perspectives (Units 1 and 2)	Social and moral issues	Methodology	**Ethics** Debates: nature/nurture; is psychology a science?	

AS level

Unit 1:
• The cognitive approach
• The social approach
• The cognitive–developmental approach

Unit 2:
• The learning approach
• The psychodynamic approach
• The physiological approach

Unit 3:
• One practical piece of work, submitted as coursework and marked by Edexcel.

The A2 part of the course

Unit 4: a choice of two of the following applications:
• Clinical psychology
• Criminal psychology
• The psychology of education
• The psychology of work
• Sports psychology

Unit 5 (part a): a choice of one of the following applications:
• Child psychology
• Environmental psychology
• Health psychology

Unit 5 (part b):
• A compulsory research methods question including ethical issues.

Unit 6:
• Issues, perspectives and debates in psychology. You will need to draw on material that you have studied for the AS examination, and material from other areas. Issues include comparing the approaches, the 'nature/nurture' argument, ethical issues and methodological comparisons and queries.

Suggested plans

Plan one

Work your way through the textbook in this order:
• Introduction and study guide
• Chapter 1 – The cognitive approach
• Chapter 2 – The social approach
• Chapter 3 – The cognitive–developmental approach
• Chapter 7 – Methods in psychology
• Chapter 8 – Ethics in psychology and coursework
• Chapter 4 – The learning approach
• Chapter 5 – The psychoanalytic approach
• Chapter 6 – The physiological approach

An alternative approach to your studies

The six main chapters are divided into sections:
• Key assumptions
• Research methods
• In-depth areas of study
• Two studies
• Key application
• Contemporary issue

You could choose to read all the key assumption sections, as that would give you an overview of the history of psychology, and what it is about. Then you could read all the research method sections, as that would give you an overview of how methods in psychology are used. You should read Chapters 7 and 8 at the same time.

You would then be in a good position to study each chapter separately.

An introduction to psychology

You may have signed up for a course in psychology without being completely sure of what this entails. For this textbook I am following the Edexcel specification completely. However, no specification at this level is going to cover everything in the subject. One area that is not covered is 'perception' – yet this area of study tells us a lot about ourselves. It seems a pity to miss out such a fundamental area, and so I am including it here as a brief introduction to the sorts of things that are covered in psychology.

Perception

Students of psychology do better if they have an open mind and this is a very difficult thing to keep. In this textbook I have tried to keep 'an open mind'; however, I have also been able to choose some of the material, and I have obviously chosen what I think is interesting.

The whole point about humans is that we do not have open minds. Our brains are full of information and it is hard to see how we could make any judgements about anything without taking previous information and knowledge into account.

One way that is often used to demonstrate how we don't have an open mind is to use illusions. An illusion is where our perception is fooled in some way. Although the examples I am going to use are about our vision, we are also fooled when we mishear something, and we are fooled about people too, sometimes.

Visual illusions

Look at some of the well-known illusions, and you will see how our perception is guided and how much we put into our perceptions. We receive information from our senses – sensations. This is not perception as such. These sensations appear to be translated into perceptions. See how far you agree with this.

The Necker cube

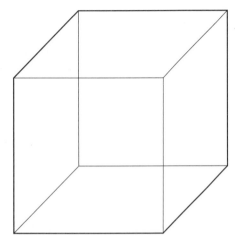

The Necker cube

Focus on the cube above. Look at it until you can see two cubes that alternate, first one and then the other. The idea is that your brain does not know which cube to look at, as it has no hypothesis (instruction) to go on. If you put a dot onto the front face of one of the cubes, and you tell yourself to focus on that one, then you probably can. This shows that we need to know something about what we are looking at. Faced with two conflicting explanations of what we see (two cubes) we can see first one and then the other until we tell ourselves what we are looking at.

Rubin's vase/faces

The Rubin vase

If you focus on the Rubin vase figure you should be able to see vase and faces, but not at the same time. As with the cube, you will see first one and then the other. In one instance the black is the background and the white is the figure. In the other instance, the white is the background and the black is the figure. You have no hypothesis to work on, as there is nothing to say whether you should be looking at a vase or at faces. Given context, it is possible that you would see the faces or the vase only.

A case of context

In Chapter 1 you will find the following figure and an explanation for it. I have shown it here too as it helps to show how important context is. We need a hypothesis for what we see, otherwise we may be unsure. If the context is letters, the figure is seen as a 'B' and if the context is numbers the identical figure is seen as '13'. This shows the importance of what is around us, and demonstrates how sensation (the information coming into our senses) is not the same as perception (making sense of the information).

The Muller–Lyer illusion

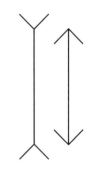

The Muller–Lyer illusion

The Muller–Lyer illusion (above) is a well-known one and has more than one explanation. The explanations are interesting, however, and suggest that we use our previous experiences when making sense of our world.

One explanation is a bit complicated although it is interesting. When you look at the illusion you should see one line as longer than the other, even though the lines are the same length. The line with the outward-facing arrows should seem longer. I hope this works for you. The line with outward-facing arrows is like the corner of a room that is far away from you. You need to think like an artist to understand this. The laws of perspective mean that a corner far away from us has the ceiling and floor lines facing upwards. A corner that is facing us has arrows facing downwards (see below). Our experience of walls, corners and perspective would teach us that near corners have pointing down arrows and far corners have pointing up arrows (so to speak). When we look at a building scene we would expect the corners that are near to us to be shorter (being closer) than the corners that are in the distance (being further away). According to the laws of perspective, corners that are near are shorter than those that are far away. So we would expect a line with outward-facing arrows to be further away. We would, therefore, expect it to be longer, and in the illusion we see it as longer. We see the line with inward-facing arrows as shorter, because according to our experience we see it as a front-facing corner, which should be shorter because it is near.

There are criticisms of this explanation. However, we don't need to go into these too much here. The main point is that our previous experiences do seem to affect what we see. Our perception is more than the sensation – or the input from our senses.

Perception – more than sensation

The above illusions and their explanations will have given you experience how your own mind is not 'open' but filled with experiences and assumptions.

Perception and stereotyping

There can be more to interpersonal perception too. Interpersonal perception refers to how we perceive other people. We make judgements about them based on previous experience. You can try studies for yourself. You could try asking people to describe certain people – for example, a judge, a docker and a student. If you ask a few

people and they write down their answers, you should find that their answers are very similar. Since you have not even specified the age, gender or ethnicity of the 'people' it is surprising that the answers are so alike (assuming that they are). We use our previous experiences and what we learn about people from others to draw conclusions. These conclusions are not always correct.

I have seen this example in more than one book, so I am not sure where it comes from, but try this 'riddle' – which you may have heard before.

A father is killed and his son is badly injured in the same accident. The son is rushed to a hospital where the surgeon immediately says 'I cannot operate on this person. He is my son'.

This may seem impossible to you – or it may not. Can you see what the problem is, if you have a problem with it? The surgeon is the boy's mother. Many people assume that a surgeon is male. You could try this out on a few people to see if they do make this assumption.

Students of psychology and ethical guidelines

This is only the introduction to this book, yet already I feel I ought to mention ethics. Ethical guidelines are outlined in Chapter 8. I have suggested that you try a few things out on other people. You must stick to ethical guidelines if you do this. Psychology experiments and tasks can be very threatening to other people. As soon as you become a student of psychology you must learn about ethical issues. I am sure you will treat people with respect, and they must be given rights. They can say they don't want to take part at any stage and you must explain what the study is all about. This may sound a bit over the top, considering I have only suggested you try out a 'riddle' or ask people to describe a 'judge' and so on. However, we all get anxious on being asked to do things, especially in front of others. We don't know what the right answer is, or whether we will look foolish. Please be aware of these issues from the very beginning. We need others to help in our studies, and we need their cooperation.

Keeping an open mind

In this book you will probably read things you don't agree with. I suggest that you read without thinking about this at first. You need to understand what is being said. Then you will be able to evaluate. You should aim to be critical, but you need evidence for your criticisms. You will find the study of psychology quite difficult if you bring too much of your own 'knowledge' with you.

However, the claims of psychology ought to be the same as our common-sense ideas. We are all psychologists and we have all learnt about people. Try to read about a particular theory, assess the evidence for and against it, consider whether it seems likely and if it has real-life application – and keep an open mind.

For example, if you have strong religious views, you might find it impossible to accept the idea of evolution by means of survival of the fittest. You would not be the first to reject this explanation of our 'creation'. You might reject the whole theory. However, before doing so, you would have to thoroughly understand it. Then you could reject it – on the grounds that there is insufficient evidence perhaps, or for some other reason.

You are not asked to accept everything that is claimed. The book gives lots of evaluation and criticisms of its own. However, you will need to be ready to be 'open minded' as you read the information. If you cannot have this open mind in some cases – and sometimes our beliefs do not allow this – then you may need to learn the alternative theory for the purposes of writing about it, even if you are not going to accept it for yourself.

A brief history – approaches to the study of psychology

The theory of behaviourism – the learning approach

In the early 1900s, mainly in America, behaviour was studied in terms of stimulus (something happens to an animal or person) and response (the organism responds). Both the **stimulus** and the **response** can be measured, and this appealed to the 'scientific' minds of that time. (For more on learning theory and behaviourism, see Chapter 4).

The figure below shows the stimulus–response approach. There is, however, the question of what happens between the stimulus and the response. Behaviourists did not consider that question, as they could not measure those processes. They focused on what was measurable.

The basic stimulus–response approach

The advantage of studying the input (or stimulus) and the output (or response) is that from measurable, controlled experiments, scientific understanding can grow. This basic assumption is still held today, and the scientific method could be said to be the basis of psychological research.

It was soon realised that behaviour is more complex than a simple stimulus followed by a response. Animals being studied in terms of stimulus and response were shown to be using **cognition** in their behaviour. Rats, for example, used cognitive maps when learning mazes in laboratory studies (Tolman et al, 1946). The rats held a map of the maze in their brains and used it. In one experiment they learnt a particular route through a maze to some food. They ran this route a number of times, being **reinforced** to do so by the food at the end. Then the maze was blocked at a certain point, and food left elsewhere. If all the rats had done was to learn the original route, then they would have to learn the new route in the same way – by trial and error. However, they were able to use a short cut to the new food position. This could only have been done if they had a map of the maze in their heads somehow, to which they could refer. Also, if the maze was rotated, they could find the food from different starting points. Thought processes could not be ignored, or so it seemed. These thought processes are the subject matter that cognitive psychologists study.

The theory of cognitive development

From the 1930s Piaget in Switzerland was studying children (Piaget, 1932). He was very interested in their **maturation** processes. His theory of cognitive development is outlined in Chapter 3. He (and others) emphasises how thought processes develop as a child matures physically. A child is not simply a miniature adult. Younger children have different types of moral reasoning to older children.

For example, children might be asked a question such as who is the most naughty – a boy who has broken a lot of cups when helping his mother to clear up, or a boy who has broken one cup when disobeying orders and helping himself to a drink? A young child will say that the one who broke the most cups is the naughtiest, whereas an older child will take the situation into account – the one who broke the most cups was trying to help, whereas the other boy had been told not to get a drink. Therefore, for the older child, the one who was the most naughty was the one who broke only one cup.

Here it is clear that cognitive processes are being examined, although currently cognitive development is a different field to that of cognitive psychology. Think of it as being about development first, and cognition second, whereas cognitive psychology is all about cognition.

The theory of social cognition, within social psychology

From the 1950s research has been carried out into how people understand their social worlds. Our thinking processes influence how we see others. For example, **stereotyping** is used in making judgements about other people. The study of cognitive processes is important because it suggests that we use **schemata** to make sense of the world. This means we use past experiences and previous knowledge. For an illustration of why this is important, read Box 1.

Box 1

Using stereotyping as a short cut when making decisions

Someone is following you along a lonely footpath late at night. You hear their footsteps and realise they are hurrying to catch you up. Should you wait for them to keep you company? Do they need help? Should you hurry away?

You might glance around and use short cuts such as stereotyping to help you in your judgement. If you are female, and the other person is a female of around the same age as you, you will probably wait for them to catch you up. If you are female and the other person is a young male of scruffy appearance, you would probably hurry off. If, however, you were being followed by an older man dressed in a suit and carrying a briefcase, you might not worry. Of course, in any of these situations you could make the wrong judgement.

You could test this idea for yourself by writing some stories similar to this, and asking people what they would do. However, read Chapter 8 before you carry out any such tasks, as the above story might well itself lead to stereotyping, or might frighten a participant.

The study of social cognition is clearly about thought processes. It falls, however, within the field of social psychology, which is explored in Chapter 2.

Developments in the understanding of the physiology of the brain

Psychology is a relatively new discipline. Physics, chemistry and biology take a scientific look at how things and people work. Philosophy examines areas that are outside the sciences. For example, within philosophy there is the field of metaphysics. This means looking at things 'above' physics – areas that we cannot access (yet) in a measurable way.

In the 1900s and during the Industrial Revolution, physics, chemistry and biology were making discoveries, and

philosophy was widely studied. Sometimes science and philosophy overlap. Language was in the area of philosophy, until people like Broca (1864) and Wernicke (1874) made discoveries about which parts of the brain were for speech and language. Box 2 gives a brief explanation of what was discovered.

Box 2

Particular areas of the brain are for particular purposes

Both Broca and Wernicke discovered that specific parts of the brain were responsible for specific language skills. For example, Broca discovered that there is a part of the brain for speech. It is this very part which is often completely damaged by a stroke, and that is why many people who have had a stroke have problems with their speech. Although they know what word they want to use, they say a different word.

Wernicke pinpointed a special area for the understanding of sentence construction, and for understanding language. Those with damage to this area can speak perfectly well but their understanding of complex sentences such as 'the bird that the cat watched was hungry' is faulty. They might well 'understand' from the above sentence that the cat is hungry (Blakemore, 1988)

Gradually, as knowledge has been built through scientific method, areas that had been studied 'philosophically' have come into the realm of one or other of the sciences. There is still plenty of room for philosophical discussion, of course, as we still have a lot to learn.

Psychology arose from both biological discoveries and philosophical thinking. It has been defined as the study of brain and behaviour. Those who prefer to separate the brain and the mind might still look to philosophy for the study of the mind. Those, however, who focus on the study of the brain (and cognitive psychologists could be said to do this) will need to look at developments in biology. As understanding of the **physiology** of the brain develops understanding of thinking processes will improve. You will see in Chapter 1 that early cognitive psychologists used **models** to represent how the brain might process information. As knowledge of physiology grows, these models may no longer be needed. Neuroscience is often used as a term to cover the study of the physiology of the brain, and cognitive neuroscience may replace cognitive psychology as an area of study. Currently, knowledge of the physiology of the brain is used within cognitive psychology, and so is part of what cognitive psychologists study.

The development of computers

Babbage, who died in 1871, is credited with being the first to attempt to build the modern computer. Turing (1950) first described a machine that could perform calculations and print out results. In just a short space of time, computers have developed at a tremendous pace. First-generation machines have now given way to fifth-generation machines, and as well as simple adding devices, there are now **neural networks** and multi-purpose tools.

In the basic computer, information is input into the computer's central processing unit (from a keyboard, for example) and then 'something is done' (depending on the calculation required) and there is an output of some sort (perhaps on a screen, or via a printer).

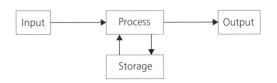

Simplified model of a computer system

The architecture of a computer, including the concept of the central processing unit (CPU), is based on John Von Neumann's 1930s design. The computer is defined as having five basic parts: the input, the output, memory, an arithmetic unit and a control unit.

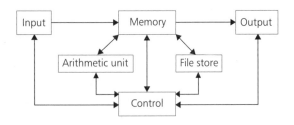

The basic parts of a computer

The links between cognitive psychology and computers are discussed in Chapter 1.

Summarising the historical view

- Criticisms of the stimulus–response approach of the behaviourists led to further examination of what was called the black box – this is the area between the external stimulus and the resulting response.
- Those who examined the processes that take place between the input and the output are cognitive psychologists.
- Computers have input, output, storage and something is processed in between the input and the output.
- Knowledge about the physiology of the brain has helped cognitive psychologists in their understanding of brain processing.

It is interesting that cognitive–developmental theorists maintain a separate discipline, as do those whose research is in the field of social cognition. Although they too examine processes within the brain and mind, they are not cognitive psychologists themselves, and this is an important distinction.

The future – cognitive science?

Cognitive psychology, social psychology, learning theory, cognitive–developmental psychology, and neuroscience have remained separate disciplines, whilst all contributing to a discussion about cognition.

There is a growing field called cognitive science. Not everyone agrees with this multidisciplinary approach, and indeed the separation of the approaches into chapters in this book show there are still divisions between disciplines. However, there are growing numbers who do think that disciplines can learn from one another.

Cognitive science covers areas such as artificial intelligence, perception, language, memory, and neuroscience, and illustrates well the basic assumptions of the cognitive approach. In the study of cognitive science, computer programming is taught, together with knowledge of how the brain functions. The aim is to pull together biological knowledge and progress in the field of artificial intelligence. Cognitive scientists also use evidence from cognitive psychology to bring together the interdisciplinary elements in order to make new discoveries about cognitive functioning. Engineers can take ideas from how the brain works, and cognitive scientists can learn from engineers. Box 3 outlines how disciplines can learn from one another.

Box 3

An example of cognitive science as a multidisciplinary approach

An example of how engineering and cognitive science can learn from one another is in the field of computer vision. Cognitive scientists learn about the neurological processes involved in vision. These might be used in the field of medicine or therapy, to help people with problems with their vision.

There is also tremendous interest at the moment in computer vision. For example, speed cameras take photographs of vehicle number plates. Computers can 'recognise' these numbers and find the car owner in a very short time, even sending them a letter just after they have sped past. Computer vision programs are used in this recognition process. There are standard ways of pattern matching, but these rely on letters on number plates being the same size and appearing at roughly the same place on the car.

For the computer to search the whole picture for the number is much harder. This sort of problem does arise in the field of engineering – for example, if the program was spotting numbers on trains. Train numbers appear at different places on carriages, are painted on in different colours and using different fonts.

It is useful to apply what is learned about biochemical processes to help in developing new ways of programming a computer to 'see'.

How to use this book

- Each chapter is written separately and stands alone. You don't have to start at Chapter 1, although it might be a good idea.
- References are at the end of the book.
- The glossary/key terms at the end of the book would make a good revision list.
- Study aids should help in your organisation and with study skills.
- After completing each chapter, turn to the exam questions in the appendices and test yourself.
- Terms that are in the glossary/key terms list are in **bold** in the text.
- Coursework suggestions are given at the end of each chapter.
- Reading is an enjoyable experience, and reading psychology should be interesting in itself.
- Active study is often best. As you are reading, make lists of terms and draw diagrams of key points. Make lists of names and summarise what each researcher says.
- Revision means seeing something for a second time (at least). Plan your revision by making suitable notes as you study.
- Use other textbooks to supplement your reading if you can. A GCSE book can be very useful, or another 'A' level textbook.
- There are other studies and examples that could have been included. Research some of these – use the Internet (a list of useful Internet sites is included as an Appendix).
- Key skills are included and activities suggested.

1

The cognitive approach

The aims of this chapter

The aims of this chapter are, with regard to the cognitive approach, to enable the reader to:

– *appreciate some of the general assumptions*
– *discuss research methods used*
– *describe and evaluate theories of how memory might work*
– *describe and evaluate theories that focus on forgetting*
– *describe and evaluate some relevant studies*
– *understand research into eye witness testimony*
– *explain one contemporary issue or debate.*

Self-test 1

After reading this chapter, test yourself on each of the above points. Use the points as exam questions and make notes accordingly. Then see how much you can write on each.

This chapter covers

KEY ASSUMPTIONS
1   The information-processing approach
2   A computer analogy
3   Empiricists v. nativists

RESEARCH METHODS
1   Laboratory experiments
2   Case studies of brain-damaged patients
3   Scanning techniques

IN-DEPTH AREA OF STUDY: MEMORY
1   Theories of memory
2   Theories of forgetting

STUDIES IN DETAIL
1   Levels of processing (Craik and Lockhart, 1972)
2   Context-dependent forgetting (Bouton et al, 1999)

KEY APPLICATION: EYE WITNESS TESTIMONY

CONTEMPORARY ISSUE: THE ACCURACY OF RECOVERED MEMORIES

Introduction

The term **cognitive** means 'thinking and knowing'. Descartes, a famous philosopher, tried to prove existence by claiming *cogito ergo sum*, which translates as 'I think, therefore, I am'. Cognition is thought by many to be central to human existence.

Cognition involves thinking, remembering, problem solving, using language, perceiving, and paying attention.

> ### STUDY AID
>
> As you are now studying a different approach, remember to start a new section in your folder, or a new folder.
>
> Key Skill LP3.1 – Agree targets and plan how these will be met, using support from appropriate others. You need your tutor for this, and you will need a record of the discussion, to use as evidence. Discuss organising your work and develop a time plan for working through this textbook. It is tempting to leave everything to your teacher, but you should be reading the Chapters as you study each approach, and do this alongside the work your teacher gives you. Make a note of dates and what you will have achieved by then, so that you can review your progress for Key Skill LP3.3.

If you have not already read the Introduction and Study Guide, it would be useful for you to do so now. Psychology is a collection of approaches, and some idea of these different approaches will help in understanding what follows.

Key assumptions of the cognitive approach

Key assumption 1 – the information-processing approach

The stimulus–response (S–R) approach to studying learning rests on the basic assumption that information comes into the brain via the senses, and then a response is given – that is, behaviour takes place. Cognitive psychology is interested in examining the processes that take place between the input of the information and the resulting behaviour.

This idea of processing information came from the S–R approach. Information was said to flow from external stimuli and result in a response. The information-processing approach, which underpins cognitive psychology, took this idea of input–process–output as its basic principle. There are clear links with the second key assumption, outlined below – the use of the computer analogy in cognitive psychology.

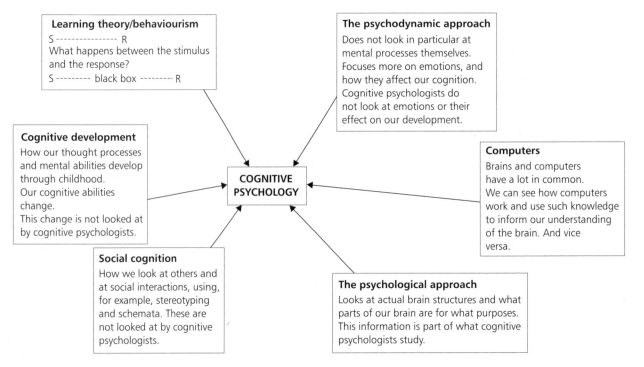

Figure 1.1
Linking cognitive psychology to other approaches

As an example of the information-processing approach in cognitive psychology, consider research into selective attention, some of which is outlined in Box 1.

Box 1

Selective attention research using information-processing models

According to Broadbent's (1958) model, information comes from the senses through a **sensory buffer**, where information is filtered through a selective filter. Then, through a limited-capacity processor, a response is generated. Long-term memory is involved in the process too.

Treisman (1964) built on Broadbent's work. This happens often in psychology. One person comes up with a model based on experiments, and someone else studies the model, does more experiments, and then adds to the model.

Broadbent's model suggests that information is either selected or it is not. However, we know that we are monitoring information whilst dealing with other stimuli. For example, if someone were to call your name now, you would probably look up from this book, even though you are engrossed in it!

Treisman's model takes the above phenomenon into account. She suggests that information is attenuated, rather than lost. So some information is selected for attention, and other information is 'turned down' but is still monitored (attenuation is basically monitoring).

Other models suggest that selection takes place much later. For example, Deutsch and Deutsch (1963) thought that all information is processed and then, after seeing what is relevant (or pertinent, in their terms), we select at this later stage.

Evaluation

- The models are built around the basic assumption that we are information-processing machines. We receive stimuli through our senses, something happens to do with attention, memory and so on, and then we respond. This is a fundamental assumption of the cognitive approach.

- Note the methods that are used. A model is suggested which fits studies that are done. Others use this model and test it. Some suggest amendments to the original, to fit new discoveries, and sometimes the whole model is rejected, when evidence no longer supports it.

Broadbent (1958) developed a filter model to show how we attend to certain stimuli rather than others (Figure 1.2).

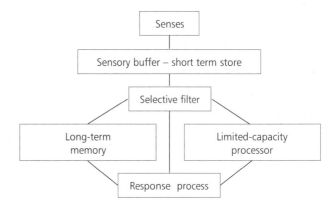

Figure 1.2
Broadbent's filter model of how we attend to certain stimuli

Self-test 2

1 How does information 'come into' the brain according to the information-processing model?

2 Information could be said to be 'pure' input for a computer – e.g. new information is entered via a keyboard or a disk. In what way might it be claimed that information 'input' into the brain is not pure? (See below for a suggested answer.)

Evaluation of the information-processing approach

A linear model
Does information enter our brain from outside (as sand, cement and water enter a cement mixer), to be processed and then there is an output? The linear models so far presented suggest that this is the case.

If we accept that information comes directly via sense data, this is called **bottom-up processing**. Bottom-up processing refers to input from the outside coming purely through vision, sound, taste, touch and smell.

However, the brain is not a *passive* receptor. We have moods, previous knowledge, and complex cells 'preprogrammed' in many different ways – and these all affect the input, perhaps even before we receive it.

A number of studies illustrate that **top-down processing** takes place. Top-down processing refers to intervention from our brains, coming from our previous experiences.

Gregory (1966) uses illusions to show how we use past experiences and expectations to make sense of information before it is input. A brief explanation of how perception is more than sensation is given in the Introduction and Study Guide to this book. An example is given by Bruner and Minturn (1951), and is illustrated in Figure 1.3.

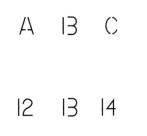

Figure 1.3

You see a letter B if the context is the alphabet. You see a number 13 if the context is numbers. However, the input is the same in both cases.

Asking whether processing is bottom up or top down suggests that it is either one or the other, and information-processing models tend to be linear, in having a starting point (the input of information), processing, and then an end point (the output).

A cyclic model

Neisser (1976) developed a cyclic model (Figure 1.4), which could be said to better represent the idea that information does enter the brain but that we in turn affect that information. This is different from processing in a computer, which does not have an effect on what is input (not until the input reaches the central processing unit, that is).

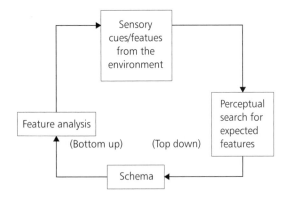

Figure 1.4
Neisser's (1976) analysis-by-synthesis model

The cyclic model demonstrates the importance of information processing, but shows that bottom-up information via the senses is only one part of the process. We also use past experiences, context, emotions and moods, which affect how we interpret the input and how we respond.

Parallel processing

Both linear and cyclic models assume a single flow of information, or at least step-by-step processing. Our brains, however, may use parallel processing and do more than one task at the same time.

Activity 1 asks you to think about when you might use parallel processing.

ACTIVITY 1

WHEN CAN YOUR BRAIN COPE WITH MORE THAN ONE THING AT A TIME?

Read any passage and say the word 'and' over and over again as you read. Now try reading without speech. Did you find it difficult to read and speak at the same time? Most people do. This suggests that reading and speaking use the same parts of the brain. Audiotypists, however, can type and listen at the same time, which suggests these two activities use different processing areas of the brain.

Think of other times when parallel processing seems to be used – that is, when you can do more than one thing at a time.

Key Skill C3.1a – when you have done the task and are thinking about other times when we might use parallel processing, this would make a good group task. Remember you need evidence for your portfolio.

Key assumption 2 – a computer analogy

The development of the computer has been very important in the development of cognitive psychology. The information-processing approach takes its cue from computers. Researchers want to learn more from computers about how the brain works. You can find some information on how a computer works in the Introduction and Study Guide to this textbook.

Similarly, there has been great interest in how knowledge of brain processing can inform work on artificial intelligence. Activity 2 asks you to think about whether the brain is like a computer.

ACTIVITY 2

IS THE BRAIN LIKE A COMPUTER?

Make a list of things computers can do, things people can do, and things chimpanzees (humans' near relatives) can do. Compare them.

This exercise will help you see why the brain is sometimes seen as being like a computer.

Compare your list with the one in Box 2.

> Key Skill C3.3 – this activity lends itself to a writing activity. You can either write an essay with a title such as 'Is the brain like a computer? Discuss' or you can write an article as if it were to be sent to a newspaper. Remember in either case to use the arguments for both sides.

> Key Skill C3.1a – this activity would also be good for a group discussion – if you are working in a group.

There are many other categories that you might have considered. You probably came up with different examples.

Evaluation of the computer analogy

You might not agree that computers, humans and chimpanzees can make choices, at least not in the same way. You might not agree that each can solve problems in the same way, or can recognise objects to the same extent. Although computers can do the same things to an extent, there are **qualitative** and **quantitative** ways in which they are often different. Computers can use language, but in a way that is artificial, perhaps. Searle (1980) looked at the difference between computers and humans. He tried to explain what 'real' understanding is, by telling the story of the Chinese Room (Box 3).

Computers can manipulate symbols, but they don't have 'real' understanding. This seems a simple difference. The problem is that with the use of neural networks, it is clear that computers can learn to draw conclusions, and can learn to build a body of understanding.

Neural networks involve computers learning from experience. An example of their use comes from the railway industry. A computer has been taught to recognise a full platform, a half-full platform and an empty platform: pictures of full, half-full and empty platforms were taken and the information input into the computer, which was told which picture represented which state (full, half-full or empty). After a little while the computer started to estimate what was being shown. It does very well and can learn to judge whether a platform is full, half-full or empty with a high degree of accuracy.

Box 2

Comparing the abilities of computers, humans and chimpanzees

Computers	*Humans*	*Chimpanzees*
Have language	Have language	Have language
Can talk	Can talk	Cannot talk
Have no emotions	Have emotions	Have emotions
Are very good at adding	Are good at adding	Can add simple sums
Can make choices	Can make choices	Can make choices
Can recognise objects	Can recognise objects	Can recognise objects
Can solve problems	Can solve problems	Can solve problems
Can selectively attend	Can selectively attend	Can selectively attend
Can develop knowledge	Can develop knowledge	Can develop knowledge

---

┤ **Box 3** ├

The Chinese room analogy

This analogy is a famous one, outlined by Searle (1980). What follows is a brief summary.

You have to imagine an enclosed room. Someone is in the room. Surrounding this person, there are symbols written in Chinese, but the person does not read Chinese. Once the person is in the room, the only access from outside is through a slot like a letterbox. The person in the room is given rules, written in English, which they do understand. They are told what to do when given one set of symbols, and can 'respond' by giving another set from the symbols in the room by way of a reply. There are different batches of symbols. People from outside can 'post' in symbols in a certain order. The person inside, using the rules, can choose symbols from inside the room, and can send back a reply. Those outside receiving the reply would be able to understand it. It would seem to them that the person inside the room was understanding what they were being asked (in Chinese, by way of the symbols posted into the room), and was replying. It would seem that there was understanding, but the person inside is simply correctly manipulating symbols according to instructions that they understand.

Searle claims to have shown by means of this example that there is more to understanding than manipulating symbols. Others would argue that usually we are not 'locked in rooms'. We interact with our environment, so understanding involves more that manipulating symbols. It involves gathering information from the senses about objects, as well as learning to attach labels to them.

From the examples of the Chinese room and neural networks, you can perhaps see how compelling the computer analogy is. The Chinese room example says that humans are different; however, the neural network example suggests that perhaps humans and computers learn from experience in the same way. The discussion about the ways in which the brain is like a computer, and the ways in which it is different, is still continuing.

Key assumption 3 – nativists v. empiricists

The empiricist view

Empiricists believe that what we know comes from the outside world. If you are asked to give empirical evidence, then this means 'give data gathered via the outside world'. The assumption is that there is a world 'out there' separate from us as individuals and as groups.

The nativist view

Nativists believe that we are born with some knowledge and some capabilities. The computer is built by us and appears to be what Locke (1690) called a *tabula rasa* ('a blank slate') on which knowledge can be drawn. The computer has capabilities; for example, an arithmetic logic unit that can add and do sums (given data), and memory where storage can take place. Data then has to be input. We have capabilities too, from simple cells to complex cells, we have an area in which to store knowledge, and areas for problem solving.

There are differences, however, between humans and computers. Many would argue that we are born with emotions, a temperament, some knowledge from our life in the womb, and genetic blueprints which can shape us in many ways (see Chapter 6). Our brain is a biological living thing, unlike a computer. This difference is of great importance to some.

Evaluation

An interactionist view has been proposed. This view claims that the properties we are born with and the data our senses receive work together and interact. It is not that we can separate **nature** from **nurture** but that the product which develops grows with the interaction. We are products of our inheritance and our environment. Activity 3 asks you to consider examples of bottom-up and top-down processing in your own perceptions.

ACTIVITY 3

TOP-DOWN AND BOTTOM-UP PROCESSING IN ACTION

Recall the distinction between top-down processing and bottom-up processing. The question was asked whether information comes in purely through our senses, or whether our past experiences are used in interpreting the information. Think of an example of when you have made a mistake in your perception. Perhaps you thought you saw someone you know, when it turned out to be a stranger.

Note down what part of your perception was from sense data, and what part was from past experience. In the above example, your senses would have told you the height, weight, length of hair, clothes, style of walking and so on of the person you saw. Your experience would have given you the idea of your mother, or a close friend who is a close match to the person you see. Then you might have mistakenly taken the picture from your past experiences, and 'matched' it to what you were seeing.

Key Skill C3.1a – as you will find with many of the activities in this book, this would make a good group task where you could share information and ideas. Remember to keep evidence for your portfolio.

UNDERSTANDING THE SCIENTIFIC APPROACH

Imagine that you want to boil an egg, and you have never done it before. Write down what you would do.

Compare your answers with those in Box 4.

Bottom-up processing might combine with top-down processing, not as one adding to the other but as a more complex multiplication of the two sets of information. This might explain how we consistently make mistakes in our cognition.

There is a general theory about the topic (in this case boiling eggs) and some knowledge is already present. Then predictions are made about what will happen (these are called **hypotheses**). Referring to real data in some way tests these hypotheses – the prediction is found to be either true, and the theory is updated, or false in some way, and the hypothesis is amended.

Research methods used in cognitive psychology

Chapter 7 deals with research methods in detail. Please refer to the relevant section for a discussion of each method, its advantages and disadvantages, as well as when each method might be chosen when researching in psychology.

Laboratory experiments

Self-test 3

List some of the areas that cognitive psychologists study, and in each case suggest a way in which this area could be studied. When you have read this section, compare your list with what has been suggested here.

Cognitive psychologists are interested in brain processes. In the early years introspection was used: participants were asked to carry out mental tasks and then to say how they had done them. It was not easy to compare people's answers when they were using introspection.

Other sciences offered a method that could be tried – take an idea, test it, and then see if you find what you predict. Activity 4 asks you to try out something, to better understand the scientific approach.

Box 4

The basic scientific method – form a hypothesis based on a theory, and then test it. Amend your theory according to what you find.

First, get an egg. You know things are boiled in saucepans, so find a saucepan or something similar. You know you need water, so fill the pan with water. You want boiling water, so heat it, either by gas or electricity. Most of this you will probably know from watching others.

1 You may drop the egg straight into the cold water before you heat the water. However, you will probably quickly find out that you don't know how long the egg has been cooking for.

2 You probably decide next time to drop the egg in when the water is boiling. However, perhaps the egg cracks when you drop it in.

3 You may decide next time to lower the egg in with a spoon. However, you still don't know how long to boil the egg.

4 You might find a timer. However, you still cannot tell what the finished egg will be like.

5 You have to go through the process more than once until you find the finished egg is to your taste.

Two experiments within cognitive psychology

Held and Hein (1963) – the kitten carousel
Held and Hein used kittens in an experiment.

Evaluation of the use of non-human animals

- In this case animals are used because they are going to be deprived of something. We cannot deprive human babies in this way, so animals are used. Some would definitely argue that we should not deprive animals either. The use of animal experiments has been criticised on ethical grounds (see Chapter 8).
- Animals and humans cannot directly be compared, because they are different. However, much has been learnt from animal experiments.

The study. Held and Hein were studying the development of perceptual abilities. Kittens were kept in darkness for the first 8 weeks after their birth. Then for around 3 hours each day they spent time in a special piece of apparatus built for two kittens – called a 'kitten carousel'. This was like a roundabout. One kitten could walk, and was attached to a harness on one side of the roundabout. The other kitten was carried around in its harness, and could not walk. So one kitten walked around 'towing' the other one. The carousel was round, and was surrounded by a circular wall covered in vertical stripes (Figure 1.5). Each kitten simply saw the vertical stripes as they circulated in the carousel and had the same visual experience.

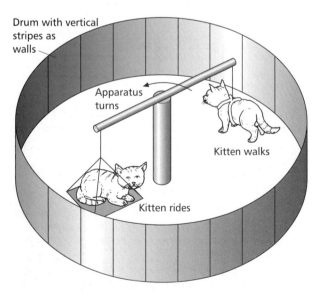

Figure 1.5
Held and Hein's kitten carousel

Labels in figure:
Drum with vertical stripes as walls
Apparatus turns
Kitten walks
Kitten rides

Apart from the 3 hours in the carousel the kittens were kept in darkness. After some weeks, the kittens' coordination was tested. Could they put paw to floor successfully, for example, even after having been reared in darkness or in this unnatural 'vertical' world? One kitten had had no activity in light. It had been in the 'passive' state of being towed around by the other one. The other kitten had had the opportunity to be active, even though in a very limited way.

This was an experiment. The controls were that each kitten was kept in darkness for the first 8 weeks, and for all the time afterwards, other than the 3 hours a day. Each kitten had the same visual experience. Each kitten was the same age. The only difference was that one kitten could actively move the carousel, the other one could not.

The result was that the active kitten did stretch its paws out when tested by being dropped gently onto the floor. The passive kitten did not do this. The active kitten blinked in response to approaching objects, and the passive kitten did not do this. The passive kitten did learn normal responses quite quickly, however.

Evaluation

- It was originally concluded that the passive kitten had not learnt perception, for example of objects, or depth perception. However, the passive kitten had had little opportunity to practice movement along with perception. It looks as though this took a little while. The conclusion was that the kittens needed to coordinate their movements with what they saw, but not that they needed to move around in the environment to learn to perceive.

Gray and Wedderburn (1960) – hearing and the use of meaning of words
Refer back to Broadbent's (1958) information-processing model of selective attention. Broadbent suggested that each ear is a separate channel. Whatever we hear in one ear we hear separately from what we hear in the other ear. Activity 5 asks you to conduct an experiment similar to Broadbent's.

In the tradition of experimental psychology, others tested Broadbent's claims, and tried modifications to his studies. Try a different task to test his claims (Activity 6).

Broadbent and Gray and Wedderburn used experimental methods. They used controls and the only difference between the tests is whether numbers were given on their own, or whether some meaning is introduced to the information to be fed to the participant.

ACTIVITY 5

TRY YOUR OWN EXPERIMENT, BASED ON A SPLIT-SPAN TASK

Broadbent (1954) used headphones for this. If you can, prepare two tapes. The participant uses the headphones, with one tape playing into one ear and the other into the other ear. A quicker way of doing this is suggested below.

Sit in groups of three, in a row. The person in the middle is the participant. The two on either side are going to feed in the messages. The person on one side must have three numbers ready, say 3, 9, 8, and the one on the other side has a different three numbers ready, say 4, 7, 2. They must be trained to say the three numbers at the same time, turning towards the participant in the middle. This is called the split-span procedure (Figure 1.6).

The participant recalls numbers, either pair-by-pair, which would give 34, 97, 82, or ear-by-ear, which would give 398 and 472.

Ear-by-ear recall often gave more accurate answers, so Broadbent thought each ear was a separate channel. Try asking your participants what they recall. Usually they will recall ear-by-ear, not pair-by-pair, supporting Broadbent's claim.

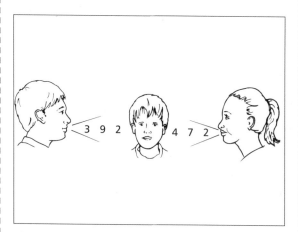

Figure 1.6

Key Skill C3.1a – this activity would make a good group task (you will need other people for this experiment in any case).

ACTIVITY 6

A MODIFICATION OF BROADBENT'S STUDY

Gray and Wedderburn (1960) tried using meaning in the information that was fed into the participant's two ears using a split-span procedure similar to that outlined in Activity 5. Instead of feeding the numbers into each of the middle participant's ears, try giving some meaning to the information.

They chose to feed into one ear 'dear 2 jane' and into the other ear '6 aunt 9'. This has to be carefully timed. Those feeding the middle participant should practise as they must say the three separate items in unison.

Figure 1.7

According to Broadbent's study, your participant should hear 'dear 2 jane' and '6 aunt 9'. This would be ear-by-ear. However, Gray and Wedderburn found that participants heard 'dear aunt jane' and '629'. So meaning seems to have affected how they processed the information.

Key Skill C3.1a – again you should be in groups for this experiment, and you should make sure that everyone contributes. If you are studying alone, you may need to imagine this experiment as you need people to help you.

Evaluation

- An advantage of experiments is that, because of the strict controls, we can be reasonably sure that if we do the experiment again we will get the same results. In other words, this method is **reliable**.

- These controls give an advantage, but they also lead to a disadvantage. This is that experiments, especially those carried out in the laboratory, are not natural. They make people do what they don't usually do. So they don't really measure 'reality', or what they say they measure. In other words they are not **valid**. They are not 'real' in their setting, and they are artificial. This sort of validity is called **ecological validity**.

Case studies of brain-damaged patients

In some cases, experiments are not suitable. Another way of discovering what areas of the brain serve which functions is to look at humans whose brains have been damaged. As these studies are in-depth investigations of particular individuals, they are **case studies**. In practice these individuals are often asked to carry out experiments, to see what they can and can't do, but the overall research method is case study.

Case studies within cognitive psychology

The case of H.M. (Blakemore, 1988)

H.M. underwent an operation for epilepsy, and his hippocampus was removed on both sides of the brain. He had severe amnesia, in that he had difficulty in laying down new memories, even though he could remember things from before the operation. He could not transfer information to long-term memory (see below). H.M. has been extensively studied over 25 years. Tasks have included learning short lists to test short-term memory, which is found to be normal, or asking questions about people H.M. has just met.

From this sort of study, it has been concluded that the hippocampus is needed for memories to be transferred to long-term memory, or at least to some permanent store. Such evidence also supports that claim that there is a short-term and a long-term memory.

Evaluation

- An advantage of the case study is that it is in depth and thorough. It measures what it claims to measure, and is valid.

- However, because it is a study about a single person, it cannot easily be said to apply to everyone. H.M. had specific surgery that affected his hippocampus, but we cannot say what else was affected.

The case of Clive Wearing

Note that the participant in this case study is named, whereas H.M. is not named. Box 5 explores this ethical issue.

Clive Wearing suffered a virus which attacked and destroyed his hippocampus. The virus is common enough, but very rarely does this sort of damage. Other parts of his cortex were also damaged. If we look at what he can and can't do we can get a good idea of what the damaged areas of his brain were for.

The hippocampus seems to be needed for laying down new memories in long-term memory. Information enters the brain as it did before the damage, and this is the case for this participant. When his wife walks into the room, he feels he is seeing her for the first time. If she leaves the room for a short while and then re-enters, he sees her for the first time again. It is like living with snapshots of time. He can play patience, because the cards are there for him to look at each time. He can remember who his wife is, because some of his long-term memory is intact. He can play the piano and conduct as before. This is because these sorts of skill memories are stored elsewhere in the brain (areas like the cerebellum, at the base of the brain).

Evaluation

- This sort of case study gives evidence to support the models. It is from these case studies that such knowledge is developed.

- There are problems because the area of damage is not simply the hippocampus. However, in general, if there is damage to the hippocampus and some parts of the cortex, we would expect amnesia, which Clive Wearing suffers from.

Colin Blakemore (1988) presented a series of videos called *The Mind Machine*. These videos are available, and one, called *Amnesia*, features the case study of Clive Wearing.

Scanning techniques

Brain scanning has been used mainly for medical purposes. However, scanning has led to a great increase in understanding the brain because it enables us to see the living brain in action.

The use of scanning within cognitive psychology

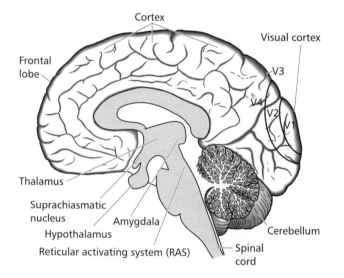

Figure 1.8
The human brain

MRI scanning involves the use of magnetic fields. John Tchalenko, who carries out research on drawing and cognition, Humphrey Ocean, who is a portrait painter, and Robert Solso, a cognitive psychologist, have recently used it in a particular study (Sunday Times magazine, 24 October 1999). Ocean was the participant, and whilst in the scanner he had to draw pictures from symbols flashed up in front of him. Computer images were generated of his brain at work. Other participants (non-artists) carried out similar tasks, and the areas at work in their brains were compared with Ocean's.

Ocean used much more of the frontal and parietal cortex, as well as the hippocampus, than did the others, who were simply using their visual cortex. The non-artists seemed to be copying the images, whereas the artist was thinking about the portrait and using his memory. This example could be given as a contemporary issue.

There are different kinds of scanning. MRI scanning is one type, and CT scanning is another. They use different ways of generating pictures. Scanning is looked at in more detail in Chapter 6.

As scanning becomes more routine, perhaps more controlled studies can be undertaken and more can be learnt.

In-depth areas of study – memory and forgetting

Cognitive psychology covers many areas of thinking, including perception (Held and Hein), and selective attention (Broadbent and Treisman). This chapter will focus on memory and forgetting. This area has been chosen for a number of reasons. Firstly, from the study of memory you will be able to generate many research ideas of your own, for your coursework. Secondly, you will be able to carry out some of the studies yourself, and can test your own memory. Thirdly, you can learn from memory studies how to improve your own memory. Lastly, it is hoped that you will find the study of memory interesting because applied research in the area has importance. Police interviewing has been affected by cognitive psychology, and the cognitive interview is now widely advocated, as will be seen. Clinical psychology, which is the area that looks at mental health, uses knowledge from cognitive psychology to help people to cope with amnesia, for example.

Theories of memory

The multi-store model

One of the best-known models of how memory works is that proposed by Atkinson and Shiffrin (1968), also known as the dual-process model. Box 6 discusses the use of models, to emphasise that you are not reading about hard and fast rules, but about ideas of what might be the case.

Box 6

Models

When learning, for example, a new subject like psychology, it is tempting to think that everything you learn is the truth.

Take a few minutes here to recall something of what was said earlier about cognitive psychology. Models are representations about what might be true. As more evidence is gathered by various means and from different sources, models are amended and changed, so some models become more accepted than others. However, a model is only ever an *idea* of what might be the case.

The student of psychology needs to develop the skills of gathering the knowledge, and then, most importantly, of looking at the evidence and deciding how far what is suggested can be accepted.

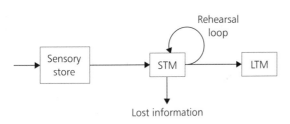

Figure 1.9
The Atkinson and Shiffrin dual-process model

Figure 1.9 illustrates the focus of cognitive psychology on information processing. Information first comes into a sensory store and some reaches short-term memory (STM). If the information is rehearsed, it enters long-term storage, but if it is not maintained, then the information is lost before it reaches long-term memory (LTM).

The sensory store

Experiments have shown that at this stage the information is in the form in which it enters the store. So if visual information is being received, it is in a visual form, or a visual mode. There is a term for this idea of data being in the same form in which it is received – **modality specific**. Lots of data are being received in the sensory store all the time, and cannot be held for very long. Information is maintained in this form for a very short time indeed, before some is lost, and some enters STM. Box 7 gives more information on the sensory store.

Box 7

Properties of sensory storage or sensory memory

Sperling (1960,1963) studied sensory storage. He showed people an array of 12 letters in a 3 × 4 table. With 12 letters available for processing, he wanted to see how many people could recall. He found they recalled on average around four letters. He let them see the array for only a very short time, so they did not have time to get the information into STM.

Then he tried another experiment. He showed people more arrays of 12 letters in the 3 × 4 table. However, this time he asked them to recall a specific row – top, middle or bottom. The participants now had only four letters available for recall out of the original 12, because there were four letters in each of the three rows. He found that participants could recall on average three or four letters.

So there was very similar recall whether 12 letters or four letters were available. Sperling concluded that the letters were available only for a very short space of time. Even with 12 letters, the participant had to search through them in their minds one at a time. So they managed around four letters, and they managed only three when searching the whole array for a particular line. It seems as if the letters are fading as the person looks at them, and four is the maximum number they can scan before the image fades.

Activity 7 suggests ways in which you can test Sperling's ideas.

ACTIVITY 7

TESTING SENSORY MEMORY

With some help you might be able to program a computer to flash up an array like Sperling's for about 50 milliseconds (one-twentieth of a second). A tachistoscope can also be used. This is a piece of equipment where a card slides into the back of a large viewer. The participant looks through the viewer and presses a button to illuminate the back of the viewer for a timed period.

Alternatively, print different arrays on overhead transparencies and switch the overhead projector off and on quickly.

An example of such an array:

D	G	K		F
L	X	R		B
P	M	Y		H

Flash up the 12-letter array for a very short time, and have many different arrays available. The participant might take a little while to realise that you are showing letters. Eventually the participant will be able to call out the letters that he or she recognises. If you take an average, you should find the participant can recall four or five of the 12 letters.

*The second part of the experiment is to do the same thing again but this time, instead of allowing the participant to call out any of the letters (**free recall**), ask them for a particular row. For example, wait until you have shown the array, and then say 'top', and the next time say 'middle', and so on. Do a number of trials for each participant. Box 7 outlines what you should find.*

Key Skill C3.1a – you will need to work in a group in any case for this study, and a group discussion about what is needed would be very useful.

Key Skill N3.1 – if you carefully record the data from this study you could keep the results as a large data set and plan and interpret information. You could then do calculations for Key Skill N3.2.

From Sperling's (1960) study we can conclude that the information available immediately quickly fades, and cannot be recalled.

Evaluation

- Note the connection here with research on selective attention. Look back to Broadbent's filter model, and you can see that there is a similarity between the way sensory memory is said to work and the claim Broadbent makes that information is filtered out in some way.

Short-term memory

Data that is retained on entering the sensory store is said by the Atkinson and Shiffrin model to pass into STM.

Evaluation

Remember, this is only a model. However, through the H.M. case study it was decided that the hippocampus was the area of the brain needed in order that memories could be laid down and held. So the hippocampus is possibly involved in STM. This sort of evidence supports the multi-store model. Other models have alternative explanations, as will be seen later in the chapter.

Studies Experiments have been carried out to see what happens in STM.

ACTIVITY 8

TESTING THE NUMBER OF ITEMS THAT CAN BE HELD IN STM

You need to work in pairs, if possible. Get your partner to write down 13 different numbers in a row, without showing you. Ask them to make sure that the numbers are 'random' and that they have no pattern or meaning. For example, use: 7, 3, 9, 2, 8, 5, 4, 6, 7, 1, 5, 4 …, not 2, 4, 6, 8, 1, 3, 5, 7, 9 …

The numbers should be fed to you individually but you must repeat the numbers aloud as they are fed to you. For example, in the above set, someone reads to you the number 7: you say 'seven'. They give you the next number, 3, and you say 'seven, three'. Then they read you the number 9, and you say 'seven, three, nine'. You have to keep going until you make a mistake. At that point you have discovered your memory span – the most numbers you can recall in sequence before going wrong.

Key Skill N3.1 – you could gather the data from this study, especially if you are studying in a class and all the class do the task. Then you will have a large data set ready to work on for this key skill and Key Skill N3.2.

From Miller's experiments (see box 8), it was concluded that STM has a capacity of 5–9 items.

However, what is an item? You might already be thinking that you can recall more than nine items quite easily. Indeed, you may have done so in carrying out Activity 8. For instance, telephone numbers are more than nine digits long, and yet you probably can recall several.

Box 8

The number of items held in STM is limited

Miller (1956) claims that the number of items that can be held in STM is seven, with an allowance of two either side. This claim can be tested. First, look again at the diagram of the multi-store model (Figure 1.9), and focus on the rehearsal loop. Imagine a real loop of tape, which is used again and again. It could be a large loop, where lots of information could be stored before being passed into LTM, or it could be a short loop. It was assumed that STM is a short temporary store, and that the loop was reused quite often. If something is well learnt, then it is in long-term memory. Therefore, if we stop someone from learning something well, and we don't give them long to learn it, we can test what happens in STM. We might be able to see the size of the loop.

If you carry out Activity 8, Miller's work predicts that you will get up to five numbers in a row right, and that you might reach nine numbers, but you will probably go wrong at that stage. In other words, you should be able to recite seven, plus or minus two, numbers correctly.

LTM, and you are no longer testing STM. You should find that the best recall is from those reading the meaningful groups.

2 With two groups of participants, create a long list of letters that have no meaning by writing down a meaningful sentence and taking the first letters of each word. For example, the sentence 'I like to travel to Paris because it is very beautiful and there are a lot of interesting buildings to explore' gives the letters I L T T T P B I I V B A T A A L O I B T E. Each participant is asked to recall the same list of letters. One group, however, is given different instructions. They are given the sentence at the same time as the list, whereas the other group are not told the sentence when learning the list. The group with the sentence to help them chunk the list into words should recall more of the letters.

> Key Skill C3.1a – for this experiment you may need the help of others. Before carrying out the study you might need a group discussion so that all controls are considered.

> Key Skill N3.1 – when collecting data for any of these activities, keep the results and take the opportunity to interpret them. Do some calculations for other Key Skills in the Application of Number area

---

Miller accounted for the fact that we can get more than nine items into our STM even if we don't have time to rehearse the material to get it into LTM, by saying that the nine items can be nine **chunks**. So if you make a longer list of numbers – say 123 456 789 234 567 789 345 678 and so on, you could manage all these numbers because you could group them into chunks.

ACTIVITY 9

CHUNKING HELPS TO EXTEND THE CAPABILITY OF THE LOOP IN STM

You can carry out a number of experiments based on the claim that chunking helps to extend STM.

*1 You could use **trigrams**. Trigrams are groups of three letters that have no meaning: 'cat' has meaning but 'gar' does not, and is a trigram, or nonsense syllable. Find two groups of participants. Show one group a list of trigrams, and the other a list of meaningful three-letter words or acronyms (an acronym is a group of letters with meaning – e.g. FBI, CIA). Which participants would recall most letters? It is important not to let the task last more than 20 or 30 seconds, otherwise the material goes into*

Self-test 4

Write down at least 10 important points to note when carrying out the study discussed in Activity 9. Think about what you need to control, and how to treat your participants. Check your list with the one below.

Some methodological points to note when carrying out Activity 9:

- treat your participants ethically – see the next seven points
- explain to them afterwards (debrief them)
- let them stop at any time (give them the right to withdraw)
- ask for permission and explain a little (consent)

- say you will fully explain at the end (informed consent)
- say they can withdraw the use of their data if they wish
- say you will not use their names (confidentiality)
- explain that this is not a test of individual abilities
- use the same letters in the trigrams as you did in the meaningful chunks
- use the same number of letters overall
- give all participants the same length of time to look at the stimulus materials
- give all participants the same standard instructions, so they get told the same thing.

Other experiments have tested the Atkinson and Shiffrin model. One looks at the rehearsal loop itself. If we need to rehearse information in order for it to get into LTM, then presumably if we block rehearsal in some way, we would recall fewer items than if we allowed people to rehearse. Box 9 examines research where the loop is tested by preventing rehearsal.

Box 9

Testing the existence of a rehearsal loop

There is a well-known technique used in this area of research, called the Brown–Peterson technique. Brown (1958) and Peterson and Peterson (1959) developed the idea of blocking rehearsal by such tasks as counting backwards. These were two separate groups of researchers, so the technique was jointly named after them.

Participants learnt trigrams such as BHK. Once they had been given the trigrams, however, rehearsal was blocked by making them count backward in threes, for example 57, 54, 51 … The number of trigrams they could recall was recorded. Participants forgot a great deal of the information after only 9 seconds and almost all of it by 18 seconds.

It was concluded that information stayed in STM (without rehearsal) for a maximum of 18 seconds.

ACTIVITY 10

TESTING THE REHEARSAL LOOP FOR YOURSELF

Prepare a list of trigrams or a list of consonants (if you use vowels you might give words by mistake) for each participant to try to learn. Give them about 20 seconds to look at the list. You need quite a few more than nine items, or your participant will recall them all.

There are two different **conditions**. *In other words, the two groups do different things. One group will look at the list, wait 25 seconds rehearsing it, then recall the list in order. The other group will look at the same list for the same amount of time but, instead of waiting 25 seconds and rehearsing, they will be asked to count backwards in threes from a high number (say 598) for 25 seconds, then they too will be asked to recall the list in the right order.*

You should find that the group that counts backwards is having their rehearsal time blocked, and so will find the task very difficult. The other group has time to rehearse. Indeed some material has perhaps reached LTM, so their recall should be much more successful.

Key Skill C3.1a – you might like to discuss this in a group before carrying out the study. It would be useful to use others in the class in any case.

Key Skill N3.1 – take the opportunity to plan and interpret the information. When you have gathered a large data set, you could do calculations too, for other Key Skills in this area.

STM thus has a capacity of seven (plus or minus two) items. Chunking can be used. STM lasts for a little more than 18 seconds, but less than 30 seconds. Rehearsal is needed or material is lost. You will have noticed whilst carrying out the activities that, on being asked to learn material, you are often saying it over in your mind. STM is often thought to use acoustic coding. This means that we seem to hear the data when learning it.

Evaluation

- Many of the studies use numbers, letters and words. It is likely that for this we will use acoustic coding. Experiments can lead to unnatural studies, and could lead to false conclusions.

Long-term memory

LTM is harder to pin down than STM. Apart from the immediate sensory store (which is said to be very brief) and STM, which lasts a very short time and shows that we need to rehearse material to lay it down in LTM, the rest of what we recall is in LTM.

ACTIVITY 11

THE CONTENTS OF YOUR LTM

Make a list of things that you can remember. Check your list with the one below.

> Key Skill C3.1a – after you have made your own list (and this is best done on your own) then you could discuss each other's lists in small groups. Extend the discussion by sorting things into lists, and deciding whether they are stored by sight, sound or meaning (or some other way).

You probably came up with events that you recall, such as a past birthday. You might have listed things such as languages or academic knowledge. You may have come up with remembering how to do things such as riding a bike, or swimming. You may have listed 'facts' such as the names of your brothers and sisters, or other family members. LTM stores all of these. Some things are stored visually, some are stored as sound (e.g. a favourite song), and some are stored semantically (according to meaning). LTM seems to have some order to it. Many studies have been done to look at organisation in memory, and in particular LTM. For example, it seems that categories aid recall. Activities 12 and 13 suggest ways you can test this.

ACTIVITY 12

CATEGORIES AID RECALL

This is an experiment that works well for coursework. There are a number of variations, and you could think of your own. The basic idea is to give one group of participants a list of 20 words to learn in four 'random' sets of five words. The other group has four 'meaningful' sets of five words. The best idea is to work out the four sets of five meaningful words, and then use the same words but put them into four sets where they are not grouped. For an example see the lists below:

Organised list

Red	Table	Crisps	Train
Orange	Chair	Potatoes	Van
Green	Desk	Bread	Bus
Purple	Piano	Carrots	Aeroplane
Blue	Stool	Cheese	Lorry

Random list

Red	Green	Cheese	Piano
Desk	Bread	Bus	Chair
Purple	Table	Lorry	Potatoes
Carrots	Blue	Orange	Stool
Crisps	Train	Van	Aeroplane

The categories are 'colours', 'furniture', 'food', 'transport'.

You could try this study with a number of variations.

> Key Skill N3.2 – if you gather a large data set in this way, use the opportunity to do calculations like the ones you will need for your coursework. Chapter 7 explains what is needed.

Tulving and Pearlstone (1966) did a study similar to the one in Activity 12. The participants were given the same stimulus materials to learn (the grouped words with headings). The conditions in their study were whether they were given the category names on a piece of paper when recalling, or whether they free recalled on a blank sheet of paper. Tulving and Pearlstone found that the cues (the category headings) helped recall. They had to give participants more than 20 words to notice the difference. Also when the group who were given free recall were later given the cued recall, they too could remember more. This suggests that the memory for the words was there all along, but the participants needed the cues to remember the words.

ACTIVITY 13

Think of some variations for the study in Activity 12 and note down what you would do. Read or recall Chapter 7 and note down the hypothesis in each variation, and the independent and dependent variables. Also write down which design you would choose and why.

One suggestion of how to do this:
- *Use an independent groups design (different participants do each condition).*
- *Conditions are **a** one group has the categorised list to learn and **b** the other has the random list.*
- *The independent variable is whether the lists are categorised/grouped or not (the independent variable is the variable you set up to be different in the two conditions).*
- *The dependent variable is how many words*

are recalled by the participant (the dependent variable is what you are measuring, which results from what you have set up).

- *The experimental hypothesis is 'There is a difference in the number of words recalled depending on whether the stimulus list is categorised or not, and participants will recall more words from the categorised list than from a random list using the same words'.*
- *The null hypothesis is 'There is no difference in the number of words recalled, and participants do not recall more from a categorised list. Any difference that is found is due to chance or some other factor'.*
- *The recall of the words could be better for the categorised list or better for the randomised list – but the hypothesis says that the categorised list is better, so it has a direction predicted. By predicting direction, and saying that the categorised list is better, we have made this a one-tailed test (with no direction, it is two-tailed).*

The theory says that LTM is organised, and that cued recall is best. Although the suggestion asks not for cued recall but for cued learning, we could claim that cued recall is also best.

Another variation would be to give cued recall. Or you could decide to give everyone the randomised list, and only one group cued recall. You probably came up with these sorts of variations. Remember, for coursework, take only one hypothesis and don't test more than one variable at once.

Key Skill C3.1a – if you are studying in a group, a discussion would work well for this activity.

Box 10

The primacy and recency effect – testing the existence of a separate STM and LTM

Glanzer and Cunitz (1966) tested the Atkinson and Shiffrin model using a list of words that people had to learn. The participants were allowed to recall the words in any order. This is called free recall. The idea was not to see *how many* words they had recalled: the important thing was *which* words had been remembered. Glanzer and Cunitz wanted to see if the words at the beginning of the list had been recalled

well, with those in the middle of the list recalled badly, and those at the end recalled quite well again.

They found that people did indeed recall the first and last words well. The words in the middle were recalled least well. Think of what the Atkinson and Shiffrin model would predict. Where are the words that come first in the list (in terms of STM and LTM). Where are the last few words?

It is claimed that the first words have gone into LTM and the last words are the STM rehearsal loop. The middle words are in the process of being laid down in LTM. The first words are well learnt (in LTM). The last words are fresh in the participants' minds, and so would be better recalled than the middle ones. They are still in the STM loop.

The **primacy effect** is when the first words are learnt well, and the **recency effect** is when the last words are well recalled. The existence of a primacy and recency effect supports the Atkinson and Shiffrin model because it strongly suggests that there is a separate STM and LTM.

LTM lasts forever and has unlimited capacity – potentially. This does not mean we do not forget things. Box 10 describes an experiment which gives evidence for STM and a separate LTM, and Activity 14 suggests a way in which you can carry out this experiment.

ACTIVITY 14

TEST THE PRIMACY AND RECENCY EFFECTS

You can carry out a study similar to that of Glanzer and Cunitz. Write down a list of 20 words. These must be 'random' and have no meaningful links (table, tree, yard, chair, horse, plant, bus, white and so on). These are your stimulus materials, and all participants will be asked to learn and recall the list. Give your participants 30 seconds. This is important as they will be using both STM and LTM. They are not allowed to look at the whole list – you have to feed them the words by either reading them out steadily (and at the same speed for each participant) or by having the words on cards and showing them one at a time (take around 30 seconds to do this).

Once you have fed the words to the participant, he or she must recall the words in any order (free recall). If you plot a graph giving the percentage recall of each word against the

▶

position of the word on the list, you will draw a serial position curve (Figure 1.10).

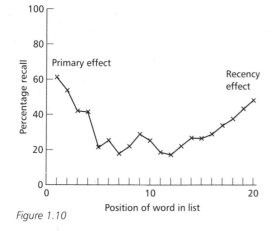

Figure 1.10

To test the findings you have a number of options. You could take the middle ten words as the middle list, and the first five plus the last five words (the outside ten) as the list of words that should be better recalled. Then you can compare recall of the middle ten for a particular participant with their recall of the outside ten. However, this does not take into account the fact that recall of the first five words might be better than recall of the last five. You could test this.

If you carry out the above experiment you should find evidence of a primacy and recency effect, replicating Glanzer's and Cunitz's study.

> Key Skill N3.2 – once you have a large data set you can take the opportunity to do calculations on the data for Key Skills in the area of Application of Number.

Evaluation

- Evidence such as this is taken to support the two-process model. It is claimed that we recall best what we learn first – the primacy effect. We also recall best what we have just seen – the recency effect. The existence of a primacy and recency effect is said to show that we do have separate short and long-term memories.

Other ways of looking at LTM – expanding on the Atkinson and Shiffrin model

Episodic, semantic, procedural, and declarative memory

Episodic memories are personal to you, and are things or events that happened to you. Your birthday party is an episode in your memory.

Semantic memories are 'facts' and knowledge. Tulving (1972) says that your semantic memory is like a dictionary. It was Tulving who distinguished between episodic and semantic memory. Semantic memory tells you that birthdays are special days which happen once a year on the date that you were born, and episodic memory lets you recall particular birthdays.

Tulving (1985) claimed there is also a **procedural memory**, which is where we remember how to do things like riding a bicycle.

Cohen and Squire (1980) distinguish between **declarative memory**, which is about knowing that something is the case, and **procedural memory**, which is about knowing how to do something. Declarative memory joins episodic and semantic memory into one. This information about our memories can also be used to help others.

ACTIVITY 15

APPLYING SOME OF THE INFORMATION LEARNT SO FAR

Different researchers come up with different, but similar, ideas. Declarative memory is neither episodic nor semantic, just another way of dividing LTM up into something that can be studied and understood.

Note down areas where you think this information might be used to help others.

You may have come up with ideas such as improving one's memory for examinations or helping people with brain damage. Cohen and Squire were looking at people with problems in just this way.

> Key Skill C3.1a – this activity would make a good group discussion. You could also consider doing more research in this area for Key Skill 3.2 or doing a presentation for Key Skill C3.1b.

Levels of processing

The levels of processing (LOP) model explains memory in a different way from the multi-store model, and can be used to evaluate and comment on the Atkinson and Shiffrin model.

Craik and Lockhart (1972) saw memory as part of the information processing that takes place, but not as important in itself. They claimed that if we process some information better than we process other information, we will recall best the information that has been most processed. The deeper the level of processing, the better the storage, and hence the better the recall. Activity 16 suggests a way you can test this yourself.

ACTIVITY 16

TEST THE LEVELS OF PROCESSING THEORY

With a list of words we can do three different tasks:

- *we can simply try to learn the list*
- *we can think of words that sound like the main word and use them to help us to learn the list*
- *we can generate words that describe the main word, and use this to help us learn the list.*

For example, a list could include 'car', 'cat' and 'jam'. One set of participants could try to learn this list in a given period and then recall it, giving us scores to use as a baseline. This group sees the words, and they are visually presented.

Ask a different group of participants to learn the same words, but to think of a word that rhymes, for example 'car – jar', 'cat – mat', 'jam – slam'. These people have processed the list more, because they have actively thought about the sounds of the words.

Finally, ask a third group to learn the list, but to generate verbs linked to the words (for example 'car – drive', 'cat – purr', 'jam – eat'). This last group processes the meaning of the words.

Those who process the meaning of the words (use semantic processing) process to a deeper level than those who think of the sound of the words (use auditory processing). The first group, who used visual processing only, should have lowest recall rate.

Key Skill N3.2 – if you generate a large data set from this activity use the opportunity to calculate measures of central tendency. You will need to practice doing these calculations for your coursework. Chapter 7 explains more.

If you found that deeper processing led to greater recall, you have supported Craik and Lockhart's claim that memory is a by-product of information processing.

Evaluation

- The model can be criticised because if we say that deeper processing gives better recall, and then prove it by looking at good recall and saying this means the processing is deeper, we are using a circular argument – and prove nothing.

- In favour of the level of processing model, however, is that it supports the assumption of cognitive psychology that information is processed. It is an appealing claim that the better the processing the more secure the information. Also the multi-store model claims that information that is not rehearsed cannot pass into LTM – rehearsing could be said to be the same as processing more deeply.

- Using a similar argument, it could be emphasised that experiments to test whether STM is improved by chunking involve adding meaning. Adding meaning could be claimed to be another way of saying the information is more deeply processed.

Working memory

A third model extends the multi-store model by focusing on STM, or at least looking at similar issues. This model is the **working memory model** suggested by Baddeley and Hitch (1974). The working memory model breaks into different parts what the multi-store model considers only as STM (Figure 1.11).

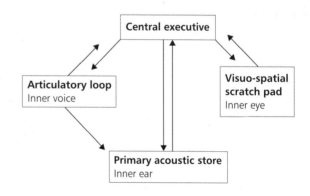

Figure 1.11
The working memory model

The **central executive** is in control in allocating attention and directing operations. It can operate on any data – visual, sound, touch etc. (This is called being **modality free**. Compare this with **modality specific**, which is true of the sensory store.)

The **articulatory loop** is what we use when we say a phone number over and over again, trying to keep it in our minds before making the call. When discussing the rehearsal loop of the multi-store model, it was claimed that STM used an acoustic code, based on this idea of inner speech when rehearsing. In the working memory model, this part of memory is called the articulatory loop. It can also be called the inner voice.

The **visuospatial scratchpad** is also used in rehearsing. This time instead of language being used in rehearsal, visual or spatial information is being rehearsed. If you were a racing driver, you might rehearse a particular racetrack, checking out all the bends and the racing line. This is the inner eye, and uses a visual code.

The **primary acoustic store** can either receive information from the articulatory loop, as you are saying the information over and over again, or can receive sound information directly. This is known as the 'inner ear'. Visual information must be translated into sound for it to be received in the primary acoustic store. For example, you could see the racetrack in your mind, and then translate into words, just as the navigator translates for the rally driver.

In Activity 1 you were asked to try to read a passage and repeat the word 'and' over and over again – a very difficult task. One explanation would be that the articulatory loop is being used for both these tasks, which makes the two things extremely difficult to do at once.

Evaluation

- The sort of evidence gained from doing such tasks as trying to use one of the parts of the model twice (and finding this difficult) is used to say that the working memory model is useful because the evidence supports the model.

- The working memory model is widely accepted, partly because it makes sense to us to think of these different parts to STM.

- Although the multi-store model is supported by evidence, this evidence comes largely from experiments using numbers, letters and words, which test only one part of memory. Memory for visual or spatial information is not tested or explained by the multi-store model. For this reason the working memory model is accepted as a more in-depth explanation of the processes within what is known as short-term memory.

- However, little is known about the central executive. Think back to the discussion on information processing earlier and Treisman's model of selective attention. She claimed that the information that is not directly attended to is attenuated, not lost as Broadbent's model originally

proposed. She used this idea to explain how we monitor our surroundings, so that, however much we are concentrating on a task, we can still hear the word 'fire' and react quickly to it. The problem for her model is the question of who is doing the monitoring. Who is attending to the 'rest', separately from the individual who is focusing on the 'important' task? There would need to be something like a hidden observer in our brains. The working memory model seems to need this hidden observer too, to allocate tasks and control things. It is difficult to study this hidden observer.

Theories of forgetting

Forgetting in STM

It is convenient to use the multi-store model when discussing different ways of forgetting, but don't forget that this is only a model of what might happen. If we take STM to be where memories are either passed into some more permanent store or lost, then forgetting is usually said to be through interference or displacement. **Trace decay** is a theory of forgetting that could apply to either STM or LTM. Other theories of forgetting do not link to the multi-store model.

Trace decay

Forgetting seems to increase over time. The longer the time between laying down the memory and attempting to recall, the more likely forgetting is to have taken place. A memory is actually a change in the brain. Hebb (1949) looked at the brain and showed that a memory occurs when a group of nerve cells excite one another. Think of this as one cell in the brain triggering or activating another cell, by some sort of electric current. Chapter 6 looks more at the actual biological processes involved. If these nerves trigger each other more than once, an actual physical change takes place.

These physical changes may decay over time. If decay occurs because no repetition of the neural activity takes place, then trace decay as a theory of forgetting applies only to STM. However, researchers other than Hebb have claimed that such decay can also occur through disuse, so trace decay would apply also to LTM.

Evaluation

- The problem is that we do recall things we have not thought about for a long time. We can reactivate lost memories, particularly if the cues are right. We can ride a bike after a long period, for example; we can understand a foreign language after many years. We have not been renewing the physical memories in the interim, but the memory is still there.

Activity 17 suggests a way that you can test whether trace decay is a good explanation of forgetting.

ACTIVITY 17

TEST THE THEORY OF TRACE DECAY AS AN EXPLANATION OF FORGETTING

Jenkins and Dallenbach (1924) found that people who slept between learning a list and recalling it recalled more than those who did not sleep. This is a study you could do yourself.

Find some willing participants. Ask one group to learn a list of ten nonsense syllables (like the trigrams referred to earlier) before they go to sleep. They should recall as many as they can when they wake up. Assuming this is after 8 hours, ask a second group to learn the same material in the morning. After 8 hours they should be asked to recall as much as they can.

If trace decay accounts for forgetting, then both groups should have the same amount of trace decay, and should recall the same number of nonsense syllables.

Key Skill C3.1a – you could discuss this activity in a group and plan and share the data collection.

Jenkins and Dallenbach found that people who had slept recalled more than those who had not. It is tempting to conclude that interference from the day's activities caused the forgetting in the 'day' group, whereas those who were asleep had no conflicting information to process.

There are many problems with the study suggested in Activity 17, in terms of methodology. If you choose to do Activity 17 for coursework, you will have to work hard to put right many of the problems.

ACTIVITY 18

SOME METHOD PROBLEMS

List some of the problems with the study suggested in Activity 17, and make suggestions for improving the study.

Key Skill 3.1a – this activity would make a very good group discussion as you could share ideas.

One problem you might have pointed out is that you would need a sleep laboratory to add controls. Jenkins and Dallenbach supervised the learning of the stimulus materials, then let the participants go to sleep but woke them up 2, 4 and 8 hours and asked them to recall. You would probably not be able to do this, and could not control how long participants learnt the list for at night. Similarly, Jenkins and Dallenbach asked their day participants, after having supervised their learning, to report back to them at 2, 4 and 8-hourly intervals. You would find it difficult to do this.

However, even poorly controlled studies using few participants can demonstrate what other researchers are claiming. If you are using one of the suggestions for coursework, you do need to implement as many controls as you can.

Interference

Trace decay sounds a sensible idea – that actual physical changes in the brain decay over time unless they are renewed – but it does not fit all we know about forgetting.

Interference is another way in which we might forget. It has been suggested that the day's activities interfere with retaining memories. When looking at STM an experiment using the Brown–Peterson technique was outlined. If rehearsal is blocked by tasks such as counting backwards, then these tasks seem to interfere with rehearsal, and participants who have to do an interference task recall fewer items than those who have rehearsal time. It does seem that some forgetting in STM is due to interference.

In LTM there are two types of interference. For example, material that you have already learnt – perhaps German words – can interfere with material you are now trying to learn, such as Spanish words (you may have had this experience with languages yourself). **Proactive inhibition** occurs when learning the first list (the German words) gets in the way of learning the second list (the Spanish words). **Retroactive inhibition** is when the learning of the later list (the Spanish words) gets in the way of remembering the first list (the German words). Inhibition is another word for interference.

Self-test 5

What would you do to improve your memory when learning a subject like psychology? (Remember the advantage of rehearsal, and of using categories to aid recall.)

Key Skill C3.1a – although this is a self-test and you might prefer to test yourself first, it would also make a good group discussion task. By discussing in a group you could share ideas.

Evaluation

- A problem with interference as an explanation of forgetting is that is has limited application. Experiments using words and lists of letters may show interference, but in 'real life' we don't usually learn lists of words and letters. Most of what we learn is meaningful, and meaning seems to improve recall.

- Categorising lists in LTM appears to help recall. Giving cues like a sentence to help remember a list of letters seems to help. Other studies have found that imagery aids recall, and **mnemonics** are used to help people to remember. An example often given is that of the colours of the rainbow – red, orange, yellow, green, blue, indigo and violet. Some people find acronyms work (shortening what has to be recalled), for example, ROYGBIV. Others have found elaboration works, for example, Richard Of York Gave Battle In Vain.

STUDY AID

Note that these strategies are memory aids, and you should make use of them for yourself. Make up acronyms to help you in your studies. Remember the Atkinson and Shiffrin model, the working memory model and the LOP model. When you make notes, write them in a shorthand that you understand. Group things into categories and draw diagrams.

If all the above strategies aid memory and prevent forgetting, it is hard to see how forgetting can be caused only by interference. Interference may be *an* explanation of forgetting, but is not likely to be *the only* explanation. We tend to assume that forgetting is one thing, because there is one word for it. Probably, however, this one word is used to cover many different types of forgetting, with different causes.

Displacement

A different explanation for forgetting in STM is **displacement**. Remember we suggested that the rehearsal loop was like a real loop of tape, which holds between five and nine items. Say it holds exactly nine items. On the tenth item, you would be overwriting the first item, and forgetting could occur.

This is a bit simplistic, but is a good way of imagining the model. You could argue that traces for the first items were starting to decay, so the traces for the later items were stronger. This would be moving back to trace decay as an explanation of forgetting. Also note that there was a

recency effect in the Glanzer and Cunitz study. Early items were safely stored in LTM and were recalled much better, so the displacement explanation only works for STM before the items have been successfully stored. Or you could argue that the later material interferes with the earlier material. This is moving back to interference as an explanation of forgetting.

Evaluation

- Displacement can be explained by either trace decay or interference, and because it is difficult to test these separately, displacement is not a very useful explanation of forgetting.

Forgetting in LTM

Cue-dependent forgetting

Cue-dependent forgetting links closely to the claim that categories in LTM aid recall. Tulving and Pearlstone's (1966) study showed that participants given the category headings on their recall sheets were able to recall more words than those who did not have such cued recall.

Tulving (1974) referred to two types of cue-dependent forgetting. If the cue is the state or condition the person was in when the learning took place and this state is absent, then there is **state-dependent forgetting**. Alternatively, the cue could be the place where the person was when learning took place. If they are in a different place cues are absent, and so **context-dependent forgetting** can occur.

Godden and Baddeley (1975) studied divers. It is important to note, from an ethical point of view, that they used people who were already divers! If the words were learnt in 15 feet of water, and were recalled in the same context, the recall was better than if the words were recalled on land. The learning was under water, and something about the context of being under water must have aided the recall.

Baddeley (1995) repeated the study, using recognition instead of recall. For example, subjects learned a list of words but, instead of having to recall them, they were asked to point out words that were on the original list amongst other words that were not. They had to recognise what they had learnt, not recall it. Activity 19 suggests a way that you can study the difference between recognition and recall and Activity 20 suggests how you can study context-dependent forgetting.

ACTIVITY 19

RECOGNITION OR RECALL?

Plan a study that compares recognition and recall. Ask all the participants to learn the same set of words. One group must recall the words on a blank sheet. The other group is given a list of words that includes all the stimulus words and some other words, and has to tick the words that were on the stimulus list.

You should find that recognition is easier than recall.

Key Skills N3.1, N3.2 and N3.3 – you can use activities like this one, where you are going to gather large data sets, as evidence for Application of Number, depending on how much you interpret and represent the data. You may only carry out all these calculations and operations for the piece you will present as coursework, but practising the skills is a very useful thing to do. See Chapter 7 for what skills are needed.

ACTIVITY 20

TEST CONTEXT-DEPENDENT FORGETTING

You need two groups of participants. Place some objects on a table. Ask the participants to study the objects and then leave the room. One group will recall the objects in the same room, the other will recall them elsewhere. Those in the same context should recall the objects better.

You could decide whether the objects should suit the context (for example, office equipment in an office) or should be randomly chosen. These sorts of decisions can make a study very interesting. If you choose to use office equipment in an office, do the participants 'recall' office equipment that was not on the table? They might use their schema, or idea of what is in an office, to help them in their recall.

Key Skill C3.1a – this activity needs quite a bit of planning, and discussing the decisions in a group would be very productive.

State-dependent forgetting could be tested by asking people to learn something when drunk, but this would not be an ethical thing for us to do. You could argue that the divers were not only in the context of underwater, but were also in the state of diving. Their emotions and feelings would be the same when diving each time, perhaps, so the Godden and Baddeley study outlined above could as much be a test of state-dependent forgetting as context dependent forgetting.

You could use this theory to suggest to your school or college that you ought to take the exam in your classroom. Make sure that you have at least been to the examination room, so that you are familiar with it.

Motivated forgetting

This approach developed from Freud's ideas, and you will learn more in Chapter 5. You might like to look at the assumptions of the psychodynamic approach before reading further.

Briefly, Freud believed that all forgetting is motivated: there is a reason why we forget. Freud claimed that we use defence mechanisms unconsciously. We don't know we are doing it; in fact we would hotly deny any such thing. Defence mechanisms are there to defend our conscious selves from knowing things we can't cope with.

One defence mechanism is repression. We simply deny all knowledge of something we don't want to know about. This repression is, for Freud, forgetting. These things are not really forgotten, just not acknowledged. The psychodynamic approach claims that problems stem from such a defence mechanism.

Levinger and Clark (1961) tried to test the existence of motivated forgetting. In free association, where participants respond to words fed to them, emotionally charged words took longer to respond to, and also gave more arousal as measured by galvanic skin response (GSR). GSR is a measure of skin resistance, and is a way of assessing stress. Then participants were given the words again and asked to recall the associations they had given. They did worse when remembering the 'emotional' words, which is what Freud would have predicted. This is **motivated forgetting**.

Evaluation

- Anderson (1995) points out that traumatic experiences disturb our memories; this is well known.

- However, it is difficult to prove the existence of repressed memories. Parkin et al (1982) looked at Levinger and Clark's study and carried out a similar one. This time they delayed the recall of the words and the associations. When recall was delayed, participants had no more trouble in remembering the associations for the 'emotional' words. Higher levels of arousal prevent recall if recall is immediate but seem to improve recall if recall is delayed. This is an interesting finding, and means there must be more than repression at work. Arousal is a physical state. Stress is a biological thing – part of our nervous system is activated in preparation for action. If this readiness continues for too long without the body being 'stood down', stress occurs. Arousal, not motivation, may cause the forgetting. Findings from one study can thus be interpreted in different ways.

One of the contemporary issues described later in this chapter concerns false memories, and links to this discussion on repressed memory and motivated forgetting.

Amnesia

Amnesia is usually taken to mean forgetting because of brain damage. The case studies of H.M. and Clive Wearing have already introduced you to forms of amnesia.

Repression is said to be a part of some types of amnesia, for example, multiple personality disorder. In multiple personality disorder, which is very, very rare (in fact some say there is no such thing), a person moves from one personality to another, and often the one in control forgets the existence of the others. There is usually one personality who does know about the others. Multiple personality disorder is not accepted by everyone, but there are some famous cases. One case, written about by Flora Rita Schreiber, concerns a young woman called Sybil. A film has been made about her story – rent the video and watch it.

Also there is event-specific amnesia, when people forget what happens in a particular time span, perhaps during a violent crime where they are involved. Motivated forgetting could explain this.

Studies within cognitive psychology

Two studies are presented here in detail. However, you have sufficient detail in many of the others to use them as examples.

Craik and Lockhart (1972) – levels of processing

The LOP model of memory has already been outlined. Craik and Lockart's study is a review that outlines the model in more detail. Recall the short-term and long-term stores. The Atkinson and Shiffrin (1968) multi-store model is the model that most research has been based on and

itself came from ideas of researchers such as James, who in 1890 distinguished between primary and secondary memory. So there is a long tradition of studying memory by means of these stores.

Craik and Lockhart claim that the LOP approach was the first challenge to the multi-store model. The LOP model starts with the idea of information processing and sees memory as a by-product of that processing, rather than something in itself. According to the LOP approach, it is not rehearsal that is important in allowing information through into long-term memory. It is what is done during rehearsal that is important.

In favour of the multi-store model

Broadbent (1958) and others have used the concept of stores in explaining perceptual processes, and others have used similar ideas when explaining the processes of memory. The idea of there being a sensory memory, then a short-term store and then a long-term store, is widely accepted. Information can enter the 'system' via the sensory memory, whether the individual is attending to it or not.

The short-term store lasts a maximum of 30 seconds, is mainly acoustic in coding, has a limit of seven plus or minus two items. The long-term store lasts indefinitely, uses meaning in storage quite a lot, and receives information that has been rehearsed in the short-term store.

The case against the multi-store model

There have been arguments against this idea of a clear information flow. Craik and Lockhart point out that the exact capacity of the short-term store is far from clear. The multi-store model is based on a computer analogy, and it is not clear if the actual capacity of the short-term store or the speed at which operations can be performed is limited. The capacity is not clear.

The capacity of the short-term store is usually taken to be between five and nine items; however, when the words form a sentence, participants can remember far more words than nine. Even the idea of chunking to explain this extended capacity does not help, because chunking must allow for semantic analysis, and that is not usually attributed to the short-term store. To encode the chunks, you need to note the meaning. The multi-store model does not explain how this is done.

There is also an argument that coding cannot always be acoustic or articulatory in the short-term store – not everything that goes into the short-term store can be encoded by sound or speech. Some meaning is encoded, and sometimes visual material must be encoded. Craik and Lockhart prefer to look at the level of the processing of the information, rather than the coding that is used in a short-term store.

Levels of processing

Craik and Lockhart discuss selective attention models (these were briefly outlined much earlier). Firstly, sense data is analysed to perceive information 'coming in' to the brain. Then, meaning is looked for and past experience used in interpreting the information. This idea of there being some basic analysis of the information in terms of lines, angles, brightness and so on, and then some 'higher' analysis, matching the information to past experience, is sometimes called **depth of processing**. The greater the depth, the more the cognitive analysis. Once the information has been analysed briefly further analysis can take place.

One of the results of this analysis is that there is a memory trace. Craik and Lockhart claim that the length of the trace depends on the depth of analysis. The deeper the level of analysis, the more long lasting the trace. If the analysis has been deep enough, it is worth us storing the trace, because we may need it, having extracted its meaning. If the trace is superficial, with little analysis, then we may not need to store it.

Anything that is familiar or meaningful must match existing cognitive structures. When something is processed to a deeper level (matches), it is retained (remembered). The amount of attention given to the input, how far it matches previous inputs and the processing time all affect how well the material is retained (remembered).

Craik and Lockhart look at perceptual processing. Information comes in and is processed. This processing starts with sensory analysis (the features of the input), then moves on to pattern recognition (matching with previous experiences) and goes on to stimulus elaboration (finding more about it by continued processing). They don't think of these as three stages, but rather as a continuous process. Memory is the same thing: some memories are involved in the sensory analysis; others are involved in the pattern recognition; yet others are involved in stimulus elaboration. Memory is also involved in another process, which is when we recycle items, keeping them in our consciousness.

Craik and Lockhart accept that the processor is of limited capacity, and that we can't do everything. At a superficial level the processor can handle a certain amount of information. As the level of processing deepens, the processor makes use of previous knowledge and rules, and can operate more efficiently, allowing more

information to be retained. Some items like words are particularly easy to remember because they are very familiar. Other items, such as pictures, can be very difficult to process (and so are less well recalled).

There is an acceptance that continual repetition in some sort of short-term store will help to keep the material in consciousness, but it will not improve retention of the material unless it is more deeply processed (by adding meaning and linking to experience).

Incidental learning

Craik and Lockhart then address the issue of incidental learning. If memory relies on deep processing, how could we learn material 'by accident'? They explain this by saying that people can use good strategies for encoding information, even if it is not deliberate. Similarly, they can use poor strategies even when they are deliberately trying to encode information. So sometimes incidental (not deliberate) learning is more effective than deliberate learning.

Tresselt and Mayzner (1960) performed a study using three types of task. In the first, participants crossed out vowels, in the second they copied the words and in the third task they had to judge if the word was an instance of the concept 'economic' (this is the sort of task you could do for coursework.) If the participant does not know they will be tested (incidental learning) they can do as well in the deep processing task (involving the meaning of the words) as they can if they try to learn the words, knowing they will be tested.

Craik and Lockhart conclude that memory performance has to do with the level of processing needed for the task, although the way the memory is tested is also important. Recognition, for example, is better than recall.

Returning to the multi-store model

The studies that show that STM involves acoustic coding do so only because that is the coding useful for that task. Some studies look at the last words in a list, and try to show that the type of coding (or level of processing) used decides whether these words are recalled or not. It is not the case that the first words are in LTM, so well coded, and the last words are in STM, so still available from the rehearsal loop – it is just that the first words are likely to have been deeply processed, whereas often the last words have not been deeply processed (this would also make an interesting study). This goes against the idea of the serial position curve, where the first and last words are best recalled. The idea of the serial position curve is supposed to be evidence for the multi-store model but Craik and Lockhart claim that the last words are *not* always well recalled.

They also look at rehearsal – the fact that items that are rehearsed are better recalled is also taken as evidence for the multi-store model. However, Craik and Lockhart claim that recall depends on the type of rehearsal. If the rehearsal just involves verbal repetition, the items are not better recalled: it is only if repetition involves deeper processing that recall is better.

Conclusion

The important parts of processing are the sensory input, the pattern recognition and analysis of meaning by linking to past experiences. Memory happens because of these processes. The more the information is processed, the more likely the trace is to be retained. Deeper analysis involves more study time, and more effort. The aim of the review here is to try to focus attention away from the multi-store model and towards a different interpretation.

Evaluation

- The LOP approach has been called a theory – and indeed is presented as such earlier in this chapter. However, it is really an approach rather than a theory. It is a different way of interpreting the data from studies. One problem is that it is hard to find tasks where we look at words and do not note the meaning. Although some experiments try to give participants tasks where they don't look at meaning (for example, crossing out the vowels), it has been shown by other studies that you can't help but look at meaning. An example is the Stroop effect. A list of colour words written in the correct colour of ink is given to participants, who have to call out the colour of the ink the word is written in. They are timed doing this. In another condition, they have a list of the same words, but written in the 'wrong' colour ink (for example, the word 'red' is written in blue ink). The participants have to call out the colour of the ink again, and again are timed (you could try this; it is an interesting study). It takes longer to call out the colour of the 'wrong' words (for instance, you say green because the ink is green, but the word is 'blue'). This is explained by saying that the reading of the word is automatic. Even when you don't want to, you read it. You are looking at the ink colour, but can't help reading the word. This effect can be used to criticise the levels of processing theory. Clearly, you can't help but attend to meaning.

- Another problem with the LOP approach is how you measure depth of processing separate from time and effort. We can only really measure deep processing by saying how many words are recalled, and this is a circular argument. Parkin (1993) discusses criticisms of the LOP approach, and points out that deep processing could simply be longer processing. So a study was carried out where one task involved analysis of meaning. A second task took longer, but did not involve analysis of meaning.

If better processing was simply 'longer on task' then the longer task should lead to better recall, even if there was no analysis of meaning. This would go against the LOP approach. The findings were that the shorter task that needed meaningful analysis led to better recall. So the study supported the idea that it was depth of processing that was important and not time on task.

- Some of the studies that have been done, and have used different tasks, have been queried because it is not clear how to measure depth of processing. Hyde and Jenkins (1973) used five different tasks. Participants had to (a) rate words for pleasantness (needs meaning), (b) estimate how often the words appear in English (needs meaning), (c) find the number of 'e' and 'g' letters in the words, (d) decide if the words were nouns, adjectives and so on and (e) decide if the word fitted into a sentence. The participants recalled more in conditions (a) and (b), where meaning was needed. However, others have claimed that the fifth condition also needed an analysis of meaning, so this study has been criticised. You can see how difficult it is to define 'depth of processing'.

- The LOP approach only really describes the processes. There is no explanation of what is happening.

Bouton et al (1999) – context-dependent forgetting – a modern research approach

Forgetting may happen for a number of different reasons. This study starts by reviewing some of these explanations. The memory trace can decay over time, or there can be interference. This particular study focuses on retrieval failure. It is not that the material is not available in a store; it is not accessed by the individual. He or she fails to retrieve the memory.

Usually retrieval is best when the circumstances for recalling the information are similar to those when it was encoded. Recall the discussions on context-dependent and state-dependent forgetting (people forget more when in a different context to when learning took place, and they forget more when in a different state). Even time can change the context, and so retrieving the memory becomes more difficult as time passes. In this study the idea of time changing the context is called the **context-change account of forgetting**.

Bouton (1991, 1993) has done some work on conditioning and memory. Here is a brief example – conditioning a dog to salivate (drool) when a bell is rung. Normally, dogs salivate when food is presented. Now ring a bell a few times when the food is presented. In a short while the dog will salivate at the sound of the bell. To extinguish this response, bring the food in a few times without the bell. Bouton points out that this is not unlearning – the dog stops drooling to the sound of the bell, but change the context, and the conditioned response returns. The behaviour appears to be extinguished, but it is just that the context has changed (the bell has been removed). So extinction depends on the physical context for retrieval.

Bouton et al are saying that it is not that we forget things, but that we don't recall them because the context is wrong. They also suggest that the passage of time can be a change in context in itself. Extinction could mean forgetting over time, as well as being due to the change in physical context. This is the context-change account of forgetting.

Another concept from the learning approach is then used. **Generalisation** is when, using the above example, the dog salivates to different tones of bell. In the example, the dog was conditioned to salivate to a bell by pairing the bell with the food (to which the dog naturally salivates). If the dog generalises, it will salivate to different bells, not just the one presented. It has been claimed that generalisation takes place over time in both non-human animals and humans. It is generally accepted that the more the stimulus presented differs from the original, the less likely we are to generalise to it. In other words, the dog might salivate to bells with similar tones, but the less the sound is like a bell, the less the dog will salivate.

As time goes by, it is more likely that generalisation will occur to a stimulus that is less like the original one. One recent study in this area has been carried out by Estes (1997), who suggests that items in memory are in arrays with features and attributes (arrays are used a lot in computer programming, so this is an interesting analogy). Over time the features and attributes blur and this could cause increased generalisation. It is as if the original stimulus is being forgotten over time, and something like it can trigger the response.

The context-forgetting paradox

Two contradictory claims have been made above.
1 We need context to help retrieve memories, and lack of context is one reason for forgetting. Time is part of the context.
2 There is more and more generalisation over time, so the specific stimulus should not be needed – something like it should do.

These two things are contradictory, because one says that you need specific context for recall and the other that you use more and more general context (or stimuli) for displaying the behaviour. When claims are contradictory it is said that there is a **paradox** – both things cannot be true.

Responding to the paradox

Responding to this paradox is what this study is all about.

Bouton et al look at the idea of generalisation to see if it does mean that the context-change account must be wrong.

Firstly, they say that forgetting will occur in any case, so response to the stimulus will start to decrease in any case. (In the evaluation we need to examine this claim. You could argue that not all remembering is to do with conditioning, and you could argue that classical conditioning leads to a more permanent change. Otherwise we would 'forget' things like phobias, and I am not sure if this is true or not.) There is no problem in using the idea of conditioning to explain forgetting. It makes sense to say that the context changes. Responding less to the stimulus means forgetting.

Secondly, they suggest that memory would increase over time, if stimulus generalisation occurs. In other words, more stimuli would trigger the response so you would remember more often. Bouton et al argue that the context-change account says that forgetting occurs because of changes in background context (including time), whereas generalisation means responding to things different from, but like the original stimulus – but things that are in the foreground. Most studies of generalisation involve foreground stimuli, whereas most studies that say that context acts as a cue for remembering are talking about background context.

Information about generalising over time

Thomas and Lopez (1962) trained pigeons to peck at a key that was lit with a certain colour of light. When the light colour is systematically changed, the pigeons stop performing as the colour gets less like the original. This generalising happened over one day, but did not change with time. What generalising to different colours there was stayed the same, whether the time delay was one day or more than one day. (In evaluation we must look at whether a failure to generalise is the same thing as forgetting.)

Another study had a different result. Shocks were paired with a certain tone and then, even after years, the specific tones were quite well remembered. In other words, not much generalising took place (Hoffman et al, 1966). (In evaluation you can say that a difference was that the pigeons in the Thomas and Lopez study were rewarded for pecking when the coloured light was on, whereas the pigeons in Hoffman's study were punished when a certain tone was heard. Perhaps the punishment formed a stronger connection, so generalisation did not take place.)

The important point is that, if generalisation continues over time, context cannot be a factor in forgetting. Change of context would not affect recall, because generalising from specific stimuli to more general examples of such stimuli would be taking place. There should be *more* remembering, in fact.

Perkins and Weyant (1958) studied rats that were trained to run for food down a runway. Half had a black runway and a black food box, and the other half had a white runway and a white food box. The start box was always grey. The rats were tested – some after 60 seconds, and some after one week – either in the same colour of runway as the learning took place in or in a different coloured runway. When the testing was at 60 seconds, the change of colour slowed the rat down. However, when the testing was at one week, the change of colour did not slow the rat down. The rats seem to have generalised more (to the different colour runway, or different context) after one week.

Tests with human participants

McAllister et al (1965) showed students a 50 mm line on a piece of cardboard. After 30 seconds or 8 minutes subjects were shown lines of 50, 54, 58 or 64 mm and had to judge if the new line was longer than the first line. The judgement worsened with length of delay. This suggests that forgetting is affected by time delay.

Bahrick et al (1967) showed students 16 line drawings of common objects one, three, nine or eighteen times (to different groups). Students then had to pick out an item (one of the 16) within other similar items not in the original 16. The participants had 8 seconds to pick the correct drawing. The drawings were very similar – for example, a row of cups of slightly different sizes and markings – and students had to pick the one they saw. Some were tested immediately, some after 2 hours, some after 2 days and some after 2 weeks. Performance decreased over time. There was little difference in the success of the participants to choose the 'right' picture regardless of the number of times they were shown the picture: ability to pick out the picture declined over time in more or less the same pattern. Therefore, it seems to be time that causes the decrease in remembering, rather than training time.

One point in evaluation is that these studies all have slightly different methods. Some use an independent groups design, and some use a repeated measures design. Some use non-human animals and some use humans. Therefore, it is hard to draw strong conclusions. This field of testing forgetting by looking at conditioning is an interesting one.

Conclusion – generalisation and the context-change account

Bouton et al go into a lot more detail about changes in context. Even though there is generalisation over time and responding occurs in different contexts due to generalisation, there is a paradox. If context is needed as a cue to remembering, then it must be specific; yet remembering occurs more (at least responding to a stimulus occurs more) due to generalisation, and occurs more over time and with changes in context. So there is more remembering within a specific context, and more remembering with a more general context.

Bouton et al do look more closely at the paradox. However, their studies are more detailed that we can go into in this chapter. There is insufficient room for all the evidence here, and in any case their resolution of the paradox is only partial. At least you have had the opportunity to explore an area of research in forgetting that is being studied at the moment. This was a useful study to choose, as it links two main approaches – the cognitive and the learning approaches (this helps you to see that psychology is not just one approach). Once you have finished the AS part of the course you will be in a much better position to see how the approaches fit together, and can move on to apply psychology in the A2 part of the course.

I have not outlined the whole of Bouton et al's account. It is more like a meta-analysis of many different studies. I have picked some out for you, to give you a flavour of their views. I have also picked out some points in evaluation of their points about context-change forgetting, and their defence of such an explanation of forgetting.

Evaluation

- **Animal studies** – Much of the research Bouton et al look at when defending the context-change account of forgetting is done with non-human animals and they generalise their findings to humans. From a method point of view a lot can be learnt from the study of non-human animals; however, you can always argue that humans are not like non-human animals (different non-human animals are not the same as each other either). They do use research with humans to try to link the findings from the two different areas but the work with non-human animals is in the area of conditioning and the work with humans is in the area of memory (of different line drawings and so on), so you could say these are different 'cognitive' skills.

- **The learning approach and the cognitive approach** – You may have started with this first chapter, in which case you have not yet studied the learning approach, which is outlined in Chapter 4. However, you have read about the assumptions of the cognitive approach, and how interest is in brain processing. The assumptions of the learning approach include that measurable external behaviour is examined, without much reference to brain processes. Here Bouton et al are taking studies from the learning approach, looking at conditioning, and then linking it to memory. The argument seems to assume that all learning is by conditioning, and this includes concepts within the learning approach such as generalisation. The evidence is about behaviour that is conditioned via stimuli, whereas you could argue that not all memory is about such behaviour. We don't just remember actions like salivation or responding to stimuli.

- **Is a failure to generalise the same as forgetting?** If a pigeon generalises only a bit from the colour it is supposed to be pecking, does this mean that as it generalises to other colours it is forgetting the 'right' one? Maybe it is hopeful that pecking at a similar colour will still give the reward? Perhaps the pigeons cannot see the difference between all the shades of colour (although other studies do suggest that they can).

- **Methodology** – The experimental method is being used in all the studies mentioned and could be said to be not valid. The studies outlined involve artificial tasks, and you should ask whether they represent 'memory' or 'forgetting'. Also you have read about other explanations for forgetting, including Freud's idea of repression. The studies cited here seem to be assuming that there could be one explanation for forgetting (lack of retrieval cue because different context), rather than many. You can criticise this view by mentioning other 'sorts' of forgetting.

Key application – eyewitness testimony

Reconstructive memory

This section aims to apply a theory within cognitive psychology to a real life situation. The chosen situation is that of being a witness to something.

ACTIVITY 21

ARE YOU A GOOD WITNESS? ARE OTHER PEOPLE GOOD WITNESSES?

Do some investigating of your own. Firstly, think about something that happened to you earlier in the day, or yesterday. Pick an incident when you were outside, with people you don't know. Perhaps you went shopping, or rode to school or college in a bus.

Can you describe other people on the bus? Can you even describe whom you were sitting by (if not a friend)? If you were shopping, could you describe people you passed? Could you describe one of the shop assistants who served you?

You could do some investigations in this area. Do you think some people are better witnesses than others? If so, it would be interesting to find out why.

Key Skill C3.1a – as with many of the activities in this chapter, this would benefit from group discussion. You could pool ideas, go out to gather information separately, and then return to discuss findings.

To understand why it is claimed that people are not accurate witnesses, you need to think back to the discussion about bottom-up processing (information comes from the senses) and top-down processing (we interpret what we perceive using previous knowledge and experience) earlier in the chapter.

What we see, hear, touch, taste and smell seems to come directly from the outside world. However, it was suggested earlier that this is not as 'direct' as it seems. We bring our own representations of the world, and we have **schemata** or ideas of what happens and what goes with what. Activity 22 should show you the importance of schemata.

ACTIVITY 22

THE IMPORTANCE OF KNOWING THE SCRIPT

Read the following passages.

Passage 1:
When Mary arrived at the restaurant, the woman at the door greeted her and checked for her name. A few minutes later, Mary was escorted to her chair and was shown the day's menu. The attendant was helpful but brusque, almost to the point of being rude. However, her meal was excellent, especially the main course. Later she paid the woman at the door and left.

Passage 2:
The procedure is really quite simple. First you arrange items into different groups. Of course, one pile may be sufficient depending on how

much there is to do. If you have to go somewhere else due to lack of facilities that is the next step, otherwise you are pretty well set. It is important not to overdo things. That is, it is better to do too few things at once than too many. In the short run this may not seem important but complications can easily arise. A mistake can be expensive as well … After the procedure is completed, one arranges the materials into different groups again. Then they can be put into their appropriate places. Eventually they will be used once more and the whole cycle will then have to be repeated (Bransford, 1979).

Did you find one easier to understand than the other?

Most people find the story about the restaurant much easier to read and to understand. This is because you have a script or a schema for a restaurant. When you are reading the passage, you use all your previous knowledge and your expectations of what happens in restaurants, and you probably even visualised the scene and the people.

However, there was no script for the second passage. Read the second passage again, but this time I will tell you that it is about washing clothes. It should make much more sense for you now. Introspect a little (remember, introspection was an early method used by psychologists to find out about thinking). Think about what you were thinking about when reading the passage. Did you actually visualise the separate piles of washing and perhaps even the washing machine in your own home?

We use scripts and schemas when interpreting information about the world.

Bartlett (1932) discussed reconstructive memory. Memories are not pure representations of what we encode, but are reconstructed taking into account schemata and scripts. As we encode information we seem to sort it and make sense of it. Bartlett claims that we make sense of it when we recall it. He used a story called

The War of the Ghosts in his studies. Box 11 gives the story in case you want to use it for coursework.

Box 11

The War of the Ghosts

You could use this story to carry out a study of your own. Read it through carefully.

One day two young men from Egulac went down to the river to hunt seals and while they were there it became foggy and calm. Then they heard war-cries and they thought: 'Maybe this is a war party'. They escaped to the shore and hid behind a log. Now canoes came up and they heard the noise of paddles and saw one canoe coming up to them. There were five men in the canoe and they said: 'What do you think? We wish to take you along. We are going up the river to make war on the people'. One of the young men said 'I have no arrows'. 'Arrows are in the canoe', they said. 'I will not go along. I might be killed. My relatives do not know where I have gone. But you', he said, turning to the other, 'may go with them.' So one of the young men went but the other returned home. And the warriors went on up the river to a town on the other side of Kalama. The people came down to the water and they began to fight and many were killed. But presently the young man heard one of the warriors say: 'Quick, let us go home; that Indian has been hit'. Now he thought: 'Oh, they are ghosts'. He did not feel sick but they said he had been shot. So the canoes went back to Egulac and the young man went ashore to his house and made a fire. And he told everybody and said: 'Behold I accompanied the ghosts and we went to fight. Many of our fellows were killed and many of those who attacked us were killed. They said I was hit and I did not feel sick.' He told it all and then he became quiet. When the sun rose he fell down. Something black came out of his mouth. His face became contorted. The people jumped up and cried. He was dead.

Now take a blank piece of paper and write down what you remember about the story. Compare what you recall with what Bartlett and others have found (Hunter, 1964).

Bartlett asked people to recall the story. He used a technique called serial reproduction, where one person tells the story to another, who then passes on to the next person. This is a bit like the game 'Chinese whispers'.

ACTIVITY 23

CHINESE WHISPERS CAN SHOW YOU RECONSTRUCTION IN ACTION

With a group of people, play Chinese whispers. Start off with a sentence that involves items and numbers, as this works best. Write down what you start with, and then what you finish with. You might be able to trace back the changes, and learn something about the reconstructive nature of memory. Someone will have misheard, and will substitute something that not only sounds similar but also makes a sort of sense. Usually the final sentence has little to link it to the original one, but in its own way it will make sense. There will usually be a proper sentence, in any case.

Key Skill C3.1a – this activity would make a good group discussion, after the task has been completed. The group can discuss the findings and relate them to the theory.

Hunter (1964) repeated Bartlett's work and found similar results. The story gets shorter, details are omitted, but starts to make more sense. The story Bartlett chose is deliberately not very clear for people from our culture, and participants interpret it so that it makes sense to them. People tend to make it more conventional too – for example, they say that he died at sunset, which seems more logical.

Bartlett refers to **efforts after meaning** to explain the idea of reconstructing our memories to make them make sense.

The effect of culture on memory

Not only do we reconstruct our memories to make more sense but our culture affects our memory. In the next chapter you will look at social representation theory. This expands on the idea that our perceptions of the world, and of people, are guided by our culture and society.

Bartlett emphasised how we use our experiences and schemata when reconstructing our memories (you could understand the restaurant story in Activity 22, but the one without a script was difficult). You can imagine that in a different culture, where customs are strange, you would often have difficulty in understanding, because you would be lacking a script.

Box 12

Cross-cultural studies as a method

Cross-cultural studies are useful in psychology, because we can look at other cultures to find out how much of human behaviour is innate, and how much is learnt. If something occurs in all cultures, then we could suggest that it is in our human nature (smiling is an example). However, if behaviour differs in different cultures, we could suggest that it is a learned behaviour. If you do the A2 part of the course, you may learn that child-rearing patterns differ in different cultures, so probably child raising is a learned behaviour.

Evaluation of using cross-cultural studies

- The problem with cross-cultural studies is that the researcher usually comes from one culture and visits another. If this researcher does not understand the language they need an interpreter, and have to rely on the interpreter's 'interpretation' of what is going on. Also, even if the researcher understands the language, he or she may not understand what is going on in. You can understand words, but you need the cultural setting in order to understand fully.

- For example, in some cultures babies are kept indoors for a very long time, and we might consider that a poor way of stimulating a young child. However, in that culture there may be good reasons for such behaviour – perhaps to protect the child from illness.

- You could argue that if you are doing a cross-cultural study you need to be completely comfortable in both cultures before you can really understand all the subtleties of the behaviour being observed. Remember to give these sorts of criticisms when commenting on studies in psychology. Whenever there is a cross-cultural study, question the fact that the observations might be reconstructed according to the researcher's ideas, and so the data might be biased.

Mistry and Rogoff (1994) point out the importance of culture when a person is remembering. For *The War of the Ghosts*, people tend to think the person died at sunset, because that fits what we recognise as usual. Swazi cattlemen recall their cattle individually, but the ownership and care of cattle is very important to them, so they are likely to pay attention to cattle as individuals. So in a story about cattle, Swazi cattlemen might pay more attention to detail than we would. Try comparing sub-cultures to look for differences in their memories.

ACTIVITY 24

COMPARE SUB-CULTURES AND LOOK FOR MEMORY DIFFERENCES

You could try your own example of comparing memories in different cultures. You might find it hard to get participants, but think of sub-cultures. Find participants who are very interested in some particular topic, perhaps a form of popular music, and some who have no such interest. You should find that, given a story about their special interest, people will recall fine detail, but those without the special interest might recall fewer details.

Key Skill C3.1a – after doing this study you could compare notes in groups and discuss findings. Alternatively, you could plan the study by group discussion and split the task up to be more efficient. In either case group discussion would be useful for this activity.

ACTIVITY 25

TEST THE EFFECT OF LEADING QUESTIONS

Do an experiment similar to the one described above (avoid showing too worrying a film clip, however, and remember ethical issues – participants could have just had a car accident themselves, so choose a different subject). You could choose any film clip, and ask questions about any of the details. Change one word to make the questions slightly different and see what effect this change has on recall.

For example, show a clip of some action, perhaps someone buying something in a shop. Then ask 'Did you see a bicycle?' or 'Did you see the bicycle?' – if this seems a reasonable question (and if there is no bicycle in the clip).

Key Skill C3.1a – group discussion would be useful when planning this study.

Eyewitness testimony

Elizabeth Loftus has carried out a lot of research in the area of eyewitness testimony and argues that it is unreliable. She uses the idea that memories are reconstructed. Loftus and Zanni (1975) showed participants a film of a car accident. They then asked half of the participants 'Did you see a broken headlight?' and the other half 'Did you see the broken headlight?' This was the only difference in the conditions. There was no broken headlight in the film but 15% of participants asked about 'the' broken headlight said there was (only 7% of those asked about 'a' broken headlight said there was). The word 'the' implied that there had been one, and this small difference swayed some of the participants into believing what had not been there.

Loftus and Palmer (1974) did a similar study. They asked, after showing a film about an accident, 'About how fast were the cars going when they hit?' and 'About how fast were the cars going when they smashed?' The word 'smashed' suggested going faster and having greater impact, and produced an estimate of a faster speed than the word 'hit'. Activity 25 suggests a way of testing the effect of leading questions.

Evaluation

- If the misinformation is *obviously* not correct (perhaps if you asked 'Did you see the elephant?' in the activity), then the participant will not be deceived. People are more likely to be misled if the information was not central at the time, and if there is a delay before recall.

- Note as well that these studies are experiments. Experiments can be criticised for lack of validity. If a study is valid, this means it is measuring what it claims to measure. The above tasks are artificial, so there is doubt about whether they measure 'real life' eyewitness memory or not.

The cognitive interview

The police use information learnt through such studies as the one above in a technique called the **cognitive interview**. This involves taking the witness back, either in reality or in their minds, to the situation they were in at the time of the incident. You will be familiar with reconstructions of crimes. These are intended to jog people's memories.

If you are asked directly about what you recall, leading questions are likely to be involved. However, if you are allowed to recall in your own time, your recall should be more accurate. You could be taken back to the actual place or you could be asked to retrace your day, which also works. Usually you would be asked to start remembering before the incident. Then the scene is set. Then you could be asked to go over exactly what happened, using your own words. This is a safer form of recall, although you will probably still reconstruct the scene to make it make sense.

Contemporary issue: the accuracy of recovered memories

There have been many examples of adults remembering sexual abuse as children, and accusing their parents of such abuse. Psychotherapy involves encouraging people to reflect on their childhood experiences. Freud believed that the groundwork for a person's personality takes place between the ages of 0 and 5 years, which is the important time when **fixation** may occur (see Chapter 5). Fixation is when someone does not pass successfully through a stage of psychosexual development, and energy is used in defending their conscious thoughts from knowing about problems in those early stages.

Repression of memories is an explanation for forgetting. Psychoanalysts allow a safe place and a listener, and the person feels able to go back to those early years to look for possible problems. If there were such problems, and if they were severe enough to have been repressed, then this repression could be causing problems for the adult. The task of the analyst is to free the memories. Once they are conscious they can be dealt with, whereas when they are unconscious they cannot be faced. So when people remember child sexual abuse the analyst is not surprised, because this is the sort of trauma that is likely to be repressed and forgotten.

However, accused parents have sued therapists and hospitals. Some of those who accused their parents of child sexual abuse have since withdrawn their allegations, and they too have sued. In 1994, Gary Ramona received damages because it was concluded that therapists had planted the idea of sexual abuse in his daughter's mind. In 1992 The False Memory Syndrome Foundation was set up in the USA, and one in Britain followed in 1993. The British Psychological Society reported on false memory syndrome in 1995. One important point is that if child sexual abuse happened before the age of four years, then it probably cannot be recalled verbally, so this is evidence for these memories being false ones.

Young children as witnesses

Early psychologists thought of children as poor witnesses (Stern, 1910; Piaget, 1928). Freud thought children fantasised certain events (Freud, 1905/1953). Goodman et al (1991) discuss judges' reluctance to accept children as witnesses, as their testimony is considered unreliable.

There is current debate about the reliability of child witness statements (Ceci et al, 1987). The questions are:
- How good are children's memories?
- How far can their memories be changed by suggestions from other people?

Children seem to remember facts quite well, but not the timing of the events. Nelson (1978) found that children answered truthfully when they had information but, when asked questions to which they did not know the answer, they used their own scripts to guess what the answer might be. When someone questioning a child says something false (maybe not deliberately), the child is likely to incorporate that detail into their 'knowledge' of the event. This new memory can block the old one.

A child may also think that adults know better. So when presented with suggestions, the child might believe that this is the true version, and will answer accordingly, perhaps to please the adult asking the questions (Siegal, 1991). Poole and White (1993) say that children are particularly open to pressures to change their memories because they have limited ability to remember, lack experience in legal situations, and want to please adults.

Linking the contemporary issue to concepts in cognitive psychology

The accuracy of recovered memories

The issue on the accuracy of recovered memories clearly links to the idea that forgetting is motivated. It does not consider other explanations of forgetting such as interference or trace decay. Cognitive psychologists concentrate on information processing and the mental processes involved. Work on recovered memories does not consider physiological issues or emotional issues such as the pressure on the individual to 'please' the therapist. Mental processes themselves are largely ignored, except for the tension between the unconscious and the conscious personality.

False memory syndrome can be explained by reference to the power of the therapist, or by thinking about what the therapist is looking for. It is probably not that the therapist is deliberately suggesting false memories, but that he or she is expecting memories of trauma such as child sexual abuse. The patient will be motivated to accept any explanation for their distress which is not their fault, perhaps, and both therapist and patient have much to gain from such a revelation (in the short term anyway).

Many of the concepts in cognitive psychology, for example the idea of information processing or the idea of thinking of the brain as a computer, are not relevant for this contemporary issue. The work on memory is, however, relevant.

Freud was himself a doctor. He was interested in helping others, in particular those who were mentally ill. He listened to them, and heard a great deal about their childhood and their problems. His case studies seemed to show that adult problems do often stem from childhood problems. It is thought by some that those he studied did experience child sexual abuse. Freud did not accept that this could be true – he could not accept it. Therefore, he thought that the young child had sexual fantasies (you will read more about this in Chapter 5). Perhaps he was not hearing about fantasies, but about real abuse?

Those who experience false memories in therapy suffer tremendously because of it, and so do their families. However, it would be a mistake to think that all adult claims of child sexual abuse are false. Those who claim to have recovered false memories in therapy are people who have never mentioned child sexual abuse, and have never thought of it (this is the whole point: the memory is repressed). These are not all those who claim to have been sexually abused as a child, and it is very important to note the difference.

Children as witnesses

When considering the accuracy of recovered memories, and looking at children as witnesses, there are clear links to the work of people like Loftus on eyewitness testimony. Also Bartlett's idea of reconstructive memories is clearly relevant. It is said, for example, that when children can't remember the answer to a question, they draw on scripts they know about. This links to the idea of the development of schemata or scripts from our experiences, which we then use when needed to make sense of the world. Children are shown to be suggestible to ideas from adults. Just as the participants in one of the studies were more likely to remember if the word 'the' was used instead of 'a', so children can be 'guided' in their memories by the words used in the questions.

Coursework suggestions

1 Broadbent's split-span procedure showing an ear-by-ear preference when recalling numbers (Activity 5, p. 9).

2 Gray and Wedderburn's modification of Broadbent's study (Activity 6, p. 9).
3 Sperling's experiment to test sensory memory (Box 7, p. 12).
4 Chunking experiments, to see if chunking does improve recall in STM (Activity 9, p. 14).
5 The Brown–Peterson technique to block rehearsal (Activity 10, p. 15).
6 A serial position task, using the work of Glanzer and Cunitz (Activity 14, p. 17).
7 A study looking into levels of processing (Activity 16, p. 19).
8 A study based on the idea that categories aid recall (Activity 12, p. 16).
9 Test whether recognition is better than recall (Activity 19, p. 23).
10 Try to find context-dependent forgetting (Activity 20, p. 23).
11 Tell *The War of the Ghosts* to a group of people, and then ask them to recall it a few times over a few weeks. Note how the story changes over time (Box 11, p. 30).
12 Look at the Tresselt and Mayzner (1960) study outlined briefly in the study by Craik and Lockhart (1972). You could do a similar task. Participants are in three groups with the same list of words: one group crosses out the vowels; one group copies out the words; a third group has to decide if the word has to do with 'economic'. The three tasks involve different levels of processing. The deeper the level of processing, the better the recall should be.
13 Write your own story with details about a special topic. Find participants who share interest in this special topic and compare their recall with those who are not interested (Activity 24, p. 32).
14 A study around eyewitness testimony and leading questions, based on Loftus's work (Activity 25, p. 32).

Suggested further reading

Blakemore, C. & Greenfield, S. (1988) *Mindwaves*. Oxford: Basil Blackwell.

Eysenck, M. (1996) *Simply Psychology*. Hove: Psychology Press.

Gross, R.D. (1998) *Psychology, the Science of Mind and Behaviour*. London: Hodder and Stoughton.

Hardy, M. & Heyes, S. (1999) *Beginning Psychology, a Comprehensive Introduction to Psychology*, 5th edition. Oxford: Oxford University Press.

Myers, D.G (1998) *Exploring Psychology*, 5th edition. New York: Worth.

Wade, C. & Tavris, C (2000) *Psychology*, 6th Edition. New Jersey: Prentice Hall.

Weiten, W. (1995) *Themes and Variations*, 3rd edition. Pacific Grove: Brooks/Cole.

2

The social approach

The aims of this chapter

The aims of this chapter are, with regard to the social approach, to enable the reader to:

- *appreciate some of the general assumptions*
- *discuss research methods used*
- *describe and evaluate theories of obedience, in particular Milgram's work*
- *describe and evaluate theories that explain prejudice*
- *describe and evaluate some relevant studies*
- *understand research into prejudice reduction*
- *explain one contemporary issue or debate.*

Self-test 1

After reading this chapter, test yourself on each of the above points. Use the points as exam questions and make notes accordingly. Then see how much you can write on each.

This chapter covers

KEY ASSUMPTIONS
1 Individuals and groups affect our behaviour
2 Culture and society affect our behaviour

RESEARCH METHODS
1 (Field) experiments
2 Surveys
3 Discourse analysis

IN-DEPTH AREA OF STUDY: OBEDIENCE AND PREJUDICE

STUDIES IN DETAIL
1 Prisoners and guards in a simulated prison (Haney et al, 1973)
2 Group identity and intergroup prejudice (Ruttenberg et al, 1996)

KEY APPLICATION: PREJUDICE REDUCTION

CONTEMPORARY ISSUE: CROWD BEHAVIOUR

Introduction

The social approach involves examining social issues when looking at behaviour. The Introduction and Study Guide explains that social cognition involves the study of our mental processes when we are interacting with others – for example, our use of stereotyping. Any area that involves **interactions** between people is in the field of social psychology.

STUDY AID

As you are now studying a different approach, remember to start a new section in your folder, or a new folder.

Key Skill LP3.1 – agree targets and plan how these will be met, using support from appropriate others. You need your tutor for this, and you will need a record of the discussion as evidence. Discuss organising your work and develop a time plan for working through this textbook. It is tempting to leave everything to your teacher, but you should be reading the chapters as you study each approach, alongside the work your teacher gives you. Make a note of dates and what you should have achieved by then, so that you can review your progress for Key Skill LP3.3.

The historical setting

Social psychology involves looking at people as they behave towards other people. It is a relatively new field within psychology – and psychology itself is relatively new: much of the research in social psychology started in the 1950s and 1960s. Often people choose to study psychology because it looks at how people behave towards others. Examples of research include looking at relationships and friendships, attitudes, crowd behaviour and conformity, helping behaviour, leadership and many other areas. This chapter is just a small taste of what social psychologists do.

Social representation theory

Currently interest in social psychology has turned to cultural aspects of interactions between people. There is a focus now on a relatively new theory, **social representation theory**, which Box 1 outlines.

Looking for general laws

Most psychologists at the moment still look for general laws about behaviour. They think that we can use these general laws to predict behaviour and to learn about people. What follows in this chapter mainly concerns

---

> **Box 1**
>
> ### Social representation theory
>
> Some psychologists are very keen to emphasise that anything we learn about others, and ourselves, must be set within a particular culture and a particular time. We have our own ways of representing the world in our heads. Since culture and society guide representations, ways in which we represent the world are social representations. It is argued that humans can know nothing 'outside' these social representations.
>
> Hopefully, obedience means the same thing to you as it does to me. Obedience in some countries, however, means something different. It can be seen as threatening and bad, or as comforting and good. We could be freedom fighters against obedience, or we could be law enforcers in favour of obedience. Our views colour how we 'see' obedience.
>
> Social representation theory looks closely at how people make judgements and discover things about people. This means that, as in our roles as teacher and student, our representations of the world are likely to be different. Social representation theory claims that there is no such thing as knowledge that is not within a culture. Studies within social psychology should not be said to lead to a discovery of general laws, because there are no such things. Knowledge is relative, in the sense that we can only ever interpret what we know within our own social representations. Studies looking into obedience can only be interpreted within the culture they are studied in and conclusions can be claimed only about that particular culture.

research where general laws are expected. It is worth noting, however, that more and more social psychologists are accepting the claims of social representation theory, and they accept that there is no such thing as 'pure' knowledge about individuals, separated from their culture, roles, norms and customs.

Key assumptions of the social approach

Key assumption one – individuals and groups affect our behaviour

Assumptions are underlying 'facts' that are often taken for granted. The assumption that there are scientific truths to be discovered about people has recently been challenged.

Organising yourself, and managing your own time

You need to keep your notes in order. Make sure you use headings, and have somewhere for everything to go. When you do homework, either keep it in the right place in your notes or keep it carefully separately. Make notes for yourself, and keep them in an ordered format.

If you are at school or college, there may be people who can help you with your time management and organisation of folders. If you would like some advice, ask for help.

The general assumption that individuals and groups affect behaviour may seem too obvious to state. However, at some stage in the development of psychology it was recognised, and so individuals and groups became areas for study. Before that time, no one would have studied social psychology. Probably, even though this assumption is fairly obvious, none of us realise the extent to which it is true. We usually see ourselves as making our own choices and leading our own lives.

ACTIVITY 1

LEARN ABOUT YOURSELF AND THE SELF-FULFILLING PROPHECY

Note down a few things you think you are good at, and some things you think you are not so good at. Now consider how you know what you are good and/or bad at. Did someone tell you this at some stage? If you have said you are bad at maths, for example, did your teacher tell you so? Presumably you have received bad marks, and you will take this as evidence. However, before that there was probably a time when you had made no judgement about your maths abilities, or perhaps you were quite good at it?

People affect us to a very great extent, as illustrated by the study described in Box 2.

Think of how you behave with people. Are you confident, shy, interested or bored? Does it depend on the individual or group you are with at the time? The cognitive

---

Box 2

The self-fulfilling prophecy

Rosenthal and Jacobson (1968) gave a class of schoolchildren a test and scored their individual ability before the start of a new school year. At the start of the school year they told the teachers which children were about to bloom, and led the teachers to believe that this information came from the tests. The children said to be about to bloom were actually chosen at random, and this information was not guided by the test results. The teachers then taught the class for a year. At the end of that time the whole class was tested again, and the test score compared with the score gained at the start of the year.

The children who were pinpointed were those who improved the most, even though there should have been no reason for their improvement. It was concluded that they received more attention somehow. They were thought of as about to bloom, and so they bloomed.

You can link your answers in Activity 1 to Rosenthal and Jacobson's findings. Perhaps you were thought of as bad at maths (or whatever you listed) and then became bad at it due to the type of attention you received (or did not receive).

Key Skill C3.1b – contribute to a group discussion about a complex subject. Working in a small group, pool your ideas about the self-fulfilling prophecy and your own examples. Plan tasks within the group so that someone prepares a list of the group's examples, someone researches the theory from other textbooks. Give the two pieces of information to other group members, who prepare material that links the examples to the theory.

Someone must write up the work (that person could use this as evidence for IT Key Skills) and make a presentation (which can be evidence for Key Skill C3.1b) – he or she must make sure to include at least one image, which could be a diagram giving the various studies into the self-fulfilling prophecy and their findings.

If you have done the textbook research, and include an image, this could be evidence for Key Skill C3.2. Remember to note down which two (or more) extended documents were used.

psychologist might look at your mood, or the effect of your memories of past experiences. The social psychologist looks at the interactions between you and others. For example, consider helping behaviour – it is not so much whether you are a helpful person, as whether you help in given situations. Social psychologists have found that we help more often if the cost is low, or if we are on our own, for example. Activity 2 suggests a way in which you can test helping behaviour. This is a useful example of social psychology.

ACTIVITY 2

TESTING HELPING BEHAVIOUR

Try a simple field experiment. Ask people the time, or something not too time-consuming, and see if they answer you. Then ask people to do something more time-consuming – for example, to show you the way to the nearest post office. Avoid asking too many people, as you don't really want help, and it would not be ethical to put participants in the position of having to help in this way. Just try it briefly.

If you decide to do something like this for coursework, you should debrief the participants fully, and make sure the tasks are reasonable. Chapter 8 outlines ethical guidelines that you must follow.

You should find that low-cost altruism is more often offered than high-cost altruism. Altruism is helping behaviour but at some cost to the helper. Low cost means that helping is not much trouble, and high cost means it is quite a lot of trouble.

An alternative is to use a questionnaire. Ask if people would help if they came upon a car accident. You could list some possible answers, and ask participants to tick those that apply most to them. Examples of answers might be: 'I would help'; 'I would help if I had time'; 'I would help if someone was with me'; 'I would help if no one else was about'; 'I would not help'.

Studies suggest that we help if we have time, and if no one else is available. We help less if we are in a hurry or there are others about. One study you could read is that of Bierhoff and Klein (1987) who showed 'time is money'. In another study Darley and Batson (1973) *studied students going to a theology lecture on the Good Samaritan (so you'd think that they'd be tuned in to help someone in need). Some students were told they were going to be late for the talk, some were told they were on time and some were told they were ahead of schedule. They all passed someone slumped in a doorway, looking in need of help, but they did not all help. Helping depended on how much time they had. However, Brown (1986) and McGuire (1995) agreed that low-cost helping, such as giving a stranger the time, was commonly found.*

This morning I drove past an accident, whereas I usually stop. If this happens to you, note your thought processes, and see if they are about low-cost and high-cost altruism. My thought processes included 'I will miss my train', 'Others are about', 'It does not look too serious' and 'My car would be in the way anyway'. These are all excuses or reasons for not stopping.

> Key Skill N3.3 – interpret the results of your study, present your findings and justify your methods. Use one chart, one graph and one diagram. If you carried out a questionnaire like this, you could analyse your results for this Key Skill. Remember to use charts, diagrams and graphs.

A final example of how we are affected by groups is to consider crowd behaviour. Studies have shown that those in uniform behave differently. This is called being **deindividuated**. In this state you might do bad things 'out of character'. *Mississippi Burning* is a film about the scapegoating of Black people in the southern USA. Those who were lynching and torturing the Blacks were disguised in uniforms (you probably know about the Ku Klux Klan) – during the day the torturers had normal jobs, and behaved normally. This film is not very pleasant but well worth watching. One of the causes of prejudice is scapegoating in times of economic hardship, and the failure of cotton crops was just such a time (Hovland and Sears, 1940). So films like this can be of great relevance when studying psychology.

When in uniform you can do good things too. Participants in nurses' uniforms were less prepared to punish others than if they were in uniforms that were like those of the Ku Klux Klan (Zimbardo, 1969).

In any case, when you are in a crowd you might do things you would not do on your own. One reason for this is deindividuation.

Key assumption two – culture and society affect behaviour

The assumption that culture and society affect behaviour has been partly addressed by looking at social representation theory. People behave differently in different cultures.

One of the areas of social psychology that you will study in depth is that of obedience. Often psychologists start investigating an area of research following a particular study, and Milgram's obedience study is said to be the most famous in psychology. His first study into obedience was carried out at Yale University. He repeated the study in a rundown office block, and found the results were affected. In the office block he found less obedience than he found at Yale. Milgram's study is outlined in detail later in this chapter.

It did not take long for others to use Milgram's idea to do similar studies in other countries. This method of reading about a study, and then testing it, perhaps in different circumstances, is what psychologists do. It is what you will do in your coursework. Comparing studies across different cultures is called **cross-cultural** research.

If you consider that changing from the university to the office block made a difference, you can imagine that changing culture completely will also make a difference.
- Milgram (1963) used both men and women volunteers and found 65% obedience
- Both Rosenhan (1974) in the USA and Ancona and Pareyson (1968) in Italy used students and found 85% obedience
- Mantell (1971 – Germany) used men and found 85% obedience
- Kilham and Mann (1974 – Australia) found 40% obedience in men and 16% in women
- Burley and McGuiness (1977 – UK) found 50% obedience in male students
- Meeus and Raaijmakers (1986 – Holland) found 92% obedience

These results are according to Humphrey's article in *Psychology Review*. The article is worth reading in full. Most school and college libraries have copies of *Psychology Review*.

Care is required in making these cross-cultural comparisons because the studies are often carried out differently. The above studies were all about obedience, but did not exactly reproduce Milgram's procedures.

When drawing conclusions, we need to be aware that the studies were not identical. It does seem, however, that different levels of obedience are found in different countries, so you could claim that culture and society do affect our behaviour.

Social psychology assumes that our behaviour is affected by our culture at all levels. Even if no differences are found in a particular behaviour between societies, it is still likely that our social groups and cultural patterns affect us. In the example given earlier it is surely not the uniform itself that guides our behaviour, but what it symbolises. If we act differently within a crowd, it is the rule of the crowd that we are following. We learn about social roles through **socialisation** by our family, by education and by the media. We are not simply individuals acting as individuals. Social psychology assumes we are individuals **socialised** into a culture and taught rules, **roles**, **norms** and expectations. In turn we have expectations of others.

Research methods used in social psychology

For a full discussion of the various methods used in psychology, read Chapter 7. What follows uses examples to show you some of the methods used in social psychology, but does not go into great detail.

Experiments

Researchers in the field of social psychology often set up novel situations where they can isolate a particular sort of behaviour to study it. They use field experiments and laboratory experiments to do this. Sometimes they can use a naturalistic experiment, which is rather different.
- **Laboratory experiments** take place in a setting that is not natural for the participant. Milgram used Yale for this purpose. Milgram's study (outlined below) is an example of a laboratory experiment.
- **Field experiments** take place in the participant's natural setting, in other words 'out in the field'. You could argue that Milgram's study in the office block was more of a field experiment, because the setting was more natural. Hofling et al's (1966) study, which is also outlined later in this chapter, is a field experiment.
- **Naturalistic experiments** can be confused with field experiments, but they are quite different. In a field experiment the participants are still given some artificial tasks to do, such as the tests given to participants by Milgram. A naturalistic study does take place in a natural setting, but there is more to it than that. In a naturalistic experiment the researcher does not have to set the study up. Whatever is being looked at occurs naturally.

Box 3

An example of a field experiment

Piliavin et al (1969) conducted a field experiment in a New York subway. They had a lot of different **conditions**, and controlled the **variables**. They were looking at helping behaviour. They had someone who was 'drunk' and needed help, someone who was 'lame', and someone with a 'facial scar', and used Black actors as well as White ones. They wanted to know how helping behaviour would be affected by all these different conditions.

They found that more help was given to the lame person than the drunk person, for example.

This was an experiment because the researchers controlled the situation, and carefully set up the conditions. It was a field experiment, however, because they went to a natural setting – the subway.

ACTIVITY 3

TRY LOOKING AT HELPING BEHAVIOUR

You could see if someone helps you if you set up a situation where you need help. However, remember ethics (see Chapter 8): you could get yourself (or others) into difficulty if you are not careful. There is a story of students who pretended to snatch a female student's bag (she was in on it), and she was helped to such an extent that her helpers attacked the 'snatchers'.

However, you could perhaps drop a file or two to see who helps. You could see if there are differences in helping depending on the sex of the person needing help. Remember to pick up any paper afterwards, and to thank any helpers.

Key Skill PS3.1 – plan an activity with others, agreeing objectives, responsibilities and working arrangements. You need to work as a group if you do try this sort of field study, because you need someone to watch who helps you, and to record the data. Also, if the class attempt this on the same day, you need to plan where you are going so that the groups do not overlap. This planning and the results of the study can be evidence for key skills.

Box 4

A naturalistic experiment

Naturalistic experiments are quite rare because you need to find the conditions you wish to study already existing. If they already exist, you observe them or ask questions about them. For example, you could watch helping behaviour by sitting in a busy shopping precinct and watching whether men hold doors open for others more than women do. The behaviour is occurring naturally, but you are not doing an experiment; you are making an observation.

Sometimes, the strong controls of an experiment will be available in a situation. For example, Williams (1968) studied communities with and without television. He did not have to deprive a community of television – they naturally did not have it.

Williams studied three communities: one had no television and, of the other two, one community had one channel and the other one had four channels. He wanted to look at the effect of watching television, and specifically the effect it had on children's gender roles. He wondered if watching roles on television would make the children act in a more gender-stereotyped way. Of those who had television, would the boys be more 'boyish' and the girls more 'girlie'? By the end of the study the towns had changed, and the one with no television now had television and so on. At the start of the study those with television demonstrated more stereotyped behaviour, but by the end the children in the town who originally had no access to television were also showing stereotyped behaviour. So television does seem to affect us.

Evaluation

- An advantage of a field experiment is that it can keep control over variables to a large extent but is also more natural than a laboratory experiment.

- However, it is still unnatural to the extent that the situation itself (the setting up of the study) is artificial.

- An advantage of a natural experiment is that is uses a naturally occurring situation. Therefore it is **valid**.

- However, it is difficult to control such a situation. For example, Williams could not control what the non-television watchers were doing instead of watching television. They presumably learnt their social roles somehow.

- An advantage of a laboratory experiment is that there are quite strict controls over things such as the temperature of the room, the instructions given to participants, the actual tasks they do are the same, and the experimenter can act in the same way to everyone.

- However, this makes the task very artificial, and some say that nothing useful can be learnt about social interactions by doing laboratory experiments. They are **reliable**, but not valid.

Self-test 2

1 What is the term for a study that, when carried out again achieves similar or the same results?

2 What is the term for a study that measures what it claims to measure?

Use the key terms/glossary to find the answers.

Surveys

Surveys are also used in social psychology. Surveys can be done by interview or by questionnaire. It was suggested earlier that if you did not like the idea of asking people the time when looking at helping behaviour, you could use a questionnaire.

ACTIVITY 4

PROBLEMS WITH QUESTIONNAIRES

Make a list of problems you think you might encounter when doing a questionnaire.

Key Skill PS3.1 – recognise, explore and describe the problem, and agree the standards for its solution. This activity can provide evidence as you need to recognise the problems with questionnaires, describe them by making a list, and consider how they could be overcome.

You may have come up with some of the following:
- Avoid leading questions. For example, you should not ask 'surely you would not pass someone by without helping?' as this suggests the answer 'of course I wouldn't'. If you let the participant know in some way what you expect (in either a survey or an experiment) then there will be what are called **demand characteristics**. These are characteristics of the study

that demand a particular answer or give clues as to what is required.
- Avoid personal questions that are not necessary. You should be careful not to offend your participant. Give them the option of declining to answer.
- How can you know the answers are truthful? You can't really be sure about this.
- The answers could be what people *say* they will do, not what they would *actually* do. What you are really looking at is attitudes to something like helping behaviour, not actual helping.
- The participant might say what they think they ought to say. This is called **social desirability** and is difficult to avoid. If you ask someone if they are racist, they may say 'no' but this does not mean they are not. They know what they ought to say.

You may have thought of even more difficulties with questionnaires. Even so, questionnaires can gather a lot of information quite quickly and can yield interesting results, which are relatively easy to quantify. See Chapter 7 for more details of using questionnaires.

Discourse analysis

Social representation theory suggests that the only knowledge we have, especially concerning people, depends on the culture being studied. **Discourse analysis** places similar emphasis on social representations. It is a 'modern' method in the sense that early social psychologists did not use it.

Surveys and experiments collect **quantitative** data. This means that the data are measurable and comparable. We might count the number of letters recalled, or see what percentage of older people help others. We might rate people for attractiveness on a scale of 0–5, or we might record what level of 'shock' is given when a participant is expected to obey. In all these examples the results are measurable. The responses of one participant can be compared with those of another because they are measured on similar scales.

Case studies and other methods gather **qualitative** data. This means that the data are unique in some way, and give information on quality rather than quantity. We are not asking someone to rate their attitudes on a scale of 0–5 (for example on being asked how much they agree to women being in the front line in a battle): a question asking for ratings would give quantitative data. If a questionnaire included asking a participant to write about how they feel about women being in the front line in a battle, then this question would give qualitative data. These data types are not comparable. One person's attitude could not really be compared with another's, except to say perhaps that they had similar views.

Discourse analysis tends to yield qualitative data. The trend towards social representation theory means that 'scientific truths' are not looked for. Rather it is claimed that there are many 'realities' which come from each separate society, and which exist because of that society or culture. Arranged marriages are a tradition in some societies, and can be understood only within those societies. The method of discourse analysis is preferred by some because it examines 'real' interactions within people. It looks at people in a specific culture and society, and there is no attempt to **generalise** from the study of a particular **discourse** to another.

A discourse is a conversation. Language is involved but not only the spoken word. Communication between people is studied by analysing such discourse. The main focus is on the meaning of the communication, and what function it serves – what it is for. We frequently ask 'How are you?' without waiting for a reply. This is discourse serving a function, but is not a real question. We don't really want to know how a person is; we are offering communication.

We think words convey meaning clearly, but they frequently don't. Box 5 gives an example of misunderstanding.

Box 5

An example of not communicating

After the weekend a couple who are not getting on very well talk separately to a family friend. The friend talks to the husband first, without his wife being present. The husband says that they have had a bad weekend and he thinks his wife is about to leave him. He explains that she has said 'we can't go on like this', so he thinks there is no point in them talking about their problems any more.

The friend then talks separately to the wife. She is very upset. She says that there is no point in them talking, because her husband is not prepared to do anything to solve their problems. She explains that when she said to her husband 'we can't go on like this', he did not respond. He made no effort to talk to her. She assumed, therefore, that he was not interested in trying to sort things out and that he wanted her to leave.

The same wording was interpreted differently, according to the perceptions of the individual.

Breakwell et al (1995) suggest that language is a way of giving a reasonable view of events. The speaker constructs their own version but there can be no claim that it is the only truth. If you have already studied the cognitive approach, you could link the idea presented here to the criticisms made of eyewitness testimony. Think of the *War of the Ghosts* story in Chapter 1, where it was said that we reconstruct the story to make it make sense to us. This is more or less the same thing. When we are talking we are reconstructing events, and our words must be understood with this in mind.

You can use discourse analysis as a method, although for the coursework you must use a method where quantitative data are gathered. You *might* be able to pick out themes as suggested below and then count them in some way to yield quantitative data, but usually qualitative data are given by this method.

In order to analyse discourse, you have to record some data and carefully analyse it, perhaps by picking out themes. For example, if you have recorded interactions between people in a shop, one theme might be 'greeting' one another, another theme might be 'health', and another might be 'family' (it will depend if you are in a large city shop or a small country store). You might be able to see patterns in the communications, for example women might use different themes than men. You could make a list of the functions served by the communication – what it is for. One function might be 'defence' (avoiding confrontation), and another might be 'sociability' (exchanging greetings).

At the moment discourse analysis is not a central method in social psychology. However, it is becoming more popular, so it is included here so that you are ready for such changes in trend.

Evaluation

• There are problems in using discourse analysis.

ACTIVITY 5

SOME METHODOLOGICAL PROBLEMS WITH DISCOURSE ANALYSIS

Make a short list of possible problems with discourse analysis. Consider such issues as ethics, generalisability, reliability and validity. In case you are still not comfortable with these terms:
• *Ethics: what is right and wrong about doing a study on other people.*
• *Generalisability: can you analyse data and transfer the results from one situation, say conversations in a local shop, to any other situation, say conversations in an office?*

- *Reliability: if you did the recording and the analysis again, would you get the same results?*
- *Validity: are you really measuring what you say you are measuring – e.g. that one of the reasons for the conversation was to be sociable?*

Key Skill PS3.2 – compare at least two options that could be used to solve the problem, and justify the option you will forward. You need to look at problems when using discourse analysis (Key Skill PS3.1). You could also think of solutions for solving the problems. Imagine that you still want to use discourse analysis, as you can see its value. Think of ways of solving the above problems; this is your evidence.

You may have come up with some of the following:
- Lots of work involved in analysing the data.
- Concentrates on language and does not focus enough on other forms of communication such as body language.
- Artificial in recording one conversation at one moment in time outside the setting and circumstances.
- Bias in interpretation is possible, as it will be by one person who has their own society and culture, so is wrapped up in their own world view.
- Not reliable because each situation would be different (this could be said to be an advantage, because the method has validity).
- Valid in the sense of being a real recording of real interactions.
- Not generalisable because it is an individual case (but again this is the main point of doing it).
- Ethical if full permission is sought for the recording and the analysis.
- Ethical if right to withdraw is given.
- Ethical if confidentiality is ensured.

In-depth areas of study – obedience and prejudice

Of the many areas that are studied within social psychology two will be looked at further here. These two areas have been chosen because they are interesting and relevant, not because they are any more important than the many other areas that could have been included. Obedience is one of the most well known areas of social psychology, and studies can be applied to real situations. Explanations of prejudice are also interesting and useful. The key application (outlined later) examines how prejudice can be reduced, so this area of study is linked to the chosen key application.

Obedience

Some background material – conformity

Milgram's studies of obedience arose from studies of conformity. Conformity is where someone does the same as others in a group, and obedience is when someone obeys another person – they are *not* the same thing.

Asch (1956) carried out a well known study into conformity. (Note that Western culture tends to stress independence, not conformity. It is interesting that when, as you will see in Box 6, people conform to the opinions of others even when those opinions are clearly wrong, we are critical of this conformity. In another culture, independent thinking might be criticised.)

Conformity means going against your own ideas and beliefs, and doing what others are doing. There are two different types of conformity. You can go along with what the group is doing, knowing that you don't agree with it. This is complying, rather than actually agreeing. The other type of conformity involves agreeing with the group's views, and internalising them. Kelman (1958) discusses these differences between **compliance** and **internalisation**.

Asch was not the first to look at conformity, but his studies are central in social psychology, and started off a whole area of research called social influence. Box 6 outlines Asch's study.

Box 6

Asch's (1956) 'lines study'

Asch's study is a laboratory experiment. Picture a room set out like a classroom. The participant sits with a group of others, at the end of the row. He or she will not know that the others in the room are **stooges**, which means that they know all about the study, and have been briefed on what to do.

The experiment then starts. The group is asked to look at a display of four lines (Figure 2.1).

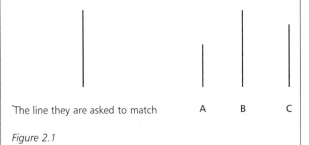

The line they are asked to match   A   B   C

Figure 2.1

For a number of trials, the stooges and the participant give accurate answers. If the single line is the same length as line A, they all answer A. The participant, being at the end of the row, hears the answers of the others, and then gives his or her own answer.

The next part of the experiment is important. The single line is shown (for example, it is the same length as line B). The first stooge in the row says 'A'. The participant would be surprised because the answer is clearly 'B'. Then the next stooge also answers 'A', and the next, and so on. When it comes to the participant's turn, will he or she give the correct answer (B), or will he or she conform to the group answer, and say A?

When this study was done, people were surprised at how often the participant agreed with the group, even though the group answer was so obviously wrong. Around a third of the participants conformed most of the time; about a quarter remained independent; the rest conformed some of the time.

Activity 6 asks you some questions about this study, and suggests how you could study conformity.

ACTIVITY 6

TESTING CONFORMITY

Using Asch's tests will cause distress to the participant, who would probably feel foolish on being told how he had conformed. You also have to deceive the participant, who does not know that the others are stooges. Deceit and distress are listed in the ethical guidelines (see Chapter 8), so you can't do an Asch-style study.

However, you could consider using a questionnaire to look for factors affecting conformity. Make statements which you can score using a Likert scale. An example is given below.

SA = strongly agree; A = agree; DK = don't know or unsure; D = disagree; SD = strongly disagree

	SA	A	DK	D	SD
1 I let others into the stream of traffic whenever I can	☐	☐	☐	☐	☐
2 I don't agree with queuing	☐	☐	☐	☐	☐
3 I tend to agree with others when I am in a group	☐	☐	☐	☐	☐
4 I like to stand out in a crowd	☐	☐	☐	☐	☐

Statements 1 and 3 are scored thus: SA = 5; A = 4; DK = 3; D = 2; SD = 1
Statements 2 and 4 are scored thus: SA = 1; A = 2; DK = 3; D = 4; SD = 5

Think about the scoring. Why are the statements scored differently? Statements 1 and 3, if agreed with, show conformity but statements 2 and 4, if agreed with, show independence. If you want a conformity score, you need to score all the statements with regard to conformity.

Key Skill C3.1a – if you are studying in a group, you could use this activity as a group discussion. Then you could extend the questions, decide on what personal data are required, and think about problems with doing the study.

Many other conformity studies have been performed. Asch's study has been outlined here because it led Milgram to devise studies of obedience, and in this section it is obedience that is of interest.

Evaluation

- Ethical criticisms have been made (see Activity 5). Asch deceived his participants, and caused them distress.

- Asch's methods can be **evaluated**. Asch used laboratory experiments, so can be criticised for drawing conclusions from work that lacks **ecological validity**. This means that he took people away from natural settings but claimed to look at conformity in real groups. His groups were artificially formed, and in a laboratory, so conclusions cannot be extended to real-life situations.

- Asch's work has also been criticised because it lacks validity with regard to the tasks (we don't judge length of lines in this way). Also there was no pressure on the participants to give the right answer. It was hardly a matter of life and death.

- Note, however, that Asch used strict controls. This makes his work repeatable. If someone does the same thing again, they are likely to get the same results, which means that his work has reliability.

Setting the scene for Milgram's famous study

Milgram is a very well known social psychologist. Asch was criticised because his task was trivial. Milgram set out to do a similar study, but one where the participant's responses would be important to them. Milgram decided to use Asch's task, but to get the participant to shock a stooge if the stooge gave a wrong answer. This stooge would be the only one giving the answers, and would be given instructions by Milgram. The participant would observe other experiments where other stooges, this time acting as participants/experimenters, doing the same study, would give shocks to the person giving the answers, even when the answers were right. The participant would watch the stooge experimenter asking questions and giving the answering stooge shocks even when the answers were correct. The question was whether the participant would conform and give shocks even when the person giving the answers got the answer right.

Milgram did not carry out this study. He would need a **control group** because he needed to know how willing the participant was to shock someone, without the stooges being there. This control group became the focus of his interest.

In the meantime, Adolf Eichmann was being tried in Jerusalem for crimes committed against the Jews in the Holocaust (when Nazi officials slaughtered 8 million Jews, Gypsies, gays and others) – Eichmann was the officer most responsible for the Holocaust. Reports of the trial showed that Eichmann did not appear to be evil. He was a mild character, who looked ordinary. He kept saying over and over again that he did it because he was ordered to. This was very frightening to other people. Was everyone capable of such crimes if ordered to carry them out?

Milgram's famous experiment resulted from his thinking about Asch's work, and his reading about Eichmann. He could ask people to give a shock to other people and see how likely they were to do it, and under what conditions.

Obedience – Milgram's famous study

Conformity is agreeing with group responses; obedience is responding to direct orders.

Box 7

Milgram's basic obedience study (1963)

Milgram advertised for participants, and told them they were taking part in an experiment on human learning. The experimenter, Milgram, had a helper, called a **confederate**, who was the learner who would 'receive' the (fake) shocks. There was one actual shock of 45 volts, which the participants received to convince them that the machine was real. The confederate-learner was middle aged and pleasant looking. The participant, who would be the teacher, heard the confederate-learner tell Milgram about a slight heart condition. Remember the confederate-learner was primed. The participants took part in the study one at a time.

Participants arrived at the laboratory and waited in a room with the confederate. They were led to believe that the confederate was a participant too. The two of them drew lots to decide who would be the learner, although it was rigged that the confederate was always the learner, and the participant always the teacher. Milgram reassured the participant that the shocks would be painful, but that there would be no permanent tissue damage. The participant-teacher watched the confederate-learner being strapped into a chair and wired up so that the 'shocks' could be felt.

Milgram took the participant-teacher into another room. There was a long counter in front of an array of switches and an impressive looking machine. This was the generator. The switches were in a long row and were labelled as running from 15 volts to 450 volts. Along the length of the machine, above the switches, were comments such as 'danger', 'slight shock' and so on. This left the participant in no doubt that the shocks would be increasingly painful and dangerous as the voltage increased. The participant sat in front of the 15-volt switch and began the experiment, having been given instructions by Milgram. He or she was to move up one switch at a time each time the learner gave a wrong answer.

The task required the participant to read out word pairs such as blue-box, nice-day, wild-duck, then read out the key word and four possible pairs. For example, he might read out blue-sky, ink, box, and lamp. The confederate-learner had four buttons and had to press the right one. In this example, the correct answer is 'box'. A wrong answer was given a 15-volt shock, and each successive wrong answer was given a shock 15 volts higher: 30 volts, then 45 volts and so on.

At first the learner gave correct answers, then a few wrong answers. Up to 75 volts there was no indication that the shocks were causing distress. However, the learner then gave some grunts, and at 120 volts shouted that the shocks were becoming painful. The question was: when would the participant stop carrying out the task?

Milgram and the confederate were working to a script, so that each participant had the same experiences. At 150 volts the learner shouted out that the shocks were becoming painful and that he did not want to go on with the study. These shouts became agonised screams at 270 volts. At 300 volts the learner refused to give answers. The experimenter, Milgram, calmly told the participant to treat the absence of a response as no response and ordered him to go on with the shocks. If they reached 450 volts, they were to continue with that switch. The experimenter was in the room with the participant, so the participant would think no one was with the learner, who was now silent and could be in a bad way. It was pointless to continue with the study as the learner was not responding – no learning would be taking place. Would participants continue simply because they were ordered to? They were free to leave, after all. It is worth noting that Milgram had a script too. On occasion he prompted the participant to continue, by saying things like 'you must continue', or 'it is absolutely essential that you continue'. These prompts were called verbal prods, and may have affected the outcome.

Box 8

Milgram's expectations

Milgram expected participants to refuse to go up to 450 volts. He thought he would have to modify the pattern of screams and responses, because the participants would never agree to carry on. Before carrying out the study he asked students and colleagues what they thought. They thought 2 or 3% would continue to the end. When people were asked what they would do, none said they would continue to the end.

However, the results showed that 26 out of the 40 men who did the study did continue to the end, as did 26 out of the 40 women who did the study. Those who went to the end continued to give 450 volts until the experimenter told them to stop.

Similar studies have been carried out in other cultures, as outlined earlier, and in all cases participants obey more than would be expected (although the studies and the results vary).

From the results we can conclude that:
1 Social influence is strong, and we obey.
2 We don't think we will obey, so this obedience is not generally known about.

Explanations

Slippery slopes. One reason why everyone who was asked thought that the participants would not obey is that they did not take into account the experimental procedure. This asks participants to go from a small harmless shock and to progress very gradually. The participants did end up giving 450 volts, but they did not do this straight away. Those judging what would happen did not take the concept of a slippery slope into account, and how this affects us. Having started small and worked up to higher levels of shock, it was perhaps easier for the participant to continue than if 450 volts had to be given straight away.

The manner of the experimenter. The experimenter was very calm and clear. He said things like 'you must continue' or 'it is absolutely essential that you continue'. He was calm at all times. He acted as though the experiment was of great importance, and took it for granted that the participant, a paid volunteer, would carry out his moral obligation of carrying on with the study. As he started the experiment, the participant had a good idea of what level of shock was acceptable. As the study progressed, the participant was faced with the experimenter's idea of what was acceptable. The question was, would the participant go along with his own ideas, or accept the moral obligation of going along with the experimenter's ideas of what is acceptable? Many appeared to go along with what the experimenter thought was acceptable.

Also the study was at Yale University, which lends authority to the experiment and to the experimenter. Milgram wore a lab coat, which also lends authority. When the study was moved to a rundown office, fewer obeyed to the end.

Agency theory. The participants who obeyed to the end said things like 'I was just doing what I was told', and 'I would not have done it by myself'. Having agreed to take part, the participant would continue to do as ordered. This is called being in an agentic state. It is as if the participant felt that he or she had no choice. The agentic state is the opposite of being autonomous – being under one's own control and having power. The experimenter's grey 'official' coat and the university setting reinforced this agentic state. The experimenter had the power. The commands were seen as coming from a legitimate authority.

Milgram (1974) suggested that it was our social system that led to such a degree of obedience. When people see themselves as individuals, and not as part of a social system, they might normally respond to any threat by avoiding aggression. It is suggested that we have evolved with this tendency to avoid aggression: avoidance of conflict, in earlier times, would have been more likely to have led to survival. This is the idea of natural selection, where any tendency that meant surviving would remain in the human gene pool, and would be passed on through the generations. It is claimed that individuals now have this tendency to avoid aggression when they are in the autonomous state (when they have power over themselves). However, early humans had a stronger chance of survival if they lived in social groups. We have inherited our tendency to be social animals. We now have social systems where there are leaders and followers. Our social systems are hierarchical, which means that we learn to obey those 'above' us in the system. We see ourselves as agents acting for someone else – this is the agentic state that led Milgram's participants to obey.

In the autonomous state, when individuals are acting for themselves, they see their actions as voluntary, and in their own power. In the agentic state, they see themselves as agents of others, and of society; their own conscience is not in control. Milgram thought that we learn this agentic state from early childhood: parents tell children what to do; schools have a hierarchical organisation, and it is clear who has power. In Milgram's experiment, the experimenter has the power, so the participants pay attention to him. The learner has no power, so his distress is ignored. In the agentic state people don't feel responsible for their actions, and tend to think that what they are doing is not wrong because they are not under their own power (autonomous) but acting under orders for someone else (in the agentic state). When the learner was nearer to the participant, they obeyed the experimenter less, as if, by being more visible, the learner became more important. The participant acted more as an individual.

Social power. French and Raven (1959) described five different kinds of power. Legitimate power is held by those in particular roles, such as a head teacher. Those who control resources and distribute rewards, such as bosses and parents, hold reward power. Those who have the power to punish hold coercive power, and those who have specialist knowledge (such as doctors) hold expert power. Finally, those who can win people over (this comes from personality to an extent) hold referent power.

It could be argued that in the experiment, Milgram had some of these types of power. He was the experimenter, which gave him legitimate power; he could give reward to the participant, so had reward power; he may have been seen has having the power to punish (since the participant thought a colleague was receiving shocks), so had coercive power; he had specialist knowledge because he worked at Yale, so had expert power.

So participants were in the agentic state because of the power held by Milgram. It would have taken autonomous thinking – the individual would have had to have had the power – to disobey the experimenter. However, for the reasons given above, the participant was not autonomous, but in the agentic state, so he or she would not disobey.

Milgram's variations on the original study

Table 2.1

Situation	Result
Original study	26 out of 40 continued to the end (65%)
Two experimenters, not one. At 110 volts, one tells the participant to stop, and the other tells him to continue	All participants stopped
Three teachers (two are confederates). One confederate-teacher stops at 150 volts, and the other stops at 210 volts	Only 10% of participants continued to the end
Experimenter's instructions are given by tape and the participant can speak to the experimenter, who is not in the room, by phone	Nine subjects continued to the end out of the 40 (22.5%)
Moving the victim closer, until the participant held the victim's hand down to receive the shock	Twelve out of the 40 obeyed (30%)
Held in Research Associates of Bridgeport offices, in a fairly rundown office building	Of the 40, 19 obeyed (47.5%)

Milgram carried out a number of variations on the original study (Table 2.1). With the variations listed, obedience reduced (although when someone else 'gave' the shocks, the participant obeyed more). Without the experimenter in the room, there was no need for a reason to stop, whereas with the experimenter there, a reason had to be given. If the victim was visible, it seems to have made it harder to administer the shock. If another person stops, it is easier to conform and to stop as well.

When asked why they obeyed, many participants said it was because it was 'fair'. It is supposed that this means that, because the participant thought that as they drew lots it was pure chance as to who was receiving the shocks and so it was a 'fair' experiment. Milgram tested this idea out. by changing the procedure slightly. The confederate-learner told the experimenter about his 'heart condition' and insisted that the experiment was stopped when the learner had had enough. However, 16 participants obeyed to the end, even though they had agreed to stop the shocks when the learner requested it. It does not appear that obedience was just down to fairness.

ACTIVITY 8

ETHICAL ISSUES IN MILGRAM'S STUDIES

Draw two columns on a sheet of paper and make a list of ethical guidelines (see Chapter 8)

in the first column. In the second column comment on whether Milgram's studies obeyed these guidelines. Note, however, that the guidelines were drawn up after Milgram's studies. It could be claimed that they were drawn up because of his work.

Key Skill C3.1a – this would make a good group task and discussion. You could also look at other criticisms of these obedience studies to extend the group task.

Evaluation

- Baumrind (1964) criticised Milgram on ethical grounds:

  - Milgram deceived his participants. He said the study was about learning, whereas it was about obedience.

  - He did not give them the right to withdraw. Indeed, he even pressed them to go on, using verbal prods.

  - He did maintain confidentiality, in that the names of the participants were not published, although the area they came from was.

  - He did obtain consent from participants, but it was not informed consent, because he deceived them.

– He caused participants distress, and they had to come to terms with obeying to such a high level, when they would not have expected to.

– The actual experiment was very stressful.

• However, to give Milgram credit, he did ask colleagues and others what they thought would happen, and no one thought the participants would go so far. Milgram also had a psychiatrist contact 40 of the participants, and there was no evidence of harm having been done. The participant was in fact free to leave at any time, and did give consent to an extent. In a follow-up questionnaire, most of the participants said they were happy to have taken part. However, Milgram could have explained that there would be some short-term stress involved without spoiling the study by saying too much. This would have been better from an ethical point of view.

• Since the main study and most of the variations were laboratory experiments, the usual criticisms about validity apply. We don't usually go about giving shocks to other people. However, there were careful controls, and Milgram took care to vary only the **independent variable** each time, so the study was well conceived and well executed, in spite of its ethical short comings.

Obedience – a prison simulation (Haney et al, 1973)

Haney et al (1973) also studied obedience and brutality. They used the basement of the Psychology department at Stanford University. They set up a mock prison and simulated the situation of prisoners and guards. The 70 volunteers knew what was to happen, were genuinely allocated randomly to be a prisoner or a guard, and were paid for a 2-week long study. Some were 'rejected' when Haney et al screened them to make sure they were 'stable', and 24 young men remained. To get them in the 'mood', the volunteers were arrested, searched, deloused and so on, as if they were real prisoners. They were stripped and given gowns. Haney et al were trying to degrade them. The guards wore reflective sunglasses, uniforms and carried night-sticks.

This study is usually called Zimbardo's study, and there are many different references for it. Zimbardo was the superintendent in the study, and played the senior role.

Results

The guards began to act the role of guards, and the prisoners became like typical prisoners. The prisoners rebelled, the guards withheld food and made the prisoners do push-ups and similar tasks. They made the prisoners clean toilets. The guards became more and more brutal. After six days Zimbardo had to stop the experiment as the prisoners became so demoralised.

Explanations

The prisoners did rebel, so it is not surprising that the guards punished them. But why so brutally? To an extent the guards worked up to a high level of cruelty – the slippery slope explanation given to show why Milgram's participants delivered the high shocks can be used here too. Also the less we allow people to be human, the more degraded they become, and the easier it is to be brutal towards them.

A real-life example of this is shown by the behaviour of American troops at My Lai. The troops were ordered to kill women and children in Vietnam and did so. There were a number of different circumstances that led to the massacre, as it was called. However, one of them was said to be that the troops were taught to call the Vietnamese names like 'gooks', and to degrade them, even before they arrived in Vietnam.

It is interesting that in Zimbardo's study the prisoners, when asked, explained that there were three types of guards – good guards, average guards and bad guards (the brutal ones). This has been reported by 'real' prisoners of war too. How do guards have so much power? Conformity studies show that we tend to make decisions based on group norms. This means that we go towards the majority opinion, and tend to come to a group decision that is somewhere in the middle of the views of the individuals. So those with extreme views would meet in the middle. However, this only happens if we can express our views, and discuss them. In the prison, it is doubtful whether the guards actually discussed their behaviour. They probably just got on with it, as they were told to. So the bad guards would have perhaps acted more clearly and more definitely. They would have shown the other guards their opinion of what should be done, so perhaps the others took their lead from the bad guards.

Hofling et al's (1966) study of obedience

> ### STUDY AID
>
> In case you have not read this elsewhere, 'et al' is short for *et alia*, which means 'and others' in Latin. It is very useful, because it means you don't have to remember the 'others'. Hofling did the study with Brotzman, Dalrymple, Graves and Pierce, as you can see by the reference at the end of the book.

This study is interesting because it was carried out in a real hospital and was a realistic task. It is an example of a field experiment. A doctor talking over the telephone separately told 22 nurses to give a patient a dosage of a drug that was twice the permitted amount. The question was whether the nurses would obey. The nurses had to fetch capsules that contained no real drugs. However, the capsules were labelled as containing 5 mg of Astrofen. A maximum dose of 10 mg was stated on the capsules but the nurses were told to administer 20 mg. The doctor asked them to give the drugs immediately and that he would arrive to sign the forms in about 10 minutes. Three basic rules were broken here: the nurse should have checked that this was a real doctor, should not have given 20 mg if the maximum permitted was 10 mg, and should have obtained the doctor's signature before giving the patient the drug. Of the 22 nurses 21 obeyed without question, and 11 said they had not noticed the dosage problem.

Evaluation

- This study is a field experiment that takes place in a real hospital with real nurses. The task also has realism, so it could be said to be valid. It can be repeated, because the procedure is clear and controls are good, so it could be said to be reliable. Nurses are trained to obey doctors, and this is what they did. So this study does show real obedience. Of course one difference between Milgram's and Hofling et al's experiments is that Milgram's participants were asked to harm someone, whereas the nurses were trying to help someone. They both, however, show how power leads to obedience.

- Whilst noting that Hofling et al's study had merits, it is worth commenting that Rank and Jacobson (1977) could not replicate it – a similar study did not get similar results.

- You could say that this study was not ethical. The nurses did not give consent and were not given the right to withdraw. They were debriefed, and the study might have been useful in showing them the importance of the rules. However, the nurses might also have been upset by the study because it showed them that they might have done something dangerous for their patient.

Prejudice

Milgram's study arose in part because people at the time could not understand what was done to the Jews and minority groups such as gypsies by the Nazis. Some suggested that Germans were different; however, Milgram's work strongly suggested that this was not the case. When faced with obeying instructions, given the right circumstances, anyone might obey.

It seems that what happened to the Jews was because orders were obeyed, not because of prejudice. However, it is hard to see how prejudice was not an issue. Stereotyping and prejudice are other areas of social psychology.

Stereotyping

Stereotyping involves carrying over an idea about someone and applying that idea to a whole group. So we might see one woman as weak, and then stereotype all women as weak. Katz and Braly in 1933 looked at stereotyping. Others repeated their work in 1951 and in 1969. It was interesting to see differences in the studies as times change. Box 9 outlines the studies.

Box 9

Studies of stereotyping

Katz and Braly (1933) devised a way of studying stereotyping. They gave 100 university students in the USA a list of ethnic groups, which included Americans, Jews, Negroes, Turks, Germans, Chinese, Irish, English, Italians, and Japanese. There was also a list of words from which the students had to choose six traits they thought were typical for each group. It was interesting that the students described the groups using stereotypical traits, and often these were bad characteristics.

The students even attributed characteristics or traits to groups when they did not know a member of that group. For example, they described Japanese without knowing anyone from Japan. Gilbert (1951) found less agreement when he did the same study, and found fewer unfavourable traits – students did not want to do the task. In 1969 Karlins et al repeated the study and this time there was a willingness to stereotype – however, the chosen traits were more favourable.

Carrying out studies on stereotyping is difficult, mainly because of ethical issues.

ACTIVITY 9

CARRYING OUT STUDIES ON STEREOTYPING

*It is not ethical to repeat Katz and Braly's study for coursework. By asking people to stereotype, you could suggest prejudice to them. Perhaps it is reasonable to try it in class, however. Remember that even if the whole group refuses to stereotype by nationality, they could be displaying **social desirability**. This means that they know they must not stereotype. It does not mean that they are not prejudiced, however.*

Stereotyping can be a useful shortcut, when trying to make sense of incoming information, and trying to make judgements. We don't have time to gather lots of data when making judgements, and we probably cannot avoid stereotyping.

Prejudice and discrimination

Prejudice is more than simple stereotyping: we allow our stereotypes to affect our attitudes. Prejudice usually means a hostile learned attitude, although you can be prejudiced in a positive way. If you always pick tall people as your friends, you might be prejudiced towards tall people.

In social psychology the prejudice that is studied is usually the hostile sort. When the prejudiced attitude leads to prejudiced actions, this is called **discrimination**. Discrimination is a behaviour that stems from prejudice, although you can actually discriminate without having prejudiced attitudes. Usually discrimination is assumed to be deliberate. If you are prejudiced against older people, then you don't like older teachers. You are discriminating against older teachers when you choose younger ones. Employers would be discriminating on the grounds of racial prejudice if they rejected someone who applied for a job because of their race.

Institutional racism is when institutions discriminate, but not directly through prejudice. Institutional pressures cause the discrimination, rather than direct racism. For example, if a shop will not employ Black people because the shop managers think customers would stay away, this is institutional racism.

Rose and Platzer (1993) discuss how nurses tend to be prejudiced against gay patients, mainly because of their assumptions. They give the example of a patient who had a cervical smear. The patient was asked if she was sexually active, and she replied that she was. She was asked what contraceptive was used, and she replied that she used none. She was then asked if she wanted to become pregnant. The point is the questions made the assumption that the patient was heterosexual. The patient had to explain she was gay, before the nurses understood. Another patient had 'high risk' written clearly on their notes, so that everyone could see. This was because the patient was gay, and it was assumed there was a high risk of HIV.

An individual can be prejudiced, and so can a group.

Causes/explanations of prejudice
Prejudice is caused by personality variables
One of the earliest explanations of prejudice that is given is the claim of Adorno et al (1950) that prejudice comes from an **authoritarian personality**. Once again, the Nazis were studied. Why were they so anti-Semitic (against the Jews)?

By questioning a lot of people about their prejudices, different scales were developed. These scales included one for **ethnocentrism** (ethnocentric means focused on our own culture), and one for anti-Semitism (meaning anti-Jew). There were other scales to do with being authoritarian or being weak or strong (these are outlined below). An analysis was done to see if those who were weak, were also ethnocentric and so on, and to see what answers went with each other. Adorno et al found, amongst other findings, that those who were authoritarian were also ethnocentric.

Box 10

The authoritarian personality

People with an authoritarian personality are against anyone they see as inferior. They don't tolerate weakness or uncertainty. They believe in being conventional and follow rules. Adorno et al used Freud's theory to help to explain how those with an authoritarian personality tend to be prejudiced towards minority groups. They also tried to explain how they became 'authoritarian' in the first place.

Authoritarians have often been brought up in a harsh and disciplinarian manner. They are often hostile towards their parents, although this is likely to be hidden. This hostility, which is hard to accept consciously but is strong in the unconscious, is displaced onto minority groups.

The psychoanalytic approach with Freud's theory is outlined in Chapter 5. Very briefly, we are strongly affected by experiences and desires that are hidden in our unconscious. We are not aware of these experiences and desires but they are strong enough to guide our behaviour, and in some cases can give symptoms of mental illness and depression. The psychoanalyst will encourage free association, or will analyse dreams, in order to find out what is hidden in the unconscious.

Most of the time we use defence mechanisms to help in our daily living. We have these hidden desires and experiences, but we repress them. This idea was also outlined in Chapter 1, in the context of forgetting. One of these defence mechanisms is displacement. If there is something we cannot admit to ourselves, then we displace the feelings onto something else. Often this is the opposite of the real feelings. We would have to choose a minority group, or a group of which we are not a member, so that we can protect ourselves.

You can test for yourself if those who have an authoritarian personality are more likely to be prejudiced.

ACTIVITY 10

TESTING THE CLAIM THAT THOSE WITH AN AUTHORITARIAN PERSONALITY ARE MORE LIKELY TO BE PREJUDICED

You need to do this very carefully, paying attention to ethical guidelines. Use a questionnaire to create items that will allow you to decide if someone has an authoritarian personality or not. You need a second set of items that will help you to decide if someone is prejudiced or not.

You might like to draw up two separate questionnaires of one side each. You will need to know the participant's age and gender. You might be interested in their job, but it is up to you what details you ask for. Your main interest is to give a score for prejudice and a score for authoritarian personality, and to compare the two. If you ask for more than just 'yes' or 'no', and get scores from the questionnaire items, then you have a correlational study.

Here is an example.

- *Standardised instructions are written at the top of the questionnaire. You should ask the participant to help with your study, inform them that their name is not required, and that they are free to leave the questionnaire unanswered at any time. Everything will be explained to them after they have completed the questionnaire, and they can ask for their results not to be included.*
- *Start with a question about gender ('m/f – please tick'), and one about age group ('under 16; 16–24, 25–34, 35–44, 45–54, 55–64, 65+'). Any questions asking for personal data must be justified and carefully worded.*
- *Then you want to ask them to give you some information regarding their personality. You could decide to list different words and ask them to tick those that they feel apply to them. For example:*

Law abiding	☐	Strong	☐	Not religious	☐
Liberal	☐	Relaxed	☐	Strict	☐
Weak	☐	Religious	☐	Confident	☐
Follower	☐	Shy	☐	Independent	☐

- *In this list there are some 'authoritarian' traits and some opposites. This is not a perfect list – you will need to generate your own for coursework – but it gives you an idea. Someone who says they are strict, law-abiding, strong and possibly religious could be said to have an authoritarian personality. If they say they are liberal, relaxed, weak and not religious, then this suggests they are not authoritarian.*
- *You could get an authoritarian score by giving your participant a scale on which to mark their level of, for example, strictness. If they judge where they fit on a scale of 0–10, then you can give them an authoritarian score.*
- *You then need a 'prejudice' score. This time you could give your participant statements to agree with or not. For example:*

	SA	A	DK	D	SD
1 Women should not be allowed in the front line	☐	☐	☐	☐	☐
2 The age of consent for homosexuals should be reduced	☐	☐	☐	☐	☐
3 Different cultures don't mix together well	☐	☐	☐	☐	☐
4 We can all learn to live together	☐	☐	☐	☐	☐

- *You could score each statement 5, 4, 3, 2 or 1 based on 'prejudiced' views. Statements 2 and 4 are scored SA = 1; A = 2; DK = 3; D = 4; SD = 5, and statements 1 and 3 are scored SA = 5; A = 4; DK = 3; D = 2; SD = 1. (Scoring on a Likert scale was explained in Activity 6).*
- *You would need more statements, but this should give you an idea. Some ideas for statements can be found below, using Peterson et al's (1993) research. Then you can take each person's 'authoritarian' score, and compare it to their 'prejudiced' score. You could claim that the more authoritarian (the higher the score), the more prejudiced (the higher the score), which is showing a positive correlation.*

Adorno et al (1950) used statements to find out about personality. Some examples from their 'anti-Semitism scale' are shown in Box 11.

Box 11

Some items from Adorno et al's (1950) anti-Semitism scale

1 One trouble with Jewish businessmen is that they stick together and connive, so that a Gentile doesn't have a fair chance in competition.

2 Persecution of the Jews would be largely eliminated if the Jews would make really sincere efforts to rid themselves of their harmful and offensive faults.

3 Jewish leaders should encourage Jews to be more inconspicuous, to keep out of professions and activities already overcrowded with Jews, and to keep out of the public notice.

Adorno et al did not just look at anti-Semitism, because they thought there was a wider issue of ethnocentrism: in other words, prejudice was not just against Jews. They did not only use a questionnaire either. They developed an E (ethnocentrism) scale. Then they chose 80 participants from the many who carried out the questionnaires, and carried out clinical interviews: 40 of these 80 had very high scores on the scales, and 40 had very low scores. From the interviews they did find a personality attracted to prejudice, and then they developed a new questionnaire, which they called the California F (fascism) scale.

When Adorno et al (sometimes called the Berkeley group) marked the same participants on the E and the F scales, they found a correlation of 0.75, which does seem to suggest that authoritarianism is related to prejudice.

Evaluation of the 'authoritarian personality' being an explanation for prejudice

- Even if you do find that an authoritarian personality and prejudiced attitudes go together, you cannot claim that having that sort of personality causes prejudice. It may be that they go together because there is some other cause. Adorno et al (1950) claimed that the personality caused the prejudice, which is hard to test.

- It has been suggested that the research gave levels of authoritarianism in the USA because of the high level of international threat to the country at the time. This was tested out. From 1978 to 1982 there was said to be a high level of threat to the USA from other countries, and from 1983 to 1987 there was said to be a low level of

threat. Authoritarianism did seem to vary, with less when there was a lower threat (Doty et al, 1991). This links to the realistic conflict theory, which is another explanation for prejudice. So the explanation is not that there is an inborn (innate) personality trait, but that events in the country at the time lead to certain views.

- Recent research (Peterson et al, 1993) has looked at what the authoritarian personality is like, and has found an attitude that people with AIDS should be punished. They also found the view that there should be very harsh treatment for those dealing in drugs.

- Other views of the authoritarian personality included opposition to the right to have abortions, and the belief that the homeless are lazy. You could consider using some of these statements in a questionnaire if you decide to do one. These ideas seem to represent the culture of the USA, but the question is, would they represent personality in a different culture? If the authoritarian personality is innate, then it should be found across different cultures. If, however, it is not found elsewhere, then it seem that prejudice is caused in some way other than there being an innate 'prejudiced' personality.

- McFarland et al (1992) did a study in Russia (just before Yeltsin was elected), and found an authoritarian personality linked to conservatism, and people not liking change. It seems that the authoritarian personality is linked to not liking change. It is not likely to be an in-built trait, but arises out of the situation the country is in at the time. The claim that this personality is also prejudiced does seem to stand, however.

- Adorno et al used questionnaires and clinical interviews, so any evaluation could include commenting on their methods. Questionnaires might not be reliable, because the answers depend on the mood of the participant at the time. In-depth interviews might be biased, because the views of the interviewer might affect what is said. However, Adorno et al did ask very many people, so in some ways bias is less likely. Studies carried out after theirs did support their results. Even a study in a different country, Russia, found such a personality. So overall, their methods do seem to have been quite sound.

- Evaluation can also include ethical issues. You can see that the statements on the scales were strongly prejudiced. Please do not use the examples given in Box 11, as they might themselves make participants prejudiced. Firstly, you can criticise the method if the statements seemed to suggest an answer, and, secondly, you can criticise the ethics, if you think that the tasks would lead to the participant becoming prejudiced.

Prejudice is caused by 'realistic conflict'
Realistic conflict theory. There seems to be prejudice when a country is under threat from other countries, or at times of great change (like the change from communism in Russia). **Realistic conflict theory** suggests that when groups are in conflict, they become prejudiced towards one another. The conflict is real, and

groups change in the face of this conflict. They start thinking of others outside the group as the **outgroup**, and of themselves as the **in-group**. They stereotype the outgroup and behave towards them in ways that their individual moral codes would not allow. Ethnocentrism is this hostility to the outgroup and loyalty to the in-group.

A famous study was carried out by Mustafer Sherif and others, to see if real conflicts do lead to prejudice.

Box 12

The Robber's Cave experiment

Sherif et al (1961) wanted to test the idea that if you create an in-group/outgroup situation (ethnocentrism) by creating groups and then creating conflict between them, prejudice will arise. They thought a hierarchical structure would develop (e.g. power would go from a leader down through 'lieutenants' to the followers), and that there would be loyalty to the in-group and hostility to the outgroup. Also, the in-group would stereotype the outgroup. Sherif also thought that if the two groups were set a goal that needed their co-operation to achieve, then prejudice would be reduced. A goal that neither group can achieve separately, but can achieve together, is called a **superordinate** goal.

This study is often called the 'Robber's Cave' study, because it was carried out in Robber's Cave State Park, Oklahoma. 20 boys stayed at the camp for 3 weeks and were carefully selected to be normal and ordinary, that is typical of their age, sex and class. The camp counsellors let the boys choose their own activities and do what they wanted.

The boys were randomly divided into two groups, which the boys named the 'Rattlers' and the 'Eagles'. For the first week the two groups did not know about each other, and passed the time normally and separately, doing what they chose to do. The 'Rattlers' were tough guys, whereas the 'Eagles' did not allow swearing. Then they discovered each other, and both groups felt that the other was invading their territory.

Sherif introduced real conflict at this stage by having a tournament between the two groups. The teams got points, and the member of the team with the most points got a prize. This indeed led to loyalty to the in-group, and hostility to the outgroup, as was predicted.

The hierarchy that had developed when the groups were separate (leaders and so on) became more rigid

and set as the conflict developed. There was negative stereotyping of the other group. The camp counsellors counted the negative words used when referring to the outgroup. Each group thought the others were 'sneaks, smart alecks, and stinkers', whilst their own members were 'brave, tough and friendly'. Each burned the flag of the other group, and carried out raids.

Then the researchers set about trying to reduce the prejudice. They tried simple contact, by bringing the groups together. However, this made things worse. Then Sherif organised superordinate goals, where the boys had to work together to overcome problems. Firstly, the camp water supply 'failed'. At first the groups set off separately to find the problem. They met up at the water tank, where the problem was, and co-operated to fix it, getting on better in the process. Secondly, a truck got stuck in the mud, and they all had to pull it out. This reduced hostility and indeed led to a friendly atmosphere. The counsellors noticed less name-calling, and the boys used fewer negative traits when describing the others. Prejudice had been reduced.

Sherif (posing as the camp handyman) also asked the boys who their friends were. In the 'hostility' phase, 93% had friends in their own group; however, after the co-operation phase, 30% had friends between the two groups. This shows the reduction in prejudice.

Evaluation of the Robber's Cave study

- A very strong point in favour of this study is that it is a field study, which gives it validity. Sherif wanted to look at realistic conflict, and for it to be as realistic as possible. He tried to set up real groups, and then real co-operation.

- The study used American boys, and it could be claimed that ethnocentrism is a part of American culture, but not of other cultures.

- The groups were hostile immediately, even before Sherif introduced the tournament as competition. They wanted to defend their territory as soon as they knew about each other. So it may not be the case that competition for material (real) goods is what leads to ethnocentrism. Simply being two groups may be enough.

- The participants were all 12 years old, and white middle-class American boys, so generalisation to the American population as a whole is not possible. Sherif's results are often quoted as evidence that prejudice can be formed by ethnocentrism, and reduced by co-operation, but generalising from this study to all people would not be wise.

The jigsaw classroom study. Another study that looks at realistic conflict as a cause of prejudice was carried out by Aronson et al (1978). They chose to look at an American classroom, where there is a lot of competition. They introduced the jigsaw classroom technique: in small groups, each individual contributes one section to the whole solution and the only way of arriving at the complete solution is to combine each individual's efforts. The groups were made up of people from different cultures. They had to co-operate, just as the boys did in Sherif's study, when faced with a superordinate goal (one which needed co-operation).

Evaluation

- The study was carried out in a natural setting, so was valid.

- However, the task itself was artificial, so the study can be criticised.

- It was carried out on children, so we don't know what the effect of such co-operation would be on adults.

- We cannot tell what long-term effect the study had on the reduction of prejudice.

- Aronson (1992) points out that the technique works best with young children, before they can become too prejudiced. This shows the dangers of generalising, as the participants were young. Another point is that, although the individuals liked each other better, this did not always generalise to all members of that group.

Social identity theory

Tajfel and Turner (1979) suggest that prejudice is caused by the creation of groups, not by realistic conflict – just creating two groups will cause conflict. There does not need to be real conflict over real material goods. Tajfel created minimal groups to see what would happen. A small group of students (up to 16) was asked to pick which painting they preferred from two modern abstract artists, Klee and Kandinsky. They didn't know which artist they chose, because the paintings were not labelled, and are similar in style. Then some were told they preferred Klee, and some that they preferred Kandinsky. The groups were actually randomly split, so although students thought they chose either Klee or Kandinsky as they were told, they might not actually have chosen their 'allocated' artist. The groups were not supposed to talk to one another. They were minimal groups and stayed that way, as they could not confer. They were not in conflict, but believed they were a group who chose the same artist

The researchers had to find a way to see how the participants would act towards a person they thought was a member of their own group, and one who was a member of the other group.

One study asked participants to say how much two of the other students should be paid for a subsequent experiment. The participant could tell that one of the students was from his or her own group, and one was from the other group (they could tell by numbers allocated to all the students on the basis of their group). Typically, the participants said the person from their own group should receive more than the person from the other group. This demonstrated prejudice, even between groups that were formed for a reason as trivial as liking a certain painting (Tajfel et al, 1971).

Tajfel (1981) looked at many studies that had been done using this procedure for creating minimal groups, and concluded that in-group favouritism was very common. The studies tried different ways of measuring favouritism, such as rating personality of the others using a list of traits, and in many cases in-group loyalty was found.

Social identity theory suggests that participants want to promote members of their in-group over the outgroup members, because it enhances their own status (Tajfel and Turner, 1986). If you are in a group, thinking of that group as the best will enhance your own self-esteem.

Crocker and Luhtanen (1990) showed that those who think highly of the group they are in have high collective (or group) self-esteem, and show loyalty to the in-group in a minimal group situation. This supports social identity theory, and suggests that supporting the group lifts self-esteem. However, it is interesting that even within in-groups where there is low collective self-esteem (for example, where a team is losing every match) there seems to be in-group loyalty. Lalonde (1992) studied a poorly performing hockey team. They had to admit other teams were better than them regarding skills but they claimed that the other team was 'dirtier' – they claimed moral superiority – so there was still in-group favouritism. Lalonde took the trouble to watch the matches, in case the other teams were indeed 'dirtier' (in which case they would have simply been telling the truth). However, he concluded that the losing team he was studying were by far the 'dirtiest', so there was bias in their outgroup prejudice.

These examples have all involved rewarding the in-group. Other studies have looked at what happens if punishment is involved. For example, if a person has to expose both their in-group and the outgroup to a loud noise, they are much more fair. However, if they were told that their in-group was in the minority (20% of the whole group) and were not very good at a task, then they were more biased in allocating punishment (in the form of the noise). It seems that if we know we are in the minority and we know that our group has low status, then we are more willing to deliver punishment to the outgroup (Mummendey et al, 1992).

Another interesting effect has been found doing minimal group research – the black sheep effect. Members of the in-group are willing to say bad things about one member of their group. It is as if, by identifying one weak member, the group are enhancing their own self-esteem, by showing that they can be critical of their own group (Marques and Yzerbyt, 1988)

Evaluation

- Tajfel's study was done in Britain.

- Social identity theory does go against the idea of realistic conflict leading to prejudice. However, it could simply be claimed that status can be the cause of real conflict, just as other issues like competing in a tournament. So in many ways Tajfel's research backs up Sherif's. Social identity theory expands and amends the claims of the realistic conflict theory.

- Because research was carried out both in Europe and in the USA, it does not seem that the attitudes were specific to one culture.

- Most of the situations that were studied, including the hockey team and the false groups formed by being told which painting was preferred, are fairly realistic. The hockey team was a real team, for example. So the studies are fairly valid compared with studies carried out in a laboratory.

- The minimal groups set-up has also been repeated in different cultures and by different researchers, so the studies are reliable. (Reliable means if you do the study again you get the same results, and valid means something is measuring what it claims to measure.)

Prejudice is caused by frustration–aggression

An alternative view regarding the cause of prejudice is to look at the individual concerned. It has already been suggested that individuals with an authoritarian personality might be more prejudiced. Perhaps prejudice is caused by an individual's mood or situation at the time, rather than their personality, or their group membership. Dollard et al (1939) developed a frustration–aggression theory that was used to study prejudice.

The frustration-aggression theory started with the idea that a child is frequently frustrated during the socialisation process. This idea comes from Freud's view that problems arise for the child, firstly, by waiting to be fed, and, secondly, by learning to control its bladder. Problems continue as the child struggles with learning the rules of becoming a social being. It is suggested that the child feels very frustrated with its parents at this stage, because they are imposing the rules. However, parents are too big to attack, and the child also loves its parents, so it is not appropriate for the child to turn on the parents. The child's frustrations can be displaced onto another target, and prejudice can result.

Hovland and Sears (1940) found that as the price of cotton fell in the southern USA, lynchings rose. The whole economic system of the south rested on the price of cotton so, when the price fell, everyone's livelihood was threatened. It seems that they turned their frustrations onto the minority and low-status group at the time.

However, Berkowitz (1959) did a study to see if frustration leads to general aggression, or whether it leads to prejudice. Female college students were given a questionnaire on anti-Semitism to get an initial measure of their attitude to Jews. Half of the participants were then insulted (to annoy them) and the other half were not. Then they had to work with another person (a confederate). In one condition this other person was called Miss Johnson, and in the other condition, she was called Miss Cohen. If the anti-Semitic participants were frustrated, and if this led to prejudice, then they should have rated Miss Cohen less favourably than they rated Miss Johnson. However, this did not happen. The participants were all asked to rate the confederate by ticking a list of traits. The 'frustrated' participants did rate the confederate more harshly, but there was no difference in their ratings of Miss Cohen or Miss Johnson. So it seems that frustration does lead to aggression, but not specifically prejudice.

Evaluation

- The frustration–aggression hypothesis does not explain specific prejudice very well. It does seem that there is more frustration in times of economic hardship, and people do seem more easily incited then, as shown by the Hovland and Sears study. However, the aggression is more general than specific, and the theory does not explain the ethnocentrism found in the in-group/outgroup situation.

Summary of what leads to prejudice

Theories concentrating on the individual:
- Hostility can be displaced onto minority groups and lead to prejudice. This can be hostility from an authoritarian personality, or hostility due to frustration leading to aggression.
- It is not likely that there is an inborn authoritarian personality; such a personality probably develops from reaction to harsh upbringing.
- Similarly, frustration as a reaction to strict socialisation seems to lead to aggression of some type. However, this aggression is more general, and not necessarily focused on minority groups.
- Scapegoating, in times of hardship, is found, however. It seems that the general aggression that arises from frustration can be focused onto minority groups quite easily, and can lead to scapegoating.

The creation of groups can lead to prejudice:
- Real conflict can lead to prejudice as people compete for real rewards.
- However, it might be simply that the creation of an ingroup, which is bound to have an outgroup, can in itself lead to prejudice.
- Merely identifying with a group, and therefore seeing others as the outgroup, can lead to prejudice, according to social identity theory.

Studies within social psychology

Social psychology is a very large field, and there are many different studies that could be chosen to look at in depth here. The Edexcel AS examination will ask you to know two studies. Some are detailed here, but of course you could choose different ones if you wish (Milgram's study has been carefully outlined above, as have others, so you could use them).

Haney et al (1973) – A study of prisoners and guards in a simulated prison

This study was been briefly outlined in the context of obedience.

There was a military side to the study, as the intention was to see what the effects of imprisonment were, so that soldiers could be trained to withstand thought control and indoctrination, for example. Haney et al got approval from the Office of Naval Research before carrying out the study, and they were the sponsors. So there was a real practical aim to the study.

The question was: why do prisons lead to such brutal behaviour? The actual study was carried out in 1971, although references range from 1971 to 1973. I will use the Haney et al reference, but call the study Zimbardo's, as he was the person in charge.

The intention was to find out whether guards are brutal and insensitive people by nature. Perhaps there is something about people who choose the job that makes them the sort of people they are? Haney et al expected to find that it was not the individuals who were to blame for the brutality, but the conditions inside the prison. If they could show that this was the case, then prison conditions should be improved. If, however, it was the personality of the guard that was the problem, then there was no need to change the prison conditions. It was decided that they would choose people to act as guards who would not have chosen the role, and could not be expected to have any special sort of personality that goes with the job. The researchers could watch the participants' behaviour and see if the chosen guards became brutal or not. If they did, it might be claimed that this was not a result of their personality.

A special prison was created in the basement of Stanford university. Participants were randomly assigned to be either prisoners or guards. The hypothesis briefly is that there is a meaningful difference in the behaviour of the prisoners and the guards. The researchers would measure how each person coped and adapted to the situation.

Self-test 3

1 What experimental design is this?

2 What is the independent variable, and what is the dependent variable?

This is an independent groups design as different participants are in each condition. The independent variable is whether the participant is a prisoner or a guard and the dependent variable is the type of coping they adopt.

If you found the self-test difficult, this is not surprising. This is a social psychology experiment, and is not as clear cut as other experiments. Although it is called an experiment, because variables are manipulated, as is the situation, really Zimbardo is observing the behaviour of the guards and the prisoners and is gathering qualitative not quantitative data. As often happens in psychology, identifying the method is not easy. If you called this an observation, it would be hard to argue with you. Often this study is simply called a simulation.

A total of 75 men replied to Zimbardo's advertisement for participants. They were paid $15 per day. They were given questionnaires and interviews to test their suitability and their 'normality', and 24 were eventually chosen. All were normal, healthy college students, mainly middle class. They did not know each other at the start of the study. Two of the 24 were stand-by prisoners, and one guard did not take part on the day, so the study involved 10 prisoners and 11 guards.

The simulated prison had three small cells with steel barred doors, and the only furniture was a cot. A very small toilet (two feet by two feet and seven feet high) was across from the cells. There were also guard quarters and a bedroom for the warden. There was a yard too, and in various positions there were video cameras and observation places. The prisoners were in the prison 24 hours a day, with three to each of the three cells and the others on stand-by at home. The guards worked three-man shifts of 8 hours a day and only stayed at the prison whilst they were on shift.

The participants were fully informed about the study, and were told that they would be randomly allocated to be a prisoner or a guard. They were given no instructions as to how to behave, but prisoners were told they should expect to lose some of their civil rights. The guards were told that they had to maintain a degree of order and had to be prepared for anything to happen. They were not told what they had to do to maintain order, however. The guards thought that the researchers were interested in observing the prisoners, and even helped set the prison up. The only instruction they had was that they could not use physical punishment. Both guards and prisoners had uniforms, and each prisoner had a toothbrush, soap, towel and bed linen. No personal belongings were allowed. The guard uniforms were khaki and military-style. The prisoners had smocks with numbers on them, which were designed to be humiliating. They also wore a stocking cap to make them as similar as possible (for example, to hide long hair), and to simulate the shaving of heads that takes place in some prisons and in the military.

Real policemen 'arrested' the prisoners and charged them, advising them of their rights. They were handcuffed and searched, often in front of neighbours. They were fingerprinted and blindfolded at the police station, before being driven to the mock prison. At the prison the prisoners were stripped and made to stand alone naked in the yard. Then the superintendent gave them the rules of the prison (for example two visits per week, and movie rights) and the observations began.

Both guards and prisoners developed many negative attitudes. They were free to be nice to one another, but they were not. Prisoners became passive quickly, whereas guards took a very active role in interactions. Verbal commands were the most common, and interactions were very impersonal. Verbal insults were used. Five prisoners had to be released because of depression, anxiety and crying. This pattern began in the second day for four of the prisoners; the fifth had a psychosomatic rash (a rash caused by psychological/mental factors, rather than physical ones). The whole study was ended after six days, even though it was planned to continue for much longer. The prisoners were very pleased that the study was over, but the guards were not. They seemed to have enjoyed the power the role gave them. One guard did say he had been upset by the prisoners' suffering and said he would swap roles, but he did not do so. None of the guards were ever late for their shift.

There were differences in the ways the individuals reacted to the situation. Half of the prisoners coped and some of the guards were not hostile.

Evaluation

- Zimbardo himself admits that the situation was hardly natural. The prisoners knew that they were only there for a short time, and what was required. Demand characteristics were evident, as they could guess what the study was about. However, even when the prisoners thought they were not being watched, they talked about the prison and the situation for 90% of the time, and not about their own lives. So Zimbardo concluded that they were immersed in the situation. The researchers also found out that when guards were alone with prisoners and thought they were not being observed, they often harassed the prisoners even more. There was a lot of evidence to show that the participants were caught up in their roles. The guards went on playing the role even when the prisoners were clearly suffering emotional distress. The prisoners who were offered parole if they would give up the money they had been promised were willing to do so, even though they had initially only taken part for the money.

- The guards seemed to enjoy the power of the role. Some were leaders, and the other guards followed their lead. Power seemed to be the reward in itself, and this could be the case in real prisons.

- The prisoners adopted various coping strategies. Firstly, they showed disbelief at what the guards would do. Secondly, they rebelled. They also tried to set up a grievance committee to work within the system, and then self-interests emerged as they stopped co-operating. Some prisoners became good prisoners and sided with the guards. The prisoners had lost their identity and power, so they may have been seen as fair game by the guards.

- Haney et al thought they had enough evidence to show that their 'guards' took on the role of the brutal guard because of situational factors. It was not the personality of the individuals, because they had been carefully chosen, but it was the situation they were in that led them to such behaviour. This means that the study has application to real life, and the excuse cannot be given that prisons are brutal places because the guards are like that naturally.

- However, the participants were merely acting out roles using their ideas of what the roles were like. They were using stereotyped explanations, which casts doubt upon the validity of the study. However, you could argue that in 'real life' we rely on stereotypes to play our roles. Zimbardo himself thought that, even if they were role playing initially, the participants were 'real' prisoners and guards at the end of the six days. Also, even if the guards were playing roles according to stereotypes, it is harder to see how the prisoners knew how to act. The role of being a prisoner is perhaps not so clear.

- Zimbardo himself says that the study needs careful ethical scrutiny. He says that the volunteers suffered a great deal of pressure and stress. Savin (1973) argues that the findings do not justify the distress caused. Zimbardo defends criticisms by saying that there was no deception, except that the actual arrest was a surprise. In all other ways the participants were fully informed, and so informed consent was given. This is an advantage of using a simulation. The participants even signed contracts agreeing to the violation of their civil rights. Also the study was stopped as soon as it was realised that there was intense suffering. Approval had been officially sought, including from the University Committee of Human Experimentation. It was just that such extreme reactions were not anticipated (this was similar to Milgram's experiences). The researchers also looked for an alternative methodology, although none was found. Debriefing sessions were held, including follow-up questionnaires at yearly intervals. There was even an unbiased observer on hand to stop the study if necessary.

- The study is valid to an extent, because such great effort was made to make the mock prison realistic; however, it was still an unnatural situation, so the study must be criticised to an extent. This is not the sort of study that is easily repeated to see if it is reliable. There were different shifts of guards, however, who did not meet or compare notes, and they all acted in similar ways, so there is some evidence of reliability within the study. It is hard to generalise the study as only white middle-class male college students were used. These findings might not apply to any other group. Certainly care should be taken in generalising the findings to other cultures or countries.

ACTIVITY 11

THINK OF SOME MORE CRITICISMS OF ZIMBARDO'S STUDY

Note down some criticisms of the mock prison experiment. You could think about reliability (if it was done again, would it get the same results) and validity (was it real-life behaviour?). You could consider generalisation (could you generalise to everyone, from the 24 participants?). Also, consider ethical issues, and compare this study with Milgram's.

Key Skill C3.1a – this would make a good group activity.

Ruttenberg et al (1996) – group identity and intergroup prejudice among Jewish and Arab students in the USA

This is a study of in-group and outgroup relationships between Jewish and Arab students. The idea of belonging to a group involves group self-esteem, religious involvement and involvement in ethnic organisations. The idea of minimal groups is outlined earlier in this chapter. Studies that show that groups with low self-esteem are less likely to denigrate others are outlined here. This study

by Ruttenberg et al goes against previous findings and suggests that those involved in in-group activities who think that their group is not well viewed by the outgroup may say things against the outgroup in an attempt to boost their own self-esteem.

One way to get high in-group self-esteem is to denigrate (put down) other groups. High collective (group) self-esteem is what is aimed at. Ruttenberg et al chose Jews and Arabs because of their history of conflict and negative intergroup attitudes (Bizman and Amir, 1982). Crocker and Luhtanen (1990) found that groups with high self-esteem react protectively, but not those with low group self-esteem. Those with low group self-esteem played down group differences to try to protect their own low self-esteem.

On the other hand, there were also findings that suggested that groups with low self-esteem would want to denigrate the outgroup to boost their own self-esteem. These findings are a bit contradictory. This is why Ruttenberg et al set out to test the ideas, and they also think that experiments are rather unnatural, so it would be good to test in-group/outgroup prejudices outside the laboratory setting.

There is also the psychoanalytic view that prejudice reflects personal inadequacies. As there is a clear correlation between personal self-esteem and group self-esteem (as personal self-esteem of members rises, so the group self-esteem rises), it might be that the group will be prejudiced because of the inadequacies of those in the group. This is an interesting view, and relates to the material in Chapter 5.

There is quite a lot of evidence to say that groups with members with low self-esteem are likely to be prejudiced, even though some of the laboratory minimal group studies suggest the opposite. This is what this study is all about.

Hypotheses

Ruttenberg et al looked at religious attitudes because a high religious attitude in Christians has been shown to predict anti-Semitism and other prejudices (Batson and Burris, 1994). So one prediction was that a high religious attitude in Jewish and Arab students would predict prejudice. Membership of ethnic organisations tends to predict prejudice (Yogev et al, 1991), so another prediction was that membership of such organisations would predict prejudice. Ruttenberg et al, having weighed the evidence, also predicted that low group self-esteem would mean more prejudicial attitudes towards the outgroup. These were the main three hypotheses.

Method

Participants

A total of 42 Jewish and 49 Arab college students studying in Washington, DC were chosen, all aged between 18 and 24. They volunteered and the study took place in Spring 1994. The Jewish students were at a private university and more than half of them belonged to the Hillel organisation. Most of the Arab students attended one university, the rest were from the youth group of the Arabic Baptist Church. The youth group were Christians not Muslim, but this was thought to strengthen their ties to Arab culture. Of the Jewish students 97.1% were born in the USA, whereas only 17% of the Arabs had been, most originating from Kuwait, Saudi Arabia or the United Arab Emirates.

Measures

- Ruttenberg et al measured self-esteem using the scale devised by Luhtanen and Crocker (1992). They looked at personal judgement of how good their own group was, their judgement about how good they were for the group, judgement of how others view their group and how important their own social membership was for their own self-concept. However, the study was changed so that the participants focused on their social identity as it related to ethnic origin. They also used a five-point Likert scale, whereas Luhtanen and Crocker used a seven-point scale.
- They measured organisational involvement by giving the participants points for membership of different groups.
- They measured individual religious involvement by asking about religious attitudes, attendance at services, affiliation with a mosque or synagogue (according to which was relevant) and frequency of prayer. They used a points system for the scoring of answers.
- They assessed prejudice against the outgroup by adopting the anti-Semitism scale and ratings of ethnic humour of Levinson and Sanford (1944). They took out any items that might cause offence and removed items that they considered too stereotypical. They gave an anti-Jewish scale to the Arabs and an anti-Arab scale to the Jews. The items on the scale focused on materialism, power and clannishness, for example. To get additional measures they also asked the participants to evaluate disparaging humour – there were jokes and cartoons that showed Jewish and Arab stereotypes. Arabs were portrayed as incompetent in war, threatening, unhygienic, controlling of women and uncharitable. Jews were portrayed as obsessed with making money, warlike, duplicitous – for example, manipulating the media, refusing to accept peace and misrepresenting military strength. The

participants were asked how far they thought the joke or cartoon was funny, and how accurate the portrayed traits were. The researchers averaged the scores to give each participant a Jewish humour score and an Arab humour score. The participants were then asked if they thought the stereotypes were accurate, and were given a Jewish stereotyping score and an Arab stereotyping score.

Procedure

Participants were assured that answers would be confidential. The study was said to be an investigation of the perception of social groups. The scales were administered as outlined above.

Results

- The Jewish students had higher public group self-esteem.
- The Jewish students were more 'religious'.
- The Jewish students were no more involved in ethnic organisations than the Arab students.
- The Jewish students were less negative towards the Arab students than the Arab students were to them.
- The Jewish students found the Arab humour funnier than the Arab students did.
- The Jewish students thought the Jewish jokes were less representative of the Jewish people than the Arab students did.
- The two groups did not differ regarding perception of Arab stereotypes.
- The two groups did not differ regarding ratings of Jewish humour.
- The Jewish students found outgroup humour funnier and more accurate than in-group humour but the result was not statistically significant.
- The Arab students found jokes about the outgroup significantly funnier than jokes about the in-group.
- The Arab students found outgroup humour to be more accurate than in-group humour.
- Being in an ethnic organisation linked to high group esteem in the Arabs, and meant that they found the Jewish jokes, but not the Arab jokes, amusing.
- The Jewish students who were most religious were least anti-Arab and the Jewish students who were most religious also had high group esteem. However, the Arabs who were religious had low group esteem and were more strongly anti-Semitic. The Arabs who were religious agreed with both Arab and Jewish stereotypes. Those Arab students with high group esteem did find the Arab jokes less funny and less representative of Arab traits.
- So it seems that the Arabs were more prejudiced than the Jews.

- Ruttenberg et al do present some criticisms of their study. The sample was small and the people in the Arab group had two religions and were culturally different. However, they did all identify with 'being Arab'. The findings might have been different if the participants had been living in the Middle East, and it is interesting that the title of the study emphasises that it was done in the USA.

- Some of the scales used were adapted, so they were not tested thoroughly. Also there might have been social desirability in the answers. This means that the participants might have said what they thought they ought to say.

- The researchers say they are pleased that they did not use a laboratory study, but used participants involved in real-life conflict, as they claim this improves their study and makes the results more valid.

- You could criticise the ethics of the study: they do say they give confidentiality but they don't actually tell participants what the questions or the study are about. Of course, if they said too much the results would be biased. Perhaps they should have said more about debriefing and the right to withdraw, to counter any problems of not getting informed consent. The participants were volunteers, although it's not clear how they were found.

Conclusions

It was not found that groups with high esteem get their esteem by denigrating outgroup members, because the Jews (who had higher group esteem) were less denigrating. It did seem that low group esteem and high organisational membership (in ethnic organisations) was more likely to lead to prejudice. The Jews who were more highly religious were more tolerant, and this goes against research that found that religious Christians were more prejudiced. More study is needed to look at religiosity and prejudice.

It is possible that the Arab students were more involved in the Arab–Israeli conflict because many of them were not born in the USA, whereas most of the Jews were. This might explain the higher level of prejudice in Arabs. Alternatively, they might be more frustrated than the Jews – for example, in economic terms.

Key application – prejudice reduction

Ways of reducing prejudice have been outlined when considering causes of prejudice, and are worth summarising (see Figure 2.2).

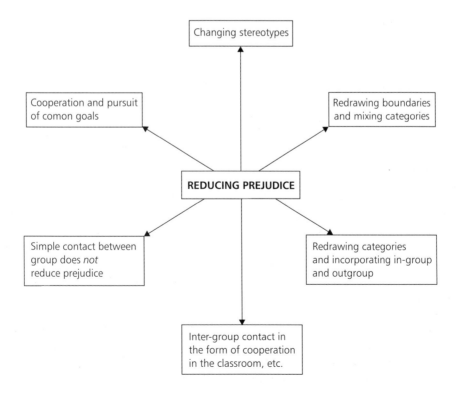

Figure 2.2
Ways of reducing prejudice

ACTIVITY 12

WAYS OF REDUCING PREJUDICE

Note down ways of reducing prejudice that have been suggested by the second area of study above. This is not an easy task, so if you do think of them, you have done well.

Key Skill C3.1a – If you are studying in a group you could use group discussion for this activity. Widen the discussion by recalling the causes of prejudice mentioned earlier in the chapter. Draw from these what you think ways of reducing prejudice might be.

- **Co-operation over superordinate goals reduces prejudice – pursuit of common goals.** Sherif et al (1961) created prejudice by setting up competition between two groups. The two groups were allowed to get to know one another separately, and to become 'real' groups. Then Sherif et al created a tournament with real prizes, and this 'realistic conflict' led to prejudice. In fact, it was claimed that the prejudice arose immediately the two groups knew about one another, and before the competition, so there is criticism of the realistic conflict theory. Sherif then went on to create superordinate goals – situations that can be solved only when groups work together. Sherif's groups did have to work together (to free the camp bus and to sort out the water supply) and prejudice was reduced considerably. However, only 30% mentioned friends from the other group at the end of the study. Admittedly, this figure was 7% before the co-operation phase, but even so 70% still kept their friends within their in-group.

- Worchel et al (1977) made the point that in Sherif's studies co-operation succeeded in solving the problems and achieving the superordinate goal. They showed, however, that if co-operation followed competition, and the co-operation did not achieve the goal, then there was even less liking for the outgroup.

- **Simple contact between groups does not reduce prejudice.** In the Sherif study, simple contact was not enough. The boys were in conflict when they were put together, and it was only the need for co-operation that led to the prejudice reduction.

- **Co-operation in the classroom reduces prejudice – intergroup contact.** Aronson's jigsaw classroom study was shown to reduce prejudice. Multi-cultural groups were formed, and individuals had to work together. Each had to contribute for the group to achieve the task. This did lead to reduction in prejudice, although perhaps only for that particular task.

- **Redrawing the categories can reduce prejudice – incorporating outgroup in with in-group.** Turner (1991) noted that if with the superordinate goal the groups redefine themselves as one group (the one needed to achieve the goal), then they all become an in-group. Gaertner et al (1993) did a laboratory experiment that showed this to be the case. When two groups became one group to solve a problem, reactions between individuals was more favourable than when they were left as two separate groups.

- **Redrawing the boundaries can reduce prejudice – mixing categories in the groups.** Alternatively categories can be redrawn if two social categories (e.g. race and gender) cut across the groups. If the groups are a mix of gender and racial groups, and quick categorisation using these categories is not possible, prejudice is reduced (Deschamps, 1977). This study was laboratory based, and so some of the complexities of real groupings was missing. Hewstone et al (1993) looked at real-life groups with mixed categories. The categories were religion (Muslim and Hindi), nationality (Bangladeshi and Indian) and language (Bengali and Hindi). The study, carried out in Bangladesh, showed that the categories were not 'equal' in that religion had more importance when the individuals were evaluating each other. They did not seem so concerned about what language was spoken, or even their nationality, but the other person's religion did affect their judgements. Language and nationality had some importance, so if the other person was of a different religion and also spoke a different language, liking for them was even lower.

- **Simple contact does not reduce prejudice, but equal status contact can.** In Sherif's study, when the boys came into contact with one another prejudice grew, if anything. However, if people focus on individuals in the two groups, rather than on a task, it does seem that prejudice is reduced (Miller et al, 1985). Contact with typical members of the other group has been found to improve relationships between the two groups (Desforges et al, 1991). If the interaction with the 'typical' member of the outgroup goes wrong, however, then this reinforces the negative attitude held about the outgroup, so the status of the person is important.

- Aronson (1980) suggested that the contact that Whites have had with Blacks in America is to see them in low-status jobs such as dishwashers and servants. Amir (1994) makes a similar point and suggests that the actual contact with other groups should be examined carefully. Deutsch and Collins (1951) did an early study looking at contact between different groups in two housing projects. One project involved segregated housing for different racial groups, and the other involved integration. There was less prejudice in the integrated housing project, so contact does seem to reduce prejudice. Presumably the people in the housing were of equal status. Minard (1952) studied miners, where groups of mixed races worked well together underground, but when they came to the surface at the end of a shift, they did not mix. It seemed as if the miners were of equal status as miners, so got on underground, but the norms that were used above ground did not allow this mixed contact to continue.

• The problem with these studies is that within these groups individual friendships may have occurred, but this does not mean that being friendly with one member of a different group makes you friendly with them all. The formation of groups is different. While the miners constitute the in-group, there may be reduced prejudice, but above ground different group structures would be operating.

• **Changing stereotypes can reduce prejudice.** Aronson and Osherow (1980) reported an experiment where a class teacher called Jane Elliott tried to give her pupils the experience of being discriminated against, so that they could learn about it, and possibly change their stereotypes. She told her class of 9-year-old students that the brown-eyed children would be the ruling class for the day, and the blue-eyed children were to be kept in their place. The blue-eyed children began to do badly in their school work quite quickly, and became depressed. The next day Elliott told the children that she had lied, and that it was the blue-eyed children who were the ruling class, so the brown-eyed were inferior. The brown-eyed children were quickly discriminated against. Then she debriefed the children and explained to them the idea that if they had experienced prejudice and discrimination, they would not be so likely to be prejudiced themselves.

Contemporary issue: crowd behaviour and social identity theory

This issue is taken from an article in the *Daily Telegraph*, 19 January 2000, which is about religion and violence in the Spice Islands.

There were 4 days of fighting and 250 people were killed, in what was said to be a 'war' by one of the youths involved. The violence spread as Muslims heard about attacks on 'their religious brethren'. Christian gangs and Muslims were involved in the fighting. Muslims in the military joined in, as did Christian policemen.

It is said that the Christian and Muslim communities had lived peacefully for centuries but are now polarised. Neighbourhoods are now one or the other as they have

been 'cleansed' of the 'other group', whichever was the minority.

It appears that Muslims are not having equal access to education and health care because most schools and hospitals are in the Christian centre. Both sides say that the cause of the violence is a conspiracy to do with a former dictator wanting the military to have more power. Parts of the army loyal to this dictator have supposedly started up the violence and there are also radical Muslim leaders who are opposed to the moderate form of Islam found currently.

There is a picture to accompany the article, and the caption refers to a 'Muslim mob'.

Linking the contemporary issue to concepts in social psychology

Emotional contagion

Studies of crowd behaviour go right back to Le Bon (1895), who suggested that there was such a thing as emotional contagion. In other words, emotions are catching. For example, in a crowd if someone shows fear when seeing someone with a knife, it is likely that others nearby will 'catch' that fear. Social psychologists are now looking again at this idea of emotional contagion (Hatfield et al, 1994). It is suggested in the article that the violence has been brought about by 'evil hands' and a conspiracy against the government. So it is possible that some people are inciting the riots and that the 'mob' has come about through emotional contagion.

Density and crowding

When we discuss crowding, we mean what it feels like to experience density, and density refers to the number of people in a given space. You might be in an enclosed space with one person and feel more crowded than when you are at a concert with a lot of people.

ACTIVITY 13

THINK OF TIMES WHEN YOU FEEL CROWDED

Think of times when you feel crowded and note down whether you think it was due to emotional contagion or to density.

Key Skill C3.1a – this might be a bit small-scale for this key skill, but you could discuss this activity in a group. You could widen the discussion to bring in football crowds and other crowds.

You might have chosen a situation where density was the cause of the crowding, for example in a lift, or you might have chosen a case of emotional contagion. An example of emotional contagion is when you feel crowded and swept along by the crowd, for example at a football match. There is no mention in this article of crowding, but as the violence spread and the crowds became larger then crowding would become an issue.

Animal studies of crowd behaviour

Animal studies have been done to study the effects of crowding in the sense of an over-dense population. Animal behaviour seems to be regulated by crowding, as in the case of lemmings. Their population increases quickly, and then a malfunction of the adrenal gland leads to hyperactivity (and sometimes accidental drowning). The increase in population has a direct effect on the behaviour of the animals. Stress due to overcrowding in Sitka deer has shown to increase the size of the adrenal glands, and this causes the death of many of the deer, so that the population stabilises (Christian et al, 1960)

A well-known study of crowding in animals is that of Calhoun (1962). He placed rats in a crowded space and watched what happened. The dominant rats took up the space and left others to fend for themselves. The less dominant rats were more aggressive, poor nest builders and poor rearers of young, so this strain of rats died out. This was a way of regulating the population.

Studies with humans

Studies with humans have also shown that overcrowding leads to stress and arousal. Overcrowding is also linked to poor health. Saegert et al (1975) found that in overcrowded situations people were less able to give directions and to use cognitive maps (see Chapter 1 for an explanation of cognitive maps). Karlin et al (1979) found that high-density living at university correlated with lower grades. Rodin (1976) found that children raised in high-density living conditions found it more difficult to make choices. So these three studies all suggest that cognitive ability is affected by overcrowding.

The stress caused by overcrowding may have been a factor that explains the bloodshed because the violence was very bad. A Christian gang leader was said at one stage to have walked down the street holding a sword in one hand and 'dragging a headless corpse behind him'.

Social identity theory

There is evidence in this article of in-group/outgroup behaviour. The Muslims and the Christians have become two gangs just like those in Sherif's study outlined earlier. They need a superordinate goal in order to overcome their prejudice. There will be stereotyping of the outgroup, and only instances that reinforce the in-group/outgroup ideas will be noted, for example, every instance confirming how 'bad' the other group is. Outsiders like the military were said to have joined the Muslim gangs because they belong to the country's 90% Islamic majority, and Christian policemen joined the Christians. Each were drawn into 'their' group as tensions rose.

Realistic conflict theory

The groups were fighting over territory because they were being pushed into segregated areas. It is suggested that they were fighting over things like education and health facilities. These are real goals, and this links to realistic conflict theory. The problem seems to be concern about the moderate government, and the worry over the loss of military power. This explanation fits better with the idea of whipping up of crowd behaviour and emotional contagion being the cause of the violence, rather than the groups fighting over real goals.

Conclusion

Perhaps it is wrong to look for one cause for such violence. On the one hand a powerful ex-dictator seems to be causing the violence because of his own views, and then emotional contagion and in-group/outgroup pressures seem to be doing the rest. On the other hand, it seems that one group is not getting as much as the other group, so there is competition over actual goals such as access to education and health.

Coursework suggestions

1 Devise a field experiment to test helping behaviour (Activity 2, p. 38).
2 Observe helping behaviour (Activity 3, p. 40).
3 Compose a questionnaire about conformity (Activity 6, p. 44).
4 Do not try to repeat Milgram's studies, as this is not an ethical thing to do. You could, however, observe behaviour and look for obedience. Supermarket checkouts are places where people queue and obey norms. You could watch for examples of conformity, and where people do not conform. Perhaps an employee will ask people to move, and you can watch their reactions.
5 Devise a questionnaire to look at the possible correlation between personality and prejudice (Activity 10, p. 52).

6 Create a questionnaire to look at in-group/outgroup like and dislike. This would have to be carefully worded, but you could choose a certain sports team and analyse their attitudes to members of other teams.

7 Look at overcrowding. You could try asking directions in two conditions, one where there is crowding and one where there is not, and think of a measure to see how easily the participant gives directions (perhaps you could measure how long it takes them to tell you the way to the Post Office, and use a crowded and a less crowded shop).

Suggested further reading

Deaux, K. & Wrightsman, L.S. (1988) *Social Psychology,* 5th edition. Belmont, California: Brooks/Cole.

Eysenck, M. (1996) *Simply Psychology*. Hove: Psychology Press.

Gross, R.D. (1999) *Key Studies in Psychology,* 3rd edition. London: Hodder & Stoughton.

Hardy, M. & Heyes, S. (1999) *Beginning Psychology, a Comprehensive Introduction to Psychology,* 5th edition. Oxford: Oxford University Press.

Hewstone, M., Stroebe, W. & Stephenson, G. (eds) (1996) *Introduction to Social Psychology – a European Perspective,* 2nd edition. Oxford: Alden Press.

Myers, D.G. (1998) *Exploring Psychology,* 5th edition. New York: Worth.

Pennington, D.C., Gillen, K. & Hill, P. (1999) *Social Psychology*. London: Arnold

Sabini, J. (1995) *Social Psychology,* 2nd edition. London: Norton and Company.

3

The cognitive-developmental approach

The aims of this chapter

The aims of this chapter are, with regard to the social approach, to enable the reader to:

– *appreciate some of the general assumptions*
– *discuss research methods used*
– *discuss Piaget's theories of child reasoning/stages of development*
– *discuss one theory other than that of Piaget*
– *discuss relevant studies*
– *understand how the approach links to issues within education*
– *explain one contemporary issue or debate.*

Self-test 1

After reading this chapter, test yourself on each of the above points. Use the points as exam questions and make notes accordingly. Then see how much you can write on each.

This chapter covers

KEY ASSUMPTIONS
1 The importance of cognition and cognitive abilities
2 The focus on development over time (and stages)
3 The use of different frameworks

RESEARCH METHODS
1 Case studies
2 Observations
3 Experiments
4 Clinical interviews
5 Longitudinal studies

IN-DEPTH AREA OF STUDY: THEORIES OF COGNITIVE DEVELOPMENT
1 The theory of Jean Piaget

2 The theory of Vygotsky
3 The theory of Bruner

STUDIES IN DETAIL
1 Does the autistic child have a theory of mind? (Baron-Cohen et al, 1985)
2 The influence of classroom peers on cognitive performance in children with behavioural problems (Bevington et al, 1999)

KEY APPLICATION: INFLUENCES ON EDUCATION

CONTEMPORARY ISSUE: CHILDREN'S COGNITVE LEVELS AND PERCEPTIONS OF PAIN

Introduction

Developmental psychology looks at all areas of how we develop, from babyhood to adulthood. At first, most researchers did not look further than when we reach adulthood. However, they did later take what was called a **'life span' approach**, and people like Erikson were interested in how people develop right up to old age (see Chapter 5).

The cognitive-developmental approach focuses particularly on how we develop in a cognitive sense. Think of cognition as 'thinking'. It means looking at mental processes, and the cognitive-developmental approach involves looking at how our mental processes develop.

> ### STUDY AID
>
> This may seem obvious, but as you are now studying a different approach, remember to start a new section in your folder, or a new folder.
>
> Key Skill LP3.1 – agree targets and plan how these will be met, using support from appropriate others. You need your tutor for this, and you will need a record of the discussion, to use as evidence. Discuss organising your work and develop a time plan for working through this textbook. It is tempting to leave everything to your teacher, but you should be reading the chapters as you study each approach, and do this alongside the work your teacher gives you. Make a note of dates and what you will have achieved by then, so that you can review your progress for Key Skill LP3.3.

A brief historical setting

The developmental approach

If you decide to continue your study of psychology, and you take the full 'A' level, in the A2 choices you could study more of developmental psychology. However, this chapter focuses on one specific part of the developmental approach – theories of cognitive-development.

An Introduction to the cognitive-developmental approach

There are many influences on us as children, and our development depends on these influences. You could say that everything about us comes from inherited characteristics, but this is not accepted because even identical twins, who share 100% of their genes, are not identical in every way. It is usually accepted that both **'nature'** (characteristics we are born with) and **'nurture'**

(how our environment affects us) are important issues that affect how we turn out.

Theories of cognitive development consider both our biological inheritance (nature) and the effect of the environment (nurture). The main focus of the initial theory at least (Piaget's) is, firstly, how our development unfolds in a predetermined way (nature), and then, secondly, how our development is affected by the interaction of our nature with our experiences in the environment.

From the 1930s Piaget in Switzerland did a lot of work in the area of studying children growing up. He focused quite a lot on his own children, and was very interested in their thought processes. He noticed how young children do not think in the same way as older children do (see later).

Other main theorists in the field of cognitive development are Bruner and Vygotsky. Vygotsky worked in Russia and focused much more on social interactions than Piaget did. He recognised the importance of others in the development of mental processes, and so did Bruner in Britain. For Piaget, language was not a central issue, but other cognitive-developmental theorists give much more emphasis to the effects of the development of language. Research is still continuing in the field of cognitive development, and one interesting area is called 'The Theory of Mind'.

Key assumptions of the cognitive-developmental approach

Key assumption 1 – The importance of cognition and cognitive abilities

Cognition refers to all the mental processes including memory, perception, problem solving and thinking. From the 1950s **cognitive** psychology gained in importance.

The behaviourists had been focusing on the stimuli (things – usually in the environment) that start an action, and the type of action that is produced. They were working on what they could measure – I hit you (stimulus), then you cry (response). However, you might not cry – you might hit me back, and it was not long before cognitive psychology developed – interested in the thinking processes that took place as part of the learning.

Neither those studying learning theory nor cognitive psychologists stopped to look at how mental processes develop. They concentrated on things as they found them, and this tended to mean they looked at adults or animals. Children are not specifically mentioned in most other approaches, although the psychodynamic approach does have a focus on children, and often ideas from the psychodynamic approach are included in developmental psychology in general. If children are the focus of attention, usually this means that the study would come under the heading 'developmental psychology'.

Early interest in physical development

During the nineteenth century, as children started to be employed in factories and so on, interest grew in how children developed. Also, Darwin's (1859) book *The Origin of Species* showed how humans were related to other species. This suggested that children were not just little adults. Children could be compared with other animals, such as chimpanzees. They could be seen as different. Later, these interests led researchers to look at a child's cognitive development.

Stages of physical development were written about at this time. It was probably easier to observe noticeable changes. For example, they looked at when a baby learns to crawl (one stage), walk (the next stage), and so on. Language development was studied in stages. There was the one-word stage, and the two-word stage. It is not surprising that cognitive development was also studied stage by stage.

Researchers take the thinking of their time and simply go with it, and this is why this sort of background understanding is important. They take current understanding and use this basic understanding as grounding for research. They share basic assumptions, such as that humans have evolved from basic life forms, and that families are the right way to bring up children. It is very hard to make a list of basic assumptions, because we are so involved in our own culture. (Read or recall the arguments presented by social representation theorists outlined in Chapter 2).

You may have come up with some of the following ideas:

- Babies cannot stand up (true, although they have a walking reflex at first, which disappears)
- Babies need stimulation and playing with (true)
- Some children are born naughty (probably not true, and learning theory can help to explain 'naughty' behaviour – see Chapter 4)
- Boys are more aggressive than girls (well maybe not naturally, but could they learn to be more aggressive because this is expected?)
- Mothers naturally love their babies (probably not. You could ask around!)
- Fathers play with their children, but they are not good at physical care (early studies did show that mothers and fathers had different roles, but there is no evidence that fathers cannot do the 'mothering')
- Children should be talking by the age of two years (usually, a child will start talking by this age, but there are those who don't talk by two years, and develop completely normally)

Not all of these are correct, and you will almost certainly have come up with different ideas. Your ideas are, however, probably quite similar. We do have basic assumptions that we have learnt through our own **socialisation**. You might like to reconsider your list of what you think about children, once you have studied more about development.

In our culture, with its emphasis on education and skills, we value the development of thinking. We value those, who have a good memory, and envy those with a 'photographic' memory. Qualifications are valued too. We see the development of cognitive processes such as language, thinking, memory, and perception as very important. These are some of our basic assumptions.

A 'Wild Child'

One way of looking at the importance of thinking patterns is to look at what are called feral children. The Wild Boy of Aveyron is an example of such a child. Victor was a twelve-year-old boy who emerged from the forest, could not speak and acted like a wild child. He did not learn much, even when taught, so it is concluded that socialisation is needed for a child to be 'human'. Box 1 outlines the case study of Victor.

ACTIVITY 1

LIST SOME BASIC IDEAS THAT WE HAVE ABOUT HOW CHILDREN DEVELOP

Think about babies and children in general. Write down what you know already. This will be a good basis for your study of cognitive development in this chapter. You could work with someone else and pool your ideas.

Key Skill C3.1a – as is often the case when learning psychology, group work here would be very useful. You can share ideas.

Box 1

Victor – The Wild Boy of Aveyron

Victor appeared in a French hamlet in 1800, simply coming out of the woods. It was thought that he was about twelve years old. He tore clothes off when they tried to put clothes on him, and he ate potatoes, roots and nuts. He made no sounds and did not respond to human voices. He acted like a wild animal, and it was concluded that he had lived alone, and had not been **socialised**. He moved on all fours and it was thought by many that he was 'mentally deficient'.

Jean-Marc Itard took the boy in and tried to teach him to be 'human'. Itard did not think the boy was 'retarded', but thought that he had simply lacked socialisation. It was quite common for children to be rejected for one reason or another at that time.

The important conclusion drawn from the above story is that a child will not be 'human' if not brought up in society in some way. It was discovered that language was not natural, and that social norms, such as what and how we eat, have to be learnt. Itard thought that the necessary skills could be taught to the boy. If these skills could be taught, then much of what we 'are' comes from nurture, not nature.

Victor did learn basic communication and could write a few words, but he did not learn to speak or interact well with others.

Evaluation

- There is always the possibility that Victor did not have normal mental capacity, so it is hard to draw strong conclusions from this one case. Other evidence does support the claim that socialisation is important, however. Much of the research on language development suggests that, after the age of twelve, it would be very difficult to develop language, and this supports Itard's claim that Victor needed teaching. In turn, Victor's story gives support to those who claim that we need to have developed language by the age of twelve. Key Assumption 2 looks at the importance of development over time, and the evidence from the case study of Victor strongly suggests that timing is important.

The importance of cognitive abilities

There were two ways in which the 'Victor' story was interpreted:

1 Many people thought that Victor was mentally impaired, and that accounted for his lack of social abilities and his lack of ability to learn when taught.
2 Itard, however, thought that Victor was in fact quite able – since he seemed to have survived on his own in the forest for a long time. Itard thought that he must have been alone from a very young age, or he would have had some language and social abilities.

In the first example (1) many said he was not human because he lacked cognitive abilities. In the second example (2) Itard said that he had good cognitive abilities, but needed to be taught what was required. In both cases it was assumed that cognitive abilities are of great importance for us to develop into social beings.

Cognitive abilities include perception, memory, problem solving, language, attention and thinking. None of those who looked at Victor's story said that he lacked the ability to perceive, to remember, to attend to certain things, or to solve problems. All these abilities were needed for him to survive, and Itard understood that. It was language that was the missing ability, and the other things he lacked, such as knowing how to eat, or how to walk, seemed to be social norms. This underlines the importance of language in human development.

At the time (1800) people had not started looking at the development of cognitive abilities as we have today. Most of those who heard about the story just thought that there was something wrong with Victor. However, it was from these sorts of examples that people began to look at how children develop their abilities, especially their ability to fit in with society. Itard was one such person, and it is from his initial interest and experiments on Victor that people began to look at how cognitive abilities, like language and thinking, develop.

Language and thought – Bruner, Piaget and Vygotsky compared

Bruner, Piaget and Vygotsky are the three main cognitive development theorists, on whose work the approach is based. Here they are compared to show that cognition is very important in the cognitive-developmental approach, but that the main theories do differ.

It was seen, from stories such as Victor's, that the development of language is very important for us to become social beings. In the field of psychology there was also discussion about the relationship between language and thought. Was it just that we needed to learn language or do we need the cognitive ability of thinking before we can learn language? This is worth looking at here, as the main cognitive-developmental theorists differ as to the role of language.

Activity 2 asks you to think about the question of whether you need language to have thought, or whether you need thought before you can have language.

ACTIVITY 2

WHICH COMES FIRST, LANGUAGE OR THOUGHT?

Some say that you need thought before you can use language, and others say that without language you cannot think.

▶

Try thinking about going on holiday. Note down some of your thoughts. Did you need language for these thoughts? Well, probably you did, because I asked you to write them down. You might have thought about when you go on holiday, or where you go on holiday. Places have names, and if you think about when, then you will have words in your head. So you might conclude that you need language to have thoughts.

However, try thinking about something without words. You might be able to think of a colour, but probably you would have to try to name it to think of it clearly. Try thinking about a favourite photograph or a picture. Perhaps the Mona Lisa is best thought of in picture form rather than in words. There are things that are best pictured. Also there might be sounds that you can think about without needing words.

Key Skill C3.1a – again this activity would make a good group discussion. You could set up a debate with two sides. One group would say you need language in order to think, and the other group would say you need to be able to think before you can develop language.

Even with the few ideas above of how you can think without language, people usually use words when they think. Perhaps some people, like artists, can think better without words, and others find they use language a lot when thinking. There might be an idea for some coursework here – to see whether some people can think without words better than others.

Thought needs language – Bruner

One group of psychologists claims that you need language to have thought. They go so far as to say that our language guides our thinking. If you live in a culture where there are lots of words for 'snow', you would think differently about snow. The Inuit have lots of words for snow. We mostly use the words 'slush', 'sleet', 'soft snow', 'real snow' – but not many more. However, a skier would have lots more ways of describing the different types of snow. The claim is that these different words for snow actually make you think differently about snow. You could use the example of colours. A non-artist would use the main colour words such as 'brown', 'green', 'red', and so on. An artist might refer to 'burnt umber' or 'burnt sienna' to describe different types of brown.

Bruner, who is one of the main cognitive-development theorists, thought that we need language so that our thinking can go beyond what we can learn through our actions and what we see. He suggested that there are three main stages in cognitive development. In the first stage we learn through actions. In the second 'stage' we learn through images, and it is in the third 'stage' that we need language. Then we can move from knowing things from actions and pictures, and can start using symbols (words). Bruner's theories are discussed more fully later, but note that he gave language a central role in the development of cognition.

Language only appears as a result of our being able to think – Piaget

Another argument is that we need thought to develop language. This is the opposite of saying that thought develops from language use. Bruner says that if we did not develop the use of symbols for objects (words) we would not develop beyond learning from what we do and what we see. However, Piaget holds the view that a child must be at the right level of cognitive development before it can use language. So two of the main researchers you will be studying have opposite views about language and thought.

Language and thought are separate, at least for the first few years – Vygotsky

Vygotsky held that language and thought are both important for the young child, but that they do not link at first as closely as Bruner thought. Up to the age of about two, the child is doing two separate things as far as language and thought are concerned. What they do and what they see are being registered as thoughts, and they are learning about the world. Also, they are getting ready to use language, by babbling and crying. They are using early communication, but this is separate at first from their experiences of the world. It is only later that the babbling is converted into words, for example, 'cup', and their perception of a 'cup' is linked to this word. At first, the two things are separate. From the ages of two to seven (roughly) the child uses language both to communicate to others ('want cup') and to think internally ('hmmm – want drink'). Vygotsky thought that the child cannot separate these two uses, which is why they will often think aloud.

Summary – the importance of cognition (thinking)

Although the three main theorists differ in the way they think that language and thinking develop, it is clear that there is an underlying assumption for all of them that language and thought are important cognitive abilities without which we would not develop into socialised people.

- Bruner thinks we need language for our thinking (cognition) to develop. Language is necessary for thought.
- Piaget thinks we need the right level of thinking (cognition) before we can use language. Thought is necessary for language.
- Vygotsky thought that before the age of two the child is separately learning about language (by babbling and so on), and is learning to think about the world (by experiences). Then these two gradually come together.

Key Assumption 2 – The focus on development over time (and stages)

So for us to develop into socialised humans, we need cognitive abilities, and language is perhaps particularly important. It was found from the study of Victor, and from other research, that we need to develop language before the age of twelve. This suggests that the time period over which we develop is in itself important. This is another basic assumption. Before studies were carried out within the cognitive-developmental approach the child was thought of as a little adult. It was not realised that certain experiences had to take place within a certain time span in order for a particular skill or ability to develop 'normally'.

Current areas of interest rest on our views of how children develop over time

Current areas of interest reflect this emphasis on development of abilities over time. For example, young children are often not allowed to give evidence in court because we now acknowledge that their thought processes and memories may be unreliable (see Chapter 1). Also decisions about whether to allow children with particular learning difficulties into mainstream schools are affected by assumptions about how we think 'healthy' children develop. We want to see how the children with learning difficulties would fit in with others of the same age, and we assume that at a certain age, children will have reached a certain stage. The age at which we teach children to read depends on when we think they are ready to read. Attitudes towards divorce depend on what people think children can understand at certain ages.

Children develop physically over time, so it is assumed that they develop their thinking abilities over time too

In the introduction it was said that the first area of interest regarding children was in their physical development. It was only later that cognitive development was studied. These days developmental psychology is interested in people from birth to old age, but the early cognitive-developmental approach concentrated on the period from babyhood to adulthood. It was assumed that we have developed our cognitive abilities by the time we reach adulthood.

Continuous development or development by stages?

Babies go through certain physical milestones; and cognitive-developmental theorists, starting with Piaget, thought that they also go through mental milestones. These are set out in stages, and the child passes through one stage before moving on to another. Actually, whether these are really stages has been disputed, and this too we can look at later, but the early theories were what is called **stage theories**. Freud's theory (outlined in Chapter 5) is a stage theory, as is Piaget's.

Behaviourism, however (see Chapter 4), is not a stage theory. Behaviourists say that we develop by means of reinforcements and punishments, in a *continuous* way. If we are positively reinforced for doing something (for example, a child might make his or her own bed and be praised for doing so), then we do it again. If we are punished for doing something (for example, the child pulls the baby's hair and is told off), then we don't do it again. So according to behaviourists we are continually learning and changing, and we do not develop by stages at all.

Ontogeny refers to how we develop over our lifetime, and involves both our inherited characteristics and our experiences. **Phylogeny** refers to how we have developed as a species, so basically refers to our inherited characteristics. Developmental psychologists are interested in ontogeny. At first sight we seem to develop in our lifetime by adding more and more experiences to what we know. We add memories and knowledge. This seems to be **quantitative** change in that the quantity of what we know changes. This would be continuous development with continuous change.

Those who think that we develop in stages, however, think that these stages show **qualitative** changes. One stage is different in quality from another stage, as well as in quantity. For example, if language development is thought of as continuous, then there will be quantitative change in the number of words a baby knows, and in what it can say. However, if language development is thought to be staged, then there will be a qualitative change from when the baby can babble to when the baby can use one word. As another example think of sponges, which grow continuously, getting bigger and bigger, compared to flowers, which grow discontinuously in stages from seed to sapling to flower (Cole and Cole, 1996).

Flavell (1971) listed four things that are needed for something to be called a developmental stage. These are listed in Box 2.

> **Box 2**
>
> **Flavell's (1971) list of what makes a 'stage' in development**
>
> For something to be called a 'stage':
> 1 There must be a qualitative change. For example, walking does not lead from the skills of crawling – there are new skills involved, and these are different in quality.
> 2 From one stage to the next there must be a number of these sorts of changes, and they must happen at the same time. For example, children don't just learn to use grammar, they also learn to talk about themselves, and to pretend that dolls can talk, and so on.
> 3 The change from one stage to another must be quick. For example, the growth at puberty is rapid compared with the slow growth up to then.
> 4 There must be a pattern to the physical changes and the changes in behaviour that characterise a stage.

If it is accepted that development in childhood is by stages, then at each stage the whole way the child experiences the world will change. For example, when a child learns to use language (if this is claimed to be a stage), its whole experience changes. Kagan (1984) suggests that these changes are necessary for the child to face the next set of tasks ahead. It also means that they can leave the past behind. Note that this is a different idea to the psychodynamic view. Freud and others thought that early experiences up to the age of five shape our whole experience of life, whereas Kagan is suggesting that we move on.

Others criticise the whole idea of us developing in stages. The behaviourists think change is continuous. Siegler (1991) points out that children's thinking is continually changing, and it is hard to argue with this. One problem with stage theories is that it is often not the case that a child can either do something, or cannot do it. For example, a four year old may use language in a fairly sophisticated way, but is able to talk more simply to a younger sibling. Activity 3 suggests a piece of coursework that you could do in this area.

ACTIVITY 3

TESTING THE CLAIM THAT DEVELOPMENT IS IN STAGES

This is a very complex area, and all you could do would be a small-scale study.

1 If you have access to young children, and if full consent can be given, then you could test the idea that 12–18 month-olds may be in one stage of development, but may not be at this stage at all times.

Use a measurable example, such as language. Let's say that babbling is one stage, and using 'one word' is another stage. For an example of the 'one word' stage, think of a child saying 'car'. This could mean 'mummy is coming home (I can hear the car)', or 'look at my toy car', or 'are we going out in the car?'.

You would need to see if those children who could use one word successfully in this way had stopped babbling. Is the change qualitatively different? Use Flavell's stages to help you to decide whether there is a qualitative change from babbling to the 'one word' stage or not.

If you decide to do this for coursework, you will have to do some research to look up the stages of language development, as they are not dealt with by the cognitive-developmental theorists. Some information is given in Box 3.

2 Another idea for coursework is based on material that is outlined later in the chapter. One of the main ideas of Piaget is that young children cannot take the view of another. Piaget tested this by building a model of three mountains. By positioning a small toy doll on the model opposite to the child's viewpoint, you can ask the child what the toy doll can see. The mountains mask the doll from the child's view (Figure 3.1). Young children usually give their own viewpoint when saying what the doll can see, not the right answer. Piaget used this as evidence that a young child is unable to take the view of another. He said they cannot 'decentre'.

However, another study says that a young child is perfectly capable of 'decentring'. If you build a model out of Lego bricks and you can position a 'policeman' behind one wall, and another doll behind another wall, you can ask the child if the policeman can see the doll (Figure 3.2). If the child can answer correctly, then we assume the child can take the view of the policeman – in other words, can 'decentre'.

This later study found that indeed the young child can do this more meaningful task. You could see if the child can decentre on one task (which perhaps is more easily understood) and not on another task. This is evidence that stages are not all or nothing – or it is evidence that Piaget was wrong.

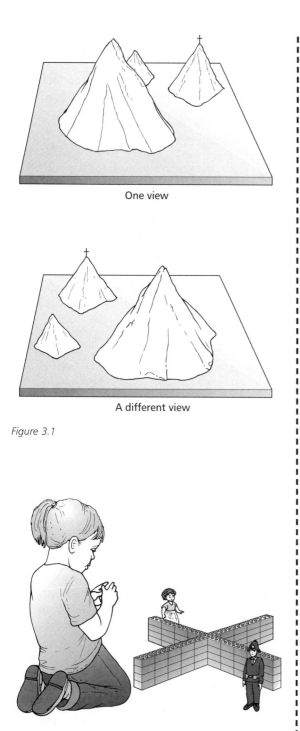

One view

A different view

Figure 3.1

Figure 3.2

Key Skill C3.1b – you could gather additional information by looking up these studies in other textbooks and using other resources. Then you could try the tasks out – this might be useful following group discussion, so you might get evidence for Key Skill C3.1a here too. Then do a presentation and the images you could use are drawings of the two pieces of equipment (the mountain task and the policeman–doll study.

A brief outline of the stages of language development as an illustration of a stage theory

1 Pre-linguistic (0–12 months) – firstly, cooing and making sounds, and then babbling between six and nine months. It seems that at first all babies babble using the same sounds whatever the language of their culture. Then, after about 9 months, the baby babbles only using the sounds used in 'their' language.

2 The one-word stage (12–18 months) – this stage also occurs in all cultures. The words can be invented, or are sometimes clear words. If there is a consistent label for the same thing, then it is assumed that the baby is communicating and using one word. Sometimes one word is used but only in one situation, for example, when the word 'car' is only used for one particular toy. The one-word stage is often called the holophrastic stage, where one word is used for lots of sentences, and gestures are used to complete the sentence.

3 The stage of two-word sentences – itself in two stages from 18–30 months and from 30 months onwards. The first stage here is often called 'telegraphic' because the child's message is in a form like that of a telegram. For example, 'Joe drink' means (for a child called Joe) 'can I have a drink?'. The second stage starts at around 30 months and involves grammar. Often the child gets it wrong, so they talk about 'geeses' and 'shoppies'.

Chapter 4 gives a discussion of how we might learn language, and why children might use words like 'shoppies'.

You can see from the above arguments that development is thought of as stages, but probably things are not as clear cut as that. Children move into these different stages or abilities at different ages. They probably don't simply go from one stage to another in one step, but the change is more likely to be gradual. Also it is important to remember the alternative view that development is continuous. There is another view of language development that says it continues, with skills in language use as well as vocabulary improving and increasing all the time.

STUDY AID

These initial sections on the key assumptions are very useful as evaluations of the material that follows. If you need an evaluation point about Piaget, for example, whose theory is a stage one, then you can argue that a child's development is not in such clear-cut stages at all.

At what time/age does the ability have to develop?

Another assumption mentioned earlier is that there are special times in a child's development when something is best learnt or experienced. Victor never developed proper language use, but it was said that he was about twelve years old when discovered, so he was past the time when language develops.

There are two suggestions, one that there is a **critical period** when something has to be experienced or learnt. The second suggestion is that there is a **sensitive period**, when something is best experienced or learnt, but can still be developed, even if this sensitive period is missed. One example is in the development of language. Some claimed that there was a critical period when babies had to experience language and to practice its use, whereas it is now more accepted that there is a sensitive period when language should develop. Although it is accepted that children should have language use by the age of twelve, the main age limit where children should have experienced language is by the age of six or seven.

Methodological problems in finding out about time limits in development

One problem with finding out about age limits when looking at cognitive development is that there are so few children who do not experience, for example, language. Socialisation of children occurs in all societies, even though the social ideas and norms are different. We need to look at those who have not been exposed to 'normal' influences in order to find out the answers as to what is necessary for development. If everyone is exposed to language, then we have no way of knowing the age at which this is necessary. Also, if everyone is exposed to some kind of stimulation and socialisation, then we have no way of knowing what would happen without these experiences.

This is why the discovery of children like Victor is so interesting. Another child, called 'Genie', was subjected to similar experiments. The case study of Genie is outlined in Box 4.

Box 4

The case study of Genie, a child who lacked socialisation, a bit like Victor

Many psychologists studied 'Genie' (not her real name), but Curtiss (1977) wrote up the case study. Unlike Victor, Genie's history is known. She spent eleven years chained to a potty in the day and tied up in a sleeping bag at night. She was not spoken to, although her father did bring her food, and tied her in for the night. She was thirteen when she was found. She did not make sounds and did not walk normally. She was very malnourished and was not toilet trained.

Psychologists started tests with Genie, just as Itard had done with Victor. They found she had normal powers of perception and could think about spatial relationships. Some cognitive abilities seemed intact, so perhaps these are inborn or innate. Genie did learn to walk better, and became toilet trained, but, like Victor, she did not learn normal language use. She developed emotions, and some social interactions, although these were far from normal.

One conclusion drawn from the case study of Genie was that there needs to be some exposure to language for language to develop. In spite of a lot of training, Genie did not learn proper language use. She was thirteen by the time she was exposed to language, so perhaps there is a time beyond which we cannot learn language.

Ethical issues in the case of Genie

There was a lot of criticism of the way Genie was treated as a research object. Rymer (1993) wrote a book about Genie and thought that Genie did not get all the help she could have had, because the scientists were so keen on their experiments. The scientists, however, argued that they gave Genie excellent care. They did try to teach her what she needed, and they did care for her in their homes. The scientists said that the point was that what Genie needed, which was training to live a normal life, was just what the scientists wanted to try to do, so there was no real conflict. It was argued, however, that the scientists over-emphasised language development (for their own interests), and this was not in Genie's interests.

There was dispute amongst the scientists themselves over Genie's care. In the end the 'problem' was solved because the funding for the 'project' was withdrawn. The National Institutes of Mental Health funded the study of Genie, but eventually withdrew support mainly because this was a single case study and no strong scientific knowledge could be learnt. When the funding was withdrawn Genie was returned to her mother, and then placed in foster care when her mother could not cope. She lives in a home for mentally retarded adults in California and still cannot talk normally or behave 'normally' in social interactions.

Like Victor, Genie might have had mental difficulties from the beginning, so they could never prove anything about the need for exposure to language at an early age.

There is a very good video about Genie, in the *Horizon* series. If you can get a copy, it details all the above, and the scientists explain their position. Genie's story is briefly outlined again in Chapter 8, where ethical issues are discussed.

The case study of Genie adds evidence to the conclusions drawn from the study of Victor, the 'Wild Child'. Early exposure to language does seem very important. However, just as Victor was said to have 'mental problems' and this accounted for his being abandoned, so Genie might have had similar problems, and this accounted for her father's behaviour. (Out of interest, her father committed suicide not long after she was discovered, so it was hard to investigate this issue.)

Key assumption 3 – use of different frameworks (Cole and Cole, 1996)

Within these different approaches, there are often different frameworks too. There are many different questions asked and answered in psychology. The main approaches are one way of dividing up such a large area of study. The frameworks described here are another important viewpoint. The frameworks are really ways of separating questions. What follows is taken from Cole and Cole (1996).

The biological maturation framework

This framework says that our development is **endogenous**. This means that the changes come from within. In Chapter 6 it is said that our body clock, which governs our patterns of sleep and waking, for example, is endogenous. This means that it is a real physical area (the suprachiasmatic nucleus) within the brain, triggered by light falling on the retina through the eye. Not only do causes of change come from within the body, but also they are genetically given.

In this framework **maturation** is said to cause development. Maturation is a biologically programmed sequence that is inherited through genes and that reveals itself as we develop. Within this framework, theories usually assume stage-like development following biological stages. Pinker (1994) says that the ability to use language appears with maturation, and Plomin and McClearn (1993) say that intelligence and personality may well have a strong genetic basis. These are two examples of research within a **biological maturation framework**. In all cases where the biological-maturational framework is used, there is some importance given to 'nurture' too, though.

The environmental learning framework

Just as the biological-maturation framework allows room for environmental influence, so the **environmental learning framework** allows for genetic influences on development. However, the main causes of development are said to be **exogenous**. Exogenous means having a cause in the environment. Just as there is an endogenous (built-in) body clock, so it is triggered by daylight, and daylight is exogenous (in the environment). In Chapter 4 these issues about the effects of the environment are dealt with in more detail.

The constructivist framework

The **constructivist framework** has more relevance to the cognitive-developmental approach, because Piaget worked within it. He thought that maturation was very important, and he was a biologist in the first place, not a psychologist. He linked the development of thinking to physical growth. However, Piaget (1973) also thought that an individual's social environment played a very important role in shaping the person. Every interaction the individual has with his or her social environment changes them. This means that Piaget works within a constructivist framework that lays equal emphasis on both nature and nurture.

The cultural context framework

Those who work within the **cultural context framework** agree that nature and nurture are important in shaping the individual. They agree that the individual is constructed from the interaction between these two factors – that is they agree with all three frameworks given above. Where they differ is that they also think that the **cultural context** within which the individual develops has great importance. Both Vygotsky (1978) and Bruner (1990) think that it is the culture within which the genes and environment mix that is important in the child's development. A culture is a set of designs for living including language, rules of the society, customs and values, and the knowledge transmitted down generations within that culture. So a child does not just learn knowledge out of context and culture. Saxe (1994) in a study of the Oksapmin of New Guinea found that their maths learning consists of counting body parts. This would not be very useful for a Western child who needs to deal with a Western money economy. However, it is good enough to teach children number concepts and it teaches them what they need to know. This is an example of how culture affects learning and shapes the individual.

Evaluation

- Both those within the constructivist framework, and those within the cultural context framework (and this includes the three main early cognitive-developmental theorists – Piaget, Bruner and Vygotsky) agree that development takes place through stages (or stage-like phases). Both frameworks also assume that the child is an active participant in their development – it is not just something that happens to them. However, the cultural context framework suggests that both children and adults have a role in the development, which is, therefore, co-constructed, whereas those within the constructivist framework put the emphasis on the child.

- Also those within the cultural context framework can allow for lots of variation in development, since there is wide variation in each individual's experiences. There is also a great emphasis on cultural history, and its effect on development, so the stages themselves might depend on cultural context, so again individuals may differ a great deal.

STUDY AID

Evaluation

Note that Piaget falls in the constructivist framework, and the other two are within the cultural context framework. So when you want to evaluate one of these three early theorists, you can use these more general statements about them, and give similarities and differences.

Research methods used in cognitive-developmental psychology

Chapter 7 deals with methodology in detail. What is presented here is a brief outline of the methods used in the cognitive-developmental approach.

Case studies

Case studies are used in the study of cognitive-development, and two have been outlined above. Box 1 outlines the case study of Victor, and Box 4 gives the case study of Genie. Case studies are in-depth studies of individuals or small groups. They are very useful in giving a lot of detail, but the problem is that, because they are studies of individuals or small groups, we cannot **generalise** the findings to everyone. This is not the most central method used in the cognitive-developmental approach, but since I have given some examples of case studies above, it is worth mentioning here.

The case studies given above focus on language development, rather than on the development of thinking. Piaget used his own children when developing his theory about cognitive development, but he did not really write these studies up as case studies.

Evaluation

- Since most researchers in the development of cognition are looking at stage theories where all children are said to pass through the same stages, it is unlikely that case studies will be useful. This is because they focus on individual differences, rather than things that all children have in common.

Observations

There are participant observations, where the observer also has a role in the situation, and non-participant observations, where the observer has no role. There are covert observations, where the participants are not aware of the observation taking place, and overt observations, where the participants are aware that they are being observed.

Observations are sometimes difficult to pick out, because you could claim that all experiments involve observation. Here, however, we are mainly talking about naturalistic observations, which mean observations in the participants' natural setting. These are 'true' observations, whereas experiments are situations that are deliberately set up, and then what happens is observed.

Naturalistic observations

In the study of cognitive development, children are observed in their everyday lives. This method gives **validity**, because the children's actions and situations are real. There is a problem with validity if the observer is noticeable and will affect the children's behaviour. Therefore, the observation is often carried out by someone already in the situation, for example, a teacher. This is participant observation.

Baby biographies

In another form of naturalistic observation, some nineteenth-century scientists kept baby biographies of their own children, including Darwin (1877). Piaget also kept detailed accounts of the cognitive development of his own children. Baby biographies are still used in the area of language development, because they are a source of data; however, they are not used apart from this. This is because they are not **objective** enough. It was thought that people such as Piaget would not be able to list their children's achievements without some **subjectivity** and in scientific research objectivity is necessary.

A frequent criticism of Piaget's theory is that much of the data was gathered using his own children. Not only was there a question of subjectivity, but also he had only three children, so there is the same problem with generalising the results to a wider population as there is with case studies.

Ethology

Ethology is another form of naturalistic observation. This is the study of non-human animals in their natural setting. It is thought that if we want to know about non-human animal behaviour, then we should study them in their everyday settings, in natural behaviours. Ethologists focus on the biological side of behaviour and look at it from an evolutionary point of view.

You could say that ethology is done where children are concerned. For example, children can be studied in the classroom to look at their social interactions and friendship groups. These would form naturally, without intervention from the teacher, and so the study of these patterns is the study of children in their natural setting, and can be called ethology.

Observation of context – of the child's ecology

When research involves a number of different settings and contexts, it is studying the child's ecology. Studying ecology involves looking at people's roles in all situations, including the problems with such roles. In a biological sense, ecology means the non-human animal's natural habitat. The ecology includes the relationships within the population, as well as the environment. So where people are concerned, ecology means the situations where people are actors.

When psychologists studying child development point out that the child's community is of great importance in their development, they are emphasising the child's developmental niche, and are looking at the child's ecology. The developmental niche includes physical and social context, as well as the child-rearing practices and customs of the community. It also means looking at the parent's biological characteristics. Barker and Wright (1951) studied the natural ecology of school children in the USA. For example, they chose one individual and

wrote down everything they could about him from constant observation. You can choose one child and get in-depth information, or you can choose a particular situation and focus on more than one person and more than one example of that situation. Either way, you need to gather a lot of detailed information, because it is necessary to focus on this whole ecology – physical setting, social setting, cultural practices and customs. Rogoff (1981) did such a study in Guatemala. It was not possible to look at everything, so time sampling was used. This meant taking 'snapshots' at certain times and gathering data in that way.

Time sampling

If you decide to do an observation, you may need to use **time sampling** – see Activity 4.

ACTIVITY 4

USING TIME SAMPLING IN NATURALISTIC OBSERVATIONS

Here are some ideas for coursework with some advice on using time sampling in your study.

1 You could observe children at play in a school playground. There are always problems with using children, because you need to be sure to get proper consent, and you need to follow the ethical guidelines outlined in Chapter 8. However, in some cases such studies are ethical, if carefully planned and carried out.

You would need to make sure that you do have full consent. Then you would need some role in the playground perhaps. Also, you might make the children anxious, and this cannot be allowed. If you think you can approach such a study sensitively, and if the proposal is accepted, you could consider such a piece of coursework.

You need to have an hypothesis in mind. You could decide to study gender differences in play behaviour, and you would need to do some research on this area first. Make sure you find some background studies on which to base your own study. If you read about aggression, you will find the suggestion that boys are more aggressive than girls. So you could watch for aggression in boys and girls, to see the difference. First, you have to decide what is aggressive behaviour. Then you have to make sure it is measurable (remember that for

►

the coursework for the Edexcel AS examination, you must collect quantitative data).

You may decide that physical contact is aggression, and so is shouting if it is at someone. Pushing is aggression, perhaps, and so is chasing if it is not play chasing. Then you have a few categories:

- *shouting at another*
- *pushing another*
- *chasing if not laughing.*

Spend the first observation making a note of types of behaviour you would call aggression. Then you do another observation, this time using your list. On the second observation you put a tally mark against each behaviour and you note the gender of the child.

Time sampling is useful because you can't watch everyone at the same time. You will have to look away to do the tallying in any case. So make a mark every few minutes, and you are time sampling. You may need longer between marks, or less time, depending on what you have decided to observe.

2 Another way in which you might use time sampling is if you decide to use content analysis. Content analysis is not quite observation, because you will be looking at something like a television programme that has already been prepared. You might have a video of children at play, however, and then you would be doing content analysis of the programme.

You will probably not be able to watch the whole programme recording every action. So use time sampling. Record the actor's behaviour, whoever is acting, and whatever the action, every few minutes or so. You will not have observed everything, but you will have sampled the actions, and you should be able to give a fair picture of the overall activity. This will be fairer than simply recording what you think is of interest, and it will force you to note down all behaviours, whether you think they are useful or not. It may help to avoid subjectivity, as you will objectively note down whatever is happening in the particular time slot that you have chosen.

If you are doing a content analysis of gender behaviour in the media, for example, you should really choose to collect data on different days of the week and at different times of day, as well as using different channels. So you might watch for 10 minutes three times a day on more than one day in the week and using all main channels. The times of day need varying and so on.

Content analysis is useful for looking at gender behaviour in the media, or at children's play behaviour. It is useful in social psychology, as well as in developmental psychology.

Time sampling is useful when doing observations, because it is very difficult, probably impossible, to observe everything. If you choose what to observe, you may not be objective. If you use time sampling, this is a less biased way of deciding what to record, and it gives you time to record the data.

One other way of avoiding bias in naturalistic observations is to use more than one observer using the same scale. So more than one person is trained to use the same list of actions or whatever is being observed. They then separately observe at the same time. If the two (or more) observers agree on their data, then the study is said to have **inter-observer reliability**. This means that, for example, if you say that the boy in the green jumper has been aggressive three times, and I agree, then we have inter-observer reliability. Remember, reliability means if the study is done again we get the same results. You may hear the term '**inter-rater reliability**', which is the same as inter-observer reliability, but the researchers are rating behaviour rather than just tallying the number of incidents.

Rogoff (1981) used time sampling using the same principles as those outlined in Activity 4. She could not observe everything, so she chose to look at each child for about 10 minutes several times a day, and on different days of the week. Rogoff noted what the child was doing, and who with. She found that Mayan children, like US children, spend much of their time apart from adults. However, when they are with adults, their experiences are different from those of US children; for example, the Mayan children help the adults with their jobs.

Evaluation

- One problem is that the observer has expectations about what they will find. One of the ways to avoid such subjectivity is to use more than one observer, but often this is not possible. Also it might be less ethical to have more than one researcher with the children, and might disrupt the child's natural behaviour even more.

- Another problem is the way that the child's natural behaviour is likely to be affected by being observed. It is not ethical to covertly observe without letting anyone know. However, individuals are unlikely to behave naturally if they know they are being observed. Graves and Glick (1978) asked mothers in a laboratory study to help their children do a jigsaw puzzle. The children were between 18 and 25 months old. The researchers told half the mothers that a recording was being made, and the others were not told this. Those who were told there was a recording were more helpful. This shows that people do behave differently when they think they are being watched.

- Another difficulty is that an observer cannot write down everything, so data are lost. Time sampling can help to overcome this difficulty, but it still means lots of data are lost. It is useful to have a list of behaviours to look out for, but this means that other behaviours cannot be recorded, even if they seem to fit. Making the data quantitative is useful because the study is more likely to be reliable. However, deliberately choosing some actions and leaving out others makes the study less valid.

- A further difficulty with observations is that they can only really say that there is a relationship between two factors, for example boys and aggression. The data from an observation do not show a cause for this relationship. For the cause, the researcher has to look elsewhere. The studies tend to find patterns, but then further study is needed to look for reasons for these patterns.

Observations and cognitive development

Piaget and other researchers in the field of cognitive development did a lot of observing, but it was the type of observing that follows experimentation. For example, they set up situations to see what would happen, and then observed the children, but this was not really using naturalistic observation. This method has been included here because you may well find that you can use naturalistic observation to study cognitive development. Naturalistic observations are also widely used in developmental psychology, and in this chapter the cognitive-developmental approach is representing developmental psychology.

Experiments

Experiments are used in the study of cognitive development. Situations are set up and the children are asked to carry out certain tasks to see what happens.

Field experiments

However, studies in cognitive-developmental psychology are not really standard experiments. For one thing, they are usually **field experiments**. The study of children in a laboratory would not be very useful, because it is their everyday thinking patterns that we want to study in the cognitive-developmental approach. So experiments take place in the child's natural setting. This can be a playgroup, the child's home or at school or any other natural setting.

Experiments in the cognitive-development approach

Piaget did carry out field experiments (see Box 5). However, he was often more interested in the reasoning processes of the child than in the actual answer to the task, so he is more often said to use clinical interview than experiment. If you decide to repeat his tasks, however, and you accept a simple right or wrong answer as the data, then you might say you are doing an experiment.

Box 5

An example of a field experiment carried out in the field of cognitive-developmental psychology

Piaget looked at a child's ability to conserve. A child can conserve when it is able to say that something has stayed the same, even when it appears to have changed.

Conservation of liquid

A young child of about four years old is asked to watch a demonstration and then answer a question. The demonstration involves three drinking glasses and a jug of water. Two of the glasses are short half-pint tumblers, and the other is also a half-pint glass, but taller. The demonstrator pours water from the jug into the two short glasses. They make sure that the child understands that the level of water in the two short glasses is the same. The next step is for the demonstrator to pour the water from one of the short glasses into the taller glass. The important question is then asked – is the water in the two glasses (the tall and the short glass) the same?

The four year old, generally, says the amount of water is different – there is more in the tall glass. The eight year old, generally, says the amount is the same. The older child understands that when water is poured from one glass into another, the amount of water remains the same.

When the child understands that water poured from one container into another remains the same in volume, he or she is said to be able to conserve volume.

Piaget concluded from such experiments that young children are in the stage of not being able to conserve, and older children have passed through that stage, and can conserve.

Experiments involve **independent variables** and **dependent variables**. The independent variable is what is manipulated by the experimenter. In the above case the independent variable (IV) is age. The dependent variable (DV) is what is measured as a result of the manipulation; in the above case it is whether the child can conserve or not (depending on their age).

Evaluation

- There is an argument that Piaget's work (and that of others) is not exactly experimental. He is asking the child questions, and this method can be more precisely called interviewing. His studies are like field experiments, and there are strict controls, but he is often relying on what the participant says, rather than what they do. So Piaget's methods are sometimes called clinical interviews. What is said is not a very exact measure, because all sorts of misunderstandings can occur.

- Also the usual evaluations of experiments apply. The strict controls mean the studies are often not valid. How do we ask the question in the experiment given in Box 5? Questions can be quite misleading. One criticism of Piaget's conclusions about conservation of liquid is that the younger child might have thought there ought to be a change. When faced with an adult pouring out two equal glasses of water and then pouring the contents of one of the glasses into another glass, the child might well reasonably assume that there was a reason for the task. Having made this assumption, the child might respond to the experimenter's question about the amount of water by saying that there has been a change, because they assume that is the right answer. Why would the task be done if there were no change? You will see that others have tested this criticism and found that the younger child can conserve if the task is given a reason. So the experiment lacks **validity** because it is not really measuring the child's understanding as such, just their understanding of what answer the experimenter wants.

Although the experiments lack validity, they are useful because they are **reliable**. Self-test 2 asks you what it means to say that experiments are reliable.

Self-test 2

Outline briefly what it means to say that the experiment outlined in Box 5 is reliable.

Good controls make the procedure easy to repeat with other children. When it has been repeated the same results have been found. In practice, Piaget's work has been very well replicated, in spite of the above criticisms.

Clinical interviews

Usually, when discussing Piaget, it is said that he used clinical interviews, not experiments. Clinical interviews are completely different from experiments, because they are designed to get data from individuals, and not to gather results that apply to everyone. Clinical interviews gather **qualitative** data. Interviews are outlined in more depth in Chapter 7.

The word 'clinical' implies a problem in terms of health. Freud used clinical interviews (see Chapter 5). He carried out case studies, using such interviews, and gathered in-depth data about individuals. He was interested in health issues. Piaget, however, used clinical interviews because he needed to be able to follow the lead of the participant, and was not looking at health issues. Although Piaget used field experiments, he based his studies on clinical interviews with children, from which he learnt about their thinking patterns.

Evaluation

- Clinical interviews are a good way of collecting qualitative data. They allow the researcher to gather data that might be missed if using a more controlled method, and are good for initial data gathering – even though experiments are a good way of following up the initial findings, because experiments are more reliable.

- However, a great deal rests on what the participants say. What they say may not match what they do, and also communication can be misunderstood. Social representation theorists claim that we cannot find 'facts' outside our own way of looking at the world. So interpretation of the interviews can be subjective and biased. What the participants say is not only open to question but also is interpreted, which is another source of bias.

Clinical interviews in the study of cognitive development

Piaget used clinical interviews to investigate different aspects of cognitive development, and spent a lot of time asking children questions. When looking at moral development, for example, he wanted to know how an older child's moral development differed from that of a younger child. So he investigated how children perceive rules. He asked about games like marbles, to see if the children thought it was okay to change the rules, and for what reason. He interviewed the children about this and used their answers as his data.

Longitudinal studies

One key assumption of the cognitive-developmental approach is that the concept of development over time is important. So participants have to be studied over a period of time, to see how they change.

Longitudinal studies, and their 'opposite', cross-sectional studies, are outlined in some detail in Chapter 7, but you need to note now that longitudinal designs are those where the same participants are studied over a long(ish) time period. Cross-sectional designs are the opposite – different participants are studied at the same moment in time.

For example, assume we want to do the study outlined in Box 5. We need four year olds to check that they cannot conserve volume and eight year olds to see if they can conserve (and say that the volume of water in the same). Self-test 3 asks you to write down how you would do this using a longitudinal design, and how you would do it using a cross-sectional design.

Self-test 3

How would you do the above study (based on the one outlined in Box Five) as a longitudinal design?

How would you do the above study as a cross-sectional design?

> Key Skill C3.1a – although this is a self-test question, once you have thought about it yourself, if you are working as part of a group, this task would benefit from group discussion, and you could use the evidence for this Key Skill. Widen your discussion to include ideas of how you would actually go about doing some of these studies, and look at what needs to be controlled. You could try giving the hypotheses too, as this is good practice.

If you said that for a longitudinal design you would test the four year olds then wait until they were eight before testing them again, then you are right. For a cross-sectional design, you could do the study at the same time, testing a group of four year olds and a group of eight year olds.

Evaluation

- Longitudinal designs are very good because they test the same individual. With the cross-sectional design suggested above, you would be comparing a four year old with an eight year old and they would be different individuals with different experiences.

- However, there are problems with using longitudinal designs. Self-test 4 asks you to write down some problems with longitudinal designs.

Self-test 4

Note down some problems with longitudinal designs. Think of about three before reading on.

One difficulty is that you have to wait a number of years. There are a number of problems associated with this wait.

- The researcher(s) may have moved on, and no one else might want to continue with the study.
- You cannot control what happens to the participants in the meantime. Something in the culture might happen to affect all seven year olds (this is called a **cohort effect**), and this might be the reason for the study's results. It is hard to give an example of what might happen – perhaps a war and evacuation procedures, or some specific television programmes focused at the particular area of study.
- Longitudinal designs are also expensive and time consuming.
- After the first collection of data parents may refuse permission for their child to continue with the study.
- Children may move away, and a good-sized sample may become a very small one, so data are lost and generalising becomes difficult.
- You could argue that certain 'sorts' of parents withdraw their children from a study, or certain 'sorts' of parents move away, so the sample might become biased.
- Participants may become used to the study and the methods. They may learn what it is they are supposed to do, rather than give natural behaviour.

Cross-sectional designs are better in that they are quicker and cheaper. Fewer participants drop out, and they are all available at one moment in time. There is the problem with individual differences (individuals are compared, but are different, so their individual differences must be taken into account), but, as in many methods used in psychology, the researcher must weigh up the good and bad points about different designs and then make a choice.

Longitudinal designs in cognitive-developmental studies

Piaget based a lot of his initial conclusions on the study of his own children. He had a son, Laurent, and two daughters, Jacqueline and Lucienne. He followed their development and logged down in detail various things they could and could not do. Since he used the same participants over a period of time, he used a longitudinal design.

Most studies within the cognitive-developmental approach are cross-sectional, because the researchers use different participants at the same moment in time – mainly due to problems with longitudinal designs mentioned earlier.

In-depth areas of study

The theory of Jean Piaget

Review of what has been said about Piaget so far

Maturation is a pre-programmed pattern of development that is in all of us, and refers to changes that occur as we grow. One example would be our readiness to pass through the stage of puberty. This stage is ready from the beginning of our life.

Piaget thought that thinking processes (cognition) were ready to develop and mature, just as physical aspects are ready to develop. What he set out to do was to look at what stages of development these thinking processes would go through, and to answer such questions as 'will everyone go through the same stages at the same time?'

Activity 5 asks you to summarise what you already know about Piaget, from what you have already read in this chapter.

ACTIVITY 5

WHAT DO YOU KNOW ABOUT PIAGET'S THEORIES ALREADY?

Note down all you already know about Piaget's views. He has been mentioned quite a lot already.

Key Skill C3.1a – this would make a good group discussion.

Here are some of the ideas that have already been explained.
- Piaget's theory was a stage theory, not one suggesting that development is continuous.
- Piaget was Swiss and his theory was developed from around 1930 to 1980, so what is presented here is a summary only.

- Piaget thought that language developed from the development of thinking. In other words, without development of our cognitive abilities we would not develop language. It is not the case, according to Piaget, that we need language in order to develop.
- Piaget's views fall within the constructivist framework, which means that he lays equal emphasis on the nature side and the nurture side of our development. Both our inherited characteristics and our environment are important in our development.
- Piaget used baby biographies in that he focused a lot on his own children, and his work has been criticised because of this.
- Piaget used clinical interviews a lot too, so that he could delve into what children were saying without being restricted by only being able to ask certain questions. This can be criticised, because the interviewer can bring a subjective element when interpreting.
- Piaget did experiments too, such as the one using a model mountain. He said that young children cannot 'decentre', which means they cannot see what someone on the other 'side' of the mountains would see – they cannot take the viewpoint of another. This has been criticised by another study using a policeman and a doll.
- Another of Piaget's claims was that young children (for example, four year olds) cannot conserve volume. When water is poured from a small half-pint tumbler into a taller half-pint glass, young children do not realise that there is still the same amount of liquid in the taller glass – they are apparently swayed by the fact that the level in the taller glass is higher.

Introduction to Piaget's cognitive-developmental theory

Piaget's central theme – that cognitive development is in stages and each child progresses through these same stages – is a fundamental approach to understanding children, and has had wide implications, for example, in the field of education. Piaget did not spend time applying his views to education, but others have. Anyone who has done teacher training will have come across Piaget's views. Not only is Piaget's work very important in this sense, but his way of testing children lends itself to further study. Piaget must be credited with doing so much himself, and also leading the way to even more knowledge in the area of cognitive development.

His conclusions have attracted many criticisms; however, it is important not to forget his contributions. Many have replicated his studies, and found exactly what he found and it is hard to be too critical. However, others have tested his claims and come to different conclusions.

Cognitive development in early infancy

Piaget looked at a baby's reflexes and started from the basic constructivist viewpoint that development involves both nature (genes and inheritance) and nurture (environmental and social influences).

Schemas, assimilation, accommodation, adaptation – equilibration

Piaget's claim is that the baby's reflex is its first **schema**. A schema for Piaget (this word is used elsewhere in psychology too) is a mental structure that gives a model for what happens when the baby does 'this'. Imagine the baby moves its hand (without knowing what a hand is, or what moving means). It develops a schema for what happens when it does a certain muscular action, even though it does not have words for this.

Gradually, through interaction with the environment, the baby develops schemas ('schemata' is often used as the plural of schema) that tell it something about its world. These original schemas will be modified as the baby finds out more. It gets more sophisticated perhaps at moving its hand, and the schema is more sophisticated too. The baby may move its hand deliberately in different directions, for example. In this case the schema is developed.

The way in which the schemata (or schemas) are developed is by assimilation, accommodation and adaptation. Remember these three 'A's.

Assimilation means adding information to existing schemas, strengthening them. For example, babies suck as a reflex. This sucking is one of the initial schemas. Then the baby may be given a dummy. It sucks the dummy. However, it has to assimilate this new shape to suck and this becomes part of its sucking schema.
- Assimilatng is changing the input information to fit the schema.

Then the baby may try to suck on something else, and this cannot be assimilated, because sucking on it does not work in some way.

Accommodation means amending an existing schema to suit a new situation. In the above example, the baby will modify the way it sucks to include sucking on a blanket. New experiences are included in the existing schema and it develops.
- Accommodating is changing the internal schema to take the new information into account.

Adaptation is the term used for these two processes of assimilation and accommodation. As the baby assimilates and accommodates, building its schemas, then it is adapting.
- Adaptation is the way the baby adapts to its environment through the processes of assimilation and accommodation.

Equilibration refers to when there is a balance or equilibrium and adaptation has taken place. For children, this balance does not last long. Maturation (biological development) and the changing environment mean that the process of assimilation and accommodation keeps going.

Piaget's first stage in early infancy – the sensorimotor stage (0–2 years)

Piaget's is a stage theory, which means that each new stage brings qualitative as well as quantitative changes. It is not just that the child learns more through adapting and changing its schemas – the experiences are different altogether.

During the adaptation process in infancy, it is mainly sensory and motor processes that are being 'learnt' about. The infant mainly moves and senses – and does little else – hence this stage is called the '**sensorimotor stage**'. Of course from 0–2 years a lot changes, and Piaget did discuss six substages within this main stage. Box 6 outlines the six main substages.

Box 6

The main substages of the sensorimotor stage

Substage 1 – up to about one and a half months old

The infant is mainly learning about reflexes and this is the first substage. It brings with it its pre-programmed maturation processes, the first of which is the reflex, and with the environment that will surround it this is where the adaptation process starts.

Substage 2 – from one and a half to four months

The infant starts using actions that it repeats just for the pleasure of them. For example, the baby might repeatedly blow bubbles. These actions that are repeated just for the pleasure of it are called **primary circular reactions**. Also adaptation is taking place, and, for example, the baby may suck its thumb because it has assimilated this from its sucking reflex. From sucking its thumb, it may enjoy its own saliva, hence the blowing of bubbles. The actions are called 'primary', because they involve the baby's own body, and 'circular' because they lead back to themselves.

Piaget sees the infant as an active being, exploring and interacting with its environment. It is not that the environment acts on it without a two-way process taking place. Problem solving is going on. The infant is constructing its own world using its maturation processes (for example, reflexes) and its environment.

The social environment is also important, and changes in the carer's actions towards the baby are important. For example, Kaye (1982) investigates the 'jiggle' that mothers give to the bottle or breast if a baby stops feeding. This 'jiggle' seems to start the baby feeding again, but this renewal of feeding does not seem to be a reflexive action. These sorts of interactions are affecting the adaptations of the baby.

Substage 3 – from four to eight months

Primary circular reactions become secondary circular reactions as the baby interacts more with the environment. Actions can now bring changes in the environment. An example of secondary circular reactions is when the baby kicks a bar and a bell rings on a toy. They do this repeatedly. The baby kicks deliberately, but does not really understand what it is doing.

Substage 4 – from eight to twelve months

This is the early form of problem solving when schemas can be combined to get an effect. Now actions are for a reason, rather than accidental. Piaget's own example (1952b) is from observation of his ten-month old son Laurent. Laurent combines dropping a tin to make a noise with banging the tin on a sink to make a noise. This is an example of combining schemas. **Object permanence** (see below) is a way of seeing a child combine schemas.

Substage 5 – from twelve to eighteen months

Now the baby can use tertiary circular reactions, where it can experiment to see what will happen.

Substage 6 – from eighteen months to twenty-four months

Images and words start to be used and new problem solving can occur using symbols for objects.

So the infant moves through the six substages, each time learning more about interacting with its environment, and each time using both physical maturation and environmental and social stimulation.

Box 7 discusses object permanence in more detail. You might be able to study object permanence yourself, and an idea of how to do this is found in Activity 6.

Box 7

Object permanence

Piaget thought that it was in substage 4, within the sensorimotor stage, that infants showed they knew that an object has permanence. The main technique to investigate this is to interest a baby in an object. Then hide the object behind a screen, or cover the object with a cloth. Then look to see if the baby searches for the object (visually) under the cloth or behind the screen.

At around eight months old the baby will search for the object in the same place as it was before it was hidden. It seems to know that the object is still there (under the cloth, or behind the screen), and knows that the object has permanence.

By 18 months, the child will search for the object, even if it has been moved from behind a screen, for example. The child knows that the object still exists somewhere.

The stages of object permanence correspond to the six substages listed above, as the one and a half month old child does not search for objects at all, and the four month old, whilst knowing that the object has disappeared, still looks at the place from where it disappears.

Piaget thought that by around eight months old, babies had started to learn that objects have a permanence, that is they exist. If the baby was interested in a toy that was then hidden by a screen, the eight-month-old baby would look at the screen as if looking for the toy, whereas a younger child would look away as if confused.

Evaluation

- Other studies, for example Baillargeon (1993), have shown that babies as young as three and a half months old seem to know that objects exist when they are hidden. This contradicts Piaget. Piaget's work involved the infant actively doing something to look for the object, whereas other researchers allowed the baby to be more passive (that is not take part).

- One experimental technique used by those who claim that object permanence is achieved by babies younger than eight months old is outlined in Box 8.

Box 8

An experimental technique to look at object permanence, where Piaget's views are queried

The baby was set to watch a rotating screen, to get used to it. The screen rotated towards the baby, and was hinged to a table. There is a diagram below. Across the middle of the table is a hinged board that can be lifted to an upright 'screen' position blocking the baby's view. It can be pushed back flat away from the baby, pulled up to the upright middle position, and pulled forward flat towards the baby. This rotation is automatically done, and the baby watches it until it is bored with it.

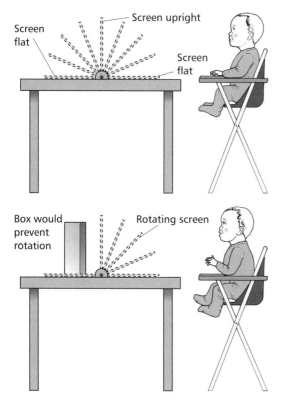

Figure 3.3

The next stage is when the screen is flat towards the baby. The baby sees a box being positioned where the screen, being rotated, would hit it. The box is just behind the upright position of the screen. In practice the box is moved as the rotating screen reaches the

---

upright position. The baby does not know this. So if the screen rotates past the place where it would have hit the box, the question is 'Is the baby surprised?'

If the baby is surprised, then we assume it knows the box should be there, and that the baby has object permanence.

As has been stated, those like Baillargeon (1993) find that as young as three and a half months, the baby seems to know about object permanence using techniques like the one described in Box 8.

INVESTIGATING OBJECT PERMANENCE YOURSELF

If you are sure that you can get full consent for observing babies, and if you can get access to that age group, then you could replicate Piaget's studies. Interest a child in a toy by playing with them. Then hide the toy under a blanket and watch if the child reaches for the toy or not.

Have someone else observing too, and you could have inter-observer reliability. Watch where the child looks, as well as where they reach.

Use babies of around eight months, as they should reach for the hidden toy, because they have reached the stage of object permanence. Then use younger babies to see if they reach for the toy. Your hypothesis, following Piaget, is that the eight-months-old (or near enough) babies have object permanence, but the younger babies do not.

While techniques favoured by those like Baillargeon shows that younger babies have object permanence, this does not mean that Piaget's observations are not correct. So you can still do Piaget's tasks, even though others have criticised his conclusions.

Key Skill C3.1a – you might like to use group discussion to plan the above study, checking for controls, writing out the hypotheses and the type of design and so on. This is good practice for the coursework part of the course.

So Piaget's observations are reliable, and young babies do not have object permanence according to his techniques. However, others have shown that using different techniques, babies as young as three and a half months have object permanence. Clearly the difference is the different technique used. Piaget watched eight-month-old babies reach for the toy, whereas the other technique simply watches the babies without the babies having to do anything.

Diamond (1991) looks at Piaget's claims and the differences between the two conclusions.
• Perhaps Piaget's eight month olds forgot, in the few seconds it took to move the object, and so looked in the wrong place. It is memory that they lack, not object permanence.
• Perhaps they can't stop themselves reaching for the toy, even if it is in the wrong place.
• They may have problems in reaching for the blanket covering the toy, for example, not problems with object permanence.

Therefore, it is not always the study itself that is at fault if another study comes up with different conclusions. It is often the case that the method used leads to other conclusions being possible, but they are not considered.

Cognitive development in early childhood

By the age of two then, the child has object permanence, uses tertiary circular reactions to experiment and learn about its world, is interacting with others so uses their reactions in building new schemas, and is using symbols (usually words) for solving new problems.

Piaget then looks at the older child. Now that the child can use symbols and develop language, it can represent things when those things are not present. So it can use 'pretend play' and extend its experiences.

Mental operations
Around the age of about seven years, the child has built enough on its experiences, and has representations in its mind about things in the world. So children become able to use **mental operations**. Mental operations are activities like combining ideas, separating ideas and applying logic (mentally) to various issues in the world.

Piaget's second stage in early childhood – the preoperational stage (2–6 years)
The whole point is that the child in the **preoperational** stage is pre (before) - operational (it can use mental operations). So at this stage the child cannot use logic or transform, combine or separate ideas. The child's development consists of building experiences about the world through adaptation and working towards the stage when it can use logical thought.

So children in the preoperational stage have limited thinking. The types of limited thinking are outlined below. You will be able to test some of the ideas for yourself, although remember it is always difficult carrying out studies involving children because of special ethical issues (see Chapter 8).

Centring on one side of things
Centring on one side of things is one main limitation that children in the preoperational stage have. Recall or re-read the outline of the experiment using three glasses and a jug of water in Box 5. Briefly, young children watch as two short tumblers are filled to an equal level with water. Then the experimenter pours the water out of one short tumbler into a taller glass. The important question is whether the child says that the volume of water in the two glasses (tall and short) is still the same (as it was in the two short glasses).

Young children think that the tall glass has more in it, and Piaget concludes that they cannot conserve volume. They do not appear to have the mental operations or mental processes to see more than one side of things. Piaget thinks the young child looks only at the level in the two glasses (which is different) rather than at the volume (which is the same). Later, in the next stage, the child can **decentre**, and focus on more than one side of things, so can think about the height and the amount at the same time, and an older child can conserve. The older child says that the volume is the same, and seems to be able to think about pouring the liquid back into the short glass, when it would be the same again (this is called reversibility).

In a different example, looking at this same point of the younger child centring on one side of things, Piaget uses beads of different colours. Box 9 outlines the experiment.

Box 9

Another of Piaget's experiments looking at the inability of the preoperational child to decentre

The child is shown wooden beads. Some are brown and some are white. They have to keep in mind the main set (wooden) and the two subsets (brown and white). They are asked 'which are there more of, brown beads or wooden beads?' The preoperational child says there are more brown beads. Older children can successfully think of the 'wooden' classification at the same time as the 'colour' classification.

Evaluation

• The question is said to be a bit confusing. Some studies that criticise Piaget's work focus on asking different questions.

Activity 7 suggests that you adapt the above study, or carry it out as it stands, so that you can test Piaget's claim for yourself.

ACTIVITY 7

DOING THE 'WOODEN BEADS' STUDY YOURSELF

You need to use preoperational children (who can't decentre, so will say there are more brown beads) and those in the next stage (who can decentre, so will say there are more wooden beads).

You must be sure that ethical principles are followed. Your teacher must accept that the study is okay, so check first.

The hypothesis is that there is a meaningful difference in the number of children who say there are more brown beads, and the number who say there are more wooden beads, on being asked the Piaget-style question 'are there more wooden beads or more brown beads?' when being shown brown and white wooden beads. The difference depends on whether the children are in the preoperational stage (say around four years old) or in the next stage (older than seven, for example). Those in the preoperational stage are more likely to say that there are more brown beads, whereas the older children are more likely to say that there are more wooden beads (the correct answer).

You could try asking a different question, such as a question about cars. Show the child a lot of cars, including quite a few of one colour. As an example, say you choose quite a few red cars as well as some blue cars. Then ask the child whether there are more red cars, or more cars. Will this slightly more realistic task make a difference? (I have no idea – I have never tried it. One exciting thing about doing psychology is that you have the chance to find something out for yourself that no one else has tried.)

> Key Skill C3.1a – you could discuss the difference between the 'beads' study and the 'cars' study and work out what the likely results would be. Plan the study in your group, and perhaps you know a few children of the right age so you can test it out. If you are doing the study for coursework, of course, you would need more participants.

Egocentrism

Egocentrism refers to when the child cannot see anyone else's viewpoint. Piaget thought that the preoperational child not only cannot decentre, but is also egocentric. Recall the experiment outlined in Activity 3. A model of three mountains was used (Piaget & Inhelder, 1956), and the child had to try to take the viewpoint of a doll that was placed at the opposite side of the mountains to the child. The doll could see a different view of the mountains than the child could see, but the preoperational child will give its own view when being asked what the doll can see. It is concluded that a young child cannot take another person's viewpoint, and is egocentric.

Another way of looking at egocentrism is to ask a preoperational child to describe an arrangement of blocks to another child who has to build the arrangement with blocks provided. This study has been done. The second child cannot, of course, see the arrangement that must be built, and has to rely on instructions from the first child. A preoperational child does not give enough information, but an older child can do this task. It is concluded that the preoperational child cannot put itself in the 'builder's' shoes, so cannot think what information the second child needs. (This is another study that could be done for coursework perhaps.)

Theory of mind

Modern research in cognitive development often focuses on the theory of mind. Some researchers are Astington (1993) and Hirschfeld and Gelman (1994). The idea comes from Piaget's ideas about egocentrism. One of the techniques used is outlined in Box 10.

Box 10

One technique used to look at egocentrism and the theory of mind

This experiment was on an Open University video about autism. Simon Baron-Cohen is carrying out the experiment, and is a well-known researcher in the field of theory of mind and autism.

He is carrying out the study on autistic children. He uses two dolls, Anne and Sally. He talks to the autistic young person and shows that one of the dolls hides something under a beaker. Both dolls are 'present'. There are other beakers there too. Then one doll 'goes out of the room', and the participant is told this – it is also demonstrated, as the doll 'walks away'. Now the remaining doll moves the counter from under the beaker and places it under a different beaker.

▶

The important question is whether the doll that returns will know where the counter is. Of course we know that the doll will not know – because that doll was 'out of the room' at the time.

The autistic child is most likely to say that the returning doll will know that the counter has moved. This is said to be because the child itself knows that the counter has moved.

Up to the age of about three years, a child will be egocentric and will say that the returning doll will know (because the child knows). In other words the child cannot take the view of another. However, young children do learn quite quickly that anyone 'out of the room' cannot know what happens after they have left. Autistic children do not seem to be able to take the view of another in this way, and this seems to be a characteristic of autism.

Tasks like the one outlined in Box 10 have been carried out in other cultures (one example is the study done by Avis and Harris (1991), who researched the Baka people). Cross-cultural research is useful in finding out whether something is true of all peoples, or is only true in certain cultures. The Baka people are hunter-gatherers with no formal education, and stories are handed down to teach the children. They live in West Africa, and move around according to the seasons and where the food is. They are very different from people from Western cultures, so if their children learn to decentre at a similar age, using such techniques as the one given in Box 10, then this is of great interest. Avis and Harris found that the Baka children do indeed decentre at the age of between three and five years, as Western children do.

Self-test 5

1 If something is only true in certain cultures, is it more likely to be brought about by nurture or nature?

2 If something is true in all cultures, is it more likely to come from nature or nurture?

Cross-cultural studies are very useful because if something is found to be true in many cultures, it is likely to be from an inherited characteristic (nature). Much of Piaget's work has been repeated in other cultures, and they have found the same results. This is evidence to show that Piaget's stages are universal (found everywhere) and it suggests that they are 'biological' in basis, as he thought.

Precausal reasoning and confusion of appearance with reality

There are a few other characteristics of a child's thinking in this preoperational stage. I am going to summarise them briefly, as you already have a lot of information.

Confusion of appearance with reality characterises a preoperational child. For example a child might think that a mask changes the person's identity in a real sense, or a stick is really bent in the water. Precausal reasoning is also found, for example where a child thinks a graveyard is a cause of death because dead people are buried there. Both these examples come from Cole and Cole (1996).

Evaluation – horizontal déalage

- **Horizontal décalage** means that the child does not have to do all the things in a stage at the same time. The theory of mind example, where the child learns that someone out of the room cannot know what has happened in the room, even though the child knows, is an example of what a child can do early in the preoperational stage. Conservation may come later (remember, conservation of volume, for example, is knowing that the volume stays the same, even if the level of the water in a taller glass is different). Décalage means misalignment, so it is okay for the different aspects of the stage to be misaligned (and occur at different times through the stage). Conservation of volume occurs late, but conservation of number is earlier. Activity 8 outlines an experiment showing how children in the preoperational stage cannot conserve number.

ACTIVITY 8

AN EXPERIMENT SHOWING CONSERVATION OF NUMBER

This is based on the same idea as the conservation of volume study. Here you get two rows of six counters (such as in the game Connect 4). Arrange the counters in two rows where they are all lined up, and the child can see clearly that there are the same number of counters in each row.

Then move the counters in one row, so that they are closer together, and that row is shorter.

The important question to ask the child is whether there are now the same number of counters in each row. There are still six, but one row is shorter. The preoperational child is likely to say that there are a different number of counters once the row lengths have been changed. However, a six or seven year old, still in the preoperational stage, may well be able to conserve number (by saying that there are still the same number of counters) when they cannot conserve volume.

If you do the study yourself, you must be very careful with ethics when using children.

Flavell et al (1990) say that there are two ways of looking at whether a child sees another's point of view. One is when the child must realise that someone else cannot see what the child can see at all (for example, in the theory of mind tasks), and the other is when the child has to realise that its own viewpoint is different from that of someone else. These are two different abilities, so it may be that the child can do one before it can do the other. This has the appearance of there being a misalignment.

Case (1992) argues in support of Piaget that if a child is asked to use the same reasoning on two different tasks, and they do this, then they could be said to be at the same stage of reasoning. He tested this out, and it worked. He asked about the juiciness of a drink and the happiness of a child. It does look as if there is some stage-like change, as Piaget thought.

Evaluation

Recall that with a different technique for testing object permanence, younger babies were shown to have that ability. Similarly, although you will be able to do Piaget's tasks and usually you will find what he claims is the case, you can vary them a little and you will find different results. Piaget's claims about a child's reasoning, and that there are differences in cognitive reasoning ability as the child grows, are probably right. However, much of what he found does seem to rest on how he asked the questions. When different tasks are used, or different questions asked, people come up with different interpretations and times for certain thinking abilities to occur. In some ways these researchers are simply refining Piaget's views, rather than saying that his basic claim about stages and needing to build certain thinking abilities is false. It is probably the case that we can challenge the age when children can do these things, such as conserve.

So here are some examples where Piaget's conclusions have been criticised.

- The mountain task that showed that a preoperational child is egocentric

Borke (1975) made a model like the model of the mountains. However, she used a small lake, a horse and cow, and a building. Grover (from *Sesame Street*) 'drove' around the landscape in a car and stopped sometimes to look at the view. Children as young as three could correctly give Grover's viewpoint, but they could not do the mountain task. It is concluded that Borke's task made sense. Remember we looked at the policeman–doll scenario and said that younger children could correctly say whether the policeman could see the doll too.

- Theory of mind and children's ability to understand the intentions of others – also looking at egocentrism

Meltzoff (1995) let 18 month olds watch adults. The adults either tried to pull the ends off a wooden dumbbell, or tried to hang a wooden necklace over a cylinder. In half of the trials (times that they did the task) the adults completed the task. For the other half, they did not complete the task. The eighteen month olds copied the tasks. They went on copying and showed that they knew what the adult was trying to do, even if they had not seen the completed task. This was taken as evidence that they knew what the adult was trying to do, and could understand the intentions of others.

- Conservation – earlier than Piaget thought

Some studies have shown that children can conserve earlier than Piaget found. For example, McGarrigle and Donaldson (1974) used a 'naughty teddy' to rearrange the counters in a standard Piaget task. Remember I suggested using Connect 4 counters (or any other games where brightly coloured counters are used) and lining up 12 of them in two rows of six, side by side. Then the experimenter pushed the counters in one of the rows together, making one row shorter. What if 'naughty teddy' does this?

Given a reason for the rearrangement of the counters, (teddy was being naughty), the children were able to say that the number of counters remained the same in the two rows. In other words, the children could conserve number.

In another study, Light et al (1979) in the conservation of volume task, instead of simply pouring the water from the short half-pint tumbler into the taller glass, suggested to the child that the reason for doing this was that there was a crack in the glass. Given a reason, the younger child was able to conserve volume (said that the volume of water was the same, even if the visible levels were different).

These two examples suggest that although children's thinking does seem to be different according to their age, it may not be as Piaget says. It may be that younger children are more trusting of adults, and expect them to do sensible things. So when an adult pours water from one glass to another, he or she is expected by the child to have a reason. When the adult then asks if the water is the same in amount, the child might well say it is not, thinking that that is the 'right' answer (the answer the adult expects). Given a reason by the adult, for example a cracked glass, the child thinks that the 'right' answer is that the water is the same. There could be similar reasoning behind the child's ability to conserve number if naughty teddy messes up one row, whereas the child cannot conserve number if the adult does it.

Siegal (1991) suggests that children believe that when an adult asks a question for the second time, the child thinks the answer must have to change.

Piaget's third stage in middle childhood – the concrete operational stage (6–12 years)

Briefly, in the following stages the child develops the capabilities it lacked.

The child up to the age of six or seven is having difficulty in decentring, cannot conserve, is egocentric, and is preoperational so cannot use the mental operations of separating categories and so on. In the concrete operational stage, these abilities are developed.

Concrete operational thinking

Concrete basically means something that exists, so concrete thinking means you need the objects you are thinking about in front of you, or you need to have actual objects to imagine. A child in the concrete operational stage can answer a question where they are asked to add (mentally) two apples and two oranges, and say how many pieces of fruit they have. However, they need formal reasoning (the final stage) before they can imagine abstract things and do mathematical calculations. Thomas (1992) gives an example of formal reasoning by asking the following question: if we imagine a whole made up of two quantities, and we increase the first quantity, but the whole remains the same, what has happened to the second quantity? Answering this question successfully means using formal operational thought (the fourth of Piaget's stages).

Here are some more features of the **concrete operational** thinker:
- Decentring – the child can decentre – they can consider more than one category at a time (for example, wooden beads and brown beads, so they can pick out the brown wooden beads)
- Conservation – the child can conserve – even when some things are altered, the child can understand that certain properties, for example, the volume of water, remain the same
- Reversibility – the child can understand that when an action is reversed, you get the same thing back again – that is when the water is poured back into the short tumbler, the quantity will be the same again
- The child is no longer egocentric, and can see things from another's viewpoint
- Knowledge of categories means that the child can learn about a new category – this is important in learning. So you can say to a child 'This is a pog' and show a picture. The child will be able to go to someone else and tell them things about 'pogs'

Cross-cultural studies of concrete operations
- Dasen and Heron (1981) found that in non-Western cultures children reach the concrete operational stage about a year behind 'Western' children
- Dasen (1982) found some cultures where twelve and thirteen year olds could not conserve
- Greenfield (1966) tried the 'water' conservation task with children in Senegal and found only about 50% of the eleven to thirteen year olds could conserve
- Dasen (1977a, 1977b) found (reviewing other studies) that adults in central Australia, New Guinea and the Amazon jungle had not reached the concrete operations stage

Evaluation

- Jahoda (1980), however, says the adults could not function without concrete operational thinking, because they would need to know about new categories, and would need to decentre and so on. Probably the cross-cultural studies were done in such a way that the adults did not understand what was expected. Perhaps there were problems with communication, or with the tasks themselves. These are problems with cross-cultural studies in general.

Training in concrete operational reasoning does help

Dasen and others thought about the cross-cultural studies that seemed to suggest that Piaget's stages are not universal at all – this means that, because other cultures give different findings, it cannot be the case that the stages are biologically given. If they were biologically given, they would be found in all humans – and the studies given above suggest that this is not true. This suggests that the stages are culturally given.

So Dasen tried training those in other cultures to see if they developed concrete operational thinking. He thought that if they did, this suggests that the studies showing lack of such thinking were done in such a way that the participants did not understand the tasks. A study was done using Australian children (Dasen, Ngini & Lavallee, 1979). They used both Australian children with European background and those with Aborigine background. With a small amount of training those with Aborigine background showed concrete operational thinking. They were, however, behind those with European background in the sense of developing concrete operational thinking later, so it was concluded that their environment did not provide the stimulation and information needed for such thinking to develop.

This conclusion suggests, firstly, that training helps children to reach certain stages, and, secondly, that environmental influences have a large role to play.

This can be a 'racist' argument, so please be aware

Note that there is a strong argument from many psychologists that the problem is nothing to do with other cultures lagging behind 'us'. What is true is that the tasks and the methods are more suited to Western cultural experiences than to other cultures.

Are the stages universal (do they apply to everyone in all cultures)?

Berry et al (1992) think that they are. Once you have taken into account all the criticisms of the cross-cultural studies that showed that in some cultures concrete operational thinking is not reached, it does seem that concrete operations does apply everywhere. It is the case, however, that we must take care when taking studies from one culture into another.

Piaget's fourth stage in adolescence – formal operational thought (12–19 years)

At this stage the individual can move from having to think about concrete things and objects, and is able to think in abstract terms too. The young person is able to test things in a scientific way by looking at all the possibilities.

Activity 9 suggests how you could play a game and also look at the difference between concrete and formal operational thought. This idea comes from a video about cognitive development, and the video is referenced at the end of the chapter.

ACTIVITY 9

THE DIFFERENCE BETWEEN CONCRETE AND FORMAL OPERATIONAL THOUGHT

One example that you could try is the game 'Twenty Questions'. If you do this game with younger children, they are likely to guess what the answer is by going through items individually. Older children will try to narrow the answer down more skilfully. For example, imagine that you are in a kitchen, and you choose at item to think about. The people guessing what you have chosen have 20 questions in which to guess it. They can ask any question, but it has to let you say only 'yes' or 'no' in reply. Children not yet in the formal operational reasoning stage may start guessing by asking 'is it the fridge?' However, those in the formal operational stage might ask 'is it made of metal?' or even the usual question asked (as you will know if you know the game), which is 'is it animal, vegetable or mineral?'

In this stage young people also start to look at other people and their judgements, and to take them into account. Social categories become important. Politics and the law become of interest, and logical principles are applied in these areas too.

Logical operations are mental actions and require the person to consider many alternatives, and to balance arguments.

The combination of chemicals problem

The combination of chemicals problem is an example of a Piaget-type task to look at the logical operational stage. The task is outlined in Box 11.

Box 11

The combination of chemicals problem – to show formal operational thinking

There are four bottles of clear liquid – all four are different liquids, but they look the same – and two beakers. Then there is also an indicator bottle. When a drop from the indicator bottle is added to some of the clear liquid, the clear liquid turns yellow, but at other times, added to other combinations of the clear liquids, a drop from the indicator bottle turns the now yellow mixture back to clear again. The beakers are used for mixing things together.

The experiment starts with one beaker having a mix from bottles 1 and 3 in it, and the other beaker has some of the liquid from bottle 2 in it. Adding a drop from the indicator bottle to one beaker turns the mixture yellow, and adding a drop from the indicator bottle to the other beaker leaves the liquid clear.

The task is to try out all the combinations and see what turns yellow and what remains clear.

A young child of around seven, if given this task, is likely to take first bottle 1, then bottle 2 and so on. He or she is not likely to think of combining the liquids unless prompted to do so. A young adolescent, however, will quite quickly realise that combinations of the liquids are required, and is more likely to be able to do this systematically until the right answer is found.

This study is a good example of Piaget's method. This is clearly an experiment, but the data is found by clinical interview. In other words the information from the experiment is the reasoning the child gives. It is this reasoning and how the solution is found that is of importance. So although this is an experiment in many ways, it is the interview that yields the data.

Doing chemical experiments needs some expert knowledge! However, you might be able to think of another task that needs systematic trial and error, and then you could test whether an individual has reached the level of formal operational thinking.

- You can criticise Piaget by criticising the idea of stages and by by saying that development is continuous. You can criticise his method, because he took a lot of his data from his own children. Not only was this a limited sample, but he may also have been biased.

- You can talk about his theory as being one complete explanation of cognitive development, or you can discuss his theories. If you are asked for more than one theory, use the ideas of egocentrism, object permanence, conservation, or adaptation, as these could be called separate ideas.

- There is a lot of material that has been left out of this account of Piaget's work. This is a very large area and has generated a lot of research. For example, it is generally thought that males are more successful at formal operational thinking than girls; this has led to a lot of research. Linn and Hyde (1989) have looked at research in this area, and claim that males are better at spatial and mathematical thinking. This idea has also been supported by more recent evidence. Peskin (1980) suggested that these tasks were more boring for girls, and this is the reason for their poorer performance.

- There is also research looking at formal operational thinking in non-literate cultures. Hutchins (1983) looked at studies of navigators in the Caroline Islands. It had previously been thought that they did not use logical thinking about the system they used, but Hutchins thought that the system was indeed logical. It was quite logical for a Western thinker to think that the canoe moves across the water and the island remains still. The islanders, however, thought that the boat stood still while the island they were using as a reference point moved. This was logical to them. This shows the problem with using 'Western' methods in other cultures, and it appears that all cultures do use formal operational thinking of one form or another.

- A further way of evaluating Piaget's views is to use the views of those with different theories. The ideas of the two other main theorists, Bruner and Vygotsky, are outlined below. Remember to use one theory to evaluate another, by saying that there are other viewpoints that oppose Piaget's.

The theory of Vygotsky

Vygotsky pays more attention than Piaget did to the social and cultural influences on a child's cognitive development. Both his and Bruner's work fall within the cultural context framework outlined earlier. Not only is the child active in its own development (as Piaget thought), but it is interactive. This lays more emphasis on the effect of the cultural context on the actions of the child.

Vygotsky was Russian and lived from 1896 to 1934. It is interesting to include some psychologists from other countries, as so much of what we learn in British psychology seems to come from Britain or America.

Think of Vygotsky as having a 'social' theory. He emphasised the social aspects of a child's development much more than Bruner or Piaget did. Vygotsky thought of language as much more social than cognitive. Of course it is cognitive, as it involves thinking, but the reason for language is a social one – to communicate with others.

Vygotsky emphasised language to such an extent that he claimed thought is just inner speech or thinking in words. We cannot do anything for ourselves at birth, and it is only through interacting with other people that we develop as we do. Through being social, we become independent and able to function as individuals, and part of this is our cognitive development, according to Vygotsky.

Problem solving is continually taking place, and is a process that happens between adults and the child. The child takes this problem solving in as an internal action (a mental one), and this is what thinking is, and this is how it develops. One important point here is that Piaget saw the child as an active scientist learning about the world (given the tools to learn), whereas Vygotsky saw the child as a participant, learning from the social world around it.

Vygotsky (published 1978) discusses the act of pointing; the baby reaches out for some object, and at this stage is not pointing. However, the caregiver interprets this act of reaching out as pointing. The object is then given to the baby, as the person looking after the baby thinks this is what is wanted. So the baby learns to use the act of pointing, having found out that it produced desirable results. At some stage this pointing gesture becomes communication with the caregiver, rather than reaching for an object. So you see that interaction with others is what is teaching the child. Other people are, therefore, very important in cognitive development. The children are there to learn, and they need people around them to guide them.

Scaffolding

Whoever is taking the role of the tutor for the child is said to be providing **scaffolding** for them. This can be a teacher, or a peer. It just has to be someone who knows more than the child. The scaffolding is the context (like giving the desired object) and allows the child to achieve whatever they want, or to solve the problem. Without this scaffolding the child is unable to learn. The term 'scaffolding' is useful. It was not Vygotsky who used the term 'scaffolding' but it is based on his ideas about cognitive development. 'Scaffolding' suggests that the structure can be taken away. As the child gets more competent, the tutor can withdraw support gradually, until the problem is solved, or the skill is achieved.

There is no need for the child to do everything for itself, as it can learn from those who already know. Piaget's child has to adapt itself to all new experiences, whereas Vygotsky suggests that we learn from others too. Meadows (1995) suggests that mature learners are scaffolding themselves and have the skills to do so. They usually work just within their own competences.

Wertsch et al (1980, cited in Durkin, 1995) suggest that if Vygotsky's ideas are correct, then any new skill or problem-solving ability should be able to be done socially first, and then individually. This can be tested. The task was to build a model truck and there were different coloured shapes ready to complete the task. There was a model and then the task was to build a truck like the model. The children had to look at the model a lot, so that it could be copied. Their mothers were present, and the researchers checked if the child looked at the model after the mother had. The question was whether the child was learning from the mother's example of looking at the truck. Wertsch et al found that in 90% of the cases, the child's looking at the model was just after the mother had looked. When they looked at older children, these followed the mother's example less, which is what you would expect if the idea of scaffolding is true. So this study supports Vygotsky's ideas.

Collaborative learning

Collaborative learning means using others to help us learn. Reciprocal teaching is a similar idea. Scaffolding outlines a way of collaborative learning. Those who know can support those who do not, until the support (scaffold) is no longer needed. Wood et al (1976) also did research in this area and looked at what sort of help worked best. Some mothers gave specific instructions on how to complete a task of building something. Others simply gave words of encouragement. The most successful were those who gave more specific instructions when needed, but less help as the building progressed. This is what Vygotsky thought, that is that more help is needed at first, but that it is important to keep withdrawing help in the interaction, and passing control over to the individual. At first the learning is social, and then it becomes individual, as Vygotsky believed. One approach is to start with general instructions and then wait to see where help is needed. That help must be given, and then support withdrawn again, until needed again.

Meadows (1995) shows that the way adults and children interact with regard to language supports Vygotsky's ideas too. There is close support as adults use 'child-like' words, and then the adult lets the child develop on their own as they get better at it. From the 'child-like' words, the adult moves on to using the 'proper' word. So the adult offers support, works within the child's own abilities, and then pushes the child forward to develop better and better language abilities.

Zone of proximal development (ZPD)

The child's **zone of proximal development** (ZPD) is the area where it is about to develop, but has not quite reached that stage. It is what is nearly within the child's reach. The child is at a certain level of development, and the ZPD is what the child is about to move on to. Children at the same level of development cannot be said to be about to develop at the same rate. This is because one of the children could have a different ZPD, which basically means one might be more ready to move on to the next stage than another child. 'Proximal' more or less means 'near'.

Durkin (1995) looks at evidence for this ZPD. The evidence that scaffolding works, and that language development moves forward by giving support and then withdrawing a bit, is taken as support for the existence of this ZPD.

Collaborative learning, reciprocal teaching (outlined below), the ZPD, and scaffolding all converge around the main point that the child is the learner and gets on better with some teaching. However, this teaching has to be pitched just above the level of what the child can do, and must be such that the child can be actively seeking the answers. The support must be where needed, but not where it is not needed. The child must be allowed to push forward individually, until another bit of support is needed.

Using Vygotsky's theory in education

The idea of reciprocal teaching is outlined below, and can be linked to Vygotsky's idea of the ZPD. Also collaborative learning and learning in groups would be supported by Vygotsky's views. Peer teaching should work just as well as having an adult teacher, as long as the child gets help when needed, and not when it is moving to the stage of making that knowledge internal.

The theory of Jerome Bruner

Bruner's three modes (ways) of representing the world

The enactive mode

In the **enactive mode**, the baby represents the world through actions. There are no thoughts, as yet. The baby's knowledge grows from what it learns by experience through these actions. Think of something you have learnt through actions, even walking. It is very hard to describe walking using words, but you know how to do it. As we carry out actions and repeat them, they become more and more automatic and well learned.

Evaluation

- Bruner, like Piaget, sees the achievement of object permanence as a major event for the baby. The enactive mode is very similar to Piaget's sensorimotor stage.

The iconic mode

Icons are images, so think of the **iconic mode** as a way of thinking about the world where pictures are used. The world is represented in the child's mind using pictures and mental images of things that it has experienced. The images include past events where objects have been 'met', and, rather than being exact pictures of particular situations, the images are usually generalisations.

Evaluation

- In Piaget's sensorimotor stage schemas are being adapted and built up. The iconic mode is very similar to Piaget's idea of building up schemas (which are really mental images). The child cannot think anything other than that things are what they seem to be (or look like).

The symbolic mode

This is where there is a major jump for the child. Bruner differs from Piaget here, because he emphasises the importance of language. Both Piaget and Bruner agree that at around six years of age there is a major change regarding cognitive development. For Piaget the change is to concrete operational thought, and for Bruner the change is that language starts to have a great influence on thought.

The child at this stage (or mode of thinking) can go beyond information presented in front of them and can think about other issues too.

Bruner and Kenney (1966) did an experiment to show the difference in the thinking of a child in the iconic mode, and one in the **symbolic mode**. This study is outlined in Box 12.

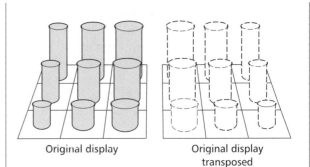

Original display   Original display transposed

Figure 3.4

There were two tasks for children to perform. One was to look at the arrangement and to reproduce it (this was called the reproduction task). The other task was to reproduce it, but this time in reverse. If the smallest and narrowest piece was originally on the left-hand bottom square, the child started reversing the display by putting that piece on the right-hand bottom square, for example (this was called the transposition task).

The reproduction task involves the iconic mode, because the children can reproduce the visual image. The transposition task involves the symbolic mode, because they have to reason verbally in order to reverse the display. So those who can reproduce but not transpose are using the iconic mode, not the symbolic mode.

The results of Bruner and Kenney's study showed that children could generally reproduce the display before they could transpose it, and this supports Bruner's claim that the iconic mode comes before the symbolic mode. 79% of seven year olds could do the transposition task, whereas none of the five year olds could; 60% of five year olds and 80% of the seven year olds could do the reproduction task.

Evaluation

- This is quite a well-thought-out study, and can be quite easily reproduced. It does seem to be the case that the one task is simply to visually reproduce the display, whereas it is a lot more complicated to produce a mirror image of it. The evidence supports the hypothesis.

- However, this is an experiment, and the criticisms of experiments do apply. You can claim that the task is not a valid one. It may be the case that children have reproduced something before, but they are unlikely to have produced a mirror image of such a display. Perhaps they did not understand the task. It is quite difficult to

---

Box 12

The transposition task – showing what it means to think in the symbolic mode

Bruner and Kenney (1966) tested the change from the iconic to the symbolic mode of thought. They used a board like a chessboard with nine squares altogether. Then they prepared materials – you could do this using playdough or plasticine. They prepared cylinders and arranged them in order of height and width.

explain to someone, so five year olds may have been more confused about what they had to do than unable to do it. As an experiment, it is reliable and can be replicated, so this is in its favour. However, observing children doing what they naturally do might produce more valid results.

Using language helps understanding

Piaget thought that language came along as a part of the development of thinking processes. However, Bruner thought that language plays a crucial role in cognitive development, as outlined earlier. So Bruner tested this idea, using Piaget's conservation of liquid task. Recall this task, which was outlined earlier.

Bruner took this experiment and looked at what happened when the children could not see the level of the liquid. There was a screen, which meant that they could not use the iconic mode, which is the visual image of there being a higher level of liquid in the taller glass.

Bruner used two short tumblers and one that was wider still. So if the liquid is poured from one of the short ones into the even wider glass, the level is lower. The children saw the three glasses and then watched the liquid being poured from one of the short ones into the wider one. The difference between this and Piaget's task was that the children could not see the level of liquid in the glass, due to a screen. Half the four year olds asked, and almost all the five to seven year olds, could conserve when there was a screen stopping them from seeing the changed level. When it is said that they could conserve, this means they were able to say that the amount of liquid remains the same. When the screen was removed, the four year olds did start 'not conserving' again, but the others did not. Furthermore, when the researchers then did a standard task without the screen, the four year olds tended to start giving the wrong answer again (and could not conserve). However, the five to seven year olds tended to give the right answer. It looked as if they had learnt what the answer was.

Bruner concluded that the four year olds were using iconic mode, and, although some of them managed to say that the liquid was the same (in other words they conserved) when there was a screen, without the screen they went back to using iconic mode. However, the five to seven year olds, having said that the level was the same, did not revert to the iconic mode. It looked as if they had been forced to verbalise what the answer was, and this use of the symbolic mode had taught them to use it again in a similar situation. So five to seven year olds were more likely to conserve in the standard Piaget task if they had said the right answer previously in the modified task using a screen.

The spiral curriculum

The **spiral curriculum** reflects Bruner's ideas and is examined below too, because applying these theories of cognitive development to education is the key application of the approach.

'Spiral' suggests working upwards but not in a straight line. 'Curriculum' refers to what is taught in school. So the spiral curriculum means that what is taught helps the child to progress and move forwards, but not by a straight route. The idea is that the levels of difficulty that the child encounters in what it learns are progressively more difficult. As the child can do one thing, it moves on to another. It is not that the child has to be ready to move on to the next stage, as Piaget suggested, but that the child can be taught to move forward too. There is much more of an interaction between adults and children than Piaget thought. Piaget's idea was that the individual child had to be ready to move forward, and would learn actively. Bruner thought that the child needs to be shown the underlying principles of what is to be learnt, so that there is deeper understanding that leads the child forward. It is not that the facts have to be taught to the child. If the child understands the principles, the child can extend these to other areas, so does not have to be taught every 'fact'. Smith and Cowie (1991) talked about teachers making links and relationships between subjects, to help the child to transfer their understanding skills to other situations.

Evaluation

- One way of evaluating theories in psychology is to look at how useful they are when being applied to real life. So Bruner's contribution in suggesting ways of teaching means that his theory can be praised as being of practical use. His ideas about scaffolding and the spiral curriculum are not really different from Vygotsky's ideas about scaffolding and the zone of proximal development. They both say the same thing – that children can be taught, but their learning depends a bit on their own level of cognitive development. How the above theories are applied to education is the subject of the key application, outlined below.

Bruner's developmental theory (1966)

Bruner was influenced by Vygotsky, and agrees with the idea of using scaffolding in education. Bruner (1983) says that the best way of giving a child help in learning is to watch the success of the child, and leave it to continue, and then watch where things go wrong, and intervene. This is a form of scaffolding, and is based on the ideas outlined above when looking at Vygotsky's theory. Bruner thinks that adults need to intervene so that the child can develop successfully, so in this sense Bruner emphasises the need for education. This is unlike Piaget, who thinks that providing the means of stimulation is important, but the child must actively explore for itself, in order to learn.

For Bruner, teaching and using language are both essential in the scaffolding process, whereas Piaget does not emphasise either of these.

Bruner was, however, also influenced by Piaget. He agreed that cognition develops over time, and he agreed that there is a biological process that matures and allows the learning and development to take place. Bruner also emphasises the inquiring nature of the child, just as Piaget does. It is the exploring child who develops, and it is not true that the child's environment shapes it without the child's active intervention.

Piaget's is a stage theory, and he has four stages, as you have learnt. Bruner has three 'stages'. They are not really stages as such. They are called 'modes' and these are ways of thinking about the world. It is true that these 'modes of representation' (ways of thinking about the world) happen at different ages and that each child reaches them in sequence, one at a time. So in many ways they are like stages. It is just that they are not usually called stages but are called 'modes of representation'.

Comparing Bruner, Piaget and Vygotsky

One way in which the three main theorists, Bruner, Vygotsky and Piaget, differ is their emphasis on language. Piaget thought language just happened as a result of the maturing cognitive processes of the child. Vygotsky thought that language and thinking were separate to the age of two, and then begin to come together. Bruner thought that it was language that moved cognitive development forward, and there is a central role for language.

Piaget worked within the constructivist framework, thinking that biological maturation and environmental learning worked together to influence the child. Vygotsky and Bruner, however, fit more within the cultural context framework, and emphasise interaction (actions between people) more than actions (which emphasise simply the one individual).

Bruner and Piaget are more like stage theorists, although Vygotsky too emphasises a kind of stage-like development. The information processing approach, and behaviourism, are two approaches that see development as continuous.

Studies within cognitive-developmental psychology

Does the autistic child have a 'theory of mind'?

This is an outline of a study carried out by Baron-Cohen, Leslie and Frith (1985) to look at **theory of mind**, and to test whether autistic children do not develop a theory of mind.

Why this study?

It is hard to decide which studies to include in this section, as there are so many. You will be able to choose other studies if you wish. I have chosen this one because it looks at cognitive development in a different way.

Linking the cognitive, cognitive-developmental and physiological approaches

There is a video on autism produced for the Open University, and Simon Baron-Cohen demonstrates the study outlined here in the video. Baron-Cohen also spoke on a programme about synesthesia. Synesthesia is a peculiar phenomenon. Some people, when they hear sound, also see shapes, and synesthesia is the word for this idea of 'crossed senses'. Others see colours when they see letters, for example, a letter 'A' for one person could be purple. This is another example of synesthesia. Baron-Cohen explains the 'condition' by showing how this could literally be 'crossed wires' in the nervous system. People really could be seeing shapes when they hear sound. It is interesting that the cognitive approach, the physiological approach, and the cognitive-developmental approach are all linked here. Baron-Cohen is interested in cognition and thinking, he is using physiological explanations in his studies of how we think, and he is involved in looking at the causes of autism where there appear to be problems in the development of cognition. You can see how, when you study psychology, you need to knit these approaches together, if you want to aim for these sorts of explanations.

What is autism?

Autism was first recognised around the 1940s, and usually it is noticed in a child when it reaches about four years old. It is the child's behaviour that is diagnosed. The child appears cut off from others, and autism is often called a psychosis. Neuroses are problems that the individual recognises, and psychoses are problems where the individual is not in control enough to know that they have a problem. The autistic child is very cut off from other people. *DSM-IV* (1994), which is the American book used for diagnosing mental disorders, mentions the following difficulties:

- poor eye contact
- poor turn-taking abilities
- language development is poor, including non-verbal communication
- lack of friendships
- inflexibility and a tendency to rely on rituals
- lack of make-believe play, and lack of creativity in play.

The autistic child is not easy to describe, because not all children with autism are alike – there are wide differences in them. However, autism is characterised in all as showing poor imagination, lack of social interaction, and problems in communication. An interesting feature of autism is that autistic children often have one outstanding skill.

Autistic children can learn and their difficulties do change with this learning; however, their autism does not go away. It affects between one and two people per 1000 of the population, with about twice as many boys being affected as girls. Dustin Hoffman in *Rain Man* shows that autism is not restricted to childhood. Frith (1993) gives a good account of autism. Currently Baron-Cohen's (1990, 1993, 1995) explanation of autism is widely recognised. He focuses on a core problem for all autistic people, and that is that they have problems in understanding mental states. This is where there is the link with cognitive-developmental theories.

A theory of mind

Work with chimpanzees led researchers to look at how they viewed mental states. Soon researchers looked at young children to see how they looked at 'mind'. They wanted to see if young children could see things from another's mental state. A false belief task is used. Earlier the experimental method was outlined. This is the idea of using two dolls, hiding a counter under a beaker, and then pretending with the observing child that one doll 'goes out of the room'. The counter is moved to another beaker. The researcher and child know this, and one of the dolls 'knows' it too. The question is, will the child think that the other doll (who is 'out of the room') knows that the counter has been moved? A very young child of about three years old will be egocentric, and will not understand that anyone not in the room when the change was made cannot know about the change. The child knows, so other people know too. However, an older child, even of about four years old, can say that anyone not present when a change is made cannot know about the change. This four year old has a 'theory of mind'.

Remember, we said that this sort of task has been done in other cultures, and there too, very young children do not have a theory of mind, whereas by the age of around four years old, they do. Since the same results are found across different cultures, it looks as if this theory of mind

develops through maturation, and is 'natural' and inborn. The idea fits nicely into Piaget's theory, although was not his idea.

Baron-Cohen et al's (1985) study

Wimmer and Perner (1983) carried out a false belief task. There were two dolls, Maxi and his mother. Maxi puts chocolate in a green drawer, and then goes out to play. His mother moves the chocolate to a blue drawer, whilst he is playing. The child with a theory of mind will know that Maxi will look in the wrong drawer for the chocolate, whereas the child who has not developed a theory of mind, will say that Maxi will look in the blue drawer (where the child knows the chocolate is).

Baron-Cohen et al's study is based on this earlier one. They used dolls called Sally and Anne, and moved a marble from a basket to a box. Wimmer and Perner used 'normal' children, whereas Baron-Cohen et al used three groups. They used 20 autistic children, 14 Down's syndrome children and 27 'normal' children. The control group of normal children were of preschool age, but the children in the other two groups were older. The word 'normal' is used here because it is quicker than saying children without autism or Down's syndrome.

The dependent variable was whether they had a theory of mind (knew that Sally, who was 'out of the room' when the marble was moved, would look in the wrong place for it) or not. The independent variable was whether the child was autistic, Down's syndrome or neither. This independent variable occurred naturally and was not manipulated by the researcher, so this is a quasi-experimental method.

What they wanted to find out was whether autistic children do lack this theory of mind. Do autistic children remain egocentric, and unable to take the view of another or to predict other people's behaviour? If this is the case, then autistic children will indeed have problems in relating to others. If the Down's syndrome children do have a theory of mind, then it is not just that the autistic children are 'mentally impaired', but that there must be a specific difficulty.

Procedure

Firstly, the child was introduced to Sally and Anne and asked to name the dolls, to check that there was understanding. Sally placed a marble into her basket, then left the scene. Anne moved the marble and hid it in a box. Sally returned. Then the experimenter asked the main question 'where will Sally look for her marble?' This is testing for a false belief – Sally will have a false belief, because Sally will think the marble is still in her basket. If this child understands Sally's false belief, then the child has a theory of mind.

There were two control questions. The researcher asked 'where is the marble really?' This was to check that the child had noted the transfer to the box, and understood what had happened. The other question was 'where was the marble at the beginning?' This question was to check the child's memory, to make sure that forgetting was not a problem.

Results

All of the participants passed the two control questions and the naming question. This suggests that they all understood the scenario and the task. Most of the normal and Down's syndrome participants passed the false belief question too. In other words they knew that Sally would have a false belief. Twelve out of the 14 Down's syndrome children, and 23 out of the 27 normal children did have a theory of mind.

However, 16 out of the 20 autistic children did not correctly say that Sally would think the marble was in her basket still. These 16 children did know where the marble really was. The conclusion was that there was something about autism that links to theory of mind and taking the view of another. Note, however, that four autistic children did have a theory of mind.

Differences between this task and Piaget's mountain task

Although it looks as if the autistic child cannot take the view of another, and this is very similar to Piaget's ideas about egocentrism, it is worth noting that in Piaget's mountain study the child has to say what the other one sees. The mountain task involves visuo-spatial skills, and these are not the same as attributing beliefs to others, which is what Baron-Cohen et al's study shows. Autistic children can do the perception task – that is they can say what other people see. So the cognitive skills needed for taking the perceptual view of others are not the same as those needed for taking the viewpoint of another in terms of their beliefs. It might be worth noting, then, that Piaget's task seems only to show how we perceive, rather than to demonstrate different mental states.

Evaluation

- The theory of mind is, according to Leslie (1987), a demonstration of some underlying mental mechanism which starts to mature from 12 to 18 months and should be present at the age of four years. This mechanism allows the child to think about thinking, so to speak. The child can have a belief about a belief, including someone else's. Therefore, the child can think about what Sally believes, apart from the child's own beliefs. This is one explanation of the theory of mind.

- Another explanation links theory of mind to egocentrism, and suggests that the child must have reversible mental

processes before being able to understand that other people have different beliefs (Bryant, 1998). One problem with explaining the development of a theory of mind as either an underlying mechanism that develops, or decentring as the child develops at a cognitive level, is that this assumes that the child is an isolated explorer in its own world. In reality, the child is a social person, interacting with others. The first problem, that the child is seen as an isolated explorer, but is not, is also a criticism of Piaget's theory, and it is just this criticism that is addressed by Bruner's and Vygotsky's theories. It is in social interaction that the child develops understanding of others, and it is this understanding of others that is missing in the autistic child.

- A criticism of the Baron-Cohen et al study is that it may not be looking at a problem with theory of mind in autistic children, so much as at a problem with lack of imagination. It is already known that autistic children have problems with imagination and pretend play, so nothing new is learnt here. Also, Sally is only a doll and has no mind or belief. Another problem is that, even when the study is done again, some autistic children do succeed in the task, so we cannot say that all autistic children lack a theory of mind. When, however, they extended the task, and asked where Anne thought Sally thought the marble was, all the autistic children were unable to answer correctly.

- This study has a practical application in teaching autistic children. Teachers can be aware of the child's limitations, and can make sure tasks do not ask the child to think about the beliefs of others. As in most studies in psychology, a practical application of the findings is usually the goal. A better understanding of autism is itself a goal too.

The influence of classroom peers on cognitive performance in children with behavioural problems

This is a study by Bevington, J. and Wishart, J.G. (March 1999), printed in the *British Journal of Educational Psychology*, Vol. 69, Part 1, pp 19–32.

Why this study was chosen

This study links in well with the idea of collaborative learning and with the key application for this approach, which looks at education. Also the study examines factors that look at underachievement, and this of interest in itself. It was thought that looking at children with behavioural difficulties would be relevant, not only for the AS but also for the more applied areas of the A2 part of the course, which you might be going on to study.

This study looks at the effect of peer presence on classroom performance – especially where children with behavioural difficulties are concerned. The hypothesis was that as the number of peers increased, so cognitive performance would decrease. This goes against the idea of collaborative learning, and suggests rather that peers lead to loss of concentration perhaps. These are the sorts of questions the study aims to examine. If these questions can be answered, then the results can be used in classroom management, and perhaps can be used to help such children.

Introduction

The study begins by claiming that underachievement is not always due to low intelligence (Jensen, 1967). If there are other factors, these need to be discovered, so that something can be done to avoid at least some of the underachievement. The study cites other studies that show that behavioural problems and underachievement go together, and an example of such a study is that of Smith and Rutter (1995). It is possible that underachievement and behavioural problems go together, but that there is no causal link; however, the study summarised here claims that this is not the case. There are three possibilities. Firstly, the underachieving may lead to problem behaviour. Alternatively, the behavioural problems might result in underachievement. Another alternative is that behavioural problems and underachievement both come from another common cause such as a poor social environment. However, when social environment is controlled for, the link between behavioural problems and underachievement still remains.

Smith and Luckasson (1993) find links between temperament and school achievement. High distractability, attention deficits, motivational problems and disorganised approaches to learning are factors that tend to go with low achievement. Hyperactivity and impulsiveness are also characteristics that link to academic underachievement. However, the authors of this study claim that it is not temperament in itself that leads to low achievement, it is rather the way that the child's temperament interacts with the environment. Therefore, we must study the environment and see what can be done to avoid such low achievement.

Bevington and Wishart assert here that the obvious environment to start with is the classroom. Rewards in the classroom setting go to those who can sustain attention independently and who will persist even when the task is unstimulating. Therefore, those children who are more active or who cannot focus their attention so well will be at a disadvantage in such an environment. Some children are more easily distracted. Distractions in the classroom can be physical (such as seating arrangements) and social (such as classroom dynamics and which children work together). Rogoff (1990) has investigated the effects of working in groups. Refer to some of the material in this chapter on collaborative and reciprocal learning to find

out more about this. Generally research has found that peer interaction improves learning and that collaborative learning is good.

However, although research suggests that children who help one another learn more, in practice this does not seem to be the case. Some say that group learning can prevent progress (studies cited include one by Messer et al, 1993). In a real classroom, even with some group work, much of the time children are learning independently without help even from the teacher. Research usually focuses on the collaborative side, and not on the independent learning that children do.

This study looks at children with emotional and behavioural problems and studies the effect on their cognitive performance according to how many others are present.

Method

Sample
Twenty-four children aged between nine and 14 are used. These are taken from four classes in two special schools. Each class had six children in it – and this is how the 24 were obtained. One school was a primary school, which was non-residential. The other school was a residential secondary school. There were more males than females in the sample.

Procedure
Teacher ratings were taken and the children were each assessed in the areas of non-verbal intelligence, academic achievement and performance on a cognitive task. The performance of the cognitive task was done by the child in three conditions. In one condition the child was alone. In a second condition the child worked with one other child present. In a third condition the child was assessed when all six children were present.

a) For non-verbal intelligence Raven's Standard Progressive Matrices were used (SPM: Raven 1977). Basically children see an abstract pattern or design with an element missing and they have to choose the missing element.
b) Academic achievement was measured using three achievement subscales from the Kaufman Assessment Battery for children (K-ASC: Kaufman & Kaufman, 1983). The scales involved reading/decoding; reading/understanding; arithmetic.
c) Cognitive task performance involved perceptual/conceptual matching exercises from the SPM. Even though the children saw these before, to prepare them, it was not thought that they had remembered how to do them all.

d) Levels of behavioural problems used the Child Behaviour Checklist and Teacher Report Form (Achenbach & Edelbrock, 1986). Items included antisocial behaviour, distractability levels, attention-seeking behaviour and response to discipline. Teachers rate the child's behaviour.

Design

The design was a within-subjects or repeated measures design. The independent variable was whether the child was alone when doing the cognitive tasks, whether the child was with one peer, or with five peers. The dependent variables were the mean score on the tasks and the mean time the tasks took.

Results

Non-verbal intelligence was average or below average for the child's age (chronological age). The group were also underachieving regarding academic attainment; again all were below average for their chronological age. Younger children did seem to show more behavioural problems than the older children, but not with a significant difference.

The table below shows scores of completion of the cognitive tasks within the three conditions. The mean score and the mean times are given.

Scores are higher when children are alone and decrease as peers are present. However, the difference was not so great for the younger (primary) group. In groups the tasks were done more quickly, although more slowly with one person present than when alone. This was true for both the younger and the older children, and was an interesting finding.

Discussion

Performance was found to vary depending on whether children were alone, with one other or in a group of six. Scores varied, as did the time taken. As far as time is concerned, they were slower if with one other and quite a lot quicker if with a group of six. It is interesting to ask why. Perhaps with one other present, the distractions were social and off task, but in a group they all focused on the task and were quicker (and made more mistakes).

Links to social facilitation theory are possible. Zajonc (1965) says the mere presence of another increases the likelihood of a dominant response. The dominant response is the one the child is most used to. Since typical classroom behaviour is disruptive in these settings, the behaviour facilitated by another child being present may have been the dominant response – disruption. Triplett's (1898) work may help to explain why a group of six were faster. Triplett's research showed cyclists went faster in a group when competing. Therefore maybe with five other children they saw themselves as competing. Some say in groups people may work faster but less well, and this supports these findings (Davies, 1969).

The child's behaviour was also noted during the study. The researchers logged such incidents as the child shouting out, and positive or negative verbal or non-verbal exchanges. They noted disruptive behaviours such as throwing possessions, chanting or damaging classroom equipment. Problem behaviour, except for shouting out, was found much more when there was only one other child there than when the other five were present. Since the disruptive behaviour was found when one other child was there, this might account for the longer time the tasks took in the condition when one other peer was present.

Evaluation

- It would have been useful to have looked at the relationships between the children and the group dynamics. Dodge et al (1990) found that highly aggressive boys were angry and reactive when with other highly aggressive boys. However, when highly aggressive boys were with low-aggression boys, their behaviour involved proactive bullying. It seems as though group dynamics is an important factor, and this was not looked at in this study.

- One school was residential and one was not, so this could have made a difference. The older children were in a residential setting. Richards et al (1995) found that children who are inattentive often do worse in an environment where there is intensive learning, and this is more likely to be the case in a residential school. A longitudinal study would have been better because these sorts of factors could have been looked at.

N=24	Solitary condition		With one peer		With five peers	
	Score (max.12)	Time (seconds)	Score (max.12)	Time (seconds)	Score (max.12)	Time (seconds)
	8.75	122.94	8.29	133.98	7.83	82.98

- The study looked at specific cognitive tasks rather than classroom learning, and it is not known how these tasks relate to classroom learning. Therefore, it is difficult to conclude that collaborative learning leads to less successful learning. The task was a structured problem-solving task done in the classroom, so there is some validity here.

- The common finding that low achievement goes with low intelligence was supported by the findings of this study, although these measures were not the central ones, and the cause of this connection was not looked at. It might be that behavioural problems go with a cognitive deficit; however, this is not proved in this study by any means.

- In praise of the study, it is important to note that other studies in the area do not look at the presence of peers, and the hypothesis that the presence of others will lead to weaker performance on cognitive tasks was supported by the results. Sylva (1994) reviewed information on the influence of school on a child's development, and the influence of peers was not mentioned. There is a lot of work on collaborative learning and on integrated learning. However, the finding from this study suggests the opposite – that children learn better without others present. Note that the sample involved only children with behavioural difficulties, however.

- If accuracy is required, then children with behavioural difficulties should work alone. If speed is required, they should work in a group. These are the sorts of conclusions we can draw from the study.

- You can also evaluate the method itself and the measures used. The children may have performed better on their own because they felt important and were part of a study – if they knew this. Ethical issues are not mentioned, but it is assumed that proper permission was sought and granted. As the authors of the study themselves say, they did not take into account the group dynamics. Perhaps some of the groups of six got on well, and others did not. Twenty-four is a small sample, and the study would need to be done again to test reliability. The four classes were from different schools, and the schools and teachers may have had different classroom practices in the first place. As the authors say, one school was residential and the other was not, so this may have made a difference.

Key application – cognitive-developmental theory and education

Education, in our society at least, is seen as very important. We think that our children must be educated, and their time spent in education seems to be getting longer. In some societies there is no formal education. The Baka have already been mentioned, and they pass on knowledge by means of stories. Their needs are such that their children need to have special knowledge about food gathering, their own safety and medicines – and their 'education system' reflects their needs.

In our society, it is thought that we need a formal system, because of what children have to learn. The implications for our society are that we need as many people as possible to be educated, mainly perhaps for economic reasons, but also for social reasons.

Here we want to look at how the theories of cognitive development have made a difference to the way we educate children, and what we can learn from the theories.

Learning difficulties

Before looking at 'normal' education, it is worth looking at how the theories have affected how we 'deal' with learning difficulties. The list of learning difficulties is growing, and this is itself partly a result of the study of cognitive development. There are learning difficulties, such as when a child is blind or deaf, and when a child has behavioural difficulties or is emotionally disturbed. There are other learning difficulties that are now widely recognised, such as dyslexia. Then there are the less obvious learning difficulties that are becoming recognised. These are difficulties with mathematical concepts, short-term memory difficulties, and thinking disorders.

The way in which we find out about learning difficulties often includes using intelligence tests. These are tests that have been carried out on a lot of children of a certain age. From these initial tests, we find a 'norm' of what a child of that age can do. Based on this 'norm' we test all children, and those who cannot do certain items in the test may be thought of as 'below average' in that ability. Probably teachers or parents have highlighted a problem in the first place, for the tests to be given.

Often, learning difficulties are said to be due to abnormalities in brain development. This seems to be true of dyslexia, those who have problems with mathematical concepts, those who have memory difficulties, and those with behavioural disorders. Regarding problems with reading, for example, there could be problems in the processing of information, or problems in the auditory cortex (Miller & Tallal, 1995).

The usefulness of using the information-processing approach to explain some learning difficulties

Using the information-processing approach to the understanding of cognitive development can be useful when trying to pinpoint problems certain children have, and, perhaps more importantly, trying to solve these problems. The information-processing approach (see Chapter 1) is another way of explaining the development of cognition (Figure 3.5).

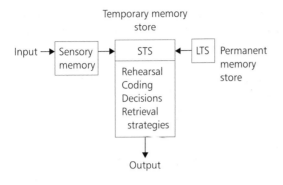

Figure 3.5
The information processing model

Tallal et al (1993) looked at the idea of there being an information-processing deficit in some children. These were children who found it difficult to acquire language. If bits of information were input very quickly, the children found it difficult to process them. Tallal et al used two groups of children, the ones with difficulty, and a group with no difficulty. They presented the children with two tones, one after the other, and asked the children if the tones were the same or different. If the interval between the tones was more than half a second, both groups could do the task, but with a shorter gap between the tones, the group with language difficulties had problems in doing the task. They also did an MRI scan on the children with language problems, who were shown to have fewer cells in the language area of the brain. However, this latter bit of information needs expanding for strong conclusions to be drawn. It is interesting, though, that Tallal et al backed up their experiments with biological evidence. So it looks as if one type of language difficulty is a problem in the necessary speed of processing the information. So the information-processing approach can be used to explain such difficulties. The easiest solution would be to make sure these children had the necessary time gap between the presented information so that it could be processed, but this might be harder in practice than in theory.

Computers in schools

Crook (1994) gives three ways of looking at the use of computers in education, and these link to the different ways of approaching the study of cognitive development.

1 There is the idea of computer-aided Instruction, where the computer becomes the teacher. Items are presented, the child responds, then the computer marks the answer, and gives feedback. This idea *links to the information-processing approach*, as it assumes that the child is such an information processor. Information is fed into the brain, is processed by the child, there is an output, and then the output is considered from the computer feedback.

2 There is the idea of using a computer more actively. This *fits in with Piaget's view* that we develop cognitively by interaction with the environment as well as through

biological maturation. The child needs to actively explore the environment, according to Piaget's views. The computer, therefore, is programmed to do interesting things, and the child can produce drawings and design exercises. Harel and Papert (1991) have done work in this area. In Papert's design, the child teaches a turtle, and in doing so teaches itself.

3 The computer can be used to give a variety of experiences. This view is *within the cultural context framework* outlined earlier in this chapter. Networks between schools can be established, and these can be in different parts of the world. Children have to work in small groups and gain a lot of academic skills when working on joint projects. Along the same lines, children can use CD-ROM technology in the classroom and can enter into virtual adventures, where they can have lots of new and different experiences.

Child-centred learning and readiness – Piaget

Piaget, as has just been stated, thought that learning should focus on the child. Schools needed to provide the necessary materials, so that each child could explore and build schemas. The child would adapt, reach a state of equilibration and then move into a state of disequilibrium as it learns yet more. This process requires an active enquiring child, and the materials the child needs to explore its surroundings. A teacher is not really required, as there is no place for training. This goes against the views of Bruner and Vygotsky, who both thought that training did help learning.

Piaget's views are taken into account especially in primary schools. Piaget took each individual child into account. To an extent you could say that a seven year old should be in the concrete operational stage, but the actual age depends on the individual child. Piaget's theory suggests that if a child is not yet in the concrete operational stage, then no amount of teaching will be any use if that stage is needed to understand what is being taught. So children need to work at their own level. It is this thinking that led to whole class teaching being abandoned in favour of small group teaching. Sitting a whole group of children facing the front with a teacher explaining 'facts' was thought to be no help to those children not in the required stage. So primary school classrooms were redesigned to have small tables with children in groups working on different subjects at different levels. This is child-centred learning. The child reaches a stage of readiness and can then move on to the next stage.

Piaget himself did not actually apply his theory to education; however, it is clear that his ideas can be applied to teaching.

Discovery learning – Piaget

The term 'discovery learning' is often applied to the way that Piaget's views can be interpreted as being applied to education. The child needs the materials, and then can discover things. This is different from being taught things. The child needs to construct its own knowledge (Smith & Cowie, 1991). There is a good way to structure the curriculum, in that teachers need to recognise that young children are not likely to use formal operational thought, and will not understand logical arguments. They can discover for themselves, but within limits.

Following Piaget's claims, the teacher must:
• Assess the individual child's stage of development and see what the child is ready to do. Tasks must be interesting enough that the child will explore
• Teachers must create disequilibrium so that the child is forced to assimilate and accommodate new information. Although providing the materials is essential, the teacher should direct some of the child's thinking according to Thomas (1985)
• It is the learning process that is important, not the content of what the child learns. This idea is similar to that of Bruner, who wants to emphasise understanding the principles, rather than learning 'facts'
• Small group work is useful. Firstly, it has social value and social experiences are important in building schemas. Secondly, interacting with peers can help to move the child beyond egocentrism
• The curriculum needs to fit individual children, rather than being prescribed for everyone

Reciprocal teaching – links to Vygotsky

Palincsar and Brown (1984) developed a method called **reciprocal teaching** to help children to decode written material and to understand it. Firstly, the teacher and a small group of students read through the text. Then there is a discussion leader who summarises the content of the text. The group either agrees with the summary, or they re-read it and discuss it again. The discussion leader is not always the teacher. The important skills are to ask questions, summarise and clarify.

Links to Vygotsky's 'zone of proximal development'

The zone of proximal development idea is that children can be involved in such activities as reading for meaning, even though they do not have all the abilities needed. Reciprocal teaching can allow such students to be involved in reading, and in discussing meaning, even if

they don't understand everything in the text. So reciprocal teaching is a way of putting Vygotsky's ideas into practice (Brown et al, 1992).

Studies summarised by Rosenshine and Meister (1994) show that reciprocal teaching is effective in increasing children's reading skills.

Collaborative learning – Vygotsky

According to Vygotsky's ideas, teachers should guide, extend and challenge, but there is no room for the traditional, teacher-centred approach to education, especially in primary schools. Not only do teachers help children to move forward, taking their zone of proximal development into account, but also their peers help. Collaborative learning means that those who do know can help those who do not. Reciprocal teaching is a similar idea. Sutherland (1992) discusses collaborative learning. It is interesting that this idea seems to come from the idea that cooperation is important, not competition. In Western schooling competition seems to be important, and this can be seen by the grading and testing that we do. In other cultures, however, cooperation is important, and children are encouraged to help each other. Remember that Vygotsky was Russian, and from a non-Western culture. Foot (1994) suggests that collaborative learning can help older children too, although research tends to take place in primary schools.

The spiral curriculum – Bruner

Bruner suggested that one way of training children is to teach a subject at increasing levels of difficulty so that the child has time to move from the iconic to the symbolic mode of representation. The symbolic mode of representation is very important, because the child learns to understand the principles behind what is learnt, not just the 'facts'. With this understanding, and using verbal reasoning, the child can then understand other similar 'facts'. This means the child is reasoning and learning for itself, and can move forward without being taught everything. This is not the same as reciprocal teaching, which allows a child to experience things just outside its own understanding, but within its reach (or ZPD). However, it is a similar idea. Both Vygotsky and Bruner thought that training helped a child to develop in a cognitive sense. Both thought that this had to be a gradual training, within the child's reach. Both thought that the child could be led to a higher level of understanding by interaction with others (adults or peers), and this is contrary to Piaget's view that the child has to be ready to explore and learn for itself.

Contemporary issue

Children's cognitive level and perception of pain

Introduction

This article was in the magazine *Professional Nurse*, October 1998, Vol. 14, No. 1, pp 35–37 and links very clearly to Piaget's theory of cognitive development. This makes it a good choice for a contemporary issue. The article is written by Alison Twycross and is part of a series about children and pain. The aim is to help nurses to provide appropriate care. It is, therefore, written with a practical purpose in mind.

A practical application of Piaget's theory

Just as it was suggested above that teachers should find out the level of cognitive development of a child, and plan their learning accordingly, so this article suggests that nurses need to be aware of the level of cognitive development of the child so that they can assess their pain. The article explains this notion.

Perrin and Perrin (1983) are quoted as saying that communication is needed, and that knowing the level of communication depends on knowing what the child can understand. There is a need to know how children think about illness and pain, including what they think the cause of pain is. Only by understanding the child's view can nursing and pain management be successful.

It is claimed that most nurses and doctors address the child as if they were in the concrete operational stage of cognitive development. Rushforth (1996) found that nurses did not put into practice their understanding of cognitive developmental stages, even though the child's anxiety could be reduced if communication was better.

Muller et al (1986) suggest that nurses, if they took into account the stage of the child, could improve explanations, provide better reassurance, understand better what the child is saying and see how the child is interpreting events. The article presents a table showing how Piaget's stages link to the child's perception of illness. The table is summarised below.

Linking Piaget's stages to the child's perception of pain

Preoperational stage (2–7 years)

The cause of the illness is seen as something real that happened at the time of the illness. The child does not see the direct connection between this perceived external cause and the child, and the link is just that this perceived cause and the illness are near each other – the child does not actually work out how one causes the other. The child is egocentric so is likely to blame someone else for their pain. They may hate the nurse giving the treatment. They cannot link treatment to the removal of the pain.

Concrete operational stage (7–11 years)

Now the perceived cause is still something or someone close to the child, but this time the child thinks there is physical contact or that the child is doing something wrong. At this stage a child might, however, think that the illness is in the body, even though the cause can be external. They need reassurance. They can also think about death at this stage.

Formal operational stage (12 years and over)

Now the child describes the illness as a malfunctioning organ and they can describe the illness as a sequence of things happening. The child also realises that psychological attitudes can affect health. They can think logically about the illness, and in abstract terms.

So children develop a perception of illness that follows Piaget's stages of cognitive development. McGrath (1990) says that children cannot take themselves out of the environment in the preoperational stage, and this links to egocentrism, where they focus on their own viewpoint. By the concrete operational stage, however, the child can separate themselves from their environment and they can look for external causes for their illness. In the formal operational stage they can think in more abstract ways, and so can think about psychological reasons for their illness.

Other factors that may be involved in the child's perception of pain

Yoos (1994), according to the article, points out that other views of cognitive development look at changes in knowledge rather than development by stages. So another view would say that knowledge changes rather than the type of thinking. Even so, the article says that nurses need to take this level of knowledge into account, just as they would take into account the child's developmental stage.

Thompson and Varni (1986) say that pain is an abstract concept in any case, so the child who cannot think in abstract terms, that is who in Piaget's terms is not in the formal operational stage, will probably not understand what pain is in any case. Nurses need to be aware of this. Also the child's level of language ability will affect what they say about their pain, because what they say may not actually reflect what they feel. So nurses need to look at non-verbal clues and watch for a child's pain by watching their behaviour. The role of play is important too. Firstly, the child's play may give a clue about their pain, and, secondly, they may be able to understand what is happening to them if their play centres around their illness (Doverty, 1992).

There are other issues concerned with the child's perception of pain, such as their experience of pain. If the pain is chronic, then the child seems to have a more mature perception of it (Unrah et al, 1983). This suggests that there is more to it that Piaget thought, because, if it was just a case of what stage the child was at, the type of pain should not affect the maturity of the child's perception of their pain. Also the stress of an illness might lead the child to give the responses of an earlier stage than the one they are at. Therefore, these factors (the type of pain, or the amount of stress) seem to affect the response to pain just as much as the cognitive-developmental level of the child. Also individuals differ, and children's experiences affect how they perceive pain.

Practical advice to nurses

The article gives a list of factors to take into account when dealing with a child's pain:
- Note that if the child has been ill for some time or in hospital, this might affect their perception of pain
- Children do not become desensitised to pain, if anything they become more sensitised to it
- Explanations need to be appropriate for the child's age
- The preoperational child needs to be reassured that the pain is not punishment
- The preoperational child may hate the nurse (being egocentric, they may blame the nurse for the pain)
- The preoperational child may not see the connection between treatment and relief of pain
- The concrete operational child needs reassurance about death
- The concrete operational child needs appropriate explanations
- The formal operational child needs to be able to discuss fears
- The formal operational child needs information about the illness and the treatment

Conclusion – links to Piaget's theory, to the information-processing explanation of cognitive development, and to the discussion of stages v continuous development

The above example of a contemporary issue clearly shows how knowledge of cognitive development can help in a practical sense, in this case by helping to deal with a child's perception of pain. Other issues besides Piaget's stages are looked at, for example, the child's own experience, the type of pain, the amount of stress, whether the pain has continued for a long time, whether

the child has been in hospital, and the length of their illness. The child's language ability might be a factor, and the nurses can also use play, both to find out about the pain and to help the child to deal with it. So on the one hand Piaget's stages are made use of when knowing how to deal with a child, and on the other hand the article is saying that there are a lot of other factors to consider.

Piaget seemed not to consider such issues, and this point can be used as a criticism of Piaget. Indeed you could link the above arguments about a child's perception of pain to the information-processing explanation of cognitive development, and see how the child's processing of the information takes place. Another concept that you can link in to this contemporary issue is whether cognitive development is stage-like or not. Most of the article is about the links to Piaget's stages, so the stage theory is supported; however, there are also indications that the level of knowledge is important, as well as the level of stress. This seems to point to development being continuous, adding knowledge and skills steadily as the child ages, and so the argument as to whether cognitive development is continuous or in qualitatively different stages is relevant here.

Coursework suggestions

1 Test a young child on the three-mountain task, and then use a Lego model to see if the child can take the viewpoint of the policeman. Studies using young children must be done with particular attention to ethics, and full consent must be obtained (see Activity 3, p. 72).
2 Test the idea that once a baby has passed the babbling stage, it will move to the one-word stage, and the change will be qualitatively different. Test whether a child in the one-word stage ever babbles. Studies using young children must be done with particular attention to ethics, and full consent must be obtained (see Activity 3, p. 72).
3 Carry out a naturalistic observation of play behaviour in a school playground, looking at gender and aggression – provided that full consent can be obtained and the study is approved (see Activity 4, p. 77).
4 Carry out a content analysis of gender behaviour in the media, using time sampling (see Activity 4, p. 77).
5 Carry out the suggestion in Activity 7. See if young children can't answer correctly that there are more wooden beads than brown beads, and older children can. Don't forget the ethical problems when using children.
6 Carry out the study outlined in Activity 8, to see if young children can conserve number. You could use the same children, and see if they can conserve number before they can conserve volume (do the 'water' study too). This would be testing the idea of horizontal décalage.

7 Produce some materials using playdough and a chessboard and replicate Bruner and Kenney's (1966) study to see if young children can only reproduce a display of graded items, and older children can transpose the display.

8 There are lots of variations of Piaget's studies. Simply vary the way you ask the questions, or change the materials that you use. Consider using a cracked glass in the 'water' study to see if younger children can conserve if given a reason, for example.

9 Study object permanence in babies (see Activity 6, p. 85), but don't forget ethical issues.

Suggested reading

Cole, M. & Cole, S. (1996) *The Development of Children*, Third Edition. New York: W.H. Freeman and Company

Eysenck, M. (1996) *Simply Psychology*. Psychology Press

Gross, R.D. & McIlveen, R. (1998) *Psychology, A New Introduction.* London: Hodder and Stoughton

Gross, R.D. (1998) *Psychology: The Science of Mind and Behaviour*, Third Edition. London: Hodder and Stoughton

Hardy, M. & Heyes, S. (1999) *Beginning Psychology, a Comprehensive Introduction to Psychology*, Fifth Edition. Oxford: Oxford University Press

Uniview Videos, PO Box 20, Hoylake, Wirral CH48 7HY

4 The learning approach

The aims of this chapter

The aims of this chapter are, with regard to the learning approach, to enable the reader to:

- *appreciate some of the general assumptions*
- *discuss research methods used*
- *describe and evaluate theories of classical and operant conditioning*
- *describe and evaluate social learning theory*
- *describe and evaluate some relevant studies*
- *understand how learning theory helps to explain deliberate alteration of human behaviour, for example, in therapies*
- *explain one contemporary issue or debate.*

Self-test 1

After reading this chapter, test yourself on each of the above points. Use the points as exam questions and make notes accordingly. Then see how much you can write on each.

This chapter covers

KEY ASSUMPTIONS
1 Emphasis on stimulus and response – the process of learning
2 The importance of the environment

RESEARCH METHODS
1 Laboratory experiments
2 Non-human animals in experiments on learning
3 Ethology

IN-DEPTH AREAS OF STUDY
1 Classical conditioning
2 Operant conditioning
3 Other forms of learning

4 Observational learning and social learning theory

STUDIES IN DETAIL
1 Imitating aggressive models (Bandura et al, 1961)
2 Conditioned emotional response (Little Albert) (Watson and Rayner, 1920)

KEY APPLICATION: DELIBERATE ALTERATION OF HUMAN BEHAVIOUR

CONTEMPORARY ISSUE: THE EFFECT OF VIOLENCE ON TELEVISION

Introduction

This chapter concerns the learning approach to psychology. This title really covers conditioning, behaviourism and social learning theory.

STUDY AID

This may seem obvious, but as you are now studying a different approach, remember to start a new section in your folder, or a new folder.

Key Skill LP3.1 – agree targets and plan how these will be met, using support from appropriate others. You need your tutor for this, and you will need a record of the discussion, to use as evidence. Discuss organising your work and develop a time plan for working through this textbook. It is tempting to leave everything to your teacher, but you should be reading the chapters as you study each approach, and do this alongside the work your teacher gives you. Make a note of dates and what you will have achieved by then, so that you can review your progress for Key Skill LP3.3.

An historical account

In the learning approach, there is no mention, at least at first, about the mental processes that happen between the stimulus that sets off a behaviour and the final response. Cognitive psychologists took up this issue and started to look in detail at those mental processes.

So the learning approach should be thought of as coming before the cognitive approach. In the early 1900s Wundt, James and Freud (separately, and differently) looked at consciousness and (in Freud's case) unconsciousness. It was then decided that what was needed was something that could be measured, as data in science can be measured. So focus was on the outside stimulus, that is what prompts the action, and then on the outside response, that is what happens. You can't measure consciousness, and looking inside our heads to see how we are thinking was thought to be a very unscientific approach, so they decided to look at what they could measure – external behaviour.

Key assumptions of the learning approach

Key assumption 1 – Emphasis on stimulus and response – the processes of learning

Psychology – the science of behaviour

At the beginning of the twentieth century psychology moved from the 'mental' emphasis of consciousness to a 'practical' emphasis on behaviour. Psychologists could then have a respectable 'profession' because they would be scientists, and would study what was testable and measurable. Psychology became the science of behaviour. If mental processes were to be looked at, it would be as physical things that could be measured and tested. From around 1897, when Wundt and James (and others) were using **introspectionism** to look at man as a conscious being, to around 1913, when behaviour was what was being examined, there was this important change.

Psychology became a profession around 1892, when the American Psychological Association (APA) was started.

STUDY AID

The APA website

Note the APA still exists, and has a very useful website that you could access – www.apa.org. Why not take a break and log on? There are menus that you can follow, and you could look up whatever interests you. It would make a change from reading.

Key Skill IT3.1 – use of the Internet, where you plan and use different sources to search for, and select, information required for two different purposes can be shown here. You would need to search for an article to update your knowledge of a particular issue, for example, and then, for another purpose (perhaps coursework) you would need to search again. Keep evidence for your portfolio.

At that time it was said not to be a science, and in response to this sort of criticism, William James (1892) said that psychology should be practical, of use to people, and a branch of biology. These changes took place within a cultural context which wanted to look at issues such as how humans adapt to changing environments. Darwin had helped to shape these questions with his explanation of evolution through natural selection and survival of the fittest (see Chapter 6).

James was an experimental psychologist at Harvard, but soon wanted to move more towards philosophy. He and others used a model of human action like the one outlined below.

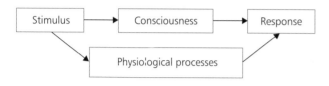

Figure 4.1

It was seen that consciousness had to involve some physiological processes, and could not be studied easily, and possibly consciousness does nothing to affect behaviour in any case. As these views took over, there was increasing interest in behaviour, and in the reasons for behaviour, and less interest in consciousness, and in introspection. Experimental method moved from introspection to a more **objective** method where the stimulus (what starts an action) is related to the response. Introspection is a subjective measure, and so very unscientific. Objectivity is a requirement of doing science.

ACTIVITY 1

TRY A BIT OF INTROSPECTION

You could try introspection. One idea they used was to set a metronome going, ask people to listen to its rhythm, and then with the metronome off, get people to think about their own mental processes. You probably don't have a metronome handy. You could, however, clap hands in a rhythm or get someone else to do it. Then 'look' inside your head to see if you are retaining the rhythm, and what you hear. When you are thinking about your thinking, you are introspecting. You can probably see that this is not a very scientific thing to do, but it does have some value. At least what you are examining are real mental processes.

Key Skill C3.1b – if you are working in a group, you could all try introspection, and then make a presentation about what you learnt. You could compare introspection with laboratory experiments used now, and compare the different methods and their strengths and weaknesses in certain situations. You must use at least one image – perhaps a diagram of the different methods – and you would need evidence, for example, a video of the presentation, and a copy of a handout that was generated, or an OHT produced.

The study of animals and psychology

In animal psychology at the time, experimentation was taking over from simply watching animals – at the same time as experimentation was taking over from introspection in the study human psychology. Thorndike and Pavlov (see later) used animals and strict experimental procedures. There were naturalistic experiments and laboratory ones, and these are discussed more fully in the section on research methods that follows. The aim of studying animals was to produce a natural science.

Thorndike, the law of effect and connectionism – towards operant conditioning

Thorndike's work took place around the 1900s. He was a student of James's at Harvard University in America. Thorndike called his approach '**connectionism**'. He was referring to the stimulus–response approach, where a stimulus was given to the animal, and the response was monitored. Thorndike was interested in human behaviour, although he used non-human animals because he could more easily and ethically set up the situations he required, with the required controls. The use of non-human animals in research is considered in the following research methods section. A very basic outline of Thorndike's work is given in Box 1.

Box 1

The puzzle box and what it tells us about learning

Thorndike used a puzzle box and watched non-human animals open it by trial and error. Thorndike set up a complicated system of pegs and string so that the animal could nudge the string and so on to open the door and escape, but this had to happen by accident. Eventually the animal, trying hard to get out of the box, did do the right thing by chance (trial and

▶

error). Having escaped, it found food, which was given as a reward. So getting out of the box was desirable.

The animal, when placed in the box again, this time had learnt how to escape, and was able to do so quite quickly, and even more quickly the time after. Thorndike argued that the animal has learnt, by trial and error, to escape, and then did this again because of the reward. The animal did not work out how to escape, and the mental process of reasoning was not there. It simply did things until, by accident, it did the right thing. Then, getting the required response, it did it again when faced with the situation again.

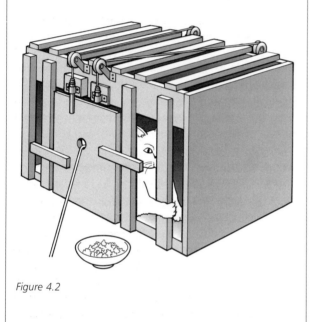

Figure 4.2

Evaluation

- We can criticise experiments because they are not natural. We have said that valid behaviour is not measured in an artificial setting. A study is valid if it can be said to be measuring what it claims to measure, and for this to be the case, the behaviour must be a natural one. Even in the early 1900s (and Thorndike published his findings in 1911), Thorndike was criticised because the behaviour of the animals was not natural, and, therefore, the results of the studies were said to be not useful (Mills, 1899). Köhler (1925) thought that an animal penned into a box would not think about how to get out, but would fall back on trial and error to escape, whereas an animal in a natural environment could think and reason. Köhler talked about insight learning, and gave examples of primates who solved problems. It is true that Thorndike's animals were not showing 'normal' behaviour, and this is a problem with laboratory experiments.

Law of effect

Thorndike talked about the **law of effect**. He said that learning takes place because of what happens after an action. If we like the consequences of our actions, that is if we are rewarded, then we repeat the action. Thorndike thought that the greater the reward, the greater the connection made between the action and the consequences. Thorndike talked about connections, and his theory is called connectionism. Punishment would reduce the connection.

Law of exercise

Thorndike also had another law, the **law of exercise**. This says that the connection is stronger if the two events (action/stimulus and consequence/response) have been connected a number of times.

These two laws were thought by Thorndike to apply to all behaviour. Even language is learnt in this way, with the 'right' things rewarded, and the 'wrong' things ignored, according to the law of effect. Human reasoning is automatic and acquired through habit.

Evaluation

- The basic problem with this simple stimulus–response (S–R) explanation of the processes of learning is that stimuli are different and also do not usually occur one at a time. So in real life it is not easy to see which stimulus behaviour is responding to, because more than one thing will be going on. Also, with something like reading, there has to be some adding up of responses to give an overall response. There has to be something happening between the stimulus and the response, and this is where other approaches like the cognitive one come in. It is interesting that within cognitive psychology, and thinking of the computer analogy, there is a theory called connectionism, which addresses Thorndike's problem. This time, however, the connections are within the brain, not outside, and they are between an action and a consequence.

Pavlov's dogs and classical conditioning

Pavlov was a Russian physiologist (which means studying the physical side) who was studying digestion. He was not a psychologist, although his work led him to study psychology. He based all his conclusions on the **objective** method. He used systematic methods, and in doing so developed the idea of classical conditioning. Whilst he was studying digestion, and when he had dogs attached to an apparatus that measured their salivation (mouth watering), he noted that the dogs would salivate when a stimulus was present (like his laboratory assistant) that had been associated with food. This led him to outline the idea of classical conditioning (see later). Imagine that you ring a bell every time you give a dog food. The dog will associate the ringing of the bell with the food. The dog will naturally salivate when the food is given. So the salivation becomes associated with the ringing of the bell too. Soon the dog will salivate to the ringing of the bell, even without the food. This is classical conditioning.

At first the food is the stimulus that gives salivation. Then the bell becomes a stimulus that gives salivation as a response. This theory is also concerned with the stimulus and the response, and you can see again that this idea of stimulus–response is a key assumption of learning theory.

Pavlov concentrated completely on scientific method, and had no interest in the workings of the mind when studying behaviour. He looked for general laws about behaviour, and took a positivist viewpoint.

STUDY AID

What you need to know when studying psychology

Psychology is not a difficult subject in some ways, because what you are reading about is people and their actions regarding other people. We know a lot of that already, and all you need to do is make sure that you relate what you learn to real life behaviour.

On the other hand, you have to learn all the studies that lead us to our conclusions. This is because otherwise you may be giving false claims. Some of what we think we know is not shown to be true by research. For example, if you ask most people if they believe that someone is born or becomes a leader, most of them will say that people are born leaders, but actually this is shown not necessarily to be the case. So you have to learn the necessary studies to prove your point.

Then, not only do you need the studies, but you need to be able to evaluate or criticise them. This is because the strengths and weaknesses of the study will show you how far you can believe what it said. In this way we can start to build some ideas about our behaviour – these ideas are what psychology is about.

So you need common-sense real-life examples, research studies, and a thorough understanding of methods, so that you can look at strengths and weaknesses.

Finally, psychology is difficult, because you are asked to look at underlying principles too. So concepts like 'positivism' are explained here.

Positivism

If you are also studying sociology, you may already have come across the term '**positivism**'. Positivists basically believe in using the scientific method to gain knowledge of the world. They look for real truths about the world. Science often offers us such truths, for example the temperature of our bodies.

The way that these sorts of facts are known is by testing using animals and humans, and building knowledge. It is assumed that there are general laws that apply to everyone. The search is for these general laws. As evidence builds, scientists make assumptions and test them. If they keep finding the same results, and the evidence starts piling up, then they start claiming real knowledge. Until we find something out that puts all their evidence into doubt, we accept that what they say is true.

Social constructionism

There are other ways of looking at the world, however, and not everyone agrees with the positivist approach. In Chapter 2 social representation theory is outlined. **Social constructionists** dispute the idea that there are general laws about behaviour to be discovered at all. They point to our culture and differences between people, and say that any knowledge can only be understood and useful in the society it applies to. So we might find that anyone can be a leader, for example, but we might only want to say that that is true in a certain culture. After all, the studies are done within certain cultures, so it is reasonable to say that conclusions from such studies should only be about the same culture. The idea is that we socially construct our reality and it is shaped by the society that we are in. There are not general laws about everyone, but only particular bits of information about particular situations.

Therefore, for some, all these 'scientific' theories that come from scientific method are not any use, since they assume that there are truths to be discovered. In the learning approach the underlying view is a positivist one – claiming that there are laws about people that can be discovered. Therefore, methods will be scientific. Whereas, in the social approach, other methods can be used by those who take a social constructionist viewpoint.

Watson's behaviourism

J.B. Watson studied animals and their behaviour. Around 1913 he was working in the field of animal psychology, examining the behaviour of non-human animals, and using the objective scientific method. He was the person who used the term '**behaviourism**'. The behaviourists were looking for answers so that behaviour could be predicted and controlled. Watson thought that the term 'animals' also included humans.

Watson did not want to look at mental processes at all and even thought that thinking related to the movement of muscles rather than any brain processes. His goal was to make behaviour predictable and controllable, and he saw no role for the mind and consciousness in this. 'Thinking' for Watson is still behaviour, but not observable – well it would be observable, being linked to muscle movements, but he did not have a way of observing it. Mental processes, for Watson, have no role in guiding or affecting behaviour.

Evaluation

- Many agreed with Watson's criticisms of introspection; however, many thought he went too far when rejecting the role of the mind in guiding behaviour. Others criticised Watson because they said he was not studying psychology at all, but biology. At that time many wanted to stay with using introspection because they wanted to study consciousness and did not know how otherwise. Think about what would have happened then if they had had the scanners and means of studying the brain that we now have (see Chapter 6). Also, Watson claimed that thought was linked to movements in the larynx/throat, and these movements were like silent talking. However, others had lost their larynxes (naturally, because of illness) but they could still think, which suggests that there is more to thinking. On the positive side, Watson is credited with being at the start of the change in psychology – from using introspection to study consciousness, to looking at measurable and observable behaviour.

Behaviourism after the First World War

The First World War led to the use of tests to measure soldiers' ability, and objective scientific procedures were needed – behaviourism was the natural way to continue.

Behaviourism was defined by Watson as the study of the association between a stimulus and a response. We need to look more closely at what behaviourism is. There was even disagreement at the time. We have already looked at Thorndike's and Pavlov's work, and both looked at behaviour by examining the response to a particular stimulus.

After Watson, behaviourists tried to redefine behaviourism, and focused on the experimental method that behaviourism demanded, rather than on what behaviourism was. The problem was that there was still this need to look at people as conscious beings with minds. Behaviourists thought that psychology should look only at physical data, as did other sciences, and then they could look at other issues like consciousness by linking to other subjects such as sociology. Activity 2 asks you to list what you know about behaviourism already.

Here are some points about behaviourism that you may have come up with:
- Watson started the term 'behaviourism'
- The start of behaviourism was at the beginning of the twentieth century
- It is not exactly the same as Pavlov's ideas about classical conditioning, although those ideas fall under the overall term 'behaviourism'
- Behaviourists focus on the stimulus of an action and the following response
- Behaviourists do not focus on mental processes
- Behaviourists leave the study of consciousness to others
- Behaviour is studied using the scientific method, looking at what is measurable
- Humans are animals, so non-human animals can be studied, and conclusions about humans can be drawn

It is hard to give a complete definition of behaviourism because, even at the time, there was argument over what causes our behaviour. Generally, however, behaviourists think that all human actions, including mental actions, involve physical responses that are in a way conditioned. Take the idea of Pavlov's conditioning.

Classical conditioning explains how we associate different things (like a bell) with reflexive actions (like salivation), and so reflexive actions (salivation) start occurring in response to different stimuli (like a bell). However, most of our actions are not reflexive. Think of behaviourism as extending the idea of association of stimuli with responses. Then imagine that everything you do has been learnt in that way. Box 2 suggests an example, then Activity 3 asks you to think of examples for yourself.

Box 2

An example of how human behaviour is learnt by *association*

When at primary school you probably had a system of rewards. These rewards could have been gold stars or special privileges. If you did something that the teacher wanted, for example, a very good piece of writing, then you might get a gold star. Assuming you want gold stars, then the teacher is thinking that you will do another good piece of writing because then you might get another gold star.

If you then do a piece of work that is not so good, and you do not get a reward in the form of a gold star, then you might stop doing what you did wrong that time.

The assumption that is made is that we learn all our behaviour by this system of rewards and punishments.

Think of some behaviour and explain it by using the idea of rewards and punishments. You should be able to apply this idea to any behaviour. Remember to avoid any mention of biological or genetic causes.

Key Skill C3.2 – read and synthesise information from two extended documents about a complex subject. One of these should include an image. This task could be carried out by researching 'handedness'. This is a complex topic, and involves both research and summarising the information. You will find extended documents in, for example, *Scientific American* or *New Scientist*. You could also try using the Internet in your research (don't forget to claim any Key Skill here too, e.g. an IT Key Skill). You will find images easily enough, because diagrams of the brain are almost always involved. It is an interesting area of research, and also contributes to the 'nature–nurture' discussion.

ACTIVITY 3

GIVE YOUR OWN EXAMPLE OF LEARNING BY REWARDS AND PUNISHMENTS

According to Watson, everything you have learnt is by this system of rewards and punishments. So you should be able to think of anything you do, and explain it in the way described in Box 2.

One other example might help. Watson looked at the way people used either their left or their right hand most often, and how most people used their right hand most. These days we know more about the brain and how 'handedness' (which hand is the preferred one) is governed by brain structure. Remember that Watson, however, did not look at mental structures. So he explained 'handedness' by saying that it is learnt through a system of rewards and punishments. For Watson, if children are taught to hold a pencil by someone placing it in their right hand, then they are likely to become right handed, because they are being rewarded for using their right hands.

According to behaviourists, you can't say that someone is good at cricket because their father was good at cricket, and they have the 'genes for it'. You have to say that a boy with a cricketer as a father is likely to pick up and play with a cricket bat very early in life. The father is likely to be delighted that his son shares the interest, and so there will be lots of rewards for the boy if he is good at cricket. Rewards include someone praising you. So for the behaviourist it is true that a cricketer father is likely to have a son who is good at cricket, but it is not because of any inherited ability like having a good 'eye' or having good reflexes.

Watson did a study with Rosalie Rayner in 1920 and it is widely used as an example of how a child might learn. Basically a young child known as 'Albert' was conditioned to show a fear response to a rat. Originally Albert liked the rat and used to stroke it. Watson used a hammer being struck on a metal bar to make a frightening noise, and Albert had a natural fear response to the frightening noise. Then when Albert stroked his pet rat, the bar was struck. Soon Albert showed the fear response on seeing the rat. Watson claimed that this showed that even emotional responses like fear are learnt through conditioning. There are lots of ethical criticisms of this study, and it is linked to the key application in this chapter too, so the study is discussed more fully later.

Key assumption 2 – The importance of the environment

You can see that if Watson is right in claiming that all our behaviour comes from conditioning between certain stimuli in the environment, then it is the environment that shapes us, and not inherited characteristics. This is another key assumption of the learning approach.

Inherited characteristics and the nature/nurture debate

Our behaviour is often said to come either from inherited characteristics (our nature) or from our experiences in our environment (our nurture). You will probably have already come across this question of whether certain actions are caused by '**nature**' or '**nurture**'.

The learning approach, by studying what causes an action (the stimulus) and the action itself (the response), assumes that behaviour arises from experiences around us, not from forces within us. Therefore, for behaviourists, inherited characteristics do not cause behaviour, or at least behaviourists don't focus on genetic factors. Actions do not come from brain activity, or from our inherited abilities, but from experiences that we have. So another major assumption is that our environment is important in governing what we are like.

The environment

Our environment is just about everything that we experience. The term covers our everyday experiences, our actual surroundings, the climate, the type of school we attended, our friendships and so on. Activity 4 asks you to make a list of what you would include when thinking about your **environment** as the cause of behaviour, and what you might include when thinking of genes or brain processes as causes of behaviour.

ACTIVITY 4

NATURE OR NURTURE?

Think about as many actions as you can that you have 'done' today. Make two lists. One list should give a list of environmental causes for your actions, and one list should make a list of 'other' causes that can loosely be called 'nature'.

Nurture	Nature (possibly)
_____	_____
_____	_____
_____	_____
_____	_____

Key Skill 3.1b – since you are making two lists here, this might be an ideal topic for carrying out a presentation. This is assuming you are working in a group, or have access to an audience. You have to use at least one image. You could ask your audience to try to come up with some things themselves, before you produce your list. You would need to include some of the background theory, and you could prepare handouts so that the other students would have notes from your presentation.

If you think about something like typing, you can see that we can be more sure about what is learnt from experiences in an environment than about what is due to inherited characteristics. It was this ability to test scientifically what responses would arise from what stimuli that led to the growth of behaviourism. The whole point is you can study how we type, how we hold cutlery, what we cook and where we live. These are measurable things. However, studying the reasons for abilities, speed of moving fingers and colour choice can be more difficult.

Tolman's operational behaviourism (1936)

Others worked within the field of behaviourism, and had a slightly different view. However, the importance of the environment was still emphasised. Tolman took behaviour as the dependent variable in what was studied within psychology. The dependent variable is what is measured after doing a test of some sort. Tolman was looking at what is measured in psychology, and he took that to be behaviour.

The **independent variable** is what is manipulated to cause the resulting behaviour (the **dependent variable**). Tolman took that to be things in the environment. Tolman did recognise that there are internal things that cause behaviour too, but not mental things. For Tolman, the internal causes of behaviour were physical, just as things in the environment that cause behaviour are physical. This was the start of realising that there were internal factors, including things like hunger, that caused behaviour. Even inheritance was mentioned at this stage. So you can see that the learning approach is going to lead to the cognitive approach (see Chapter 1).

Tolman used the term 'operational' to discuss behaviourism. This was partly because we operate on our environment when acting, and partly because he operationalised the variables. When variables are said to be **operationalised** it means they are made measurable. Box 3 discusses the operationalisation of variables.

Box 3

The operationalisation of variables

Operationalising means making something measurable. The glossary of terms explains this idea. You might have some good ideas for coursework, but quite often you will find you cannot measure what you want to look at. For example, you might want to look at helping behaviour. However, it is easier to go out into town and count how many people hold doors open for others, and what their gender is, than to measure helping behaviour in general. With such general ideas as 'helpfulness' you need to operationalise and say what you are actually going to measure.

Behaviourists use a positivist approach, which means they use a scientific approach in their research. You can only use a scientific approach if what you are looking at is measurable. So to study behaviour, they had to operationalise what they were looking at. This is another reason for them not looking at unmeasurable mental processes.

Skinner's behaviourism

I have jumped a bit here, because there were other people in the learning approach who had other ideas around the 1930s; however, Skinner's name is one you need, and I am sure you have enough of the background now.

Skinner (1904–1990) was a very influential figure in psychology. His psychology is scientific, as you would expect of a behaviourist. His views rested on Darwin's ideas about evolution, and he focused clearly on the environment as a cause of human behaviour. Skinner did not think people acted for moral reasons, for example. That would involve mental processes. Skinner thought people just acted in response to their environment. So I might do a good thing, but not for moral reasons. I would simply do this good thing because I had some reward for doing it. I had learnt to do it by being rewarded in the past, perhaps. Mental states are irrelevant when explaining human behaviour.

Links to Darwin's ideas about evolution

You need to recall the basic ideas of natural selection here. The main point is that any behaviour that is useful in terms of reproduction and survival is likely to mean that the organism survives. If the organism survives, it will reproduce and pass on useful characteristics that are likely to lead its young to survive and reproduce. Darwin is talking about survival of the fittest, and 'fittest' means the most 'fitting' in that environment.

So useful characteristics survive, and others die out. Think of Skinner's views in this way. Any behaviour that leads to a reward of some sort is likely to be repeated. Any behaviour that either does not lead to a reward or is punished is not likely to be repeated, and so should die out.

There is a bit of a problem in the above reasoning, since Darwin's views rest on the idea of behaviour coming from inherited characteristics that are passed on via genes by reproduction. Skinner's views ignore genetics and look at behaviour in the life of the organism. However, the idea is the same. For Darwin's organisms useful behaviour means survival. For Skinner, rewarded behaviour survives in the organism's lifetime.

Skinner's operant conditioning

Pavlov discussed the conditioning of reflexes, which involve involuntary behaviour, which is behaviour over which we have no control. Tolman talked about 'operant', referring to the way we operate on our environment. Both Tolman's and Skinner's conditioning is about voluntary behaviour, over which we do have control. Skinner's conditioning is **operant conditioning**, where we operate on our environment. Thorndike's puzzle box experiments have already been mentioned. The cats escape through trial and error learning. This learning involves operant conditioning, because the cats operate on their environment. Watson and Rayner did the experiments on Albert, creating a fear response to the rat. The fear response is involuntary, and Albert had no control over it. So Watson and Rayner's study involves classical conditioning and involuntary behaviour.

Self-test 2

Here are some examples of conditioning. Sort out which involve classical conditioning (the conditioning of involuntary behaviour – reflexes) and which involve operant conditioning (the conditioning of voluntary or operant behaviour).

1 A beautiful girl eats a chocolate bar in a television advert, the man likes the girl, so he comes to like the chocolate.

2 Someone goes to a different supermarket and the weekly shop is cheaper, so she goes there again.

3 Two friends are stuck in a lift and are frightened. From then on they won't go in a lift.

4 You eat chicken in a restaurant one evening and a little later you are sick. You now don't like eating out.

5 You write your first psychology essay and get good marks, so you enjoy psychology.

Statements 1, 3 and 4 involve classical conditioning because men liking a girl, feeling fear when in an enclosed space and being sick because of bad food are all involuntary responses. Statements 2 and 5 involve operant conditioning because going to a certain shop and writing a psychology essay are both voluntary behaviours.

You can see that operant conditioning involves interacting with the environment in some way, and this emphasis on the environment as the cause of our behaviour, rather than on mental processes of some sort, is one of the key assumptions of the learning approach.

Social learning theory

Social learning theory also explains how we learn and is included in the learning approach. Social learning theory moves on from behaviourism. Behaviourism suggests that everything we learn is by conditioning. However, once the baby has learnt to drink from one cup, it can then generalise to other cups, so it does not have to be reinforced at every stage. Similarly, social learning theorists suggest that we model and imitate those around us. This also saves having to be reinforced every time. When copying the behaviour of others, these others are part of our environment and our nurture. So for social learning theorists, the environment has importance, and it is nurture that is being looked at, not nature. Social learning theory is outlined in more detail later.

Research methods used in the learning approach

When studying each approach it is important to have a good idea about the methods used in that approach.

The learning approach is one area where you are unlikely to do a piece of research. Few ideas for coursework are given. This is because the learning approach is about conditioning behaviour, and we don't want to alter someone's behaviour just for our own interest. It would not be ethical to do so (see Chapter 8). There are ethical guidelines concerning the use of humans in research, and concerning the use of non-human animals. What follows discusses methods that you might not approve of (see Chapter 8).

Laboratory experiments

Laboratory experiments are used within the learning approach. Behaviourists often studied non-human animals in their experiments, and their methods are considered below, where the use of non-human animals is considered. Laboratory experiments have also been carried out on humans, however, especially within the social learning theory approach. Examples of these experiments are to be found later.

Laboratory experiments were chosen for their strict controls. It was thought that a scientific approach to the study of learning was best, and science involves laboratory experiments. However, the use of laboratories to carry out studies relating to how humans learn has been widely criticised. Laboratories are not natural places, and are not likely to lead to natural behaviour. In practice experiments on humans were done, but the settings were made as natural as possible, and usually observation of behaviour was involved.

You can learn about the advantages and disadvantages of doing laboratory experiments by reading Chapter 7, and you will be able to use the strengths and weaknesses outlined there when you discuss methods used in the learning approach.

An example of a laboratory study using humans and looking at learning is the study done by Bandura, Ross and Ross. There were a number of studies in fact. Basically two groups of children were used and their play behaviour was observed for signs of aggression. In one condition, one group of children watched a film showing adults punching what is called a Bobo doll. This is one of those plastic dolls that are quite tall and that rock if hit. The question was whether the children (having watched the film) would go into a room where there was one of these dolls and would punch it. The other group was a control group, in other words they played in the room with the Bobo doll, but had not seen the film. From studies like this Bandura developed the idea of social learning. It was claimed that children imitate others, like the adults in the film, and their behaviour is a result of this imitation.

Evaluation

- The usual criticisms of laboratory studies apply. The situation is unnatural, so we are unlikely to measure natural behaviour. With the study outlined above, you can see that the children had been shown a film of an adult hitting a doll. Then the children find themselves in a room with the same doll. They might think they are supposed to hit it, and their behaviour might be more a result of the experiment than showing their true behaviour. So the findings are not valid.

- Also you could question whether hitting a plastic doll when it seems okay to do so is the same as showing violent behaviour.

The use of non-human animals in experiments on learning

Behaviourists use non-human animals in their work. Activity 5 asks you to give reasons why they use non-human animals, drawing from what you have read so far.

ACTIVITY 5

REASONS FOR THE USE BY BEHAVIOURISTS OF NON-HUMAN ANIMALS

Write down anything you can remember about why behaviourists choose to use non-human animals in their studies. Why would social learning theorists not use non-human animals?

Key Skill IT3.1 – at this stage you could use either a CD-ROM or the Internet to find out more about the use of non-human animals in studies relating to humans. You could go beyond their use in the learning approach. Either find some examples of actual studies, or find some comment about the ethics of animal use. You need information for two different purposes, so one purpose could be to find examples, and the other purpose could be to see what people think of the use of non-human animals in research. CD-ROMs would give you information from newspapers, and you should be able to find articles about the use of non-human animals in research. Don't forget you need printouts for evidence of your research.

Key Skill IT3.2 – the BPS have just issued new guidelines concerning the use of non-human animals in research so you could explore these issues. You could e-mail the BPS to find out more information (one purpose) and e-mail other students to exchange views (another purpose). Mail@bps.org.uk is the BPS e-mail address, and their website is www.bps.org.uk. Website comments to webmaster@bps.org.uk. Information requests to enquiry@bps.org.uk

---

- Since measurable stimuli and responses were needed, these needed to be isolated from all other experiences
- Studies with non-human animals are fairly easy to repeat and quite cheap (you can get more animals)
- Darwin's ideas suggested that you could study non-human animals and transfer the finding to humans
- Laboratory studies with careful controls are objective

Activity 6 asks you to consider problems with using non-human animals in laboratories to learn about learning.

ACTIVITY 6

PROBLEMS WITH USING NON-HUMAN ANIMALS IN LABORATORY STUDIES

Make a list now of difficulties when using non-human animals in laboratory studies.

If you have just done Activity 5, keep the two lists together and you will have a useful checklist when considering methods and ethics, and the use of non-human animals in the study of psychology.

Key Skill IT3.3 – you could keep a database of useful resources and include a list of websites and e-mail addresses. I have included more websites elsewhere in this book. You could explore these when you have the chance, and I am sure you can come up with more. You need to maintain the database and keep it as evidence. You should sort in alphabetical order, and you should have separate databases for websites and for books/articles. You could also keep lists of CD-ROMs or magazines whenever you find them useful. You could even try to catalogue these according to topics, for example, one for each approach. If you know how to, you could set up a relational database to make links between items.

Here are some reasons why behaviourists choose to study non-human animals in laboratory experiments:
- They are fairly easy to handle
- You can do things with them that you can't do to humans, in ethical terms
- They can learn something new, and you know they will have no experience of it, so no previous learning
- Behaviourism was developed by those who were already studying non-human animals
- Laboratory studies mean strict controls

Here are some possible problems with using non-human animals in research:
- There are brain differences in humans, so it is hard to **generalise** from non-human animals to humans
- Ethically, you can't ignore the rights of non-human animals and do what you like with them
- You can't be sure that human learning is done in the same way as non-human animal learning
- There could be other factors involved, other than the stimulus the researcher sets up, and the response that follows

- Non-human animals don't have the same emotional responses as humans, so the findings might not mean much when related to human behaviour
- Not all animals can be conditioned to every stimulus, and it might be the same for humans, so again generalising is difficult
- Laboratories don't give natural behaviour, even of animals
- No allowance is made for chance factors

Chance factors

Those who research within the learning approach take a scientific view and want to find general laws about behaviour. They don't tend to look at chance factors. There is the assumption that every action has a cause, and the cause can be found. Most studies don't look at chance factors. However, there was a study by Collins in America. He reared mice that were genetically identical so that there were no variations in their gene structure. He then reared them in an identical environment, with all the same sounds, smells and so on. These mice were identical and their 'nature' and 'nurture' were controlled. Then the researchers observed the mice, who had to scoop their food up with one paw and hold on to the wire of the cage with another in order to reach the food. Almost exactly half fed with the right paw and held on to the wire of the cage with the left paw. The other half did the opposite. So half were left-handed, and half were right-handed. There was no 'nature' reason for this and no 'nurture' reason, as far as the researchers could tell. So they concluded that 'handedness' arises by chance.

Actually, the behaviourists' studies were repeated lots of times, and they were careful with their controls. So it is not likely that their results were due to chance, but you might like to remember the above study, and use it in criticism of laboratory studies. There is always this element of chance, perhaps.

Examples of non-human animal experiments

You have already come across examples of non-human animal experiments carried out by behaviourists. Activity 7 asks you to recall some of them.

ACTIVITY 7

EXAMPLES OF STUDIES USING NON-HUMAN ANIMALS IN THE STUDY OF LEARNING

Note down examples of the use of non-human animals when studying learning. If you are working in a group, you could all pool ideas.

Key Skill C3.1a – if you are working in a group, a discussion works well here, because you can all contribute what you can remember. You could make a list of the non-human animal studies you remember, and then you could discuss their strengths and weaknesses. Remember to keep notes and keep these as evidence. You might even like to video the discussion.

One example of the use of non-human animal experiments is Thorndike's studies using the puzzle box. Another is where Skinner uses rats to press levers for food. Skinner used a Skinner box (Figure 4.3). In the box he could set up various experiments. In one, for example, there might be a disc at which a pigeon can peck and release food pellets. Then the experimenter can choose what stimulus will be used to train the pigeon to peck at the disc. The pigeon can learn to peck the disc when a red light is on, for example, but not when a green light is on. These are the sorts of animal studies that are done within the learning approach. Watson studied non-human animals himself, but often his method was observing them in their natural setting.

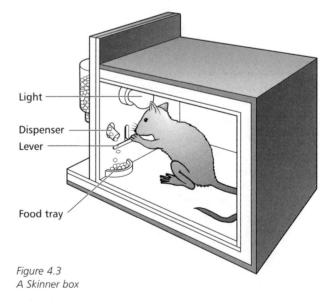

Light

Dispenser

Lever

Food tray

Figure 4.3
A Skinner box

Ethology

Ethology is the study of animals in their natural setting. Watson observed birds and carefully noted down his results. He did do some experiments in the sense of moving the bird's nest, for example, and seeing what happened. However, the experiments were carried out in the natural setting, and were intended to cause little disruption. Watson used the scientific method, and chose to alter one thing in the bird's environment in order to study what effect moving it would have.

Usually observation of non-human animals in their natural habitat involves very little manipulation of the environment. The whole point is to get the natural behaviour and the interactions between members of the species. Ethologists are different from those who study non-human animal behaviour in laboratories. This is because the surroundings are part of the study for the ethologist. If we want to look at predator–prey relationships, for example, then we need to see such relationships in action, and these interactions are hard to reproduce in laboratories.

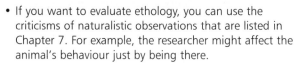

Evaluation

- If you want to evaluate ethology, you can use the criticisms of naturalistic observations that are listed in Chapter 7. For example, the researcher might affect the animal's behaviour just by being there.

- The researcher must interpret what is happening, so there is an element of **subjectivity**.

- It is difficult to observe and record everything that is happening, so the researcher probably has to choose what to record, and this is also likely to affect the objectivity of the study.

An example of behaviourists using ethology

As an example, here is a study of J.B. Watson's. He studied sooty terns – their nesting habits and behaviour. He spent time watching and recording. He tried a few experiments too although the birds themselves were not interfered with. What he did was carefully alter something in their setting to see what they did. If he changed only one aspect of their environment and recorded their behaviour, he could learn something about their activities. For example, when a bird was away from its nest, he might carefully raise the nest on four twigs so that it was a few centimetres off the ground. Then he watched to see what effect this might have. In fact the bird returned to the nest without problem. Then he moved the nest a small distance, and watched to see what effect this might have. This time there was a problem. The bird returned to the old nest site. It did eventually go to its nest, but Watson was interested in how it found its nest. After all, all the nests seemed to be the same. As the bird had no problem with a raised nest, but had difficulty in finding a moved nest, Watson concluded that the birds used clues in their environment to find their nest again.

These were the sort of carefully controlled studies that Watson carried out. You can see he is measuring carefully, and only varying one thing at a time so that he can look

for the effect of the change. When he sees the effect, he assumes that it is the thing that he has varied that has caused it.

In-depth areas of study

The learning approach is made up of the ideas of classical conditioning, operant condition and social learning theory. You need to make sure you know what each theory is about. Then you need to be sure that you can evaluate each theory. Finally, it is quite important to be able to give the differences between the three ideas, as they are basically different explanations of how we learn. Although the focus in often on non-human animals, you need to know examples of such learning in humans.

Classical conditioning

Classical conditioning came from Pavlov. Pavlov (1849–1936) won the Nobel Prize in 1904. Some of his ideas have already been outlined in the key assumption section, as his theory comes under the 'stimulus–response' explanation of learning. Pavlov was studying the digestion of dogs. He was measuring the amount of saliva (mouth-watering) produced by the dogs. He noticed that the dogs were salivating when they saw his laboratory technicians. These technicians brought the dogs their food. So Pavlov reasoned that the dogs were salivating because they made the association between the lab assistant and the food.

Box 4 outlines the processes of classical conditioning in more detail.

Box 4

The basics of classical conditioning

Firstly, there must be a natural stimulus followed by a reflex response. Classical conditioning only applies to reflexive response, not to other sorts of behaviour. In Pavlov's original discovery about dogs' salivation, the natural stimulus is the food, and the reflex response is the salivation. A natural stimulus is called an **unconditioned stimulus** (UCS) and the reflex response is called an **unconditioned response** (UCR).

In classical conditioning a new association is made. In Pavlov's example, this new association is between the lab assistant and the salivation. This is not a natural connection. Normally, there is no reflexive response (salivation) to a lab assistant. The stimulus that will give the new association is the **conditioned stimulus** (CS). In Pavlov's example the CS is the lab assistant.

▶

To establish an association, all that is needed is to pair the UCS with the CS a few times. The UCS (food) will give the UCR (salivation), and soon the CS on its own will give the UCR. At this stage the UCR becomes a **conditioned response** (CR).

The following diagram should help with this explanation:

UCS (food)   UCR (salivation)

UCS (food) + CS (lab assistant)   UCR (salivation)

CS (lab assistant)   ———→   CR (salivation)

                          ———→

                          ———→

The self-test task below asks you to try some examples, to make sure that you can apply Pavlov's ideas. In some texts you will see the term 'conditional' used instead of 'conditioned'. You can use either.

Self-test 3

Some questions to test your understanding of classical conditioning

Using the terminology (UCS, UCR, CS, CR) draw the diagram like the one in Box 4 above, but this time using the following examples:

1 A child sneezes when there are flowers about. She often visits her grandmother's house, where there are flowers. Even when there are no flowers at her grandmother's house, she still sneezes.

2 A dog's owner always rings a bell when the dog's food is put down for the dog. One day the dog's owner accidentally knocks the bell, and it rings. The dog drools as if ready for the food.

3 A child is afraid of spiders. One day he is in a lift and notices a spider. Now he is afraid of lifts. (I am assuming that the fear is a reflexive and natural response to a spider, and that the child did not learn this fear.)

Here are suggested answers:-

1 UCS (flowers)   ———→   UCR (sneezes)

   UCS (flowers) + CS
   (grandmother's house)   ———→   UCR (sneezes)

   CS (grandmother's house)   ———→   CR (sneezes)

2 UCS (food)   ———→   UCR (drools)

   UCS (food) + CS (bell)   ———→   UCR (drools)

   CS (bell)   ———→   CR (drools)

3 UCS (spiders)   ———→   UCR (fear)

   UCS (spiders) + CS (lift)   ———→   UCR (fear)

   CS (lift)   ———→   CR (fear)

Pavlov went on to study the processes of classical conditioning more fully. Some of what he suggested is outlined below.

More of the mechanisms of classical conditioning

Higher order conditioning
In the above example of the dog being conditioned to drool to a bell (the second example in Self-test 3), imagine that the dog was further conditioned into drooling to a buzzer. This is done, firstly, by conditioning the dog to drool to the bell, as was suggested in the example. Then do the conditioning again, pairing the bell with the buzzer. The diagram of this process is given below:

First CS (bell)   ———→   UCR (drool)

First CS (bell) + Second CS (buzzer)   ———→   UCR (drool)

Second CS (buzzer)   ———→   CR (drool)

Generalisation
Generalisation is a term in classical conditioning that means the extending of the original association to include similar stimuli. This means, for example, that if a dog becomes conditioned to salivate to a particular bell, then it might generalise, and salivate to other sorts of bell. If you have studied method, recall that generalising from a sample to a whole population means taking something that is true of the sample, and saying it is true of the whole population. Similarly, generalising in classical conditioning means the response that occurs to one instance then occurs to other similar instances.

Discrimination
Discrimination in classical conditioning is the opposite of generalisation. Take the example of the dog salivating

to a bell. You can get the dog to salivate only to one particular tone of bell, rather than generalising (salivating to any tone of bell). If a researcher does experiments with an animal and asks it to discriminate too closely, the animal behaves in a neurotic way.

Activity 8 suggests that, if you have not already done so, you now consider the arguments for and against using non-human animals in studies, as you may wish to explore these arguments and decide how you feel.

ACTIVITY 8

THE CASE FOR AND AGAINST USING NON-HUMAN ANIMALS IN STUDIES

The argument surrounding the use of non-human animals in research is given in Chapter 8. You may be upset by some of the examples of non-human animal studies given above, in which case you should read the arguments and make up your own mind.

It is worth noting that non-human animal studies are limited by all sorts of laws and ethical guidelines. In your study of psychology for this course (and in most cases at least up to degree level) you will not be doing experiments using animals.

Key Skill C3.3 – for this key skill you need to write two different types of document about a complex subject. One piece of writing must be extended and use at least one image. You could write an article suitable for a newspaper, and you could choose to write either against or in favour of the use of non-human animals. This could be an extended article with one image. Or you could write an essay 'Discuss the use of non-human animals in psychological studies'. You would have to present the arguments for and against their use.

Key Skill IT 3.3 – if you write the newspaper article, and use word processing, then you could also prepare a presentation using overhead transparencies. Remember to use an image. You also need an example of numbers, and you should be able to get enough information about the use of non-human animals (both in psychological research, and in cosmetic testing, for example) to make some tables or graphs. You could consider a Powerpoint display.

Self-test 4

Which of the two following examples is discussing discrimination, and which is discussing generalisation?

1 A baby has started sneezing when playing with a particular furry rabbit, because the toy was originally the cat's rabbit, and the baby sneezes when cats are around. The baby now sneezes whenever it is given any furry animal.

2 A man has a fear of entering a particular garden shed because a very large spider once fell on his head when he walked into the shed. He is fine with other garden sheds.

Extinction
Extinction refers to when the association is no longer there. So when the association is extinguished, then, for example, the dog no longer salivates to the bell. Box 5 explains this very briefly.

Box 5

How extinction of an association (in classical conditioning terms) occurs

Think of ringing the bell when you give your dog food, and wait until the dog is conditioned to salivate (which it naturally does when the food arrives) to the bell. Then you would ring the bell a few times and check that the association is there, by seeing if the dog salivates. You might at this stage (in your imagination) ring a different tone of bell to see if the dog salivates then (this would be generalisation). If the dog does not salivate to the different bell, it has discriminated.

Then you decide that the dog should not be used to do tricks. So you want to extinguish the salivation response. You have to bring the food without the bell for a little while. Eventually you should be able to ring the bell and get no salivation response. Extinction has taken place.

Spontaneous recovery
You need to understand extinction, to understand **spontaneous recovery**. In a little while, after the response has been extinguished, you might find it suddenly reappears for no obvious reason. To continue with the

example in Box 5 above, after some time, you might ring the bell (for some reason) and the dog might salivate. The response would come back for no apparent reason. This return of the response is called spontaneous recovery.

Conditioned inhibition

Conditioned inhibition is another way to extinguish a response. You can pair the conditioned stimulus (say, the bell) with another conditioned stimulus (say, a smell of lavender). This is done without the unconditioned stimulus (say, food). Originally, in this example, the dog would be salivating to the bell because the bell had been paired with the food. So now the new pairing is the bell and the lavender smell, rather than the food and the bell. Soon the response of salivating to the bell should disappear, and the dog will not salivate to the lavender smell because it was not paired with the food.

Types of classical conditioning

1 Delayed conditioning is when the conditioned stimulus (for example, the bell) is presented and maintained whilst then presenting the unconditioned stimulus (for example, the food). The conditioned stimulus remains until the response appears. This type of conditioning works well for laboratory studies with non-human animals.
2 Backward conditioning is when the conditioned stimulus is presented after the unconditioned stimulus. So the bell would be rung after the food had been brought. Non-human animals don't learn very well using this sort of conditioning; however, advertising uses this type of conditioning. First the scene is set with the beautiful girl, or whatever is chosen, and then the product is introduced.
3 Simultaneous conditioning is when the conditioned stimulus and the unconditioned stimulus are presented at the same time, and this can happen in real life.
4 When the conditioned stimulus (the bell) is presented and then stopped before the unconditioned stimulus is produced (the food), then this is called trace conditioning as only a memory trace remains. This is not a very successful form of conditioning.

Evaluation of Pavlov's work and classical conditioning as an explanation of learning

Activity 9 asks you to list some points of evaluation.

ACTIVITY 9

EVALUATION OF CLASSICAL CONDITIONING

List some points evaluating Pavlov's ideas concerning classical conditioning.

You might like to divide a sheet of paper in two and use half for 'strengths' and half for 'weaknesses'.

Key Skill C3.2 – you will find lots of textbooks with accounts of classical conditioning. You could find two extended documents with such information and prepare a piece of written work that takes information from both documents. Note down and reference the sources, and you will need a copy of your work as evidence. You will be reading about operant conditioning soon. You could make notes on both types of conditioning and then include an argument about their differences and similarities in your written work.

- We should start by giving Pavlov credit for his very careful experiments leading to some very sound conclusions. If his ideas are tested, the same results are found, and this means that his work is reliable. His findings are also valid, in that the ideas outlined above can be used when studying people, and can be useful. He does seem to have been measuring something interesting, and his studies, whilst being laboratory ones, do link well to real life examples.
- His work has led to treatments for those with problems, so it deserves credit for having practical application(s). Classical conditioning principles are used in therapies like aversion therapy. Therapies linked to learning theory are discussed in the key application of this approach.
- The main criticism would be that Pavlov studied non-human animals and then applied his finding to humans. You have already looked at the advantages and disadvantages of using non-human animals in research, so use those points as evaluation of Pavlov's work. It is not easy to criticise the idea of classical conditioning, as it has been seen to work so often. You will read later in this chapter about Watson and Rayner's study where they conditioned a young boy they called Albert to be afraid of rats. They used classical conditioning, and it does work.

Examples of classical conditioning in humans

For the Edexcel specification you need to focus on examples of classical conditioning in humans; however, since these are given elsewhere in this chapter, they are not repeated here, but are summarised.

Some examples of classical conditioning in humans have already been given. For example, Watson and Rayner's study mentioned above. This study is given in more detail later. It shows how young Albert became afraid of his rat, and generalised his fear to other furry objects. Aversion therapy is referred to when looking at the key application for this approach. The key application looks at learning theory and behaviour change, and so examples of both operant and classical conditioning in humans are given then. Also, advertising has been mentioned, and there are examples of classical conditioning in advertising too.

Operant conditioning

Operant conditioning has already been briefly outlined in the discussion on key assumptions at the start of this chapter. There are differences between classical and operant conditioning. Activity 10 asks you to give any differences between classical and operant conditioning that you can remember.

ACTIVITY 10

THE DIFFERENCES BETWEEN CLASSICAL AND OPERANT CONDITIONING

List differences between classical and operant conditioning. You could refer back to Self-test 3 to refresh your memory if you wish.

Key Skill C3.1b – you could choose to do a presentation on the differences between the two types of conditioning (or you could take part in a group discussion, and use that for Key Skill C3.1a). You need to use at least one image in your presentation. Remember that if you use overhead transparencies or a power point presentation you may be able to use these as evidence for Key Skill IT.3 (although you would need to present numbers too).

The main difference between classical and operant conditioning is that classical conditioning involves involuntary behaviours or reflexes, whereas operant conditioning involves **voluntary** behaviours. Voluntary behaviours are those that cannot be elicited (made to happen). This means you can't get at these behaviours until someone carries them out. **Involuntary** behaviours such as fear, salivation, breathing quickly, the startle response and feeling or being sick can be elicited. This means you can do something that will produce an involuntary response.

Note that operant conditioning can be called instrumental conditioning. The term 'instrumental' is used because the behaviour is instrumental in getting the required response (which means it has the effect of getting the response).

Box 6 outlines an interesting point about Skinner and the use of statistics in psychology

---

Box 6

Skinner and statistics

You don't have to do statistical analysis for your piece of coursework for the Edexcel specification. However, you do have to learn about statistics for the A2 part of the course. You may, therefore, be asked by your teacher to learn about statistical analysis for the coursework – indeed this is a good way to learn. If you are going to analyse your own data using statistics – and you will do so if you go on to study psychology at degree level – then you might like to remember the point about Skinner and statistics.

Skinner thought there was no need for statistical analysis when studying behaviour. His point was that behaviour is something that is measurable and testable. There is no element of chance, and no likelihood of other variables causing the behaviour that is being measured. So there is no need to test using statistics to see to what extent the results might be obtained by chance.

You might like to use this argument at some stage during the course – many students do not enjoy having to do statistical analysis on their data. You will still have to know about statistics though!

The use of non-human animals in developing the ideas of operant conditioning

Evaluation

- It is important to note that Skinner's theory was built around the use of non-human animals in experiments. He used rats and pigeons, for example. He used non-human animals because there could be strict controls. As we have already said, you need to read the section in Chapter 8 on the use of non-human animals in research, and you also need to consider ethical issues. If you have not yet thought about the good and bad points of using non-human animals in experiments, you should do so now.

Explaining how we learn language, using the principles of operant conditioning – an example of operant conditioning in humans

Skinner used the principles of operant conditioning to explain how we learn language. He wrote a book called *Verbal Behaviour* in 1957. Skinner did no experiments on language development. He drew his conclusions from non-human animal experiments, and he claimed that the principles of learning for both non-human and human animals are the same.

In learning speech, the listener is important in two ways. The listener reinforces some behaviour and acts as a stimulus too. For example, the listener might understand some speech and not other speech. So the reinforcement is the understanding (perhaps involving the listener in doing what the person wants because of this understanding). If what is said is understood and acted upon, then it is done again. If, however, there is no understanding, the person must try again, perhaps in a different way. So language can be shaped in this way – by reinforcement. The listener is also a stimulus, because the listener also speaks, and may speak differently to different people, so stimulating certain speech instead of other speech.

So when a young child says 'doll', and the parent understands and passes the doll to them, the reinforcement is the receiving of the doll. For Skinner, this is exactly like the rat pressing a lever and gaining food. The food is the reinforcement and the rat presses the lever to get the food. So language is completely learnt by reinforcements. Whatever is reinforced in some way is repeated. Whatever is not reinforced is discontinued.

Skinner talked about 'mands' and 'tacts'. When the reinforcement is that a child gets what it asks for, this is what 'mands' are. When the reinforcement is the repetition of a word or sound by an adult, this is what 'tacts' are. These are called selective reinforcements.

Evaluation

- You might already have thought of criticisms to Skinner's claim that all language is learnt by reinforcements.

- Adults do not seem to correct the child's grammar or their pronunciation, so how would correct language be learned by reinforcement? Tizard et al (1972) found that correcting grammar had little effect. Slobin (1975) found that children learn grammar but this is learnt some other way, as parents do not reinforce correct grammar.

- If the child is simply imitating, they would only use 'adult' language, whereas this is not the case. Also people produce sentences all the time that they have never heard before. You could say 'the car walked over the hill'. I

would have difficulty understanding how the car could walk, but I do know what you mean. This sentence could not have been understood by reinforcement.

- Skinner's idea is that everything relies on nurture and the environment. Others, however, note that 'nature' also has a part to play. For example, there is evidence that all babies babble, and that this babble involves the same sounds, whatever the language of that society. Then at some stage the relevant sounds for the language are maintained, and other sounds are lost. The fact that necessary sounds remain does suggest that the baby has been reinforced to make particular sounds ('dada' for example) and not others. This does back Skinner's claim. However, the fact that all babies are capable of all these other sounds, means that there is some inborn capability for making the sounds in the first place, and this is an important point that Skinner did not investigate.

- Similarly, only humans have the special capacity for learning and using language that we call language. Other non-human animals are capable of language to an extent, and indeed some can learn to use human language using signs; however, only humans develop language in the way that we do. This strongly suggests some inborn capability for using language and grammar. This inborn capability is likely, and evidence is that all cultures have some form of language.

- Chomsky (1965) thought that humans have a language acquisition device (LAD) which enables all humans to learn a language. He noticed that children tend to use their own type of grammar; for example, the plural of 'sheep' is 'sheepies' and the plural of 'shop' is 'shoppies'. This is a logical and sensible way of using grammar rules they have learnt, for example, that you add an 's' for a plural. However, the child could not have learnt these words from adults by reinforcement, so Chomsky's views criticise Skinner's.

- However, Skinner's ideas about learning language by reinforcement of certain sounds is a useful explanation of the way we learn a particular language, including the dialect and accent. It is just that it may not be the whole story.

More mechanisms of operant conditioning

Types of reinforcement
We have claimed that praise is a reinforcer, as are gold stars in school. However, there are different **types of reinforcement**, and these need outlining now.

1 **Positive reinforcers** are those that have been given as examples up to now, and are the most straightforward to understand. You give something positive and it reinforces the behaviour so that it is repeated. Whatever is positive depends on the receiver. If you want gold stars, then they can be positive reinforcers, but not if you don't want them. In prisons, sometimes, a token economy programme (TEP) is used, and this is discussed later in this chapter. The TEP is another example of the

use of operant conditioning in humans. Prisoners are given tokens if they do something right. They collect the tokens and can exchange them. Often they exchange tokens for cigarettes. This system would only work if you enjoyed cigarettes, or if there was something in the 'shop' that you wanted. So you do something for the reward of something pleasant. Positive reinforcers encourage the behaviour.

2 **Negative reinforcers** are not punishments. This is a most important point. When you do something to avoid something unpleasant, then negative reinforcers are being used. So if you go to a shop, and you don't like the background music then you might not go to that shop again. Not going to the shop means you avoid something unpleasant, and this is responding to negative reinforcement. Negative reinforcers encourage the behaviour.

3 Punishers are probably obvious. This is when you do something and are then punished for it, so you don't do it again. This is not the same as learning by negative reinforcement. Punishers stop the behaviour.

Self-test 5

Here are some examples of learning. There is one example each of positive reinforcement, negative reinforcement and punishment. Decide which is which.

1 John continues with his driving lessons because the instructor is nice to him.

2 Jenny stops going to her driving lessons because the instructor is too critical of her driving.

3 Jean's driving instructor shouts at her for going through a red light so she does not do it again.

Primary and secondary reinforcers

Most reinforcers in our society are probably what are called 'secondary' ones. This means that they are not reinforcing in themselves. So money can be a strong reinforcer, as most people who work would agree. However, it is not reinforcing in itself. It is desirable because it buys us things.

Primary reinforcers are those that are desired for themselves, for example, heat, food, water and sex. These could be called basic needs. **Secondary reinforcers** are usually things that lead to primary reinforcers. Kind words and praise must be primary reinforcers I think, because they are reinforcing, and don't always lead to anything else.

Schedules of reinforcement

Skinner looked at how often a reinforcement is needed for the learning to take place. He wondered if the reward had to be given on every occasion, for example. To explain **schedules of reinforcement**, let's use the example of a rat who is being trained to press a lever for a food pellet only when the green light is on (see Figure 4.3). Let's assume that the rat enjoys the food pellets.

1 A continuous schedule is when the response is always rewarded. This is usually when the first learning is taking place. So in the first place you will give your rat a food pellet every time he presses when the green light is on. For humans, an example might be being thanked every time you wash the car for your parents. This schedule gives a good response rate, but the learning is easily extinguished.

2 A fixed interval schedule means that at regular intervals of time you give a reward. So no matter how much the rat correctly pressed the lever, he would only be rewarded every few minutes, assuming the correct response has been given at least once in that time. For humans, an example might be your monthly pay, which is given at regular intervals, no matter how many correct responses you have given. This is not very successful — at least in rats. They speed up their responses just before the next reward is due. Extinction is quite quick too.

3 Variable interval schedules are where rewards are given at varied times, although the average is set. So there is no real way of predicting when the reward will come. Rats tend to go on pressing, because they don't know when the reward will come, so this schedule is successful. Extinction is slow too.

4 A fixed ratio schedule means that a reward is given for a fixed number of correct responses. The rat might be rewarded after every ten correct responses, for example. Rats, once they have learnt the schedule, tend to pause between rewards, knowing that nothing will happen in the middle. Extinction is quite quick.

5 A variable ratio schedule means that the reward is given after a number of correct responses, but the number varies. On average the rewards are steady, but they might come more quickly at certain times. For example, you could reward an average of eight correct responses, but you could reward four quickly, and then have a delay before rewarding some more. This sort of schedule is successful and resistant to extinction, so the learning lasts.

If you look at the various ways of giving rewards, you will see that the unpredictable or variable schedules are the most effective. This is interesting when considering human behaviour. The example of fruit machines is often given. If payment came after so many goes, the regulars in the pub would sit waiting until they know the machine is about to pay out. If, however, payments are variable, then you are likely to keep trying as you don't know when it will pay out.

Shaping

Another interesting feature of operant conditioning is that we can shape the desired behaviour. This is just as well, because we could wait a long time for a certain behaviour to be found. We need the behaviour before it can be rewarded.

There was a well-known advertisement showing a squirrel running an 'assault course' to James Bond music. The squirrel would never, of course, have completed the whole course in one go to reach the reward of the nuts. So the behaviour had to be shaped. You have to reinforce successive approximations. This simply means that as the required behaviour is approached, you reward until you get what you want. Those creating the advert would have to get the squirrel to do the first bit and find the nuts. Then the nuts would be moved on, and the squirrel had to conquer another bit of the puzzle until finally it could do the whole thing. This is **shaping**.

Punishment

Punishment is not as successful as giving a reward. After all, you do things again for a reward, and all **punishment** does is to stop you. It does not show you what you should be doing, so it is not very useful in learning. You could say, however, that actually punishment is stronger and more likely to lead to very strong learning – not to do something. Probably the best thing is to combine punishment with reward. The wrong behaviour is punished and the right behaviour is rewarded. One other problem with punishment is that it makes the person anxious and stressed, which may not help learning at all, so probably strong punishment should be avoided.

Escape and avoidance learning

Escape learning is when a rat learns to escape something unpleasant, for example an electric shock. This is a form of negative reinforcement, not punishment. The rat does not get the shock (which would be punishment) but is acting to avoid it.

Avoidance learning is when the rat learns what to do to avoid the shock and has warning. It is a bit more complicated than escape learning, because the rat is not sure what it has to avoid until a warning is given. When avoidance learning is studied in laboratories, the equipment used is a box split into two. Both separate floors can be 'shocked' but only one at a time. The rat has to learn that a signal means the shock is changing to the other floor. So the rat has to learn to jump from the non-shocked floor each time.

The warning signal is paired with the shock and gives anxiety (this is the first stage). Then the rat learns how to avoid the anxiety by paying attention to the signal. Jumping to the safe floor is the way out. This is learnt by negative reinforcement and is the second stage. This explanation of avoidance learning is outlined by Gray (1975) and is called the two-process theory. It is also given by Mowrer (1960) and called the two-factor theory.

Preparedness

It is important not to think that any non-human animal can be conditioned into doing any behaviour. Rats and pigeons have been mentioned. Rats can be taught to press levers, as can pigeons. However, you cannot stop pigeons going into water, and rats don't like water. Rats press levers for food, but they are not good at pressing levers to stop a shock. Species seem to be 'prepared' or ready to do certain things rather than others. Seligman (1970) talked about **preparedness**. He claimed that some actions are useful for certain animals when it comes to survival, and others are not. It seems that through the idea of survival of the most fitting animals for the environment, certain behaviours are more likely than others. These behaviours are able to be used in conditioning, other behaviours are not.

Although when we talk about phobias we should be discussing classical conditioning (the fear response is a reflexive one), phobias are useful as an example when explaining preparedness, so are discussed here. Some phobias in humans are more common than others. Activity 11 asks you to make a list of what you think is likely to give a phobia and what might not.

ACTIVITY 11

PREPAREDNESS FOR CERTAIN PHOBIAS

Make a list of phobias you have heard of. Think about what gives phobias. Then, if you know anyone with any strange phobias, make a list of these. Can you think of reasons why the most common phobias are found in humans?

You might be able to try some coursework in this area, but you need to be aware of ethical issues. You could ask people to rate their liking for certain creatures, and then rate their fear of them. These two rating activities would have to be done separately, in two lists, so that the participants could not recall one rating when doing another. You might find that the creatures people think are repellent or unattractive are those they fear most. Ladybirds are generally thought of as attractive, for example, and people do not usually fear them. An explanation might be the amount of harm the unattractive creatures might have brought to humans in the past. Therefore, the fear might be a survival trait that has been passed on through genes.

Key Skill N3.1 – if you decide to do this particular piece of coursework, you will have two different sets of data. If you can ensure that the data sets are large, then you can plan and interpret information from the two data sets and you will have the chance to get this Key Skill.

Key Skill N3.2 – you could carry out calculations on the above data sets, for example, a correlation and working out percentages. Remember you need to keep the evidence. You will need to carry out calculations for your coursework in any case. Don't forget to claim the relevant Key Skills.

Key Skill N3.3 – you will also have to present your calculations and graphs for the results part of the coursework.

Note that depending on the level of your calculations, you may only be able to claim level 2 key skills here.

Discrimination
Discrimination happens in operant as well as in classical conditioning. If a pigeon learns that food is given when it pecks the disc and the green light is on, but there is no food in response to pecking when the red light is on, it has learnt to discriminate.

Generalisation
Generalisation in operant conditioning is like that in classical conditioning. If the pigeon pecks at a yellow light and gets food, it may also peck at similar colours, thus generalising beyond the yellow colour.

Evaluation

- Again you can evaluate studies done when looking at operant conditioning by criticising the use of non-human animals. You can criticise on ethical grounds, or because of the problems in generalising from non-human animals to humans.

- The idea of reinforcement learning is widely accepted; however, you can criticise Skinner and those like him who claim that all learning is by conditioning. Other forms of learning involve elements of mental processing. Rats were taught to run a maze and they found food at the end. The food was the reinforcement for running the maze. They took a particular route. If, however, the researchers blocked the learnt route and the rats had to go another way through the maze to reach the food, the rats could still do it. They did not have to learn the new route. It seemed as if they had built a cognitive map of the maze. They could refer to the map in their heads and could find the way immediately. This type of learning was called latent learning, and it suggests that there are cognitive elements to learning that need exploring. Behaviourists can be criticised for ignoring these cognitive elements. Similarly, insight learning suggests an element of cognition in learning. Both insight and latent learning are looked at below, and you can use these other forms of learning as criticisms of the behaviourist's ideas.

- Also, too, the arguments against Skinner's theory as an explanation of how we learn language can be used here. Whilst not denying that some learning is by reinforcements and punishment, the argument about how we learn language also points to there being innate processes involved. This argument could be extended to be a criticism of operant conditioning in general – in other words it is not a complete explanation when it comes to learning. Also social learning theory is outlined later. This explanation of learning can also be used to evaluate Skinner's ideas.

Other forms of learning

It is useful to know a bit about other forms of learning as you can use these to evaluate the two forms of conditioning. Both latent learning and insight learning are ideas that suggest that there is a cognitive or thinking element to learning, and so both criticise the behaviourists' claim that conditioning accounts for all learning.

Latent learning

Latent learning has been outlined briefly above, using Tolman and Honzik's (1930) study of rats running mazes and learning more about the maze than just the route they needed at the time. Activity 12 asks you to think about your own examples of latent learning.

ACTIVITY 12

EXAMPLES OF LATENT LEARNING IN HUMANS

You will need to think of something you know a bit, but not well. I will suggest one example.

Think of a supermarket where you have shopped quite often, but that you don't know thoroughly. What if I asked you where the self-raising flour was. Do you know? Think about it and see if you can find the answer. What did you do? Presumably you scanned some sort of cognitive map in your head. You might have visualised the aisles and mentally roved up and down them. You might have worked out that flour is usually near sugar, and you might know where the sugar is. If you have watched Supermarket Sweep, you might have noticed that this is what the shoppers on the programme do.

Key Skill C3.1a – you could get into groups, if you are working in a group. You could each come up with an example of latent learning in humans, and then feed back to the rest of the class. Remember you need to keep evidence.

The example of learning given in Activity 12 shows latent learning because you did not know you knew it. You had learnt where the self-raising flour was while you were learning other things.

Insight learning

Another type of learning suggests that learning is cognitive. There is a school of thought called the Gestalt school. The term 'Gestalt' refers to the idea of studying in a holistic way, and not using a reductionist approach. Briefly, reductionist research means looking at all the parts of a problem, and trying to discover what is happening by building the whole thing from the parts. So you might look at language by discovering what parts of the brain are for what bit of language production. Holists, however, argue that to look at language use, for example, you have to see someone using language. You can't find things out by looking at parts, because you miss the relationship between the parts that make something 'whole'.

The Gestalt idea is like that of the holists. You have to study the whole thing. Learning cannot be broken up into bits, like stimuli and responses. Learning must be looked at as a whole process. Box 7 outlines an example of insight learning, an idea from the Gestalt school.

Box 7

An example of insight learning

Köhler (1925) gives an example of **insight learning**. He talks about a chimpanzee in a cage wanting to get a banana that is just out of reach outside the cage. Köhler points out that the chimpanzee does not use trial and error learning (unlike the cat in Thorndike's puzzle box). Köhler watched the chimpanzee. Picture the scene. The chimpanzee seems to realise that the banana is out of reach. The banana is outside the cage, and the chimp's arm is not long enough. It does not keep trying with its arm. There is a stick outside the cage too. The chimp suddenly reaches out for the stick and uses it to rake in the banana. It is as if the chimp has an insight into the problem, and then solves it.

The chimp suddenly solves the problem, often after a period of inactivity. It is as if there is an understanding of the problem and a realisation of how to solve it. This is nothing like conditioning.

Evaluation

- You might like to criticise the above example of insight learning, however. The tools to solve the problem (like the stick) tend to have to be near to hand. Chimps have to be able to see the tools they need, whereas people can represent them in their heads and solve problems in the abstract (mentally). Also the chimps in the above sort of studies had had previous experience. They may not have solved that particular problem, but they had had experience of sticks and bananas. So they might have been using previously learnt knowledge when showing the insight.

- It does seem, however, that without something like insight learning, we would never be creative. We probably need experiences to do problem solving. However, often a particular problem needs a different way of using these experiences, so to this extent we are having 'insights' and learning from these insights.

- Harlow (1949) suggests that insight learning is not a different sort of learning to the stimulus–response ideas of the behaviourists. It is just a step further on. By trial and error, and linking stimulus to response, a set of things is learnt, and then these experiences can be used in further learning. It may look as if, when using these learnt experiences, the person is using insight, but it is just using previous learning. In this way, Harlow believed, we build up learning sets. The chimp described in Box 7 had a learning set for how to use sticks as rakes.

- However, the new learning still involves insight, because it is using previous experiences in a novel way. Therefore, cognitive or mental processes are still needed in learning. It does look as if stimulus–response learning does not explain all learning. This idea of using previous learning and transferring the understanding to new situations is called transfer of learning, and is used in education. Howe (1980) thinks that this transfer of learning is like generalising to other stimuli. Just as the pigeon might learn to peck to a different tone of bell, we might transfer simple learning to other situations.

Observational learning and social learning theory (SLT)

Social learning theory (SLT) started in the USA in the 1950s and linked the behaviourists' approach to the psychodynamic one. An important part of Freud's theory is the idea of identification (see Chapter 5). According to Freud, the boy identifies with his father, and the girl with her mother. Here 'identifies' means becomes the father or mother, and models on them – and the reason for this is examined in Chapter 5. Social learning theorists build on the idea of identification.

Bandura developed social learning theory. His aim was to examine the idea of identification using scientific methods to obtain objective data. Social learning theorists agree with other learning theorists about how we get our knowledge via principles such as conditioning. However, they are more interested in looking at acquiring understanding of moral and social behaviour, rather than any behaviour. Social learning theorists do accept that there are mental processes involved in such learning. In this they differ from the behaviourists.

One problem with conditioning is that the behaviour has to occur before it can be reinforced or not. However, this means that we have to wait for the required behaviour, or some form of it, to occur before we can give the appropriate response. Bandura (1965) pointed out that we actually watch others and model our behaviour on them. We do not behave in some random way and then wait to be rewarded or not.

The mechanisms of social learning

Observational learning
Observational learning is different from conditioning because it involves modelling and imitating. Learning just happens through this modelling, and there is no planning

or thinking involved. There is more to it than simple modelling, however, because not all behaviours are modelled, and not all models are imitated. It depends on the model, and also on what the consequences of the observed behaviour are. If behaviour is punished, then it might not be copied, for example. So reinforcement is important because it can determine whether a behaviour is copied or not. We not only watch people, but we watch what happens when they do things. The person we model on is important, and the consequences of their actions are important too.

Reinforcement is, according to Bandura, motivational, because we are more likely to imitate the behaviour and to be motivated to do so, if we like the consequences or reward for the action. Bandura (1974) does think that thought is important in the process of learning.

Five cognitive functions in observational learning:
- When observing, the learner needs to be able to pay attention to the important parts of the action, and not to the incidental bits
- The learner has to record the information in memory, and younger children might find this harder than older children. You could link this to Piaget's views about cognitive development (see Chapter 3), where it was claimed that children need to reach the right developmental stage for certain types of reasoning. It is possible that children would model the behaviour straightaway, whereas, as they get older, they may be able to store the information up, and act in that way only when it was appropriate
- Those who used memory aids and could organise their memory well would benefit most from observational learning
- Motivation is important, as the consequences decide whether the behaviour will be carried out
- The child must be able to carry out the action, so must have the necessary physical control

A study by Bandura et al (1961) tests out the idea of memory use in learning. Children watched a film. There were three groups. One group described the actions in the film, another group just watched the film and the third group did an interfering task whilst watching the film (they counted backwards – see Chapter 1). The first group, those who described the actions, reproduced the model's actions best when asked to. They could talk them through. The group who had interference did least well, as you would expect.

Who is imitated?
Activity 13 asks you to think about who would be imitated in observational learning. Would it be just anyone?

ACTIVITY 13

THINK ABOUT WHO WOULD BE IMITATED

Make a list of pretend people of different ages and gender, and then think about likely models. By pretend people, I mean 'a five-year-old boy whose father is a mechanic and who likes watching East Enders' or 'a teenage girl who wants to be a fashion model'. You could take models from public life, from the media, or from family.

For example, not long ago a ten-year-old girl might have imitated one of the Spice Girls.

> Key Skill C3.3 – you could write about a complex topic here. You could research the literature on social learning theory and find material on the influence of television. Look in sociology books as well as psychology books. Then write an essay / extended piece of writing on social learning theory, giving your examples.

You need to know about the age group and the gender. You can probably give models for people of your age group. You could watch children at play and see them imitating their favourite heroes. Young aspiring footballers probably model on Michael Owen. Notice that he has started appearing in adverts and promotional videos. Advertisers use this idea of imitation. Of course, children also model on their parents, and on brothers and sisters, and you probably noted this too.

The model has to be appropriate, relevant, similar to the observer and consistent. Examples are given below showing some of Bandura et al's (1961) findings.
- They found that aggressive male models were imitated more than aggressive female ones were. Apparently it is more appropriate for males to be aggressive.
- Boys were more likely to imitate the aggressive male model than girls were. This shows relevance. The boys saw the male model as relevant to them.
- Consistency is important. Parents who tell the child not to be aggressive and then are aggressive themselves are more likely to find the child behaves aggressively. This is because the actions of the model are more likely to be imitated than the words. This sort of parent is likely to get exactly the behaviour they don't want.

Evaluation of social learning theory as an explanation of human behaviour

- Overall social learning theory seems to offer a more complete explanation of human behaviour than do the two types of conditioning. It is not that social learning theory denies the conditioning explanations, so we probably need all the above explanations to understand learning. Social learning theory does start to involve cognitive issues such as imitation and modelling, so the criticisms that behaviourism is all about external behaviour are answered by social learning theory.

- However, much of the evidence comes from laboratory studies, and these can be criticised. Bandura et al's study is outlined in quite a lot of detail below. Criticisms of that study can be taken as being criticisms of social learning theory in general.

- Remember too that Skinner's explanation of language development was said not to be sufficient. Evidence was presented that there is some 'nature' element in our ability to learn language. Chomsky pointed out that all cultures have some form of language, and this cross-cultural evidence by itself strongly suggests a genetic element in our ability to develop language. So when we give social learning theory as an explanation of learning, we might need to add that there are some innate, inherited mechanisms that are at work too. For one thing, we would need an innate device to enable us to model and imitate in the first place.

Social learning in humans

Examples of social learning in humans have been given, for example, modelling on television characters and learning behaviour from them. Usually social learning theory is used to explain moral behaviour and aggression. Aggression is often linked to violence on television, and behaving in a moral way is often linked to watching 'pro-social' programmes on television. Therefore, social learning theory is usually explained by reference to television and its example to those (especially children) in our society. One of the main studies is outlined in detail below. Therefore, you will find below an explanation of social learning in humans.

Studies within the learning approach

Bandura, Ross and Ross (1961) – Imitating aggressive models

Background

Recall the way social learning theory explains learning. Bandura proposed the idea of observational learning, and this study is one of the main ones from which he got his ideas. This study is also important because if Bandura and others can show that we learn by observation and modelling, then we might say that children who watch violent television might well become violent. There have been instances of violent crimes carried out by children, where films or television programmes have been mentioned as a possible cause.

ACTIVITY 14

THINK ABOUT THE LINK BETWEEN VIOLENCE ON TELEVISION AND REAL-LIFE VIOLENCE

You might be able to recall some of the examples where violent crimes have been said to come from watching violence on television. If you are in a group, discuss this issue. You might recall actual crimes. If you cannot, think of violence on television and what influence it might have. Consider how young children might model themselves, for example, on The Joker in the Batman films. Make a list of aggressive characters on television, and consider which children might model on these characters.

Key Skill C3.1a – if you are working in a group, break into small groups and discuss violence on television and the effect it might have on those watching, particularly children. A debate giving both sides is interesting and useful, where half of a group say there is no effect and the other half say there is an effect.

Key Skill C3.3 – there is quite a lot of literature on violence on television, so you would have plenty of scope to research. Then you could write a piece of extended writing on the subject, giving arguments for and against there being such an influence. You need to include at least one image.

Key Skill IT3.1 – you could use CD-ROMs and the Internet to research the above. The APA website (www.apa.org.) has some material on violence on TV and the current situation. Also newspapers are on a CD-ROM which you are almost certain to have in your library, and they often print stories of how violence on TV is linked to a particular crime. So you can use these sources for your piece of written work. One purpose can be to research the argument, and another purpose might be to present a debate.

One thing you might have noticed is that the 'villains' tend to be male, so you might have thought that it would be mainly boys who would model on them. This does tend to be the case. You might have argued that it takes more than one example of violence on television to make a boy aggressive. This also does tend to be the case. Research has found that there are many other factors, including the modelling the child has in the home. For example, a boy with an aggressive father, who also watches violence on television, might be more likely to go out and commit a violent act. This type of research has a **practical application**.

Bandura et al's study outlined here focused on the modelling of aggressive behaviour. This does not mean that it is only aggressive behaviour that is learnt by modelling. However, aggressive behaviour is of interest and is also measurable and observable. Studies have been done to see if prosocial (helping) acts on television are modelled, but prosocial behaviour is not so clearly observable. This study does look a bit at how the non-aggressive models were copied.

The study

Seventy-two children (36 boys and 36 girls) were shown both aggressive and non-aggressive adult models and then their behaviour was observed without the models being there. The children were around four years old. This study focused on the child's behaviour when the model was no longer there. It was expected that the children who had watched aggressive models would show more aggressive behaviour than the ones who had watched non-aggressive models.

There was also a **control group**, who watched neither the aggressive nor the non-aggressive models. It was thought that those who watched the non-aggressive models might be even less aggressive than the control group. It was also thought that boys might copy the aggressive models more than girls. The final idea was that boys would copy male models more than female models, and girls would copy female models more than male models. Some of these ideas came from previous research. Activity 15 suggests a piece of coursework you could carry out.

ACTIVITY 15

COURSEWORK TO LOOK AT SOCIAL LEARNING THEORY

You cannot ethically find a group of children and show them a violent film, so we cannot copy the above study. However, you could try a questionnaire to look at violence on television,

▶

and you could ask adults to complete it. The idea is outlined in the section on coursework suggestions. You could only do a correlation, and this would not show that violence on television causes aggressive behaviour. You could see whether males watch more violence on television than females, and whether males seem to show more aggressive behaviour. Note that if you measure aggressive behaviour by asking participants to rate their agreement to statements, then you are only measuring what they say they would do, and not what they would do. However, you are still measuring aggression in attitudes, and this can be of interest.

You could use children in the survey, but this is more difficult when considering ethical guidelines. Studies have been done where you ask the children what television programmes they like and then observe their behaviour in the playground and score it for aggression. You might find that those who like watching more 'violent' television also play more aggressively, but you would need to take care in categorising play behaviour, as well as in categorising 'violent' television.

> Key Skill N3.1, N3.2, N3.3 – these key skills tend to go together, because they go with the coursework. Firstly, you have to plan and interpret information, then you have to do some calculations, and then you must present the data. This is more or less what happens in your coursework, so whenever you do your coursework or a study, you should be able to claim these skills.

Participants

The 36 boys and 36 girls were from the Stanford University Nursery School. These were not, therefore, a random sample, so the sample might be biased. They were three to five years old. There was one male and one female model. The children's 'normal' levels of aggression were noted from information received from the school, and the participants were matched on this basis to try to make sure that not all the 'naturally' more aggressive children were in one group. The way they were rated for aggression was by noting physical activities, verbal aggression and the way they treated inanimate objects. The experimenter and a teacher at the school rated them, and both these people knew the children well. These ratings were carried out separately by

the two judges, and then compared, and the ratings showed a high correlation when they were compared. This means that both the experimenter and the teacher tended to rate the same children in the same way without comparing notes, so it was thought that the ratings were 'accurate' and reliable.

Design

There were eight groups with six children in each group, and then the other 24 children were in the control group. Of the eight groups, half watched aggressive models, and half watched non-aggressive models. Also some boys watched the male model, and some watched the female model, and it was the same with the girls.

The study was carried out by first settling the child in a corner to design pictures, and then the adult model was brought into the room and sat in another corner. There were materials for the adult model to play with, and these materials were the same in all conditions. The non-aggressive model assembled toys quietly. The aggressive model also assembled toys for one minute. However, then the aggressive model started behaving aggressively towards a five-foot high Bobo doll placed in the model's corner. A Bobo doll is one of those inflatable dolls that you can hit and bounces back.

So that the actions could be easily measured once the children were left to play without the model there, the model was instructed to carry out some very clear actions. For example, the Bobo doll was sat on and punched on the nose. Also there was a mallet that was used to hit the model on the head. The model also used verbal aggression such as 'throw him in the air' as this was done. This would give actions that could be watched for and measured.

The child could not imitate the acts, because there was no Bobo doll in the child's corner, so the learning could only be observational. The whole situation lasted for ten minutes.

There was a little more to the study. At the end of the session, before the children started to play and were observed, they were put into an aggressive state. This was for a number of reasons. The experimenters knew from other studies that watching aggression tends to reduce aggression (Rosenbaum & deCharms, 1960). So the children who watched the aggression might have been in a less aggressive state than the others in the study. This could be a factor, so the experimenters wanted the children to be at the same level of aggression as the observation of behaviour began. Another reason for making them a bit aggressive was that those who had watched the non-aggressive model might be seen more easily to be calmed by this behaviour if they actually reduced from this slight aggression to no aggression. This change would not be apparent if they were not a bit aggressive to begin with.

So the children were taken to play with some 'interesting' toys and then, just when they became interested, they were stopped by the experimenter saying they were her best toys and she did not let just anyone play with them. They were then allowed to play with different toys. The experimenter stayed in the room for the observation, because the children would not have wanted to stay alone, but she tried to remain inconspicuous.

The room they played in was arranged in the same way all the time. The Bobo doll was there, as was a mallet and other materials, including drawing materials. Each child spent 20 minutes in the room and their behaviour was rated by judges using a one-way mirror. Observations of the play behaviour were recorded every five seconds using an electronic timer. At times there were two judges, so that inter-rater reliability could be looked for. Activity 16 suggests that you refer to Chapter 7 if you have not already looked at the description of observation as a method.

ACTIVITY 16

You need to be familiar with issues like inter-rater reliability, so if you have not already read the appropriate section of Chapter 7 – on observational method – then you could do so now. This will help in evaluating this study.

The judges rated such behaviours as sitting on the Bobo doll, or hitting something else with the mallet. Types of aggression other than the acts that the aggressive model performed were scored, because they were acts where there was non-imitative aggression. In these cases the children were aggressive, but not copying the model. The researchers needed to record these acts.

Results

The children in the non-aggressive or control conditions showed practically no aggressive behaviour; however, those who watched the aggressive model did carry out a lot of aggressive acts imitating those they had seen. Of those in the other two conditions, not the one with the aggressive model, 70% had zero aggression scores. Children in the 'aggressive' condition showed both physical and verbal aggression. Not only did the children who had watched the aggressive model carry out more aggressive acts, but these acts were directly modelled on the acts they had seen.

Those in the non-aggressive condition did the least aggressive acts with the mallet, which tends to suggest that the non-aggressive model did in fact have a calming effect on the children. This was especially true for girls, who were much less aggressive in the 'non-aggressive' condition than in either the control group or the 'aggressive' condition. So perhaps girls are calmed even more than boys by a non-aggressive model?

Boys were more physically aggressive – that is they copied more of the physically aggressive acts carried out by the 'aggressive' model. However, there was less difference between boys and girls when measuring verbal aggressive acts. The conclusions were not quite straightforward. It was not, for example, concluded that only the boys were aggressive. The girls who watched the female model showed more verbal aggression that was copied from the model, and showed more non-imitative aggression than the boys.

In general it did seem that the aggressive male model was more imitated than the aggressive female model.

The main overall difference between those in the 'non-aggressive' condition and the control condition was that those in the control condition used the mallet more, and in this way were more aggressive. However, this seemed to be the only difference. However, when looking at the influence of the male model, those in the 'non-aggressive' condition did show fewer aggressive acts in all senses than those in the control group. Where the control and the 'non-aggressive' group did not differ was when there was a female model. So when we said that females seemed more calmed by the non-aggressive model than males, it must have been the male non-aggressive model that did the calming.

Also those who observed the non-aggressive models spent more time not playing at all than did those in the control group. Also girls spent more time playing with dolls than boys did.

Overall then, it was clear that there was imitation of the aggressive model. It is important to note, however, that in general there was also imitation of the non-aggressive model, in the sense that often those who watched the non-aggressive model were even less aggressive than might be expected normally (as shown by the control group). Also there were some gender differences, and boys seemed to be physically more aggressive than girls, if not verbally more aggressive. Also the male model seemed to be imitated more than the female model did.

Discussion

It seems that imitation is a form of learning, and that the learnt behaviour can be displayed at a later date. Not all behaviour has to be reinforced to be learnt. Observational learning seems to have been shown. There were gender differences, and male models seem to be imitated more than female models. Also boys seemed to imitate physical aggression more than girls. When it comes to verbal aggression, the girls did imitate this behaviour, but they seemed to imitate the female model more. Also the boys imitated the male model more where verbal aggression is concerned.

You can see from the variety of results that this is a complex area. It does seem that we learn by observation. However, the behaviour that is repeated seems to depend on a number of things. From this study it does seem that one of the issues is the gender of the model, and especially when compared with the gender of the observer.

Evaluation

Evaluation can take more than one form. You can evaluate the method in general, the ethics and the study itself. Carry out Activity 17 before reading on.

ACTIVITY 17

LIST SOME EVALUATION POINTS CONCERNING THE ABOVE STUDY

If you are working in a group, get together to list as many criticisms and evaluation points as you can. You might like to make three lists. One list could concern the method (see Chapter 7). A second list could concern ethical issues (see Chapter 8). The third list could concern the actual study itself, and criticisms of particular methodological issues.

Remember that evaluation can include good points about the study.

Key Skill C3.1a and C3.1b – you could do both the small group discussion and the presentation for this topic. You could work out details of your presentation in a small group discussion, and the prepare the presentation for the rest of the group. Don't forget you need evidence.

• Method in general
This study was an experiment carried out in a laboratory-style setting. It was carried out in the school, but the setting was not really natural, as it would be in the child's home.

So you could criticise the unnatural situation, where the child sits in one corner and plays, and then an adult is taken to another corner to play. This does not usually happen. Experiments are well known for their lack of ecological validity (real-life application).

Within the experiment, there was observation. Observations can also be criticised. For one thing no one can observe every action. In this study records were made every five seconds, which must have been difficult. However, they did have another observer, so there was an attempt made for inter-rater reliability, which is a good thing from a method point of view.

• Ethical issues
I don't know what sort of consent was given. Presumably parents agreed, although it is tempting to think that as the university nursery school was used, there was some power over the granting of permission, and perhaps it was difficult to say no. There could have been detailed permission granted. The study was done in 1961 before the strict guidelines that we have today, so it is possible that permission was not sought.

Another ethical problem that you might have come up with is that the children were made to feel aggressive by the withdrawal of the toys when they were taken to play in between the watching of the models and the playing afterwards. They were presumably distressed by being told they could no longer play with these 'best' toys – as this was the intention. This is against the ethical guidelines.

You could also argue that those exposed to the aggressive model were being taught to behave in an aggressive manner. Indeed those who were in the 'aggressive' condition did behave more aggressively. You could argue that research should not lead to this sort of teaching.

• The study itself
There were many points about the study that were well planned, including the use of inter-rater reliability. The sample was quite well selected in the way they matched the participants for aggression. However, you could criticise the sample, as you could argue that the Stanford School had a particular class or type of child, from a particular area. We don't actually know the exact details, but we do know the children were American, so we could at least say you can't generalise beyond the make up of the sample.

Also, only aggression was being studied. So we can only really conclude that aggression or non-aggression is imitated. This does not show anything about other sorts of behaviour, although we might assume that observational learning applies to other behaviour too. This study also suggests that aggression is a learnt behaviour, whereas there are other theories that link aggression to biology and inheritance. It has been claimed, for example, that males are more aggressive, and this could help to explain some of the conclusions from this study, where the boys were more physically aggressive. Social learning theory emphasises learning, whereas 'nature' could be a factor.

When looking at the actual study you could criticise the role of the Bobo doll. Children who are not familiar with a Bobo doll might be more likely to imitate an adult's treatment of it because that is what they think they should be doing. This would have little to do with aggression, even though it looked like an act of aggression. The children might have been showing obedience, rather than aggression. A similar point is that no one was hurt, as all the aggression was towards toys. So perhaps it is wrong to call this behaviour aggression.

• Practical application
You could evaluate a study in terms of how useful it is. This study is useful to society, because it suggests that we model both on aggressive and non-aggressive models. This suggests that aggression on television might be a bad thing for children to watch. However, non-aggression, or prosocial behaviour, might be a good thing. This study can be praised as leading to real-life applications. The contemporary issue that follows looks at the issue of violence on television.

Not only might you apply the study to the effect of violence on television, but you could, for example, claim that children who have been victims of physical violence might be more likely to be violent towards their own children when they become adults. One problem with this claim is that not all adults who have been the victim of such abuse when they were children then abuse their own children, so imitation cannot be the only factor.

Conditioned emotional reactions – the Watson and Rayner (1920) 'Little Albert' study

The Little Albert study has already been briefly mentioned. Recall that Watson and Rayner were using the principles of classical conditioning and conditioned Albert to fear his previously loved pet rat. In Chapter 5 you will read about the psychodynamic approach, and there is a very interesting case study about Little Hans. Don't confuse these two studies. Little Albert is the conditioning study and Little Hans is the Freud case study.

Watson and Rayner wanted to show that emotional responses could be conditioned. They were using Pavlov's principles. Recall that he noted that the laboratory assistant brought in food for the dogs, then the dogs, who salivated naturally due to the food, learnt to salivate when they saw the lab assistant (even when he was without the food). The dogs had learnt to associate the lab assistant with the food. The unconditioned stimulus (the food) produces an unconditioned response (the salivation). Then the conditioned stimulus (the lab assistant) with the unconditioned stimulus (the food) gives the unconditioned response (the salivation). Soon the salivation occurs in response to the conditioned stimulus (the lab assistant) alone, and then the salivation is called a conditioned response.

In this study the aim is to condition a fear response in Little Albert. Think a bit about how they will do this.

This is a laboratory study involving one participant, an eleven-month-old child called Albert. This is called a single subject design. Albert's mother worked in the hospital where Watson and Rayner were working. This is also a diary study, because they kept notes on Albert's responses over more than a month. Most diary studies involve noting down lots of different information, but here the two experimenters noted only Albert's fear responses.

The researchers describe Albert as normal and stolid. He was thought to be quite placid and not easily upset, and this made him a suitable participant for the study. The two researchers thought Albert would not be particularly upset by the study. They spent some time wondering whether to do the study at all, then decided that Albert would have to face frightening noises at some stage, so the study was not too unethical.

Phase One

The first thing they did was to make sure that Albert was not afraid of such things as rats, rabbits and fur. He never seemed to show fear, and almost never cried. So they had a base line measure for their study. Then the researchers tried hitting a metal bar to make a loud noise behind Albert's head. They observed that first he showed a startle reaction, then his lip trembled, then he started to cry. So they had their two measures – Albert was normally not afraid, but he did show a fear reaction to a loud noise behind him.

The researchers wanted to test four things. Could they condition a fear response, for example to a white rat, by pairing the frightening noise with the rat? Would Albert generalise this fear response to other things besides white rats? How long would such responses last and could they be extinguished?

The conditioning then took place, and as Albert reached for the rat and touched it, the researchers made the frightening noise on the metal bar. Albert did show a fear response. They repeated the noise when Albert touched the rat again, then left it for a week so that they did not disturb him too much.

Then a week later they watched Albert reach for the rat. This time he did not quite touch it before he withdrew his hand. The two trials did seem to have led to some conditioning. Then there were some more trials. As the rat was reached for, the noise was given. This happened four or five times. On the first time, Albert jumped and fell to his right. Then this happened each time – Albert showed a startle response and then fell to the right. Finally, after another five trials, the rat was presented without the noise and Albert crawled rapidly away from it.

This first phase showed a conditioned fear response after seven trials.

Phase Two

Having shown that an emotional response can be conditioned, they then wanted to see if it would generalise to other objects. They had been giving Albert blocks to play with between the previous trials, but with no conditioning. So after another five days, they tried the blocks, and found that Albert showed no fear response. They tried the rat again, and each time he saw the rat he showed a fear response. The trials of showing the rat, and then the blocks, and then the rat, and so on, all showed that Albert was afraid of the rat, but happy to play with the blocks. So they knew that the fear response had lasted.

Then they tried various other animals. A rabbit made Albert afraid. A dog made him a bit fearful, but not as much as the rabbit. A fur coat made him afraid. He did not like cotton wool, but was not as afraid as he was with the animals.

So they concluded that there was some generalising of the fear response to other furry objects.

Phase Three

In the next set of trials, after another five days, although Albert was still a bit fearful of the rat, he was not so afraid, so they decided to do the pairing of the rat and the noise again. They included trials of giving Albert blocks to play with, and each time they did this he played happily. In between, however, he showed fear responses to the rat and the rabbit as they were presented on different trials.

Up to now they had been using a small room and Albert was seated on a mattress. They wondered what would happen if he was in a larger room, to see if a change in the setting would make a difference. Firstly, in the original room they conditioned Albert to fear the rabbit and dog too, by pairing them with sound. Then they moved to a large lecture hall. Here they presented the rat, the rabbit, the dog and the blocks – in single trials. Albert showed fear at the sight of the rabbit, the dog and the rat, but always played happily with the blocks.

Phase Four

For a little while no further tests were done. Then at nearly thirteen months, they tried some more tasks. They used a Santa Claus mask and a fur coat, and both produced some fear reactions, such as withdrawing from them. Albert let the rat approach him, but was still upset by it. He still played with blocks as before. These trials involved the fur coat, the blocks, the rat, the Santa Claus mask, the

dog and the rabbit. All these were presented one at a time. Each time he played happily with the blocks, but he showed some fear response in all the other cases.

It was concluded that conditioned responses continue after one month, and they can be generalised beyond the original object.

Phase Five

This would have been the extinction phase, but Albert was taken from the hospital at that time. Watson and Rayner did not have the opportunity to reverse the conditioned fear responses.

Evaluation

- Watson thought that our emotional reactions are built in this way, through conditioning and associations made with things in the environment.

- Note that Watson's work can be criticised for gathering quantitative measurable data, but not looking at the differences in the emotional responses. Emotions are qualitative (to do with quality), and not easily measurable. It is unlikely that conditioning accounts for all adult emotions, as they are more complex than a simple adding of experiences.

- Looking at the method used in this study, you can be critical because there was only one participant. They would have done more, but Watson lost his job around that time. There is also some doubt about the results, since they were published in more than one paper and sometimes there were differences in what was claimed. Some accounts claim that Albert was 'de-conditioned' before he left the hospital, and this seems likely since the researchers did know he would be leaving.

- Watson was involved not long after the Little Albert study in the 'unconditioning' of a child called Peter. Peter was afraid of rats, rabbits, fur coats, and cotton wool, amongst other things. They used systematic desensitisation (it was called this much later, and supposedly started by Wolpe, as outlined elsewhere in this chapter). Little Peter was slowly introduced to a caged rabbit, and gradually the rabbit was moved nearer and nearer to Peter until Peter was relaxed with it very near.

- There are ethical criticisms of the Little Albert study. The researchers did say that they thought it was okay to frighten Albert as he would be exposed to such stimuli at some stage in any case. However, it is not really likely that he would have a metal bar struck in order to frighten him. Also, they said that he was quite placid in any case, but this hardly justifies their actions.

- The main criticism, however, seems to be that when the data are examined, it seems that it was quite difficult to condition Albert to be afraid of the rat, and that the fear did not last long. They had to repeat the pairing to strengthen the association from time to time. Textbooks seem to suggest that it was easy to condition Albert to fear the rat, and then easy for the generalisation of the fear response to other animals to happen. However, analysis of the data seems to suggest that this was not easy, and was not that clear cut. Harris in 1997, and Cornwell and Hobbs (1976), examine some of the above issues and present the arguments criticising the Watson and Rayner study.

Key application – the deliberate alteration of human behaviour

Below you will find examples of classical and operant conditioning in humans.

The compensatory reaction hypothesis and drug tolerance

The compensatory reaction hypothesis is concerned with classical conditioning, and drug tolerance is explained by looking at this hypothesis. Injecting drugs is an attempt by the user to deliberately alter their behaviour and experiences. Usually psychologists are talking about the deliberate alteration of human behaviour by others. However, taking drugs is a way in which we deliberately alter human behaviour, so this issue has relevance here. It is an interesting addition to the understanding of classical conditioning, and you could use it as an example of a contemporary issue.

The compensatory reaction hypothesis tries to explain why some classical conditioning works in exactly the opposite way to that proposed by Pavlov. For example, those who inject themselves with insulin do so to lower the blood sugar level. Therefore, insulin is the unconditioned stimulus that naturally produces the unconditioned response of a decrease in blood sugar level. The needle should be paired with the insulin, and classical conditioning principles predict that the sight of the needle itself should decrease the blood sugar levels (this would be useful and save on insulin!).

However, this does not happen. The sight of the needle actually raises the blood sugar level. Siegel (1977) reports that there is a compensatory reaction. It is suggested that this is because the body is anticipating the drop in blood sugar level and so compensates ready for it.

If you think about those taking drugs such as heroin, which gives a feeling of, amongst other things, happiness and euphoria, you would think that soon the sight of the needle would give the same feelings. However, it does not. The sight of the needle (or any of the other equipment needed) actually leads to depression and other such feelings. It is as if the body is ready for the euphoria, and so compensates with the depression.

Perhaps this is why the addict will need to take more and more of the drug. This is one explanation of drug tolerance, which means needing more and more of the drug. If you continue to the A2 part of the course, you may choose the application that looks at issues like drug tolerance, and you could recall this issue then.

If the addict moves to another environment (where the environmental triggers may not be present), there is a risk of overdose. The addict will inject more, having experienced the low prior to the injection. However, the conditioned depression response will not occur if the environmental triggers are not there, and then an overdose could occur. This is because the addict is injecting more, to compensate for the low, but the low will not come, because the stimulus is not there.

Behaviour therapy and the use of principles of classical conditioning

Both classical and operant conditioning have given rise to methods of deliberately altering human behaviour. Some of these you have already come across. For example, the teacher can award gold stars for good work, and by doing this reward good work. Hopefully, the pupils will then be encouraged to produce more good work, and this is operant conditioning and positive reinforcement in action. We have also already mentioned aversion therapy, where someone can 'unlearn' a liking for something undesirable. Aversion therapy uses the principles of classical conditioning. Any therapy that works on classical conditioning principles tends to be called behaviour therapy, and therapies that work on operant conditioning principles tend to be called behaviour modification.

This section looks at behaviour therapy, and the section below looks at behaviour modification.

Systematic desensitisation

Wolpe (1958) was most involved in developing the idea of **systematic desensitisation**. This therapy helps people with phobias. The basic idea is that no one can be both anxious and relaxed. Two opposite emotions cannot exist at the same time. Those with a phobia are very anxious. If relaxation can replace the anxiety, this should get rid of the phobia. The principles of classical conditioning are used to pair relaxation with the phobic object instead of anxiety.

The therapy is systematic, because it is done step by step and in a sequence. I will use the example of a 'spider' phobia. Imagine you were using systematic desensitisation for someone afraid of spiders. First, you need the person to relax, and you may have to instruct them in how to do this. Assuming they are relaxed, then you could ask them to imagine a spider, or you could introduce a picture of a spider. When the person was relaxed enough with a picture, you could systematically work through tiny spiders to large ones, each time checking that the person was sufficiently relaxed to move on. The patients have to think about spiders before the next session, and have to do a lot of work on their own, practising the relaxation and putting themselves in anxious states by imagining spiders (in this example) and so on.

Evaluation

- Systematic desensitisation does seem to work. It does seem to work better for small phobias, rather than for agoraphobia. Agoraphobia tends to mean not wanting to go outside, not wanting to meet people, having lots of obsessions and rituals each day, and so on. This is much harder to tackle by systematic desensitisation. You also need people with good imaginations, and who can learn to relax. Also it may be difficult for those who use mainly imagination to defeat their phobia to then transfer that learning to a real life situation.

Implosion therapy and flooding

Implosion therapy means confronting the person with what makes them anxious, but with no gradual introduction. They have to imagine the worst situation (or most frightening spider) straight away. The principles here are that the person cannot maintain anxiety for long. Physically they would run out of energy. So if you make them as anxious as you can, their physiological response should at some stage start reducing. They can then interpret that reduction as them getting used to the stimulus (the most frightening spider) and they will start to associate a more calm reaction to that stimulus.

Flooding is only different from implosion therapy in that the actual large spider would be presented to the person. Implosion therapy involves imagining the worst case scenario, and flooding means it actually existing.

Evaluation

- Flooding is considered to be more successful than implosion therapy (Marks et al, 1970). Flooding has also been used with those with agoraphobia with some success. There is a famous example of Wolpe taking a girl who was afraid of cars on a car ride, and driving around for hours. The girl did become hysterical, but the fear did disappear by the end of the journey. You might want to say this sort of therapy is unethical – even though it does seem to have worked. One of the problems in evaluating therapies is that it is difficult to know if the treatment will work forever, and you can usually say that there is no guarantee of this.

Aversion therapy

Aversion therapy is best explained by example. Someone might want to be cured of alcoholism. Therefore, instead of the 'pleasurable' response to alcohol, there needs to be an aversive response. One way is to pair alcohol with an emetic drug. An emetic drug is one that makes a person sick. After a few trials where the individual drinks the alcohol and takes the drug, he or she will then pair the alcohol with feeling sick, and will (hopefully) not wish to drink any more. It is important to give people something to drink, even water, without the drug. This stops them generalising. You don't want to condition them to pair the sickness feeling with all drinks, or they may stop drinking altogether. The person is given an emetic drug, like Antabuse, in salt water. Just before they are sick they are given the alcohol (whisky, for example) to drink.

Evaluation

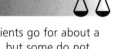

- This is not a miracle cure. Some patients go for about a year without drinking alcohol again, but some do not transfer their learning to their home situation. Aversion therapy has some effect, but probably needs to be part of the patient's treatment, rather than the only treatment.

- Aversion therapy used to be used widely to condition homosexuals to becoming 'straight'. Many criticise any attempts to change a person's sexual preference. This is on ethical grounds. Even if the person wants to change their sexual preference, this could be due to social pressure, and it is thought they are under pressure to want to change. Many feel that therapists should refuse to help homosexuals change. Then again, you could argue that this is also refusing to agree to the desires of the patient, and this would not be right either. Aversion therapy is also used with those with fetishes. One example of aversion therapy used with homosexuals is to show them lots of slides. Some of the slides will be of naked women, some of naked men. The individual has control over the slides. If he or she takes a long time staring at a particular slide, an electric shock will be delivered. So the sight of a naked male (in the case of a male homosexual) will be paired with the shock, and the individual should become conditioned against naked males. This type of aversion therapy has not been used very much since the 1970s, and is hard to evaluate, as follow-up studies are difficult. It does seem effective in the short term, in that the homosexuals will report a change in sexual preference. However, some may be prisoners or in an institution, and they may have something to gain by reporting such a change. There is no evidence that such a change would last. Marks et al (1970) did report a change for up to two years, so the therapy seems to have limited success.

Covert sensitisation

This is similar to aversive therapy, but the problem and the aversive stimulus are imagined, rather than being real. You might like to try this carefully. For example, if you really do not like snakes, and really do like chocolate, imagine a favourite type of chocolate bar wrapped in a snake. Is it enough to put you off chocolate? You could try something similar, but don't be hard on yourself! We tried it and it did work in the short term but you had to keep imagining it all over again as the image faded.

Behaviour modification and the principles of operant conditioning

Baddeley (1990) suggested that behaviour modification of any sort follows the same steps. Think of the process of shaping that was outlined earlier. The behaviour to be changed should be small and manageable. You need to know the normal reactions of the person, so that you can measure the change. You must decide what to reinforce, and what to ignore.

Shaping behaviour

One example of such behaviour shaping is in teaching autistic children to speak. Lovaas et al (1967) were involved in this procedure. First, you get the child's attention by rewarded eye contact or attention to the therapist speaking. The reward can be some form of food that the child enjoys. Then you want to give the food only when there is some sound made. Gradually the therapist waits until the sounds come near to speech, reinforcing bit by bit and shaping the behaviour.

Evaluation

- This process takes time and patience. Also the child is likely to speak only in the setting where the teaching has taken place. They do not always generalise the learning to their homes, for example. Also their speech is often not very good. Having said that, it is an improvement. Parents are trained to use such shaping techniques at home, and have noticed improvements. Shaping can be used for behaviours other than speech.

Token economy programme

The **token economy programme** has been mentioned earlier. Tokens are used as secondary reinforcers for the required behaviour, and then can be used to purchase whatever is wanted. This therapy came from Ayllon and Azrin (1968). The system is used in institutions and can be very successful in producing the required behaviour. Tokens can also be exchanged for special privileges.

Evaluation

- Tokens can be given immediately, which is an advantage, and also you can be very consistent in their use. The system has been used with those with schizophrenia with

quite a lot of success. Social skills are improved. The programme meant that some institutionalised people could be released into the community. Davison and Neale (1994) see the results as very successful, especially considering the poor behaviour of the chosen people in the first place. However, the token economy system was not simply using the principles of operant conditioning. At least the rewards were not just the tokens because the patients got more attention. Also they may have watched the behaviour of others and some social learning may have taken place. This is no cure, but if the person's behaviour is more 'acceptable' then they may be said to have a better quality of life. There is a problem again when the person moves from the institutional setting, because these therapies do not seem to transfer well to other settings.

Ethical problems in the deliberate alteration of human behaviour

For the types of behaviour therapy and modification outlined above you can also evaluate them by reference to ethical issues. The question is to what extent should people have their behaviour altered, and for what reasons? Activity 18 asks you to consider these issues.

ACTIVITY 18

SHOULD WE DELIBERATELY ALTER THE BEHAVIOUR OF ANOTHER?

If you are working in a group, this question would be a useful discussion question. You might like to organise a discussion with half on each side. Think of as many arguments for and against such intervention as you can. Some of the arguments are suggested above.

Key Skill C3.1a – take part in a group discussion about the rights and wrongs of deliberately intervening in someone's behaviour. Remember you need evidence.

The discussion about using aversion therapy with homosexuals should have given you some material for the above discussion. Homosexuality used to be considered deviant behaviour, but is not now thought of as deviant (by most people in any case). Therefore, these days there is less desire to change the behaviour of a homosexual by using therapy. However, some do ask for intervention and for help to change their behaviour. The question is: should we offer such intervention?

The token economy programmes can also be abused. Patients may be refused facilities like television unless they earn enough tokens to watch it. Someone has to decide whether watching television is a right or a privilege. The best way of ensuring fairness is by having an open-door policy where visitors are welcomed and can see what is going on. Also, if the idea were used in schools, you may find that children only do what is needed to get the token, and do no more. This might lead to less, not more, learning.

There are Guidelines for the Professional Practice of Clinical Psychology (1983) and they must be followed. However, these guidelines are not very useful in individual cases, as they require the practitioner to give the care the patient is thought to need, which is not very specific advice. Clinicians have problems because they are agents of social change.

One problem faced by therapists is in choosing the 'right' therapy. The scientific nature of the research in psychology tends not to see the clients as humans; however, the clinician needs to consider them in that way. The clients too see themselves as 'ill' because that is how they are seen in society. So they are seen as having little power. The client is likely to accept the suggestions of the therapist, which gives the therapist even more responsibility. Many of the therapies are not proved to work in every case, and, as has been shown, do not 'last' forever. This means that the choice of whether to deliberately alter someone's behaviour is a difficult one.

There is also the issue of control, as tokens, for example, can be used to control someone's behaviour. In some cases, such as in systematic desensitisation, we can see the benefits in releasing someone from their fear. Also we can see the benefits for the autistic child and the family if they can communicate using some form of speech. However, you could argue about whether behaving in a socially acceptable manner in an institution is necessary control or not.

It is difficult to come up with answers. You need to be aware of the issues and the problems. Although I have given 'medical' examples of the deliberate alteration of human behaviour, you could also use 'educational' examples. Then you should consider how far we should alter a child's behaviour and shape the sort of person they are.

Contemporary issue

The effect of violence on television

This issue is taken from an article found on the Internet on the APA (American Psychological Society) website. The reference is http://www.apa.org.uk/publinfo/violence.html.

The title of the article is 'Violence on television: What do children learn? What can parents do?'

A 1982 report by the National Institute of Mental Health says that violent programmes on television lead to aggressive behaviour in children and teenagers. In 1985 the APA passed a resolution informing broadcasters and the public of the potential dangers. The research shows three major effects of seeing violence on television:
• Children may be desensitised (become used to and so less sensitive) to the suffering of others.
• Children may be more afraid of their world.
• Children may be more aggressive to others.

Children watching a lot of violence on television are less aroused that those who watch only a little. For example, these children after watching a violent film are less likely to call for help when they see younger children fighting. A study at Pennsylvania State University looked at 100 children. Some watched cartoons with violent acts in them, and some watched non-violent TV. There were real differences in their behaviour afterwards. The ones who watched violence were more likely to hit out, argue, disobey rules, and leave tasks unfinished (Huston et al, 1992).

Eron did a longitudinal study, which means following the same group of children over time. Children who watched many hours of TV violence when young showed more aggressive behaviour as teenagers. At 30 years old those who had watched a lot of TV at eight years old were more likely to be arrested and prosecuted for crimes as adults.

Some argue that there is no evidence for the link between aggressive acts and watching violent television, but in 1992 the APA published another report showing that the harmful effects of TV violence exist.

Most scientists say children learn aggressive behaviour from TV but parents can moderate the behaviour – by limiting the number of hours they watch, for a start. Parents should also watch what their children watch, or at least one episode. They can discuss violent incidents with their children and explore non-violent solutions. They can encourage other hobbies, and encourage the watching of programmes showing helping behaviour.

Links to concepts in social learning theory

The above issue is clearly linked to social learning theory, because it arises from studies within that explanation of learning. It is from such studies as Bandura's that people started to think that watching violence on television might link to aggression in 'real life'. It was thought that children, in particular, imitate models, including those they see on television. So the concepts of imitation and modelling are useful in the above issue, for example to explain the possible link between watching violence on television and being arrested and prosecuted for crimes later.

When looking at social learning theory above, it was also claimed that children use others as models as well as those on television. They also model, for example, on their parents. Therefore, above it is suggested that parents can do something to reduce the likelihood of their child modelling on TV aggression. The parent can suggest alternative solutions to a problem being portrayed on television, for example. The parent can explore what is being said and done, and can present other arguments.

Bandura et al's (1961) study showed that the children who watched the prosocial (helping) behaviour on television seemed to be less aggressive than a control group of children who watched no programmes in the study. So it is suggested that parents could encourage their children to watch helping behaviour on television. These suggestions as to what parents can do come directly from the studies that Bandura and others carried out, and are examples of practical applications of the social learning theory.

Coursework suggestions

1 Try making a list of creatures, including attractive ones like ladybirds, and ugly ones like cockroaches. Then ask participants to do two tasks. Give them the list and ask them to rate the creatures for attractiveness. Then give them the list again (perhaps putting the creatures in a different order) and ask the participants to rate them for how afraid they are of them. See if the two scores are related – do we fear what we find unattractive?

2 You could carry out a questionnaire to look at violence on television. The problem is that you will not be able to draw firm conclusions, but you could test viewing habits, and then ask questions about behaviour. For example, you could ask (ethically) what people watch, perhaps by listing types of films and asking them to suggest preferences. Then you could make a few statements such as 'if someone drove into a parking place just as you were going to reverse in would you (a) be very annoyed (b) just find another space ... and so on. You could then find a 'violence on TV watching score' and compare it with an 'aggressive reaction' score. You might find that those who tend to have an aggressive reaction also watch more TV violence. It will not prove that the two are linked, because those who have aggressive reactions might simply prefer that sort of television, but it could be an interesting study. You could also look for gender differences, and add some background material on gender and aggression.

Suggested reading

Eysenck, M. (1996) *Simply Psychology*. Hove: Psychology Press

Gross, R.D. (1999) *Key Studies in Psychology*, Third Edition. London: Hodder and Stoughton

Gross, R.D. (1998) *Psychology: The Science of Mind and Behaviour*, Third Edition. London: Hodder and Stoughton

Leahy, T. H. (1997) *A History of Psychology*, Fourth Edition. New Jersey: Prentice Hall

5

The psychodynamic approach

The aims of this chapter

The aims of this chapter are, with regard to the psychodynamic approach, to enable the reader to:

- *appreciate some of the general assumptions*
- *discuss research methods used*
- *describe and evaluate Freud's theories*
- *describe and evaluate one other theory from psychodynamic psychology*
- *describe and evaluate some relevant studies*
- *understand mental health issues in relation to psychodynamic concepts*
- *explain one contemporary issue or debate.*

Self-test 1

After reading this chapter, test yourself on each of the above points. Use the points as exam questions and make notes accordingly. Then see how much you can write on each.

This chapter covers

KEY ASSUMPTIONS
1 The importance of the unconscious mind and motivation
2 The importance of early childhood experiences

RESEARCH METHODS
1 Clinical interviews
2 Slips of the tongue
3 Free association
4 Dream analysis and the analysis of symbols
5 Case studies

IN-DEPTH AREAS OF STUDY
1 Freud's theory
2 Erikson's theory

STUDIES IN DETAIL
1 The case study of Little Hans (Freud,1909)
2 The usefulness of dreams during pregnancy (Ablon, 1994)

KEY APPLICATION: UNDERSTANDING MENTAL HEALTH ISSUES

CONTEMPORARY ISSUE: FAMOUS PEOPLE AND IDENTIFICATION

A warning to the reader

Much of this chapter is written as a story. There are not many activities I can offer, and coursework in this area is difficult. There are a few difficulties you should be warned about.

1 We cannot really discuss the psychodynamic approach, and Freud's work in particular, without talking fairly explicitly about sexual matters. The whole point is that our basic instincts guide us, and this includes sexual instincts. This approach is interested in therapy, and so the main focus is on those who have neuroses like anxieties. Therefore, the focus tends to be on those with problems, and their problems will be, according to Freud, grounded in sexual problems.

2 You can't really do a lot yourself. If you start doing dream analysis, or trying free association, you are likely to come up against problems. We can't go around analysing other people when we are not trained to. Think of the ethical principles in Chapter 8 – one of them involves competence, and we are not competent to analyse people. Also you might reveal something about yourself that you don't want to know. We have defence mechanisms, according to the psychodynamic approach. Admittedly analysts try to break these mechanisms down, but they do so carefully, and would have support. This is just a chapter written for you to learn the theory. You will not have the support you need. I have made a few suggestions for you to explore the issues a bit, but don't go too far, and don't be tempted to be amateur analysts. Hopefully, you have chosen to study psychology because of your interest in people, so you will respect both others and yourself.

This does mean that this chapter is more about reading than about activities. However, I hope it is interesting because it is different.

Historical background

Freud was thinking scientifically when developing his theory. He was a medical doctor, and wanted to help others. Many criticise his ideas as being unscientific, but this is not what he intended. The problems of psychology wanting to be a science were problems for Freud. Scientific ideas have to be testable. If you have read Chapter 4, then recall how those within the learning approach looked for things that were measurable and testable. They thought that then they could build more certain knowledge. It is precisely because many of Freud's ideas are not testable that he is widely criticised. However, just because something is not testable does not actually make it wrong.

You need to read this chapter with an open mind. You may be starting it with negative views about Freud's theories, or you may be starting enthusiastically. Whatever your previous assumptions, I suggest you open your mind to his views. You will probably read some of what follows with scepticism; however, there is no doubt that Freud is one of the most well-known figures in psychology. Some researchers in psychology dismiss Freud's views, and others embrace his ideas as the complete truth. You need to decide for yourself.

A little about Freud himself

Freud worked around the turn of the twentieth century, and he was trained as a doctor. He worked in Vienna, and you need to imagine the situation at the time, if you can. People who were 'mentally' ill were given little treatment, because little was known about their illnesses. Alternative treatments were fairly horrific. They were cared for to an extent, and then when they died, their brains were examined so that people could learn about such illnesses. Learning was taking place at the time; for example, Broca examined the brain of someone who could not speak, and found damage to a certain area of the brain. This area was called Broca's area, and is now known to be the area needed for us to actually speak words. People who have a stroke often have damage to Broca's area, and when they do, their speech is affected. However, doctors did not have enough knowledge at the time to solve the problems.

Doctors like Freud could do little for patients with mental illnesses. Freud toured mental hospitals and began to wonder about these sorts of illnesses. Little was known about what could cause them in a physical sense, and Freud, as well as others at the time, began to think about other causes. Breuer was someone who was looking at such problems. Breuer also talked about hysteria, and how physical symptoms could arise from non-physical causes. Someone else who influenced Freud was Charcot, who was working in Paris. Freud attended a lecture there given by Charcot, where he listened to Charcot talk about hypnosis. Freud came to reject the use of hypnotism to uncover the causes of problems, but he was greatly influenced by people like Breuer and Charcot.

Freud was a Jew, and this is important because he lived at a time of persecution of the Jews. He was ambitious and wanted to be a saviour. He saw himself as a daring explorer, and he wanted to be known for some famous discovery. You might be interested in the fact that he used cocaine – some have wondered if this affected his thinking. In any case, he had the necessary motivation to build a whole new theory about behaviour and what guides us – and this is what he did. He was not a scientist in the sense of building knowledge painstakingly. He was just the sort of person to make 'shocking discoveries', and form a theory on the basis of very little real solid research. Nevertheless, this does not make his theories wrong.

Freud was quite vain. He thought that the first blow to humans' view of themselves as all-powerful was to learn that the earth is not the centre of the universe, but goes around the sun. The second blow was Darwin's claims that humans are part of nature just as other animals are. The third blow, he thought, was his own idea that we are guided by strong unconscious urges and not by our rational thoughts.

Many academic psychologists often do not accept Freud's ideas about what motivates us. If you have read previous chapters you will know that the behaviourists, cognitive psychologists and those working in the field of social psychology were all working within the scientific method of looking for general laws about behaviour. They did not make leaps of judgement about the role of unconscious urges, and, since these cannot be proved, they did not investigate Freud's claims as they investigated other issues.

As I said earlier, there are those who embrace Freud's views and there are those who dismiss them. Gay (1989) points out, however, that all of us use Freud's views in our everyday lives. We talk about his ideas, as you will see. Many people are interested in the meaning of our dreams, and many people think that we are strongly affected by our very early upbringing. So probably you need to learn more about his views and then decide what you think.

I ought to point out too that his views are translated into English. Some say that they may have been mistranslated and misunderstood. Certainly it is easy to make generalisations about what Freud said, and often these generalisations are not completely accurate. In what follows there may be such inaccuracies, as I am giving you a short and general version of what Freud claimed. This is, however, true of many theories in psychology. If you want exact knowledge, then it is necessary to go straight to the source. This is not possible in a book such as this. I have, however, tried for exactness as far as possible.

Key assumptions of the psychodynamic approach

Key assumption 1 – The importance of the unconscious mind and motivation

Physical symptoms might have non-physical causes

Freud focused on the unconscious mind. If people had physical symptoms, but there seemed to be no physical cause, as in those with 'hysteria', then these physical symptoms might come from the unconscious mind. The conscious mind of the person was telling them that, for example, they could not use their arm. The doctors were examining the arm, and finding no physical problem. So those like Breuer and Freud were investigating the idea that the cause of such problems was not physical at all. It could not be a problem in the conscious mind, since, when examining the patients, it seemed quite clear that they were puzzled themselves, and could not understand what the problem was. So it might be that there was a problem in the unconscious mind. It was because people like Freud wanted to solve these patients' problems that they began investigating these areas.

Freud studied **neuroses**, and these days we think of neuroses as being mental problems. However, Freud was thinking of neuroses as neural disorders (disorders to do with nerves/neurons). Hysteria is now known as when a physical symptom seems to have a mental cause. However, in Freud's time, hysteria was thought to have a neural cause. Freud thought the cause of hysteria was sexual, and 'real' rather than 'mental'. Treatment was physical, because they thought the cause was physical. Also, remember that the word 'hysteria' was derived from the word for the 'womb' and they thought only women could suffer from hysteria. Doctors at the time were male, so there was also a problem with the relationship between the doctor and the female patient. This is important later, when Freud talks about transference, as you will see.

It should be noted that at the time the treatments for 'hysteria' were what we would call barbaric. Treatments ranged from icy showers and ridicule to suffocation and 'abuse'. Psychoanalysis must have been seen as a much better idea.

Aiming for a scientific theory

Freud started asking such patients lots of questions to try to find out what was causing their problems. He used different methods to those that have been examined in previous chapters. These methods are outlined in the section that follows and are a central focus of Freud's views. He could not use experiments, observations or questionnaires. What he wanted to know was buried where even the patient could not find it, so he had to devise ways of tricking the conscious mind to reveal what was in the unconscious one.

Freud was interested in therapy and in helping his clients; however, he was also very interested in building a whole scientific theory. His data consisted of his client's words, and he then analysed them in a way he thought of as just as scientific as using an experiment. The therapy was another way of showing his claims to be true. One of the reasons for the criticisms of Freud's ideas is that he used what was really a **subjective** measure (being the analyst's viewpoint) and then claimed that the data was scientific and **objective**.

Freud as a doctor trained in **physiology**. His training was scientific. He would have thought of a physiological cause as being measurable, and he would think about finding general laws about human behaviour. The problem was that he was looking at individual case studies of people with individual problems. If he wanted to publish a complete theory – and there is evidence that he did – then he would look for general laws about behaviour that he could find from analysis of these individual problems. It would be in the physiology and nature of people that he would look, because, if you draw conclusions about people's underlying nature, then you can talk about everyone, and apply that theory to everyone.

So Freud gathered his data from case studies, but he generalised his conclusions to cover everyone. When he thought that physical problems without obvious physical causes came from problems in the unconscious, he meant that we are all governed by our unconscious. If some people's problems stem from unconscious urges – and he thought they did – then he concluded that all of us were guided by our unconscious. He would come to this conclusion partly because he was looking for general laws about human behaviour.

The unconscious

One problem with claiming that unconscious desires when not released can cause hysteria is in finding out what these desires are. Freud needed to come up with some interesting methods in order to collect such data. He thought that slips of the tongue and the content of dreams revealed hidden desires. His methods are

discussed later in this chapter. A good way of explaining the role of the unconscious is to outline one of the case studies used by Freud when building his theory. This case study is actually about a patient of Breuer's. It is outlined in Box 1.

Box 1

Breuer's case – Anna O

It is said that the case of Anna O, who was a patient of Breuer's, started psychoanalytic therapy. Her real name was Bertha von Pappenheim. She was a young middle-class woman who had had to nurse a sick father. She had difficulties in hearing and speaking, and had some minor paralyses – these were typical symptoms of hysteria. Breuer found that if Anna talked and uncovered previously forgotten memories, she seemed to get a bit better. One example was that she could not drink water from a glass, but when discussing this she remembered an incident where a dog had licked a glass. Once Anna had remembered the incident, she could immediately drink from a glass again. However, Anna did not get well, even with these treatments. Breuer used hypnosis with Anna, although Freud rejected this method, as is explained later.

Anna herself gave **psychotherapy** the name 'talking cure' and organised her treatment herself. She was not cured by hypnosis and talking, although she did get some relief from it, as outlined in Box 1.

From this general beginning, that talking could offer some relief, and that previous memories might be part of the problem, Freud and Breuer (1895) developed the idea that repressed memories could be the problem for those with hysteria. These memories remain in the unconscious and the problem shows itself as some physical symptom. You can see that what is needed is for the memory to become conscious and then the problem should resolve itself, just as when Anna could drink from the glass. The effect of the buried memory is then 'unstrangulated' or 'abreacted' – in other words it becomes conscious and is released.

Freud moved away from hypnosis, and moved towards a talking cure where people were awake and aware. He named this procedure '**psychoanalysis**'. Freud and Breuer parted company, probably because Freud, in his search for a publishable grand theory, wanted to generalise from these few findings to apply the theory to everyone, whereas Breuer was more cautious.

Where is the unconscious?

Most people agree that we are not aware of all our conscious thoughts, but this is not the same as saying that there is a separate space that is the **unconscious**. Freud thought that all thoughts start in the unconscious and then are allowed into our **conscious** mind if they are suitable. These ideas may be allowed through and then remain in the **preconscious** until made conscious. So there are some thoughts we are conscious of, some we can become conscious of, and others that we cannot reach. The preconscious is an area where there are thoughts we can make conscious if we wish to.

Those ideas that do not get through into the preconscious are the powerful ones, and the ones that must be forcefully repressed. This repression is **dynamic** and active and the thoughts that are not allowed through keep trying (so to speak). Therefore, there are active attempts for these thoughts to break through and we can look for these activities. Slips of the tongue might reveal these hidden thoughts, as might dreams and neurotic symptoms. These thoughts are not locked away in the unconscious and safely forgotten. The whole point is that they are actively being repressed and this takes energy. This is the 'dynamic' part of the psychodynamic approach. Sometimes these thoughts are sublimated, which means they are channelled into another, more acceptable form. So we have to look at dreams, slips of the tongue, neurotic symptoms and our other behaviours in order to try to uncover these unconscious wishes, thoughts and desires. These are often sexual, as is explained below.

So the unconscious is real and exists, and the energy used up in repressing thoughts that cannot be allowed into the preconscious is real too. At first Freud thought of the mind as having these three spaces – the unconscious, the preconscious and the conscious – but later he divided the mind up differently. Note, however, that the unconscious is not only the place where our unacceptable ideas are kept, trying to escape, but it is also an irrational, emotionally unstable area, out of touch with reality.

Freud replaced the idea of these three areas with a more structural idea of three parts of the personality. He saw the innate, irrational part as being the **id**, and this was the unconscious part. The second part was rational and focused on reality, and was called the **ego**. Finally there was the censor that gave moral behaviour; this was the **superego**. These ideas are outlined later.

Key assumption 2 – The importance of early experiences

What we learn in our lifetime can be passed via genes to our children – the importance of childhood

Freud thought that our early years were where we developed our personality. He was guided by theories of his day. There was an idea based on Darwin's views, that *phylogeny recapitulates ontogeny*. They thought then (although no longer do) that a baby's development from fetus onwards took the same form as the human's evolution over the years. So if humans go from a fish-like state to standing on two legs, then so does the baby. You can see that this seems right, but it has been shown to be wrong. It is an interesting idea, though. Freud took the idea and applied it to psychosexual development. His five stages of psychosexual development (which you will read about soon) include a latency stage when not much happens. This is supposed to be like the Ice Ages, when Freud thought not much changed. He followed Lamarck's idea of development, not Darwin's. See Box 2 for an explanation of this.

Box 2

Lamarck and Darwin

Lamarck thought that we could learn something in our lifetime and then pass it on through our children via genes. Well, genes weren't actually known about, but the idea was suggested that known things could be passed on. So, for Larmack, giraffes had long necks because they stretched them to reach leaves. They would then have offspring and pass on the stretched necks, so their young would have long necks.

Darwin's ideas contradict Lamarck's. It is not now accepted that genes can hold learnt information. Darwin explained the giraffe's long neck by suggesting that long-necked giraffes could reach leaves. They had an advantage in that sort of environment. The long-necked giraffe survived because it lived to reproduce. The genes for long necks survived, because the long-necked giraffes survived to breed, whereas their short-necked cousins did not. Any mutation – like an individual with a long neck – that helped survival was likely to survive in itself.

Chapter 6 outlines more about genes.

Freud found Lamarck's ideas useful. In his theory, drawn from his case studies, he suggested that young boys had castration fear – and more is said about this later. Freud was criticised because it was said that children would need to know that opposite-sexed people have different genitals, and that children at that time did not see adults naked. Freud could counter this criticism by saying that boys inherited this knowledge.

So the early years are important, but some of the knowledge children have could have been inherited from their parents. Now that Lamarck's views are not accepted, these sorts of ideas from Freud must be criticised too.

The sexual instinct

Not only are the early years important, but it is the sexual instinct that is the most important. Remember Freud was looking for a physiological and scientific theory. Freud wanted a theory that would apply to everyone of every culture (he was searching for an all-encompassing theory) and the sex drive was useful as an overall motivator, because everyone everywhere has a sex drive (or so Freud assumed). Freud looked at drives in animals and saw them as being hunger, thirst, self-preservation and sex. His patients were not starving, thirsty or in physical danger, so the sex drive had to be important. Freud was looking for a physical theory, so drives such as producing works of art or appreciating nature were not important according to him. He wanted to see what would motivate people to hold something in their unconscious that would lead to things like physical illnesses, and only the sex drive seemed to be there as a suitable motivator.

Freud realised that most human societies try to regulate the sex drive, and this made him more sure that the sex drive was causing problems. Childhood sexual fantasies seemed to appear in his patients' stories too, so he thought that it was in the repression of the sex drive that people had problems, and that this occurred at a young age. The middle classes in Europe were his patients also. Other classes had fewer possessions, but were more free when it came to sexual matters. The middle classes did not like the poverty of the lower classes, but they envied their sexual freedom. Freud saw the 'neuroses' in the middle classes, and he saw that sex in the lower classes was uncomplicated and pleasurable. At the time, the middle classes, and this included Freud himself, deprived themselves of sexual pleasures, and saw this as giving integrity. It was the same in Victorian England, where it was 'noble' to deprive oneself of pleasure in all forms. At the same time temptation meant that there was a lot of sexual abuse. It is important to understand Freud's theories within the setting in which they were developed.

Men (especially middle-class men) loved women and idolised them, so put them out of reach. Sex could be had with prostitutes because that was accepted. However, there was a lot of impotence and problems between married couples because of this reverence that men had for women. Women were seen as in need of protection.

It is important to remember that times have changed – probably because of Freud himself. If you think Freud's views are all about sex, then you need to take yourself (mentally) back in time, and think of the situation then. Freud was probably right that many of the problems his patients had stemmed from repressed sexual instincts.

Childhood sexuality

Hopefully you have understood Freud's reasoning and have grasped his main points. We have yet to outline his theory, but you know that it rests on the idea of a strong unconscious where strong desires are kept, all striving to escape. You can also see that Freud thought that a lot of these desires would be sexual ones.

At this stage you may start to question Freud's assumptions, because now he looks at child sexuality. We have already mentioned castration fear. Freud thought that the first five years were very important, and that a child goes through various stages that must be successfully negotiated. If these stages are successful, there will be few repressed urges; if, however, things go wrong, then the child will use a lot of energy as a grown person in repressing these unresolved urges.

One of the crucial phases takes place in the phallic stage. This happens somewhere around the age of five. A boy will have sexual feelings for his mother, and has to resolve them because he also feels guilt. He will see his father as competing for the attentions of his mother, and he will also love his father, hence the guilt. We will look more at this later. For now, you can probably see that if the boy can successfully resolve the guilt by identifying with his father (becoming him), he can move on without problems. If, however, he cannot successfully resolve the problem, then he might have urges in his unconscious that will lead to neuroses later in life. There is more to it than this, and I will go into more detail later, but you can at least see the importance of the first five years when looking at a person's development.

Did problems come from seduction by fathers?

At first Freud had thought that later problems stemmed from seduction by the father, but later he decided this could not be the case. One reason why he thought there had been no real seduction was because psychoanalysis did not work, in other words the discovery of this by his patients did not cure them, as it should have done if the unconscious urges had been released into consciousness. Another reason was that he thought all fathers could not seduce their children. He thought about his own, and decided it could not be true. Thirdly, he realised that the unconscious was itself irrational and would not stick to reality. Finally, he also found that mad patients did not reveal the idea of seduction by the father. When they had stopped repressing, because of the madness, then the truth should be revealed, but they did not talk about seduction.

The Oedipus complex

Freud turned down the idea that fathers were seducers, and that childhood sexuality came from the father. He then used his own experiences to come up with the idea of the **Oedipus complex** to explain childhood sexuality. He recalled an incident in his own past where he remembered being attracted to his own mother. He remembered being in love with his own mother and jealous of his father. He then assumed this was true of everyone (remember his desire to build a grand theory).

So Freud thought that adult neuroses came from buried unconscious urges that come from childhood sexual events. At first he thought these events were real seductions, and then later he thought they were sexual fantasies.

Evaluation

- The above story – of Freud's move from thinking that childhood sexuality came from real seduction, to deciding there were sexual fantasies – has been criticised. Sulloway (1979) argued that Freud borrowed a lot of his ideas from Fliess, with whom he worked. Some think that Fliess had the idea that children are 'sexual' and that there is such a thing as the id. Fliess and Freud (like Freud and Breuer) did fall out, so it is possible that it was indeed Fliess who had the original ideas.

- Others claim that Freud either persuaded his patients into admitting childhood seductions or created the stories himself. Freud thought of his analysis as being objective and scientific; however, it is likely that he guided his clients. He thought that the sexual drive was important in any case, so would be looking for confirmation of this view. He interpreted his client's stories, and they could not argue, as he was claiming to be revealing the unconscious, and they could not know their own unconscious. His patients resisted his interpretations, but

he was able to show that this is likely, as they would not want to have their unconscious desires revealed. In fact the more they resisted, the more he claimed he was getting to the truth. When Freud came to think that not everyone could have been seduced, the only way he could rescue his theory was to use the Oedipus complex as an explanation.

In another version Masson (1984), a critic of Freud, says that Freud was right to believe that his clients had been sexually abused. Masson claims that Freud discovered how widespread the sexual abuse of children was (and is) and then walked away from it. Masson thinks that one reason was to avoid the displeasure of the establishment at the time. Masson also criticises Freud for, firstly, not seeing that there was real sexual abuse, and then, secondly, not realising that not all child abuse was sexual. Surely children who were starved and beaten would have demonstrated neurotic symptoms in later life too, and it seems odd that Freud only concentrated on sexual abuse.

Research methods used in the psychoanalytic approach

Clinical interviews

Freud regarded his talks with his patients as being scientific data. He thought of his analyses as being scientific, just as experiments are scientific. He understood that there were some problems in generalising from case studies to a whole theory, but his aim was to build such a theory. His main aim was to reach into the unknowable unconscious of the person. In order to do this he had to get the patient to talk, and then analyse such talk. He would then put this interpretation to the client and if it was accepted, then what was unconscious would become conscious. There was **catharsis**, which means the emotions that were being repressed would be released.

The urges and wishes in the unconscious must be ones that cannot be allowed into the preconscious. This idea is outlined above. If these urges are not allowed through, then they must be strong and unwanted. Energy is taken up in keeping these unconscious wishes away from the preconscious. When these wishes are released and known, then the problem can go away, and the energy is released and the person is free from the repressed urges.

So hypnosis is not used. In hypnosis the analyst may hear what is being said, but the patient cannot. It is important that the information comes from the unconscious into the conscious, so the person must hear it for themselves and must acknowledge the analysis.

The interview, then, takes the form of the client talking and the analyst listening. In theory the listener is non-directive, in other words suggestions can be made but the person must accept explanations. In practice, however, it appears that Freud did direct his clients in their interpretation of stories and problems. In practice, the more the person resists an explanation, the greater the temptation to think that this explanation is getting near to the truth.

Activity 1 asks you to think of a situation where you might resist an explanation about yourself. Don't get too personal!

If you are vehemently against pornography, and cannot stand anything along those lines, Freud might well suggest that you are hiding sexual desires, and perhaps desires about taking your clothes off in public and so on. You could look (privately and carefully) at what you feel strongly about and see if your real feelings are the reverse of what you are saying. For example, imagine someone who persistently claims no one likes them, even though they seem to have a lot of friends. Perhaps what they really might mean is that they don't like anyone else.

Box 3 makes a few points about becoming a psychoanalyst, to make sure that we all remember that we are not trained in this sort of analysis (at least I am assuming you are not).

ACTIVITY 1

Think of a situation where you might find a Freudian explanation of your behaviour unacceptable.

For example, imagine that you hate the idea of pornography. So when you find a pornographic magazine lying around in your school or college, you rush indignantly to a tutor and demand an enquiry into who is bringing such 'disgusting rubbish' into school. Imagine that you are very upset by the incident, and protesting loudly.

Think about what Freud would have said about your behaviour.

Now think of an example for yourself. If you are working in pairs or groups, make up a similar story, and then ask one of the others to act out the role of analyst. Don't forget to make up the stories – you need to protect yourself from real analysis at this stage. If you don't want to take part, then please don't.

Consider ethical issues too, and please don't do coursework in this area, however much it interests you. Remember the ethical principles of conduct and competence. I am assuming you are not a psychoanalyst; neither am I, so we are not competent to carry out analysis. Box 3 talks a bit about becoming a psychoanalyst

Key Skill C3.1a – as suggested, this would make a good group discussion and you could explore Freud's ideas actively.

Box 3

About being a psychoanalyst

To become a psychoanalyst (in the Freudian sense) you have to undergo psychoanalysis yourself. This takes years. In Freud's style of psychoanalysis, he used to see his clients every day for six days. This went on all the time, and there was no time limit. There are modern versions where there is a time limit and the person is seen less frequently each week; however, it is a long process.

The analyst stays out of sight of the patient – picture the couch and the analyst at the head of the couch, behind the patient. This contrasts with counselling, where the counsellor is visible and taking part in the process.

Transference is when the client transfers emotions onto the analyst. At first these tend to be positive emotions (like the child has for the parents) and later these emotions become negative (like the child when he or she starts resisting parental control). The analyst has to be prepared for these feelings, and indeed transference is part of the analysis. There is also **countertransference**, which refers to the feelings the analyst will have for the client. These feelings also form part of the analysis. The analyst has to be ready for them, however, and it is not an easy task. Training concentrates on such issues, as well as how to recognise and deal with resistance, which is when the client resists the analyst's interpretations.

Ethical principles say that we need to be competent when doing research in psychology. Don't go into psychoanalysis too deeply, as we are not qualified to do so.

Evaluation

- If you have read Chapter 3, you will have read about Piaget, who used clinical interviews too. However, his methods were not like those of Freud's. Piaget asked children questions and then explored with them what their answers were. In a way Freud does that with people too. However, Piaget did no analysing. He was trying to find out how children think. Piaget looked at cognition (thinking) where Freud looked at emotions. There are ways in which their methods are similar, however. They both use interviews. However, Freud's method is more aptly called 'clinical' because clinical implies a medical or therapeutic intention. Piaget borrowed his method from these ideas.

- Clinical interviews have the problems of case studies. If you have already have studied Chapter 7 you can stop to make a list of such problems here. Case studies tend to get at valid data, in that the person is giving the information. However, when you look at one person you cannot really generalise from that information to everyone else. Freud did tend to do that. Later you will read the case study of Hans. You will see that Hans' story fits Freud's '**Oedipus complex**'. However, this does not mean that everyone goes through such a complex in the **phallic** *stage*.

- Case studies are also not reliable. You have probably read some of the other chapters so you probably know what 'reliable' means in psychology. A study is said to be reliable if you do it again and get the same results. It is unlikely that you will do a case study again and get exactly the same results. You will perhaps ask different questions, or follow a different route.

- Similarly, there is a problem in that Freud's case studies were **retrospective** in the sense that they involved people remembering their early years. You could argue that you cannot reliably remember your early years, and many have criticised Freud's methods because of this.

Slips of the tongue

Freud was interested in occasions when clients said one word and meant another. The usual example of this is when someone giving a biology lecture uses the word 'orgasm' instead of 'organism'. Think about what Freud would have said about that. Imagine someone talking to their boyfriend or girlfriend and calling him or her by their last partner's name. Freud might say that they have not forgotten their previous partner. Similarly, if you forget your mother's birthday, Freud might think of this as **motivated forgetting**. His ideas about forgetting have been discussed in Chapter 1, so you may have already come across them.

As well as slips of the tongue, Freud was interested in when we become absent minded, and he thought we forget about things we don't want to do. Again, this is motivated forgetting, and not accidental forgetting. Next time you make a slip of the tongue, look closely at what you said and why. Freud would say the slip revealed your unconscious

desires. Freud did not claim that absolutely everything we forget was due to motivated forgetting, but he was interested in forgetting, because some of it revealed the unconscious desires that he was trying to learn about.

Evaluation

- Many have said that you can make simple mistakes without revealing any innermost emotions. In Chapter 1 there were many other explanations given for forgetting, besides it being motivated. You could forget a birthday because you had other things on your mind, for example. You could be so used to saying one name, you could call a new friend by that name. If you have brothers and sisters I would be surprised if your mother or father had not sometimes called you by the wrong name, but I am not sure we should then conclude they think less of you.

Free association

Free association is not really a new method, but part of the clinical interview. During his interviews Freud asked his patients to use free association. This involves them saying anything that enters their mind, no matter what it is. Freud was trying to uncover what was hidden in his patient's unconscious, and he did not want conscious monitoring of thoughts. So he persuaded his clients to say whatever came into their heads, to avoid this cognitive monitoring. All embarrassing and trivial comments were needed.

When the patient started to resist, claiming that certain things were not important, this is when Freud became interested. It would be those things that you don't want to say, or consider are not important, that would be most likely to lead to uncovering unconscious wishes.

Evaluation

- Patients found it difficult not to resist saying certain things. Activity 2 suggests that you try this for yourself. This would be better if you are alone.

ACTIVITY 2

TRY FREE ASSOCIATION FOR YOURSELF

I suggest you do this when you are alone. You may not believe all that Freud suggests, but it is likely that some of what he claims is right – at least it could be. You are likely to say quite revealing things when free associating. Usually you monitor what you say. Think about removing that monitor. So, when you try it, I suggest you say things aloud, but alone.

It is quite difficult. You think at first that you are thinking nothing. Then you start thinking about free association. You might need to relax and let your mind wander a bit first.

You can see how difficult this is to do. Imagine letting yourself go with someone you don't know very well. It would not have been easy for Freud's clients. Some might have started to say what he wanted to hear, or what they thought he wanted to hear.

Dream analysis and analysis of symbols

Freud used dream analysis. Later in this chapter you can read about the case study of Hans, where dream analysis was used in understanding the problems of Hans. Freud thought that dreams were the way into the unconscious, when the waking mind was monitoring less. There was the problem of making the thoughts conscious. If in your dreams you make thoughts conscious you would wake up. So dreams may give a clue about unconscious wishes, but they are revealed through **symbols** rather than directly. This is to protect our sleep.

Everyone should really have their own symbols, because each dream should be a revealing of each individual's unconscious wishes and urges. However, Freud came to believe that there were some symbols that were universal. They are nearly always sexual in imagery. Lots of things can be a penis, for example. However, you need to understand the dream in the context of that person's experiences in order to understand the dream fully, which is why you should not attempt quick dream analysis based on common symbols.

For Freud there is the **manifest content** of a dream, which is what the person will tell us the dream is about. The defence mechanisms have censored the dream, and the manifest content seems harmless. Then there is the **latent content**. This is what the dream is 'really' about, and the content comes from the unconscious. It needs interpretation.

Evaluation

- There are other explanations for why we dream, and they could be used to argue with Freud's ideas about dreaming. Perhaps we dream to restore brain functions, or perhaps we go through the day's thoughts that are left as neurotransmitters in our brains. You need to relate this argument to the material given in Chapter 6, about the physiological approach. Other explanations do seem to make sense. Often when we dream we can explain the dream quite well by going through what happened the day before. Activity 3 asks you to review your dreams.

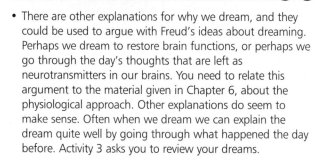

ACTIVITY 3

REVIEW SOME DREAMS – CAN THEY BE EXPLAINED BY THE PREVIOUS DAY'S ACTIVITIES?

Many argue that their dreams are easily explained and don't seem to reveal unconscious wishes. However, many others say that their dreams do recur and do seem to be symbolic. People do dream about falling down stairs, or about symbols that could represent the penis.

If you are in a group this might work better. I am not suggesting you start analysing your dreams. Firstly, remember from Chapter 6 (if you have studied it) that not everyone remembers their dreams. So some of you cannot take part in this activity. Then, remember that there are many explanations for dreams. Also you need to protect yourself at this stage. Avoid telling the whole class about a dream that could say things about yourself you would rather keep private. I am sure you will know the dreams to avoid telling!

Now try writing down a recent dream. Can you explain it by thinking about what you did the day before – for example, by thinking of a film you watched? I am sure many dreams can be explained in this way.

> Key Skill C3.1a – again, this activity makes a good group discussion. Remember to keep evidence for your portfolio.

So we are saying that many dreams can be explained by looking at what happened the day before. However, you notice that I want to warn you about 'those other' dreams. If you asked people in the street (we probably should not do this) whether they think dreams are symbolic and represent hidden desires I think they would say that they are. We do seem to accept this nature of dreams. The fact that so many people are interested and do think this suggests to me that there is something in it.

There are other problems with dream analysis, besides saying that there are other explanations for why we dream. One important problem is the difficulty of interpretation. If the manifest content of the dream involves symbols where the meaning is hidden, you could say that almost any interpretation could be used. It is not difficult to look for sexual imagery in dreams. Some imagery is clear enough. You might dream of being lost in a forest, and this could symbolise you feeling lost in your self. Dreaming about a journey may mean we feel we have reached a staging post in our lives. If we are a passenger in a speeding car, then this might mean we have lost control over our own life. The house is usually said to represent our selves. The kitchen might be where we work, and the bedroom scenes might be about more intimate things. Water can be about life, and if we dream about being 'out of our depth' this might mean that we have lost control of our life.

Not all of the above come from Freud's views, as some would relate to Jung's ideas. However, these are examples of using dreams as symbols and analysing them accordingly. This is an interesting area, and for your interest I have listed some ideas that go with colours. However, you should note that dream analysis as used by the psychoanalyst involves knowing the client and all the background. A quick analysis of one dream probably will not do.

An outline of what colours in dreams might mean – not to be taken too seriously!

White – purity and innocence. However, it can represent a colourless drab life.

Black – death and a period of mourning. However, it can represent receptivity and motherliness.

Red – physical energy and strength. It can mean renewed vigour or warn against danger.

Orange – means looking at social relationships. It can also mean adding cheerfulness.

Yellow – denotes clear thinking and intellectual reflection. It can also mean cowardice.

Green – a relaxing colour meaning 'take more time off'. It can also mean jealousy.

Blue – means protection (as from the sky) and restored hope. It can also mean coldness.

Indigo – looks at instinct and intuition.

Violet – is the colour nearest to heaven and means things spiritual.

Brown – devotion to duty. It can also represent depression.

Gold – sunshine and happiness.

Symbols in literature

Analysis of symbols in literature can also be done. Later in this chapter an explanation of the fairytale *Snow White and the Seven Dwarfs* is given. This demonstrates how **psychodynamic** concepts are often used in literature to understand what is being said. There are many examples of this sort of analysis, including an analysis of parts of the Bible. The way psychodynamic concepts can be used to explain tales in literature can be taken as evidence for these concepts being a good explanation. Freud looked at Shakespeare's *Hamlet* and Jones (1954) elaborated on Freud's analysis. One of the important points of the play is Hamlet's decision to wait so long before he finally avenges his father's death. This delay eventually causes Hamlet's death, and the death of many of the others in the play. Hamlet's problem is that he has to kill a man who has killed his father and married his mother. This is, according to the Oedipus complex, what Hamlet himself unconsciously wishes to do. Freud and Jones thought that the audience was gripped by the play, because they too had this unconscious wish and it uncovered conflicts within the members of the audience.

Later in the chapter you will read more about the Oedipus complex. Freud used literature to help when drawing up his 'grand' theory. It is worth very briefly outlining the Oedipus complex here, as analysis of symbols in literature usually centres on this. When describing the Oedipus complex, Freud is talking about boys; however, he does extend his ideas to include girls too, and he does this by outlining the **Electra complex**.

There is a Greek legend about Oedipus. Oedipus kills his father Laius and marries his mother Jocasta, although he didn't know at the time that she was his mother. Freud was interested in the way the story still gripped audiences as it had so many years ago. Freud thought that a plot that could stand the test of time must have some underlying appeal, and must be representing something people could relate to. He suggested that boys in the phallic stage (any time around the age of five years) developed sexual feelings for their mother and jealousy of their father. They had this wish to kill their father, although this led to guilt. To resolve this guilt and to solve the problem of the feelings for the mother, the boy identifies with (becomes) the father. In this way the boy learns masculine behaviour and a moral code – by taking on the views of his father. There is a similar conflict for girls, called the Electra complex.

Since, according to Freud, everyone in the audience would have had these feelings – the desire to kill one parent and so on – they would identify with Oedipus. They would be horrified when watching the play, because their fantasy is fulfilled by Oedipus. Most boys learn to repress the wish to kill their father and marry their mother. So in adulthood a person would recoil from such an idea. Masson (1985) suggests that the force of the horror would match the strength of the repression.

Freud was also fascinated by Shakespeare's Hamlet. Hamlet should have taken revenge on the man who killed Hamlet's father and married Hamlet's mother. He was unable to do so, and so turned against himself. Freud seemed to have thought that it was Shakespeare's own unconscious motives (to kill his father and marry his mother) that were found in Hamlet's dilemma (Brill, 1983). Freud thought it was interesting that the Greeks acted out their fantasies in stories like that of Oedipus. However, later writers suppressed these desires, as Shakespeare showed in Hamlet – who could not carry out the killing of the person who had done what Hamlet (according to Freud) unconsciously wished to do himself. The audience only learn of the problem for Hamlet because of what Hamlet will not do. However, in *Oedipus* the plot is clear.

Freud thought that unconscious wishes and motives led to creativity as well as to neuroses, so it is not surprising that symbols in literature are thought to be an important method of uncovering unconscious thoughts and wishes. Poets allow themselves to freely associate and poetry is likely to demonstrate the preoccupations of people.

It is interesting that Freud's analysis of Oedipus and of Hamlet helped to lead him to the conclusion that everyone goes through this Oedipus complex (a bit different for girls, but similar enough). The important point is that such plots are found fascinating by people, and this fascination (and revulsion) leads Freud to conclude that it uncovers some repression in us. Freudians used literature to develop the theory, and then psychoanalysis was used (and is still used) when analysing literature.

Another example of Freud's use of literature and writers to back his theory is when he looked at Dostoevsky and suggested that Dostoevsky's epilepsy was a neurosis. Dostoevsky saw his father murdered, and Freud assumed the seizures then grew stronger (Dostoevsky was aged 18). Dostoevsky's guilt was because of his earlier wish to see his father dead (during the Oedipus complex). This guilt explains Dostoevsky's attitudes to God and his obsessive gambling. It also explains Dostoevsky's sympathy towards criminals.

An article on *Hamlet* has been written by Robert Silhol (1999) and can be found on the Internet (http://web/clas/utl/edu/ipsa/journal/articles/psyart1999/silhol01.htm). Silhol examines the play and its significance. Much of the argument covers more depth than you will need, although you might like to have a look for yourself. Some basic points are, however, outlined here. Silhol shows how the first and most basic question in the play is the question 'Who's there?' (asked by one of the soldiers). This is the question we all want answered, and only those undergoing psychoanalysis are likely to have it answered. A little later, when the soldiers are still talking, someone asks if the person there is Horatio, and the answer is 'A piece of him'. Silhol suggests that these first questions are about identity, and this is a central theme in the play. Silhol sees the fact that Hamlet's father is also called Hamlet as significant too. He suggests the play is about identity. When Hamlet is asking the ghost (the dead father) to speak (as others ask it to speak) it will not. Hamlet asks 'What may this mean?' and Silhol suggests this question is asking what our hallucinations and dreams mean, as well as our nightmares. He suggests that this is a question we all ask. The ghost will not speak to Horatio, because the ghost (Hamlet the father) will only speak to Hamlet alone. The ghost is the mirror or the parent and this has to do with identification, and how we identify with our same-sex parent (remember the Oedipus complex).

You may read more about the above issues, and the material is quite complex. The problem is that the analysis of symbols in literature involves interpretation – and a lot of it at that. I hope you have read enough here to realise a few points.

- The main part of Freudian theory that you will use in the analysis of literature is the Oedipus complex.
- Freud used literature and the grip of certain plots to show our underlying repressed wishes and desires.
- Repressing unconscious wishes and urges, usually focusing on our parents, but not always, is also an important focus when using psychoanalytic ideas to interpret literature.
- Some writers have written their work knowing about Freud's ideas, and sometimes believing in them. Therefore, it is possible that you could use psychoanalytic concepts in analysing literature when it was precisely these concepts that gave rise to the story.

Activity 4 asks you to choose a fairy story, or another short story. You can then try these sorts of analysis for yourself.

ACTIVITY 4

Choose a fairy story and try analysing it using some of the concepts used in the psychodynamic approach.

You may need to study more of this chapter before doing this activity. Later you will find a brief analysis of the story of Snow White.

Choose a different story and see if you can link in some of the concepts you will read about.

Focus on the Oedipus complex – see if the plot centres on the relationship between a parent and the child. Focus on unconscious desires – see if the plot revolves around dreams, fantasies or desires and if these are fulfilled, and at what cost.

If you are working in a group, this would make a good group exercise. You might not succeed in finding a story that exactly matches the concepts, but you should find you learn a lot by trying – and by discussing the issues.

Key Skill 3.1a – this activity would be the basis of a good group discussion.

Evaluation of analysis of symbols in literature as a method within the psychodynamic approach

Before Freud outlined his theory, writers would not have known about it, of course. Therefore, when Freud looked at Shakespeare's plays, or at Oedipus Rex, he was able to look at the plots and at what interested audiences, and draw conclusions from them.

However, once his views were known, many writers would have read about them. The idea of the Oedipus complex and of the importance of dreams became part of cultural knowledge. Writers might well have incorporated such ideas into their writing, but the problem is we cannot use their writing as evidence for the existence of the concepts. Those very concepts might have given rise to the ideas in their writing.

Freud's claim that the fascination of some plots stands the test of time, and, therefore, these plots have great underlying signifance for us, is an appealing one. There certainly does seem to be a revulsion felt for anyone who kills their father and marries their mother, even if this is done unknowingly. Freud looked at this revulsion and assumed it hid something of great relevance to us. He assumed that it was not straightfoward revulsion, as this would be short-lived and not so strong. The very strength of the feeling shows to Freud that it hides something in our unconscious. This something is the desire to do just what we are revolted by – kill our father and marry our mother (if we are male). His argument lacks evidence – however, we can understand it.

The problem is there is no evidence to be found in this sort of analysis of literature. It is interesting, and many plots that

interest audiences do involve ghosts, dreams, hallucinations, incestuous relationships and so on. However, this is not evidence for the existence of Freud's concepts. Also, after Freud's ideas were made known writers might well have incorporated them deliberately, so after that time the analysis of such literature (and finding examples of Freud's concepts) cannot be taken as evidence.

Case studies

Freud used clinical interviews, dream analysis, free association and slips of the tongue. He realised that analysis had to be of an individual, and had to be thorough. He therefore had to use case studies. He would not have considered collecting his data by questionnaire. His was not a theory that would look at people as all the same. He looked at people as individuals. Admittedly, he then used his findings to generate an overall theory that he claimed applied to everyone. However, in gathering the data he used in-depth studies of individuals. He gathered his data over a period of time, and recorded a great deal of information. Clinical interviews really have to lead to case studies if you want the required depth. One of Freud's case studies, the story of Hans, is outlined in quite a lot of detail later in this chapter, and a study of this one does show Freud's methods well.

Evaluation

- You could use the general evaluation of case studies (see Chapter 7). Case studies tend to be valid because they gather data immediately from the individual. They tend not to be reliable, because if you did them again, you would probably get different results. This is because an individual researcher does a case study, and another researcher might gather different data. Also the case study is at that moment in time, and people change over time, so you might not get the same information at another time.

- Freud's case studies are slightly different, however, because they do involve a lot of interpretation. They could be accused of lacking objectivity. Indeed this is a problem with case studies. They do rely on the interpretation of the researcher. Freud would claim that the interpretation was part of the method, but this does not fit with the usual methods found in psychology.

In-depth areas of study

Freud's theory

Freud's ideas have been outlined when discussing the basic assumptions of the psychodynamic approach, because his were the foundation ideas of the approach. Basically, recall that Freud thought that it is our unconscious, with the wishes and desires that we do not allow ourselves to know about, that guides our actions. He also thought that the first five years of life, where childhood sexual thoughts are of great importance, prepared us for our future. If we turn out to be neurotic and sexually perverse, then Freud thought this was because of problems in those first five years. Those are the problems that we repress in our unconscious. Closely linked to these ideas are Freud's ideas about the instincts.

The 'instincts'

Freud had studied human physiology. When he started looking at people's problems and seemed to be finding in his clients either sexual abuse when they were young or sexual fantasies, he thought that instincts were underlying the problems. It was thought that the basic 'instincts' (it is claimed that Freud's term is mistranslated as 'instincts') for humans were hunger, thirst, warmth and sexual drive. He considered that his clients were comfortable in terms of basic needs, so he thought that it must be the sexual drive that was causing them problems. Remember he was looking for a physiological cause for the problems.

However, the problems he was uncovering whilst listening to his patients were emotional and psychological ones. Even so, it did seem that there were problems that seemed to be linked to sexual matters, and these problems did seem to link to the time before the client was five years old. Once Freud had started to think in this way, it is possible that he found instances to support his thinking. At one stage he thought he was listening to stories of real sexual abuse, often by the father; however, later he came to think that he was listening to sexual fantasies. It has already been pointed out that people now (including Masson) think that he may well have been right to think that the abuse was real.

Once Freud was focusing on instincts, he had to look for an explanation for the sexual fantasies his clients seemed to have. So he claimed that young children do have sexual feelings, and if these are not fully resolved when the child is young the repression involved will cause problems for the adult. So the Oedipus complex was developed to explain the child's sexual feelings towards the opposite-sex parent, and then to explain the resolution of these feelings – by identifying with the same-sex parent.

If the child does not identify with the same-sex parent, and the sexual feelings towards the opposite-sex parent are not resolved, then these feelings become problems and are repressed in the unconscious. Note that Freud had more to say about boys, but I am interpreting the Oedipus complex as applying to girls also at the moment.

Actual energy sources

Freud needed some actual energy source for the child to keep these feelings repressed. For Freud there is an actual

unconscious and the repression takes up real energy. In 1915 Freud wrote about there being two primal instincts. The first of these is the self-preservation instinct, and the other is the sexual instinct. The ego represses the sexual instinct, and there is a struggle between the two.

Then, in 1920, he revised this idea, and he began to think about the death instinct. He saw instincts as drives. Drives motivate us to behave in certain ways, and Freud saw humans as motivated to satisfy urges and wishes. Urges and wishes put us in the state of arousal, and when they are satisfied arousal is reduced. Arousal is a physiological concept. Box 4 explains a bit about arousal.

Box 4

Physiological arousal

Our nervous system consists of the central nervous system (brain and spinal cord) and other systems. One of these is the autonomic nervous system, which is 'automatic' in the sense of not being consciously controlled. There are two parts to the **autonomic nervous system**. One of these parts is the sympathetic part. It prepares us for fight or flight. Some say it prepares us for fight, flight or frolic, and that might suit Freud's theory quite well. Frolic is probably not a word widely used these days, but it suggests dancing and larking about happily!

Humans probably developed the fight or flight response to react quickly to danger. Imagine you are a caveman (or cavewoman) and are faced with a man-eating (person-eating!) lion. You would survive well if you had an immediate fight or flight response. Someone else nearby who did not have this response might well be eaten. So you and your genes survive, and you reproduce. Your genes with their good fight or flight response survive. It seems that we have inherited this fight or flight response, and it is very useful.

The other part of the autonomic nervous system is the parasympathetic part. If you the caveman had not had the ability to calm your fight or flight response down, you would have carried on using up important blood sugar, and your heart would have carried on its quick beat. Eventually your immune system would have given up, since you could not have kept up that level of energy. So you would only have survived if you also had the parasympathetic bit that put everything back to normal. (Note that you need to allow your body to go back to normal. If you maintain a fight or flight response, that is what is called stress.) Arousal is the cutting in of this fight or flight response. It can actually be pleasurable, and people visit places like Alton Towers just to experience it.

Freud thought that one of our drives was to reduce arousal. So he worked out that one way to reach this state of non-arousal was death. He quickly added 'death' as another of the instincts. So for Freud there are two main instincts – the instinct for life and the instinct for death.

'Eros' was Freud's term for the life instincts, which were the self-preservation and sexual instincts. 'Thanatos' was Freud's term for the death instinct. Thanatos provides the energy for the ego to repress the sexual wishes, and Eros provides the energy to prevent the instinct that leads to death. Freud thought that aggression was a good thing, because the death instinct could be sidetracked onto more positive drives like sport and anything aggressive.

The importance of dreams

Freud is famous for saying that dreams are 'the royal road to the unconscious'. It has already been explained how the unconscious holds our repressed urges and desires. It is almost impossible to know what these are as they cannot, by definition, become conscious. So we have to trick ourselves into revealing what is in our unconscious. One way of doing this is to study our dreams. Some of this has been outlined when looking at Freud's methods earlier.

Evaluation

- The topic of sleep is studied in Chapter 6, and when you have studied both Chapter 6 and this chapter, you might like to consider how different Freud's idea about what dreams are is from that of other theorists. The differences should show you clearly how different the approaches are. When looking at analysing dreams, you ought to remember that there are many other explanations of why we dream, and that not all of them think that the content of a dream tells you something about your innermost thoughts and desires.

- However, most people are attracted to the idea that our dreams have meaning. You could argue that if individuals are so willing to accept that their dreams have meaning, then it might indeed be true. Why would we go along with such a claim if we did not think it was true?

Self-test 2

1 There are three types of 'consciousness', mentioned earlier when explaining the basic assumptions of the psychodynamic approach. What is the third besides the conscious and the unconscious?

2 It was said that the unconscious is dynamic – what does 'dynamic' mean in this context?

3 Why would the analysis of dreams be useful?

I think you will have answered why we might analyse dreams. The third type of consciousness is the preconscious. 'Dynamic' means active, in the sense that the urges are not simply put into the dungeon that is the unconscious, but are actively trying to escape. During waking moments, the ego is on guard and is busy repressing our unconscious desires. However, during sleep, there is less monitoring, and the thoughts can find a way out.

The repressed thoughts cannot completely reveal themselves, or we would wake up. So to protect sleep, the repressed desires find a way to show themselves, and to fulfil themselves, but they are disguised. For Freud every dream is a wish fulfilment. So if we can understand these hidden messages, then we can turn a light on our desires, make them conscious, and so release ourselves from them, so to speak.

Therefore, analysis is needed, and psychoanalysts do analyse the dreams of their patients to try to uncover the cause of their problems. Note that Freud did not think that only those with problems (neurotics) needed their dreams analysed to uncover their unconscious wishes. He thought that this applied to all of us.

Free association was the method Freud used to analyse dreams. The clients use free association when considering their dreams, and hope to find out what the dream 'means'. It was later that Freud came to think that there were universal symbols in dreams. He thought that certain symbols meant the same for every dreamer. For example, walking up a flight of stairs symbolises sexual intercourse. Psychoanalysis was also applied to myths, legends and stories, examining the symbols used in the same way as outlined here. It was not far to go then to say that everything is not what it appears to be. Slips of the tongue were never just that. For Freud they always had meaning. Forgetting was not just forgetting, but had to be motivated, and to have meaning.

Evaluation

- One important point about Freud's views, no matter whether you criticise them or not, is that they led to our acceptance of sexuality as important. This is hard to grasp now, but you need to remember the attitude to sexual matters at the time. It occurs to me, however, that you might well be wondering even now whether all this talk about sex is a suitable topic to put into an AS textbook. Freud would probably have smiled at this – perhaps we do repress our feelings, and this is his point. If we were discussing art or philosophy, this would probably be considered to be more suitable. Freud discussed this sort of sublimation. Sublimation is when we put our feelings about one thing onto something else. So we may have a lot of sexual energy we cannot admit to, so we put all this energy into art appreciation.

Psychoanalysis and science

One of the biggest criticisms of Freud's ideas is that they are not testable. In the world of science ideas are tested against reality. The problem with Freud's idea of reality – including the unconscious and the meaning of dreams – is that it is not testable. His concepts are not measurable.

To be scientific, a theory must be falsifiable. This means it must be possible to test it in such a way that if it was not true you could find out. However, Freud's ideas mean that almost anything can be interpreted using his concepts. One of his case studies demonstrates this quite well, and is briefly outlined in Box 5.

Box 5

The case of little Hans

One of Freud's case studies – which is outlined in more detail later in the chapter – concerns a young boy called Hans. To be precise, Freud actually spoke to Hans's father, not to the boy himself. You can read about the study in more depth later, but basically Hans was afraid of horses.

When Hans's father describes the boy's fear, he describes a fear of being bitten by a white horse. The father and Freud are both involved in analysing the boy's anxieties. They decide that the horse represents the father, and Hans is really afraid of the father. However, there is a story about Hans's mother taking Hans out one day. There is an accident and a horse drawing a heavy bus falls over. Hans thinks the horse is dead. Freud thinks the real issue is that Hans wishes the father to be dead, so that Hans can take his father's place with the mother.

There is an alternative explanation. If you have studied Chapter 4 you will have learnt about classical conditioning. You can probably see that the unconditioned stimulus is the noise or startle of the accident that gave a fear response. The horse is the conditioned stimulus, and gives a fear response. Actually, Hans is afraid of loaded carts and so on as well, so he probably generalised his fear to include loaded carts drawn by horses, as well as buses.

The terms used here are explained in Chapter 4, but hopefully the meaning is clear. Hans developed a phobia about horses because he experienced a frightening incident involving a horse.

A problem with case studies and interpretation is that there is often more than one explanation.

When you read the case study you might well think that some of the explanations are a little far-fetched. There is a dream about two giraffes, where Hans dreams one of the giraffes is crumpled and Hans (in his dream) sits on it. The father interprets this dream by saying that the two giraffes represent the mother and father, and that the dream is of the bedroom scene. You can probably work out for yourself what the crumpled giraffe means, and this is explained in more detail later. This is quite a leap of faith, and you can see why people say that Freud's concepts can explain most things.

Freud's model of the personality – the id, the ego and the superego

Freud's view of the personality links to his basic claim that our unconscious urges are 'dynamic' in that they are trying to reach our consciousness. Freud thought we had three conflicting tendencies that make up our personality. We have three different reactions, and he gave these 'names' but they are not real 'things'.

The **id** is the primitive bit, and is the basic part of our make up. Biological urges are what drive us, and these were discussed earlier. The id works on the **pleasure principle**, and its aim is to get us gratification and satisfaction. The id does not distinguish between reality and fantasy, or between wishing something and having something. It is involved in a blind pursuit of pleasure now. It is the 'I must have' part of our personality. The baby is all id and no reason.

The **ego** is where reality sets in. The baby soon learns that in reality not all its desires are immediately gratified. The infant has to cry to get fed, and the ego is the part that tries to work out how to satisfy the id. Sometimes we have to wait, for example. The ego obeys the **reality principle**. When the ego learns to satisfy the id, then there is a whole working system, and this is the self. At this point there is an 'I' not just an 'it'. 'Ego' means 'I' in Latin. 'Id' means 'it'.

The **superego** develops later. The young child, up to at least three years old, has the ego serving the id. Soon, however, the ego also has to listen to the superego. The superego develops at around four years old. The superego gives us our morals. It is the 'you can't have' part of us. The ego is between the id ('I want …') and the superego ('you can't have …'). The superego gets its moral code from society and parents, and can administer punishment. The small child may even smack its own hand for doing something wrong. The superego gives us guilt too. In Latin superego means 'above I'.

Problems can start because if the ego obeys the superego, then it has to do something about the id's demands. This can lead to **repression**, as the ego represses the demands of the id (or the superego).

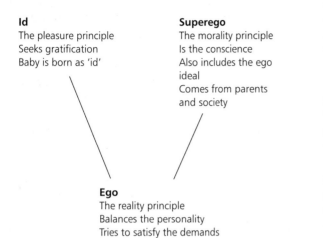

Figure 5.1
Freud's model of the personality

Defence mechanisms

The **defence mechanism** of repression has already been explained. Also, sublimation has been mentioned. The ego has to resort to defence mechanisms in its job of keeping the peace between the demands of the id and the orders of the superego. Don't think of the id, the ego and the superego as existing. Think of the id being biological demands, the ego being the rational self, and the superego being the controlling rules of society. The individual is caught between these often-conflicting orders, and so has to resort to things like defence mechanisms in order to avoid stress.

Repression is often not enough. The ego might try to ignore the urges and not allow them through into the preconscious or the conscious, but it needs other defence mechanisms.

Displacement

Displacement is another defence mechanism. Repressed urges that break through show themselves as something different. They cannot be recognised for what they are, otherwise the ego would not be able to keep the peace between our biological urges and our cultural demands. Displaced aggression is an example. You can be angry, then turn round and kick the cat (either literally or figuratively). Recall the discussion on prejudice in Chapter 2. It was argued that scapegoating was one symptom of prejudice. In times of problems, cultures turn against minority groups and blame them for the problems. This is a form of displacement.

Reaction formation

In **reaction formation**, the urge that is leaking out of the unconscious because it is not successfully repressed is seen as the opposite of the 'truth'. If a boy shows his brother great love and affection, this could show strong jealousy and feelings of hatred. If the brother feels overcome by the feelings and they seem too much, then they might not be real, and might be an example of reaction formation. It seems that Freud's views can explain anything. Even strong feelings can mean the opposite. You might like to think of a friend (or yourself) who has said she or he hates someone. It is often not long before they are going out together.

Rationalisation

Rationalisation means interpreting feelings in a different way that makes the individual look good. So a father might say he is beating his son 'for his own good'. When being 'dumped' we tend to say we did not like the person anyway. This is an example of rationalisation.

Projection

Another defence mechanism is **projection**. Here the feelings are clear enough, for example, hatred and love. However, the person receiving the emotion is the wrong person. The emotion is projected onto someone else. You might say you hate someone, and you mean you hate someone else. Again, you can see that Freud can explain anything. Even if you protest about something, he can argue that this shows defence mechanisms.

Isolation

Isolation is a further defence mechanism. You can recall detail and allow memories through from your unconscious, but you isolate yourself as regards the emotions that go with them. So if someone is relating some horrifying experience and seems to be calm about it, they may be using isolation as a defence mechanism.

Defence mechanisms are keeping urges in the unconscious and this can cause neuroses. Freud thought that these feelings needed to be released into the consciousness, where they could be understood. Catharsis would take place as the emotions are released. So, for Freud, defence mechanisms are bad. Activity 5 asks you to make your own list of these defence mechanisms with an example each, to help in your revision.

ACTIVITY 5

Make a list of some defence mechanisms and give an example.

This would make a good group activity. List the defence mechanisms. Then discuss them, if you are in a group. You need to have a clear list, a brief definition and then a real-life example that you come up with by group discussion. If you have your own examples, you will understand better. If you are in a class where you can divide into small groups, you should feed back your ideas to the other groups. Then you should have a good list with some good examples, and better understanding.

Key Skill C3.1a – this is a useful group discussion where you can find evidence for this key skill

Psychosexual stages of development

So far we have looked at Freud's ideas of:
- the instincts and how sexual urges are of great importance
- unconscious urges guiding our behaviour
- dream analysis and ways of reaching the unconscious
- three parts of our personality shaping our self
- defence mechanisms where the ego tries to protect us from conflict between the id and the superego, by keeping our urges in the unconscious.

All the above takes place during the child's development, and the first five years are very important. Freud thought there were **critical periods** during the child's development when certain things happened, and these either led to successful development or led to problems.

The child starts life as the 'id' seeking pleasure. Freud concentrated on areas he thought gave pleasure to children as they developed, and these became the focus of his stages. He used data gathered from his case studies to form his theory. The child moves through the stages partly as it biologically matures, and partly through the reaction of those around it. The stages are the oral stage, the anal stage, the phallic stage, the latent stage and the genital stage.

Fixation

Freud thought many adult problems could be caused by problems in passing through these stages. Each stage involves frustrations and these may lead to future problems. One reaction to frustration is **fixation**. Fixation means holding on to an earlier stage of pleasure when it should have been passed through. Older children may still suck their thumbs, for example.

Reaction formation

Instead of fixation and clinging to the stage, the child may use reaction formation to display the behaviour that is the opposite of what it wants to do. For example, a child may become constipated because of undue anxiety over relaxing the bowels. It is not allowed to relax the bowels whenever it wants to, and so becomes constipated.

The oral stage is the first stage of development. This would last from birth to about two years old. The pleasure is centred on the mouth. If someone is fixated at the oral stage, then he or she develops the oral character. In later relationships, these people will be passive and dependent, just as they were when being fed by their mothers.

The anal stage is the second stage of development, when the pleasure is centred on the anus. This stage occurs between two and three years of age. The anal character (fixated at this stage) develops his or her character from conflicts and the potty-training stage. This person may become obsessively clean, because the reaction formation as in not relaxing the bowels becomes transferred onto cleanliness in the home. Alternatively, the anal character can be obstinate, as when holding back when sitting on the potty. An anal character can also be mean with money, which is another form of holding back. This person would hoard possessions and be obsessed with their rights (especially ownership). The anal character is orderly, mean and stubborn.

The phallic stage is the third stage of development, and starts at between four and five years of age. This is the stage that Freud thought was the most important. It is in this stage that the Oedipus complex is found. The family triangle of mother, father and child brings with it jealousies and strong feelings. During the phallic stage these feelings have to be worked through. By working them through, the child develops its understanding of morality and gender. It learns about gender behaviour by identifying with the same-sex parent, in other words it 'becomes' the same-sex parent, and so acts out the 'appropriate' gender role. It learns about morality also through identification. It is at this stage that the superego develops, bringing the notion of an ego ideal (the child learns what it is supposed to be like) and a conscience (it learns what society and parents expect).

Oedipus was a mythical king who killed his father and married his mother. Freud thought this drama was worked through in all families – for boys there was the wish to kill the father and marry the mother.

In the phallic stage the boy becomes interested in his penis, and his urges become focused on his mother as the obvious available female. However, the boy has a rival – his father. The boy wants his father out of the way. The son starts to be afraid of his father, because he somehow thinks the father knows about this wish (for the father to go away). The boy starts to think he will be punished, and he thinks of a fitting punishment – castration. So the son develops castration anxiety. He needs a defence mechanism and instead of thinking he hates his father, he thinks that his father hates him. Eventually the father is completely hated and feared. To resolve these very strong feelings, the boy solves the problem and identifies with ('becomes') the father.

In the girl, there is no Oedipus complex, but instead there is what is called the **Electra complex**. This is like the Oedipus complex, but the girl focuses on the father, hates the mother, and then identifies with the mother. The girl does not focus on the penis and turn to the mother for satisfaction, as the boy does. So the girl's preoccupation with her father is explained using the idea of penis envy. The girl feels unworthy, and thinks of the mother as unworthy too. She focuses on her father, who does have a penis, and she thinks he can help her to get a penis substitute, which seems to be a child. (This is a bit confusing.) There is a lot of criticism of this part of Freud's theory as there seems to be no good reason why the girl would want a penis, although it might be understandable to think she wanted male power.

The latent stage is the fourth stage. In sexual terms there is little development. Boys play with boys, and girls play with girls. Freud is often criticised for thinking that there is no development between the phallic stage (around five years of age) and the **genital stage** (at puberty).

The genital stage is the fifth stage. If there are no fixations, and all the stages have been successfully resolved without frustrations, then at this stage the child is strongly attracted to someone of the opposite sex. However, those strong feelings of the phallic stage mean that, for example, a boy is attracted to a female but feels all the old anxieties associated with the Oedipus complex. So adolescence is an anxious time. If the Oedipus complex has been resolved, then the boy will successfully accept himself as male, and the girl will accept herself as female.

An analysis of a fairy tale – to show psychoanalysis at work

Brown (1940) analysed Snow White in psychoanalytic terms. You might like to try this, and Activity 6 suggests you do the analysis yourself.

ACTIVITY 6

ANALYSE SNOW WHITE USING PSYCHOANALYTIC PRINCIPLES

Snow White is persecuted by her stepmother, who is jealous of Snow White's beauty and

---

tries to have her killed. Snow White goes to live with the seven dwarfs, but is found by her stepmother. Her stepmother tries to kill her with a poisoned apple, but instead of dying Snow White falls asleep for seven years. The dwarfs leave her in a coffin for this time. Then a handsome prince finds her, and opens the casket with a sword – they live happily ever after.

Key Skill C3.1a – this would make a good group discussion.

You might have done well in analysing the Snow White story if you used the idea of the Oedipus complex. Snow White is jealous of her stepmother, and projects her hatred onto the stepmother. She comes to fear her stepmother. The erotic feelings are then hidden in the unconscious, and during the latency period (which lasts seven years) there is calm. Then along comes the prince ready for the genital stage. You can interpret the opening of the coffin with the sword in any way you wish!

Evaluation

• Some evaluation of Freud's theory has already been offered. Activity 7 asks you to offer some criticisms yourself.

ACTIVITY 7

EVALUATE FREUD'S THEORY

Make a list of points in favour and points against what Freud claims about development. Even if you do not agree with what he claims, you should be able to find plus and minus points. Some of these have already been made. You need to look at both strengths and weaknesses when evaluating.

Key Skill C3.1a – this task would be a good group activity. You could widen this task. You could research Freud in other texts and using the Internet. Then you could gather information from various sources. You could then do a presentation and include an evaluation of Freud. The task could be used as evidence for more than one communication key skill.

You probably found quite a few points in evaluation.

Strengths of Freud's theory	Weaknesses of Freud's theory
Focuses on the individual's own experiences	Explains everything after the event
Allows the individual to talk freely	Does not allow prediction (see below)
Accepts what might be the unacceptable (e.g. the importance of sexual matters)	Analyst is not objective and interprets too much
	Biological factors over-emphasised, should be social
Forces society to focus on the 'unacceptable'	He never studied children directly
Provides a framework for explaining neuroses	He based a whole theory on a few case studies
	His clients were not a random sample

The above table outlines some evaluative points that you can hopefully expand because they have already been discussed. Two points need perhaps to be further discussed.

The criticism that there is no predictive power in Freud's theory is an important one. A theory really needs to tell us what will happen, so perhaps we can avoid problems. Freud's theory is good for explaining things retrospectively (after the event). However, he can either say that when I say I hate my mother it means I think she hates me, or he can say that I have said I hate my mother, and that supports the idea of the Electra complex. The theory can explain most things. Anything I dream about can be interpreted as a symbol, for example.

Also, Freud's theory is criticised by some psychoanalysts who are called neo-Freudians. This is because they have tended now to focus on psychosocial stages, and not psychosexual ones. Some say that Freud laid too much emphasis on the biological, including the focus of his psychosexual stages. The focus should be on social factors, and Erikson's theory (see below) shows what this emphasis on social factors means. Sexual matters are important, but only because they are socially, not biologically, important.

Some more evidence in criticism of Freud

Examining the oral and anal characters
Zigler and Child (1972) could find no evidence that the way the infant is fed affects its later personality, so they find no evidence for the oral character.

Fisher and Greenberg (1977) do find that neatness, obstinacy and meanness do tend to go together. Therefore, there may be an anal character. Activity 8 suggests you try a questionnaire based around these factors.

ACTIVITY 8

A QUESTIONNAIRE TO SEE IF NEATNESS, OBSTINACY AND MEANNESS GO TOGETHER

I don't think you can go to people and ask about their potty training. However, you could ask carefully about their personality. You could ask some simple questions about their neatness, for example. You could generate statements about 'neat or messy bedrooms', for example. Then you could ask about their stubbornness, again generating statements about what they would do in certain situations. Finally, some questions about savings or spending would be quite straightforward.

From Freud's views, your hypothesis is that there is a meaningful correlation in that the neater you are, the more obstinate you are. A further hypothesis might be that the more obstinate you are the meaner you are.

You need to obtain a 'neatness' score, an 'obstinacy' score and a 'meanness' score, so when you generate your statements, use the Likert scale. This means scoring 5, 4, 3, 2, 1 according to strongly agree, agree, neither agree nor disagree and so on. Read about the method in Chapter 7 if you need to know more.

When Fisher and Greenberg did their study they asked mothers to complete a questionnaire and they found that if the participant was mean and so on, so was the mother. They did not always ask people to rate their own traits, they also asked their friends to rate them, so their study is not exactly like the one suggested above.

Beloff (1957), however, compared the age that children were toilet trained with their meanness, obstinacy and neatness and found no pattern. So Beloff's findings do not support Freud's views.

Brazelton (1962) suggests that leaving toilet training until later does tend to make for less bedwetting, so you might conclude that it makes the child less anxious. This does support Freud's views. However, there seem to be no long-term effects from different toilet-training schedules, according to Orlansky (1949). Cohen (1953) looked at different cultures and found no relationship between toilet training and economic competition, so there seems little evidence that toilet-training practices affect later personality, as Freud claimed.

The main finding that supports Freud is that the cluster of traits go together, and a child with such traits (meanness, obstinacy and neatness) tends to have a mother with those traits. This, however, can be explained by looking at the way values are passed down from parent to child. We don't need Freud's theory to explain this. Social learning theory (see Chapter 4) underlines how we model on our parents and those around us.

Examining the Oedipus complex

According to Freud, the Oedipus complex should be found in all cultures. Malinowski (1927), however, pointed out that the Trobriand Islanders brought children up very differently, but did not have problems by doing so. For the Trobriand Islanders the biological father is not the head of the household. He plays with the children but has no authority over them. The 'father' role is played by the mother's brother. According to Freud the biological father should still be seen as the rival for the mother's affections. However, there was no evidence of this amongst the Trobriand Islanders. However, there was some hostility towards the uncle, who played the disciplinary role. In their myths, the Islanders have the mother's brother as the villain, not the wicked father. So, although some of this supports Freud's ideas, the crucial difference is that it is the authority figure that is hated, and not the biological father.

Examining the importance of dreams

It does seem as though we dream about things that bother us. If we are anxious about something, it will appear in our dreams, and is often in a disguised form. You can probably think of examples yourself. Breger et al (1971) examined dreams, and gave the example of someone awaiting surgery. They might well dream about falling off bridges or about machines that need repair.

However, this is not the same as saying that our dream content is wish fulfilment and releases repressed desires. Dement and Wolpert (1958) monitored participants who went to sleep thirsty. They did not dream of drinking, but could have obtained gratification in this way. This goes against Freud's claims.

Hall (1953) argues that dreams do tell us about our desires and wishes, but these are not censored as Freud claims. They are being expressed in the dream. In some ways these ideas support Freud's, but they go against his central argument about the unconscious.

Evaluation using laboratory studies

Researchers have tried to test Freud's ideas. One way is to ask a participant to respond to words. If the response is slow, and there is anxiety produced (which can be measured using GSR – galvanic skin response – to look at physical responses), then we can assume that it is an 'emotional' word for the participant. You could argue that if the emotional words are more difficult to recall than other words, this is evidence of repression. Link this argument to the material on motivated forgetting given in Chapter 1.

I would suggest you did this sort of study as a piece of coursework, but it means you have to show people 'emotional' words and that might be unethical.

It is probably true to say that many accept the idea of motivated forgetting. However, this does not mean that Freud's whole explanation of such forgetting is accepted.

Freud's contributions

There is little doubt that Freud contributed a great deal to our understanding of neuroses. You may not accept everything that has been said so far; however, we do now investigate such topics as neurotic symptoms, family relationships, personality patterns, slips of the tongue, word association and dreams. We also tend to accept that adult problems can come from early upbringing, and that dysfunctional families can be a problem.

Erikson's theory

Erik Erikson was a student of Freud and developed his own theory, this time emphasising psychosocial developmental stages, rather than psychosexual ones. Erikson died in 1994. He used psychoanalysis, but emphasised a more social influence on development. He used other methods too, including comparing different cultures, and looking at famous figures (called psychohistories).

Identity

Erikson agreed with Freud about the importance of early childhood, and he accepted the importance of unconscious drives. He also accepted the idea of an ego trying to balance the demands of an id with the conscience of a superego. He thought our main goal in life was to establish an identity. For Erikson, identity meant having a clear, balanced picture of oneself as an individual within a social framework. One of the differences between Erikson and Freud was that Freud tended to ignore cultural pressures, whereas Erikson emphasises the cultural aspect of development.

The epigenetic principle

Our development follows a genetic plan. However, it is not simply a biologically driven development. Part of the genetic plan involves the social and cultural context. There is an **epigenetic** pathway along which we move, and this comes from our genetic structure. However, cultures are structured to help us along this pathway, and should not be ignored when trying to understand the development of our personality (or identity). We need to learn the social rules to help us develop, and society is structured to help us to do this.

Each stage comes from a biological need or an epigenetic principle, which has to take account of cultural expectations too. The problems of the stage can either be resolved well or not. If properly resolved, the individual moves on in a healthy state to the next stage. If there is the 'wrong' outcome, there might be problems for the individual later. Erikson did not believe we had to completely resolve any problems, but thought that the more positive outcome should be the most dominant one.

Crises

Erikson suggested that we have some main tasks to complete, and these tasks are listed in the eight stages he proposes. We have to learn trust, autonomy, initiative, industry, identity, intimacy, generativity and integrity. He called these tasks 'crises' because of their importance, and because they represent a conflict.

Erikson thinks there are eight stages of development. These are sometimes called the 'Eight Stages of Man'. His views are important because his is a life-span approach, which means that he is interested in the whole of our development – from babyhood to old age. Most psychologists looking at development had previously stopped when adulthood was reached. Neither Freud nor Piaget researched development after adulthood was reached. Now there is much more interest in life-span approaches, and this is to an extent thanks to Erikson. At each of his stages there is conflict that we must resolve.

We resolve these conflicts and in doing so we learn new skills and are able to develop as social beings. However, the new skills bring new conflicts for us to resolve.

These stages are outlined below.
- Trust v. mistrust – infants learn to trust those who care for them, or learn to mistrust them
- Autonomy v. shame and doubt – children gain **autonomy** and control over themselves, or they become uncertain
- Initiative v. guilt – children learn to plan their own activities, or they become guilty about trying for independence
- Industry v. inferiority – children learn to be competent in their activities, or feel inferior
- Identity v. role confusion – adolescents get a personal identity in a social group or they are confused
- Intimacy v. isolation – young adults find an intimate companion or are lonely
- Generativity v. stagnation – adults are productive at work and raising the next generation or they stagnate
- Integrity v. despair – people see their lives as meaningful or they despair of lack of achievement

Trust v. mistrust

We can either learn to trust or not. This stage covers the first year, when the baby becomes attached (or not) to its caregiver. The baby learns trust, in that someone will come when it cries, and also keeps some mistrust. When the baby learns to trust its caregiver, it can move on to the second stage. This stage is like Freud's oral stage. The infant relies completely on the caregiver, and needs to be responded to in a positive manner. Then it can develop feelings of trust. This stage occurs in early infancy, and the infant is what it is given. It learns hope.

Autonomy v. shame and doubt

This is the second stage, and corresponds to the anal stage in Freud's theory. Self-control is developed, and this includes self-control over the bladder and bowel. The child learns some independence, based on its trust of its caregiver. This stage occurs in late infancy, and the child is what it wants to be. It develops a will of its own.

Initiative v. guilt

Initiative or guilt is the third stage and is Freud's phallic stage. The Oedipus or Electra complex is to be resolved and with it the feelings of guilt. The child learns to initiate its own actions. This stage occurs in early childhood and the child is what it imagines it can be. It develops purpose.

Industry v. inferiority

This is the fourth stage and goes with Freud's latency period. The child learns things, and interacts with peers. It sees itself as competent and moves on, or it sees itself as inferior and problems develop. This stage occurs in middle childhood, and the child is what it learns. It develops competence.

Identity v. role confusion

The next stage is to develop a sense of identity. This links to Freud's genital period. Freud thought there was a resolution of sexual conflicts, whereas Erikson thought the formation of a stable identity was important. Society comes to be seen as moral and just, and society must recognise the value of the adolescent. Without mutual recognition the adolescent can have a crisis. This stage occurs in adolescence, and the person is who they define themselves to be. They learn loyalty.

Intimacy v. isolation

This is the first of the adult stages, and the young adult gets the chance to form an intimate relationship with someone of the opposite sex. There will be feelings of closeness with others, or else isolation. There has to be a balance with independence, though. This stage occurs in early adulthood, and the person is what they love. They learn love.

Generativity v. stagnation

This is the next stage. Generativity might involve helping children to reach their potential or becoming a productive member of society. Adults can have a mid-life crisis in this stage, because they may be without children or have no meaningful job. Some jobs do lead to generativity, for example, nursing and teaching. However, others do not. We should be thinking of the next generation, and not just of our own greed. Erikson thought it was a mistake for us to go on wanting more and more for ourselves. He thought it was a problem that we did not think more about the next generation in this stage. This stage occurs in middle adulthood, and the person is what they create. They learn care.

McAdams et al (1993) looked at generativity in three groups. The groups were aged 22 to 27, 37 to 42 and 67 to 72. They looked at age differences, and looked at four different sorts of generativity. First there was generative concern, which refers to how far the person cares about other generations. Then there were generative strivings, which refer to how far the person will help and nurture the next generation. Then there was generative action, which lists the actions the person has actually done, and finally there was generative narration, which measures past memories and how far they reflect generativity. These four measures of generativity were used in the study. Erikson's theory suggests that generativity peaks at middle age, and the findings supported this prediction. The young group was less generative. However, the middle and older groups were equally generative, although both were more generative than the young group.

Activity 9 suggests you could try a piece of coursework in this area.

ACTIVITY 9

LOOKING AT GENERATIVITY IN ADULTS

You could try a questionnaire to see if there are different types of generativity in adults depending on their age. You could simply ask people to complete the sentence 'I typically try to …' This is one of the statements used by McAdams et al.

Then you need to know the age of the participant, and gender might be useful too. You might decide to gather information about occupation, but you must only get the information you need. Remember, too, to follow ethical guidelines and give the right to withdraw, confidentiality and so on.

You could divide the statements up into the different types of generativity, or just score them according to how caring or generative they are. Do the statements mention children or helping others, for example? Are the statements about things the participants want for themselves, in which case they are not generative?

It was interesting, too, that those adults who showed generativity in their answers also seemed to be the happiest with their lives. You could check that out too with some carefully worded questions.

Ego integrity v. despair

This is the final stage. Older people look back over their lives and see them as meaningful and well spent. However, they may look back and feel despairing. This stage occurs at the end of one's life, and we are what survives us. We learn wisdom.

Evaluation

- Like Freud, Erikson's theory is a stage theory. Remember that these can be criticised, because you could say that no one really passes through specific stages, that there is a lot more to development than that. There is an argument about stage theories compared with theories that suggested continuous development and this is outlined in Chapter 3, so you might like to recall the evaluation given there. Behaviourists claim that development is continuous, and you can use their theory to evaluate those of Erikson and Freud, just because their theories are stage theories.

It appears that Erikson saw our lives as moving through this linear pattern, of one stage before the next. However, actually he thought of the process as a cycle. Those people beginning their lives are influenced by those at the end of theirs. The older people have integrity, and can pass on their wisdom to the younger ones. If the older ones have integrity, then the younger ones learn trust.

It is hard to get evidence to support stage theories, because it is difficult to know when someone has gone through one stage. If you use questionnaires, then there are problems in getting truthful answers. You need to use the information in Chapter 7 to help you to evaluate methods. Similarly if in-depth interviews are used, there are problems in analysing them.

Also these stage theories tend to focus on crises, whereas not everyone has crises. Mid-life can be the best time of life, not a time of crisis. Children may have left home, and yet the individual is still young enough to be active and enjoy life.

There is also the problem that evidence for such stage theories tends to be gathered at more or less one moment in time. So there might be a **cohort effect**. This means that something in the upbringing of a certain group at a certain time (an economic depression, or a war) might affect the whole group in a way that another group at another time are not affected. Therefore, the cohort effect and not the crisis could be the problem.

Studies within the psychoanalytic approach

The case study of Little Hans

This is an analysis of a phobia in a five-year old boy called Hans. It is one of Freud's case studies, and he published the account in 1909. This account is supposed to show the Oedipus complex in action, although, as has been mentioned earlier, there are other explanations, such as that of the learning approach.

This is a case study where data are collected from an individual (or a few individuals) and a story is created. Note that in evaluation you can use criticisms about case studies in general – see Chapter 7. Freud collected his data by clinical interview and there is analysis. The term 'clinical' refers to the medical context in which the study is taking place. The aim is to provide therapy, and Freud's therapy was psychoanalysis.

The method according to Freud

In the write-up of the study Freud talks about the problems with it. He does not want to accept what the father says, or to accept what Hans says in the presence of his father. He wants to take as evidence only the times when Hans is freely talking about his problems. Freud points out that there are many reasons why Hans would agree with his father, and so the data may not represent the true situation. On the other hand, when Hans resists questions, then these areas might be of special interest (linking to repression and resistance). Freud also accepts that taking information from one such case study and then saying the analysis is true of everyone is not an acceptable way to build a body of knowledge – even though this is apparently what Freud does.

One other interesting point worth mentioning is that Freud says you need to be in the situation at the time of the analysis to really understand what is happening. When writing an account, it is almost impossible to give all the details. You may have done studies with young children, for example, to test their object permanence. Imagine playing with a six-month-old baby. You interest the baby in a rattle, and then hide it under a blanket. You check to see if the baby looks for the rattle and knows it is under the blanket, showing object permanence. Although you can see that the baby is interested and follows the toy with its eyes, it is very hard to be convincing about this in words. This is where videos are useful. Freud seems to feel that he has experienced the situation, and so knows that his analysis is correct, but that he finds it hard to convince those of us who were not there. It is worth noting that Freud did consider criticisms of his work.

He also thinks that the views of children are worth listening to. He thinks they tell the truth as far as they can, just as adults do. This is important, as he has to show that the memories of Hans are trustworthy. Hans is said by his parents to be cheerful and well educated. He seems to have few problems. However, an illness (anxiety and fear) makes his parents take the problem to Freud. The case study is told through the father and perhaps words were being put into Hans's mouth, but Freud thought not. For Freud the important part is the psychoanalysis, not the scientific study. Hans is there to be helped.

The early story

Hans had an interest in his 'widdler'. Hans thought all humans had a widdler, as Hans did, even though he could see that his sister did not have one. He saw them on animals – and he thought all animals, and, therefore, all humans, had one. It seems that Hans's mother at one time threatened to cut off Hans's widdler when he had his hand on it. Hans did not seem concerned with this threat at the time, but Freud thought it might have caused later problems (being buried in his unconscious).

It is hard to see in the account where Hans's father is doing the analysis using Freud's concepts, and where Freud is commenting and analysing. The following account puts Freud as the analyst, since the father talked his ideas through with Freud.

Hans appeared to enjoy touching his penis ('widdler') and had been told off for this. It appears that he then transferred his interest onto looking at the widdlers of other people. Hans had a dream where he wanted a friend of his (a girl) to share his widdling, and Freud sees this as revealing Hans's unconscious wishes. Hans seems to have asked often to see the widdlers of his mother and father. Freud saw this as his need to make comparisons and to try to understand himself by comparing himself with others.

Hans took pleasure in his widdler and also dreamt about his bottom. He dreamt about having children and wiping their bottoms and helping them to widdle. Freud thought that Hans must have got pleasure from having this done to him. In reality, Hans denied all interest in these things, and they only came to life in his dreams. Freud thought that it was his repression that made him deny all interest in widdlers and bottoms.

Freud also reports Hans as desiring his mother in a sexual way, and wanting his father out of the way. His father seems to have been away on business, and in and out of the house during the holidays. Hans, without the father there, found he could focus his attention on his mother, and he enjoyed this. He seems to have wanted his father to 'go away'. The family moves house, and this means his father is not away so often, and then he wants his father dead. Hans's phobia is that a white horse will bite him, and Freud thinks that this could represent his fear of his father.

Freud thinks the birth of Hans's sister when Hans is three and a half years old brings back to him his own upbringing, and the feelings of pleasure. He shows jealousy of his sister almost at once, and he seems to worry about the possibility of another baby arriving in the household. Freud concludes this from a conversation with Hans's father about Hans's fear of baths. Hans says he is afraid of falling under the water in the bath, and eventually Freud and the father suggest to Hans that when watching his mother bath his sister, Hans wishes his mother would let his sister's head go under the water. Hans says 'yes' to this. So they conclude that Hans's fear of water represents his wish to drown his sister. Freud thought that Hans saw both his father and his sister as being likely to take his mother away.

More evidence, and the analysis moves on

The analysis then moves on. Hans had an anxiety attack in the street with his father. He had wanted to stay with his mother, although eventually he became anxious even when his mother was with him. At this stage he stated a fear that a white horse would bite him. Freud saw this as an outward explanation of the cause of his fear, but thought that the underlying problem was linked to this desire for his mother. Hans even said he was afraid that the horse would come into the room – this will be of significance later.

Hans was also having dreams that his mother had gone away. Freud and Hans's father gathered all this evidence whilst building the analysis. Early on when Hans's anxieties were developing, his mother had taken him into her bed to try to calm him. This, too, Freud saw as important, thinking that this left Hans in a state of sexual excitement. There was also information that his mother bathed him and powdered him, but worked around his penis, saying that it would not be proper to touch it. Hans then appears to have started masturbating. Freud thought that he should be encouraged to stop masturbating, and this was part of his therapy.

The analysis continues. It is revealed that Hans has heard the father of a little girl who had been staying with them say she must not put her finger on the white horse (drawing the cart that had come to take her to the station) because it would bite her. Freud thinks the expression 'don't put your finger on' reminded Hans of the instruction not to masturbate, so Hans connected the fear to horses. Then (it gets a bit complicated) his father seems to have convinced him that women don't have widdlers, and Hans seems to connect this to the mother's threat to cut his own penis off, made earlier. Freud links this to a castration fear. Hans seemed to be working this fear through (though it is not clear how), and then he talks to his father about a dream about two giraffes. One giraffe is crumpled, and Hans sits on it. The other giraffe just stands away. Hans's father thinks the two giraffes are the mother and father, and the dream represents the bedroom scene.

Hearing this dream and the father's interpretation, Freud then links Hans's fear that the horse will come into the room with the dream. Freud says it is time to inform Hans that the fear of horses represents Hans's fear of his father. Hans had said he was afraid of the black on horses' mouths and things in front of their eyes. Freud thought these represented glasses and moustaches of grown men. At this stage Hans, according to Freud, felt free enough to reveal details of his phobias, and he says more about his fears.

It appears that he was afraid of carts, vans and buses as well as of horses. Horses that were heavily laden or that drove quickly were particularly frightening. Hans said he was afraid of horses falling down. At this stage Freud reports Hans recalling an incident that happened just before his illness. On a walk with his mother, Hans saw a horse that was drawing a bus fall down. He thought the horse was dead.

Then Hans appears to have focused his anxiety onto faeces and baths -- or at least fantasies about being in the bath. There appears to be a mix of problems to do with Hans being born, his sister being born and his fascination with faeces. Freud links Hans's preoccupation to his fear of the loaded carts. The falling horse was his father dying, but also represented his mother in childbirth. It seems that Hans had not believed the story of the stork that delivered his sister, but had seen his pregnant mother followed by the birth of the sister and had worked out what happened.

Freud talks about Hans's bath dreams, where there is a plumber present. A further dream also involves a plumber. Hans says the plumber takes Hans's bottom and widdler away and brings new ones. The father asks Hans if this means that Hans wants a bigger bottom and penis like the father's, and Hans agrees that this is the case. Freud thinks this shows that Hans has overcome his castration fear, and is identifying with his father. For Freud the therapy is now successful and Hans's unconscious desires have been made conscious and understood. Finally, Hans's father makes one more analysis. Hans is playing with dolls and 'having children'. The father comments that a boy cannot have children. Hans says that mummy is the children's mummy, Hans is their daddy, and his own father can be grandfather. Hans's father thinks this fulfils Hans's wish to be with his mother, and solves the problem of wanting his father dead. His father can be the grandfather.

At this stage Hans is said to be cured and the illness is at an end. However, earlier, Freud does say that Hans still has a fear of horses. Hans grew up to be a producer of operas and was supposed to be perfectly normal. He could not remember the analysis, and did not seem to be upset by it.

Evaluation

Alternative explanations

- One problem is that the parents of Hans were followers of Freud. They knew his views and when they had a child they agreed to bring him up mindful of Freud's teachings. So it seems strange that the mother would threaten Hans with castration, or tell him the story about the stork. Freud appears not to have warned them against these lies when bringing up children. Fromm (1970) even suggests that

Freud turned away from the explanation that adults were abusing children, because he did not want to criticise his own society in that way. Perhaps Hans needed to be protected from his mother, who was making many threats, and he needed his father to intervene. Fromm suggests that in Freud's society men had the power in the relationship, and mothers were seen as insignificant, so Freud would not have looked to blame the mother. For him, it must have been the father who was frightening. In another extract from the father's report Fromm reports that Hans told his father he would like to beat his mother with a carpet beater, as his mother had threatened to do to him.

- There is a second explanation. The mother also seems to have threatened to leave the family, and Bowlby (1973) thought that Hans's problem was anxiety that his attachment figure would leave. If you choose to study child psychology in the A2 part of the course, you will read about Bowlby, who developed a theory about the importance of attachments in upbringing. The case study does show that the mother kept threatening to leave Hans. Bowlby noted that Hans's fear of the mother going away came before his fear of horses. Also he might have connected the incident where a young girl (who was going away) was told not to put her finger on a white horse with someone going away.

- A third explanation links the fear of white horses to Hans's fear of a surgeon, since Hans had not long before had an operation to remove his tonsils (Gay, 1988).

- A fourth explanation is one hinted at earlier, when describing Freud's concepts. Classical conditioning can explain Hans's phobia, as outlined in Box 6.

Methodological criticisms

- Freud has himself explained some criticisms of his method. For example, he was using the father's account of events, not that of Hans. The father might have had problems in analysing someone he was close to; also the parents were acquaintances of Freud and knew his work. Hans's mother had been treated by Freud before she was married. You could argue that Freud's methods did not produce a scientific account, because the data are not testable. However, you could argue that Freud's methods gave even more useful data than sciences give. We have been criticising experiments saying that they do not test natural behaviour. Freud gets his data directly from the participants, and as such it is 'real'.

- Freud met Hans only twice, so it is hard to give this case study credit for being an impartial evaluation. Firstly, Freud had the idea of the Oedipus complex before he started on the case study, so would have had an 'explanation' in mind. Secondly, as Freud himself says, a case study is unique and the findings cannot really be generalised to others.

Application of the study

- One problem with this study is precisely because it seems to back the idea of an Oedipus complex. Miller (1986) criticises this (and Freud) as going against the idea of 'real' child abuse. She asserts that there is such abuse, and this case study seems to emphasise a different interpretation. Freud has been criticised for not tackling the problem of abuse in his society. Of course, Freud said that these feelings are unconscious. The basic assumption that our unconscious desires are being repressed and causing any neurotic symptoms we display does not fit with an explanation bringing in real child abuse. Freud's rejection of real abuse as an explanation fitted with his underlying beliefs.

Box 6

Using classical conditioning to explain Hans's fear

The case study explains an occasion that might have triggered the phobia. Hans's mother and he are out and Hans witnesses a horse drawing a bus falling over. He thinks the horse is dead. This might be sufficient to trigger a phobia. Hans would feel fear after having been startled. Then the fear would be linked to horses. Wolpe and Rachman (1960) outline how classical conditioning explains the phobia.

The unconditioned stimulus of being startled would give fear, for example, being frightened by the noise. Then the horse would be the conditioned stimulus giving fear. This fear could easily be generalised to all horses, and all horse-drawn vehicles. The incident involved a large vehicle (a bus) and so large vehicles would give more fear, and this was the case. Hans would, therefore, have learnt fear after the incident, and then felt fear each time he met or thought about horses.

False memory syndrome

In Chapter 1 false memory syndrome was discussed. A brief account of Freud's theory was outlined then. You might like to turn back to that section if you have already studied the cognitive approach, as it should make more sense now.

Psychoanalysts have been accused of 'helping' patients to recover false memories. Having read the above case study about Hans, you can probably understand better how this happens. These false memories involve remembering real sexual abuse, which is an important point. At that stage, it is not a fantasy that is being discussed, which is interesting. Freud was, in fact, more likely to underline how unreliable memory is, rather than to set great store by it. Also Freud was looking at fantasy, not fact.

The usefulness of dreams during pregnancy

This case study (Ablon, 1994) has been chosen to show you an example of psychoanalsysis 'in action'. You will

need to recall some of the concepts of the psychodynamic approach. For example, the Oedipus complex, which outlines the relationship between the individual and the parents, is important. Also it is very important to think about transference. Recall that it is through transference that much of the analysis takes place. The analyst is important in the analysis, especially the relationship between the individual and the analyst.

It is quite difficult to summarise this sort of case study, because the content of the dreams represents the data. However, I did want to shorten the study, so I have outlined the dreams rather than giving a fuller account. I hope that sufficient detail is given for you to get an idea of what psychoanalysis is, and how it 'works'.

If you have not already studied the key application, you might find it useful to do so now. This case study is really concerned with therapy and with mental health, so you need the concepts outlined below, in order to understand what follows more fully.

The study

Introduction

This is a case study of a 36-year-old woman who started psychoanalysis, and then the analysis continued through her pregnancy. There have been other studies where it has been claimed that dreams during pregnancy are particularly useful in analysis (Gillman, 1968; Greenberg et al, 1992; Kestenberg, 1976). Dreams in analysis during pregnancy help to understand the challenges of pregnancy and early unresolved conflicts. Pregnancy is self-orientating and regressive, in that it takes the individual back to their own early days. There is often an increased awareness of early experiences. During pregnancy the analysand (the person being analysed) often thinks back to her own mother.

During pregnancy the individual often has 'rich' dreams that help in understanding developmental changes during pregnancy as well as helping to resolve earlier problems. It was previously thought that during pregnancy psychic energy would be focused inwards and not be available for transference. However, analysts now believe that analysis during pregnancy can be useful. During pregnancy individuals often have increased awareness of feelings from early childhood – of being cared for and abandoned. Identification with the mother, and separation from her, are also often strong feelings at this time. During pregnancy dreams provide access to unconscious conflict and anxiety. What follows is information from notes made during analysis.

Background of the analysand – Y

The analysand is called 'Y' during the case study. She is a 36-year-old married architect who is in analysis because of low self-esteem, sadness and anxiety. These feelings have stopped her progression in her job. She seems to have been unsure about having children. She is Californian and has a younger brother. Her father, a professor of engineering, was a 'precise, rigid and often tedious' man. He appears not to have attained his expected level of achievement. He was often unavailable to his family, whilst being praised for his guidance of students. Y's mother was a nurse and then gave up work to care for her children. She was devoted to the children; however, according to the information presented, she was an anxious and controlling mother. Y's mother became depressed due to her husband's domination and devaluation of her. Y felt she was a burden to her parents. She was told that she had had colic when she was a baby, and she was irritable and difficult to comfort because of this. Y was sad and lonely when at three and a half she was told she could not get into her parents' bed any more, and could not accompany her father into the bathroom and flush the toilet for him. Y was four and a half when her brother was born. Y became constipated at the time, and her mother gave her enemas.

In analysis it was said the constipation was related to her fantasies about oral impregnation and anal birth. Y remembers being jealous of her brother. She remembers fighting and worrying about injuring him. The family moved when Y was five, twelve and eighteen, because of her father's change of job. She felt loss and loneliness even though she was an outstanding student and had friends. Later, after university, she had relationships where men devalued her and were critical of her (as her father was of her mother). Then Y met and married Dave and was especially attracted to his devoted, emotionally available and nurturant personality. After four months of analysis, Y became pregnant, and the following notes were taken after she became pregnant.

Notes from analysis

Nine weeks pregnant. Y talks about smashing into a car (really, not symbolically or in her dreams). She then talks about the analyst and says things like 'I love you' and 'I'd like to smash you', and she talks too about other feelings about the car. The analyst relates these feelings to her frustration at the analyst's unresponsiveness, and he says this is like her father's coldness towards her.

Then Y tells of a dream about being on the toilet and giving birth to fetal pigs. There is a suggestion from the analyst that Y thinks her husband might leave her because she is a dirty pig. Y says that she thinks she was mixed up about having a baby and bowel movements, whereas she thought she had sorted that out a long time ago.

Three and a half months pregnant. Y dreamt of seeing her father eating dinner in a bathroom on Dave's side of the bed. Her father tried to get into bed with her and wanted to cuddle. She called for her mother (in the dream). Her father went into the guestroom. Her mother arrived and Y wanted to say how nice her mother looked, as if they were peers.

Then Y talks to the analyst about him caring about her and asking about the amniocentesis results. She seems to have said she wanted to welcome the analyst 'back with a bang'. She then reports another dream. She and the analyst were talking in the dream. When Y woke up she thought that if the analyst were in bed with her, her father would not come in bed. Someone at work talked about her pregnancy but she did not want people to know that she was pregnant, and she did not want to be pregnant. She explains why she was late for analysis.

The analyst asks if she was angry that he was not in bed with her, having a baby with her. She answers she would like to flush him down the toilet, her father too.

Y then says how being pregnant shows you have been having sexual intercourse, and she does not like people knowing this. She talks about her mother, wondering if because her mother gave her attention, her father felt he did not need to. Her father said having a baby was disrupting and her mother said that her father thinks everyone should have an abortion – he does not like children.

Thirty-five weeks pregnant. A new dream is reported. Y dreamt she had a full moon face and wondered why the medicines did that to her. The analyst wondered if she saw pregnancy as an illness, and perhaps Y was worrying about a caesarian. Later she talks about getting larger, having a scar, losing a penis, and losing virginity – and she talks of all this as loss. Also she worries about not working. Y wonders about being abandoned. Did her mother push her father away when Y was born, and push Y away when her brother was born?

Two weeks after the expected due date. Y dreams about asking if the baby is dead, not whether it has been born. She had been reading about the birth and realised what a shock it is to be born. Y wonders if she was not taken care of properly. The analyst asks if she thinks it was because she had colic that she was hard to love, and this makes Y very sad.

She says she cannot imagine being a mother. 'It feels like somebody died' – the analyst thinks she means that to be a good mother the baby has to die – he is referring to the baby in her that longs for appreciation from her mother.

After the baby was born. A baby girl was born and was healthy. The analysis continued.

Y still had dreams but not as vivid and the impact was less than during pregnancy. Y referred back often to the lack of nurturing she received due to her mother's depression and anxiety. The analyst concludes this is because of Y's disappointment at only being able to visit the analyst for five hours a week. Y felt her baby was very hungry for love. The analyst sees this as displacement. Y felt the analyst would either be more interested in the baby and push Y away or feel that the baby would be too burdensome. During analysis Y comes to see the baby as an individual in itself.

Another central theme is the unresolved feelings towards Y's enema-giving castrating mother. Y through transference sees the analyst either as the father who did not give her enough attention, or as the castrating mother. She also dreamt that she and the analyst would get together and have sexual intercourse (his wife would look after the baby).

Discussion

In the first three months Y showed anxieties about the baby and about miscarrying. She dreamt of helplessness and loss of control. Also she was afraid because she thought her father, her husband and her analyst would leave her because she was a 'dirty pig'.

In the second three-month period she focused on her body changing shape and not being able to hide having had sexual intercourse. She said she might have been mixed up about having the baby and being a baby. Dreams expressed love for her father and how the love was against the rules.

In the third three-month period she focused on fears about having the baby. She was determined to be a better mother. She worried about her career and how her father would disapprove of her not carrying on with her career.

The vivid dreams during pregnancy made this analysis easier and quicker.

Other authors have found similar themes in the analysis of pregnant women. Some themes are listed below.
• Change from being a girl to being a mother
• No turning back
• Separation from own mother
• Fear of injury
• Fear of deformed baby
• Anxiety at being 'dirty'
• Fear of being destructive towards the baby

Are there changing thought processes in pregnancy that might affect the imagery in dreams? This could account for some of the findings of this study.

Evaluation

• The findings of this study are supported by other literature, which strengthens the conclusions. Others have found useful dream imagery in pregnancy. Psychoanalysis does allow the individual the opportunity to talk about anything they want to talk about, and this could well be of use. Other forms of psychotherapy do the same, however, so it cannot be said that psychoanalysis is the only answer.

• You can criticise the study by pointing to the amount of interpretation needed. For example, the concept of the analysand being a 'dirty pig' comes from one dream. The analyst starts from the idea that there is conflict for the young child, and that the Oedipus complex must be worked through. So he will be looking for any symbols that might suggest hatred of her father, or indeed he will look for evidence of the relationship with both her mother and her father. He will be especially interested in the first five years of her life. Therefore, when she talks about the birth of her brother, and how she became constipated, he will focus on that, rather than on other subjects.

• Much of what he uses in analysis does not come from the dreams. It comes from the story of her life so far. This is true of the time when she was constipated, and the apparent concern that she might harm her young brother. Also the relationship with her father, where he takes little interest in her, is something she outlines without symbolism. The same is true when she talks about her mother, and how she felt unloved because she seems to have been a 'difficult' baby. Without some of this knowledge we cannot understand the analysis, so clearly some information comes from conscious thoughts. Not everything is buried in the unconscious, so you could ask what feelings are buried and what feelings are left conscious.

• The analysis relies heavily on the concept of 'transference'. The analyst seems to assume that Y will have feelings of either hatred or love for him. He seems to talk to the analysand as if this will be the case. For example, early in the account, Y tells the analyst about the smashed car, and he says he thought she was telling him how, like her father, his own unresponsiveness 'enraged her'. Then he said she might be worried that these feelings might drive the analyst away. Y does not say this, but this is the analyst's interpretation. It is perhaps not surprising that after many months of this sort of analysis Y does eventually dream about sleeping with the analyst. There is also a mention of how Y tried to explain why she was late. Resistance is one of the concepts used, and is thought in psychoanalysis to be when the analysand resists the analyst's interpretation because it is getting close to the 'truth'. It is immediately after Y explains why she is late for her appointment that the analyst mentions her feelings for him. This is expected given psychoanalytic concepts. She is late, and this suggests resistance. The analyst then knows that he is getting near to something important. So he examines the transference to see if he can find what this important thing is. When Y says that her baby was hungry for love, this is interpreted as showing that Y is hungry for love, and the analyst interprets that as needing to see him more often. Here the analyst would be 'standing in for' and representing her father. She could also have been thinking of the baby as needing love, it all depends on the interpretation. Also, Y talks at one stage about the loss of a penis, and this must surely have come from knowing about penis envy. Perhaps she does think about such a loss, but it seems unlikely.

- There is no way that we can test the data. I have shortened the account, and the writer was only able to select passages from the notes, so our criticism here must only be superficial; however, we cannot repeat the study. As with other case studies, the method is not reliable, because it cannot be repeated and tested. It would be possible to talk to Y, perhaps, and ask questions. However, the analysis has become part of her memories and would (as intended) have changed her perceptions of herself. Therefore, we cannot get at the data objectively to test it.

- However, case studies do yield valid data in that the information comes directly from the individual. In this case the analyst will only be able to take notes of some comments, so there is an element of selection. He does outline the 'normal' fears of pregnancy such as having a deformed baby, but there is also emphasis on the Oedipus complex and transference. This might mean he wrote down certain comments and dreams rather than others. The analyst records the dream about Y's father wanting to get into bed with her, and the comments about her sadness at not being able to go to the toilet with her father and to flush the toilet for him. With only the chosen comments to go on, it is difficult to know if there were many dreams like this, or if he recorded what was relevant in 'Freudian' terms.

- Since this is a case study, there can be no generalisation of the findings. However, the overall concepts, such as transference and the Oedipus complex, as well as the idea that dreams hide unconscious urges, are taken from a theory that was built from such evidence. Then the analyst has taken these concepts and used them when analysing Y's dreams and thoughts. In a way this is self-fulfilling, in that he is looking for certain themes and symbols, so he is likely to find them.

- The list given in the discussion, where Y is seen to have 'normal' anxieties about pregnancy, could be used in psychotherapy without the analysis of the dreams, and the 'Freudian' interpretation put on them.

- One point of evaluation, however, is that there are similar themes here to those in the Hans case study. Toilets and

such things appear in the dreams and thoughts of both individuals. There does seem to be conflict with parents, and Y's self-esteem appears to be very low. This low self-esteem seems to be to do with her parents' comments about her, and she does seem to have lacked love. Even so, we only have the data to go on. At one stage the analyst seems to accept that Y was not loved. Y says that she might not have been taken care of in the right way. The analyst replies that he wondered if 'she felt that because she had had colic she was difficult to love, and this made her terribly sad'. It is as if Y is asking whether she was loved, and the analyst seems to accept that she was difficult to love. By doing this he confirms her thoughts. It would be interesting to have the parents' view, or to ask her brother. The analyst is limited to one source of data – and that from an anxious, pregnant individual with low self-esteem. However, this is what psychoanalysis involves, and as we have said it is hard to test or to criticise.

Key application – understanding mental health issues

Freud is most well known for his use of psychoanalysis in helping his patients. It is in the field of mental health that the approach is most used, even though the contemporary issue below does show how psychodynamic concepts can be used in explaining other issues.

The aims of psychoanalysis

Psychoanalysis aims to allow repressed feelings and desires in the person's unconscious to come to light. In acknowledging such repression, the individual should release the feelings into their conscious thoughts. Then there should be no further problems, since the unconscious urges are now conscious.

Freud looked at neuroses and saw mental illnesses as stemming from underlying problems. These neuroses, which could be phobias, anxiety or feelings of depression, are seen as ways of adapting to unconscious urges. However, they are not good ways of adapting, because the person is 'malfunctioning'. The ego is trying to maintain a balance between the demands of the id and the demands of the superego. These demands often conflict. The ego may resolve the problems by repressing them in the unconscious. However, these feelings show themselves somehow, and this can be in the form of neuroses. The unconscious urges can reveal themselves as stressful dreams too, as well as in unreasonable hatred of certain people or some other similar symptoms.

So think of people who undergo psychoanalysis as having the above sorts of mental illnesses. Of course, you could say that other illnesses could be linked to these underlying unconscious urges needing expression. Usually, however, we think of neuroses and anxieties.

Defence mechanisms are there to protect the individual against these urges; however, they can themselves lead to stress and anxiety and are not effective ways of dealing with the problems. For example, if through projection you see people as murderous, then the defence mechanism of projection is not helping you.

Some disorders treated by psychoanalysis

Disorders treated by psychoanalysis include eating disorders, anxiety, multiple personality disorder, personality disorders, schizophrenia, sexual dysfunction, depression and youth disorders. Others are alcoholism, post-traumatic stress disorder, substance abuse and obsessive-compulsive disorders. Some of these are also treated by other methods, but here psychoanalysis is considered. You will find other therapies mentioned elsewhere, and for the A2 you may study the option called clinical psychology, which looks specifically at disorders and mental health. If psychoanalysis is used as a therapy, then you can be sure that a psychodynamic explanation of the mental health issue is used. So, for example, obsessive-compulsive disorder will be explained by reference to what such behaviours are replacing, and anorexia is explained by reference to not wanting to grow up.

Someone with obsessive-compulsive disorder might be compulsively checking her baby's food. This could be concealing a wish to harm the child, and checking the food is a way of stopping herself from harming the child. This guards against unconscious urges or impulses that somehow the mother recognises.

Post-traumatic stress disorder (PTSD) might be explained by looking at the stress caused because the individual cannot integrate the experience into their sense of self. PTSD has as one of its symptoms a 'numbing' and this could be explained as defence and protection against these unwanted strong feelings.

Freud defines anxiety as an unpleasant emotional state. Objective anxiety is obvious, because there is an external cause. Objective anxiety is rational fear, as when a gun is pointed at you. Moral anxiety could be caused by the superego, where the individual worries about their behaviour and its morality. Neurotic anxiety is where the person is afraid of doing something socially unacceptable or harmful, and is anxious about giving way to urges that are barely controlled. Repression should hide these urges successfully from the individual, but Freud thought that the urges were strong enough to find an outlet in consciousness.

Psychoanalysis

The therapist wants the patient to reveal unconscious wishes and desires. There is also the understanding that problems stem from early childhood. So psychoanalysis involves taking people back in their minds to their early childhood and examining possible problems.

Distinguish between psychotherapy and psychoanalysis. Psychotherapy is a wider term for all therapies like psychoanalysis, and includes counselling and other modern therapies and 'listening cures'. Here we are talking about psychoanalysis. In traditional psychoanalysis, the analyst, is out of sight, behind the couch. No emotions are supposed to be expressed by the analyst, who is 'faceless'. It is the patient who must uncover the problem and reveal the contents of the unconscious to consciousness. The doctor is a blank screen for the patient to project the problems on to. However, in practice, because of transference, counter-transference and resistance, the analyst cannot really remain anonymous, as is explained below.

Usually the treatment means the client attends for about one hour a week for several years, and this is expensive. There is an alternative version, where, over a shorter period of time, the analyst and client meet once or twice a week. Brief focal therapy is an example. This lasts for 30 weeks and is one session a week. The focus would be on a particular problem. Here the client and analyst sit opposite one another, as you might expect in a counselling situation. So the classic psychoanalysis has sometimes been replaced by these 'shorter' versions.

Transference

Transference is an important part of the process. Transference happens when the patient projects repressed feelings onto the doctor. These can be feelings of love or feelings of hatred. Usually the client transfers good feelings onto the analyst at first. These feelings become negative later, just as the child becomes hostile to its parents. Many analysts focus only on the transference, because it is through understanding the transference that is currently happening, that the childhood 'problems' can come to light.

Countertransference

Countertransference refers to the feelings the analyst then has towards the client. These can be feelings of irritation, dislike or sexual attraction. Freud saw these feelings of countertransference as a failing, but these days they are considered to be inevitable. Analysts now use these feelings as well as the feelings of the clients towards the analyst, and analyse both in understanding the issues.

Resistance

To help the client understand their childhood experiences the analyst must interpret the transference. Resistance is a defence mechanism that helps the client to resist these interpretations. They will be resisted, because they are going to be painful. Defence mechanisms are there to keep those feelings and urges unconscious. So the client will stop talking, make jokes, fall asleep or arrive late for therapy. The analyst must have enough of a relationship with the client to help them to work through this resistance, so remaining an anonymous figure is not really possible. Freud did not remain anonymous either.

Dream interpretation

Another technique used is dream interpretation. The client can outline dreams, and together the client and the analyst can interpret them. It is as if two adults are getting together to study a child. Dreams involve symbols, and these symbols are analysed. The idea is that the unconscious desires might be revealed in dreams, but they would still be disguised, and it is the analyst's job to help to uncover meanings behind dreams.

Free association

Another technique to try to uncover the contents of the unconscious is to use free association. The client says whatever comes into his or her mind, no matter how absurd or unrelated it seems. The analyst and the client then examine such associations, and again look for meanings.

Is this a cure?

The idea of a cure would be to reveal the contents of the unconscious so that the problem behind whatever symptoms are appearing would be revealed. With this knowledge, the client can deal with the problems, whereas whilst the problems were manifestations of underlying hidden difficulties the client could not deal with them. Once the 'problem' is understood, that should be the cure.

The client needs to have the motivation to continue and the insight to understand. The frustration of the analysis must be endured, and the client must be able to afford it, so overall only certain types of client would perhaps benefit from psychoanalysis. Most people who begin a course of psychoanalysis continue with it for a long time. This is not a quick and easy solution usually. The problems need to be neuroses. Recall that psychoses are mental health problems where the person is not aware of the problem, whereas neuroses tend to be problems that are 'only' a bit different from normal everyday experiences. Neuroses are understood to be problems by the person

involved, whereas understanding, because of their nature, cannot solve psychoses. Psychoanalysis is perhaps really only suitable for specific neuroses and specific people (who have insight, patience and funding).

There is no real cure, because the problems arise from underlying unconscious urges and desires, and we all have those. It is just that some people have specific difficulties in dealing with their symptoms. Even if some of the unconscious wishes are revealed and can be dealt with, this is unlikely to mean that there will be no further problems. With classic psychoanalysis, the client and the analyst might meet once a week for years, but there are shorter versions as outlined above. For these shorter versions it is hard to think in terms of a cure, but this does not mean that the psychoanalysis is not helpful. It is hard to judge how useful it is, as it is hard to find measurable effects of the therapy.

Contemporary issue

Contemporary issues within the psychodynamic approach are hard to find. We could take contemporary events and interpret them through psychodynamic concepts; however, note that there are real people involved. For example, I noticed a report about a doctor who is supposed to have used a relationship with a patient to move into a sexual relationship. We could relate concepts such as transference and countertransference to such a story. However, since these were real people, and since the newspaper article made no reference to such an interpretation, I was reluctant to offer such an explanation. I am not trained in psychoanalysis, and I would not want to force an interpretation onto these events.

Therefore, I have turned to the Internet and to 'psychoanalytic' sites for contemporary issues. Then someone else in the field has done some of the linking for me. We do need to be careful when doing our own 'analysis', especially when the stories are real ones.

Famous people and identification

This subject was taken from an article found on the Internet, and called 'The Princess, The Premier and the People: Authority in New Britain'. The reference was http://www.human-nature.com/free-associations/richards. html. It was taken off the Internet on 17.2.2000 and was written by Barry Richards. This was a paper presented to the 11th Annual Conference on Psychoanalysis and the Public Sphere, 30–31 January 1998.

The article is about the 'outpouring of grief' when Princess Diana died, and especially looks at what is said to be a new idea of Britain as an 'emotionally expressive culture breaking with tradition'. It is quite a complicated article, so it is

174 AS Psychology: Approaches and Methods

summarised and the theoretical issues are pointed to at the same time, as well as being dealt with separately.

The article says that one way of looking at the grief shown by so many at Diana's death is to say that is it realistic grief. This was the death of a good citizen. However, others have died who have been good too, so this is not sufficient explanation for such emotion from so many.

Another explanation is to look at each person's conscious or unconscious identification with Diana. Then the death becomes in part a death of themselves. There is the loss of part of the ego. Here there are clear links to Freud's ideas. Freud talked about identification as the way in which the ego makes sense of pressures from the id and the superego. It is suggested here that the ego may not only identify with parents, as in the Oedipus complex, but might also identify with famous people too. (Another explanation is that the identification takes place through social learning theory, but in this we are looking at the psychodynamic explanation.)

Diana was seen as an oppressed wife, with an eating disorder, and undergoing a struggle from being a girl to being a woman. She also identified with others who were suffering. All this gave her a victim status. There were lots of ways in which lots of people could identify with her. The specific object relation (way in which she was identified with) would give the quality of the grief. Diana is said in the article to be both damaged and repairing. Those who were 'damaged' could identify with her, as could those who were 'repairing'. However, this is not enough of an explanation in itself, as other famous people have also been identified with and died, and there was not this amount of 'national' grief.

There is a third type of grief besides realistic grief and grief because of identification. This third type is reserved for public figures. People watched Diana's smile and got vicarious pleasure from it. Public figures become part of our 'emotional neighbourhood'. We know them although cannot grieve for them in the same way as we do for those we 'really' know. These figures represent society and represent our self-understanding. Diana struggled against the old establishment (royalty) and at the same time represented openness, warmth and determination. This is said in the article to symbolise the struggle of the self. It is said that we now have a therapeutic culture and she represented this new culture of exploring feelings. Her early death symbolised the vulnerability of this culture, according to the article.

Collective grief reasserted these therapeutic values and took Britain into what the article calls an expressive or therapeutic culture.

The article then turns to looking at how those in a society learn their moral code. It says that because morality has this unconscious basis now, it cannot be passed down through parents. This links to Freud's idea of the phallic stage, where, resolving the Oedipus complex by identifying with the same-sex parent, the child takes on the moral code of the parent. It is now being said that this can no longer take place. So the moral code must come from society and from public figures.

The rest of the article deals with the Blair Labour government, showing how this new government is also linking itself to this new therapeutic Britain. Blair represents youth and talks a lot about 'heart' in his politics. Both Blair and Diana symbolise a young country. This is linked in the article to the young person breaking away from parental authority. It is like the child struggling to break free from authority, and the article suggests that we are doing that in Britain today, symbolised by Diana and Tony Blair. However, there is a contradiction, as the government is authority and has strong leadership. In Freudian terms we must struggle and then accept the authority and if we do not do this then we are in crisis. Blair does want to break away from the class and race structure of Britain, and to move away from the old authority, and Diana represented this.

The article says that we are in a sense now all adolescents. Diana's death symbolised this struggle of the new therapeutic Britain wanting to overcome old traditions.

Links to concepts within the psychodynamic approach

Identification

The article uses the concept of identification to explain some of the grief that people felt at the death of Diana. It is suggested that we identify not only with our same-sex parents, as Freud explained happened through the Oedipus complex, but also with public figures. This was especially true when the public figure has vulnerabilities that many might share, so there were many different people who could identify with Diana for many different reasons.

Symbolism

Diana is said to symbolise the new therapeutic culture of Britain where feelings can be openly explored and are important. The concept of symbols being used to represent underlying forces and feelings is one that can be linked to the psychodynamic approach. In this approach the emphasis is to look beyond the overt 'obvious' explanations, and to look for such symbols when explaining human behaviour.

Struggle against authority

It is said that Diana represented a struggle against authority, and this is like the struggle we go through as adolescents, trying to break away from the authority of parents. It is also said that the New Labour government, with its emphasis on youth and equality, also symbolises this youthful struggle. In Freudian terms we should then come to terms with authority, which we have not yet done.

Conclusion

This is not an easy article to grasp, but I think the main points and the links to the psychodynamic approach are clear enough. Within the psychodynamic approach you take concepts such as identification and the Oedipus complex, and you widen their application. Think of symbols and of things not being what they seem. Look underneath such phenomena as the huge amount of grief that was shown at Diana's death. This amount of grief has never really been seen since the death of Admiral Lord Nelson, and it seems that it might symbolise something much more than the death (however tragic) of one person. This is the sort of depth you need if you are to understand the psychodynamic approach.

Coursework suggestions

1 A questionnaire to see if neatness, obstinacy and meanness go together in one person. If there is a correlation, perhaps Freud was right about the anal personality. (See Activity 8, p. 161.)
2 A survey to look at generativity in adults. Ask people to make a list of statements in response to 'I typically try to…' and see how generative the answers are. If caring for others is mentioned, the statement is generative. If working for one's own gain is mentioned, this is not generative, for example. Compare the answers of younger adults with those of older adults. It is predicted that younger adults are less generative. (See Activity 9, p. 164.)

Suggested reading

Cole, M. & Cole, S.R. (1996) *The Development of Children*, Third Edition. New York: W.H. Freeman and Company

Gleitman, H. (1994) *Psychology*, Fourth Edition. London: W.W.Norton & Company Ltd

Gross, R. (1996) *Psychology: The Science of Mind and Behaviour*, Third Edition. London: Hodder and Stoughton Educational

Gross, R. (1999) *Key Studies in Psychology*, Third Edition. London: Hodder and Stoughton Educational

Kurzweil, E. (1998) *The Freudians: A Comparative Perspective*. London: Transaction Publishers

Leahey, T.H. (1996) *A History of Psychology: Main Currents in Psychological Thought*. New Jersey: Prentice Hall

Rybach, J.M., Roodin, P.A. & Hoyer, W.J. (1995) *Adult Development and Aging*, Third Edition. Brown and Benchmark

6

The physiological approach

The aims of this chapter

The aims of this chapter are, with regard to the physiological approach, to enable the reader to:

– *appreciate some of the general assumptions*
– *discuss research methods used*
– *describe and evaluate two theories of why we sleep*
– *describe circadian rhythms and related research*
– *describe and evaluate one physiological theory of dreaming*
– *describe and evaluate some relevant studies*
– *understand the link between physiological concepts and the effects of shift work and jet lag*
– *explain one contemporary issue or debate*

Self-test 1

After reading this chapter, test yourself on each of the above points. Use the points as exam questions and make notes accordingly. Then see how much you can write on each.

This chapter covers

KEY ASSUMPTIONS
1 The importance of genetic influences on behaviour
2 The influence of the nervous system on behaviour

RESEARCH METHODS
1 Group 1 – biological methods
2 Group 2 – genetic influences on individual differences

IN-DEPTH AREA OF STUDY: STATES OF AWARENESS

STUDIES IN DETAIL
1 The relation of eye movements during sleep and dreaming (Dement & Kleitman, 1957)
2 Effects of 48-hour sleep deprivation (Ozturk et al, 1999)

KEY APPLICATION: SHIFT WORK AND JET LAG

CONTEMPORARY ISSUE: NARCOLEPSY

Introduction

You first need to distinguish physiology from psychology. Under pressure in an examination, it is very easy to get it wrong. **Physiology** refers to physical aspects, and psychology to more mental aspects. Since this is a psychology book, you can see that psychology includes the physiology; however, think of physiological explanations as 'biology'. I am sure that by the end of the chapter you will be clear about the difference between physiology and psychology.

A brief historical account

Researchers have been interested in the physical aspects of humans for many more years than they have looked at psychology. It has not always been known, for example, that the brain is important. When interest was shown in the skull, phrenologists concentrated on the physical lumps and bumps themselves, not the brain matter inside. Phrenologists tried to map out what different areas around the skull were for. Now people still look at what different areas within the brain are for, but they do this in a much more sophisticated way.

Advances in research methods led to advances in knowledge. The advances came through biology, not psychology. Whilst cognitive psychologists, for example, were developing models for how we think (see Chapter 1), biologists and those working in related fields were learning more about physiological processes. They were building knowledge of genetics, and studying the nervous system. Often they looked at non-human animals, since

these are easier to study. Box 1 suggests that you consider the arguments for and against the use of non-human animals in research, if you have not already done so.

Box 1

The use of non-human animals in research

For a detailed argument on the use of non-human animals in research linked to psychology read or recall Chapter 8.

Key assumptions of the physiological approach

The physiological approach is referred to in different ways. For example, neuroscientists do research on the nervous system. Neuropsychologists test abilities and disabilities of brain-damaged or impaired people. Some books will refer to biopsychology. Biopsychologists and physiological psychologists look at behaviour and how it relates to the nervous system and physiology of our bodies. For our purposes, we are discussing the biology part of psychology, and you can use the terms 'biopsychology' or 'physiological psychology'.

Biological psychologists look at behaviour differently from, for example, social psychologists. Social psychology examines interactions between people, and what behaviour means to people. Biological psychologists want to see how we act in certain ways, and what the behaviour is for, when considering our chances of survival, for example. They might consider how that behaviour came about or evolved.

Some biopsychologists examine the difference between the mind and the brain, but that will not really concern us. As an example of what will be looked at in this chapter, it is interesting to consider the study of hypnosis. Hypnosis is looked at here and can be examined as a contemporary topic within social psychology. This is because there are two main theories of hypnosis. The first is the state theory that says that hypnosis is an altered state of consciousness. This basically means that state theories of hypnosis examine the state called 'hypnotised', and agree that it exists in a biological sense. Social psychologists, however, put forward a non-state theory. They claim that there is no different physical state called 'hypnotised', but that we appear hypnotised because we obey the instructions of the hypnotist. For the non-state theorist, hypnosis is an example of obedience (see Chapter 2). When we talk about hypnosis in psychology, therefore, we are not thinking of a difference in feeling, or in a difference in our minds. What is being considered is a changed physical state. Either the state exists, as some say, or it does not, as others claim.

Key assumption 1 – the importance of genetic influences on behaviour

Advances in the study of **genetics** are probably as fast as in any other field at the moment (perhaps except in the case of computing!). Many of those studying in the field of genetics choose a particular gene and study it in great depth. It is not surprising that great advances have been made.

At first, genes for physical features were examined, and this sort of study is still continuing. Alongside this, however, there are researchers who are looking for genes for less obviously physical features, for example, for genes for intelligence, aggression and particular emotions. There is a lot of discussion about these advances. If a gene for aggression or one for intelligence is found, think of the implications. It might be claimed that people are born aggressive, or intelligent. So how we treat people in education might change. This issue is returned to when the methods used in the physiological approach are considered. Activity 1 asks you to consider how we might treat people differently if we accepted that intelligence is inherited.

ACTIVITY 1

IF WE ACCEPTED THAT INTELLIGENCE IS INHERITED, HOW WOULD THIS AFFECT THE WAY WE TREAT PEOPLE?

Make a list of how we treat people if we think that people become intelligent through hard work and learning. Then make another list, this time noting down how we would treat people if we thought intelligence was inherited. Compare the two lists.

Key Skill C3.1a – this would make a good group discussion. You could also do some research in the area and consider presenting the argument. This would give evidence for Key Skill C3.1b. Alternatively, you could have a debate, if you are studying in a group. One side could argue that intelligence is learned, and the other could argue that it is innate.

In our society at the moment most people think that intelligence develops to an extent through schooling and environment. You might have thought about parents desperately getting their children into particular 'good' schools. You might have noted down the efforts teachers and others put into encouraging children to do their school work, assuming that it will lead to better qualifications, and, therefore, a better job. At the moment we do make the assumption that intelligence can be developed through hard work. If, however, evidence showed that intelligence was innate or inherited, then people would not have to worry about the school their child attended. Children who seem 'bright' would be assumed to be bright, and those who seemed slower would be treated as 'slower'. The idea of a **self-fulfilling prophecy** (see Chapter 2) rests on the assumption that intelligence is not inherited but develops and is nurtured.

Box 2 briefly outlines some information about the discovery of genes

---

Box 2

The discovery of genes

Mendel's name is well known for his careful experiments in the 1860s using, amongst other things, garden peas, which led to the discovery of genes. He chose the right plants because in garden peas each 'species' of plant is identical, but between the plants there are obvious differences. Also garden peas can **self-fertilise**.

Pollen from a plant giving yellow peas, when used to fertilise a plant giving green peas, was thought, before Mendel's discoveries, to give a plant giving a colour pea that was between green and yellow. However, Mendel discovered that this did not happen. The pollen from the 'yellow' plant, when fertilising a plant with green peas, gave a new (second generation) plant with 'yellow' peas. Then when this new 'yellow pea-giving' plant self-fertilised, a plant giving green peas was produced. Whatever made them green had returned after one generation.

Mendel also found that in this new second generation, although green peas were produced, there was a strict ratio of three plants with yellow peas to one with green peas. This suggested to Mendel that the information was coming from within the plant. In the first-generation 'yellow pea-giving' plants, the information was only for yellow peas. Similarly, in the first-generation 'green pea-giving' plants, the information was purely for green peas. Then they were **cross-pollinated**. At this stage information for green peas was mixed with information for yellow peas, so both could be produced. Something in the plant was carrying information for colour. Mendel also studied how wrinkled the peas were and so on, and found that something was carrying information for that too.

Mendel found that some **genes** (as these carriers of information became known) always led to their information (for example, for colour) being present in the plant. Other genes seemed to need more than one copy to produce the physical characteristic they were carrying. If a single copy produced the characteristic, these are known as dominant genes. If more than one copy is needed, these are **recessive genes**. If the plant carries a **dominant gene** (for example, for yellow peas), then this can mask a recessive gene (for example, for green peas). So the plant always gives yellow peas, but still carries the gene for green peas. So in a later generation green peas can still be produced.

Mendel suggested that it is the inherited message that is important, and that is passed on through generations. Now it is known that what carries the message (called a gene) is a real physical thing. There is a message written in millions of combinations of four chemical letters coded into **DNA** (see later) and carried on **chromosomes**.

Genes can be physically linked and if someone inherits one gene, they are likely to inherit a particular second one too. Genes are found on strands called chromosomes. Each chromosome participates in reproduction separately from the others. Each species has a particular number of chromosomes and humans have 23 pairs.

As an example of how genes can affect us, take the example of human chromosome number 4, which has a marker known as G8 which is visible on the chromosome. Nobody yet knows what G8 contributes; however, the gene for Huntington's disease is thought to lie close to this marker. Gusella et al (1984) report that in a parent and a child who both have Huntington's disease, in 98% of cases they both have the same form of G8 marker. This suggests that the gene for Huntington's disease lies so close to the visible G8 marker that they 'travel' together. This is an example of the sort of work that those working in genetics do.

Some genes are sex-linked, in that they 'travel' with the sex gene. This is why some diseases or characteristics are found in one sex more than in the other. Manic-depression, for example, occurs mainly in females, so the gene for such an illness might be sex-linked. Also, most colour-blind people are men.

Other variations occur. If one parent contributes two copies of chromosome 21, for example, then the child has three copies, and the consequence is Down's syndrome.

Genes do not inevitably influence physical characteristics. A gene might need certain environmental or even social conditions before it exerts its influence. Sometimes if the environment is changed, the gene does not 'function'. There is a condition called phenylketonuria (PKU) which leads to brain damage. However, if a child's diet is carefully changed and controlled, there is no problem, as the gene's effects are cancelled. All babies are tested for PKU, so that they can be treated and the gene does not cause the damage it might have caused.

A chromosome is really a double chain of DNA (deoxyribonucleic acid). Each chain of DNA consists of guanine, cytosine, adenine and thymine. All the genetic information is given by the order of these four bases. **RNA** (ribonucleic acid) picks up the message from the four chemicals that make up DNA and then take the message to the cells. Box 3 explains this in a bit more detail.

Box 3

More on RNA and passing on the message: retroviruses and AIDS

Different kinds of RNA serve different functions. tRNA (transfer RNA) transports amino acids to the ribosomes of the cell, and mRNA (messenger RNA) acts as a model for forming proteins. The order of RNA bases gives the order of the protein's amino acids. The proteins then dictate how the organism develops, and its properties, in other words what it is like. Some proteins form the physical body, and others regulate chemical reactions in the body.

A chromosome is a double chain of DNA. DNA produces RNA and RNA delivers the message. Viruses are compounds of RNA and they serve as templates or patterns for proteins, just as RNA does. However, one of the proteins produced by a retrovirus causes the formation of a new segment of DNA and if this becomes incorporated into one of the chromosomes, it will carry on producing the retrovirus. The retrovirus might even be inherited, because it is incorporated into the chromosome. So a retrovirus is very difficult to attack medically. AIDS seems to be a retrovirus, and retroviruses may also be linked to schizophrenia. This is a relatively new area of research.

The study of genes in humans is done most often using non-human animals. Hundreds of human genes, including diseased genes, are the same in humans and other animals. Mice breed quickly, and can be used in experiments that could not be done on humans (see Chapter 8). The mapping of genes along chromosomes is similar enough between mice and humans for the studies to be useful. Box 4 gives an example of how animal studies can be relevant for humans.

Box 4

An example of non-human animal studies linked to humans

White cats are often deaf (Jones, 1996) and this is because melanin, the pigment that gives skin/fur its colour, is also involved in the workings of the sense organs. People with an inherited white front forelock, and albinos, are often deaf (Jones, 1996). The same gene in mice also gives deafness. This is an example of how the study of genes in mice can be used in the study of humans. It was also discovered that the problem develops early, when cells containing melanin don't move into the ear and start working.

Box 5 briefly examines an example of the use of genetics in explaining disease. This example is taken from Jones (1996).

Box 5

Cancer as a genetic disease

The study of genetics and how it can explain our behaviour and other issues is illustrated clearly in the study of cancer. Cancer is not one disease. All cancers, however, involve damage to DNA and this damage happens as cells divide. For example, in one form of leukaemia, almost every white blood cell carries an unusually small chromosome 22. It seems that damage in the bone marrow is producing the damaged cells. Since damaged cells reproduce faster than other cells, the disease spreads. Cancer is often a disease that affects older people, because it can take some time for the cancerous cells to reproduce.

Cancer genetics shows the complications of this particular process. It seems that chromosome 22 is smaller because part has broken off and transferred to chromosome 9. This transference and joining leads to a new abnormal protein that speeds up cell division.

Sometimes cancers are caused by a virus which damages the genes controlling cell growth. Sometimes we are born with a genetic structure that makes us

---

vulnerable to developing cancer, but we need something to set it off. When both situations are present, the cancer develops. Even then, we normally have a system that detects damaged cells and puts them right, so this system has to be harmed as well. Smoking can damage this natural protection system, as can radiation. Therefore, suggested reasons why people develop cancer are:

- because of a virus
- because they have inherited a genetic structure that makes cell damage likely
- because a mutation spontaneously occurs
- because their natural protection system is not working due to smoking or for some other reason.

There are combinations of these causes, and much of the knowledge has come from work in genetics.

Similarly, there are many drugs and treatments being developed now for different cancers. These medical advances are also possible due to research into genetics (as well as research on non-human animals).

Survival of the fittest

The abilities and tendencies that we inherit seem to have been passed down to us through the mechanism called 'survival of the fittest'. This idea is very important in psychology. Darwin is the key name in this area. The basic idea is that forms of life have evolved to suit their ecological niche. This means that the **environment** – the habitat, climate, available food, predators and so on – decides which animals survive and reproduce. When they reproduce they pass on 50% of their genes to each offspring: 50% comes from the female and 50% from the male. Only those organisms that survive are able to pass on their genes. So genes that are passed on should be those that help survival.

It is in this way that different species have evolved. Whatever was useful was passed on, and whatever was not useful died out. So in one place the gorillas might be relatively small and live in trees, and in another place they may be much larger and live on the ground. Where they live in trees there are tigers, whereas where the gorillas live on the ground, there are no tigers to hunt them.

Humans have evolved in the same way. For example, humans that walked in a reasonably upright way had the advantage when places in Africa turned to desert. By walking upright, the human body was better off with regard to heat. Higher from the ground was cooler in any case, and also those who walked on all fours would have a larger area presented to the sun for it to heat.

If it were not for understanding these mechanisms of survival of the most suited to the particular environment, then we would probably not study non-human animals when looking for understanding of humans. However, because of this understanding, we now think that there are many similarities between humans and non-human animals, and so we are prepared to take findings from the studies of non-human animals and apply them to ourselves. Therefore, in the physiological approach, non-human animals are often studied and the findings generalised to humans. This is true in the search for knowledge of genetics.

Evaluation

- Some believe in the special creation theory, which says that man is created in God's image, and animals are specially created too. But those from different faiths, for example, Muslims, do not believe that this is how mankind came about. So the idea of evolution and survival of the fittest is not accepted by everyone. Also it needs the idea of mutations, and a better explanation of how these come about.

Key assumption 2 – the influence of the nervous system on behaviour

Social psychologists consider that hypnosis does not lead to any 'real' difference in physical state, but shows how people obey social norms and rules. For example, when the hypnotised person is asked to 'be' Elvis, he or she does so, because they are conditioned to obey instructions. However, biopsychologists look at the altered state of awareness that is called 'hypnotised'. They hypnotise people and then study changes in brain waves, for example. They look at the person's physical state.

One assumption of the physiological approach is that people come into the world bringing with them (in their genetic structure) lots of abilities and tendencies, as well as physical characteristics. The study of genetics is rapidly uncovering information about what we bring with us into the world. There are even those who claim that we bring with us the way in which we will die – there is so much evidence now that shows that the way we die is linked to our genes. Heart attacks run in some families, and breathing problems in others, for example.

A second assumption of the physiological approach is that our behaviour comes via our nervous system. Our genes might make us into the sort of person we are, but the way we act is through the nervous system. The nervous system is basically the brain and the spinal cord. Activity 2 asks you to think of any behaviour and consider how it is carried out.

ACTIVITY 2

HOW DO WE ACT IN CERTAIN WAYS?

Chapter 2 looked at why we act in certain ways. For example, most people only help others if there is no one else around who looks as if they might help. Here we want to look at how we act in certain ways.

Think of any simple behaviour and describe how it is carried out. Do not consider exact biological details at the moment, but focus on the physiological features of a behaviour.

Key Skill C3.1a – this would make a good group task.

You could have listed such actions as feeding your dog, writing your name or shaking someone's hand. The main point is to focus on the physical actions. To write your name you need to pick up something to write with, get some paper, put pen to paper, move the pen in the appropriate way, and so on. You would obviously have to know what your name is before you can write it, so not everything can be described in physiological terms. Soon the 'nature/nurture' debate will be examined, and you should conclude that most things about humans are partly to do with their nature, and partly to do with their nurture. So whilst studying the physiological approach, don't forget that environment is also very important.

The nervous system

The nervous system is made up of many different cells, and messages are sent around by means of these cells. Another way of sending messages is by means of hormones; however, these tend to be the slower and less immediate messages. Thoughts and instructions are generally sent by means of the nervous system. What is presented here is only a brief overview of what is known. The nervous system is really more of a chemical system than anything else. The physiological approach tends to examine single cells and individual actions, but don't forget that the whole system is much more complex than study of an individual cell can convey. Box 6 looks at two different ways of learning about things.

| Box 6 |

Reductionism v. holism

The physiological approach tends to look at behaviour in terms of small parts. Above, I suggested that you might have considered the action of writing your name. Biologically, you must pick up a pen, hold onto a piece of paper, move the pen in the appropriate way, and so on. These are the parts involved when writing your name. If you put all these parts together, you would have your name written on the paper.

The way of studying that involves taking a problem, splitting it into parts and then studying the parts to find the solution is called 'reductionism'. The scientist reduces the problem into sections, studies each bit, and then builds the answer.

However, take the example of rebuilding a car. Take a perfectly good car that is working, but that will not pass the MOT. Assume that some welding is needed, and a respray, but apart from that no new parts are needed. In order to do the car up properly, you might well take it all to pieces. Now that the problem is reduced to all the parts, you look at all the parts and start the welding and checking process. This is the reductionist approach.

The problem with this approach is that all the parts do not make up the actual car. This is because the parts are all there, but unless they are joined together in the right way, you do not have a working car. The relationship between the parts is important.

So other people argue that you can't learn everything using a reductionist approach. A **holistic** approach is needed. The whole is more than the sum of the parts. A holist might claim that experiments are never useful, because a reductionist approach will always miss out on studying the whole thing of interest.

You might look at how you write your name, by studying the biology of the actions. However, now try writing your name. Firstly, write your name as you would to a best friend. Then write your name as you would on an essay. Now write your name as you would when applying for a job.

Did you find that you wrote it differently? You probably left a little curl under your first name (which you might have shortened) when writing to your best friend. You probably used your full first name and surname when writing for the job. Your formal signature, which you might use on a cheque, is probably different again.

All the above examples are meant to show that, however much you study parts of behaviour using the physiological approach, as long as you are interested from a psychological viewpoint, you will probably need to view behaviour from a more holistic viewpoint at some stage.

When discussing the nervous system, here we mean the vertebrate nervous system, because we are discussing humans – vertebrate animals. There are other types of nervous system, but they are not discussed here. It might be worth noting this, however, for when the use of non-human animals is discussed. You might ask whether findings from the study of non-human animals (not vertebrate ones) are of use when applying them to humans.

The nervous system consists of the **central nervous system** (CNS) and the **peripheral nervous system** (PNS). The CNS consists of the brain and the spinal cord, and is looked at below.

The peripheral nervous system

The PNS consists of the **autonomic nervous system** and the **somatic nervous system**. The somatic nervous system sends messages from the sense organs (eyes, ears and so on) to the CNS and then to the muscles. So the somatic nervous system sends visual information to the brain, and then sends information back, for example, to the hand, with an instruction. If you see the word 'somatic' then remember it has something to do with physical things. 'Soma' is Greek for 'body'.

The autonomic nervous system consists of the sympathetic division and the parasympathetic division. The sympathetic part sets you up for 'fight or flight', and the parasympathetic part is the standing down from the emergency position. To understand 'fight or flight', think of our ancestors being faced with a dangerous situation. They needed all the energy they could get. So your heart pumps faster, blood sugar is required, pupils dilate, hairs stand on end. This is the emergency reaction, and you are ready for action. Then, once the danger is past, you need to calm down again. The heart rate and pulse slow and the body goes back to 'normal'. If we are in a frightening situation, the sympathetic part of our nervous system will be 'activated' and will account for at least some of our behaviour. If your body maintains this alarm reaction for too long, your immune system will suffer and you will be 'stressing' yourself.

Neurons

The nervous system consists of **neurons** and glia. These are two kinds of cells, and most of what we need to know focuses on neurons. Glial cells tend to be there to do repairs, to act as insulators, and to remove waste products from the brain. Neurons are cells that receive and transmit messages. Messages come into the cell from another cell, and then are sent on to yet another cell. The process of receiving information and sending it on takes place by chemical changes in the neuron itself. Box 7 explains a bit more about neurons.

Box 7

A neuron and the synaptic gap

Dendrites are like fingers spread out from the cell body, and these dendrites link to other cells. The way they link is very important and is explained below. An **axon** also leads from the cell body. This axon is a single 'cable', and has a sort of bulb shape at the end. This axon terminal 'meets' the dendrites from other cells. The important point is that they don't actually touch, but there is a gap, called the **synaptic gap**.

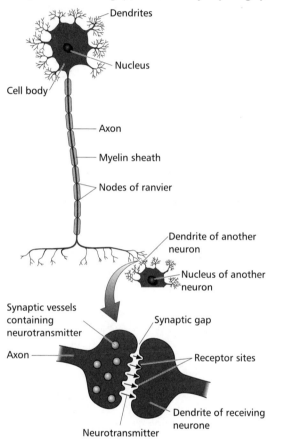

Figure 6.1

If the conditions are right, the message received at the cell body in turn sends a electrical impulse or signal down the axon. This electrical signal is called an **action potential**. The electrical signal will trigger a chemical, which is released at the axon terminal. This chemical floods into the gap, which is also called the synapse. If this chemical is 'right', it will 'fit' into the receptors that are at the end of the dendrites of the receiving cell. If the fit is right (if they match chemically), then the message continues up the dendrite to the cell body. In the right conditions, that cell body then triggers an electrical impulse, which goes down that cell body's axon to release the next chemical and so on. The chemicals that are released are called **neurotransmitters**.

There are sensory neurons, which carry information from the sense organs. There are motor neurons, which carry information to the muscles, and there are interneurons (by far the most), which do all the other work. The interneurons do all the connecting between sensory and motor neurons.

The shape of neurons does vary a lot, depending on what their job is. Neurons that carry a lot of information are wider, for example. Some neurons with widely branching dendrites receive information from lots of sources. Other neurons have short dendrites which branch a lot, and these neurons are where a lot of information is sent very quickly over a short distance.

Usually cells divide and dead cells are replaced; however, cells in the brain don't have this ability. Neurons in the brain develop their shape and their function, and then remain. However, Purves & Hadley (1985) showed that dendrite patterns do change. Some branches grow and extend, and some disappear altogether, so although cells remain in the brain, the patterns change, so the structure of the brain is not completely fixed. Alcohol affects the pattern of dendrites in rats (West, Hodges & Black, 1981) and in mice (Riley & Walker, 1978).

Evaluation

- We therefore conclude that alcohol affects our brain, thus generalising from non-human animals to humans. However, be critical of these sorts of conclusions, since the brains of rats and mice are not the same as our brains.

The central nervous system

The CNS consists of the spinal cord and the brain. The spinal cord carries messages to and from the brain by means of neurons. If the spinal cord is cut, the brain loses sensation from all parts of the body that the spinal cord below the cut serves. The brain also loses control over those parts of the body.

The brain is divided into lots of different parts (Figure 6.2), but usually it is said to have three divisions. These are the hindbrain, the midbrain and the forebrain. Research into the various functions of the different parts of the brain is still continuing, although a lot is known. In the A2 part of the course you will need to learn more about the different parts of the brain.

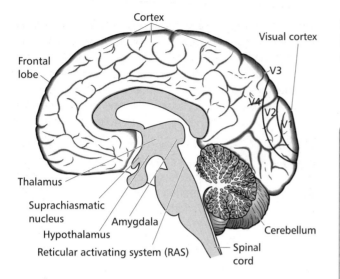

Cortex

Visual cortex

Frontal lobe

V3

V4

V2

V1

Thalamus

Suprachiasmatic nucleus

Amygdala

Hypothalamus

Cerebellum

Reticular activating system (RAS)

Spinal cord

Figure 6.2

The hypothalamus – an example of the effect of a small part of the brain on our behaviour

One particular part of the brain has been chosen to illustrate the importance of the nervous system when looking at behaviour. The hypothalamus appears to do quite a lot for us. It is found in the brain, towards the spinal cord. It seems to be important in motivated behaviours such as eating and drinking. Temperature regulation and level of activity are also controlled by the hypothalamus. This sort of information is assumed to be the case, because when the hypothalamus is damaged, problems in such motivated behaviours tend to occur.

So it is assumed in biopsychology that the nervous system plays a large part in our behaviour, and that to understand our behaviour we need to take into account the activities of neurons and hormones.

Drugs and behaviour

Another way of appreciating the importance of the nervous system on our behaviour is to study the effect of drugs. Briefly, an electrical signal is sent along the axon and triggers the release of neurotransmitters into the synapse. The synapse is a gap across which the neurotransmitter, which is a chemical, passes. If the receivers across the gap are the 'right' ones for the chemical to 'fit', then the message is successfully transmitted. The right chemicals fit into the right receivers, and these in turn trigger an electrical signal and the message continues on its way. The process of sending the electrical signal, triggering the neurotransmitter and fitting into the receiver, needs more careful explanation. However, in general you should have the main idea.

Think of drugs like cocaine, caffeine and nicotine as affecting neurotransmitters. Drug molecules are like the neurotransmitters and are similar shapes, so they can fit

into the receivers and a message can be passed on. However, the fit will not be exact. Box 8 gives an example of how a drug might work.

Box 8

One cause of schizophrenia might be an excess of the neurotransmitter 'dopamine'

Some types of schizophrenia seem to be linked to an excess of dopamine. Dopamine is a neurotransmitter (see diagram on 183). It seems likely that some people have too many dopamine receivers, so dopamine is taken up and used to send on messages. There is something wrong then with the messages received. Those with schizophrenia tend to show disorganised thinking, for example. They often make no sense and jump around from one topic to another. If manufactured drugs are taken, these can block or fill some of the dopamine receivers. When dopamine is released by the electrical charge down the axon, it flows into the synaptic gap. The receivers are opposite, waiting for the chemical. If drugs can be given, and can block some of the receivers, then some dopamine is received, but a lot is lost. The messages received do seem to be more 'sensible'. So anti-schizophrenic drugs are based around the idea of filling up dopamine receivers.

We would not be able to see dopamine activity, we would only see a person who had the symptoms of schizophrenia and we would conclude they were 'mad' since they were not talking 'sensibly'. Some people, given these anti-schizophrenic drugs, would then start talking normally again. We might then conclude that they are sane. This illustrates well the importance of the nervous system when looking at behaviour. Note that not all of those said to be suffering from schizophrenia are helped by anti-schizophrenic drugs. This suggests that the idea of excess dopamine cannot be the only explanation for schizophrenia. You might study this idea in more detail depending on which applications you choose to study in the A2 part of the course.

The drug PCP or 'Angel Dust' works by serotonin receivers being blocked. Serotonin is a neurotransmitter. Thought processes and emotions are inhibited or blocked by serotonin. If serotonin receivers are blocked by Angel Dust, then thought processes and emotions can run more freely, hence the effect of the drug.

Research methods used in the physiological approach

Methods are very important in the study of the brain and behaviour and are outlined in Chapter 7. However, 'biological' methods outlined here, that are specific to the physiological approach, are not repeated in Chapter 7 (which focuses on methods you are likely to use yourself).

Research methods Group 1 – 'biological' methods

Since we are looking at biology, you will probably guess that these are 'scientific' methods. Activity 3 asks you to come up with some of the methods used in the physiological approach.

ACTIVITY 3

List some ways in which researchers have learnt about how our physiology affects our behaviour.

Think about ways in which we can learn about our physiology. Some have been mentioned, and other ways can be guessed. Make a list before you read on.

Key Skill C3.1a – if you are studying in a group, this would make a good group activity.

- Brain scanning is much more widely used now and means we can look at active brains.
- Non-human animal studies are very common indeed, because it does seem that we can do to non-human animals what we cannot do to humans.
- We can look at problems that people have, and we can link these difficulties to any brain damage they have, and draw conclusions. Recall the case of Clive Wearing outlined in Chapter 1, showing that damage to the hippocampus meant lack of ability to pass information from the short-term to the long-term memory.

Invasive methods – lesions, ablations and surgery

This is a nice way of saying that one way of studying how we are affected by our physiology, especially the physiology of the brain, is to damage bits and see what happens. Usually this is done to non-human animals (recall the ethical arguments mentioned earlier and in Chapter 8), but sometimes humans are used. If parts of the brain are removed through cutting or burning with electrodes, this is called **ablation**. If an area is damaged but not removed, this is called **lesioning**. Another way is to stimulate a certain area of the brain, and see what effect this has. Lashley (1950) wanted to know about memories, and he systematically removed parts of the rat brain to see what effect this would have on memory. He found that it was the quantity that was removed, rather than which particular part that was removed, that affected memory, so he assumed memories are spread over the whole cortex (see earlier diagram). Studies of aggression often involve non-human animal experiments. Areas in the brains of cats and bulls, amongst others, are stimulated to see what happens. Cats can be sent into pretend rages (Bard, 1928), and bulls can be stopped mid-charge (Delgado, 1969), simply by sending an electrical signal into a particular area of their brain. In these examples it was found that the limbic system seemed to be important in aggression.

In humans some invasive surgery is used but not only to learn about the brain. Surgery is used to try to help the patient. You may have heard of pre-frontal lobotomies, which were used on many patients in and around the 1950s. Moniz used the technique and received a Nobel prize for it, even though it has been widely criticised and is no longer used. Think of something sharp being inserted so that it damages the front of your brain. Although this technique may have had a calming effect on some people, you can imagine the brain damage it caused. Some surgery is still used, but not in this crude way. The method was crude, because they did not really know what the results would be, or even why any changes occurred.

Evaluation

- Much of the research is done on non-human animals. You need to study Chapter 8 to read about the problems in using non-human animals when wanting to learn about humans. On the positive side, there are many similarities between non-human animals and humans. For example, the studies on cats and bulls, which looked at aggression, involved stimulating their limbic systems. Humans have limbic systems too, and it is not unreasonable to assume that if a non-human animal's limbic system is involved in aggression, so is the limbic system of a human. On the negative side, however, cats and bulls are not humans. A well-known example shows the dangers of generalising from non-human animal studies to humans. Thalidomide was a drug which was tested extensively on rabbits, including pregnant rabbits. However, when it was used on pregnant women, many of the babies were affected by the drug. This showed that testing on rabbits and finding that a drug is safe, does not mean that it is safe to use on humans.

- Some of the conclusions drawn from invasive techniques come from humans. The case of Clive Wearing has already been mentioned (see Chapter 1). So it seems reasonable to draw conclusions about humans from studies using humans. However, these studies are done on people with problems. When using non-human animals, the researcher can be careful that only one particular part of the brain is damaged, and then they can see what happens. This is not the case with humans who already have damage. It is almost certain that the damage will not be kept to one particular area of the brain. So it is hard to draw conclusions because there are too many things that could be causing the behaviour or problem being looked at.

- Experiments can always be criticised for not looking at natural behaviour. Although it is difficult to see what else could have caused the bull's charge to be stopped by the signal in Delgado's study mentioned above, you could always say that there was something else that could have caused it. There was invasive surgery on the bull, who must have been tranquillised, for example, so we don't know for sure that other damage was not done at the same time.

Non-invasive methods

Electroencephalogram (EEG)
Some techniques are called 'non-invasive' because they do not involve entering the brain of the human or non-human animal. The electrical activity of the brain can be measured from the outside. Electrodes are fitted to the scalp and the activity is recorded. Recall the action potential which is the electrical impulse travelling down the axon of the neuron, and triggering the release of neurotransmitters, so that the brain is actively sending and receiving messages. The EEG can measure action potentials, and the brain's activity levels are recorded. The EEG is used particularly when studying different levels of consciousness including sleep. Note that an EMG (electromyogram) records the electrical activity of muscles, and an EOG (electrooculogram) measures the activity of the eyes.

The EEG measures wave patterns, and can detect small changes. Usually the wave patterns are fairly constant, so you would not see small changes, but if the measures are done over and over again, and then a computer works out an average wave size, small changes can be seen more clearly.

Brain scanning
There are different types of scanning, but they all involve using an external machine to 'take pictures' of a brain in action. You may even had had a scan done yourself. One type of scan is a CAT (computerised axial tomography) scan. In this case an X-ray moves around the head and captures 'slices' of the working brain, which the computer can then put into a whole picture. CAT scans are generally used to detect brain damage, tumours and associated problems. Engineers work with medical experts to find a way of forming diagnoses from the CAT scan images.

Another type of scan is a PET (positron emission tomography) scan. This is very similar to the CAT scan, because the computer generates the images from the information in the same way. This time, however, instead of X-rays, a radioactive tracer is added to oxygen or glucose – something that the body uses. As the tracer is used in the body, this will show up as an area of activity. More or less glucose could indicate a tumour, for example.

There are also MRI (magnetic resonance imaging) scans. This time a strong magnetic field is passed through the head (or other parts of the body). The effect of this magnetic field on some element in the body is measured and a computer again generates images. Much clearer pictures are generated from an MRI scan than from a CAT scan.

Studies using scans include studies of what parts of the brain are for language and thinking. Hypnotised people have also been studied to try to settle the argument as to whether there is such a thing as an hypnotised state. Schizophrenia has been studied by comparing scans of identical twins, when one is schizophrenic and the other is not. If there was something different in the brain of the schizophrenic twin, then this might be a cause of schizophrenia. You might be interested to know that one such difference is in the ventricles.

Evaluation

- Well, scans do seem to be very accurate. When scans show tumours and operations are carried out, a tumour is found, for example. Similarly, if different types of scan are used, they do show the same abnormalities and absence of abnormalities. Some scans are clearer than others, because of the methods used to highlight problems. Also someone is needed to visually examine the computer-generated pictures, and these people are relied upon to interpret the results successfully. As mentioned above, research is being carried out at the moment to make sure that tumours and problems are recognised as such. Also there is a delay in getting the results of the scan. This delay can be very important. Work is being done on producing immediate images so that this delay can be removed. From a research viewpoint, as well as a medical one, scans are very useful and accurate ways of finding out what is happening in the brain.

- One problem of using scanners to do research is that they are very expensive. Even if hospital scanners are used for research, this happens rarely because they are in such demand for medical use. In the future researchers will probably have more access to scanners.

- EEG measures also seem accurate. It is not easy to criticise biological measures, because they do seem to be replicable. This means that the measurements are carried out over and over again and yield the same results.

- One criticism that you can offer of 'biological' measures like scans and EEGs is that they assume a reductionist approach to study. Recall the difference between reductionism and holism. The reductionist approach looks at a problem bit by bit, which can be successful. However, the holist approach says that, although you can learn about something by looking at its parts, you can never study the whole thing in this way. So EEG patterns might tell us a lot about sleep, for example, but we learn a lot by talking to individuals about their experiences of sleep too.

Research methods Group 2 – genetic influences on individual differences

This second group of methods used in the physiological approach involves more 'standard' psychological ways of investigating, such as interviews and questionnaires. The biological element is still there, in that it is physiology that is of interest, but the actual methods are those outlined in Chapter 7. An example of when these different methods are used, is when studying genetics. Biological measures can be used as outlined earlier. However, other 'non-biological' methods give a lot of information – for example, looking at certain characteristics in families.

Correlational techniques and twin studies

A **correlation** involves mapping a relationship between two variables, and noting that the two variables change together. A **concordance** rate is given, which means the rate of agreement between two things. So you take something measurable like diagnosed depression, and you can see if it has a biological basis. This is explained below.

Firstly, Activity 4 asks you to think about methods used in studying the influence of genes on behaviour, so that you can come up with the ideas yourself. I hope you can see that you can be a psychologist yourself, because you already have a lot of the knowledge. You will hopefully be able to come up with the same ideas as others have used, and you should be able to do successful studies yourself (always bearing ethics in mind of course).

ACTIVITY 4

HOW WOULD YOU STUDY GENETIC INFLUENCES ON INDIVIDUAL DIFFERENCES?

Think about what has been said about the influence of genes on behaviour. You will already have come across some methods used

in such studies. List as many methods as you can think of that would be useful. Most of what you have looked at so far concerns understanding of genes from a biological point of view. However, it has been emphasised that genes affect our behaviour too. In your list think of methods you could use that would look at genes from the point of view of the behaviour they might affect.

Key Skill C3.1a – if you are studying in a group this is another good topic for discussion. You could also gather evidence from other sources and do a presentation for other key skills in the area of communication.

Hopefully, you made a list that included plant and non-human animal experiments, such as those done by Mendel. Genes are isolated and examined. Where changes are made to the non-human animal or plant, the effect of those changes is carefully logged. In this way the effects of individual genes are recorded and knowledge is built. However, the other way of looking at such information is to study families. You might have come up with this idea yourself. If, for example, it is thought that schizophrenia is linked to changes in DNA then it is reasonable to think that schizophrenia might run in families. Activity 5 asks you to think of the best way of comparing families when you want to look at the effect of genes on behaviour.

ACTIVITY 5

HOW TO STUDY FAMILIES AND SEE HOW BEHAVIOUR MIGHT BE AFFECTED BY GENES

Think about families and how you might study them. For example, you would have to decide which families to study. You would have to decide which family members to study. Then think about problems with your method. Make a note of how you would choose the family, who you would study within the family, your reasons for your choices and what problems there would be in doing the study.

Key Skill C3.1a – another good activity for group discussion. You can learn a lot by sharing ideas with others in a group.

Using schizophrenia as an example

Some clues were given earlier. When discussing brain scanning it was mentioned that scans of identical twins could be compared, where one has schizophrenia, and one does not have schizophrenia. Any differences in the brain might be linked to schizophrenia. So one good way of studying genetics is to look at identical twins.

One way of choosing a family is to find one where there is a clear incidence of something like schizophrenia. There are problems with this method of investigation, as will be seen. Hopefully you have already noted some of the problems.

Gottesman (1991) showed that schizophrenia does run in families. (This is not to say that families cause schizophrenia, of course, and we need to look at problems in this area.) Gottesman and others studied twins. There are identical twins, and these are called **monozygotic** (MZ) twins. Monozygotic means deriving from a single egg. There are also non-identical twins, and these are called **dizygotic** (DZ), which means deriving from two eggs. The important point is that MZ twins share 100% of their genes (and are always the same sex), whereas DZ twins share 50% of their genes. All siblings (other than MZ twins) share 50% of their genes. Each child inherits 50% of its genes from the mother, and 50% from the father. **Siblings** are natural brothers and sisters. So DZ twins are like any other pair of siblings.

Self-test 2

Note down why the study of MZ twins is important – what can we conclude by looking at MZ twins that we cannot easily discover any other way?

Any behaviour or characteristic that is inherited, and contained in our genes, should appear more in MZ twins than in other siblings. If something is completely inherited, it should always appear in both MZ twins. It is very interesting to note that rarely is any behaviour or characteristic that is of interest to psychologists always found in both MZ twins. If MZ twins share 100% of their genes, anything totally transmitted by genes must always appear in both twins.

So by studying MZ twins we have a good chance of measuring how far something is genetically given. Gottesman and others have studied MZ twins and want to see if schizophrenia is inherited. We already know that not all MZ twins both have schizophrenia. In other words, where one MZ twin has schizophrenia it does not mean that the other one has it too. So we already know that schizophrenia is not completely genetically given.

Here is where we look for a concordance rate. To what extent are MZ twins more likely to both have schizophrenia than any other siblings, such as DZ twins? This is a useful question we can ask when using correlational techniques and twin studies.

When one MZ twin is schizophrenic, the other one has about a 50% chance of being schizophrenic too. Even when the other twin does not have schizophrenia, they seem to have other disturbances. With DZ twins, however, there is only around a 15% concordance rate. This means that in only 15% of cases where one DZ twin has schizophrenia does the other one have it too. The evidence is, therefore, quite strong that schizophrenia has a large genetic component.

Self-test 3

Although a 50% concordance rate for schizophrenia amongst MZ twins, compared with a 15% concordance rate for DZ twins, suggests a genetic element in the cause of schizophrenia, why does it look as if there are other causes, besides genes?

If genes were the only cause of schizophrenia, there would be a 100% concordance rate for MZ twins, and this is not the case. Box 9 adds a little more information about schizophrenia and about using correlational techniques.

Box 9

Handedness, MZ twins and schizophrenia

When you look more closely at that 50% concordance rate for schizophrenia amongst MZ twins, you find that there is more to it. When the researchers looked at right- and left-handedness in those MZ twins, they found something quite interesting. Where the MZ twins they studied were right-handed, there was a 92% concordance rate, which means that in almost all cases where MZ twins were right handed and one had schizophrenia, the other had schizophrenia too. However, where the MZ twins were mirror images with regard to handedness, that is where one was right handed and the other left handed, the concordance rate for schizophrenia was 25% (Boklage, 1977).

This is in a way even more evidence for a genetic link. MZ twins share 100% of their genes, but there must be more to it. If some MZ twins match with regard to handedness, and some are opposites, then they obviously have differences. Those with the same 'handedness' must share something that also is involved in schizophrenia.

Evaluation

- Correlational studies and twin studies have problems with their design. That 50% average concordance rate seems to have masked other factors. If almost all of the one group of MZ twins (both right handed) matched and only a quarter of the other group (opposite hands) matched, then these two figures when put together give the 50% average. However, the 50% does not actually mean anything.

- Imagine that you ask ten girls and ten boys what they want to do. Imagine that all the girls in the group choose to go to see a film, and none of the boys in the group choose to see the film. Overall, 50% of the group wanted to see the film (10 out of 20). If we only know that 50% wanted to see the film, then we lose the important information, which is the gender difference in the decision.

- You can also criticise correlations in general for not showing cause and effect. Just because schizophrenia runs in families does not mean that the cause is passed on through the family. Families also share their environments, so if something runs in families it could be due to something in their shared environment.

- Regarding schizophrenia specifically, you have already read about some suggested causes, besides the fact that it runs in families. An excess of dopamine receivers might cause schizophrenia, or there could be some problem in the brain, for example, enlarged ventricles. These two possibilities could be genetically given. The point is that there are often many possible causes for something like schizophrenia. The explanation could be that there is no 'thing' that is schizophrenia, but that the word simply describes a set of symptoms that could have different causes.

Adoption studies – using schizophrenia as an example

It can also be useful to study children who have been adopted. Imagine MZ twins brought up in different families (called 'reared apart'). If they were to show similar behaviour, even if brought up apart, we might claim that this shared behaviour was inherited via genes. Similarly, if the child of a schizophrenic mother is adopted, and develops schizophrenia, then we might say that schizophrenia is genetically given, because the child is brought up away from the 'influence' of the mother. It is interesting to note that 'adoption studies' do show a strong inherited factor in behaviours such as schizophrenia.

Kessler (1980) found that when adopted children with schizophrenia are studied, more of their biological family have schizophrenia than do their adopted family. This suggests that schizophrenia is genetically given. Other studies have found the same thing. A child with a schizophrenic parent who is adopted is more likely to develop schizophrenia than a child without a schizophrenic parent who is adopted by a schizophrenic parent.

One interesting study looked at records in Norway and Denmark of paternal half-siblings (children of the same father, different mother). The study looked at adopted people with schizophrenia, and found some paternal half-siblings who were also adopted. So there was no issue over shared environment. The half-siblings did not even share their mother's environment before birth. The researchers found 63 pairs where an adopted person had schizophrenia and also had an adopted half-sibling. They found that eight of the half-siblings also had schizophrenia. Eight out of 63 is above what would normally be expected, so again there is evidence for a genetic basis to schizophrenia.

Evaluation

- You need to remember that families that adopt can be remarkably similar. They have to pass an investigation, for a start, and have to want to adopt. There are more differences now, and, for example, 'same sex' couples can adopt, but when the studies that are usually given as examples were done, adopting parents were mainly middle class. So the MZ twins who were 'reared apart' could have had very similar environments. This rather spoils the conclusion that if they show similar behaviours, then these must be inherited.

- Also when it is said that MZ twins were reared apart, it is important to note that at that time (leading up to the 1960s) unmarried mothers often did not bring up their children. It was often the case that the unmarried mother's own mother brought the baby up as her own (as the unmarried mother's sister or brother). This was very common. With twins, the babies were often split between the unmarried mother's own mother and others in the family (an aunt, for example). So twins were reared apart, but often in the same family, so a similar environment – and even the same school.

- This problem of deciding what part of our behaviour is due to 'nature' and which is due to 'nurture' is going to reappear often in the study of psychology. Little seems to be completely inherited and due to 'nature'. However, from studies such as twin and adoption studies, you will also find that quite a lot of our behaviour is inherited, in other words it is not just 'nurture' either.

In-depth area of study – states of awareness

The in-depth area of study chosen to illustrate the physiological approach to the study of psychology is 'states of awareness'. You should note that throughout psychology, physiological factors are important. If you want to find out about people, it is hard to ignore their 'biological' side. For the in-depth area of study, however, discussion is limited to 'states of awareness'. You can probably think of times when you are more 'aware' than others. Activity 6 asks you to consider these different states of awareness.

ACTIVITY 6

DIFFERENT STATES OF AWARENESS

Note down as many different states of awareness as you can think of. Are you fully aware now for instance?

> Key Skill C3.1a – this would make a good group activity and pooling ideas would be useful here.

You may have come up with some of the following (or more):
- day dreaming
- fully awake
- dozing
- cat napping
- deep sleep
- dreaming
- coma
- hypnotic state
- trance
- unconscious
- faint.

The states of awareness looked at here are the more usual ones of sleep and dreaming, rather than the more unusual ones of being in a coma or unconscious.

Bodily rhythms

It seems that we move through different states of awareness during the day. Actually we have other regular rhythms or cycles besides daily ones. Activity 7 asks you to list some regular rhythms or cycles that humans and non-human animals go through.

ACTIVITY 7

SOME REGULAR RHYTHMS AND CYCLES

List some cycles that humans and/or non-human animals go through.

This would be a good group activity as brainstorming might help.

> Key Skill C3.1a – use this for a group activity. Brainstorming entails using a large sheet of paper and then everyone in the group contributes something. There is no discussion at this stage. Then you can start grouping comments, and considering them.

Here are some examples of our regular rhythms and cycles.
- **Infradian rhythms** last longer than a day. An example is menstruation.
- **Ultradian rhythms** last for less than a day; an example is sleep. Although we might sleep once a day, within our night's sleep there are rhythms and patterns.
- **Diurnal rhythms** occur during the waking day. An example is our ability to study, which seems to vary during the waking day (Adam, 1980).
- **Circannual rhythms** last for about a year, and an example is a non-human animal's hibernation and waking patterns.
- **Circadian rhythms** are daily rhythms, and each cycle lasts about 24 hours. Examples are temperature, metabolic rate and sleep/wake cycles.

Circadian rhythms, or daily bodily rhythms

Aschoff and Wever (1981) discuss circadian rhythms, and suggest that for humans these are important cycles. Heart rate, metabolic rate and temperature are at their lowest in

---

ACTIVITY 8

TESTING THE CLAIM THAT OUR DAY'S ACTIVITY AFFECTS DAILY RHYTHM

Note down how you could quite easily test the claim that it might be because we are active during the day that our heart rate, metabolic rate, temperature and breathing rate are higher in the afternoon than in the morning.

---

the morning and their highest in the afternoon. Since we are active during the day, it is likely that these rhythms will be 'high' by the afternoon. Activity 8 asks you about how you could test this.

The usual way of testing whether our daily activity affects our rhythms is to see if those on shift work, who sleep during the day, also have higher temperature, heart rate, breathing rate and temperature in the afternoon. If they do, then whether we are active in the day or not does not seem to be the cause of the changes. Activity 9 suggests you collect some data on your own changes in bodily rhythms.

ACTIVITY 9

COLLECT DATA ON YOUR OWN BODILY RHYTHMS

It would not be very ethical to use many participants but you could use 'yourself'. Over a period of 33 days keep notes about how you feel during the day. When are you tired? When are you cold? When are you most alert or most sleepy? If you work with someone else on this activity you could compare notes to see if there are common patterns. It would be useful to note down the time you go to sleep, and when you wake up.

If bodily rhythms show a similar daily pattern for people with different life styles, it seems that these rhythms are part of our 'nature', and not our upbringing or 'nurture'. The next question is whether they are completely natural, and internally triggered, or whether they rely on external cues in the environment to set them off. Activity 10 asks you to list some external cues and then to think of a way of testing the question whether they are important in the process of daily rhythms.

ACTIVITY 10

HOW COULD WE SEE IF EXTERNAL CUES TRIGGER OUR DAILY BODILY (CIRCADIAN) RHYTHMS?

There is one way in particular that has been used to see if external cues are necessary for our daily bodily cycles to exist. Firstly, list some external cues you think are important.

Secondly, suggest a way of testing the question of whether they are needed to trigger our daily cycles .

Key Skill C3.1a – this would make a good group activity since pooling ideas would be useful.

Zeitgebers

External cues are called **zeitgebers** and there are many zeitgebers that might trigger our daily bodily rhythms. You may have listed:

- daylight
- sunshine
- clocks
- smell of food
- reaction of others
- TV programmes

Some of these would give us an idea of the time itself, and others would be clues as to what was about to happen (e.g. the smell of food suggests it is lunchtime). You may also have suggested that one way of studying the effect of zeitgebers on physiological factors like body temperature and heart rate is to remove these external cues. Box 10 outlines a study that did exactly that.

Box 10

What would happen to our circadian rhythms if all external cues or zeitgebers are eliminated?

Siffre (1972) spent seven months underground to test what would happen to our daily cycles. In particular, this was to test the 24-hour sleep/wake cycle. There were no zeitgebers such as natural light or sounds. He had no way of knowing what time it was, although he did have contact with the outside world via a telephone. He had food and drink and so on. His behaviour, such as when he went to sleep, when he awoke, and when he ate meals, was monitored. It was found that he settled to a 25-hour cycle.

From Siffre's study it was concluded that our internal clocks have a 25-hour cycle. So zeitgebers must reset the clock to our usual 24-hour day.

Evaluation

- Note that Siffre's study was one study of one person so you could ask if we should then apply it to everyone. Also his body was used to 24 hours, so the 25-hour cycle may have been affected by what he was used to.

Our body clock – an endogenous pacemaker

Our body clock appears to be in the suprachiasmatic nucleus (SCN), which is in the hypothalamus. Part of the evidence for this conclusion is that when the SCN is damaged, circadian rhythms become random over the day. The SCN receives information directly from the eyes, and the eyes register day and night. The retina in the eye responds to light, and there is a link between the retina and the SCN. Therefore, it is the 24-hour day/night cycle that keeps us on this 24-hour cycle, and not on the 25-hour cycle which Siffre's study suggests is more 'natural'. The SCN is located just above the optic chiasm and this means that the optic nerve can make a direct connection between the SCN and the retina. It seems that the blind can still use daylight to reset the clock. Studies with mice, where their rods and cones are damaged so they are blind, show that daylight still resets the biological clock (Foster, 1993). So the pathway from the retina to the SCN seems separate from the 'seeing' pathways. If a non-human animal's SCN is cut away but still works, the neurons still show impulses that follow circadian rhythms, so the SCN has a rhythm of its own (Green & Gillette, 1982).

We can, however, reset our clocks. We can adapt to shift work, or adapt to a new time zone, for example when flying to Australia. Some people do take more time than others to adapt, though, and some never adapt. Some bodily rhythms adapt more quickly than others, and body temperature adapts the most quickly. So external cues do not seem to fully account for bodily rhythms, because people are different.

Internal cues are called **endogenous** and external cues are called **exogenous**. Animal studies show that if the SCN is taken from one animal and implanted in another, the receiver of the transplant changes to the donor's bodily rhythms (Ralph et al, 1990). This gives more evidence to suggest that bodily rhythms are internally governed (endogenous). Other endogenous pacemakers control our body temperature, our urine flow and so on. The sleep-wake cycle is also an endogenous pacemaker and is examined in more detail below.

Sleep – a circadian rhythm and an ultradian rhythm

Sleep is an important circadian rhythm. Within a 24-hour period (which is the definition of a circadian rhythm) we usually have one prolonged period of sleep. However, sleep is also an ultradian rhythm, because within the prolonged period different patterns are found. A class activity is now suggested (Activity 11), if you are able to find a number of people to work with. Activity 11 suggests that you study patterns of sleep to see what you can find out by comparing results from different people. This would make a good piece of coursework too.

ACTIVITY 11

Get a lot of people to note down their sleep patterns, and compare these results.

You should work within ethical guidelines here (see Chapter 8). It is a good idea to use fellow students, as you are less likely to cause offence, and also you can all help each other. If, however, you do not have access to other students, ask your friends.

You could take this opportunity to develop a questionnaire. It would be useful to know how long people sleep on average. Do they cat nap? Do they dream? Are there periods of deep sleep and periods of light sleep that they can identify? If you do this as coursework it would be useful to know about problems such as a young baby in the house, or someone on shift work, but if it is not easy to ask such a question, then just take this into account in your conclusions. If you make a note of the person's age (if they consent to give this information) and their average hours of sleep each night, you could do a correlation of hours slept against age. You might find that the older the person, the fewer hours slept.

Key Skills IT3.1 – if you do this as coursework you can look at the Application of Number key skills and your data collection/calculations should get you evidence for some of these. Also you can do research from the Internet and CD-ROM and so get some IT key skill evidence too.

Most people will say that they sleep on average seven or eight hours a day. This might be a problem with your study, as you will probably find that this is a standard answer. It shows the difficulty with questionnaires, and underlines the point that you need to know exactly how long they sleep each night.

We think that sleep is one thing that we do. However, within this long sleep, there are different rhythms, as has been hinted at above. Note that we are talking about the prolonged period of sleep, and not about naps.

Nightly sleep patterns

There has been quite a lot of research into sleep patterns. For a long time there was no way of studying sleep cycles. Then the EEG was developed, and it became possible to measure electrical activity in the brain. Loomis, Harvey and Hobart (1937) used the EEG and watched the wave patterns during sleep. These patterns changed, and the changes seemed to link to different types of sleep.

For Activity 10 you may have found that people do admit to different types of sleep. Some are more aware as they begin to wake up, for example. Other people say they dream a lot. Some people will say they never dream. As research progressed, a rolling of the eyes was thought to be linked to sleep. Aserinsky (1952) was using an EEG and wanted to test it. So he used his son, Armond, who was eight, to test the machine. He connected it up, and also used an EOG to measure eye movements. The EOG at one stage was so active that Aserinsky thought it was damaged, but he found that the rapid eye movement (REM) was related to a specific stage in sleep. This REM occurred more than once during the night. The EEG measures showed the most activity at the same time as the EOG showed REM. Dement and Kleitman (1957) investigated REM and wanted to know what sort of sleep this was. So they woke their participants up when the REM was seen. Most often, the participants said they were dreaming. When they were woken up at other times, when there was no REM (in NREM or non-REM sleep), they did say they were having dream-like experiences, but it was not the same as dreaming. The real dreams had more visual images, for example. From this study, it was concluded that REM occurred when the person was dreaming.

From EEG patterns it was seen that there were different stages of sleep, besides the REM sleep. The NREM sleep could be divided into four separate stages. Box 11 (see p. 194) outlines the stages of sleep.

Box 12 looks more closely at REM sleep.

Box 12

REM sleep

The EMG shows that during REM sleep our muscles are paralysed. However, heart rate does change and breathing becomes shallower. Also the eyes move rapidly (REM) and the brain is very active, as shown by the EEG patterns. So although muscles are paralysed, there is a lot of movement in other areas, so sometimes REM sleep is called paradoxical sleep.

Cycles of sleep

First cycle
The first cycle down the staircase, back up to Stage 2, and into REM sleep takes around 50 minutes.

Second cycle
Then there is 25 minutes in Stage 2 again, followed by a brief move through Stage 3, and into 30 minutes of Stage 4, which is deep sleep. After moving back to Stage 2, the second sleep cycle ends with another period of 10 minutes of REM sleep.

Third cycle
The third cycle includes about an hour in Stage 2 again, but no descent through stages 3 and 4. Instead one further hour of REM sleep is experienced.

Fourth cycle
The fourth cycle does not involve stages 3 and 4 either. Seventy minutes of Stage 2 is followed by another hour of REM sleep.

Activity 12 asks you to draw a table listing all the above points so that you can see clearly how someone moves up and down the NREM stages from 1–4 and back to 2, and also how REM sleep fits in.

Fifth cycle
The fifth cycle usually involves waking up. It is called the emergent cycle. The emergent cycle does not involve stages 3 or 4. Sometimes people wake from REM sleep, and sometimes from Stage 2 sleep. Notice that although you may have found that some people claim not to dream, according to the above studies, everyone does

Stages of sleep showing EEG criteria

Box 11

Four stages of NREM sleep

The EEG measures waves of electrical activity. You can see on a monitor that these look like real waves. There is the height of the wave (amplitude) and the distance between the waves (frequency). The frequency refers to the cycles per second, and this refers to the distance between the waves. The fewer the cycles per second, the further apart the waves would be on the EEG.

- When we are awake and alert the EEG shows low-amplitude, high-frequency beta waves.
- When we are in bed and relaxed, the EEG shows higher amplitude, slower frequency alpha waves.
- As sleep occurs, our heart rate slows and our body temperature drops. Then the EEG shows theta waves. This is STAGE 1 sleep, and we are easily awakened. As we go from stage 1, our bodies might suddenly jerk, or we might 'see' dream-like images and we move to stage 2.
- STAGE 2 sleep quickly follows stage 1 sleep, and the waves have a medium amplitude, with a frequency of

4–7 cycles per second. There are bursts of activity showing a frequency of 12–13 cycles per second, and these bursts of activity are called sleep spindles, but not much is known about these.

- STAGE 3 sleep has slower frequency of waves (2–3 cycles per second) and these waves are called delta waves.
- STAGE 4 sleep occurs when the frequency slows to under 2 cycles per second. In both Stage 3 and Stage 4, the person is hard to wake. The EOG shows no eye movement and the EMG shows muscles are relaxed. See earlier under 'research methods' to see what EOG and EMG are. In Stage 4 our heart rate is slow and our temperature is low. At this Stage we reach the bottom of the sleep staircase.

From the first stage of sleep to Stage 4 takes about 40 minutes (to descend the sleep staircase).

Then we climb the staircase again, but not back to Stage 1. At Stage 2 REM starts and we start dreaming.

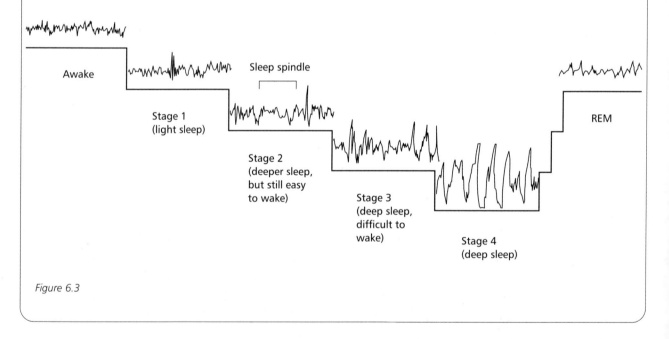

Awake

Sleep spindle

Stage 1
(light sleep)

Stage 2
(deeper sleep,
but still easy
to wake)

Stage 3
(deep sleep,
difficult to
wake)

Stage 4
(deep sleep)

REM

Figure 6.3

---

dream. It must be that some do not remember. Theories of dreaming are looked at later in this chapter.

Age and sleep

It has been suggested that you test whether there is a correlation between age and sleep, and it might be the

case that we sleep less as we get older. Sleep patterns do vary with age. Babies when they are first born sleep for approximately 16 hours a day and about half of this is REM sleep. At the age of one, the child sleeps for approximately 12 hours a day, with 30% REM sleep. When we are adults only about 25% of our sleep is REM sleep, and the elderly have even less time in REM sleep. By retirement age Stage 4 sleep has nearly gone so we are more easily woken up. Eight hours for anyone up to the age of 30 decreases to six hours at the age of 70.

Why do we sleep?

This section looks at the functions of sleep and asks why we sleep. When you go without sleep, you know how that makes you feel. Studies have been done where people are deprived of sleep to see what happens. Depriving people of sleep has even been used as a form of torture. In 1898 Patrick and Gilbert deprived three young men of sleep for 90 hours and noted that they suffered illusions and disorientation. When allowed to sleep, they slept for longer than normal. In 1959 Tripp, who was a disc jockey, did not sleep for eight days and also had hallucinations and delusions. However, Dement (1972) studied the case of Randy Gardner, who stayed awake for 264 hours. Gardner did not seem to have the same problems as were found in the other two studies quoted here. He did sleep longer when he did finally go to sleep, but was fine when he woke up.

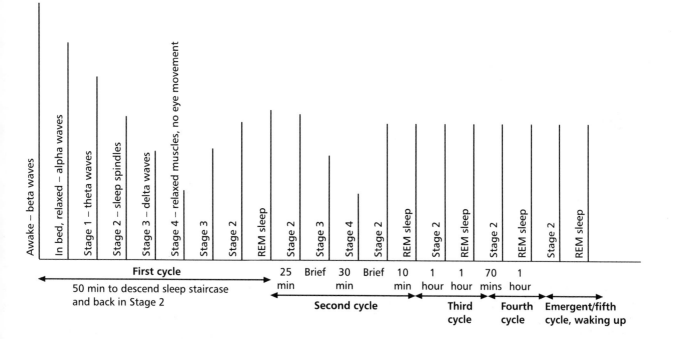

Figure 6.4
Cycles of sleep

Box 13 outlines a non-human animal study that looks at the effects of sleep deprivation.

Box 13

Rechtschaffen et al's (1983) study of rats and depriving them of sleep

Rechtschaffen et al (1983) did a controlled study to look at why we sleep. They deprived rats of sleep to see what the effects were. There was a disc sticking up from out of a bucket of water. The rat was placed on the disc and an EEG kept track of its brain activity. When the EEG pattern showed that the rat was asleep (see above for indications of which waves they were looking for), the disc was rotated. The rat had to walk with the rotation of the disc on which it was standing, otherwise it would fall into the water. Another rat on another disc was also monitored by EEG. However, when this rat's EEG pattern showed sleep, the disc did not rotate. So one rat was allowed to sleep, and the other was not. They used more than one rat, and after 33 days each time, all the rats who were deprived of sleep died, whereas none of the 'control' rats died.

It seems that sleep is vital to our survival. It seemed the rats died because they could not regulate their heat, although this was not certain. In any case, something about depriving them of sleep must have been the cause of death.

Evaluation

- Recall the arguments about using non-human animal studies to draw conclusions about humans. We could not do this experiment using humans, for ethical reasons, so it is difficult to test the above conclusions on humans. It is true, however, that if we are deprived of sleep for any reason we do start falling asleep at any opportunity and at any time of day. So it does look as if we do need sleep.

- Horne (1988) claimed that the rats were not only deprived of sleep but were continuously stimulated, and it might have been this, rather than the loss of sleep, that led to their deaths.

Hüber-Weidman (1976) – The effects of sleep deprivation

This study summarises the effects of being deprived of sleep over a period of time. For the first night most people suffer few problems, even though they might feel a bit low. After that, however, the effects grow. In the second night, the individual will have a greater desire to sleep, and this is especially true between 3 a.m. and 5 a.m. at night when the temperature is lowest. By the third night, information processing is affected and simple tasks become difficult. This is even more true for boring tasks, although more interesting ones are still not carried out so well. By the fourth night, the individual will have micro-sleeps, which mean they will stare/sleep with their eyes open. There is a tightening around the head, and the person will become confused and irritable. Night five might bring some delusions, although the intellect still functions. The sixth night can lead to loss of identity.

All the above are psychological symptoms and physiological ones are less noticeable. Heart rate, body temperature and reflexes seem to be the same, and if we are deprived of a lot of sleep we don't need to spend more and more time asleep to make this up. We don't need to make up all the hours of sleep lost, as might be expected if there were physiological problems associated with sleep deprivation.

It was also found that there are few long-term effects of going without sleep, and earlier studies that showed such problems seem not to be supported by Hüber-Weidman's conclusions.

Two theories of why we sleep – the evolutionary theory and the restoration theory

The evolutionary theory of why we sleep

Different species sleep for different lengths of time and with different patterns. It seems that their sleep patterns reflect their needs. Meddis (1979) suggested that sleep patterns evolve. Recall the explanation of survival of the fittest, which suggests that any properties we now have are a result of what has been useful in the past. It is suggested here that we sleep because it is useful for our survival, or was at one time.

Non-human animals who are at risk from predators don't sleep much, for example. Cows and sheep only nap for say 2 hours at a time. Non-human animals who have safe places to sleep and do not need to eat often sleep for much longer, even 14 hours a day. Each of these patterns would have been likely to keep the animal safe to reproduce and pass on the genes for these sleeping patterns.

Hibernation theory

Sleep can even be useful in keeping the animal (including humans) out of reach of predators, and might have stayed with us for that reason. Webb (1982) put forward the idea that sleep is useful in itself, because those animals who slept were more likely to survive. Sleep keeps us quiet. Webb's theory is an evolutionary one, but is often called the hibernation theory of why we sleep.

Evaluation

- It seems a good idea to say that sleep must serve (or have served) a useful purpose or we would not sleep. The idea of evolution has been outlined earlier, and we have said that most of our characteristics and properties have come about because they were useful. Those who fit their environment best were the ones to survive and reproduce, and so whatever they did (including their sleep patterns) was passed on through the genes.

- However, the hibernation theory has been criticised because a sleeping animal is a vulnerable one. Also you could say that animals at risk from predators sleep infrequently so that they are on guard (cows and sheep), or that animals at risk sleep for a long time to keep them quiet and safe. These two ideas contradict one another.

The restoration theory of why we sleep

The evolutionary theory says we sleep to keep us safe and to conserve energy. This seems reasonable. However, a theory that gives sleep a more active role is restoration theory. Perhaps sleep survived because it was useful, but there may have been other reasons for sleeping that were also useful. One such reason is given by Oswald (1966), who claimed that whilst asleep our bodies could repair cells and restore energy, amongst other things. Some say that neurotransmitters are restored during sleep (Webb & Campbell, 1983).

There is evidence that in Stage 4 sleep the pituitary gland releases a hormone that is important in tissue growth, and we do sleep less as we age, so both these pieces of evidence do suggest that the restoration theory might be right. Some people suggest that sleep restores us on a psychological level too. Those suffering from insomnia seem to have more psychological problems, and we usually need more sleep when stressed (Hartmann, 1973).

Evaluation

- This seems logical when you think that the more we do in the day, the more we look forward to our sleep. Shapiro et al (1981) found that after running a marathon, people slept over an hour longer than they usually did, which is evidence for the restoration theory of why we sleep.

- However, lack of exercise does not mean we sleep less. Ryback and Lewis (1971) found that normally active people who stayed in bed for six weeks resting did not change their sleep patterns. Activity 13 suggests you could test this to a limited extent yourself.

- Saying that those suffering from insomnia have more psychological problems does not prove that we need sleep to restore us. The psychological problems could be causing the insomnia. Horne (1988) looked at various studies and said the body does not restore itself during sleep any more than it does awake, except in the brain.

ACTIVITY 13

TESTING THE RESTORATION THEORY – DOES EXERCISE LEAD TO MORE SLEEP?

You could test this out on yourself over a few days and measure the time you sleep (if you don't have to wake to an alarm clock). Or you could devise a questionnaire to see if people think they sleep more if they exercise. One way is to choose those who exercise compared with those who don't, and see the differences. Alternatively, you could find people who sometimes exercise and compare the differences between their sleep patterns when they exercise and when they don't. This is only a rough guide, as you will probably find that they have to wake at a certain time anyway. You could ask if they feel they want to go to bed earlier, or questions like that.

The restoration theory of why we need REM sleep in particular

Protein synthesis seems to occur in REM sleep and this could lead to cell growth. Also, depriving animals of REM sleep seems to affect their learning, so protein synthesis might be linked to forming memories.

Evaluation

- Babies spend a long time in REM sleep, whereas adults do not, so this supports the idea that REM sleep, with its synthesis of proteins, is needed for cell growth and development. Also, if someone takes a drug overdose, which impairs brain functioning, they do then spend a lot more time in REM sleep. This again supports the idea that REM sleep is needed for restoration purposes.

Why do we dream?

Related to the question of why we sleep is the question of why we dream. This area is studied a lot and is only briefly presented here. It was because of the EEG patterns, and the realisation that REM sleep was when people dreamt, that a lot was learnt about dreaming. When participants were woken up in REM sleep, they described their dreams, so there was a lot of data to go on.

The activation–synthesis model – a physiological explanation of dreaming

According to the activation–synthesis model, during sleep various parts of the brain are active and some sort of story is built up to make sense of what is happening in the surroundings (Hobson & McCarley, 1977). One version of the activation–synthesis model is that in REM sleep the brain is aroused and ready to make sense of external stimuli, but there are few external stimuli around – not much is happening. So the brain starts using memories and starts making sense of them (Antrobus, 1986). So if you dream about floating or flying, the idea could come from movement of your body in some way. In REM sleep you might dream that you want to move and cannot, and this is explained by the fact that your muscles are paralysed in REM sleep.

Activity 14 asks you to reflect on your own experiences of dreaming to think about this theory.

ACTIVITY 14

EVIDENCE FROM YOUR OWN DREAMS FOR THE ACTIVATION–SYNTHESIS MODEL

Think about your dreams and see if you can explain them by referring to memories or some other events. These other events might be external, such as road traffic, or internal, such as movements in your body. Often you can explain dreams by thinking about what you watched on television the night before, for example. If you get the opportunity, compare notes with others.

You could do some coursework around the activation–synthesis model if you think you have people that you can ask about their dreams. Don't forget to follow the ethical guidelines (see Chapter 8). You could devise a questionnaire that asked people to briefly outline dreams the day after they have dreamt them. Then they are asked to pick out central points and see if they can recall something that happened the day before that fits the situation. You would need to find a way to analyse the information. You might like to count the number of incidents that are given, and then count the number of times that the individual feels they can account for these incidents by referring to the previous day's events.

> Key Skill C3.3 – you might find dreaming an interesting topic and dreaming comes up in Chapter 5 as well. So this might be a suitable topic for an essay and some extended writing. Research the different theories of why we dream, and evaluate them. You might try to come up with an answer to the question 'why do we dream?' and you could use that title as an essay title.

Hobson (1989) showed the firing of neurons in the brain of cats during REM sleep. The firing of these nerve cells activates other cells such as those involved in vision and walking. So cells are activated. In REM sleep, however, movement is prevented by paralysis of muscles. So perhaps this activation is synthesised (made sense of) by alternative interpretations from memory. In this way we experience a dream.

One reason for the firing of the cells is that the neurotransmitter acetylcholine still remains, and the brain activity continues. Once the neurotransmitter is 'discharged', the brain activity stops. When acetylcholine is available again, REM sleep starts again.

Evaluation of the activation–synthesis model

- Some say that this explanation is too vague. Also it does not account for everything dreamt about. In Activity 14 you should have found that some of what you dream about is accounted for by real things that have happened, but some will not be accounted for in this way. Also you might dream about not being able to move, and that links to the paralysis of muscles in REM sleep, but you might also dream about moving, which goes against the explanation. Also people have dreams that repeat, and some that have personal meaning (Winson, 1993). These dreams are not explained by the activation–synthesis model.

- In favour of the activation–synthesis model is the fact that dreams do not make perfect sense. If the brain is interpreting this random firing of cells, then it is likely that there will be no coherent story in the dream, and this is indeed the case.

- A criticism of the activation–synthesis model is that because we do seem to dream about the day's events, dreams are not as random as this random firing of cells suggests they might be.

- Another way of evaluating a model is to look at a different model. Then you can say that one is not a good explanation, because the other is a better explanation.

Freud's theory of why we dream – not a physiological theory

STUDY AID
Evaluation

If you are asked to give a physiological theory of dreaming, you need some biological explanation. So you might think that learning about Freud's non-biological explanation for why we dream is not useful.

However, one good way of evaluating one theory is to explain another theory briefly. Then you must say that the first theory can be criticised because there is another equally powerful theory. If the second theory explains the facts better, then it is an even more useful comment on the first theory.

An example of this tactic is given here. You can give the activation–synthesis theory as the physiological theory of why we dream. Then you can evaluate it by giving Freud's views on why we dream. You must say clearly that Freud's theory is equally useful because it explains different kinds of dreams such as repetitive ones. In other words you have to put in writing that one theory criticises another. Do not leave it to the marker in an examination to draw the links for you.

Freud wrote a book called *The Interpretation of Dreams*, which was published in 1900. He claimed that the purpose of dreaming was to release urges and wishes that the individual is not aware of. When we are awake we don't admit to these urges. They are in our unconscious,

and are not made conscious. We use up valuable energy in repressing these wishes, however. This energy can be released through dreaming. Even in our dreams, however, we do not see the content of our unconscious. The repression is still in place. So the content of our dreams is not what we are 'really' dreaming about. We have to look for the underlying meaning, and the obvious content is symbolic.

The dream analyst looks at the **manifest content** of the dream, which is what it is about according to the individual. The analyst then looks for the underlying message, or **latent content** of the dream. There are some symbols that are common across dreams, such as dreaming about apples for breasts. However, each dream should really have individual relevance. Much of what is repressed and released by dreaming is thought by Freud to be sexual in nature. Note, however, that although a broken pencil could represent impotence, even Freud thought that sometimes it is just a broken pencil.

Evaluation

- One criticism of Freud's theory about dreaming is that people do dream of impotence (Fisher & Greenberg, 1977). Also, as suggested by the activation–synthesis model, the content of dreams is often based on what happened the day before, rather than representing unconscious wishes and desires. Also the interpretation of dreams is **subjective** (the individual's own views can be used), not **objective**. Different analysts can interpret the same dream in different ways. This means that the process is not **reliable** (remember, reliable means if you do it again you get the same results).

Reprogramming theories of dreaming – physiological theories

Reprogramming theories of dreaming relate to restoration theories of sleep. They are called physiological theories because they suggest that the biological brain activity that is still present in REM sleep is interpreted by cognitive processes that are still active. Cognitive processes involve perception, language, memory and thinking (see Chapter 1).

Evans (1984) suggests that the brain needs a period of time when it is relatively inactive, and can sort out the day's information. REM sleep is when the brain sorts out memories and takes on board new information.

Evaluation

- There is support for this idea, since we seem to have more REM sleep if we have been engaged in a lot of mental activity. Also it could be argued that, since older people have less REM sleep, they also are engaged in less mental activity, and have less need to reprogramme their memories. However, this is rather a generalisation. Note the use of a computer analogy, when memories are said to need reprogramming. Relate this analogy to the material in Chapter 1.

Foulkes (1985) also put forward a reprogramming theory. It is argued that dreams are a result of activity in our nervous system. Brain activity during REM sleep may be random, but our logical cognitive processes are still working in REM sleep. These cognitive processes work to make sense of the random brain activity. One reason for dreaming may be to sort new information into our memories, taking into account past experiences. Another reason might be to update our own self-consciousness. A third reason might be to prepare us for events that might happen. Foulkes's idea is similar to that of Evans and the same evaluation points can be used.

Studies within physiological psychology

Dement and Kleitman (1957) – the relation of eye movements during sleep to dream activity

Background

This study is important, not only because of what it tells us about REM sleep, but also because of the method used. Earlier, under the heading 'research methods', the use of the EEG was outlined. It was the development of this machine that enabled Dement and Kleitman to recognise the different stages of sleep, and in particular the existence of REM sleep. Lack of sleep in general is recognised as leading to problems, some of which were discussed earlier when looking at studies where non-human animals or humans were deprived of sleep. However, lack of REM sleep seems even more important, as shown again by sleep deprivation studies. If people are deprived of REM sleep by being woken up, then their next sleep has more REM sleep, as if making up for what was lost. When people are woken up in REM sleep, they mainly report that they were dreaming, and that is what this study is about. It has also been suggested above that since REM sleep is when we dream, and since we seem to need REM sleep in particular, it is likely that we need to dream.

Hypotheses

Dement and Kleitman were testing a number of **hypotheses**. They were looking at whether dreaming is associated with REM sleep more than NREM sleep. They also wanted to know if the length of dreaming linked to the length of rapid eye movement measured – did a long period of REM mean there was a long dream? Also they

wanted to look at the actual pattern of rapid eye movement, to see how it fitted with the content of the dream. Did the rapid eye movement represent the visual experience of the dream?

Method

They studied seven males and two females in a controlled laboratory setting. Five of the participants were studied in more depth than the others, and most of the data were taken from these five people. Physiological changes were measured using an EEG to study brain waves. Eye movements were also measured. Dement and Kleitman measured the brain activity and eye movements, found out what people were dreaming by asking them, and then found a measure for when people dream. This is the basic claim of the study.

It was Aserinsky and Kleitman (1955) who first noted the link between REM and dreaming. They simply woke people up when REM was observed, and discovered that the participants reported dreaming much more often than when they were woken up in NREM sleep. Their conclusion was simple – that dreaming takes place in REM sleep.

Dement and Kleitman in the study described here found that these REM/dreaming phases occurred at regular intervals through the night. They asked participants about the length of their dreams and looked to see whether longer dreams were reported when there was longer rapid eye movement. They looked at the content of the dreams, to see whether the pattern of the eye movement matched the visual content of the dream in each case. They also avoided the experimenter being present when the participant recalled the dream, to make sure that there was no **experimenter effect**, for example the participant taking their cue from the experimenter.

The study was carried out overnight. The participant ate normally all day but did not drink alcohol or take caffeine. He or she arrived before bedtime and the electrodes were positioned around the eyes and on the scalp. The participant went to bed in a quiet, dark room. The wires from the electrodes were connected to an EEG in another room, and the speed of the measures was adjusted so that the eye movement and brain patterns could be clearly measured.

Participants were woken up during the night and asked about their dream recall. They usually took only a few minutes to go back to sleep. Overall they were woken up 21% of the time in the first two hours, 29% of the time in the second two hours, 28% of the time in the third two hours, and 22% in the final two hours of the eight-hour period.

Some participants took part for only one night, and others for 12 or 17 nights.

Results

Rapid eye movements

All participants had periods of rapid eye movement, and had periods of deeper sleep around these REM periods. There were no REM periods at the start of the sleep. They found that REM periods (where the participant was not woken up) lasted from 3 minutes to 50 minutes, and they became longer as the sleep progressed. The rapid eye movement was not continuous but in bursts, they were fairly regular through the night and were the same for each individual. They differed, however, between individuals. If the participant was woken up during NREM sleep, they never went straight into REM sleep. There was a steady pattern in spite of the wakenings. When woken up in REM sleep, the participant did not go back into REM sleep except if this was right at the end of the sleep period.

Rapid eye movements linked to dreaming

Participants were woken up by a bell and then spoke into a tape recorder. They had to say whether they were dreaming, and then say what the dream was about (if they could). The experimenter was listening and could go into the room to ask more questions if they wanted to. Participants were woken up both in REM and in NREM sleep and were not told which was the case each time. The conclusion was clear – that REM sleep showed more dreams than NREM sleep.

Note that the dream recall had to take place immediately, or there was much less recall. So it would be difficult for us to test any of this by means of a questionnaire, as people would not remember their dreams sufficiently well.

If participants did not recall having a dream, but were in REM sleep, this was almost always early in the night. In NREM sleep, participants were woken from a deeper sleep. They often felt that they had been dreaming but could not recall the dream at all.

Length of REM and length of dream

For this test, at first participants were woken up and asked to estimate how long they had been dreaming. However, this test was too difficult, and so the test was changed. The participants were woken up at either 5 or 15 minutes after the start of the rapid eye movement. Then they were asked if they thought they had been dreaming 5 or 15 minutes. From the five main participants, it was seen that four of them were very accurate when choosing 5 or 15 minutes. Also the longer the REM, the longer the participant could talk about the dream (as measured by the number of words used).

Visual imagery in the dream linked to specific eye movement patterns

The rapid eye movements within the REM period were very varied and it was thought that they might represent the visual imagery of the dream. The problem was that participants could not say where they had been looking. So they were asked the content of the dream when they were woken up at a particular time in the REM period. If the eye movements were vertical, the researchers looked at the content of the dream then, and so on. Thirty-five pieces of data were gathered from nine participants. Periods of only vertical eye movements were rare (three occasions), but on one occasion a participant was dreaming about a cliff with hoist equipment, and was looking up the cliff face. On the second occasion the participant was dreaming about going up a ladder, and on the third occasion the dream was about basketball, and looking up at the net to take a shot. There was only one occasion of pure horizontal movement, and then the participant was dreaming about two people throwing tomatoes at each other. When there was no eye movement, the dreams tended to be 'stationary' ones, where the dreamers were watching something in the distance. When there was a mixture of movements, the dreamers tended to say they were talking to a group of people, and looking at objects close to them. To test these findings the researchers measured the eye movements of some participants whilst they were awake, and the movements did match those registered in the studies by the machine. For example, there was little movement when the participants were watching from afar, but more movement for close-up watching.

Conclusions

It seems that REM periods occur regularly through the night, and that dreaming occurs in REM sleep. REM is not the deepest sleep. Those dreams that were said to be during NREM sleep could have been left-over recall from a REM sleep dream. More dreams are recalled later in the night, rather than in early REM. Some people say they don't dream, but this study strongly suggests that everyone does dream. Dream recall was best when done immediately, though, and normally people do not try to recall their dreams straight away. There seems to be physiological evidence relating the type of eye movements to the type of dream too.

Evaluation

- One very important point about this study is that physiological measures are used. These are scientific in the sense that they are **objective** measures, and should be **reliable**. It is hard to argue with data from EEG readings. Of course, the actual claim that people dream during REM sleep relies on reports direct from the participant.

These reports are subjective, and you could criticise these for being less reliable.

- Most of the data were taken from five participants. Even though the measures were quite reliable and 'scientific' you can see that five people is a very small sample. It must be hard to generalise to the whole population from a sample as small as five.

- Note that in NREM sleep participants did say they felt as if they had been dreaming. Perhaps they were dreaming but could not recall the dream, rather than they were not dreaming at all? This is suggested by Beaumont (1988). If the brain is more active in REM sleep, this might mean that recall of the dream is better, rather than that it is the only time we dream. This difference in the ability to recall dreams is a **confounding variable** – it can explain the findings as well as the explanation that we only dream during REM sleep.

- In favour of Dement and Kleitman's conclusions, however, is the fact that the other evidence, for example matching eye patterns to dream content, does seem to support their claims. Other research supports Dement and Kleitman, for example the activation–synthesis model described above. This model also asserts that the brain is more active during REM sleep and there is neuronal activity then. This supports the idea that we dream during REM sleep.

Effects of 48 hours of sleep deprivation – may increase susceptibility to illness by affecting the immune system (Öztürk et al, 1999)

Researchers in Cerrahpasa Medical School, Istanbul, Turkey, carried out the above study. It is interesting to include a study that came from somewhere else, not Britain or the United States.

Summary

Sleep deprivation increases susceptibility to diseases. This study is interested in the immune system, and they needed to test it. To do this they took blood from 17 healthy young male volunteers. Then ten of the volunteers were sleep deprived and six others were not. These last six acted as the control group. The first polysomnographic recording (checked for sleep disorders, breathing disorders, periodic limb movement and so on) was taken at 8.00 a.m. and then the participants (not the control group) were deprived of sleep for 48 hours. The second blood sample was taken at the 24th hour, and the third at the 48th hour. Then there was another polysomnographic recording done. The results of this second recording showed that all of the sleep-deprived participants showed slow wave and REM sleep rebound. The last blood samples were taken at the 72nd hour at 8.00 a.m. The results showed changes in the proportion of NK cells (they decreased) in the sleep-deprived participants, but there were no changes in the control group. The proportion of NK cells returned to normal after recovery sleep. NK cells are 'natural killer cells' and are a necessary part of the immune system. So it is concluded that sleep deprivation may increase susceptibility to illness.

Introduction

More and more people are being exposed to sleep deprivation. It is generally believed that sleep is needed in recovery from illness and that lack of sleep increases the likelihood of infections. It is interesting to carry out a study looking at the effect of sleep deprivation on the immune system. In non-human animals, sleep loss over 16 days is lethal, due to infection and septicaemia (Everson, 1993, 1995). In another study bacterial invasion caused the breakdown of gut wall in animals in the late phases of total sleep deprivation (Bergmann et al, 1996).

Deprivation studies in humans are better studies in a way, because they can be deprived of sleep by being asked to stay awake, whereas stressors must be used where non-human animals are concerned. So for non-human animals it is difficult to tell whether the stress or the sleep-deprivation gives the problems. Dinges et al (1995) reviewed studies and say that it is not certain that stress is involved in human studies of total sleep deprivation. Dinges et al (1994) studied 20 healthy young adults after 64 hours of total sleep deprivation and found quite a few changes in the blood cell measures. Irwin et al (1994, 1996) reported that modest sleep loss with partial sleep deprivation still resulted in decreases in the NK (natural killer) cells. The NK cells returned to normal after one night of recovery sleep. (There were other measures besides measuring the NK cells but we don't want to go into too much biology here. This seemed to be the most straightforward measure, and the one that was replicated in the study outlined here.)

The aim of this study is to deprive participants of sleep over 48 hours and to take measures as outlined in the summary. Then the results of the blood tests can be compared with those of the controls. Then it should be possible to see the effects of 48 hours of total sleep deprivation, especially regarding the effects on the immune system.

Methods

Participants

Seventeen healthy male participants aged 19–21 volunteered for the study. Two doctors evaluated their mental and their physical health and did complete blood counts. They were all non-smokers and they had no alcohol, caffeine or medication during the study period.

One participant had restless leg syndrome so he dropped out of the study, and this left ten participants who were sleep-deprived and six controls.

Procedure

The first thing done was a polysomnographic recording to test for sleep disorders, breathing disorders and so on. It was at this stage that one participant dropped out of the study.

Then ten of the participants were kept awake for 48 hours, and the other six maintained their usual schedule. The participants were kept under 'sedentary' (inactive) conditions and in the same environment. They were supervised by two doctors to keep them awake. Meals were provided. After 48 hours they were allowed to sleep. Recovery sleep was also monitored to show REM rebound effects. The study protocol was approved by The Ethical Committee of the University of Istanbul, Cerrahpasa Medical School.

Blood samples were taken at 8.00 a.m. every 24 hours for four consecutive days. These were taken at the beginning, at the 24th hour, at the 48th hour and at the 72nd hour. Blood samples of 20 ml were taken and they measured lymphocyte subsets with half, and then stored the rest until various measures were performed including cortisol measures. They did white blood cell, red blood cell and platelet counts, and counted lymphocytes too. The researchers give detail of how this was done. If you are studying biology, you would probably be interested, but it is not really relevant for us. Basically the researchers were measuring what they needed to know to check for a working immune system.

Statistical analysis

The results for each person over the different days were analysed by Wilcoxon Matched Pairs Signed Ranks Test (see Chapter 7). When comparing between baseline and recovery sleep (that is, the results whilst deprived compared with the results after recovery) a Student's *t* test was used.

Results

Compared with baseline sleep, recovery sleep had fewer wakenings. Amounts of delta sleep were increased during recovery, with less Stage 2 sleep. At the beginning of the study, the sleep-deprived participants and the control group showed no difference in the blood analysis.

NK cells decreased by about 37% in the first 24 hours of the sleep deprivation. The level then remained the same at the 48-hour check. The cells returned to normal after recovery sleep. However, other lymphocytes did not change. T-helper cells increased with 24-hour deprivation and returned to normal at the end of the 48th hour, which was unusual. B-lymphocytes did not change during deprivation, but they decreased a lot after recovery.

Discussion

Natural killer (NK) cells are rapidly activated and can protect the host (you) until more specific cells are activated (to fight the particular problem). NK cells are important in defending in the case of viral infections. They are also important in the prevention of the development and progression of cancer. Leukaemia is itself a problem with the red and white blood cells, and there are many types of cancer associated with leukaemia and blood cell count.

The NK cells are influenced by sleep, sleep deprivation and different stresses. Dinges et al (1994) found NK cells decreased at the 24th hour, and then increased during 64 hours of sleep deprivation. This study finds the decrease at the 24th hour, and then very little difference at the 48th hour, so the findings do not exactly match those of Dinges et al. However, other studies have shown similar effects regarding decrease in NK cells (Irwin et al, 1994, 1996) so the conclusions of this study do link with other studies and the findings are reinforced.

The article says that the actual implication of a 37% drop in NK cells is not known. However, they do have a role in fighting against disease and it seems that they are especially important. Therefore, the data imply that sleep is even more important in chronically ill people.

Evaluation

- The study was good in that there was a control group. Often with sleep deprivation studies all the participants are deprived. Öztürk et al point out that there is no established measure of lymphocyte subgroups, so they thought it was worth having the control group. By having the control group, they felt that they could justifiably claim that sleep deprivation causes a drop in NK cells.

- They realised that other studies of sleep deprivation have had the confounded variable of stress. Depriving us of sleep is likely to make us stressed, so findings like these might be caused by stress, not by the sleep deprivation. However, measures during sleep deprivation in humans do not show problems such as those given by stress. Also other studies, such as that of Dinges et al (1994), used psychosocial measures of stress and these showed that emotional distress during total sleep deprivation did not account for changes. In Öztürk et al's study they measured serum cortisol to check for stress, and found no differences between the participating group and the control group. So they thought that stress was not a factor.

- They thought there might have been a problem with taking only one blood sample, but they made sure to take this at the same time of day for everyone, hoping to isolate variables. They thought it might have been better to take the sample at night, but this would have disrupted the sleep of the controls and it would mean taking blood during different stages of sleep, which might have affected the results. Moldofsky (1995) shows that NK cells are influenced by the different sleep stages. They say that they should have actually noted down the real NK count as it would have been useful. They did not do this.

- Ethics can be brought into the evaluation, because clearly we can't go around depriving people of sleep. However, these were healthy volunteers. Also the study was passed by the University ethics committee. We certainly could not consider any study to do with sleep deprivation, so you won't be able to carry one out. However, this particular study was done at Medical School, and presumably they knew what they were doing.

- Another way of evaluating a study is to look at the application of the findings. This study is useful in finding something that can benefit us all. We now know that sleep deprivation, even minor deprivation, can lower the immune system, and so is not a good idea.

Key application – shift work and jetlag

Sleep patterns in humans are regulated mainly by daylight. The invention of electric lights has meant that humans can be active for 24 hours. Coren (1996) suggests that we now sleep one and a half hours less on average than we did 90 years ago. It seems that most people are in a state of sleep deprivation to an extent.

Shift work

There are many institutions such as hospitals, factories, airports and so on that are open 24 hours a day. Supermarkets and shops are increasingly remaining open too. Most of these institutions operate 8 or 12-hour shifts. So those workers who are not working in daylight hours are going against their biological clocks. It is interesting to see what effects this has.

Shift workers often have digestive problems and insomnia. They are often tired and irritable, and can suffer from depression. One problem might be that their temperature clock cannot easily adapt, and so physical problems are likely. So it is not only lack of sleep that is the problem, but the disruption of circadian rhythms in general.

Disasters such as that at the Three Mile Island nuclear plant and Chernobyl do occur in the night, and were associated with decisions made between 1.30 and 4.30 a.m., when the body is at its most sleepy. One of the problems for shift workers is that they change shifts so

often. Usually the shifts are moved backwards, from evening to day, from day to night and from night to evening. Also the change is usually made weekly. This means there is no time for shift workers to adjust their body clocks. Czeisler et al (1982) suggested changing shifts less often, only every 18 days, and also moving shifts forward. So workers would go from day to evening, from evening to night, and then from night to day. This led to better worker morale in a Utah chemical plant that was studied, and also to decreased accident rates in the Philadelphia Police Department (Gordon et al, 1986).

Recall the claim that we sleep because sleep led to our survival; for example, our biological rhythms were useful for fight and flight responses. However, with our industrial society and changed social patterns, these biological rhythms are no longer suitable. This is one cause of stress. The important thing is to recognise our natural rhythms and take them into account. By changing shift patterns to a forward cycle, and by doing each shift for at least 18 days, there is an improvement in morale and work output.

However, in some jobs, especially those of junior doctors in hospitals, individuals are so deprived of sleep that problems are almost bound to occur. Memory is affected and bad decisions can be made.

There are differences between jetlag and shiftwork. When crossing time zones, different zeitgebers are experienced and can help to adjust the body clock, whereas in shift work, the wrong zeitgebers are experienced. Also jetlag tends not to happen all the time (unless you work for an airline), whereas, when on shift work, the individual suffers the changes all the time. Some people are on permanent shifts and yet don't seem to be doing shift work. Postal workers, for example, are on permanent early mornings. Shift work is any regular employment outside the 'normal' working day.

There are problems with studying shift work. Employees worry that questions are being asked for the benefit of the employer, and employers worry that their working practices are being criticised. Also many people find shift work so difficult that they leave the job, so they are not there to be studied. Researchers look at three types of strain for shift workers. The first is the strain from changes in circadian rhythms, the second is strain from sleep problems and the third is social and domestic strain.

Body temperature seems to shift after three weeks of night work, and is slow to adjust. Heart rate and blood pressure adjust quite quickly, however. One of the problems with shift work is that some rhythms adjust more quickly than others, so there is internal 'disagreement' and this can be a problem in itself. Also shift workers get less sleep than day workers, and the quality of sleep is different, often because there is noise in the day. The necessary adjustment of the body clock means that at the start of the change of shift the worker is trying to sleep when his body is not ready for sleep. Also there is more noise in the day – both in the house and outside. Normal working hours are in the day, so shift workers miss out on normal activities. It is hard for them to join a team, for example, as they are working different shifts. Social life suffers, and also the shift worker can miss out on seeing his or her family.

As far as health is concerned, evidence does not show that shift workers are less healthy. Their attendance is not worse than that of other workers. It may be that if shift workers do have poorer health it is because of the changes of bodily rhythms, or it may be that they can do fewer leisure pursuits. Heart problems do seem a bit more likely to occur in shift workers, and sleep disturbances might cause more mental health problems. However, there is no real evidence of this at the moment. (Note, however, the study given above, where it is asserted that sleep deprivation affects the immune system.)

Although there seem to be a great number of accidents happening during the night shift, this could be due to poor lighting or because there is not a full number of staff on duty. It is not necessarily due to the tiredness of the shift worker. There have been studies that have showed 'nodding off' during driving, and loss of attention. Train drivers seem to miss more warning signals at night, for example (Monk & Folkard, 1992). However, there may be pleasure in working the night shift as part of a small team, and moods, although they vary, do not seem more hostile at night.

At the start of a change of shift, in the first four nights, mental performance does not seem to be at its best. This slow adjustment seems to match the slow adjustment of body temperature. However, performance does adjust more quickly than temperature. Reaction time is worse on the first day off after a series of night shifts, and short-term memory is worse too (Meijman et al, 1993).

How to help the shift worker?

Shift workers can be carefully selected, tasks can be redesigned and coping strategies can be suggested. Some personal factors that affect whether you can adjust to shift work or not include age. If you are over 50, adjustment is harder. This is also true if you are not very flexible concerning sleep times, or are physically unfit. Also being a morning-type person is a disadvantage. Some say that women find shift work harder than men, and this might be due to social pressures, looking after house and children, and so on. Women do tend to sleep more than men, but there are no gender differences in tolerance of

shift work when studies are done. Oginska et al (1993) found older women tolerated shift work better than younger women, and this might be due to the social pressures mentioned above. It is hard to see whether the cause of the differences is biological or not.

Choosing the right person for shift work is one way of improving tolerance. Also, it depends on the type of shifts. Weekly rotating shifts should be avoided. The rhythms of the workers do not get time to adjust. It has already been shown that temperature does not adjust that quickly. Some people work permanent night shifts and have no difficulties. They adjust well. Perhaps this is because they get higher wages and less supervision at night. Some people like the atmosphere. Perhaps they are the sort of people that adapt to night work; for example, they are already 'evening types'. However, there are problems because night shift workers have to train their bodies back on their days off, and this would be a difficult adjustment. Really, those on permanent night shift should follow that pattern even on days off.

Coping strategies are another way of adjusting to shift work. These involve zeitgebers. These are sleep, activity, bright light, meals and social factors. These should be worked out so that the changes in circadian rhythms work in favour of the shift. On a rapidly rotating shift, the worker needs a lot of bright light in the day and should avoid a heavy meal during the night shift. It would also be a good idea to have a short sleep during the night shift at some stage to keep sleep to that time (even if short). The problem of keeping the zeitgebers tuned so that the person keeps to a night-sleep cycle is that that person will be less alert on the night shift.

For the permanent night worker the coping strategies must be different. The daytime sleep should be in the dark and the night worker could do with bright light at work. This type of shift would be worse for families.

Jetlag

The sun rises in the east and sets in the west, as the earth spins on its axis. The time the sun rises and sets depends on where you are in the world. Greenwich Mean Time (GMT) is the baseline, and then different places have local time. Countries to the east of Greenwich are ahead, and countries to the west of Greenwich are behind. If you travel to the east, you 'lose' time, whereas if you travel to the west you 'gain' time. For those travelling to Australia, if you go in an easterly direction, you get there 'earlier', whereas if you go west, you get there 'later'. So two people could leave England and head to Australia in two different directions, arriving at these different times, but travelling about the same time.

These different times zones were not really a problem when people travelled by ship, because people had time to adjust their body clocks as they went. However, with fast jet travel there is not time to reset the body clock, and there are problems. The physical symptoms that arise from arriving somewhere with your body clock set to a different time zone are what is called 'jetlag'.

Symptoms can include tiredness in the day but inability to sleep at night, poorer mental performance, poorer physical performance, increased irritability and headaches. Loss of appetite is common too, as well as disorientation. Sleep loss affects mood and means a worse mental performance. These symptoms can be quite serious for many people – especially those whose work takes them across time zones frequently, or athletes who have to perform at their best in a different time zone.

Our body clocks resist change. Usually this is a good thing, because we would not want our clocks to readjust every time we went into a dark cinema for a few hours. However, if you fly from the UK to Hong Kong, when it is 8.00 in the morning in Hong Kong your body will think it is midnight. You will need to wake up and start the day, when your body is ready to go to sleep. Your body temperature will be low, expecting it to be midnight. Your body temperature will be at its highest when you are ready to go to sleep at night. You need a lowered body temperature for sleep. It is not only that your circadian rhythms do not match the new time, but you are short of sleep too.

Other factors contribute to the problems of jetlag. There will be new customs and new food, as well as loss of sleep whilst travelling. These factors are not the whole problem, however. For one thing they are adjusted to quite quickly. Another point is that jetlag still occurs when you fly home, but you are used to the customs and food then. Also if you fly a long way south (to Johannesburg, for example) you do not get jetlag, even though the customs and food are still different. This is taken as evidence that jetlag is connected to circadian rhythms and not just the flight, the stress and the changes in culture.

Jetlag is worse when you fly east. This is because if you fly west you only need to go to bed and wake up later and the body clock will delay. You have to go to bed and rise earlier to advance the body clock, and this is much more difficult to do. It is easier to go to bed later and later and go around the clock delaying than it is to advance the body clock. It is hard to go to bed early because your temperature is too high and you have not been awake enough to feel properly tired. Going west, however, is easier because the flight will make you tired in any case and you will be ready for sleep.

Age makes a difference in adjusting to jetlag possibly because older people have more set routines. There are also individual differences. Jetlag seems to affect differently those people who wake early (often called larks) compared with those who go to bed late (often called owls).

Solutions for jetlag

Sleeping tablets are not a good idea because it is hard to judge the amount needed. People may find they are not at their best the next day and this would not work for everyone. Naps and short sleeps can work, but they must not be too long. Naps are not very good if the body is on 'home time' because the body wants to sleep then in any case, and you are trying to adjust. Another solution is to look for clear zeitgebers in the new time zone. Make sure you are in daylight in daylight hours, for example.

Melatonin capsules have been used and are available. Melatonin marks the body clock and is secreted into the bloodstream between 9.00 at night and 7.00 in the morning. Melatonin is an internal zeitgeber and helps to reset the body clock. If you take melatonin in the evening (new time) this should 'tell' your body clock that night is coming. However, it is not known definitely that melatonin acts on the clock. It could either promote sleep or make you feel better instead. Lewy et al (1992) suggest that melatonin be taken at different times according to whether you want to advance or delay the clock. Going east needs delay, and going west needs advance, remember. Melatonin in the evening will advance the clock, and melatonin in the morning will delay the clock. Melatonin is just becoming available and the results of trials are not yet known.

Timing of meals can be a useful way of adjusting the body clock. High-protein breakfasts make you alert and high-carbohydrate evening meals make you sleepy. These effects are connected with the uptake of amino acids into the brain and their incorporation into neurotransmitters. Scientific tests to look at this idea of diet and jetlag have not really been carried out enough.

Bright light is supposed to help with jetlag, just as it helps with seasonal affective disorder. Bright light does seem to be able to adjust the body clock. Bright light in the morning will advance the clock, and bright light at night will delay the clock. Also you should avoid direct daylight at certain times, so that you don't shift the clock in the wrong direction. When bright light is to be avoided, you could take melatonin. Light boxes are now available, in case daylight is not available. 'Normal' indoor lighting is not bright enough.

Another way of adjusting is to fit in with the lifestyle of those in the 'new' place. Sometimes the daylight hours will fit with what you need, depending on whether you fly east or west. Using zeitgebers in the 'new' place is clearly a good way of adjusting but you may have to avoid them (for example, daylight) at certain times.

Contemporary issue

Narcolepsy

This illustration of narcolepsy is taken from an article in a local newspaper which appeared on 15 February 2000.

Most of us sleep more or less normally. There is a condition, however, called narcolepsy. Those with narcolepsy have frequent moments where they simply fall asleep. This can be at any time, but is often after meals and in the afternoon. Some people find it is worse if they are on shift work. There seem to be no other problems, but this condition can be very disabling, and also dangerous, for example, if driving. Those who suffer are often aged 15 to 25, and more men are affected than women. The condition seems to come from dysfunction of the sleep–wake regulating mechanism that is in the hypothalamus. The cause, however, is unknown, although there is some evidence that narcolepsy is inherited.

The symptoms are that people fall asleep very unexpectedly. They then wake up very refreshed. The periods of sleep can vary from minutes to a few hours, but are often very short. When asleep, the person can be woken up again quite easily, so you can distinguish narcolepsy from fainting. Many people with narcolepsy have hallucinations and two-thirds have cataplexy too. Cataplexy is when the head suddenly slumps and knees buckle. Emotions like anger and extreme laughing can bring on an attack of cataplexy. Also those with narcolepsy might suffer paralysis on waking, but just touching them can bring them out of it.

People suffering from another sleep disorder, called sleep apnoea, don't wake refreshed and are still weary. Diagnosis is usually made by a hospital, and people attend sleep laboratories where their sleep patterns are monitored by electroencephalography (EEG).

There is no cure for narcolepsy, but caffeine can help, as can drugs that stimulate the brain – such as amphetamines. There is a non-amphetamine drug (Modafinil) that is licensed too. Cataplexy can be helped with anti-depressants.

Links to concepts used in the physiological approach

Sleep–wake cycle
This cycle links well to theory studied above. Firstly, sleep patterns are studied in the area of physiological psychology, and this cycle shows that there are some people with different sleep patterns. It is also interesting that we would consider narcolepsy as a 'disorder' because it is not the norm. The problem seems to be in the mechanism in the brain which regulates the sleep–wake cycle. This is evidence that there is such a mechanism, and that it usually works. Also this mechanism is said to be in the hypothalamus, which is evidence for there being such a brain mechanism. The sleep–wake cycle is usually regulated and is a circadian rhythm. For those with narcolepsy this rhythm does not seem to be the same.

Nature–nurture issue
Narcolepsy also sheds light on the question of whether something is learnt (nurture) or inherited (nature). There is no exact evidence in the article, but it is said that narcolepsy might be inherited. Presumably it is likely to occur in families, although it must be more complicated than that every sufferer has a family background of narcolepsy. If that were the case, it would have been more certain that the 'disorder' was inherited. So it looks as if, like many things, there are elements of inheritance and elements of the effect of the environment. Also, as in many things, the exact cause is unknown. This highlights the fact that more research is needed when it comes to finding causes in the brain.

Neurotransmitters and messages in the brain
The idea is put forward that caffeine and other drugs might help the sufferer. There is evidence for drugs being involved in such things as the sleep–wake cycle. Messages are sent by means of neurotransmitters, and communication in the brain is by such means. It seems that if drugs – which affect the communication and the receiving and sending of neurotransmitters – help in some 'problem', then it might be safe to say that neurotransmitters have something to do with the problem. So the condition of narcolepsy reinforces the idea that messages are sent and received by means of neurotransmitters. If you alter the chemicals, then you alter the messages.

Ways of measuring what happens in the brain
The article also refers to the use of the EEG. The EEG measures brain waves and displays them on a monitor. Other studies have shown what 'normal' sleep patterns are, so it is possible to compare such patterns with those of the person with narcolepsy to learn more about it. So this highlights a real life use of such ways of measuring the brain, as well as the use of sleep laboratories. These are used not just for research, but also in medicine.

Shift work
There is also the suggestion that the condition worsens for those on shift work. This links to the key application for this approach. It suggests that our body clocks are

involved in sleep and wake cycles, and that we are adversely affected if the rhythms are upset by 'unnatural' events like doing shift work.

Coursework suggestions

1 A correlation of hours of sleep and age of participant. Is it the case that the older people get, the fewer hours of sleep they need?
2 Do people sleep more (or want more sleep) after they have exercised?

3 If you can find willing people, ask them to briefly note down dreams. Then ask them to try to relate specific aspects in the dream to the previous day's events. For example, if they dream about a boat sinking, have they just watched *Titanic* on video?

Suggested reading

Kalat, J.W. (1995) *Biological Psychology*, Fifth Edition. Brooks/Cole

Pinel, J.P.J. (2000) *Biopsychology*, Fourth Edition. USA: Allyn & Bacon

Wade, C. & Tavris, C. (2000) *Psychology*, Sixth Edition. NJ: Prentice Hall

7 *Methods in psychology*

The aims of this chapter

The aims of this chapter are, with regard to methodology, to enable the reader to:

:
- *describe research methods used in psychology (including experiments, case studies, questionnaires, observations, interviews, and content analysis)*
- *evaluate methods by means of advantages and disadvantages*
- *demonstrate an understanding of important methodological issues (such as hypotheses, designs, levels of measurement, variables, sampling, correlational designs, descriptive statistics and issues of validity, reliability and generalisability)*
- *apply the above issues when carrying out and evaluating a piece of research.*

Self-test 1

After reading this chapter, test yourself on each of the above points. Use the points as exam questions and make notes accordingly. Then see how much you can write on each.

This chapter covers

ISSUES THAT APPLY TO ALL METHODS USED IN SCIENTIFIC RESEARCH

1 Validity
2 Reliabilty
3 Sampling
4 Generalisability
5 Qualitative or quantitative data
6 Types of quantitative data – levels of measurement

MAIN METHODS
1 Experiments
2 Correlational design

3 Surveys by questionnaire
4 Interviews
5 Observations
6 Case studies
7 Discourse analyses, content analyses and analyses of diaries
8 Other aspects of methods

When we are trying to find things out, we ask questions, watch what is happening, or test things out by trial and error. The way we gather information is called the method we use, and the study of such methods is called methodology. Activity 1 asks you to think about why we need to study methods.

Some of the questions that someone should ask are:
• Whom did you ask?
• Where?
• How many people?
• In what circumstances?

• What time of day?
• How do you judge the driving behaviour?
• Were there passengers?
• What were they driving – cars, vans, other vehicles?

We cannot make claims about the behaviour, thoughts or feelings of others without justifying them. We need to be able to justify our methods very clearly if our **findings** are to be taken seriously.

The main purpose of this chapter is to look at possible methods, consider their advantages and disadvantages and end with the knowledge to carry out studies well.

Some issues apply to more than one method, and some are specific to a particular way of doing research. The general issues will be dealt with first, and then the different methods examined.

Issues that apply to all methods used in social scientific research

The following issues are going to be very useful, but this is not obvious at first sight. You need to make sure that you really understand the meanings of the following terms.

Validity

One of the questions you should ask is whether any findings from a piece of research are relevant. Once you start examining how to do a careful study, you may well find that the research loses all connection to reality. Try Activity 2.

ACTIVITY 2

Make a note of at least one study that has used careful controls. The validity of the study is likely to have been queried. For example, experiments use careful controls, and it is often said that what is being measured lacks relevance in any real situation. When a study lacks relevance to real life, it is said to lack validity. Recall one such study.

Key Skill C3.1a – if you are working in a group, you should come up with more than one study and list the problems regarding validity. Keep the notes you make in your group, because you can come back to the task when you look at other issues outlined below.

ACTIVITY 3

CRITICISE THE BOBO DOLL STUDY AND THE STUDY YOU THOUGHT OF FOR ACTIVITY 2

a *Make a note of problems with the Bobo doll study described above and compare your answers with the comments below.*

b *Do the same for the study you thought of for Activity 2.*

Key Skill C3.1b – you could prepare a presentation for this activity. Devise an OHT or some handout outlining the study, then summarise problems with the study, including problems of validity. Do this for both studies.

Box 1 desribes an experiment that lacks validity, and how this affects any conclusions that could be drawn.

Box 1

An example of how an experiment lacks validity – the 'Bobo doll' study

Bandura did a series of studies (sometimes researching with other people) often called the Bobo doll studies (Bandura and Walters, 1963; Bandura, 1965). The children studied were in an unnatural setting, and in unfamiliar surroundings. In one of the experiments, they were shown a film of an adult hitting a Bobo doll. A Bobo doll is one of those that is blown up, and can be punched. I hope you can imagine it. Once the children had watched the film they were allowed to play in a room with toys, and there was a Bobo doll in the room. The question was, would they imitate the adults and hit the Bobo doll? The results were that they were more aggressive towards the doll than were a **control group** of children who had not watched the film, so would not be expected to hit the doll.

The conclusion drawn from Bandura's study was that watching TV leads to imitation of the behaviour seen. Such modelling and imitation is a large part of learning (see Chapter 4). Social learning theory (SLT) is the name of the theory that holds that imitation and modelling are a strong influence on learning.

Think of the setting of the Bobo doll study, however. Could it be claimed that watching TV causes aggression?

- Only children were studied in Bandura's study, so we could only talk about TV causing aggression in children. Also you might have criticised on ethical grounds. However, I will emphasise the lack of validity, because that is what is being discussed at the moment.
- The setting was unnatural. The children were taken out of their own surroundings and were put into a room to watch TV. They watched an adult hitting a Bobo doll, and then taken to a room with such a doll in it. It is not surprising they thought they were supposed to hit it.
- Because the study was in an unnatural setting, it could be said it was not measuring what it claimed to measure – which was aggression in children. It only measured their reaction in an artificial setting, with an artificial task. So the study lacks validity. Their behaviour may not actually have been aggression, because they were simply copying the behaviour they had seen. The study could have been measuring obedience or conformity.

A study is valid if it measures what it is said to measure. If you claim to be measuring aggression, you should not be measuring 'copying adult behaviour'. So the Bobo doll study is perhaps not valid.

Self-test 2

From what you have learnt so far, including material from the earlier chapters if you have studied them, answer two simple but important questions.

1 Are experiments likely to be valid or not?

2 Are naturalistic observations more likely to be valid than experiments?

Experiments are not usually valid. There is much about an experiment that is artificial, including the setting and the task, so it often cannot be said to be about 'reality'. Naturalistic observations are much more likely to be valid, because they are in a natural setting, and usually mean observing 'real' behaviour.

Types of validity

There are different types of validity:

- Having **ecological validity** means actually measuring what you are claiming to measure with regards to the setting. For ecological validity, measures must be taken in a natural setting. If aggression in children is studied in a school playground, by observation, then the study is likely to have ecological validity because the children are observed in their natural setting.
- Having **face validity** means that, on the face of it, the results do appear to be a 'true' measure. So if you ask people the way to the post office, and record whether they point, on the face of it this is a good measure of helpfulness. Of course, they could point you in the wrong direction, so it might not be a valid measure after all!
- Having **construct validity** means that measures are good measures of something, for example a personality trait. This means that you have to look at the sorts of things involved in, say, being an extrovert, and check whether they do go together to make such a trait. For example, if we decide that an extrovert is outgoing and a 'party animal', then these two things must go together in someone for him or her to be called an extrovert. In this example, outgoing people must tend to be party animals to be called an extrovert. Here, extroversion is a construct. At this stage you don't need to worry too much about this type of validity.
- **Predictive validity** tends to refer to therapies and diagnoses, rather than research methods. A therapy or diagnosis might be called valid if what it predicts does happen. For example, say having schizophrenia is defined as, amongst other things, hearing voices. If you are a doctor and find that the prediction that schizophrenics hear voices is useful, then a study showing that schizophrenics hear voices has predictive validity.

Reliability

The reliability of a study refers to what happens if it is carried out again – if it is **replicated**. If a carefully planned and controlled study is repeated with the same care, it is a reliable study if the same (or similar) results are found.

Self-test 3

1 Are experiments likely to be reliable?

2 Are naturalistic observations likely to be reliable?

The clues to self-test 3 were given above: a study is reliable if (a) it is carefully planned and controlled, (b) it can be carefully repeated, and (c) the same results found. Experiments are carefully planned and controlled, so tend to be reliable. Naturalistic observations happen at a particular moment, and looking at a particular situation. Often that situation cannot be repeated, so naturalistic observations tend to be less reliable than experiments.

Notice that less reliable often means more valid, and less valid usually means more reliable. The more natural the setting, the more valid the study. However, the more natural a setting, the less likely it is that the study can be repeated in the same circumstances, so the less reliable the study. Similarly, the more you control the various factors in the study, the more reliable it will be, because you can do it again and get the same results. However, the more controlled the study, the less natural it is, and so it is less valid.

Self-test 4

Are the examples below likely to be more valid, or more reliable?

1 Recording whether men or women are more likely to hold doors open for other shoppers, by observing in a busy shopping centre on a Saturday afternoon.

2 Looking at age and reaction time in a laboratory by dropping a ruler for someone to catch, and seeing how long it takes for the participant to catch it.

3 Seeing if people sleep less as they get older, by giving them a questionnaire asking about the number of hours they sleep each night.

4 Observing children at play, and recording their play behaviour to see how it varies by gender.

There are no definite answers here, because you have only limited information. Here are some *suggested* answers.

1. In general, observations in a public place are more valid than reliable. You would be measuring real helping behaviour, which is what you are trying to look at (there is validity). However, if you (or someone else) watched on a different day, the circumstances would be different and it is less likely that you would get the same result (there is no reliability).

2. In general, laboratory experiments are reliable. Care is taken, for example, over how the ruler is held, when it is dropped, what instructions are given to participants, and how the measures are taken. So when the study is done again by someone else all the conditions can be repeated, and the same results are likely to be found (there is reliability). However, the task is not very realistic – so, as with many experiments, validity is queried.

3. In general, questionnaires are more reliable than they are valid. The problem is that people can lie or not give their answers carefully enough. They may say what they think they should say (this is called **social desirability**), or they may guess what they are supposed to say. In this case the study is said to have **demand characteristics**. If respondents show social desirability, or if there are demand characteristics, then the answers are not 'true' (there is no validity). There is some reliability with questionnaires. If the questions are clear enough, they can be asked again. If participants have been honest, then the questionnaire, when given again, should yield the same results (there is reliability).

4. In general, observations are more valid than reliable. Usually they take place in a natural setting, and involve natural behaviour, so they are measuring what they are supposed to be measuring (there is validity). However, they can be rather subjective, because the results might represent the observer's opinion as to what is happening. If done again, they might not give the same results (there is no reliability). One way around this is to have more than one observer and compare their results. If the results of the two observers are the same, this is called **interobserver reliability**. If the researchers are rating the behaviour they are observing, for example on a scale of 1–5, and there is more than one researcher, this is called **inter-rater reliability**.

Sampling

Sometimes you can study everyone in your **target population** (all those you are interested in). If comparing male and female driving behaviour, your target population would be all male and female drivers. It is rare that you have access to everyone. You *could*, perhaps study all the children under five on a remote Scottish island, if you wanted to, but usually you have to make do with a **sample** to make a study manageable.

The question is, how do you choose your sample? There are a number of different ways, depending on what you need to know and on constraints such as time, cost and availability.

Random sampling

This is probably the fairest way of choosing a sample from your target population.

Box 2

An example of random sampling – the National Lottery

Lottery numbers are chosen by random sampling. Every ball has an equal chance of being chosen each time. The machine swirls the balls around, and then one is taken out. The remaining balls swirl around again, before another one is chosen. Each time, all the remaining balls have an equal chance of being chosen.

You need to find a way of doing something similar if you want to do random sampling.

You need to be sure that all those in the target population have an equal chance of being chosen, although this is often not possible. If you do have all the names, you could put them in a box and pull names out one at a time. This is random sampling, because they all have an equal chance of being chosen.

Often, because the target populations (such as male and female drivers) are large, a particular area is chosen, for example a postcode district. The DVLC (the Driving and Vehicle Licensing Centre in Swansea, where details of drivers and car registrations are kept) could provide the names of all drivers in that area, and, armed with the list, you could randomly sample from that list. You could alot the people on the list numbers, and these could then be chosen by getting a computer to generate random numbers: whatever number is given by the computer, that person would be picked for the sample. However, there could be a problem with the idea of using a database such as the one used by the DVLC. Can you think what the difficulty is?

Box 3

Ethical problems in the use of databases

You cannot use a database to provide names. This is unethical. Not only is it wrong according to guidelines used in psychology, but also it is against the Data Protection Act (1984). There are very strict rules about how data is stored, and how it is used.

It is very difficult to do real random sampling. Certainly in your own research, it would be surprising if you did use a truly random sample. If you find yourself claiming to have used a random sample, stop and ask yourself if it *is*.

The idea of using a random sample is that, if everyone has had an equal chance of being picked, then the sample itself should be **representative** of the target population. You should have someone from each category, for example, and in the right proportion. For example, if there were twice as many women in your target population as men, then twice as many women have a chance of being picked, so things should work out fairly evenly. Even if they don't, at least you cannot have shown any bias when picking the sample.

Quota sampling

With random sampling you don't know what the sample will be like. You know it should represent the target population, but you don't know how your sample will be made up.

Sometimes you have to have representatives from certain groups, and you want to be sure that you will succeed. For example, market researchers are told to be sure to find young middle-class men, young middle-class women, older middle-class men, older middle-class women, and so on. They have these quotas to fill. They have a set number of people to find in each group or category.

You would need to decide what was important. Self-test 4 mentioned that you could do a questionnaire to look at age and sleep patterns. You might want to be sure to ask participants across a wide age range, and with different work patterns, or you might want to avoid people doing shift work. These are decisions you have to make. You might do well to use quota sampling for this sort of study. Quota sampling is specifically choosing to fit an agreed quota.

Stratified sampling

Stratified sampling is difficult to distinguish from quota sampling, because it involves making sure that certain groups are represented in the sample. It is different, however, because:

1 The number of people in each group is in the same proportion as it is in the whole population. This means that if 30% of all drivers drive small cars, you will want 30% of your sample to be drivers of small cars (if driving is your area of interest).
2 When you are choosing the sample of small car drivers (to continue with the example), you would choose randomly from all the drivers of small cars. Quota sampling does not use random sampling.

Systematic sampling

Systematic sampling means taking, for example, the fifth person you meet and giving them a questionnaire, or every third person on the register in a class and asking them to do a task. You are systematically choosing your sample.

This is *not* random sampling. It is often *taken* to be random (and is sometimes called quasi random), but actually not everyone has an equal chance of being chosen. If you choose every third person, then the second person, the fourth person, and so on, never gets the chance to be picked. Imagine an alphabetical register. If there were four people with the name Stevens, only one or two could be chosen, and this would not be random, because the sample would be picked according to the alphabet and not everyone would have the chance of being chosen.

Opportunity sampling

You will find it hard to carry out careful sampling for your coursework. You won't have access to the DVLA computer, and it would not be ethical to use such data in any case. You cannot use data or records from schools, firms or anywhere else, because of the Data Protection Act (1984). You might do quota sampling, but this is very time consuming. It is not always ethical either, as you might (like those doing market research), have to ask people and then say you don't want them because they are the 'wrong' age, for example.

Therefore, most students doing GCSE and Advanced courses use opportunity sampling. This means you take whoever you can get (sticking to ethical guidelines of course). This sort of sampling is usually quicker and more ethical. However, it will be a **biased** sample. If you choose who is available, this is bound not to be representative of your target population. If you ask anyone in your local area on a Tuesday morning, this will be a particular group of people, and everyone else will be excluded. Be sure to mention this source of bias in your coursework, if you use an opportunity sample.

Volunteer or self-selected sampling

Volunteer sampling is where your participants have volunteered to carry out the study. Milgram advertised for participants for his famous study (see Chapter 2), and because they chose to answer an advertisement, they were a volunteer sample. The problem here is that volunteers are self-selected. The participants are similar in that they have all read the advertisement, have had access to the same publication, have the time or inclination to do the study, and have similar interests, perhaps. So this type of sampling is surely biased.

On the other hand, this type of sampling is in a way more ethical. At least the participants have *chosen* to give up their time, and to take part in the study.

Generalisability

A study can be generalised to the target population, but only if the sampling is good. The problem you looked at in Activity 1 raised questions about casually observing men and women drivers and saying that what was found was true of all drivers everywhere (generalising). If only a brief observation was done at one place and at one time, we could *not* say that the findings are true of all drivers everywhere. We could not generalise to the whole population of drivers.

Generalisation refers to being able to transfer results to other people. A study has generalisability if it involves careful sampling from the target population and careful controls. In these circumstances, you could say that what you found from your study can be said to be true of everyone in the area of interest.

Self-test 5

1   Are the findings of experiments, where participants have been carefully sampled, likely to be generalisable?

2   Are the findings of a case study likely to be generalisable?

Whenever there is careful sampling, a study's results are likely to be generalisable. Case studies, however, involve looking at individuals or small groups in depth. This is not careful sampling, but choosing a specific group. So the results are very unlikely to be generalisable to any other individuals or small groups.

Even where careful sampling is carried out, the study will almost certainly be in one area or one country. So findings should only be generalised within that area or country. Often, when studies are done in one country, the findings are said to be true of all countries, and this is where you need to be very critical when studying psychology. There

are differences between cultures, so if you sample a target population from one culture, you should not generalise to a different culture, although this is often done.

Qualitative or quantitative data

Data are what are gathered from any study. Note that the word 'data' is plural, as is 'media'. However, by convention now 'data' is often used in the singular. The data are the findings. They are what we are interested in. Try Activity 4.

ACTIVITY 4

LIST SOME TYPES OF DATA THAT HAVE BEEN GATHERED

Either recall from your studies so far some examples of data that have been collected or flip through the pages of this book. Find a study and make a note of what data are being collected.

Key Skill IT3.1 – you could use the Internet or a CD-ROM to search for this information. Remember to keep evidence for your portfolio.

There are lots of different types of data. For example:
- Milgram (1963) measured the voltage of pretend electric shocks. He asked how far people would go when they thought they were giving electric shocks. His data was the highest voltage the participant would go to.
- Freud gathered data about the content of people's dreams, amongst other things.
- Bandura (1965) wondered if children who had watched a film of adults hitting a doll would, when playing, hit the doll more than children who had not watched such behaviour. The data he gathered was the number of times the children hit the doll.

Quantitative data

Data is called quantitative if it is measured carefully. You cannot easily measure the content of your dreams, but you can count the number of times children hit a doll, and counting is a measure. In what follows you will see that there are different types of data, and that some measures are more 'mathematical' than others. Reaction time is a very clear measure, but rating someone on a scale of attractiveness is not. Both, however, are quantitative data, and quantitative data tend to include numbers.

Qualitative data

Any data that is not quantitative is called qualitative. If a questionnaire asked you to write a short sentence about your attitudes to male drivers, then the data gathered would not be measurable. You could not compare your attitude with my attitude very easily. We *could* say that, if I remembered 10 words from a list of 20 and you remembered all 20, then you remembered twice as many as me – so the number of words recalled gives quantitative data. However, we could not compare our attitudes in the same way. Attitudes gathered in this way are qualitative data. If, however, we scored our attitudes on a scale of 1 ('male drivers are terrible') to 10 ('male drivers are great'), then we would be gathering quantitative data.

Testing memory by counting the number of words recalled means gathering quantitative data. Testing memory by interviewing someone and asking them to recall occasions throughout their life means gathering qualitative data.

Types of quantitative data – levels of measurement

Data can be quantitative or qualitative. Within quantitative, measurable data, there are different types of data, which are called **levels of measurement**.

Data are collected in lots of ways when doing psychological research. The way the data are collected affects the conclusions that can be drawn. For example, you could collect data about temperature. Box 4 outlines the differences between different types of data, using the example of measuring the temperature of a room.

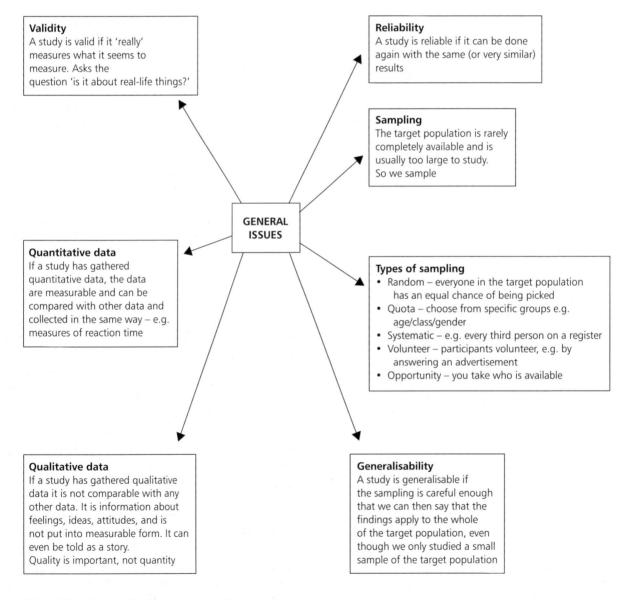

Validity
A study is valid if it 'really' measures what it seems to measure. Asks the question 'is it about real-life things?'

Reliability
A study is reliable if it can be done again with the same (or very similar) results

Sampling
The target population is rarely completely available and is usually too large to study. So we sample

GENERAL ISSUES

Quantitative data
If a study has gathered quantitative data, the data are measurable and can be compared with other data and collected in the same way – e.g. measures of reaction time

Types of sampling
• Random – everyone in the target population has an equal chance of being picked
• Quota – choose from specific groups e.g. age/class/gender
• Systematic – e.g. every third person on a register
• Volunteer – participants volunteer, e.g. by answering an advertisement
• Opportunity – you take who is available

Qualitative data
If a study has gathered qualitative data it is not comparable with any other data. It is information about feelings, ideas, attitudes, and is not put into measurable form. It can even be told as a story. Quality is important, not quantity

Generalisability
A study is generalisable if the sampling is careful enough that we can then say that the findings apply to the whole of the target population, even though we only studied a small sample of the target population

Figure 7.1
General issues of undertaking a study

Box 4

Levels of measurement

- You could say a room is hot, warm or cold. This gives three possible categories. When data are grouped into categories, the level of measurement being used is **nominal** (think of this as giving the data a name only).

- You could say that the room is hotter than it was in the morning, or that it was colder yesterday. So you are ranking the heat in the room as cold yesterday, warm the next morning, and hotter by the afternoon. The level of measurement when ranking data is **ordinal**.

- You could actually take the room temperature. You could note that it was 18°C in the morning and 22°C in the afternoon. Taking the actual temperature means taking a real measure in a way that putting things into categories or ranking them does not. Taking a real measure gives an **interval** or **ratio** level of measurement. For our purposes we can treat interval and ratio data as the same. Ratio data is only different because it starts at zero. Both interval and ratio data use measures that have equal intervals between them. Time is a good example. Time starts at zero seconds, so the level of measurement is ratio. Reaction time cannot really be zero so would be an interval level of measurement.

There are three levels or measurement, or types of data, for the purposes of research in psychology, when studying the AS or Advanced GCE ('A' level).

1 Nominal data (putting things into groups or categories)
2 Ordinal data (ranking data)
3 Interval or ratio data (assigning real mathematical measures)

Numbers are not always interval/ratio, as Box 5 explains.

Box 5

Interval data are numbers, but numbers are not always interval data

We could rank people on a scale of attractiveness (0 = not attractive, and 10 = very attractive). However, if you rated someone an 8, and I rated them as 4, it may not be the case that I think they are half as attractive as you do. I may be in a bad mood, and rate the person I think of as most attractive only as 5; you may be in a good mood and rate your least attractive person as 6. Our ratings are numbers, but cannot be compared or used as mathematical scores.

However, if your age is 20, and mine is 40, I am twice as old as you.

You can see that, with interval data where there is a 'real' measure, you can do mathematical calculations.

Self-test 6

Identify the level of measurement involved if you collected data to:

1 See if males and females are good or bad drivers.

2 Rank people on a scale running from prejudiced to not prejudiced.

3 Measure people's reaction time.

4 Decide if boys are aggressive and girls are not.

5 Rank children on a scale from aggressive to not aggressive, and see if boys are more aggressive

6 See if, on average, males are taller than women, by comparing their heights.

You will not find it easy to decide on the type of data/level of measurement you have gathered. Remember it is not always the data themselves that give the level of measurement (although male and female are always categories). Temperature could be measured at any level, as can many different sorts of data. Aggression can be measured in more than one way, as is shown in Self-test 6.

Examples 1 and 4 give nominal data, examples 2 and 5 give ordinal data and examples 3 and 6 given interval/ratio data according to how I have worded them.

Quasi interval data

Sometimes data are called interval, when the measure is not actually mathematical. For example, you may have done some memory studies and counted the number of words recalled. Although this is not really a mathematical measure like time or height, it is the case that if you recall 20 out of 20, and I recall 10 out of 20, you have recalled twice as many as I have. So we call this sort of data **quasi interval**, and it is treated as interval/ratio. It is *sort of* interval. Quasi tends to mean 'sort of and treated as such'. Earlier it was said that a stratified sample is sometimes called quasi random, and that means 'sort of random and treated as such'.

Why do we need to know about the level of measurement?

You may wonder why it is important to identify levels of measurement. The answer is that you cannot work out what statistical test is needed without knowing what type of data you have. Also it helps in deciding which **measures of**

central tendency you can use. Statistical tests are used to calculate inferential statistics. You will need to know all about this for the A2 part of the course, but not for the AS, so inferential statistics are not fully explained here. Briefly, it is important to note that you cannot do certain tests unless you have interval or ratio data. Some tests use mathematical calculations such as squares and square roots of numbers. If you don't have interval/ratio data in the first place (that is mathematical measures, where there are equal intervals between the numbers) then you cannot find the square root or square of the numbers. To choose which statistical test you need, you must be able to decide what level of measurement is being used.

Conclusion

There are three levels of measurement, for our purposes – nominal, ordinal and interval/ratio. You need to be able to work these out.

Main methods

There are a lot of different methods, and many variations. New methods are constantly being developed. Recall some of the methods you have already studied in earlier chapters. Even if you have started with this chapter, try to list any methods you already know about.

Your list might contain the following:
- laboratory experiment
- field experiment
- natural experiment
- participant observation
- non-participant observation
- structured interview
- unstructured interview

ACTIVITY 5

RECALL METHODS YOU ALREADY KNOW ABOUT

Make a list of any method you know about already, or flip through the pages of this book. Find any study, and note down the method used.

Key Skill C3.1a – this task lends itself to a group discussion. You can pool methods you know about and look up the studies. If there are enough of you, you could choose a chapter each and feed back to the group so each person contributes to the group discussion.

- case study
- discourse analysis
- content analysis
- questionnaire
- free association
- clinical interview
- dream analysis
- longitudinal study
- cross-sectional study
- cross-cultural study.

Self-test 7

When you think you know enough about methods, test yourself by writing down a brief description of each of the methods listed above.

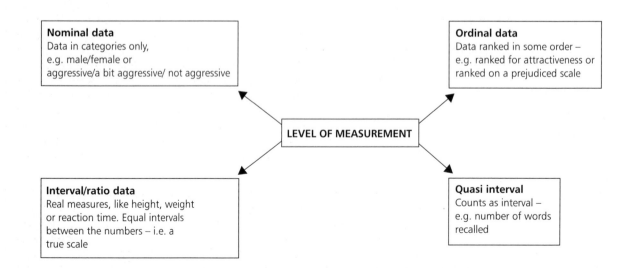

Nominal data
Data in categories only,
e.g. male/female or
aggressive/a bit aggressive/ not aggressive

Ordinal data
Data ranked in some order –
e.g. ranked for attractiveness or
ranked on a prejudiced scale

LEVEL OF MEASUREMENT

Interval/ratio data
Real measures, like height, weight
or reaction time. Equal intervals
between the numbers – i.e. a
true scale

Quasi interval
Counts as interval –
e.g. number of words
recalled

Figure 7.2
Levels of measurement

STUDY AID

Studying this chapter for the AS examination

1 **Coursework** For the Edexcel AS you are asked to submit a piece of coursework for Unit 3. You must do a piece of research for your coursework using a method where you collect quantitative data. Use this chapter to help you.

2 **Approaches** You will also need to know about the methods used within each approach. These are outlined briefly in each chapter; however, you will also need to know much of what follows so that you can answer examination questions on methods used within particular approaches. As you are reading about the relevant methods within the approach, refer to this chapter.

Experiments

Activity 6 asks you to tick what you already know about the use of experiments. This will help you to move through this section more quickly.

Research in psychology has many purposes. The reasons for doing the study often lead to the choice of method. Experiments are chosen because they are 'scientific'. If we control everything and look at only one thing, then we can perhaps come to some conclusions about it. For example, using the 'driving behaviour' example again, there will be many questions and criticisms posed about conclusions if we simply observe driving behaviour as we go along. If, however, we **control** the situation very carefully, and measure only one aspect of driving behaviour, we might be able to draw firmer conclusions. Box 6 demonstrates this.

ACTIVITY 6

TERMS CONNECTED WITH METHODS IN PSYCHOLOGY

Here is a list of terms. You may already know a lot of these so, instead of going over it all again, tick what you already know. If you don't know many of the following terms, read on. Return to this task at the end of this section to check that you now understand.

Control group ☐	Practice effect ☐	Demand characteristics ☐
Null hypothesis ☐	Order effects ☐	Fatigue effect ☐
Dependent variable ☐	Alternative hypothesis ☐	Counterbalancing ☐
Participant variable ☐	Independent variable ☐	Independent groups design ☐
Matched pairs design ☐	Situational variable ☐	
Confounding variable ☐	Repeated measures design ☐	

Box 6

A controlled experiment to look at driving behaviour (don't do this at home!)

Do *not* think of doing this for coursework – there are safety issues, for a start. This is only an example.

Think back to Activity 1 and the casual observation of driving behaviour that led us to say that women are better drivers than men (or the other way around). Think of all the questions that were asked. We need to be more careful in how we do the study. Here is an example of an experiment.

Imagine a disused airfield, or something similar, where we can gather together all that we need. Set out a track, using cones, so that the drivers all have the same task. Use one car, so that the drivers all have the same car to drive. Do the test on one day so that they all have the same conditions (and make sure the daylight is the same for everyone). Give them the same instructions, so that they all have the same information. Don't let them

watch each other, so that none can learn by watching the others. Don't let them talk to each other, so that they can't learn from each other. Choose your sample carefully, if possible (although you are likely to have to take whom you can get, i.e. use opportunity sampling). Make sure your drivers have all been driving for the same length of time. Make sure that none of your drivers is more familiar with the car you have chosen than the other drivers. Make the task realistic, but not so easy that they can all do it perfectly. Measure the number of cones knocked down. The fewer the cones knocked down, the better the driving.

You can probably already think of problems with this idea. However, it should help you to see that if you eliminate as many problems as possible, and make everything as similar as possible, you should be able to say fairly confidently that if someone knocks down more cones than someone else, he or she is not such a good driver.

If you decide to do an experiment for your coursework, Box 6 shows you the sorts of detail you need to look out for. You can also see the practical difficulties – for example, how do you know whether the participants will be familiar with the car you have chosen? How do you get people to take part? How will you choose who goes first? How can you judge if the course is fair?

I will use the above example to help explain the important terms. Once you have understood what the terms mean, you will have understood the experimental method.

Hypotheses – alternative, experimental and null

First, you start with a vague **theory**. This should come from other people's studies. My example is that gender affects driving behaviour. Insurance companies favour female drivers and offer them lower premiums, but this may mean they have fewer accidents (or cause less damage), which does not necessarily mean that they are better drivers!

You form hypotheses to test this theory. Hypotheses are statements of what you expect. I expect there to be a difference in the driving of men and women: that is my hypothesis. There are many ways of making this statement, but it must be in a formal way.

- **Alternative hypothesis** – There is a meaningful difference in the driving behaviour of men and women. (There is bound to be some difference, but it has to be big enough to be worth talking about, so I have called it 'meaningful'). More correctly, we ought to say there will be a meaningful difference in the number of cones knocked down, as that is what we are measuring.
- **Experimental hypothesis** – If the study uses experimental method, and *only* then, the alternative hypothesis is called an experimental hypothesis. This is true in my example, so my experimental hypothesis is – there is a meaningful difference in driving behaviour (number of cones knocked down) between men and women. (The difference has to be big enough to be meaningful.)
- **Null hypothesis** – This is where you make a statement which is the opposite of what you expect. You say that there will be no difference. This may seem pointless, but is explained below. The null hypothesis for my driving behaviour study is that there is no meaningful difference in driving behaviour (number of cones knocked down) between men and women. You should add that any difference there is (you are sure to find some difference) is due to chance factors or some other variable you have not looked at.

Operationalising concepts

I ought to say 'number of cones knocked down', not 'driving behaviour', because we are only measuring the number of cones knocked down, and this might not represent all driving behaviour (it might represent driving skill, but not how we deal with other drivers on the road, for example). When we make sure that we have made something measurable, then we have **operationalised** the concept. For example, helpfulness is not really measurable, but we can operationalise it by measuring how many people show us the way to the post office when we ask.

Box 7 summarises what has been said about hypotheses.

Box 7

Using the example of the 'driving behaviour' experiment, here are the hypotheses

Experimental hypothesis – there is a meaningful difference in the number of cones knocked down, depending on whether the driver is male or female.

Null hypothesis – there is no meaningful difference in the number of cones knocked down depending on whether the driver is male or female, and any difference found is due to chance or some other variable.

Test yourself by writing out the experimental/ alternative hypothesis and the null hypothesis for the examples given in Activity 7.

ACTIVITY 7

HYPOTHESES

Write out the alternative/experimental hypothesis and the null hypothesis for the following examples. In each case specify whether your hypothesis is experimental, alternative or null.

1 You want to find out whether boys or girls are more aggressive in the playground, and you think boys are more aggressive. You will observe the children.

2 You want to find out if twins are more likely to guess what each is thinking than two siblings who are not twins (siblings are brothers and sisters). You set up a laboratory experiment, where each pair has a set of the same drawings. One of the pair looks at one of the drawings, and the other (out of sight) has to guess what is being looked at. Will the

twins get more right than the non-twinned siblings?

3 You want to see if people who are prejudiced are more likely to have authoritarian personalities (briefly, an authoritarian personality is where someone is bound by rules, and is likely to be strict). You do a questionnaire. Some questions ask carefully about attitudes, to see if someone is prejudiced or not, and some questions ask about personality, to put people in the category of 'authoritarian' or not. You think that a prejudiced person will be more likely to be 'authoritarian' because this is what the theory says (see Chapter 2).

> Key Skill C3.1a – this might be a group discussion. Each group member could present some examples of hypotheses to the group for discussion. Then you could write down examples of studies – each person in the group does this secretly – and ask members of the group to come up with a hypothesis.

Suggested answers to the above activity:

1 *Alternative hypothesis* – There is a meaningful difference in how many times boys or girls shout at or hit each other in the playground. Boys shout and hit more than girls.

Null hypothesis – There is no meaningful difference in how many times boys or girls shout at or hit in the playground, and boys do not shout and hit more than girls. Any differences in such behaviour are due to chance or some other variable.

2 *Experimental hypothesis* – There is a meaningful difference in twins guessing correctly which drawing the other is looking at more often than non-twinned siblings can.

Null hypothesis – There is no meaningful difference in twins being able to guess which drawing the other is looking at more often than non-twinned siblings can. Any difference in their success is due to chance or some other variable.

3 *Alternative hypothesis* – There is a meaningful relationship in that a participant found to be prejudiced is more likely to also be 'authoritarian'.

Null hypothesis – There is no meaningful relationship in that a participant found to be prejudiced is more likely to also be 'authoritarian'. Any relationship found is due to chance or some other variable.

The alternative and null hypotheses give a clear statement about what you expect to happen.

The alternative hypothesis says what you *think* will happen. The null hypothesis is there in case your study does not work. Either there is a difference as you expect (the alternative or experimental hypothesis), or there is no difference and any difference you might find is due to pure chance or some fctor other than what you expected (the null hypothesis).

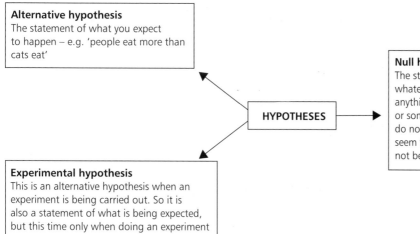

Figure 7.3

Why have a null hypothesis?

This has to do with testing whether the difference you expect is meaningful or not. You will nearly always find a difference, if you are testing people. You would not expect every driver to knock down the same number of cones (if the task is difficult enough). You would not expect all of us to recall the same number of words out of a list of 20. The important thing is, is the difference big enough to be important?

If we had two **conditions**, one where the list of 20 words is grouped and one where the list of the same 20 words is randomly produced, we might say people would recall more of the grouped list (see Chapter 1). We could have two groups of 15 people: one group would try to learn the grouped list and recall it; the other group would try to learn and recall the random list. Then we could compare the two sets of scores. Box 8 demonstrates this idea.

Box 8

The differences between the two conditions must be big enough to be important

Table 7.1 gives a set of results for an experiment. The scores are the number of words correctly recalled. A tick means that a score is higher than its partner score, which is important when we are looking for differences.

Key Skill N3.3 – use the data in Table 7.1 to interpret the results. Use graphs.

We compare the number of words recalled when the list was grouped with the number of words recalled when the list was randomised. We look at how big the differences are. We need to know if the differences are big enough not to be due to chance.

Analysis of data

Three sets of scores went against our claim that the grouped list would be better recalled, and 12 sets of scores agreed with our hypothesis (Table 7.1) (three sets of scores are higher for the random list, and 12 sets of scores are higher for the grouped list). Also, the number of words recalled is much higher in general for the grouped list. You can see that the difference seems meaningful.

Descriptive statistics

There are a few other things to be learnt from Table 7.1.

Table 7.1 – The number of words recalled depending on whether a list of words is grouped or randomly presented

Participant number	Number of words recalled from grouped list of 20	Participant number	Number of words recalled from random list of 20
1	18✓	16	10
2	12	17	13✓
3	16✓	18	14
4	17✓	19	12
5	20✓	20	13
6	12✓	21	8
7	17	22	18✓
8	15✓	23	14
9	14✓	24	10
10	18✓	25	9
11	16✓	26	12
12	11	27	15✓
13	20✓	28	14
14	14✓	29	12
15	18✓	30	11
Mean	15.87	Mean	12.33
Median	16	Median	12
Mode	18	Mode	12 /14
Range	9	Range	10

For quantitative data the mean, median, mode, and range need to be calculated. These are **measures of central tendency** and are called **descriptive statistics.** The mean, median, mode and range can only be calculated for certain levels of measurement. You cannot calculate them if you have nominal data. You can only calculate the median and mode if you have ordinal data. However, you can calculate them *all* if you have interval data. Bar charts, graphs, histograms and scattergrams are also descriptive statistics.

Calculations

The results from Table 7.1 are used in the following examples.

Calculating the mean average. Add up the scores in each condition (condition 1 is with the grouped lists, and condition 2 is with the random list). Divide the total by 15, because there are 15 scores in each condition, to give the mean for each.

The median. Find the middle score. Take the scores from Table 7.1, and put them into ascending order:
- condition 1 –
  11;12;12;14;14;15;16;16;17;17;18;18;18;20;20
- condition 2 –
  8;9;10;10;11;12;12;12;13;13;14;14;14;15;18

Here there are 15 scores, so the middle is the eighth one. If there were 14 scores, the middle one would be the 7.5th and so on. The eighth score in condition 1 (grouped list) is 16 and the eighth score in the random condition 2 is 12.

Finding the mode. The mode is the most usual score (the 'fashionable' one). In the first condition three participants remembered 18 words, so the mode is 18, because the other scores were remembered fewer than three times. In the second condition, there is really no mode: three participants remembered 12 words and three remembered 14 words. So the list has two modes, in which case it is best not to put a mode. I only did it earlier to make things clearer.

Finding the range. The range (the spread of the scores) is the top score minus the bottom score. In the first condition, the scores range from 20 to 11. So the range is 20 – 11, which is 9. For the second condition, the top score was 18 and the worst score was 8, so the range is 10.

Drawing a bar chart or histogram. A bar chart means bars drawn of any width, and representing the height of, say, the mean average. So, if the means are 16 and 12 (which they more or less are for Table 7.1) one bar reaches a height of 16 and the other 12. This gives a clear picture of the differences between the scores.

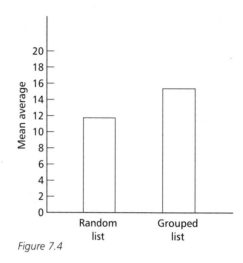

Figure 7.4

A histogram is similar, except that the bars are touching, and the widths may be different. Basically bar charts and histograms are the same thing for our purposes. However, you might represent all the scores by means of a histogram. The height of each bar represents each person's score, and the widths would be the same. If you put all the condition one scores at one end, and then followed with all the condition two scores, the heights would dramatically show the differences in the scores.

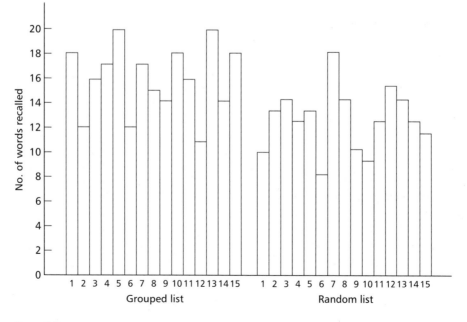

Figure 7.5

Drawing a line graph. A line graph means setting up the graph in a way similar to the histogram. Participant numbers always go along the bottom (the horizontal, or *x* axis). Scores go up the vertical, or *y* axis. Mark a cross on the graph where each participant's score is, and link the crosses to make a line. You could do this on one graph – firstly for condition one, and link the line in red then for condition two, and link the lines in blue – or, since they are different participants, you could use two graphs side-by-side for comparison.

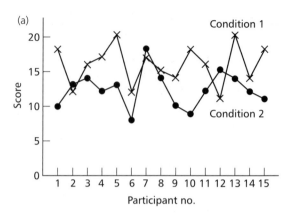

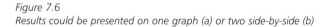

Figure 7.6
Results could be presented on one graph (a) or two side-by-side (b)

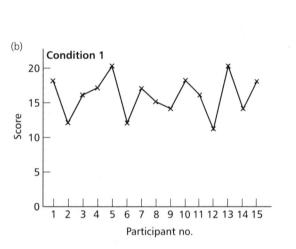

Drawing a pie chart. The scores given in Table 7.1 can't be used to produce a pie chart. An example is given below. Out of 100 people who watch television programmes:

20 said they preferred the News; 10 said they preferred wildlife programmes; 40 said they preferred 'soaps'; 15 said they preferred detective programmes; and 15 said they only watched films.

The pie chart would show 20% for News, 10% for wildlife, 40% for soaps, and 15% each for detective programmes and films (Figure 7.7).

Levels of measurement and measures of central tendency
- Levels of measurement = nominal, ordinal or interval/ratio
- Measures of central tendency = mean, median, mode, range

Not all levels of measurement allow calculation of all measures of central tendency. We get in the habit of

saying 'calculate the mean, median, mode and range', but in fact this cannot always be done. Think about it. You cannot work out a mean average score if you have just put something into categories. Box 9 illustrates this.

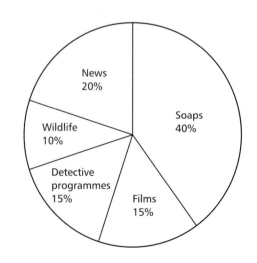

Figure 7.7

Box 9

Measures of central tendency and nominal data

	Boys	Girls	
Aggressive behaviour	10	5	15
Non-aggressive behaviour	2	13	15
	12	18	30

The above 'table' shows results when 30 children are observed and their behaviour categorised as aggressive or not (somehow). You cannot give a mean average score because the numbers in the boxes are simply showing, for example, how many boys showed aggressive behaviour (10).

For nominal data we do not calculate measures of central tendency. You should show your data in 'boxes' as in the figure.

---

1 You can calculate a median or middle score by ordering the scores (10,20,20,28,34,35) and finding the middle score. The middle is the 3.5th score between 20 and 28, so the median = 24.
2 You could calculate a mode (the most usual score). Two people scored 20, so the mode is 20.
3 However, a mean average, although it could be calculated, would not mean anything because the scores are only rankings. Adding them up and dividing them will give a number, but it won't have meaning. Your measures would not have equal intervals between them, so adding them up as if they have and dividing them by the number of participants would not be any good. Dividing is a mathematical calculation, and you can't do mathematical calculations unless your data are mathematically collected.

Similarly, you cannot work out a mean average with ordinal or ranked data. You can only give the mode and the median.

Box 10

Measures of central tendency and ordinal data

Table 7.2 shows the results of a study where six participants responded to eight statements, some of which were prejudiced and some were not. An example might be 'women should remain in the kitchen'. If the participant strongly agreed with a prejudiced statement, they received a score of 5, if they agreed they were given 4, unsure 3, disagree 2 and if they strongly disagreed they received a score of 1. (This is a **Likert scale**.) The maximum prejudiced score was 40 (eight statements answered by 'strongly agree' which got a score of 5 each).

Table 7.2 Overall prejudice score of six individuals

Participant	Prejudice score
1	20
2	10
3	20
4	34
5	28
6	35

There is no problem in calculating the mean, median, mode and range for interval/ratio data. You must do so.

I have calculated measures of central tendency in my example of results from the memory experiment. Note, however, that the data are quasi-interval, not interval. You can still calculate measures of central tendency.

Summary of analysis of results using Table 7.1

Refer back to Table 7.1. You can see that the mean, median and mode for the number of words recalled in the grouped list are higher than the mean, median and mode for those recalled in the random list. This reinforces the claim that the difference is large enough. The ranges are the same in both lists, which suggests that there is a similar spread of scores. So across a similar spread of scores, those in the 'grouped list' condition are higher than those in the 'random' condition. Therefore, everything points to the success of the experiment. The experimental hypothesis, which claimed that grouped lists are better recalled than random lists, is upheld. So the null hypothesis, which said that any difference would be only that found due to chance, is rejected.

Statistical analysis – inferential statistics

What follows is very useful, but you can get through the AS Edexcel exam without it, so bear that in mind if it gets difficult.

If you really wanted to know if the difference was big enough, you would do a statistical test. You have a choice of tests, and this choice is outlined below. You need to know about tests for the A2, but it is also useful to know a bit about it for the AS, and you won't lose marks by doing more than expected. In the study suggested in

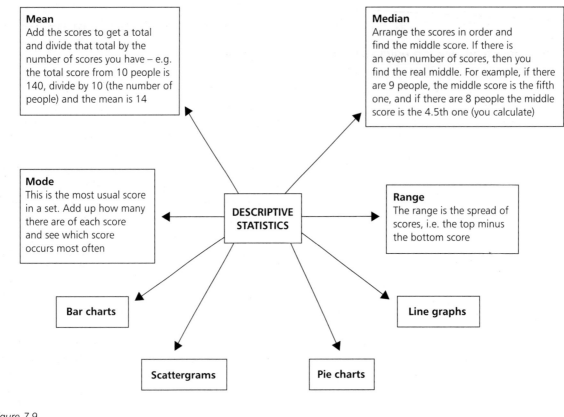

Figure 7.9
Descriptive statistics

Table 7.1 you could use either a Mann–Whitney U test or an unrelated *t* test. You don't need to go into details about how to do the test, since step-by-step instructions are easy enough to follow. You can find these instructions in textbooks about statistics (see references at the end of this chapter). However, you should still be able to understand why a test is useful.

Statistical tests look at the likelihood of the results that were found being due to chance. The question 'to what extent would these results occur by chance?' is asked. Remember the null hypothesis, which said that there would be no difference between two sets of results, but that any difference would be due to chance? Statistical tests look at how far it is the case that the results are due to chance.

You work through the right test (different tests are available for different designs, as will be seen later). You do the test and get a result. Then you look up the result to see how far it is likely to be due to chance. You will have to know how to look the results up, and you will have to know more about inferential statistics.

Some questions answered
Q Do I have to do a statistical test every time I carry out a study?

A No – if you collect qualitative data, you will not have to carry out a statistical test. You need to have nominal, ordinal or interval/ratio data to do a test.

Q Do I have to do a statistical test for the AS coursework?

A No – there are no extra marks for carrying out a test. The only thing you gain is a better understanding of method (in case you are going to study psychology at degree level) or ready for the A2 part of the exam

Q Do I have to do the calculations for a statistical test in any examination for 'A' level?

A No – you may be asked what test you need and why, but you will not have to do the test itself.

Q How do I do the test?

A Follow a step-by-step guide or the formula. I have not given you these here. There are plenty of books that do explain how to do the tests. Some computer software also makes it possible to do the tests (including, for example, Microsoft Excel).

Interpreting the results of the test
Each statistical test gives a result. So you might perform

the test (which in itself, following step-by-step instructions, is not difficult), and then find that $t = 3.45$ or rho = $+0.67$. At this stage you will need to know what to do with the result. Here is some more information.

One or two tailed?

You will need to know whether your alternative hypothesis needs a one- or two-tailed test. **One tailed** means the direction of the result is predicted in the hypothesis. Look for a directional word like 'more' or 'better'. For example, if your alternative hypothesis says that there is a meaningful difference in that more words are recalled when the list is categorised than when it is randomised, this needs a one-tailed test. **Two tailed** means there is no predicted direction. If your alternative hypothesis is that there is a meaningful difference in the number of words recalled depending on whether the list is categorised or randomised, then there is no direction predicted. You could find that the categorised list was better recalled, or that the randomised list is better recalled. You have not said which you expect.

Level of significance

You will need to choose a level of significance. Remember that the alternative hypothesis states that there will be a meaningful difference, or a meaningful positive correlation. The difference has to be big enough, and bigger than would be expected by chance.

The level of significance is the level of significance you choose which *could* be due to chance, but you would still accept the alternative hypothesis. Re-read this section a few times. It is worth grasping. It may seem a bit difficult at first, but is not really that hard.

Let's use an example. Think of identical twins and the claim that they may use some sort of telepathy. It is an interesting idea and has been tested. One of the twins has pictures or symbols in front of them. They concentrate on what they are seeing. The other one is behind a screen, so they can't see anything, and has to draw or write down what their twin is looking at. The question is, how many of the items do they get right? There is usually a control group, where siblings who are not identical twins do the same task. If identical twins use telepathy, they should get more 'right' than non-identical twins or other siblings. (This task has been done, and usually does not work. Identical twins get no more right than the control group. However, I have heard of the test working sometimes.)

Imagine the identical twin pairs have managed to get slightly more right than the control group. Say that there were 100 pairs of identical twins, and 100 pairs of siblings in the control group. Would you be happy to say that telepathy works if five out of the 100 pairs of twins got no more drawings right than their opposites in the control

group, but 95 out of the 100 pairs of twins did? Would you be happier if only one pair in 100 went against your alternative hypothesis?

If you accept that five out of every 100 people tested did not agree with your predictions (to change the example, maybe 95 out of every 100 women seemed to be a better driver, but in five cases the men were better), then this is a 5% level of significance. If you accept that one out of every 100 people tested did not agree with your predictions (maybe 99 out of every women seemed to be a better driver, but one was not) then this is a 1% level of significance.

Go back now to the twin study. I would be quite impressed if I asked 20 identical twin pairs to do the study and 15 did better than the control group (this would be a 25% (5 out of 20) level of significance, where 25% went against the alternative hypothesis). However, in psychology a 5% level of significance is the most generous that is accepted (5% here means that five in 100 might go against what you predict, and so 5% of the results might be due to chance, but you are still going to accept your alternative hypothesis and claim that the study worked).

Choosing the level of significance. You should choose this before you carry out the study. It rather depends on whether the study has been done before, or whom you are asking. If the area is well tested, you might think that you need to accept only one in 100 of the results as being due to chance. The study of telepathy, however, has not really been proven, so you might be very pleased if only five in 100 seem to be due to chance. You do not need to ask 100 pairs or 100 drivers – figures are worked out for you as if you had asked that many. You will find you can look up your result according to how many you actually asked.

Testing the null hypothesis

Recall the null hypothesis. This says that what you predict is not the case and that any difference you find will be due to chance or something else. When you do the test, you are checking how much is due to chance. If 1% is due to chance, you will probably accept that, and say that the study 'worked'. If 10% is due to chance (ten people out of every 100 did not do what you predicted), then you cannot accept the alternative hypothesis (remember, 5% is the most generous you can be).

If you find that 10% is due to chance (and how you find this is explained below), then you have to reject the alternative hypothesis and accept the null hypothesis. This means that you agree that 'there is no meaningful difference in that categorised words are better recalled, and any difference is due to chance'.

Degrees of freedom and number of participants

You have nearly all the information you need now. However, when you look up the results of the test to see what it means, you will need to know one more thing: either the number of participants, which is the easy part, and is usually represented by *N*, or the **degrees of freedom** (df).

Many students ask about degrees of freedom. You will not be expected to explain this in the AS or A2 examination, so if you are happy just to accept that you need to know what 'df' means and how to calculate it, that's fine. You will not even have to calculate it for the examination.

Degrees of freedom have to do with the number of participants. If you are using a repeated measures design, with ten participants (*N* = 10), df = *N*–1 = 9. This is loosely because when nine of the scores are in the table of ten scores, the last score has no degree of freedom to go anywhere else in the table. If you are using an independent groups design, with 20 participants (ten in each group), then df = 18. This is loosely because this time, with each set of ten, the last one has to go in the last slot, so in each case there is one score which has no choice as to where it goes. So here df = N–2 = 18. For each test, the degree of freedom is calculated differently, so you need to follow step-by-step instructions to find out the degrees of freedom.

All you need to know now is what test to choose! A table is provided at the end of this chapter, although there are still a few things you would need to know before using one of the *t* tests or the Pearson test.

Variables and controls

Each time you make a statement about what you expect, in the form of a hypothesis, you are saying that you will measure **variables**. A variable is something that you are measuring or interested in, and is something that varies. So if you are expecting to see a difference in the play behaviour of boys and girls you are interested in the variables 'play behaviour', and 'boys and girls'.

Situational variables

In an experiment you will be controlling many variables, such as heat, noise, place, light, time of day. It depends on what you are interested in. Variables to do with the situation are called **situational variables.** These must be controlled. Controlling them means keeping them the same for all the participants. If you were testing memory, for instance, and some participants had to cope with more noise than others, then this might affect your conclusions.

Participant variables

Situational variables affect your conclusions, but so might differences between or within your participants. If you were testing driving behaviour and some of your participants were tired, for example, this might affect your conclusions. These are **participant variables**, which are factors to do with the individuals taking part that might affect your conclusions.

Extraneous variables

Extraneous variables get in the way of the study and make it look as though the study has worked, when it has not. These variables give the impression we found what we expected, even though we did not, so they have **confounded** the results. Examples might be the room temperature, or the person's emotional state. We try to control all the variables, but we can only control those we know about. Milgram's (1963) study found a surprising level of obedience (see Chapter 2) and his participants seemed willing to shock a co-participant to a frightening level. However, the obedience in some cases might have been due to extraneous variables. Perhaps some of them were in a weakened emotional state in the first place, or perhaps some of them were deaf and could not hear the screams. I am only giving this as an example – presumably Milgram checked for this!

In practice, it is unlikely that in one experiment all the participants are deaf or emotionally weak. So good sampling and good controls should stop extraneous variables from affecting the results.

Confounding variables. Extraneous variables, whether situational or participant variables, are called confounding variables when they can be interpreted as causing the result. Either the variable we manipulate can have caused the result (whether a word list is categorised or not, for example) or some other variable can have caused the result (participants remembered more categorised words because the words were shorter, for example). In this case we don't know whether participants learnt more of the first list because it was categorised or because the words were shorter. The difference in word length becomes a confounding variable.

Activity 8 demonstrates the importance of controlling variables.

ACTIVITY 8

CONTROLLING VARIABLES

You want to see whether music sounds best on CD or MiniDisc. Make a list of what is important when doing an experiment to test this out. Note down briefly how you would go about testing whether a CD or a MiniDisc produces better sound.

Key Skill C3.1a – this would make a good small group discussion. You could widen the discussion by making lists of different sorts of variables in different experiments, and then discuss how these would be controlled for.

Here are some ideas you may have come up with, and there are more:
• Use the same piece of music.
• Use the same standard of equipment (this might be difficult).
• Use the same room if possible (if you played your CD at home and your MiniDisc in the car, you would not have a fair comparison.
• Have the volume and other settings the same.
• Stand between the speakers at the same distance.
• The participant should be in the same mood.
• Use the same strength of speaker.

Self-test 8

In the bulleted list above, which are participant variables, and which are situational variables? Identify a possible extraneous variable, and note down how it could be a confounding variable.

Some answers might be:
• Using the same room is controlling a situational variable.
• Having the participant in the same mood (somehow) is controlling a participant variable.
• Playing different pieces of music might be an extraneous variable.

• The extraneous variable becomes a confounding variable if differences were found between the formats because of the different pieces of music rather than because of the different formats.

Independent and dependent variables

All variables need to be controlled for so that the variables you are actually interested in (for example, gender and play behaviour) are the ones that change or vary. Everything else must stay the same.

Once all possible variables are controlled for, the researcher can concentrate on the original hypothesis. In the example given for Activity 8 an experimental hypothesis might be that there is a difference in quality of sound between music played on a CD and music played on a MiniDisc. You are interested in the music quality, which you have to measure somehow. The music quality, according to your experimental hypothesis, depends on whether the format is CD or MiniDisc.

Independent variable. The **independent variable** (IV) is what you are interested in, and what you vary. In this case, it is the format (CD or MiniDisc).

Dependent variable. The **dependent variable** (DV) is what you measure as a result of varying (or manipulating) the IV. In the above example, the dependent variable is the sound quality, because that is what you are measuring.

Practise identifying the IV and the DV, as you will need to do this for your coursework (and for the examination in the A2).

ACTIVITY 9

IDENTIFYING THE IV AND THE DV

Note down the IV and the DV in each of the examples below.

a *There is a difference in helping behaviour depending on age.*
b *Younger people are better drivers (than older people).*
c *Categorised words are better recalled than uncategorised words.*
d *Sleep patterns (sleep well, sleep poorly) vary with age.*

▶

Identify the DV first – the one which is measured and scored because of the IV. For example, we are measuring sleep patterns and age, but we are choosing people of different ages and then measuring their sleep patterns because of their age. So age is the IV we are interested in, and we think age causes variations in sleep patterns. So we measure their sleep patterns, and this is the DV. I hope this helps.

Key Skill C3.1a – this activity would be a good group task, and you could come up with other studies. First, do the ones listed. Then write down some different studies and in the group work out the IV and the DV in each case.

Answers to the activity:

a IV is age; DV is helping behaviour.
b IV is age; DV is driving behaviour.
c IV is categorised or uncategorised words; DV is number of words recalled.
d IV is age; DV is sleep patterns.

Controls

Many controls involve the variables summarised in Figure 7.10. Controls are used to keep everything the same except the factor being manipulated by the researcher.

Standardised instructions

Another important control is what is said to the participant. Each participant must be given the same instructions, so that one does not have an unfair advantage over another. So instructions must be

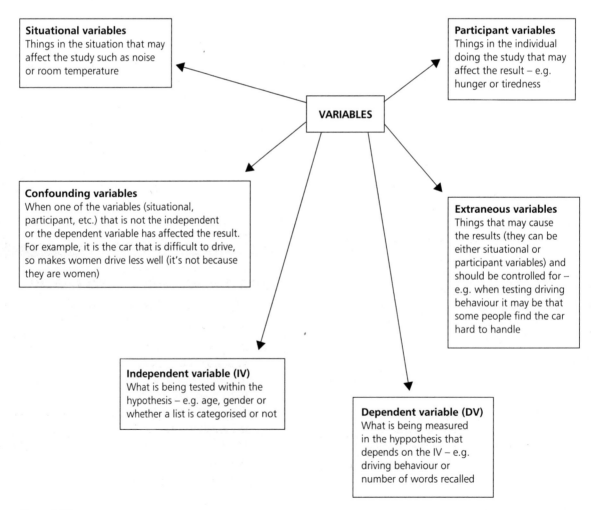

Situational variables
Things in the situation that may affect the study such as noise or room temperature

Participant variables
Things in the individual doing the study that may affect the result – e.g. hunger or tiredness

VARIABLES

Confounding variables
When one of the variables (situational, participant, etc.) that is not the independent or the dependent variable has affected the result. For example, it is the car that is difficult to drive, so makes women drive less well (it's not because they are women)

Extraneous variables
Things that may cause the results (they can be either situational or participant variables) and should be controlled for – e.g. when testing driving behaviour it may be that some people find the car hard to handle

Independent variable (IV)
What is being tested within the hypothesis – e.g. age, gender or whether a list is categorised or not

Dependent variable (DV)
What is being measured in the hyppothesis that depends on the IV – e.g. driving behaviour or number of words recalled

Figure 7.10
Types of variables

standardised. This means that everything said to the participant is written down beforehand. In this way you can control for any differences in instructions.

Ethics

Standardised instructions are also useful, as they can include advice to participants about their rights. **Ethical guidelines** are outlined in Chapter 8. You will see that important issues include confidentiality, consent and the right to withdraw. If standardised instructions are read out before the study, they can include important information about ethical issues. Instructions should include giving the participant the right to pull out of the study at any time (right to withdraw), information about how the results of the study will be used, and how confidentiality is assured. The participant should be told as much as possible about the study, so that the consent obtained after asking whether he or she is willing to take part is *informed* consent. Participants need to know, to an extent, what they are consenting to.

Types of experimental design

There are three types of experimental design. This means that there are three ways that you can do the experiment (when thinking about participants). You can get one person to do all the conditions (parts of the study). Or you can get different people for each condition. Or you can compromise and get different people, but matched in important ways.

Repeated measures design

A **repeated measures design** means asking one person to repeat all parts of the study. So you could ask someone to learn a list of 20 words presented in categories, and see how many they recall. Then you could ask the same person to learn a list of 20 different uncategorised words presented randomly, and see how many they learn. So the same person's memory is involved, to compare memory for a categorised list with memory for a randomised list.

Order effects – fatigue and practice effect. However,

if all your participants do the categorised list first, and then the randomised list, they may remember a different number of words for reasons other than that the list is categorised.

You will see that the other types of design don't involve using the same people in all the conditions, so order effects only apply to a repeated measures design. If one person does the randomised list, and another does the cagetorised list, they won't get practiced or fatigued.

Two **order effects** are the **fatigue** and the **practice** effect. The fatigue effect is that a participant may do less

well in the second condition (in the above example, the randomised list) because they are tired or bored. The practice effect has the opposite effect to the fatigue effect: the participant does better in the second condition (in the above example, the randomised condition) because he or she is used to the task and has practised it.

So order effects can affect the results, and can be the reason for any difference found when using a repeated measures design.

Counterbalancing or randomising the order of presenting the conditions. To 'cancel' order effects, you need to either counterbalance or randomise the order in which people do the conditions.

- You can toss a coin to decide in each case whether the participant does condition one or two first. This is **randomising** the order. Each time you ask a participant to do the task, toss a coin – tails could mean they do the randomised list first, and heads means they do the categorised list first.
- You can **counterbalance**. This means alternating the order in which you get the tasks done. Your first participant does condition 1 and then condition 2; your second participant does condition 2 and then condition 1, and so on.

Advantages of a repeated measures design

- Using the same person across all conditions of the experiment means we do not have problems with individual differences. The same person is used, so he or she will have the same memory ability, the same driving ability and might be said to be in the same mood. This controls well for participant variables.
- As one person does all the conditions, we have to find fewer people than for an independent groups design.

Disadvantages of a repeated measures design. The repeated measures design is good because the same person does all the conditions, so there are no differences between participants to affect the results. However, having the same person do all parts of the study also has disadvantages.

- There are likely to be order effects.
- The person might guess what the study is about. If the person gets clues from the study and can guess what they are meant to do, there are said to be **demand characteristics**. Take the example of an experiment where participants have to learn a word list in the morning, and food words are included. Then half of the people have lunch, but they know that the other half are not eating. Participants might guess that hunger is important in the study. Characteristics of the study might demand a particular answer.

Box 11

The effect of counterbalancing

Table 7.3 shows number of words recalled depending on whether a list of 20 words is in random order or in categories.

Table 7.3

Participant	Categorised list	Order: First (1) or second (2)	Randomised list	Order: First (1) or second (2)
1	16✓	1	12	2
2	18✓	2	14	1
3	14	1	15✓	2
4	15✓	2	10	1
5	14✓	1	12	2
6	18✓	2	13	1

At first sight it looks as if the categorised list is better recalled (as would be predicted): five out of the six scores are better for the categorised list than for the randomised list. However, we should look for order effects, and we use the information about the order in which the lists were carried out. This information is given in the columns headed 'Order'.

To see if there is a practice effect:

Using the scores above, rewrite Table 7.3 paying attention to the order in which the tasks were done. Firstly, the scores are rewritten with the first score first, no matter which list was being used (Table 7.4).

Table 7.4

Participant (whichever condition)	Recall of first list (whichever condition)	Recall of second list
1	16✓	12
2	14	18✓
3	14	15✓
4	10	15✓
5	14✓	12
6	13	18✓

Four out of the six second scores were best, so there *could* have been a practice effect.

To see if there is a fatigue effect:

If there is a fatigue effect, the first list would be recalled best. This is the case for only two of the participants. So there does not appear to be a fatigue effect.

In your research you need to check the effect of counterbalancing to see if order effects are present. In the above example, there could have been a practice effect but does not seem to be a fatigue effect. The practice effect was masked, and it looked as if the study had worked. (In practice, six people is insufficient – this is just an example.)

Independent groups design

If the same person does not do all the conditions, then you must use different people in each case. In an independent groups design, different people are used for each condition. Then the group learning the categorised list, for example, is independent from the group learning the randomised list because they are different people.

Advantages of an independent groups design

• There are no order effects. You simply have different people, so they don't even know what the other condition is.

• There are no demand characteristics. Participants can't compare the different parts of the study and use their knowledge to guess what is required.

Disadvantages of an independent groups design

• When you are comparing the two sets of results, you are comparing different people. You are saying that one participant recalled 18 out of 20 words when the words were in categories but another participant recalled 14 out of 20 when they are given a random list. The person getting 18 and the person getting 14 are different people. One of them might have a better memory. You have to use careful sampling, and enough people, before you can be fairly sure that the difference you found was not just due to different people having done the different parts of the study.

• Another disadvantage that you might find important is that you have to find twice as many participants to do the study.

Matched pairs design

A **matched pairs design** can appear to solve the problems encountered with repeated measures and independent groups designs. With a matched pairs design you use different people for the different conditions, but they are matched so that they are similar in many ways. You are trying to use different people but make them as similar as possible.

One way that researchers have done this is to use identical twins in studies. You are unlikely to be able to do this, and in any case it might not be ethical. An alternative is to look at what factors are important and make sure that the participants are similar in these important ways. Box 12 gives an example to discuss the different types of design.

Advantages of matched pairs design. Using different people means there are no order effects, and demand characteristics are less likely. In other words, there are all the advantages of an independent groups design. Similarly there are the advantages of a repeated measures design: the paired individuals are treated as if they are the same people, so comparisons can be made between them.

Disadvantages of matched pairs design. On the other hand, a matched pairs design does mean using different people, however hard we try to match them up on important variables. So there will be individual differences and participant variables. Even identical twins are not the same people and are subject to moods and different experiences.

| Box 12 |

Examining the three types of design

Sherif et al (1961) did a study to look at how conflict develops between groups, using boys who were staying at a summer camp divided into two groups. These two groups called themselves the Rattlers and the Eagles and they worked separately on tasks in the camp. Then tasks were set up where the two groups competed. They became rivals. Boys supported the in-group (their group) and were against the outgroup (the others). It was clear that competition led to prejudice. Later situations were set up where the two groups had to work together to solve a mutual problem. This did succeed in reducing the conflict between the groups (see Chapter 2).

A repeated measures design was not possible, as the boys could not have been in both the in-group and the outgroup. So there had to be different participants in each condition.

An independent groups study was used because the boys were divided randomly into the two groups.

A matched pairs design would have been possible, if the boys were given questionnaires about their backgrounds and interests, for example. They could have been paired off, one into each group. If there were two 11-year-old boys born in December, with middle-class backgrounds, and each with a younger sister, for example, they could have been one of the pairs – and one would go into each group. (In practice the boys had very similar backgrounds in the first place.) Some books say that a matched pairs design *was* used (presumably because the boys were picked to be similar in the first place).

ACTIVITY 10

IDENTIFY EXPERIMENTAL DESIGNS

Decide which design is being used in the following examples (remember there are three experimental designs: repeated measures, independent groups and matched pairs).

a *Using counterbalancing, participants do two conditions. In the first they recall as many as they can from a list of 15 letters, having taken 30 seconds to rehearse the list. In the second condition they recall as many as they can from a list of 15 letters, not having had chance to rehearse, because they are asked to count backwards.*

b *An observation is carried out of children in the playground. The observer scores play behaviour of boys and girls to look for a gender difference.*

c *Two types of psychotherapy are being tested. One group had one type, and the other has the other type, over a period of a week. The participants are paired up with regard to age, gender and previous therapy experiences, and then the pairs are divided carefully, one into each group.*

Key Skill C3.1a – this is a useful activity for a small group discussion. You can widen the task by each secretly writing some more examples, and then getting others in the group to decide on which design is (or should be) used, and why.

The first example in Activity 10 represented a repeated measures design. The second example was an independent groups design, and the third example was a matched pairs design.

STUDY AID

When writing up experimental coursework you need to include all of what has been said so far:
- Your introduction must end with an experimental hypothesis and a null hypothesis.
- Your method section must include details of all controls, sampling and design decisions.
- Your results must be clearly displayed in a table with suitable descriptive statistics.
- Your discussion must focus on validity, reliability and generalisability.

Types of experiment

- **Laboratory experiment** – takes place in an unnatural setting but means there can be good controls.
- **Field experiment** – takes place 'in the field', which is a more natural setting. However, this does affect the controls. The independent variable is still manipulated as it is in a laboratory experiment.
- **Naturalistic or natural experiment** – takes place 'in the field' because it means using a naturally occurring independent variable. So the researcher does not have to set up the independent variable. This is a more valid measure (because it really occurs), but controls can be difficult (because there are sure to be other things in the environment that happen with or alongside the independent variable).
- **Quasi experiment** – where the participants are not allocated to the conditions, but naturally fall into the different groups already. A naturalistic experiment is a quasi experiment because the participants naturally fall into the separate groups.

Box 13 looks at the differences between these types of experiment.

Box 13

Exploring different types of experiment

It is hard to give only one example where all types of experiment can occur, but testing for the effect of violence on TV is useful.

1 Studies have been done in unnatural settings (laboratories) to look at violence shown on TV and its effect on behaviour. (Bandura's (1965) study was outlined above). Half of a group of children watch adults on a video hitting a Bobo doll; the other half (a control group) do something else. Then the children play. Researchers count how many times the children hit the doll. This is a laboratory experiment.

2 A similar study could be done in a school. One class could watch a wildlife programme while another class watches the video of the adult hitting the doll. Then the children's play behaviour could be recorded. This is a field experiment. The study is carried out in the same way as in **1**, but in a more natural setting.

3 A naturalistic experiment similar to this was described in Chapter 2. Three areas are found. One has no TV, one has a few channels and one can receive several channels. Children are observed, to see the differences between the boys' and the girls' behaviour. As the researchers did not set up the different conditions, this is a naturalistic experiment

(If it had been a field experiment, they would have had to deprive one area of television, and so on).

4 If researchers focus on a group of people who have never had TV and a group who have had TV, so that the participants are not put into the groups by them, then this is a quasi experiment. A natural experiment is a quasi experiment in that the variables are not manipulated by the researchers, and the participants naturally fall into the groups.

Table 7.5 ends this long section on experiments by listing briefly some advantages and disadvantages. You could probably do this for yourself by now, so try first.

Self-test 9

List some advantages and some disadvantages of experiments.

STUDY AID

If in Self-test 9 you used the terms 'validity', 'reliability', 'generalisability' or 'controls', then you can congratulate yourself and take a break! If you did not, don't worry. You probably listed the advantages and disadvantages quite clearly without using the terms. However, note that for the examination you should try to use correct terminology wherever possible, and it is useful to practise it.

Correlational design

A correlation is more like a type of design than a method in itself: you might do a questionnaire and find a correlation. The main thing about a correlation is that you are looking only at things that go together, not cause one another. People used to say that the more you smoke, the more likely you are to have an illness, and this was a correlation. However, we would probably now say that smoking causes illness – it is not that smoking *correlates* with illnesses like cancer and heart disease, it is that smoking *causes* these diseases.

Think of a correlation as a co-relationship. Two things co-vary, which means they vary together. An example is age and reaction time. The older you get, the slower your reactions. Age and reaction time co-vary.

Positive and negative correlations

When two variables rise together, there is said to be **a positive correlation**. A claim that the hotter it is the more ice creams are sold is a positive correlation: the higher the temperature, the higher the sales.

If, however, when one thing rises, the other falls, this is a **negative correlation**. Age and hours of sleep are negatively correlatied: the higher the age, the lower the number of hours slept at night.

Scattergrams
One way of knowing if you have a correlation is to prepare a scattergram (Figure 7.11).

Table 7.5 Advantages and disadvantages of experiments

Advantages	Disadvantages
1 Laboratory experiments Good controls, so reliable IV can be manipulated clearly Cause and effect can be suggested Findings can be repeated by others	Lots of controls, so not valid IV is not naturally occurring so not valid Tasks are not natural, so not worth doing?
2 Field experiments More natural than laboratory experiments Still have control over some variables A bit more ethical for the participants	Lose control over some variables Less reliable than lab experiments
3 Natural experiments More natural than laboratory or field experiments Measuring naturally occurring events More ethical for participants	Lose even more control over variables Less reliable than laboratory or field experiments

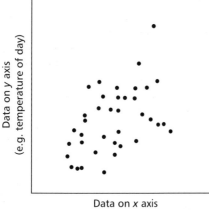

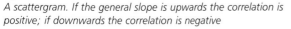

Data on *x* axis
(e.g. no. of ice creams sold)

Figure 7.11
A scattergram. If the general slope is upwards the correlation is positive; if downwards the correlation is negative

A perfect positive correlation (when one variable varies perfectly with another) is +1 and a perfect negative correlation is −1.

So, if for everyone asked it was found that the older they were the less they slept, this would be a perfect negative correlation. If for each hotter and hotter day, sales of ice creams rose and rose, then this would also be a perfect positive correlation (there would have to be no hot day when ice cream sales fell below those of a colder day).

So +0.76 is quite a high positive correlation (being near +1), and −0.52 is a reasonable, but not very high, negative correlation (being mid way between 0 and −1).

Surveys by questionnaire

Surveys using a questionnaire are a good way of finding things out, although there are drawbacks, as with every method.

Open and closed questions

Closed questions require a fixed response, for example the participant ticks whether they are male or female. There is a choice, but no opportunity to say anything else or to expand. It is usually a good idea to include a 'don't know' or 'neither' option, so that the participant is not forced too much into inaccurate responses.

Open questions give an opportunity for the participant to expand and answer in their own words. An example might be if the participant is asked about their nightly sleep patterns.

Self-test 10

Recall the difference between quantitative and qualitative data.

• What sort of data will closed questions give?

• What sort of data will open questions give?

Closed questions give quantitative data, and open questions give qualitative data.

Personal data

A questionnaire involves asking questions around an area of particular interest to the researcher. However, at the same time, the researcher needs to know personal data – the participant's age, gender, occupation, etc. – so that he or she can look at the answers (for example sleep patterns) and compare different age groups, or different genders, or those with different work patterns. The researcher needs this personal data in order to make the comparisons. You should only ask for personal data that you really need, for ethical reasons.

Standardised instructions

Participants taking part in studies should be given standardised instructions as a control, and to make things fair. When giving participants a questionnaire, standardised instructions should appear at the beginning of the questionnaire. This is not really as a control, as the instructions will simply ask participants to please answer the questions. Standardised instructions are also included for ethical reasons.

Ethics

It is very important that ethical guidelines are observed (see Chapter 8). You will see that important rights include confidentiality and the right to withdraw. The questionnaire should start by assuring participants that names are not required, and giving them the right to withdraw at any time. They must be told that they do not have to answer every question.

Constructing a questionnaire

A good questionnaire is hard to construct. It should not be too long, so that your participant does not give too much of their time or become too bored. You should not ask for personal data that you don't need. The most difficult part is wording the questions.

ACTIVITY 11

SETTING SOME QUESTIONNAIRE QUESTIONS

Imagine you want to design a questionnaire to see if sleep patterns change with age. Suggest how you would construct a questionnaire.

Key Skill C3.1a – This would make a good small group discussion – you could all pool ideas. Together you might come up with a better questionnaire. It will be a bit like doing a pilot study.

If you want to ask questions about sleep patterns, you need at least the participant's age, and there are other issues.

• Sleep patterns could be measured by the number of hours slept at night. However, there are other ways of sleeping, such as napping.
• You may have decided it is also useful to know about gender.
• Did you decide to ask the participant's actual age? You may have chosen to use age groups (16–25; 26–34; 35–44; 45–54; 55–64; 65+, for example). This might be a more ethical approach, but you will not have such precise data.
• Would participants *know* how many hours they slept at night? You might have chosen to get an average over a few nights to be more fair – the night before you ask they may have had a 'bad' night.
• We did this study and had to think hard about how we could ask people if their lifestyle meant they had interrupted sleep patterns.
• Did you decide to ask if there was a young baby in the house? Or someone ill?
• Did you ask about shift patterns or occupation?
• If you asked about occupation, what about people who are unemployed?
• We did ask participants to give an average of number of hours slept over the last three nights, and we made sure we did not ask at weekends, in case weekly patterns were different to weekend patterns.

Ethically you also need to be careful. Only ask questions that will not cause offence, and take care to phrase your questions carefully.

Pilot study

One way of making sure that your questions are understood is to carry out a pilot study. This means testing your questionnaire out on a small group to find out any problems before undertaking the main study. You can make sure your questions are clear, and that they do not give offence. You can also discover problems such as a category missing. For example, if you ask only about mothers and fathers, you will find people with step-parents, who will not know how to answer.

Demand characteristics

In questionnaires (as well as experiments) you can often ask questions that give a clue about what you expect. If your participant can guess from the questions what they are supposed to say, they could alter the answer to help you (or to go against what you expect): the characteristics of the question demand a certain answer. This will give a bias in your results, so you cannot draw conclusions from the answers.

Social desirability

Similarly, your participants may say what they think they ought to say. Few people being asked 'are you a racist?' would say they are. Your questions need to be carefully written, so that you get 'real' answers, rather than social norms. One way to measure social desirability is to include a question to which the answer is clear. For example, you could ask whether someone talks about other people. They almost certainly do talk about others, so if they answer that they don't, you might consider they are not answering the other questions honestly.

Suggestions regarding questions

Actually, questions are often hard to answer. People don't necessarily know if they are prejudiced or not, for example, so they would find it hard to answer a question asking if they are prejudiced. You probably need to be quite subtle. Direct questions are not always the best way to gather data in a questionnaire.

Statements can be quite useful. You can use a **Likert scale** asking participants to tick one of five boxes ranging from 'strongly agree' to 'strongly disagree'. Traditionally 5 points are given for 'strongly agree', down to 1 for 'strongly disagree'.

However, there is such a thing as a **response set**. If you make all the statements prejudiced, that is 'strongly agree' always gives a prejudiced response, the person might get in the habit of either agreeing or disagreeing throughout. It is a good idea to vary your statements so that people sometimes have to disagree with the statement if they are prejudiced. Figure 7.12 illustrates the use of a Likert scale.

Please respond to the following statements. You do not have to complete any you do not wish to answer. SA = strongly agree; A = agree; DK = don't know; D = disagree; SD = strongly disagree.

	SA	A	DK	D	SD
1 Women should not fight in the front line	☐	☐	☐	☐	☐
2 The age of consent for homosexuals should be lowered to 16	☐	☐	☐	☐	☐
3 Criminals and policemen have the same sort of personality	☐	☐	☐	☐	☐
4 Everyone should live and let live	☐	☐	☐	☐	☐

Figure 7.12
Using statements on a questionnaire – an example

- If agreed with, the first statement is prejudiced against women
- If agreed with, the second statement is liberal and not prejudiced against homosexuals
- If agreed with, the third statement is prejudiced against the police (or criminals!)
- If agreed with, the fourth statement is liberal, not prejudiced against others.

So, if you were scoring someone for prejudice, you would score Figure 7.12 thus:
- Statement one: SA = 5, A = 4, DK = 3, D = 2, SD = 2
- Statement two: SA = 1, A = 2, DK = 3, D = 4, SD = 5
- Statement three: SA = 5, A = 4, DK = 3, D = 2, SD = 1
- Statement four: SA = 1, A = 2, DK = 3, D = 4, SD = 5

Totalling the scores gives a possible 20 for a very prejudiced person.

There are a few problems with using statements like this. Beware awkward negative statements like 'you are not prejudiced are you?', to which the participant does not know whether to strongly agree or disagree. Also, statements *can* lead to prejudice and *can* be offensive, so need very careful consideration. However, using statements can be a very successful way of avoiding direct questions, and you might get less social desirability in the answers.

Another useful way of discovering information when using a questionnaire is using a scale, such as a **semantic differential** scale. An example might be asking people to mark on a line where they stand regarding a certain issue, or what they think their personality is like. Figure 7.13 gives an example.

Please complete this questionnaire by making a mark on the line according to how you rate your personality. You do not have to respond to every question, and your name will not be required.

Happy _____ Sad   Law abiding _____ Rule breaking

Generous _____ Mean   Bad _____ Good

Outgoing _____ Private   Unintelligent _____ Intelligent

Figure 7.13

You could use a 0–10 scale, and then you would actually have a score. You could measure someone's self-esteem in this way: if they said they were happy and intelligent, you might assume they had high self-esteem.

Using a scale like this can be a more successful way of constructing a questionnaire than asking a question like 'do you have high self-esteem?'

You can probably think of other creative ways of finding out what people think. Always be aware of ethical issues. Notice too, that the above scales do not all run from 'good' on the left to 'bad' on the right. Always try to avoid a pattern so that the participant does not get into a habit when responding. Table 7.6 looks at some advantages and disadvantages of questionnaires.

STUDY AID

You might decide to prepare a questionnaire for your coursework (you need to collect quantitative data for the coursework for the Edexcel examination). Include a pilot study, and mention in your method section how you have designed the questionnaire to avoid demand characteristics and social desirability. Questionnaires can yield useful and interesting data; however, there are lots of data to analyse, and this can be time-consuming.

Interviews

Surveys can be carried out by interview, instead of by questionnaire. Interviews can also be used as part of a case study. Structured interviews seem like questionnaires; however, questionnaires can be completed in the researcher's absence whereas interviews must be conducted in person. Also, you might ask a great many participants to complete a questionnaire, but you might only interview a few people.

Structured interviews

In a **structured interview** everyone is asked the same questions. In this way data can be compared. The problem is that the interviewer does not have the freedom to explore any issues that arise. Structured interviews usually yield qualitative data, because the questions are usually designed so that the participant can give quite a full verbal answer. However, some times tick boxes are used, and this means that quantitative data can be analysed and compared.

Unstructured interviews

An **unstructured interview** involves exploring an issue by allowing the participant to impose their own structure on what is being asked. The participant's comments are pursued. For example, a structured interview on divorce might ask set questions such as 'who do you think was to blame?' In an unstructured interview, the interviewer could pursue the point from the answer, and ask more about it. The data from an unstructured interview has more quality, in the sense that the participant has more of an opportunity to say what they like.

Objectivity v. subjectivity

In the unstructured interview a problem is that it is not only the participant who can decide the course of the interview. It is the researcher who decides what questions to pursue, and these questions may reflect the researcher's own interests. The researcher's objectivity can be questioned. Subjectivity is an important factor in methods used in psychology. Researchers have to

Table 7.6 Advantages and disadvantages of using a questionnaire

Advantages	Disadvantages
Participants can see what is asked, so can give informed consent	Participants may not be truthful, so lack of validity
Closed questions are quite easily analysed	Closed questions mean participants cannot give all information, so data are lost
Can be reliable, because can easily be repeated	If repeated on a different day, different answers might be given
Quite quick and cheap to administer	Poor response rate, especially if sent by post
	Questionnaires only find out about attitudes towards something, not about how a person would actually behave

somehow separate themselves from the situation. For example, if a researcher asking questions about divorce is also a divorced person, they may let their own feelings show, and this could bias the results. Researchers must be objective, that is they must not let their own thoughts and feelings affect the results. In practice, this is probably almost impossible. Table 7.7 looks at some advantages and disadvantages of using interviews

Observations

Observations can give useful information about people and about interactions between people. You have to be careful when carrying out an observation, as really this is just watching people, and that is not a very ethical thing to do (see Chapter 8). You will see that in the ethical guidelines there is special mention of observations. It is usually accepted that people in a public place could reasonably to be watched. So usually observations are acceptable if they take place in 'public'.

Naturalistic observations are being discussed here but some experiments involve observation. For example, Bandura's Bobo doll study involved observation of children playing after watching a film. However, this is still an experiment, even though observation was used.

Overt v. covert observations

Overt observations are ones where the participants know they are being observed. Overt means that the observation is done openly. **Covert observations** are observations that are done secretly. The participants do not know they are being watched.

Overt observations are more ethical, but the people being watched are less likely to behave naturally. Covert observations are more likely to give natural behaviour, but they are not very ethical. Also it is easier to observe overtly, as you don't have to pretend to be doing something else. With covert observations you will have to either pretend to play a different role, or actually hide. This can be difficult.

Self-test 11

Which are more valid, overt or covert observations?

Covert observations are more valid, because they are less likely to affect the participants' natural behaviour, and what is observed is more like real life.

Participant v. non-participant observations

Participant observations are where the researcher is also a participant in the group. For example, you could observe children's behaviour in the classroom, and you would be a participant observer if you were also the teacher or a classroom helper. **Non-participant observations** are when the researcher is not part of the group. So a non-participant observer would sit at the back of the class, not taking part in any activities.

Self-test 12

Which give more valid data, participant or non-participant observations?

Non-participant observations can affect what is happening. The participants usually know the observer is there, and the presence of the researcher alone can affect the participants' behaviour. So non-observation does not yield valid data unless it is covert non-participant observation. Overt non-participant observation is likely to affect results.

Participant observation does affect results in one way, because the researcher is a participant in what is happening but if the researcher is, for example, the teacher, then they would be present anyway, so the behaviour is natural. Box 14 details a naturalistic observation that you could do.

Table 7.7 Some advantages and disadvantages of using interviews to collect data

Advantages	Disadvantages
Researcher can explore in more depth	Objectivity is difficult to achieve
Participant can expand on areas they see as important	Difficult to analyse the data
Gives rich and in-depth information that other methods may not uncover	Unique to one person, so not generalisable to others

---
Box 14

An example of a naturalistic observation

Body language can quite successfully be studied using naturalistic observation. Choose a busy street, so that it is quite clear that it is a public place. Also be sure not to identify any individuals. Find somewhere to observe, where you will not affect the situation. This is an example of covert non-participant observation.

It has been claimed that men and women exhibit different passing behaviours. Women pass other people by turning away from them, and clasping anything they are carrying to their chests. Men pass others by turning towards them, and tend to open their arms to let the other person by. You might like to try observing this behaviour for yourself, or look for other differences between people.

Box 15

Using tallying to get quantitative data from observations

Suppose you want to observe differences in play behaviour in a nursery school between 4-year-old boys and 4-year-old girls.

You could spend five minutes or more watching the behaviour and noting down categories. Do not list categories before you get there, as the situation will yield its own categories. For example, there may be a climbing frame, a book corner and some dressing-up clothes. The children may spend time at these activities. You need to know what the children usually do, before you can list categories. After about 5 minutes of observation you may have a list like the one in the table below.

Now observe the children. Choose one at a time, and note down their gender. You could decide to watch each child for a few minutes (you would have to work around special times such as story times or milk time). Armed with your list, you can make a tally mark each time your chosen child plays on the climbing frame, for example. What happens if they never move off the climbing frame? You would have only one tally mark. It is a good idea to make a mark every so often (whatever is convenient) and then you would have a clearer picture of how each child spends its time. For example:

Play behaviour	Boy	Girl
Playing on climbing frame	IIII	I
Crying	I	IIII
Talking to an adult	II	III
Playing quietly with another child	II	IIII
Reading/looking at a book	IIII	I

Tallying to give quantitative data

You could simply observe situations and make notes. This would be qualitative data, and would give rich interesting information about individuals and groups. You would use this sort of observation as part of a case study, for example. However, it is also useful to gather quantitative data. These can be compared, and conclusions drawn more easily.

Tallying can be used. Observe for a little while and make notes about possible categories of behaviour. Make a list of these categories. Then observe again, this time making tally marks against the categories as you observe them. You might like to use **time sampling**. This means making a tally mark every so often, at timed intervals. Otherwise you could have problems. Box 15 gives an example of this procedure.

By using tallying you will have quantitative data, which is easier to analyse. However, you will lose some of the richness of the data. You might also like to jot down comments to enrich your research. Then you can display data using graphs and numbers, but you can also add anything else of interest. There is no reason why you should not include written comments in the results section of a coursework report.

Inter-observer and inter-rater reliability

One observer can be biased in what is recorded. For one thing, he or she can watch only one thing at a time and might miss something of interest. Also, the observer is going to be watching using their own schemata. Chapter

1 discusses schemata and how we rely on our own frame of reference when making sense of the world; Chapter 2 discusses social representation theory, and how we can gather information only via our own experiences and culture. Both these ideas suggest that whatever we record is not sound fact, but an interpretation.

If a study is reliable, we get the same results if we do it again. However, if we have bias in observation, another observer is unlikely to find the same results. So observations can be said to be unreliable. In order to overcome this unreliability, more than one observer can be used. If more than one observer is trained to observe in the same way, and they observe the same situation, we should be able to compare the results and claim reliability for the study (if their results match).

Table 7.8 Advantages and disadvantages of observations as a method

Advantages	Disadvantages
Observing a natural situation gives natural behaviour (valid)	No controls over variables, so difficult to draw conclusions
Actual behaviour itself is natural and there are no demand characteristics	Observer bias is possible
Rich data can be collected	Observer can create an unnatural situation Might miss some information

If the observers are rating behaviour, for example, as aggressive or not, then instead of saying we have inter-observer reliability, we say we have inter-rater reliability.

We would have to test for this reliability by looking at the results of each observer and seeing if they were the same. Table 7.8 considers some advantages and disadvantages of using observations.

Case studies

Case studies involve an in-depth study of an individual or small group. Where experiments aim for strict controls, leading to an examination of cause and effect (what causes what), case studies aim for rich examination of all sorts of issues. Case studies are useful at the start of a study. Until we know what variables to control, and what to manipulate, we can't do experiments in any case. A case study will examine every aspect of a situation, and might highlight areas for further study.

In some ways a case study is not a method. To carry out a case study lots of methods can be used. Researchers use interviews, questionnaires and observations. They can examine documents, or ask people to keep diaries. Anything can be of interest in a case study.

Ethnography

Some studies are called **ethnographic**. These are studies of a culture or small group, and involve describing the subject matter in great detail. In an ethnographic study you can expect to find every issue documented and examined. Researcher will immerse themselves in the area of interest. There might be participant observation, non-participant observation, interviews, and questionnaires. It is unlikely that experiments will be used, as the researcher is concentrating on validity. There is a stated intention of finding out what is really going on. Box 16 gives an example of an ethnographic study.

Box 16

An ethnographic study

This ethnographic study was undertaken at a boys' preparatory school. A class of boys was chosen. They were all 7 years old, and in the first year of the school. The idea behind the study was that the 'self-fulfilling prophecy' suggests that middle-class children seem to succeed at school because teachers are looking for the sort of behaviour these children show. These children are praised, and become 'good at work', whereas other children see themselves as less able, and become less able as a consequence. Chapter 2 gives more information about the self-fulfilling prophecy.

It was thought that, as the boys at the preparatory school were chosen by examination, and also by the fact that their parents could afford to pay for them to go to the school, in many ways they would be similar. They were all boys, all aged 7, all at a certain minimum academic standard (there was an entrance examination) and all had parents or grandparents who could pay.

There should have been no evidence of a self-fulfilling prophecy, as who would 'not succeed'? The researcher had noted, however, that some were seen as less able, and thought it would be interesting to see what actually happened in the school, and what led to some being seen as less able than others.

Since there was no previous study, and this was a specific school, the best method was to do a case study. The researcher wanted to know everything about the school. Lessons were observed using non-participant observation. Occasionally observations were by participant observation, when the researcher helped out, for example. Interviews were carried out with the boys, parents and the teachers. A questionnaire was sent to parents asking about the school. At all stages, permission was sought and granted. The school was given a copy of the study at the end. Names were never used.

The aim was to become immersed in the culture of the school, and to uncover its 'ethos', so the ethnographic method was chosen.

The findings suggested that the school used 'supersocialisation' instead of socialisation. Socialisation is the way a child learns social norms and customs (see Chapter 2) becomes a part of society. This happened at the school, but at a different level. The school had an ideal boy in mind as they were socialising their pupils, just as every school does. However, because of the selection of pupils, this school's ideal was in some sense 'higher'. So the self-fulfilling prophecy worked, but at a different level. Instead of the middle-class child being seen as brighter, the upper middle-class child was seen as brighter. This is a very simplistic explanation, but is basically what was found.

Triangulation

Although you could say that case studies look at real data, and are high in validity, there is a problem in knowing how much to believe what is claimed. It has already been shown that it is difficult for a single researcher to be objective. Usually case studies are carried out by one person. It is necessary to give evidence for any claims.

This is done by **triangulation**. One piece of evidence gathered in one way is not sufficient. However, if the same piece of evidence is gathered by more than one means, then it is 'harder' evidence. Triangulation means taking evidence from different methods and putting it together to form the story or the picture. Figure 7.14 gives an idea of what triangulation means.

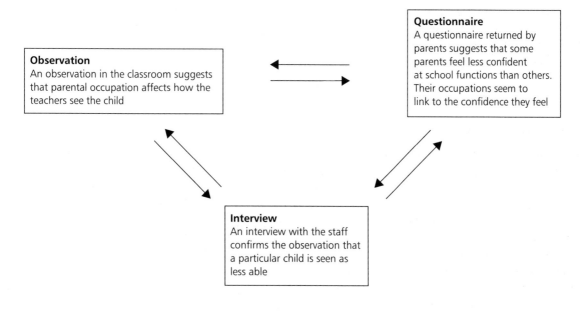

Figure 7.14
The idea of triangulation

Table 7.9 gives some advantages and disadvantages of carrying out case studies.

Discourse analyses, content analyses and analyses of diaries

The main methods used when studying psychology have been outlined. However, there are other interesting methods.

Researchers are turning more and more to methods that tell them more about interactions between people, and that give in-depth information. If you are studying sociology, you will know about the interactionist approach. Sociologists use case studies, ethnography and observations in real-life settings to find more about interactions between people. Many have realised that people cannot be studied in isolation, as they tend to be in experiments. The interactions between people themselves have importance. Similarly, questionnaires and experiments only uncover small, and perhaps insignificant, issues. There are other methods that look more directly at real people in real situations.

Diary methods

Researchers sometimes analyse historical documents and diaries of individuals to study aspects of their behaviour and beliefs. Here, however, the diary method means asking someone to keep a diary. Researchers studying sleep have asked people to keep diaries. From a therapy point of view, you can find out quite a lot of what in a person's life leads to problems such as sleeplessness or panic attacks, by asking them to keep a detailed diary. Researchers have turned to such methods in order to get rich and valid data.

Table 7.10 gives some advantages and disadvantages of using diaries to gather data.

Content analysis

Content analysis involves going directly to a source of data. This can be a newspaper or the television, for example. The content is then analysed closely and patterns are looked for. Box 17 suggests a study you could do.

Table 7.9 Advantages and disadvantages of case studies

Advantages	Disadvantages
Valid data is gathered Can generate a lot of other research Can generate a lot of data	One person or small group, so cannot generalise from the findings Not reliable, as a different situation another time, and a different researcher An element of subjectivity from the researcher

Table 7.10 Advantages and disadvantages of diary methods

Advantages	Disadvantages
Gathers real data in the sense that the participant is recording their feelings and actions Gathers rich data as the participant is free to record whatever they wish to record	Depends on the participant to tell the truth The particpiant may forget to record something Not reliable, because each individual situation is unlikely to happen again

---

Box 17

An example of content analysis

You could consider a content analysis of television advertisements, to look at issues of gender. Until recently, you could be reasonably sure that you would find males and females in different roles in television advertisements: the women would be doing household things, and the men would be doing work-related things. However, role reversal is now used in adverts. Men are seen to be using 'Flash' to clean up, and women come home from work to a meal prepared by a man.

You could look at adverts to see what roles are filled by which gender. If you stick to children's adverts, you will find traditional gender roles.

Content analysis needs planning. Think about testing the hypothesis that adverts on children's television represent what we would call 'traditional' gender roles.

ACTIVITY 12

PLAN A STUDY OF CHILDREN'S TV ADVERTS USING CONTENT ANALYSIS

- *Write down the procedure for doing such a study.*
- *How would you do the study?*
- *What are the problems, and how would you solve them?*

  Key Skill C3.1a – this would make a good group task.

You probably had to think about some of the following issues:
- What programmes would you watch?
- How long would you watch for?
- Are the programmes all at the same time of day?
- Are you watching on different days, or only on one day?
- How are you going to note down a 'traditional' gender role?
- How are you going to record your data?
- Will you include a tape recording of the adverts if you submit the study for coursework?
- How will you decide what is a children's advertisement?

There are other important questions. These decisions form part of the method section of your coursework, and are important design decisions.

Self-test 13

Test yourself on some of the method terminology.

1   When you decide what you will choose to represent a 'traditional gender role' this is said to be _____ your concepts.

2   If you decide to present your results as a written story about what you found when doing content analysis, is the data quantitative or qualitative?

3   If the researcher, when doing content analysis, allows his or her own views to affect the data gathered, can the researcher be accused of subjectivity or objectivity?

4   Does content analysis have validity as a method?

5   Does content analysis have reliability as a method?

- Deciding on a way of measuring a concept is called **operationalising** the concepts. This means making them measurable.
- Presenting the results in the form of a story means giving **qualitative** data. **Quantitative** data are measured and one person's score can be compared with another, so these are not quantitative data.
- If the researcher's own views affect the data, then there is **subjectivity**. This means the results are likely to be biased. In all research, **objectivity** should be aimed for.
- Content analysis is a valid method, because it is gathering data straight from the source. There is no manipulation of variables, and the TV adverts are directly analysed. So the results are 'real' and the study is measuring what it is claiming to measure.
- Content analysis can be reliable if the study is done using controls. If looking at adverts, for example, the study is reliable if it can be repeated. As long as the researcher states clearly what adverts were examined, when and in what way, then the study can be done again and should yield the same results.

Table 7.11 Advantages and disadvantages of using content analysis

Advantages	Disadvantages
Valid because it collects direct data Ethical because there are no participants and the situation is already present The researcher can do content analysis in their own time and without disturbing others, so relatively easy	Only looks at a particular situation, so it may not be possible to repeat the study Uses media as sources, and the facts are often biased in the media Need to use careful sampling of items to analyse – each newspaper has its own bias, for example

Discourse analysis

Discourse analysis is similar to content analysis. It involves listening to people's conversations and analysing them for meanings. Discourse analysis is a 'modern' method arising from modern theory (Chapter 2 explains how interest in discourse analysis is growing). It involves collecting qualitative data in the form of other people's 'discourses' or conversations. These conversations can be in written form, and can include texts, and discourse analysis is similar to content analysis as a method.

However, discourse analysis is interested in people talking, and in interactions between people, rather than the more sociological content of content analysis. Also it goes beyond 'just' conversations, and is more complex than this brief explanation can show. Content analysis focuses on issues such as gender roles, or helping behaviour. It looks at social behaviour in general. Discourse analysis looks more specifically at conversations and the effect of culture. One of the main features is the examination of the way we understand language, and how it can be differently interpreted by different people in different situations.

The idea is that issues examined in psychology, especially within social psychology, are not real things that can be looked at. They arise from one person's interactions with another, and can only be studied with that in mind. We can not measure self, or gender; we can only study these sorts of issues by looking at what they mean to people. The way to do this is to look at interactions between people, especially interactions using language.

Box 18

An example of discourse analysis

Gavey (1992) interviewed a small number of women and asked them about their relationships. She did not pick any particular women, as she wanted general comments – she did not choose women with problems, for example.

Gavey analysed what the women said, and consulted them again to make sure that her analysis seemed reasonable to them.

Gavey looked carefully at what the women had said, and thought that power in relationships was an important factor. She looked at what was said and picked out references to power. It was not that the women mentioned the word 'power', but that their comments referred to male power in the relationships. So power was one of the themes that came out of the analysis.

Table 7.12 Advantages and disadvantages of using discourse analysis

Advantages	Disadvantages
Just as content analysis looks at 'real data', so discourse analysis looks at real conversations. It is thus a valid method	There is almost bound to be subjectivity because the discourse between the researcher and the participant can be part of what is studied, so there is bias
The researcher can arrive at a novel way of categorising social issues	Any analysis, even of the same material, is likely to be different, so the method is not reliable
Tends to use a small number of participants, which can be easier and more ethical	It is dificult – the researcher starts with a clean sheet and has to build categories Tends to use a small number of participants and analyse in depth, so results are not generalisable

Other aspects of methods

There seems to be so much to say about methods. This section has outlined a great deal, and you will need to pay a lot of attention to it when doing research of your own. However, some important terms have not yet been discussed.

Longitudinal design

If a study is carried out on the same group of people over a period of time, it is called a longitudinal study. Even the study of babies over a few months can be a longitudinal design, if you are going to compare each baby's ability at one stage with their ability a few months later. You are comparing the same baby at each stage. Some longitudinal studies carry on for years.

Advantages

- You are studying the same person, so there are no individual differences.

Disadvantages

- So much will change over the period of time that it will be hard to know what is causing any effect you are looking at.
- People will drop out or move away.
- Even the researcher might move on, leaving someone else to continue the work.

Cross-sectional designs

If a study is carried out at one moment in time using different groups, this is a cross-sectional design. You could study babies of 3 months and compare them with babies of 6 months – but this time you would pick two different groups of babies. With the longitudinal study, you would have waited three months for the same babies to grow before testing them again.

Advantages

- You can gather all the data straight away.
- There is less likelihood of people dropping out of the study, or of the researcher leaving.

Disadvantages

- You still have the problem of individual differences because you are making comparisons between different people.
- The older group have been through different events, and there are too many variables for good controls to be possible.

Cross-cultural designs

Cross-cultural studies are those done between cultures. Chapter 3 explains Piaget's view that children pass through invariant stages. This means, for example, that they all demonstrate lack of object permanence and then develop it. Object permanence is easily understood, I think, even if you have not yet studied Chapter 3. Think of playing with a 5-month old baby. You get them interested in a rattle, then hide it under a blanket. You watch their face as it reappears. They might show delighted surprise. When they are a bit older, they will watch the blanket, knowing that the rattle is hidden under it, and will reappear. When they know that the object will reappear, they are said to have developed object permanence. When they show surprise, they show no idea of object permanence.

A cross-cultural study, for example, can test these sorts of stages and see if they are true of all babies in all cultures. If they are found to be true of all participants, then we assume that the ability is innate (inborn). If differences are found, we tend to say the ability is learnt.

Advantages

- Cross-cultural studies are useful for finding out whether something is born or learnt through experience.

Disadvantages

- The researcher won't know the culture, perhaps, so might easily misunderstand what is going on.
- The researcher might use inappropriate materials, for example, that those in another culture are not familiar with. If they use the same materials, they might be spoiling the study, and if they don't, they have lost some of the control.
- They may have language problems.

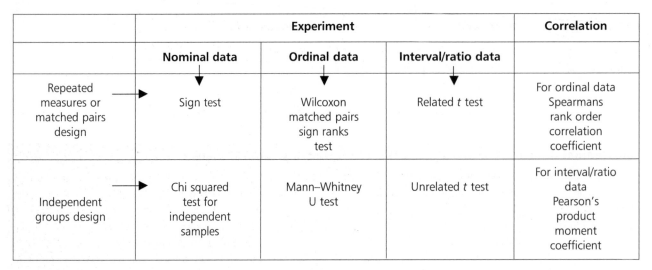

	Experiment			Correlation
	Nominal data	**Ordinal data**	**Interval/ratio data**	
Repeated measures or matched pairs design	Sign test	Wilcoxon matched pairs sign ranks test	Related *t* test	For ordinal data Spearmans rank order correlation coefficient
Independent groups design	Chi squared test for independent samples	Mann–Whitney U test	Unrelated *t* test	For interval/ratio data Pearson's product moment coefficient

Figure 7.15
A table to choose which statistical test is required

Coursework suggestions

1 Try a questionnaire to look at age and sleep patterns. Do older people sleep less than younger people? If you find out their age (even if approximately) and how many hours on average they sleep each night, then you could use a correlational design.
2 Make sure you are in a public place like a shopping precinct, and observe who holds doors open. Are men more helpful than women, for example?
3 Write out a list of 20 words, in four sets of five (i.e. grouped) – for example parts of the body, or colours. Then write the same list out again, but this time randomly presented. Do categories aid recall?

Suggested further reading

Cardwell, M., Clark, L., & Meldrun, C. (1996) *Psychology for A level.* Hammersmith: Collins Educational.

Clegg, F. (1991) *Simple Statistics.* Cambridge: Cambridge University Press.

Coolican, J. (1994) *Research Methods and Statistics in Psychology*, 2nd ed. London: Hodder and Stoughton.

8 Ethics and coursework in psychological research

The aims of this chapter

The aims of this chapter are, with regard to ethics and coursework, to enable the reader to:

- *describe ethical guidelines, based on British Psychological Society guidelines, on the use of humans as participants (including consent, confidentiality, debriefing and right to withdraw)*
- *describe ethical guidelines with regard to the use of non-human animals in psychological research*
- *apply ethical principles when carrying out and evaluating a piece of research*
- *apply ethical principles when evaluating the research of others*
- *choose a suitable hypothesis to test for a piece of coursework for the Edexcel specification*
- *write up a piece of coursework for the Edexcel specification – Unit 3.*

Self-test 1

After reading this chapter, test yourself on each of the above points. Use the points as exam questions and make notes accordingly. Then see how much you can write on each.

This chapter covers

1 Issues regarding ethics
2 Ethical issues when using human participants
3 Ethical issues when using non-human animals
4 Coursework information and advice for Unit 3

5 Getting evidence for Key Skills through coursework
6 Checklist for final submission of coursework

Rationale for this chapter

It is necessary to give information on how to write up research projects in psychology. For most psychology courses, at most levels, a student needs to carry out a piece of research and write it up in a standard format. However, before a piece of research can be carried out and written up, the researcher needs to know about ethical guidelines. So many research studies are carried out in psychology that guidelines are needed to protect those taking part in the studies.

I read somewhere that the Asch line study (see Chapter 2) cannot be carried out in the USA any more because most people have been involved in it as a participant or know about it. Soon this could be the case in the UK. There are a great many participants taking part in psychology practicals each year. Therefore, this chapter looks first at ethical issues. Although you won't be using non-human animals in your studies (the Edexcel specification does not allow this), ethical issues regarding non-human animals are also included here, because you need to know about them. As I write, new guidelines are being produced although basic rules apply.

The chapter goes on to look at how to write up a practical.

Issues regarding ethics

Ethics refers to a set of standards for behaviour. Psychologists have responsibilities towards the people and animals they work with. There are various published standards, including guidelines from the British Psychological Society (BPS) and the American Psychological Association (APA). There are other guidelines too, for example for those in clinical psychology. The Association for the Teaching of Psychology (ATP) has considered ethical issues at pre-degree level, and has published guidance based on the BPS guidelines. The ATP guidelines are the ones printed in the specification for the Edexcel course, and the ones you need to be familiar with. For the Edexcel course you have been asked not to carry out studies on animals. However, there are guidelines for animal research.

STUDY AID

This may seem obvious, but as you are now studying a different section, remember to start a new section in your folder, or a new folder.

Key Skill LP3.1 – agree targets and plan how these will be met, using support from appropriate others. You need your tutor for this, and you will require a record of the discussion to use as evidence. Discuss organising your work and develop a time plan for working through this textbook. It is tempting to leave everything to your teacher, but you should be reading the chapters as you study each approach, alongside the work your teacher gives you. Make a note of dates and what you will have achieved by then, so that you can review your progress for Key Skill LP3.3.

It is worth noting that there are two ways of considering ethical issues in psychology. The first is looking at standards of behaviour when carrying out research (both with humans and with non-human animals). The second is looking at standards of behaviour when working in psychology, that is regarding treatments and therapies. This chapter is concerned with ethical issues when carrying out research. You will need to know more about ethics and psychological therapies for the A2 part of the course. There is some discussion of these issues in the key application section of Chapter 4, since it deals with the deliberate alteration of human behaviour. In this area, you need to ask such questions as 'should we deliberately alter someone's behaviour?' and 'how do we decide whose behaviour can be altered, and for what reason?'

Why study ethics?

You need to know about ethical principles because you will be doing studies and activities while studying psychology and you must follow ethical guidelines. Another reason for studying ethical principles is so that you understand what is allowed, and what is not allowed. You may not be happy about some of the studies, and you may well want to criticise what was done. You need to know the ethical guidelines so that you can use them in your evaluations.

You may not like the idea of the use of non-human animals in psychology, and you should read the arguments for and against this use so that you can decide where you stand.

When you are asked to criticise or evaluate a study, you should always consider ethical issues, because they are useful as a point of evaluation.

Link to the chapters you have already read

It is likely that you are reading this chapter while you are studying other areas of the book. You will probably have already realised the importance of ethical issues in psychology, and will have discussed some of them. Activity 1 asks you to make a list of the issues that you think are important.

Your lists will depend on what you have already studied. A list of ethical issues might include:
- Making sure no harm comes to the participants.
- Making sure participants are not left feeling distressed in any way.
- Not using participant names, or allowing them to be identified by others.
- Giving participants the opportunity to refuse to do the study.
- Not affecting the participant so that they change because of the study – for example, not making them prejudiced because of questionnaire items.
- Not hurting animals when doing studies.
- Not using animals in studies at all.

A list of studies where ethical issues are involved might include:

- Milgram's study in which participants thought they were giving electric shocks to others and were distressed (see Chapter 2).
- Zimbardo's study, where participants acting the role of prisoners became very distressed (see Chapter 2).
- Siffre's study, where he spent a long time underground to try to find 'natural' sleep/wake patterns. He was deprived of company and other comforts (see Chapter 6).
- Memory studies in which participants have to do tasks they can't do properly (there are too many words to learn, for example) so they might become distressed (see Chapter 1).
- Piaget's studies using children, who were possibly not asked directly for consent (see Chapter 3).
- Sherif's study called the Robber's Cave, which set children against each other without asking them to take part in a study, and without telling them why (see Chapter 2).
- Watson and Rayner's study that conditioned Little Albert to fear a rat, and probably did not extinguish the fear (see Chapter 4).

There are many other studies, but these give an idea of the issues involved (you will probably have included different studies). I have used the above studies when discussing the ethical principles outlined below, so you might like to read them, so that the discussion below is more clear.

Ethical issues when using human participants

Gross (1999) says that we should see every psychological investigation as an ethical situation. This means that you should always consider ethical issues. You need to think about them when planning your own study, and when you are evaluating the work of others. In 1983, the BPS published their *Code of Conduct for Psychologists* and in 1990 *Ethical Principles for Conducting Research with Human Participants* (revised in 1993). In 1983, the BPS produced guidelines for the professional practice of clinical psychology. These guidelines were for those in practice, rather than researchers.

Guidelines need to be updated often, to keep in line with cultural and social changes: in 2000 the BPS guidelines for the use of animals in psychological research are being updated, for example. Also in 2000 the ATP, which tends to focus on pre-degree courses like this one, is reconsidering its ethical guidelines to make sure they are still what is needed. So you should think of ethical guidelines as changing with the times.

As an example, consider that until quite recently (the last 5 years or so) participants were called 'subjects'. I am sure you are reading textbooks where the term 'subjects' is used. The matter was then thought about. If you call someone a 'subject' it is as if they have no power in the situation. When the individual was called a 'subject' he or she was really more of an 'object'. So now we have 'participants', who have rights.

Consent

Participants must give their consent to the study taking place. However, this is not always possible. Consider an observation in a busy shopping centre, where you want to see who helps people. You would not be able to ask their consent. There are other ethical principles to cover these sorts of issues, as you will see. In general, wherever possible, consent must be obtained. Sometimes consent should be in writing – for example, when children are participants their parents or guardians should be asked for written permission.

Informed consent

Consent is important, but it is not enough. You really need *informed* consent. This means that, before giving consent, the participant must be fully informed about the investigation; they must be told *everything* that will happen. This is very difficult to achieve in many cases because, if you tell the participant everything, they will not be a naïve participant. They will know what to expect, and possibly how to behave, which will probably spoil the study. Imagine if Milgram's participants had known that the other person was not receiving shocks at all (see Chapter 2). There are other guidelines that tell you what to do if you cannot get informed consent.

Right to withdraw

It is difficult to get consent or informed consent, but right to withdraw is usually possible. If you are doing the 'observing in a public place' study, you might not be able to give the right to withdraw; however, usually you can – you simply say to the participant that they can stop taking part at any time. One problem is that the researcher might know the participants, so they might not feel able to withdraw. You must assure them that they *do* have that right. You might, in your own studies, be using relatives or peers as your participants and you must let them know that they have the right to withdraw. You would probably know if participants are not comfortable, so you should stop the study in any case if you think there is a problem. Some participants are paid to take part (for example, Milgram and Zimbardo both paid their participants), and this too could be a problem – they might not feel they have the right to withdraw. Any problems should be put in front of others who can act as judges for the researcher.

Consent and right to withdraw in special cases

There are special cases where consent and the right to withdraw may not be properly given. The special case of research with children is examined below, but there are others who may need special protection. For example, prisoners may feel they have to take part. A conformity study that used offenders (Perrin and Spencer, 1981) found that they are likely to conform more, because of being young offenders. They may also have felt they had to take part in the study.

There is also a problem when the researcher is seen as having power, as is often the case. Even when you are doing your own studies, you will find that you are given the power in the situation, which you are controlling (if you are doing an experiment or a survey, for example). Milgram had the power, and this affected the ethics of his study. Zimbardo also had the power. Those without the power hardly have the right to withdraw, and may not be giving consent freely.

Deception

Researchers must not deceive the participants. If you have read some of the earlier chapters, you can probably recall some studies where participants were deceived – for example, Milgram's study. For one thing, Milgram said he was doing a memory study, when he was not. Also the participants thought someone was getting an electric shock, and they were not.

Many other studies involve deception. Most memory studies require you to deceive participants, for example: if you are testing to see if categorised lists are better recalled than random lists, you can't very well tell the participants this, or they might try harder for the categorised list. This means that these studies are unethical. However, deception is also often necessary. So other guidelines are used to 'offset' the poor ethics involved in using deception.

Debriefing

A useful way of overcoming some of the problems mentioned above is by using debriefing. The idea is that you tell the participants exactly what they have been doing, and why. Then they must be asked whether the results can be included in the study. They still have the right to withdraw from the study, and this must be made clear Although we should not have done anything that at the end of the study will make the participant regret taking part, debriefing can be a useful way of making sure that the participant has not been affected by the study.

Debriefing can help in cases of necessary deception. It can also help where it has not been possible to get informed consent. It is really the lack of informed consent that is the deception.

Protection of participants

The participant must leave the situation in the same frame of mind that they brought to the situation. They must be protected from harm, both physical and psychological. Debriefing can help here too, as the researcher can make sure that everything has been understood by the participant and that he or she has not come to any harm.

In some cases there are follow-up sessions. Milgram has been criticised for his research, as you have seen, but he did use a questionnaire to follow up on the participants, and to see if they felt the study (and the deception) was justified. Many did indeed think the research was justified. Haney et al (in the Zimbardo study, where they looked at the roles of prisoners and guards) also debriefed their participants fully, followed up after a few months, and again after a year.

Some studies do not protect participants, however: the Little Albert study could be put into this group. If you have read the study though (you can find it in Chapter 4), you may remember that, although it is usually claimed that the researchers did not extinguish the conditioning, other reports say that the fear response to the rat *was* extinguished.

Competence and conduct

The issues of competence and conduct apply to the researcher. When you are researching, you must be sure that you are competent to carry out the study. If you are in any doubt, you should ask others for their opinion. This is quite usual practice. Milgram, for example, in his well known study, asked others if they thought the participants would give such high 'shocks'. If the answers had been that the participants would do that, he might well have reconsidered the study. You must be guided by your teacher who will, if he or she is in any doubt, contact colleagues to see what they think. Awarding bodies also keep an eye on studies to make sure that students are competent. Edexcel ask for submission of proposals for new studies, other than those that have already been approved.

Researchers must also conduct themselves properly. They must stick to all these guidelines for a start, and never tackle anything they are not competent to do. Researchers should not claim to know more than they do know, or to be able to do more than they can. That is why I have said we must not 'do' psychoanalysis (see Chapter 5).

Confidentiality

It is not too difficult to maintain confidentiality. You should *never* use a participant's actual name, and you can usually disguise the area in which the study was carried out. Let participants know that they will not be identified by anyone, and you should be careful to make sure this is the case.

Most of the time researchers maintain confidentiality although there is one study, the case study of Clive Wearing, where a real name is used. I am not sure why. I do know that he is a very well known musician, so perhaps it was thought that he deserved recognition for his problems. Another case widely cited in psychology, although it is not a study, is the horrific murder of Jamie Bulger by two young children. I am not very comfortable when using this young boy's name, and would be happier with a pseudonym.

Usually initials are used. In Chapter 1 we talked about the case study of H.M. You should remember not to use real names, and to maintain confidentiality.

Observing in a public place

Observations are particularly difficult because you cannot really ask for permission to observe someone. Sometimes you can get permission, but often that would upset the behaviour you want to study. Also, if you were observing helping behaviour, for example, you would not know who was going to select themselves as a participant until after the event. They would need to be a helper first. The problems of informed consent and right to withdraw are overcome if the observation is in a public place. The general idea is that in a public place you might reasonably expect to be watched. You are not likely to be doing something that you would not want watched, so it seems reasonable to observe someone on that basis.

You should not observe someone if you think they would not want to be observed, and you should be aware of cultural differences. One of the problems is that, when someone is a participant in a study and they don't know they are taking part in a study, there is no debriefing. For example, some of the social psychology experiments involve situations such as someone pretending to be drunk to see what help they get. An individual might help, and therefore become a participant in the experiment. They will not have volunteered to be a participant. You should at least go after them, after they have helped, explain what the study is about, and ask if they give their permission for the results to be included.

Often, however, we don't debrief in these situations. I have been part of a group doing a similar study, and if I explain this study, you might agree that debriefing does not always seem advisable. In groups of threes, students went into a busy town centre to drop a file of papers. The idea was that the papers would spread out a bit, and we would see who would help to pick them up. We used male and female actors to drop the papers, to see if gender affected who was helped. We made sure that we could pick up all the paper, so that no litter was left. Two of the students hid while the other one was the actor. On one occasion a very pretty girl student was the actor and dropped the papers. It was quite a wet and rainy day and one piece went under a car. A kind male helper knelt down to get this piece of paper, and his suit got a bit dirty. She decided quickly that if she said it was a psychology experiment he would be more annoyed than if she thanked him for being helpful. We all discussed this when the group got back together. I had said that they needed to debrief the participants, but on reflection I think the helper would be happier to have helped than to have possibly been made to look foolish. After this occasion we decided to be more careful about our psychology experiments. I hope this helps you see some of the problems.

Ethical standards for research with children

There are special problems when it comes to using children in psychology studies. They cannot give consent, for one thing. Even if they are old enough to give consent, it may not be *informed* consent. They may feel forced to take part. Special standards have been issued by the Society for Research in Child Development; the Ethical Standards for Research with Children.

Activity 2 asks you to consider special problems that might arise if children are participants.

Children could be more vulnerable and are likely to be more stressed by studies than adults. Also they don't have the experience to know what is being asked of them. The parents of children being studied must give their consent, as well as the children themselves. Here is a summary of some of the rules when using children in research.
- The child's rights come first, no matter what their age.
- The researcher has the responsibility for the ethics of a study.
- The researcher is also responsible for everyone else taking part in the study.
- The researcher should answer the child's questions and give them full information.
- The child must be allowed to stop taking part at any time.

ACTIVITY 2

CHILDREN AS PARTICIPANTS

Make a list of things you think might be important when children are participants. If you are working in a group, this would make a good group discussion. You could use brainstorming. To do this, use a large piece of paper (A3 or bigger). Everyone in the group has to write some useful comment somewhere on the paper. Keep circulating the paper, gathering comments. Don't discuss their usefulness at this stage. All comments are welcome. You should find that soon you can start discussing, and you could start grouping the comments into some sort of order.

Key Skill C3.1a – contribute to a group discussion. Don't forget to keep the evidence for your portfolio. You could each have a photocopy of the piece of paper with all your comments on. Or you could summarise the comments into lists or a diagram, and keep a copy.

- Informed consent of parents and others (e.g. head teachers) must be obtained, preferably in writing.
- No research operation can be used that will physically or psychologically harm the child.
- If deception is essential (sometimes it is), then a committee of peers of the researcher must be consulted.
- All information must be confidential.
- After data collection, the researcher must report the findings to the participants, unless it is more humane to withhold the information – when doing so does not harm the participant.
- If the researcher finds information that affects the child's well-being, this must be discussed with an expert in the field so that parents can be informed.
- If the experiment will lead to undesirable consequences, these consequences should be corrected as soon as this is known.
- The social, political and human implications of the research must be considered, and reporting must take this into account.
- If an experimental treatment is thought to be of benefit, the control group must be offered other beneficial treatments if available, not just 'no treatment'.

The case study of Genie and ethics

There is a well-known case study of a young girl called 'Genie' (Curtiss, 1977) (this was not her real name). Genie was locked away by her father, and given no socialisation. She could not walk properly and did not talk when she was found. The case of Genie is mentioned in Chapter 3, so you may already know the story. The whole story, including a discussion of the ethical issues, was the subject of a *Horizon* programme a few years ago, and you may be able to watch a video of the programme.

The issue is that scientists took over the care of Genie. They did care for her in many ways, but their main interest was to study Genie's language development. So, while caring for her, they tested her most of the time, to see if she could learn normal language, and how this would develop. Some of the team wanted her to be tested, others said that therapy should come first. Jean Butler was Genie's teacher at the children's hospital where she stayed at first. Then she stayed with Jean Butler. There was a battle then between Butler and the scientists.

The scientists won, in that David Rigler and his wife became Genie's foster parents and she lived with them for 4 years. David Rigler was the chief psychiatrist at the hospital, and he obtained a grant to study Genie. She lived with the Rigler family as a member of the family. She was well cared for, but she was also observed all the time. Her language development slowed down, and she was not progressing. The National Institutes of Mental Health, who had given the grant, were dissatisfied at her progress and the project ended.

There was a problem in any case, because this was one girl and one case study, so they would not be able to generalise the findings. Also there were no controls. They did not even know Genie's mental capacity at birth. This is why the project ended.

Genie was returned to her mother; however, her mother could not cope and Genie went to a number of foster homes before ending up in a home for mentally retarded adults in southern California. She is still there (or was when I last heard). She still cannot talk normally, does not walk upright and uses inappropriate social behaviours.

The question could be asked – what if Genie had had therapy instead of being observed in a scientific 'experiment'? Rymer (1993) discusses these issues in his book *Genie: a Scientific Tragedy*.

You can see that Genie did not have the right to withdraw. She did not give consent to the study taking place, and she was in a way deceived because she did not know she was the subject of a study. She may even have come to some harm because of the study.

Access to data

Although it is not mentioned much in psychology, the Data Protection Act (1984) is very important. Remember that you cannot store data about someone without their knowledge and without permission. Also you will usually have no right to access data about people. You cannot use your school or college's database, for example.

Prior consent and presumptive consent

To overcome problems with informed consent and not deceiving participants, sometimes prior consent is obtained. You can ask people if they would consent in general – in other words, they would be in a pool of volunteers. You could explain that sometimes deception might be necessary, and they would be asked to agree to this. The problem is, the individuals would not know precisely what they were agreeing to, but it is better to get prior consent than no consent at all.

Presumptive consent refers to asking others if the study is ethical. You can explain the whole thing to people who are not going to be participants, and see if they say they would have agreed to take part. This suggests that 'normally' people would not mind taking part, so you hope your participants would not mind either.

STUDY AID

You will need to know many of the ethical principles, because you will be able to use them when evaluating studies. Of course, you will also need them when doing your own studies.

It would be a good idea to get a small piece of card (like an index card) and make a brief list of the main ethical principles. Then, when you have to evaluate a study, you can glance down the list and get used to asking whether each principle was observed or not. In this way your evaluation will improve, and you will get to know the principles very well.

Ethical issues when using non-human animals

Should non-human animals be used at all?

ACTIVITY 3

POINTS FOR AND AGAINST THE USE OF NON-HUMAN ANIMALS IN RESEARCH

Make two lists, one with points in favour of using non-human animals when doing studies in psychology, and one against. You might have to consider such issues as whether the use of non-human animals is in experiments or simply watching them in their natural settings. Make a note of these questions too.

> Key Skill C3.2 – you could extend this activity by writing an essay on the topic. A possible title might be 'Discuss the use of non-human animals in psychological research'. Read two extended documents, and then use the information in your essay. You will find information on this topic in most main text books, journals and on the Internet. *The Psychology Review* is kept in most school and college libraries, and has articles on such topics.

You might want to say that we should never use non-human animals in research. Many people share that view. As far as I know nobody thinks that non-human animals should suffer pain just for the purposes of research. Some, however, think that non-human animal suffering is acceptable if the result is worthwhile. Usually, this means worthwhile to humans, but sometimes the non-human animals also gain. The argument is not really whether we should inflict pain on non-human animals, but whether it is ever justified. Many researchers claim that the end results do justify the means of getting the results. This is what the argument is about.

If you think that animals should never be used, I am not trying to argue with you. You need to read this section and decide for yourself. When there are many arguments both for and against an issue such as this, we have a dilemma (dilemma means when there are many arguments and no clear decision can be made). You may be very clear in your mind that non-human animals should never be used. I might have agreed with you once, I think.

However, I have had occasion to be grateful to many researchers, who no doubt used many live animals in their experiments. This is because people I know have had various illnesses that needed treatment, and their treatments would not have been available without the use of animals. It is much harder to make the decision that non-human animals should never be used when you start considering how you yourself have benefited from their use (even if you have only had paracetemol, or been grateful for a dentist's knowledge).

The above argument has mainly been about medicines, and we are considering research in psychology here. However, again you have to stop to think about what research in psychology has offered to people. There is a much better understanding of stress and depression now. We know more about the nervous system, how mental processes affect our physiology and vice versa. We know that stress from mental events can contribute to physical illnesses, as well as that illnesses lead to stress. We know more about the effects of overcrowding, for example, and how it can lead to violent behaviour. We have learnt how to help when someone has a phobia. Research in psychology leads to improvements in the quality of our lives, and such knowledge is often gained from animal studies.

Are humans also animals?

Before studying the arguments concerning whether we should use non-human animals in research at all, consider why I am using the term 'non-human' to describe animals in this section.

ACTIVITY 4

WHY IS IT NECESSARY TO USE THE TERM 'NON-HUMAN' WHEN TALKING ABOUT ANIMALS?

Why do you think I am using the term 'non-human' to apply to animals? It might seem unnatural. It is, however, an important thing to do. Make a few notes as to why you think it is important, before reading on.

> Key Skill C3.1a – this activity could form the basis of a group discussion. Remember to keep the evidence for your portfolio.

The main reason for using the term 'non-human' to distinguish humans from animals is that humans are also animals. This seems quite clear to me, but I do know that there are still quite a few people who disagree.

It is all because of Darwin's idea – that through **survival of the fittest** we have evolved into the species that we are. In fact, others besides Darwin put this idea forward, but he first gave the evidence. Different capabilities are needed for survival in different surroundings, and life has evolved from basic life forms into lots of different species. The process is more complicated than this, but the basic idea is that what is useful leads an organism to survive. The organisms without useful capabilities cannot reproduce, and so die out. Those 'not useful' capabilities are not passed on, because the organisms don't survive to have young and so the genes for the 'not useful' capabilities are not passed on. Therefore, mainly useful capabilities survive.

In one example, Darwin looked at finches. If their surroundings meant that there were a lot of trees, and insects needed to be dug out of bark, then those finches with beaks capable of digging insects out of bark survived better than those with blunt beaks. Those with blunt beaks would die out in those surroundings, and the finches there would have sharp beaks. Animals should become better and better adapted to their environments. In this way humans have evolved, through the same basic mechanism of survival of the fittest.

Humans are animals too, and share features with other animals, having evolved through the same processes. If people thought that humans were completely different from animals, we may never have started to experiment using animals. Some people still think that humans were separately created, and this view is called **creationism**. I am not arguing for or against either of these views. You need to be aware of them, however. The main point is that without the underlying assumption that humans are animals, it is doubtful that we would have been so interested in studying non-human animals as a way of learning about ourselves.

The case for using non-human animals

Research using non-human animals has led to improved knowledge about the way animal (and human) systems work. Improvements have been made in the quality of life of both non-human animals and humans, mainly because of advances in medical knowledge. In order to continue to study the complexities of living organisms, living non-human animals must be used. Green (1994) says that many drugs could not have been developed without the use of non-human animals.

It is claimed that there are few alternatives to animal studies.
- Some humans with life-threatening diseases do take drugs to test them; however, this is almost always only when all other medication has failed, so the individual has more to gain than to lose. Also, this is only done after the drugs have first been tested extensively on non-human animals.
- Various scanning techniques are now used on humans much more widely, and much is being learnt from this technique. However, scanning simply involves looking rather than touching and altering, whereas planned experimental testing is done on non-human animals.

Progress towards curing various diseases, and towards improving the quality of life for humans, cannot be made without the use of living non-human animals in research. If you accept this argument, then the use of non-human animals in research is both ethical and appropriate. Gray (1991) goes so far as to say that it is our duty to our species to improve our own quality of life, even if this means 'using' other species to do so. This argument is called 'pro-speciesism'.

Although psychology is not directly involved in developing drugs as cures for diseases, the same arguments apply to the use of treatments and therapies in psychology. By studying animals, we can find a lot out about the workings of the human nervous system. We can test non-human animal reactions to stressors, for example. We can test the memory of non-human animals and use the results to draw conclusions about our own memory and forgetting processes. Studies have looked at overcrowding in non-human animals, and the results have been used to draw conclusions about the effects of overcrowding on humans (see Chapter 2). Experiments can be done using non-human animals that cannot be done using humans. We can learn a great deal from such experiments, and can use the findings to improve conditions for humans.

While the aims of the studies are almost always to look at human behaviour, and to improve things for humans, some argue that animals too have benefited. For example, we know more now about the effects of overcrowding on animals, so zoos can take this knowledge into account.

Most of the above argument has discussed the use of non-human animals in experiments, but psychology also involves studying animals in a more natural setting. **Ethology** is the study of animals in their natural setting. Usually, ethology as a method is less criticised than use of non-human animals in a laboratory.

It is useful to study non-human animals

There are many reasons why using non-human animals in the laboratory is helpful. Many species have a much shorter reproductive cycle, and therefore many generations can quickly be studied. This is helpful in the study of genetics. Similarly, many species are small and easy to handle, which again makes things easier for the researcher.

The case against using non-human animals

One problem with using non-human animals is that they are different from humans. The question is, is it useful to carry out research on non-human animals when there are such important differences? What can be learnt from studying stress in non-human animals that can be *generalised* to humans? Although many non-human animals share aspects of the human nervous system and brain structure, humans are different. It may be that no generalisations should be made because of these differences.

Another issue that is widely supported is that non-human animals should not be experimented upon at all for ethical reasons. Non-human animals cannot answer back, and cannot refuse to take part. It is widely accepted that non-human animals feel pain (although there is some debate about this in the case of some creatures), and the question is whether we should be allowed to cause pain in another being just to improve the quality of our own lives.

The argument that we should do all we can for our own species was put forward as a reason for using non-human animals in research. However, we only know the value of the research after it has taken place. There may be many experiments that eventually lead nowhere, and so the animal suffered for no benefit. It is difficult to say that we need to balance the benefit of the research against the suffering of a non-human animal if we only know the benefit much later. Some people use this argument as another reason why non-human animals should not be used. Box 1 summarises a recent argument (using a *Sunday Times* article, 12 December 1999) in the debate about using animals for experiments.

Box 1

'Scientific experiments on dogs to be banned'

You can probably find many references to animal experiments in newspapers, as there is a lot of debate surrounding the issue. Most of the articles tend to argue against the use of non-human animals. The *Sunday Times* article states that the government is preventing any further experiments on dogs. There has been political pressure on the government to prevent experiments taking place on non-human animals. The Labour Party indicated before they were elected that they were against such 'cruelty', and once they were elected, they were pressed to carry out their promises.

Home Office figures suggest that 6300 dogs die a slow death each year due to painful experiments.

Activists at the British Union for the Abolition of Vivisection (BUAV) outline details of these experiments. The article mentions some of the details, and I must admit they don't bear thinking about! Jack Straw (Home Secretary at the time of writing) is about to ban the use of puppies and dogs, but the article suggests that this is just to appease the animal rights campaigners. The article points out that the Labour Party received funding from the International Fund for Animal Welfare, and implies that some action to prevent cruelty should be taken in return. In November 1998 the government announced an end to the use of non-human animals to test cosmetics but, according to the article, only 1300 animal tests were to test cosmetics, and 2.6 million tests are for scientific trials.

As only 0.3% of non-human animal experiments use dogs, according to the article, there is a suggestion that the government needs to go further than 'just' making it illegal to use dogs in experiments. For example 1500 cats are said to die in laboratories each year; most experiments (quoted as being 2.1 million) take place on mice and rats; 5200 experiments are carried out on monkeys.

Box 1 underlines some of the issues. The upsetting nature of the experiments supports the argument of groups like BUAV. If you can, look up similar newspaper articles by using CD-ROMs from a library, or by logging on to the Internet. The above article was front page news, and is written in a sensationalist way. Even so, the argument against using non-human animals in experiments is compelling.

Many people think that studying animals in their natural setting is more acceptable, and that a great deal can be learnt from this. Perhaps this is less of an ethical issue, although it could still be argued that we are disturbing their natural setting simply by being there and observing. The argument against the use of non-human animals is sometimes extended to their use in the 'wild', but in practice most people find the study of animals in their own environment is acceptable.

Guidelines for the use of non-human animals

Guidelines focus on the use of non-human animals rather than on whether they should be used at all. The guidelines assume that animals are being used, and then look at rules for safeguarding them to an extent. The research must be carefully designed and justified and the researcher must justify the use of animals.

Gray (1987) discusses the use of rats.

- Firstly, he looks at when they are deprived of food to see if this is causing them distress. He claims that this does not cause distress. They are often fed after the experiments, that is once a day. If not, their body weight is maintained at 85% of what they would be if they fed normally, and this is actually healthy.
- Secondly, he looked at when they are given shocks. The average shock allowed is one that would cause a tickling sensation in humans. So he concludes that this is not real suffering.

When Gray talks about what is allowed, this refers to Home Office inspectors. Everyone who uses animals in research needs a Home Office licence, and has to obey the rules.

Some of the important rules (these are taken from the Society for Neuroscience Guidelines for Animal Research):

- Researchers must have a Home Office licence and certificates.
- Experimenters must be familiar with the use of anaesthetics, and use them appropriately.
- Senior staff must be available to supervise studies.
- Caging and social environment must suit the particular species.
- Marking wild animals or attaching transmitters must be done with regard to stress involved.
- If the animal is to be deprived (for example, of food or drink) then this must be monitored according to the species and suffering minimised.
- Field workers should disturb animals as little as possible (for example, when observing in the wild).
- Animals must not be subjected to avoidable distress or discomfort.
- Aanesthetic must be given if at all possible if any surgical procedures are involved.
- If no anaesthetic is given, blood pressure and heart rate must be monitored to understand the pain involved and then researchers must take action to alleviate the pain (or end the experiment).
- No more animals must be used than is necessary.
- Living animals should only be used if necessary.
- Alternatives should always be sought.
- Research animals must be acquired and cared for according to guidelines published in *The NIH Guide for the Care and Use of Laboratory Animals* (National Institute of Health Publications, NO. 85-23, Revised 1985).
- General standards for looking after the animals should also be followed, as listed in the NIH guide.
- Researchers should take care after operations with animals, and should guard against infections and so on in the usual way.
- Restraints that the animal cannot easily adapt to should be used only if there is no alternative.
- There should be a reasonable time between studies where the animal can recover and rest.

The ATP guidelines mentioned earlier suggest that you should use animals in research only if you are consulting with a supervisor, and if the animals are fully respected. The methodology must be justified, and you must be trained in handling the particular species so that proper care is given.

For Unit 3, which is the coursework element of the Edexcel specification, you cannot do a practical that involves the use of non-human animals. However, guidelines on the use of animals have been included here because it is important to know about these issues when studying studies that have been done using non-human animals. You should use the above guidelines when evaluating such research, for example.

Coursework information and advice for Unit 3 – the practical element

The assessment of Unit 3 means that you have to carry out, write up and submit one piece of coursework. This must be a practical investigation and you must collect quantitative data. You can work in a small group to collect the data, or you can use class results. The specification gives you full details of what is required. You must write up the practical yourself, using your own words.

Choosing your study

Ideas are given at the end of each chapter, but your teacher must approve of your choice. Also, if you do not choose one of the studies suggested in the specification, you need to check with Edexcel that your study is suitable.

I thought you might like some more suggestions, and your teacher will probably have ideas too. The teacher guide that goes with this book gives more ideas, although not always based on material you need for this course. If you are in doubt, it is best to stick to one of the suggestions made at the end of each chapter in this book, as at least you will be studying the material for the examination, so you will be learning useful details as you do the coursework.

If you are having difficulty in deciding, here are some points that might help.

Do you have access to participants?

Do you belong to a club? Are there people at work that you could ask? Do you have access to children, in the sense of visiting or working in a playgroup or school? Are you working in a large class where you can help each other? Do you have the confidence to ask people to complete a questionnaire? Are you working alone and have no one to ask at all?

Think of the answers to all these questions, and you will have already made some decisions. For example:

- If you belong to a club, think of a task, such as a memory task or questionnaire, that suits that age group (if they agree to participate of course).
- If you work in an office, think of a task where your fellow workers can be useful and can enjoy the task, for example a survey about stress at work.
- If you have young children yourself, and have access to a lot of young children at a playgroup or nursery, then you might think about observing children, or doing a 'Piaget' task.
- If you are working alone, then you might prefer to observe people in a public place, perhaps looking at helping behaviour. If you don't feel confident enough to do this, then you could do a content analysis of how gender is portrayed on the television, for example.
- If you are working as part of a large class, you can pool class data; for example, you could all take part in a memory experiment run by your class teacher.

Pick a study that suits your lifestyle, and that you would find manageable.

Choose an area you find interesting

Turn to the chapter you found most interesting, and read through the coursework suggestions at the end of that chapter. You might get ideas from my suggestions, or you might choose one of the suggestions as it stands. Many of the suggestions come from studies that are outlined in more detail in one of the activity boxes, so you could try browsing through these boxes for ideas. Ask your teacher to run through previous studies if the course has been run at your institution before.

It is a good idea to vary the study a little bit so that it is an individual study. This will give you a bit more interest – even if you only make up the words yourself, rather than use someone else's list in a memory study. However, you don't have to do something different. You can just do a study you have read about, or do the same as someone else.

Make sure you have sufficient background research in the area

You can do a study using material that is not in this book, and not mentioned in the specification. The study must, however, use background research in psychology, so make sure that you have sufficient background research in the area. You will need to link your findings to work that has already been done, so you must already know about at least some of the previous work. Unless you are very confident, stick to something that has been suggested.

Don't try to be a psychologist yet

Most people want to learn about psychology because they want to know about people. Many people are interested in issues such as mass murder, child abuse, mental illnesses, phobias, depression, homosexuality and disorders. During the course you will indeed come across these major issues; however, these are not areas for coursework. Don't even consider tackling such issues. These areas are for psychologists to deal with. We are studying psychology as students. The areas you must choose for coursework are areas where research is being carried out, but steer clear of any sensitive topics. This may seem as if we are asking you to avoid anything interesting. However, you are not ready for such issues yet, and we cannot ethically use people with difficulties as participants.

Avoid any sensitive issues – you are not a psychologist at this stage.

Check that you are following ethical guidelines

Your piece of work will not be accepted by Edexcel if it does not clearly follow ethical guidelines. This chapter outlines these guidelines. You must not only follow them but must also clearly explain how you have done so. You must tackle this issue before you start the study. It must be part of your initial planning. For example, if you cannot get full consent for the use of children – and this includes the consent of the school, the parents, and the child – then you cannot do a study using children. The main thing, of course, is that you must get the consent of your teacher.

How to write up the practical

In this section I give you an outline of how to write up the practical you have carried out. You can get an example of a piece of coursework from the *Teacher and Coursework Guide* from Edexcel, and there is an example in the teacher guide that goes with this textbook. It is useful to have a marked piece of work to go by, although you must do your own work of course. The Edexcel specification has the mark scheme, and other advice, so is also worth referring to. The checklist at the end of this chapter should give you a good idea of what is to be included. Ideally, use a marked example piece of coursework, the mark scheme and the checklist, and then do your own piece of work with all that information to hand.

Some points to note

- Aim for at least 1500 words.
- Remember, you must collect quantitative data.
- Discuss with your teacher to make sure your choice of hypothesis is suitable.

- Discuss with your teacher to make sure ethical guidelines are followed.
- Do all the written work on your own, using your own words.
- You can work in a group to collect the data.
- If you work in a group make sure you all have access to the data.
- Use the guidelines for students printed in the Edexcel specification (pp. 64–66).
- Use the coursework guide published by Edexcel.
- Use the checklist at the end of this chapter to make sure you have covered all the points.
- An examiner appointed by Edexcel marks the work – examiner comments are included for each section in the example pieces (if you can get hold of one). Ask your teacher.
- It would be useful to read Chapter 7 as you will need to know about methods.

Getting evidence for Key Skills through coursework

Communication – Level 3

C3.1a Group discussion is possible when planning the piece of work, if it is to be a group study. Keep notes – these can be used as evidence of the group discussion.

C3.1b A presentation could be made, using diagrams and so on. This would be useful because others in the class (if you are not working alone) could offer criticisms and you could attempt to improve the study. The presentation could be made before the study is carried out (to improve the design, for example) or after the study has been carried out (to get helpful criticisms for a discussion). The material you plan for the presentation would be evidence for the Key Skill (and part of the write-up – e.g. graphs if it is after the study has been carried out).

C3.2 If you are able to use original papers as background to your study (for example, the Hyde and Jenkins study, if you are testing the levels of processing idea), then you could read and synthesise information from two extended documents – it is likely that at least one would include one image, but you would need to watch for that. Your introduction would be evidence for this Key Skill.

C3.3 For this Key Skill you need to write different types of document about complex subjects. Your coursework write up could be one of these extended documents.

Information Technology – Level 3

Note: you might not always reach level 3.

IT3.1 Plan and use different sources to get information for two different purposes. The coursework could be one of these purposes, and you could use the Internet to get information. A list of Web sites is given as an Appendix to this book, and you could start with those. Keep evidence for this Key Skill.

IT3.2 You will probably use information technology to produce your written report, and could also use graphs and spreadsheets. Evidence would come from the written report, where the graphs and tables would be displayed. Some spreadsheet packages – for example, Excel – also do statistical calculations, and this would be a useful extension to your coursework (although it is not specifically required)

IT3.3 Presenting information from different sources for two different purposes. Your coursework findings could be presented and used as evidence for part of this Key Skill.

Application of Number – Level 3

N3.1 You are likely to use a large data set for your coursework, and will plan and interpret information from it when analysing your data. For this Key Skill, you need to use different types of sources, so the practical write up may only give you one such source. However, you can use it as evidence for this Key Skill.

N3.2 You can do multi-stage calculations such as handling statistics. For the coursework you need to calculate descriptive statistics, although this might not give you enough evidence for Level 3. You are likely to be working with a large data set, and you could use formulae if carrying out a statistical test (although this is not a requirement for the coursework for Edexcel).

N3.3 You are likely to be using graphs, tables, charts and descriptive statistics when analysing your data, and these can all be used for evidence of this Key Skill.

Improving Own Learning and Performance – Level 3

LP3.1 It is likely that you will at some stage be working with others when planning or carrying out a practical. If so, then you can use the planning and target setting as evidence for this Key Skill. Make sure you keep written notes – and you could produce a written time plan, for example.

LP3.2 You could seek help when planning your coursework, and you could use others in this planning. You might not be used to using the Internet, for example, so you can seek help and use your new skill as evidence of this help. You might not be comfortable with producing graphs from spreadsheet information, such as using Excel, so you could seek help and use the final graph as evidence of your new skill.

LP3.3 Your teacher will want to mark a draft of your coursework, and you can use your target/plan in discussion with your teacher as to how your coursework is progressing. From this discussion new targets can be agreed, including action for improving performance. Keep a record of any such discussions as evidence.

Working with Others – Level 3

WO3.1 If you are going to work in a group to produce the research report and to plan an investigation, then you will need to agree objectives and working arrangements. Keep a note of your plans and your shared responsibilities, and use these notes as evidence for this Key Skill.

WO3.2 When working with others, you will need to maintain co-operative working relationships in meeting your responsibilities, and this co-operation will be useful as evidence for this Key Skill. The final piece of work will be your own write up (as required by Edexcel); however, you could add information about where there was co-opearation for the purpose of getting evidence of this Key Skill.

WO3.3 After completing your co-operative piece of work you need to review to see how far you have worked co-operatively. You could do this with help from your teacher or tutor.

Problem Solving – Level 3

PS3.1 You could recognise a problem within the planned research project, or use a problem that needs to be investigated as the research project. You have to agree standards for the solution, and this could be part of your planning and design.

PS3.2 You could perhaps consider two types of design and then give reasons for and against each one. Alternatively, you could consider two types of method and give reasons for and against each one.

PS3.3 Having chosen one particular design or method, you would plan and implement it when doing the research project.

PS3.4 After the piece of work is carried out, you need to evaluate it as part of the write up. This evaluation could be evidence of this Key Skill, as you would have to agree and apply methods to check whether the problem has been solved.

Checklist for final submission of coursework

TASK	YES	NO
1 (a) Background research		
Relevant background theory and research?	☐	☐
Concisely written?	☐	☐
Selective rather than 'all I know about'?	☐	☐
Accurate?	☐	☐
Depth?	☐	☐
1 (b) Rationale		
Rationale given?	☐	☐
Explains link from background research to study?	☐	☐
1 (c) Aims		
Aim(s) stated?	☐	☐
Clear – they say what you are doing?	☐	☐
Relevant – they say why you are doing it?	☐	☐
1 (d) Hypotheses		
Hypothesis(es) stated	☐	☐
Relevant and correctly say what is expected?	☐	☐
Stated concisely?	☐	☐
2 (a) Method and design		
Method described accurately?	☐	☐
Enough detail?	☐	☐
Reason given for choosing that method?	☐	☐
2 (b) Variables		
Variables stated correctly (usually IV and DV)?	☐	☐
Variables operationalised (made measurable)?	☐	☐
It is very clear what you are measuring?	☐	☐
2 (c) Participants		
Sampling technique correctly identified?	☐	☐
If you said it is random, is it really random?	☐	☐
Participants described (age, gender, region, etc.)?	☐	☐
Number of participants given?	☐	☐
Identified exactly how you found find them, and where from?	☐	☐

2 (d) Apparatus
Suitable? ☐ ☐
Described in detail (with diagram if appropriate)? ☐ ☐
Scoring system described, if appropriate? ☐ ☐
Details given of how apparatus was prepared? ☐ ☐
Details given of why apparatus was chosen (including word lists etc.)? ☐ ☐

2 (e) Procedure
What was done clearly stated so it can be repeated? ☐ ☐
Has someone read it to check that it can be done again? ☐ ☐

2 (f) Controls
Identified what might have caused the result, other than IV? ☐ ☐
Ethical guidelines on right to withdraw followed? ☐ ☐
Ethical guideline of no deception followed? ☐ ☐
Ethical guidelines on consent followed? ☐ ☐
Special guidelines regarding children and others followed? ☐ ☐
Ethical guideline of confidentiality followed? ☐ ☐
Other ethical guidelines followed? ☐ ☐
Ethical guidelines referred to clearly? ☐ ☐
All things besides IV controlled for and explained? ☐ ☐

3 (a) Summary table
Accurate and appropriate summary table given? ☐ ☐
Table clearly and suitably labelled? ☐ ☐
Descriptive statistics included where appropriate? ☐ ☐
Where descriptive statistics not appropriate, is this explained? ☐ ☐

3 (b) Summary table commentary
Results in table explained in words with trends given? ☐ ☐
Accurate and useful comments made about trends? ☐ ☐
Detailed comments about trends given? ☐ ☐

3 (c) Graphs, pie charts, mean, median, mode etc.
Suitable graphs included? ☐ ☐
Suitable descriptive statistics used? ☐ ☐
Where graphs not suitable, are tabled results clear? ☐ ☐
Graphs are well labelled and clear? ☐ ☐

3 (d) Commentary on descriptive statistics
Comments made about trends shown by graphs? ☐ ☐
Comments made about trends shown by descriptive statistics? ☐ ☐
Where appropriate, percentages given? ☐ ☐

3 (e) Relationship to hypothesis(es)
Hypothesis restated and linked to results? ☐ ☐
Were the expectations fulfilled (did it work)? ☐ ☐
Were the results explained in terms of the hypothesis? ☐ ☐
Was the explanation detailed and clear? ☐ ☐

4 (a) Validity
How variables were measured (operationalised) identified? ☐ ☐
Operationalisation linked to validity (real life)? ☐ ☐
Mention of ecological validity or lack of (if appropriate)? ☐ ☐
Is the study valid and reasons for/against given? ☐ ☐

4 (b) Improving validity
Suggestions made for making more valid? ☐ ☐
Suggestions detailed as a further study? ☐ ☐
Suggestions detailed as improving this study? ☐ ☐
Explanation given on how suggestions would affect results of this study? ☐ ☐

4 (c) Reliability
Reliability of this study referred to? ☐ ☐
Suggestions given as to why this study might not be repeated with same results? ☐ ☐
Problems in methodology referred to? ☐ ☐
Problems in controls (or lack of) mentioned? ☐ ☐
Problems in sampling (causing bias) referred to? ☐ ☐
Problems in apparatus referred to? ☐ ☐
Problems with standardised instructions referred to? ☐ ☐
Problems with procedure referred to? ☐ ☐
All above discussed concisely? ☐ ☐

4 (d) Improving reliability
Alternatives suggested to improve problems? ☐ ☐
More than one suggestion made? ☐ ☐
Effects of suggestion(s) outlined in detail? ☐ ☐

4 (e) Implications of study
Background research referred to again – linked to findings? ☐ ☐
Detailed discussion of findings related to theory? ☐ ☐
Implications of the study discussed? ☐ ☐

4 (f) Generalisation of findings
Results generalisable to target population? ☐ ☐
Have you explained why? ☐ ☐
Problems of generalising (e.g. poor sampling) explained? ☐ ☐

4 (g) Application to everyday life
Findings linked with everyday life situations? ☐ ☐
Have you done this in detail, giving examples? ☐ ☐

5 (a) References

All names used listed alphabetically? ☐ ☐

Complete reference (from back of book) given? ☐ ☐

5 (b) Presentation

Required headings used (see this list)? ☐ ☐

Presented clearly – pages numbered, etc.? ☐ ☐

Contents page included? ☐ ☐

Document word-processed and spell-checked? ☐ ☐

All the above elements included? ☐ ☐

Suggested further reading

Cardwell, M., Clark, L. & Meldrum, C. (1996) *Psychology for A Level*. London: Collins Educational.

Cole, M. & Cole, S. R. (1996) *The Development of Children*, 3rd ed. New York: W.H. Freeman and Company.

Gross, R. D. (1999) *Themes, Issues and Debates*. London: Hodder and Stoughton

Gross, R. D. (1999) *Psychology: The Science of Mind and Behaviour*, 3rd ed. London: Hodder and Stoughton

Appendix A

Useful Web sites

Web address	Comments
http://www.apa.org	The Web site of the APA and very useful. Lots of other sites and information can be reached from this site
http://www.sleepnet.com	Good for 'sleep' as a topic. Some interesting research can be found
http://www.psywww.com	Psychweb – a useful site for finding information
http://www.psychcrawler.com	Links to other sites – and you can search for information on a particular topic
http://www.sosig.ac.uk	A very useful site that leads you to many other useful sites. These include lots of university sites. This is a good starting place
http://fe.ngfl.gov.uk/fe/index.html	A further education site that leads to others. There are resources for tutors and students
http://ferl.becta.org.uk/index.htm	A further education site that leads to other sites and has useful materials
http://www.bbc.co.uk.education	The BBC site might be worth a visit
http://www.cti.ac.uk/centres	The cti centre at York, where materials are gathered together
http://psych.hanover.edu/krantz/	I found some brain pictures and research information on MRI scanning, as well as tutorials to go with the pictures. There is also other interesting information to be found
http://www.psych.ucsb.edu	An American university site with some interesting information
http://www.mhsource.com	Mental health information
http://www.psychnet-uk.com	Another of the search sites that gathers together information on psychology
http://www.sccu.edu/psychology/amoebaweb.html	A very useful searching site
http://info.lib.uh.edu/indexes/psych.htm	Indexes of where to find more specific information
http://www-psych.stanford.edu/cogsci/	Stanford university site
http://stange.simplenet.com/psycSite	This is a well known site for general searching
http://www.grohol.com/web.htm	Other sites are listed •

All of these sites were checked 8 March 2000. However, things do change on the Internet. You should find enough information by browsing through the above sites, because many of them lead to others. They are all fairly general sites. You will find that, once you start, the menus will lead you down many different interesting routes.

Appendix B

Suggestions, questions and exam advice

> ### In this appendix you will find:
>
> – an explanation of the assessment objectives
> – key terms used in exams
> – some tips for the exams
> – some answers to questions, so that you can see the depth required
> – exam-style questions for each chapter.

Assessment objectives

You need to know what is being looked for by the examiners, and the assessment objectives are outlined in the specification. A summary of them is given here.

For the main examination papers there are two assessment objectives. The third one involves the coursework. The assessment objectives are briefly outlined here.

AO1 – knowledge and understanding

You must:
- correctly use psychological terminology and concepts
- know and understand psychological theories, studies, methods and concepts and present them clearly
- know and understand psychological principles, perspectives and applications and discuss them in relevant contexts
- communicate the above clearly and effectively.

AO2 – Applications of knowledge and understanding, analysis, synthesis and evaluation

You must:
- analyse and evaluate psychological theories and concepts and weigh up evidence

- analyse and evaluate research and methods in psychology
- analyse and evaluate perspectives and applications.

AO1 = 'knowledge' and AO2 = 'evaluation/comment'

If you think of these two objectives as 'knowledge' and 'evaluation and comment' this is probably the best way. Knowledge is put with understanding to show that you don't just have to know something, you have to show you understand it. Analyse and evaluate basically mean commenting and giving criticisms. Evaluation can be positive as well as negative, so you can say what is good and bad about a study. Giving strengths and weaknesses is evaluation.

Applications are also important. This means being able to relate some theory or finding to a real life application such as police interviewing techniques or education. Psychologists are found in the health service, in education, in the police force, in prisons, in the workplace. All these areas are useful when thinking about applications.

AO3 – the assessment of knowledge of method and of practical work in psychology

Use the correction mark scheme given in the specification to see what AO3 marks entail. You can also use the checklist at the end of Chapter 8. If you cover all the points in the checklist, you will have covered AO3 assessment objectives.

Key terms used in exams

There are AO1 words and AO2 words and it is useful to know which are which. Here are some examples – you should be able to see what the words mean and what is needed.

AO1

- *Define* – give a dictionary-style definition. Sometimes an example is useful
- *List* – means literally say what something is
- *Outline* – similar to describe but less depth required
- *Describe* – say what something is and give depth depending on the marks available
- *Give* – as list; just say what something is
- *Identify* – means the same as give

AO2

AO2 terms cover the skills of evaluating; giving strengths and weaknesses; applying; assessing…
- *Assess* – give some points for and against, and look at a concept's usefulness. Come to some decision
- *Evaluate* – again give strengths and weaknesses or say what is good and bad about a concept
- *Apply* – link to some real-life application like health, crime, education, or even making a shopping list

Both

- *Discuss* – say what something is (AO1) and then give some criticisms, strengths and weaknesses (AO2)

Tips for the exam

- Use the key words to see what focus the examiner is looking for. There are usually some obvious points to make; however, these are not so obvious under examination conditions.
- Read the question carefully.
- Avoid your answer being triggered by one word – for example, a question on theories of memory requires a different answer to a question on studies within memory. When asked for findings, describing a study will not get the marks.
- If asked for an example, make sure you *give* an example.
- If there is more than one mark, one sentence often will not do.
- Work on the idea that you write one point for one mark.
- There are 72 marks available for 90 minutes worth of exam. Given reading time and some thinking time, this is just about one mark a minute (and some time to spare). So work on the idea that you are getting one mark per minute.
- If there are six marks available, you need to write enough. If in doubt, repeat what you have said in another way, or give an example.
- If asked to 'describe' you get no marks for evaluation.
- If asked to 'evaluate' you get few marks for description. (Sometimes you get some marks because you sometimes need to give a bit of description when evaluating.)
- Say everything clearly because there are marks for clarity.
- Avoid the temptation to elaborate if you are unsure. You might show that you don't really understand. However, if you can elaborate, do so.
- Let the number of lines available guide the length of your answer. Don't write six sentences if there is only one mark available. You might run out of time.
- On the exam paper there are usually two lines for each mark – use this as your guide.
- You can write more than the spaces available – ask for extra paper or squeeze it in somewhere
- If you make a mistake – cross it through and start again.
- If asked to evaluate and your mind is blank, think of ethical issues or method issues. For example, if an experiment is being discussed, try suggesting that the findings are not valid and say why. This may not be as good as an in-depth answer, but you should gain some marks
- Don't worry about your handwriting – try to be neat, but the examiners will do everything they can to read it. They are on your side.
- Expect there to be specific questions – for example, instead of asking for some criticisms, the question will specify *one* criticism, or perhaps *two* studies. It is not likely that you will be asked for 'many' or 'three'. So you could prepare *one* or *two* of everything. The question is likely ask for *one* strength, and *one* weakness, not 'some strengths and weaknesses'

Example questions with answers

1 Describe ONE research method used in the cognitive approach [4 marks]

Answer

There are four marks available and the key word 'describe' tells us that these are AO1 marks where we must know and understand something. You need to make four clear points about *one* research method used in this approach.

- Laboratory experiments are used in the cognitive approach
- These are controlled experiments where only the independent variable changes and the dependent variable is measured as a result of this change
- These studies take place in a laboratory or formal setting, as opposed to field experiments, which take place in the participant's natural setting – or in 'the field'
- An example of a laboratory experiment used in cognitive psychology is Tulving and Pearlstone's (1966) work on the encoding specificity principle, where they found that categorised lists are best recalled
- Laboratory experiments are often praised for being reliable, because you can do them again and get the same results, however, they are criticised for not being valid, because they could be said to have little to do with 'real life'

Although we could say more, there are four clear points here. The mark scheme would have given a list of such points for the examiner to check against. You could say that the last sentence is evaluation; however, it is a good idea to say a little more than four points when four marks are available, so I thought I would add a bit!

2(a) List **two** defence mechanisms as proposed by Freud [2 marks]

2(b) Assess the usefulness of the idea of defence mechanisms as an explanation of human behaviour [6 marks]

Answers

Part a is straightforward. There are two marks for listing *two* defence mechanisms. You could choose two from projection, rationalisation, isolation, displacement, and reaction formation. When asked for two, give just two. The two words will do for the two AO1 marks:

- Rationalisation
- Displacement

Part b of the question gives six AO2 marks (you can tell this from the word 'assess').

- Defence mechanisms, according to Freud, are useful because they help us to repress unconscious wishes that we are not allowing into our consciousness
- They allow us to function, whereas without defence mechanisms and repression these unconscious urges would find their way into conscious thought and we would have to deal with them
- Our Ego, which is the rational part of our personality,

tries to maintain a balance between the Id (the demanding part of our personality) and the Superego (our conscience). If these unconscious wishes were to be made available to our consciousess, our Ego would have problems in dealing with them. The Ego has repressed them in the first place. Defence mechanisms are useful in keeping them repressed

- On the other hand, in repressing these urges, we are using energy that could be used in moving forward. Defence mechanisms are not useful in that they do repress these urges or thoughts. If we knew about them we could deal with them. It is the goal of the psychoanalyst to release these unconscious wishes and to make them conscious. So the psychoanalyst does not seem to see defence mechanisms as useful
- Freud's views have been criticised in general as being unscientific and untestable, so it could be claimed that defence mechanisms are not useful as an explanation for human behaviour because the idea of them rests on such an uncertain theory in the first place. If we don't accept the theory, then we don't accept the existence of these defence mechanisms.
- If you look at the different mechanisms they almost contradict one another and there is an explanation for everything. For example, almost anything can be displacement, and any explanation can be said to be rationalisation. I could say I hate pornography and really hate something else (projection) or I could say I hate pornography, when I really enjoy it.

It is quite useful to use bullet points here, then you can be sure that you have given six clear points. You could get into the habit of doing something similar when you are writing, to make sure you have done enough. Write in prose style, however, not giving a list of points.

I tried to mention the usefulness of the concepts in each point, and your answer must focus on usefulness, as that is what is asked for.

Example questions chapter by chapter

These questions are for homework and for testing yourself. They are not intended to be exactly what would be on an examination paper.

Chapter 1 – The cognitive approach

1   Outline TWO general assumptions of the cognitive approach   6 marks
2   Discuss TWO research methods used in the cognitive approach   8 marks
3   Describe ONE theory of memory   5 marks

4 Evaluate ONE theory of memory 5 marks
5 Outline ONE study from cognitive
   psychology 6 marks
6 Evaluate the study you outlined in
   question 5 above 6 marks
7 Discuss research into eyewitness
   testimony 8 marks
8 Apply ONE concept used within cognitive
   psychology to ONE contemporary issue 8 marks
9 List two research methods used in
   cognitive psychology 2 marks
10 Outline TWO theories of forgetting 10 marks

Chapter 2 – The social approach

1 Discuss the influence of culture as an
   assumption of the social approach 8 marks
2 Describe surveys as a research method 6 marks
3 Evaluate Milgram's study of obedience 6 marks
4 Describe one study of obedience, other
   than Milgram's 4 marks
5 Explain TWO theories of why we obey 8 marks
6 Discuss social identity theory as an
   explanation of prejudice 10 marks
7 Describe and evaluate in terms of
   strengths and weaknesses one study within
   the social approach 10 marks
8 Outline TWO ways in which prejudice can
   be reduced 4 marks
9 Evaluate ONE of the ways prejudice can
   be reduced that you outlined in question
   8 above 6 marks
10 Outline ONE contemporary issue where
   links can be made to concepts within the
   social approach 5 marks
11 Explain the contemporary issue you gave
   above, in terms of concepts within the
   social approach 5 marks

Chapter 3 – The cognitive-developmental approach

1 Discuss how the cognitive-developmental
   approach shows the development of
   cognitive abilities over time 6 marks
2 List TWO research methods used in the
   cognitive-developmental approach 2 marks
3 What are longitudinal studies? 2 marks
4 At the foot of the page there is a table
   showing Piaget's stages with approximate
   ages. Complete the names of the stages
   that are missing, and the approximate
   ages that are missing. 4 marks
5 Discuss one study from within the
   cognitive-developmental approach 6 marks
6 Discuss the link between ONE cognitive-
   developmental theory and education 8 marks
7 Explain ONE contemporary issue using your
   knowledge of the cognitive-developmental
   approach 10 marks

Chapter 4 – The learning approach

1 Describe ONE general assumption of the
   learning approach 4 marks
2 Outline ONE study of learning that involves
   animals 5 marks
3 Complete the following table (p. 270) 3 marks
4 Give ONE example of classical conditioning
   in humans 3 marks
5 Evaluate operant conditioning as an
   explanation of human behaviour 6 marks
6 Discuss ONE study from the learning
   approach 8 marks
7 Outline ONE contemporary issue that can
   be explained by concepts from the learning
   approach 4 marks
8 Explain the above contemporary issue
   using concepts from the learning
   approach 6 marks

Sensorimotor stage	
	2–7 years
Formal operational stage	Over 11 years

UCS (food)	? (salivation)
UCS + ?	UCR (salvation)
?	CR (salivation)

Chapter 5 – The psychodynamic approach

1   Discuss the importance of early experience as an assumption of the psychodynamic approach   8 marks
2   Describe the use of the analysis of symbols as a method within the psychodynamic approach   5 marks
3   Complete the following list: 3 marks
       Oral stage
       ? stage
       ? stage
       Latent stage
       ? stage
4   Discuss Freud's theory of dreaming   6 marks
5   Evaluate ONE theory from psychodynamic psychology apart from Freud's   5 marks
6   Outline ONE study from psychodynamic psychology   6 marks
7   Taking ONE mental health issue, use ONE concept from psychodynamic psychology to explain it   6 marks
8   Outline ONE contemporary issue that can be explained by concepts from psychodynamic psychology   4 marks
9   Explain the issue you chose for the above question using concepts from psychodynamic psychology   7 marks

Chapter 6 – The physiological approach

1   List TWO general assumptions of the physiological approach   2 marks
2   Discuss the use of brain scanning as a method   5 marks
3   Discuss methods of studying genetic influences on individual differences   6 marks
4   Discuss the influence of endogenous pacemakers on the day/night cycle   4 marks
5   Describe the restoration theory of sleep   4 marks
6   Evaluate ONE theory of sleep other than the restoration theory   4 marks
7   Discuss ONE physiological theory of dreaming   8 marks
8   Outline ONE study from the physiological approach   5 marks
9   Evaluate the study you chose for the question above   5 marks
10 Discuss the effects of shift work using physiological concepts   10 marks
11 Describe ONE contemporary issue that can be explained by means of concepts from the physiological approach   5 marks
12 Explain the contemporary issue you outlined above using concepts from the physiological approach   5 marks

Glossary of terms

Ablation – removing parts of the body/brain, used as a research method to investigate with non-human animals

Accommodation – the baby changes the schema following assimilation

Action potential – the electrical impulse sent from the body of a neuron down the axon to the synaptic gap between two neurons

Adaptation – the baby adapts to its world through assimilating and accommodating, so schemas change and develop

Agency theory – the idea that people obey because they are agents of someone or society. For example, participants obeyed Milgram when he asked them to give someone an electric shock (which was not real, but the participant did not know that) because they were agents of the experimenter. They were not acting under their own moral code, but acting for the experimenter

Alternative hypothesis – the statement of what is expected, having studied previous studies and theories. An example is saying that boys are more aggressive than girls, and doing an observation.

Anal stage – the second stage of psychosexual development, according to Freud. Focus is on toilet training and such things

Analogy – a comparison of one thing with another, to help in understanding

Applied/application – a theory is understood and then related to real-life situations. If you are asked about applications, then it means you have to think of real-life situations, and say how the theory, for example, can be used in explaining such situations

Articulatory loop – the part of the working memory for speech – the inner voice

Assimilation – when a baby adds information and filters it without changing a schema

Association – learning to match things together in some way – for example, we learn to associate 'blue' with 'sky'

Authoritarian personality – refers to the type of person who is often prejudiced. Someone with an authoritarian personality often follows rules completely, and is rigid in habits

Autonomic nervous system – has two parts. The sympathetic part prepares us for action (fight or flight), and the parasympathetic part calms our body down again (resets it)

Autonomy – under one's own power, rather than the power of others

Aversion therapy – the use of classical conditioning principles to 'cure' some unwanted behaviour. Instead of the pleasure response to the unwanted behaviour (the behaviour is currently desirable), an unpleasant response is given. For example, someone addicted to alcohol, who wishes to be 'cured', might have the 'pleasure' response (of liking whisky) replaced by an unpleasant response (of feeling sick). For this to happen, a drug might be given to make the person feel sick. Then they drink whisky. They should learn to associate feeling sick with the whisky, and then won't want to drink it any more

Avoidance learning – learning to avoid something unpleasant like an electric shock, by avoiding it altogether

Axon – the thick 'cable' that takes the electrical impulse to the axon tip, where the electrical impulse causes neurotransmitters to be released. These neurotransmitters may, if they 'fit', be taken up by the adjoining dendrite and send a message back to the next cell – and so messages in the brain and body are transmitted

Behaviourism – the idea that we can study behaviour by looking at what starts it (the stimulus) and what follows (the response). These two things are measurable, and we can learn truths in this way, using the positivist approach

Biased – if a study is not fair in some way, it is said to be biased. Bias can be caused in lots of ways, for example by having a non-representative sample, or by demand characteristics in the study

Biological maturation framework – looking at development in terms of how we develop biologically. Development comes from within us

Bottom-up processing – information directly from the senses is processed

Catharsis – this refers to the way hidden forces in the unconscious can be released. You could watch a violent film and this could enable hidden violent tendencies to release themselves. The effect would be cathartic or cleansing

Central executive – the part of the working memory that controls it and allocates attention

Central nervous system (CNS) – the brain and the spinal column

Chromosome – genes are carried on strings called chromosomes. These are double strands of DNA

Chunking – putting items together in memory and so making them one item. For example, you could put together the numbers that make up your telephone number and they could become one chunk. If you were remembering a list of letters PHD could become one chunk

Circadian rhythms – daily rhythms occurring every 24 hours

Circannual rhythms – last for about a year

Classical conditioning – the idea that we learn to associate things that happen together, when one of these is a reflex. Reflexes are automatic responses that are not learnt. We also have things happen to us. When something happens to us (for example, a bell rings) at the same time as our automatic response occurs (for example, fear), then the two things become associated. That something (the bell) triggers that automatic response (the fear). You could then develop a phobia about bells

Closed questions – questions on a questionnaire where the participant is limited by having to tick boxes or say 'yes' or 'no'. They have no freedom to answer outside the limits of the question

Cognition – thinking, perceiving, remembering, using language – i.e. mental processes

Cognitive – thinking processes (cognition is thinking)

Cohort effect – a cohort is a group of people of, say, one generation that go through the same cultural experiences. So when a group of people of the same age, for example, are compared, any similarities may be due to them being part of the same cohort, having had the same experiences, rather than to whatever is being studied

Collaborative learning – using others to help us learn

Compliance – when we seem to adopt an attitude, but this is only on the outside. We know that we don't really believe it

Concordance – an agreement between two variables. For example, where two identical twins have schizophrenia, there is a 100% concordance

Concrete operational stage – the third of Piaget's stages, when a child can perform operations on things. For example, a child knows that when water is poured from one glass into another, the same quantity of water will be in the second glass as in the first glass

Condition – one of the things that happens in a study, that is one of the parts, for example, of an experiment. An example might be the 'random words' condition in a memory experiment

Conditioned inhibition – extinguishing a learnt response. For example, the sound of a bell might cause salivation. In conditioned inhibition, a different conditioned stimulus (the smell of lavender, for example) might be presented with the bell. The association between the bell and the salivation would be overridden by the new association between the bell and the lavender, so the salivation response would be extinguished

Conditioned response – a natural response (reflex), like salivation to food, is an unconditioned response. Salivation to the sound of a bell is a conditioned response created when food is repeatedly presented at the sound of a bell.

The bell becomes associated with food and causes salivation even when no food is presented.

Conditioned stimulus – something that brings an automatic response, but does not do so naturally. In the above example, the bell is the conditioned stimulus and the food is the unconditioned stimulus, because the food naturally causes salivation, whereas the bell has to be associated with the food before salivation occurs

Confederate – someone who has had instructions from the researcher, and is helping in the study. Often the participant is unaware that the confederate is not a 'normal' participant

Confounding variable – this is when a variable other than the independent variable can equally well account for the results. The independent variable is the one you are interested in (for example, REM or NREM sleep), and the confounding variable is something else that cannot be separated from the independent variable. For example, we could say that NREM sleep is deeper so may give poorer recall, and REM sleep is lighter with more brain activity so may give better recall. So we don't know if we only dream during REM sleep, or if we only recall dreams during REM sleep. We could dream in NREM sleep with the same intensity, but not recall the dreams so well. The difference in recall is the confounding variable, because it can cause the results just as well as saying we only dream in REM sleep

Connectionism – according to Thorndike, the idea that we make associations between a stimulus and a response. There is a different theory called connectionism, which has more to do with thinking of the brain as a computer

Consciousness – things in your consciousness are things you are aware of and can talk about (and presumably do something about)

Construct validity – that the construct used is real in some sense. For example, introverts are considered shy and withdrawn. If 'shy' and 'on your own at a party' go together, then you have construct validity, and 'introvert' is the construct

Contemporary – usually means up-to-date, or of the time. A contemporary issue would have to be of interest at the time, and not something that used to be of interest but where people have now moved on. Old issues can still be contemporary, as long as they are still of interest

Continuous development – happening all the time rather than in discrete steps. Discrete means that one stage, for example, is separate from another. Continuous means there are no stages, but an uninterrupted development

Control group – a group in a study who do not experience whatever is being tested. They are measured, and their score is taken as a baseline measure of what would normally happen without the intervention of the researcher. Often you need to know what the 'normal' behaviour or score would be before you can test to see if what you have done in your research will make a difference

Controls – anything put in place to keep variables the same between the conditions (except for the IV, which is deliberately varied). Time of day is controlled by doing the study at the same time of day, for example

Contructivist framework – development is constructed – and we are constructed – from the building blocks of our biology and inherited characteristics, together with our experiences and our environment. There is an interaction

Counterbalancing – is needed to avoid order effects like the practice effect and the fatigue effect. The first person does condition one and then condition two. Then the second person does condition two and then condition one. Alternating the conditions in this way is called counterbalancing

Countertransference – this is when the feelings of the analyst are transferred to the analysand. Modern psychoanalysis takes countertransference into account and uses the feelings in analysis, but earlier psychoanalysts had to avoid countertransference

Covert observations – observations in which the participants don't know they are being observed

Creationism – this is the idea that humans (and animals) were specially created 'in God's image'. This goes against the idea of evolution and survival of the fittest

Critical period – a time when something has to occur or will never occur. An example is language development; there could be a critical period where babies must hear and practice language use or they will never develop proper language. In fact most now claim that there is a sensitive period when it is best to develop skills like language, rather than there being an all-or-none critical period

Cross-cultural – comparing across cultures. A cross-cultural study is one where the same thing is done in at least two different cultures, and the results compared. Usually, if the same thing is found across cultures, it is said to be innate, but if there are differences then it is said to be learnt

Cross-pollinating – taking the pollen from one plant and brushing it onto another (to mix their genes)

Cultural context framework – our development must be understood, not only in terms of our biology and our experience but also (very importantly) in terms of the cultural context within which we are brought up

Data – the facts collected in a study. Note that 'data' is a plural word like 'media'. We should say 'the data are' not 'the data is', although 'data is' is becoming the convention

Decentre – a child can look at more than one side of things at once. The child who can decentre is able to consider the colour of beads (e.g. brown) and the type of beads (e.g. wooden) and can sort them into brown wooden beads (two categories at once). The younger child cannot decentre, and is in the preoperational stage of cognitive development

Declarative memory – knowing that something is the case. Declarative memory incorporates episodic and semantic memory

Defence mechanisms – quite a few defence mechanisms are really forms of repression. To keep unconscious urges in the unconscious, the ego uses defence mechanisms either to divert the energy or to interpret the urges differently

Degrees of freedom (df) – this is what you need to know in order to see if your result is significant. You will find out what the df is in each test, because you calculate it when doing the test

Deindividuation – refers to a person not feeling like an individual, and then, perhaps, acting differently. For example, when deindividuated, women seemed to be more willing to give someone electric shocks than when the women could be identified by a name label. Without the name label the women were deindividuated

Demand characteristics – when there are clues or cues in a piece of research so that the participants know what is required of them, and give it. Even if they go against what they see as the requirements, there are still demand characteristics, and the results are biased

Dendrites – the branching part of a neuron that collects information from adjoining cells

Dependent variable (DV) – the variable that is measured and depends on the independent variable. If you are testing to see if more words are recalled depending on whether there is interference or not, the dependent variable that you measure is the number of words recalled. (The number of words recalled depends on whether there is interference or not, and whether there is interference or not is the independent variable)

Descriptive statistics – the mean, median, mode, range, bar charts, graphs, etc.

Discourse – this is conversation really, and can be analysed to look for meanings

Discourse analysis – quite a new method in social science that tries to find out about people by analysing their discourse (conversations) to look for underlying trends and subtleties

Discrimination – **1** an action that arises either from prejudice or institutional racism. Someone can discriminate for reasons other than prejudice, but the action is still prejudiced

2 for example, a dog who is conditioned to salivate to a particular tone of bell, learns to salivate only to that bell, and not to other tones of bell

Displacement – **1** explains forgetting by saying that one piece of information displaces another

2 a defence mechanism. Repressed urges come through to conscious thought and must appear as something else (otherwise they would not be allowed through)

Diurnal rhythms – rythms that occur during the waking day

Dizygotic (DZ) twins – non-identical twins, developed from one egg each. May be boy and girl

DNA (deoxyribonucleic acid) – the chemical that makes up the chromosomes. There are four bases that make up DNA: guanine, cytosine, adenine and thymine

Dominant gene – where a single copy of the gene produces a characteristic

Dynamic – means active and not static. Things in the unconscious are dynamic in the sense that they are trying to break into conscious thought (even though they are being repressed)

Ecological validity – when the study takes place in the natural setting of the participants, it is said to be ecologically valid because, as regards the setting, the study is measuring what it claims to measure

Ego – one of the parts of the personality according to Freud. The ego is the part that is rational, responding to the urgings of the id and to the control of the superego

Egocentric – preoperational children cannot take the viewpoint of another, but are centred on themselves in terms of their view of the world. They cannot decentre

Electra complex – a psychodynamic explanation for how girls learn their gender and their moral behaviour. They have sexual feelings for their fathers and are jealous of their mothers, so they identify with their mothers to resolve these conflicting feelings. This identification for girls is not as strong as the way boys identify with their fathers, because girls don't have castration fear to spur them on

Empiricist – someone who thinks knowledge comes via our senses

Enactive mode – means an 'active' way of representing the world. The world is represented in the child's minds by means of actions only. One of Bruner's modes of representation

Endogenous – refers to cues within the body, that are internal and physical, and that guide our bodily rhythms. Our body clock is an endogenous pacemaker

Environment – refers to everything in the outside world that affects us, from the weather to our experiences at school

Environmental learning framework – means looking at development in terms of how we develop from our learning and our experiences. Development comes from outside us

Epigenetic principle – means the pathway along which we move, given by our genetic structure

Episodic memory – the part of memory where things relevant to you are stored, for example, your birthday

Equilibration – the child reaches a balance or equilibrium when the new schema has been formed and new knowledge gained through assimilation and accommodation. Children don't maintain this equilibrium for long, as maturation and the changing environment lead to more and more adaptation

Escape learning – learning to avoid something unpleasant, like an electric shock, by escaping

Ethics – what is right and wrong in the study of psychology, and how we should take care of the people and animals we use

Ethnocentric – centred on own culture and loyal to the in-group, whilst being hostile to the outgroup

Ethnography – the in-depth study of a particular group, aiming to arrive at a picture of the whole interaction, culture and meaning for the group

Ethology – this refers to the study of animals in their natural setting, rather than in laboratory conditions

Evaluation – writing about the disadvantages and advantages of something, or whether it is right or wrong. When you evaluate, you raise a lot of issues and criticisms, and sometimes try to come to a conclusion.

Evolution – referring to the idea of natural selection. Evolution occurs through survival of the fittest. Those that are the most 'fitting' (have suitable qualities) for their environment survive and reproduce. So their 'fit qualities' are passed on to their young. Change occurs in this way

Exogenous – cues from outside the body (that are external) and, for example, guide our bodily rhythms. Zeitgebers are exogenous – for example, daylight and darkness

Experimental hypothesis – an alternative hypothesis is called the experimental hypothesis if an experiment is being done. An example is saying that categories aid recall, and doing an experiment to test this

Experimenter effect – when the experimenter is in contact with the participant and asks questions, or carries out some procedure. If the participant's behaviour is affected by the experimenter giving cues (probably not deliberately) then there is said to have been an experimenter effect

Extinction – means the association (for example, between a bell and salivation) ceases, and the learning is extinguished

Extraneous variables – variables that might become confounding variables. They must be controlled so that they do not become confounding variables

Face validity – on the face of it, what you are saying has happened does seem likely. For example, if smiling and pointing to the Post Office when asked to locate it appears to represent 'helpfulness' then, on the face of it, these are valid measures

Fatigue effect – with repeated measures designs, the first condition can tire the participant, so they do the second one less well. The fatigue effect is an order effect

Field experiment – an experiment (where everything is controlled, the IV is manipulated and the effect on the DV is measured) done in the field – which means in a natural setting. An example would be a study of children done in a school. Don't confuse these with naturalistic experiments, which are when the situation naturally occurs without the experimenter setting it up

Findings – the results of a study and what is found out.

Fixation – is when a stage of development is not successfully passed through, and frustrations from this may lead to future problems. A person can be fixated at the oral stage, for example

Flooding – like implosion therapy, except that the actual phobic object is present

Free association – one of the methods used in the psychodynamic approach to uncover the content of the unconscious. The individual freely associates – says what comes into their minds, hopefully bypassing conscious control

Free recall – recalling a list of words, for example, in any order rather than in the order given

Gene – carries the genetic information from person to person. The information is coded in DNA by means of different combinations of bases

Generalisation – in conditioning, is similar to the use of the word generalising in methodology. Generalisation in conditioning means going from one conditioned stimulus (a particular tone of bell, for example) to similar stimuli (for example, other tones of bell). So a dog generalises if it salivates to a different tone of bell to the one it was conditioned with

Generalise – claiming that the findings from one piece of research using a particular sample apply to other samples. You can only generalise if the sampling is carefully done, and if the sample is representative of the population you are interested in. If the sample is different in important ways to the population of interest, then you can't generalise from it to this population

Generalisability – being able to transfer a set of results from a particular group to apply to a much larger group. This depends on good sampling

Generativity – a term used by Erikson. Briefly, where people put something back into society rather than take

Genetics – the study of genes. Genes are passed on through our parents and give us many of our characteristics, such as hair and eye colour

Genital stage – the fifth and last stage of psychosexual development according to Freud. Everything works out fine, and boys look towards relationships with girls and vice versa (if the phallic stage worked out well)

Higher order conditioning – when something that has already been conditioned (for example, a bell stimulates salivation) is then conditioned a second time (for example, the bell is paired with a man in a coat, and seeing the man in a coat then brings about the salivation)

Holism – the view that the whole is more than the total or sum of the parts. For example, there is more to a car than all its parts, because they have to be put together in a certain relationship

Horizontal décalage – this is the idea that a child in one stage might be able to do something that moves it on to the next stage before they can do one of the other things needed. For example, children can often conserve number before they

can conserve volume. It is not the case that once a child can do one of the things for the next stage, they can do them all

Hypothesis – the statement that you are going to test when doing a study. There are different types of hypothesis

Hysteria – an illness that appears to have a physical cause (to the patient) but does not. For example, someone who is blind but with no physical problem

Iconic mode – means a 'pictorial' way of representing the world. The child represents its world by means of pictures/images. One of Bruner's modes

Id – one of the parts of the personality according to Freud. The id is the part that is demanding and wanting fulfilment – it is the demanding child in us

Implosion therapy – refers to reducing a phobia by imagining the phobic object. The fear response will be present. However, it cannot be maintained as the body runs out of energy. The person will interpret the reduction in energy as calming down, and the phobia will be removed

Independent groups design – when there is one participant for each part of the study. For example, one person has the categorised list, and another person has the randomised list. The scores for those with a categorised list are compared with the scores for those with the randomised list.

Independent variable (IV) – the variable of interest. If you are testing to see if men drive 'better' than women, the main variable of interest is whether the driver is male or female. (The other variable of interest is the driving behaviour, but you are measuring how this varies 'depending' on whether the driver is male or female, so driving behaviour is the dependent variable)

Infradian rhythms – rhythms that last longer than a day

In-group – the group you are in, and are loyal to

Insight learning – suggests that we don't learn everything through conditioning. Perhaps mental processes are at work and sometimes there are insights into the problem/solution

Interactions – actions between people, which are usually viewed as a whole rather than as two separate actions. If I shake hands (one action), and you shake my hand back (another action), then we should really be looking at the act of shaking hands (an interaction)

Interference – explains forgetting by saying that one piece of information interferes with another

Internalisation – when we adopt an attitude and really believe it. It becomes part of us

Inter-observer reliability – using two or more observers, trained on the same set of criteria. They observe the same actions separately. If the two sets of data are the same, then there is inter-observer reliability

Inter-rater reliability – similar to inter-observer reliability, but this term is used if the observers are rating behaviour and comparing ratings, for example of how aggressive children are. If their ratings are the same, it is said that there is inter-rater reliability

Interval/ratio data – data measured on a true measurement scale, with equal intervals between the numbers. Height, weight, age, and time are interval/ratio data

Introspection – a method in which we reflect on how we think, remember or perceive

Introspectionism – studying human behaviour by each individual thinking about what they are thinking, and how they are processing the information. This is fairly unscientific and also difficult to do. Individuals might report experiences in different ways, and it would be very hard to build a body of knowledge using introspectionism

Involuntary response – a behaviour is a reflex and not a thought-out action

Isolation – a defence mechanism. Recall is fine, but the emotions that go with the memories are repressed, so only details are recalled, not feelings

Laboratory experiment – an experiment where everything is controlled and then the IV is manipulated and the effect on the DV is measured, done in unnatural conditions – often a room or a laboratory

Latent content – the underlying message of a dream, where the unconscious is managing to 'send a message' and break through. The manifest content is likely to be symbols that can be interpreted to find the latent content

Latent learning – when we learn something without being conditioned or reinforced. Some things are learnt without reinforcement, and latent tends to mean remaining hidden. This type of learning is not known about until the behaviour appears

Latent stage – the fourth stage of psychosexual development according to Freud – not much happens

Law of effect – refers to Thorndike's view that if we get a reward for doing something we like the effect of that behaviour, and we are likely to repeat it

Law of exercise – refers to Thorndike's idea that if a stimulus and response have been connected quite a few times, then the learning is stronger than if less frequently put together

Lesion – surgery or cutting parts of the body or brain, but without removing them

Levels of measurement – nominal, ordinal, interval and ratio are all levels of measurement

Levels of processing – the theory that there are levels of processing, and a deeper level of processing gives better recall. There are visual levels, auditory levels (hearing) and semantic levels (meaning). Semantic processing is best

Life-span approach – those developmental theories that consider us from birth to old age. Early theories only looked at birth to adulthood. The main cognitive–developmental theories look at birth to adolescence

Likert scale – a scale where the participant ticks 'strongly agree', 'agree', 'don't know or other', 'disagree' or 'strongly disagree'. Usually the scoring is 5,4,3,2,1

Linear – a straight-line model, where things occur step-by-step, one at a time

Long-term memory – is supposed to be where memories last for a long time in various forms. It is the second part of the multi-store or two-stage model

Manifest content – what a dream really seems to be about; that is, the actual story of the dream. The latent content is the hidden content

Matched pairs design – when there is one participant for each part of the study. When people are put into the two groups (categorised or randomised list to learn) they are matched on important variables. For example, they might be matched for gender, age and whether they are students or not. How they are matched depends on what is important in the particular study for test purposes. Matched pairs designs are treated as repeated measures

Maturation – patterns that cause change, and that are genetically given. Not everything about us is revealed at birth; we are also genetically programmed to develop in certain ways too – for example, during puberty.

Measures of central tendency – the mean, median and mode are all averages or measures of central tendency.

Mental operations – mental abilities, such as comparing ideas and making transformations logically

Methodological – to do with the method being used. Problems often arise because of the method, and so you can give methodological criticisms

Methodology – the study of the way in which a study is carried out

Mnemonics – cues or clues to help in memory, for example ROYGBIV can help you to remember the colours of the rainbow (red, orange, yellow, green, blue, indigo, violet)

Modality free – information can be encoded in any form

Modality specific – if information is visual, then it is encoded in its visual form

Models – representations of how things might be, without certain knowledge about this

Monozygotic (MZ) twins – identical twins. They develop from one egg and are always of the same sex

Motivated forgetting – explains forgetting by saying that we are motivated to forget, because remembering would be painful. This explanation fits in with psychodynamic theory

Multi-store model – another name for the two-stage model of Atkinson and Shiffrin

Nativist – someone who thinks that what we know comes from our natural abilities and is inherited

Natural experiment – an experiment in which the IV, instead of being manipulated by the researcher, is already naturally occurring in 'real life'. A natural experiment is done in a natural setting, because that is where the naturally occurring IV will be

Naturalistic observation – an observation that is not in a laboratory or structure. It is in a natural situation in its natural setting

Nature – refers to the properties, abilities and characteristics that we are born with, and that we have inherited

Negative correlation – when a correlation is found between two variables it means that two variables change together, even though the change in one may not cause the change in the other. A negative correlation is when one variable increases and the other decreases, for example the bigger the age, the fewer words recalled.

Negative reinforcement – when an action is done to avoid something unpleasant, and the action is repeated

Neural networks – real networks of nodes and connections, where computers mimic the way the brain works. Important information is retained as some nodes are reinforced and others not reinforced. This means that neural networks are self-teaching. For example, a neural computer is used at Bass brewery. Judgements are made based on electro-chemical information received by gas sensors and the 'nose' can detect such things as over-active yeast. Choices are made about what is 'good' and what is 'not good', and learning takes place

Neuron – what the nervous system is made up of (with glia being between the neurons). For neuron, think cell

Neuroses – problems with mental health that are not psychoses. With neuroses the patient knows that there is a problem and can talk about it. A psychotic person will not be in touch with the problem

Neurotransmitter – the name for the chemical that is released into the synaptic gap and possibly taken up by the adjoining dendrite, if the chemical is appropriate. Two neurotransmitters are serotonin and dopamine

Nominal data – data recorded in categories, e.g. whether boys or girls (two gender categories) are aggressive or not (two categories to do with aggression).

Non-participant observations – observations where the researcher is not a participant

Norms – these are the rules of a society and what is usual. Queuing can be a norm, as can kissing on both cheeks as a greeting

Null hypothesis – the statement that what is expected is not true, but that any difference that is found is due to chance or some other variable. For example, we do not recall more of a categorised list, and if it looks as if more are recalled from the categorised list, the difference is due to chance or something else (i.e. not because one list is categorised)

Nurture – refers to the environmental factors that shape us into the people we are. These factors include our parents, school, surroundings, type of area, culture, peer group and friends

Object permanence – the term for the ability of a baby to realise that an object, when out of sight, is still there. The baby realises that the object has permanence and must be somewhere. The baby (at around 8 months) will look for the object when it is made to disappear, for example, under a blanket

Objective/objectivity – a study that is not subjective. Subjective means involving the view of either the researcher or the participant. Objective means avoiding personal views, so that if someone does the same thing again they should get the same result. Science is objective, because it does not involve any personal analysis or interpretation

Observational learning – see social learning theory

Oedipus complex – this is the strong conflict (according to Freud) in which a boy comes to have sexual feelings for his mother. He also loves his father and is jealous of his father's place with his mother. So he both loves his father and wants to remove him (kill him) from his position with his mother. This conflict is resolved by the boy identifying (becoming) his father. The girl has a similar complex called the Electra complex, where in the end she identifies with her mother

One tailed – this means that an alternate or experimental hypothesis is directional – you have said which direction you expect the results to take. For example, boys are more aggressive than girls

Ontogeny – refers to our development over our lifetime, from babyhood to old age

Open questions – those questions on a questionnaire that give the participant the freedom to expand and explain by giving written answers rather than filling in tick boxes or being limited in how they can answer.

Operant conditioning – the idea that learning occurs through reinforcements. Briefly, you repeat what you get positively reinforced for doing (praised, etc.) and you stop doing what you get punished for doing

Operationalisation – this means making variables measurable. If you are testing, for example, helpfulness, it is very difficult to measure it. However, if you operationalise helpfulness as giving directions when asked, then this is something that can be measured. It is hard to measure aggression, but you can operationalise aggression as the number of times one person kicks another. You should always show in your research how you have operationalised your variables, and you should always use those variables in your hypothesis

Oral stage – the first stage of psychosexual development according to Freud. Focus is on pleasure from sucking and so on

Order effects – with repeated measures designs, the first condition the person does can affect the next one. So the order in which they do the conditions can affect the results. Two order effects are the fatigue effect and the practice effect

Ordinal data – ranked data, or data put in rank order. An example is rating attitudes to religion on a scale of 0–5

and comparing people's scores. The most religious score 5, and the least religious score 0, so the scores are ranked

Outgroup – the rest, outside the in-group, and to whom you are hostile

Overt observations – observations when the participants know they are being observed

Participant – a person who helps with a psychology study. Used to be called the subject

Participant observations – observations where the researcher is also a participant

Participant variables – things about the participant that might affect the study and need to be controlled

Passive – taking no part in what is happening. The opposite of active

Peripheral nervous system (PNS) – the autonomic and somatic nervous systems

Phallic stage – this is the third stage according to Freud, at around 4 or 5 years old, where the Oedipus complex is resolved and the superego develops

Phylogeny – refers to our development from an evolutionary point of view; that is, how our genes got to this stage, and how we evolved into the people we are today

Physiology – physical aspects of our brains and ourselves – our biology

Pleasure principle – refers to the id – Freud's term for the part of us that has urges and desires and wants them satisfied now. The id works on the pleasure principle – 'satisfy me now'

Positive correlation – a correlation is found between two variables when they change together, even though the change in one may not cause the change in the other. A positive correlation is when both variables increase together, for example the bigger the age, the greater the memory loss

Positive reinforcement – when an action is praised or some reward is given, the action will be repeated

Positivism – the idea that scientific method can lead us to the truth about things. This implies that there are truths about the world, and that they can be found by testing in a scientific manner (thinking of a statement to test and then finding a way to test it, using controls and so on). Social representation theory suggests that there are no such truths, because (especially where people are concerned) any testing we do happens in a cultural setting, and will be affected by the setting (will be part of the setting)

Practical application – this means that a piece of research is applied to a real-life situation. It is claimed that there can be understanding of the real-life situation because of the findings of the piece of research

Practice effect – with repeated measures designs, the first condition can teach the participant how to do the task, so the second one is done better. The practice effect is an order effect

Preconscious – things in your preconscious are not in your conscious thoughts, so you are not aware of them. However, they are available and you can become aware of them

Predictive validity – when you measure something, and it means you can use the results to predict something else that will happen, you have predictive validity. For example, you might do a study that shows that men help more than women, and you therefore predict that men help more than women. If you then find that men do help more than women, the original study had predictive validity

Prejudice – a hostile learned attitude, although it can be positive. For example, you can be prejudiced against people from certain cultures because of your beliefs. However, you can be prejudiced in favour of people from a certain age group because of your beliefs

Preoperation stage – when the child cannot perform operations (mental processes) on things. The second of Piaget's stages

Preparedness – suggests that both human and non-human animals have limits when considering conditioning. Some non-human animals can be conditioned to do certain behaviours and not others. It is as if evolution has prepared them in certain ways, and conditioning a non-human animal against this preparedness is not easy

Primacy effect – the way we recall best what we learn first

Primary acoustic store – the part of working memory where auditory (hearing) information is stored and processed – the inner ear

Primary circular reactions – actions that the baby (from 1.5–4 months) repeats because it is enjoying the actions for itself. This is in the second substage of the sensori-motor stage

Primary reinforcers – those that give basic needs, for example, food, warmth and shelter

Procedural memory – the part of memory where how to do things is stored

Projection – a defence mechanism. Repressed feelings surface, but are directed at someone else, so that the real feelings are repressed (the person receiving the feelings is not the right person)

Psychoanalysis/psychoanalyst – a psychoanalyst is someone who practices psychoanalysis. Psychoanalysis is the therapy that stems from the psychodynamic approach. Psychoanalysts accept Freud's theory and work on the principle that problems stem from fixations, and that there are hidden urges in the unconscious that must be released. There is a need to remove repressions and work through problems. Transference is an important part of psycho-analysis

Psychodynamic – the approach first put forward by Freud. The general idea is that much of what we do is driven by our unconscious urges, which we don't know about. We repress them in many ways

Psychoses – these are problems with mental health where the individual is not in touch with the symptoms, and cannot talk about the problem. Clearly a talking cure is not going to be useful, although some dispute this claim where 'illnesses' like schizophrenia are concerned

Psychotherapy – refers to therapies that focus on mental processes. There are different types of psychotherapy, and psychoanalysis is only one of these

Punishment – when an action is punished by something unpleasant being given, and the action is not repeated

Qualitative data – these are data that are not measured on any scale, but are attitudes and opinions. The data are things like sentences and comments

Quantitative – means measured in quantity, not quality. Your height is measured quantitatively in metres (or feet and inches), but your attitudes are measured by how you feel, which is a qualitative measure. Percentages are quantitative data, as are measurements like reaction time or number of words recalled

Quasi experiment – an experiment where everything is controlled and then the IV is manipulated and the effect on the DV is measured, but the researcher does not allocate the participants to the different conditions. Instead the participants naturally fall into groups. For example, studies of gender are quasi experimental because the participants are in the groups already

Quasi interval – sometimes when we allocate scores they are not true mathematical measures, but the scoring system does have equal intervals between the scores. For example, number of words recalled (if you score 10 and I score 20, I score twice as many as you). Although not true interval/ratio data, these data are called quasi interval and treated as interval

Rationalisation – a defence mechanism. This is putting a different interpretation on something to hide the real reason. We can behave badly towards someone and say it is for their own good, for example

Reaction formation – a defence mechanism. Unconscious urges must be repressed but are trying to find a way out. The individual can repress them by expressing the opposite wishes. For example, a man may claim to love his brother very much indeed, but this can hide actual hatred and jealousy of the brother

Realistic conflict theory – refers to the way that prejudice can arise when people are really in conflict with one another

Reality principle – is referring to the ego – Freud's term for the part of us that mediates between reality and the id's desires. The ego has to listen to the id's demands and then work on how to achieve them when faced with reality, so it works on the reality principle

Recapitulates – repeats, or goes through the same stages as

Recency effect – the way we remember quite well what we have just learnt

Recessive gene – where more than one copy is needed for a characteristic to be produced

Reciprocal teaching – where pupils and teacher get together and do a task such as reading through a text. Someone has to summarise the text – and this is not always the teacher. In this way the group learn from one another. Everyone in the group contributes after someone has summarised the details. Those that can read and understand the text help those who can only just make out the sense of it

Reconstructive memory – the idea that memory is not perfect but involves reconstructing events from what is recalled, and from previous knowledge and experience

Reductionism – the view that if we study all the parts of something, we can learn about the whole thing. For example, we can look at our physical bodies by studying neurons and parts of the brain, and learn about how we function

Reinforcement – positive reinforcement is giving something good so that behaviour will be repeated

Reliability – means when a study is well controlled so that it can be repeated, and that, most importantly, when it is repeated the same findings are reported. If a study is done again, with the same conclusions, then the study is reliable

Repeated measures design – when each participant does all the parts of the study. For example, one person learns both a categorised and a randomised list

Replicated – when you repeat a study using the same procedure, then it is said to have been replicated

Representative – if characteristics of the sample match characteristics of the target population, then the sample is said to be representative of the target population. For example, a sample might need to be representative in terms of gender, age, and cultural background

Repression – when strong feelings are not allowed into conscious thought but are kept in the unconscious by means of defence mechanisms

Response – the response to a stimulus. For example, a dog's excitement is a response to the stimulus of its chain being rattled

Response set – the participant is conditioned to respond in a certain way, for example, in a questionnaire

Retrospective – a study in which the individual has to think back to earlier times. This involves memory, and so can be unreliable. A retrospective study is usually criticised on the grounds of unreliability.

RNA – picks up the genetic message by copying the DNA and forming from it proteins as determined by the genes

Roles – within a society there are jobs and positions that people hold. These have set roles or ways of behaving and tasks to complete. Everyone has a role. Some are mothers or fathers, and are also sons or daughters, for example

Sample – part of the target population that we have chosen to study, if we cannot study them all

Scaffolding – the name for the idea of supporting a child when it is learning, but only to an extent. As the child learns, the support (scaffolding) is gradually withdrawn

Schedules of reinforcement – this refers to the timing of the reinforcement in operant conditioning. A continuous schedule is when the action is reinforced every time. A fixed schedule means regular and a variable schedule means irregular reinforcements. A ratio of reinforcements means how much reward is given considering the number of responses. The interval of reinforcements means how much time passes between giving rewards. So fixed interval means at regular time intervals, and variable interval means at irregular time intervals. Fixed ratio means at a regular number of responses, and variable ratio means at an irregular number of responses (for example, like a fruit machine)

Schema/schemata – **1** a baby's mental structure, giving basis for action in similar circumstances

2 ideas, plans, scripts and previous knowledge in our memories

Secondary reinforcers – any reinforcers that do not give basic needs (like food, warmth and shelter) but can be used to get such needs (for example, money or tokens)

Semantic – this means 'meaning'. If memory is semantic, then something is recalled by its meaning, e.g. car is recalled as 'something you drive, has more than two wheels…'

Self-fertilise – means there are no separate male and female plants, but the plant has all it needs to fertilise itself. This means there is a pureness about it, and it makes the study of genes easier, because all the genes come from the plant itself

Self-fulfilling prophecy – what is expected of us by others has a habit of becoming the truth because of the way others behave towards us, given their expectations

Semantic differential – a method used in questionnaires where someone can, for example, rate their personality between 'generous' and 'mean'

Semantic memory – the part of memory where the meaning of words and things is stored. For example, what a birthday is – rather than a particular birthday

Sensitive period – this is a time when it is best that something occurs. However, there is a possibility that the development of a specific thing can happen at another time. This is a much looser explanation of the time when certain skills and abilities should develop than the idea of a critical period

Sensorimotor stage – the first of Piaget's stages, from 0–2 years, where emphasis is on motor movements and perceptions via the senses

Sensory buffer – in information processing models this is where the first sensations from our eyes, ears and so on, are received. In the multi-store model, this is the first stage

Shaping – means gradually using schedules of reinforcements to shape a required behaviour – this is because most complex behaviours would never otherwise occur for you to reward them. You have to get there gradually

Short-term memory – supposed to be the part of memory that first registers information (after the sensory store). It is the second part of the multi-store model. Memory does not stay for long in short-term memory

Siblings – any brothers and sisters, including twins

Situational variables – variables in the situation that might affect the study and need to be controlled

Social constructionism – is like social representation theory (see positivism). Social constructionists say that we construct our world from our beliefs and customs. There are no separate truths to find out about people – separate, that is, from their culture

Social desirability – this is when the participant answers according to social rules and norms, rather than according to their own views

Social learning theory – the theory that says we learn through modelling and imitation. We use models in the world around us – parents, friends, media personalities and so on. We imitate their actions, and we learn in this way. Learning is, therefore, social

Social representation theory – basically, there is no such thing as knowing something outside the culture within which the knowledge is gathered. There are no real facts about people, because anything we find out is within cultural guidelines and must be recognised as such

Socialisation – the process of learning about our society and its rules. We are socialised first by our parents (primary socialisation) and secondly by schools, the media, peer groups and other influences (secondary socialisation)

Somatic – to do with the body, and physical. *Soma* is Latin for 'body'

Somatic nervous system – carries physical messages

Speciesism – the idea that we should protect our own species even if this means causing suffering to other species

Spiral curriculum – the idea of allowing a child to develop by means of a curriculum (which is what the child is set to learn) that builds in levels of difficulty, moving the child on to harder and harder things so that its abilities develop and improve

Spontaneous recovery – means that a previous association (for example between a bell and salivation) has been extinguished, and then reappears after a space of time

Stage theories – theories which make the assumption that during our development we pass through stages, and to get to one we have to have gone through the previous one. In Chapter 5 it is claimed that Freud's theory was a stage theory. Piaget's theory, presented in Chapter 3, is a stage theory. Behaviourism is not a stage theory, as we are changing all the time because of reinforcements and punishments. This is a continuous development, not a staged one

Standardised instructions – each participant in a study hears exactly the same instructions so that there is no bias and no person knows more than anyone else. The opportunity is also taken to explain ethical issues. For example, the researcher can let the participant know that they can refuse to continue with the study at any time, and that any results will remain confidential

Stereotyping – using small pieces of information and applying them to the whole group

Stimulus – means something that sets off an action or behaviour. For example, the sound of a dog's chain can stimulate the dog to get excited, ready for a walk. The sound is the stimulus

Stimulus list – the list given to participants, for example, in a memory study, and that is the material being tested

Stooge – someone acting for the researcher, but usually without the knowledge of the participant. A stooge is like a confederate, but the stooge is there to deceive the participant in some way

Structured interview – questions are written down and each participant is asked exactly the same questions. There is little room to explore any issues that may arise

Subjective – when a study is done from the researcher's individual viewpoint. This can have value but usually, because we aim for scientific rigour, we want studies to be objective, and free from such influences

Subjectivity – refers to the way individuals who analyse or gather data can then either interpret the data or guide what they see using their own views and frames of reference. This means that someone else might draw different conclusions or gather different data. So, from a scientific point of view, we don't want subjectivity, because the data would not be objective

Superego – one of the parts of the personality, according to Freud. The superego is the moral part, and the conscience. It is the part that puts the brakes on, and tells us what we can't do according to social rules. The ego ideal is also part of the superego and tells us what we should 'ideally' be like

Superordinate goal – a goal that a group cannot achieve on its own, but can achieve working with another group

Survival of the fittest – the idea that those most fitted or suited to their environment are more likely to survive and reproduce and, in doing so, pass on their genes. Their genes will have whatever attribute led to the survival, and so the most suited attributes should be passed on

Symbolic mode – means a child can represent things in their head by means of words and symbols. One of Bruner's modes

Symbols – things are symbols when they stand for something else. For example, if you dream about a house, the house is likely to be you

Synaptic gap – the gap between the axon tip of one neuron and the dendrite end of the next one. The gap is important – if the neurotransmitter released into the gap fits the receivers (receptors) waiting at the dendrite end, then the chemical binds to the receivers and the message goes on

Systematic desensitisation – a means of reducing phobias. The desensitising is systematic in that it is done step by step. Firstly, the person has to relax, as relaxation will replace fear as the response. Then the phobic object is introduced step by step, maybe with a picture first, for example. The relaxation response has to replace the fear response at each step

Tachistoscope – the equipment used to test things like memory. The individual peers into a box, and cards are inserted into the back of the box for the participant to see. There is a timer that activates a light. The participant can only see the material when the light is on. Things like words can be flashed up to the participant in a very short time to test processes like memory and attention

Tallying – a method of recording behaviour. You make a mark or tally each time a certain behaviour is observed

Target population – the people of interest in a study. For example, if we want to study the cognitive abilities of 4-year-old children, then the target population is all 4-year-old children.

Theory – the general idea that comes from what others have done, and gives rise to the statement of what is expected. For example, a general theory that males are aggressive can give rise to the suggestion that if boys and girls are watched in the playground, boys will be more aggressive

Theory of mind – the idea that we have the mental capability of knowing what others are thinking. If a child can correctly say that someone out of the room will not know what happens in the room, even though the child knows what has happened in the room, then the child will have a theory of mind. The child has to know that others do not know what the child knows

Time sampling – when you record certain behaviours at specific times, for example every two minutes or at regular intervals. This is to give time to record the data, and to avoid subjectivity, where the researcher could choose what they think is interesting

Token economy programme – a programme used to condition good behaviour, for example, in an institution. Tokens are given for desired behaviour, and these can be exchanged for rewards such as chocolate or cigarettes

Top-down processing – information is processed using previous knowledge and experiences

Transference – this refers to the feelings of the analysand (person being analysed). These feelings are transferred onto the analyst. At first they tend to be positive feelings (as for parents early on). Then they become more negative (as in the Oedipus complex). The analyst must use these feelings in the analysis, as they are strong clues to the problem

Triangulation – used as evidence when doing ethnographic research or case studies. If a piece of evidence is arrived at by several different means, then it is more reliable. So case studies use more than one method, and draw conclusions from data collected in different ways

Trigram – the term used for a set of three letters that has no meaning. 'Cat' is a word, but 'Cht' is a trigram

Two tailed – this means that an alternate or experimental hypothesis is not directional – you have not said which direction you expect the results to take. For example, there is a difference in aggression depending on gender (but you don't say who is more aggressive, the boy or the girl)

Types of classical conditioning – these different types are the ways in which the unconditioned stimulus and the conditioned stimulus can be put together. If both are put together at the same time, this is simultaneous conditioning. If the conditioned stimulus is presented (a bell is rung, for example), and then the unconditioned stimulus is given (the food) with the bell still ringing, then this is delayed conditioning. Trace conditioning is when the conditioned stimulus (the bell) is presented and then stopped before the unconditioned stimulus (the food) appears. Backward conditioning is when the unconditioned stimulus is presented and then the conditioned stimulus is presented

Types of reinforcement – in operant conditioning this refers to there being positive reinforcement, negative reinforcement, and punishment. All act as reinforcers

Ultradian rhythms – rhythms that last for shorter than a day

Unconditioned response – a natural response (reflex) like salivation, produced in response to a natural stimulus like food. A fear response is an unconditioned response if it happens because of an unconditioned stimulus like a sudden fall. However, a response is conditioned if it happens because of a conditioned stimulus like a bell

Unconditioned stimulus – something that naturally brings an automatic response (reflex). For example, food makes us salivate

Unconscious – things in the unconscious are not even available to be thought about. Freud thought these things were powerful and controlling. They are active and dynamic and trying to find a way into consciousness

Unstructured interview – where the researcher knows the area he or she wishes to explore, but allows the participant to follow their own thoughts and feelings, so that the issues come to an extent from the participant. There is no rigid structure

Validity – means when a study measures what it claims to measure. When findings are valid, it is because they arise from a real setting and a real situation. This means that experiments tend not to be valid

Variables – things that vary and might affect the study. Really anything can be a variable, including temperature, mood, weather and time of day

Visuospatial scratchpad – the part of working memory where visual information is stored and processed – the 'inner eye'

Voluntary response – a response that is done deliberately and with purpose

Wish fulfillment – refers to the unconscious urgings trying to surface into consciousness. These wishes are kept hidden by the individual. They can be fulfilled, however, in things like dreams, because they can find a way out through symbols. Unconscious wishes can be fulfilled through dreams, through slips of the tongue, or in other ways

Zeitgebers – external cues that trigger our bodily rhythms

References

Ablon, S.L. (1994) The usefulness of dreams during pegnancy. *International Journal of Psychoanalysis*, 75, pp 291–299

Achenbach, T.M. & Edelbrock, C. (1986*) Manual for the Teacher's Report Form and Teacher Version of the Child Behaviour Profile.* Burlington: University of Vermont

Adam, K. (1980) Sleep as a restorative process and a theory to explain why. *Progress in Brain Research, 53,* pp 289–305

Adorno, T.W., Frenkel-Brunswick, E., Levinson, D. & Sanford, R.N. (1950) *The Authoritarian Personality,* New York: Harper

Amir, Y. (1994) The contact hypothesis in intergroup relations. In W.J. Lonner & R.S. Malpass (Eds.) *Psychology and Culture.* Boston: Allyn & Bacon

Ancona, L. & Pareyson, R. (1968) Contributo allo studio della a aggressione: la dinimica della obbedienza distructiva. *Archivio di Psicologia Neurologia e Psichiatria, 29,* pp 340–372

Anderson, J.R. (1995) *Learning and Memory: an Integrated Approach.* New York: John Wiley and Sons Inc.

Antrobus, J.S. (1986) Dreaming: Cortical activation and perceptual thresholds. *Journal of Mind and Behaviour, 7,* pp 193–211

Aronson, E. (1980) *The Social Animal* (3rd edition). San Francisco: WH Freeman

Aronson, E. (1990) Applying social psychology to desegregation and energy conservation. *Personality and Social Psychology Bulletin, 16,* pp 118–132

Aronson, E. (1992) *The Social Animal.* (6th edition) New York: W.H. Freeman & Co.

Aronson, E., Bridgeman, D.L. & Geffner, R. (1978) The effects of co-operative classroom structure on student behaviour and attitudes. In D. Bar-Tal & L. Saxe (Eds.) *Social Psychology of Education,* New York: Wiley

Aronson, E. & Osherow, N. (1980) Co-operation, prosocial behaviour and academic performance: experiments in the desegregated classroom. In L. Bickman (Ed.) *Applied Social Psychology annual, Vol.1.* Beverley Hills, California: Sage Publications

Asch, S. (1956) Studies of independence and conformity: A minority of one against a unanimous majority. *Psychological monographs, 70* (Whole No 416)

Aschoff, J. & Wever, R. (1981) The circadian system in man. In J. Aschoff (Ed.) *Handbook of behavioural neurology, Vol. 4.* New York: Plenum Press

Aserinsky, E. (1952) In Gross, R.D. & McIlveen, R. (1999) *Psychology, a New Introduction.* London: Hodder and Stoughton

Aserinsky, E. & Kleitman, N. (1955) Regularly occurring periods of eye motility and concomitant phenomena during sleep. *Science, 118,* pp 273–274

Astington, J.W. (1993) *The child's discovery of the mind.* Cambridge, MA: Harvard University Press

Atkinson, R.C. & Shiffrin, R.M. (1968) Human memory: a proposed system and its control processes. In K.W. Spence & J.T. Spence (Eds.) *The Psychology of Learning and Motivation, Vol. 2.* London: Academic Press

Avis, J. & Harris, P. L. (1991) Belief-desire reasoning amongst Baka children: Evidence for a universal conception of mind. *Child development, 62,* pp 460–467

Ayllon, J. & Azrin, N.H. (1968) *The token economy.* New York: Appleton-Century-Crofts

Baddeley, A.D. (1990) *Human Memory.* Hove, East Sussex: Lawrence Erlbaum Associates Ltd.

Baddeley, A.D. (1995) Memory. In C.C. French & A.M. Coleman (Eds.) *Cognitive Psychology.* London:Longman

Baddeley, A.D. & Hitch, G. (1974) Working memory. In G.A. Bower (Ed.) *Recent advances in learning and motivation, Vol.8,* New York: Academic Press

Bahrick, H.P, Clark, S. & Bahrick, P. (1967) Generalisation gradients as indicants of learning and retention of a recognition task. *Journal of Experimental Psychology, 75,* pp 464–471

Baillargeon, R. (1987) Object permanence in three and a half and four and a half month old infants. *Developmental Psychology, 23,* pp 655–664

Baillargeon, R. (1993) The object concept revisited: New directions in the investigation of infants' physical knowledge. In C. Granrud (Ed.) *Visual perception and cognition in infancy. Carnegie Mellon symposia on cognition.* Hillsdale, HJ: Lawrence Erlbaum Associates

Bandura, A. (1965) Influence of model's reinforcement contingencies on the acquisition of imitative responses. *Journal of Personality and Social Psychology, 1,* pp 589–595

Bandura, A. (1974) Behaviour theory and models of man. *American Psychologist, 29,* pp 859–869

Bandura, A., Ross, D., & Ross, S.A. (1961) Transmissions of aggression through imitation of aggressive models. *Journal of Abnormal and Social Psychology, 63(3),* pp 575–582

Bandura, A. & Walters, R.H. (1963) *Social learning and personality development.* New York: Holt, Rinehart & Winston

Bard (1928) in Gross, R.D. (1987) *Psychology, the science of mind and behaviour*. London: Arnold

Barker, R.G. & Wright, H.F. (1951) *One Boy's Day: a Specimen Record of Behaviour*. New York: Harper Brothers

Baron-Cohen, S. (1990) Autism: A specific cognitive disorder of 'mind-blindness'. *International Review of Psychiatry, 2*, pp 79–88

Baron-Cohen, S. (1993) From attention-goal psychology to desire-belief psychology: The development of a theory of mind and its dysfunction. In S. Baron-Cohen, H. Tager-Flusberg & D.J. Cohen (Eds.) *Understanding other minds: Perspectives from Autism*. Oxford: Oxford University Press

Baron-Cohen, S. (1995) Infantile Autism. In A.A.Lazarus & A.M. Coleman (Eds.) *Abnormal Psychology*, London: Longman

Baron-Cohen, S., Leslie, A.M. & Frith, U. (1985) Does the autistic child have a 'theory of mind'? *Cognition, 21*, pp 37–46

Bartlett, F.C. (1932) *Remembering*. Cambridge: Cambridge University Press

Batson, C.D. & Burris, C.T. (1994) Personal religion: Depressant or stimulant of prejudice and discrimination? In M.P. Zanna and J.M. Olson (Eds.) *The psychology of prejudice: The Ontario symposium* (Vol.7, pp 149–169). Hillsdale, NJ: Erlbaum

Baumrind, D. (1964) Some thoughts on the ethics of research: After reading Milgram's behavioural study of obedience. *American Psychologist, 19*, pp 421–423

Beaumont, J.G. (1988) *Understanding Neuropsychology*. Oxford: Blackwell

Beloff, H. (1957) The structure and origin of the anal character. *Genetic psychology monographs, 55*, pp 141–172

Bergman, B.M., Gilliland, M.A., Feng, P.F., Russell, D.R., Shaw, P., Wright, M., Rechtschaffen, A., & Alverdy, J.C. (1996) Are physio-logical effects of sleep deprivation in the rat mediated by bacterial invasion? *Sleep, 19(7)*, pp 554–562

Berkowitz, L. (1959) Anti-Semitism and the displacement of aggression. *Journal of Abnormal and Social Psychology, 59*, pp 182–187

Berry, J.W., Poortinga, Y.H., Segall, M.H. & Dasen, P. (1992) *Cross-cultural psychology: Research and application*. New York: Cambridge University Press

Bevington, J. & Wishart, J.G. (1999) The influence of classroom peers on cognitive performance in children with behavioural problems, *British Journal of Educational Psychology, Vol. 69*, Part 1, pp 19–32

Bierhoff, H.W. & Klein, R. (1987) Prosocial behaviour. In M. Hewstone, W. Stroebe, J.E. Codol & G.M. Stephenson (Eds.) *Introduction to Social Psychology*. Oxford: Basil Blackwell

Bizman, A. & Amir, Y. (1982) Mutual perceptions of Arabs and Jews in Israel. *Journal of Cross-Cultural Psychology, 13*, pp 461–469

Blakemore, C.(1988) *The Mind Machine*. London: BBC publications

Boklage, C.E. (1997) Schizophenia, brain asymmetry development, and twinning: Cellular relationship with etiological and possibly prognostic implications. *Biological Psychiatry*, 12, pp 19–35

Borke, H. (1975) Piaget's mountains revisited: Changes in the egocentric landscape. *Developmental Psychology, 11*, pp 240–443

Bouton, M.E. (1991) Context and retrieval in extinction and in other examples of interference in simple associative learning. In L. Dachowski and C.F. Flaherty (Eds.) *Current topics in animal learning: Brain, emotion and cognition*, pp 25–53. Hillsdale, NJ: Erlbaum

Bouton, M.E. (1993) Context, time, and memory retrieval in the inter-ference paradigms of Pavlovian learning. *Psychological Bulletin, 114*, pp 80–99

Bouton, M.E., Nelson, J.B. & Rosas, J.M. (1999) Stimulus generali-sation, context change and forgetting. *Psychological Bulletin, Vol. 125, No. 2*, pp 171–186

Bower, G.H., Clark, M., Lesgold, A. & Winzenz, D. (1969) Hierarchical retrieval schemes in recall of categorized word lists. *Journal of Verbal Learning and Verbal Behaviour, 8*, pp 323–343

Bowlby, J. (1973) *Attachment and loss, Vol. 2: Separation–Anxiety and Anger*, Harmondsworth: Penguin

Bransford, J.D. (1979) *Human Cognition: Learning, understanding and remembering*. Belmont, CA: Wadsworth

Brazelton, T.B. (1962) A child-oriented approach to toilet training, *Pediatrics, 29*, pp 121–128

Breger, L., Hunter, I., & Lane, R. (1971) The effect of stress on dreams. *Psychological issues, 7 (3, monograph 27)* pp 1–213

Brill, A.A. (Ed.) (1938) *The basic writings of Sigmund Freud*. New York: Random House, Modern Library

Broadbent, D.E.(1954) The role of auditory localisation in attention and memory span. *Journal of Experimental Psychology, 47*, pp 191–196

Broadbent, D.E. (1958) *Perception and Communication*. London: Pergamon

Broca, P. (1861) in J. Kalat (1995) *Biological Psychology*, Fifth Edition. California: Brooks/Cole

Broca, P.P. (1864/1970) cited in M. Critchley, *Aphasiology and other aspects of language*. London: Edward Arnold

Brown, A.L., Campione, J.C., Reeve, R.A., Ferrara, R.A., & Palincsar, A.S. (1992) Interactive learning and individual understanding: The case of reading and mathematics. In L.T. Landsmann (Ed.) *Culture, schooling, and psychological development*. Hillsdale, NJ: Erlbaum

Brown, J.A. (1958) Some tests of the decay theory of immediate memory. *Quarterly Journal of Experimental Psychology, 10*, pp 12–21

Brown, J.F. (1940) *The psychodynamics of abnormal behaviour*. New York: McGraw-Hill

Brown, R. (1986) *Social Psychology: The Second Edition.* New York: Free Press

Bruner, J.S. (1957) On perceptual readiness. *Psychology Review, 64,* pp 123–152

Bruner, J.S. (1966) On the conservation of liquids. In J.S. Bruner, R.R. Oliver, & P.M. Greenfield (Eds.) *Studies in Cognitive Growth.* New York: Wiley

Bruner, J.S. (1983) *Child's talk: Learning to use language.* Oxford: Oxford University Press

Bruner, J.S. (1990) *Acts of Meaning.* Cambrige, MA: Harvard University Press

Bruner, J.S. & Kenney, H. (1966) *The Development of the Concepts of Order and Proportion in Children.* New York: Wiley

Bryant, P. (1998) Cognitive Development. In M. Eysenck (Ed.) *Psychology: An integrated approach.* Essex: Adison Wesley Longman Ltd.

Burley, P.M. & McGuiness, J. (1977) Effects of social intelligence on the Milgram paradigm. *Psychological Reports, 40,* pp 767–770

Calhoun, J.B. (1962) Population density and social psychology. *Scientific American, 206 (2),* pp 139–148

Case, R. (1992) The role of frontal lobes in the regulation of cognitive development. *Brain and Cognition, 20 (1),* pp 51–73

Ceci, S.J., Toglia, M. P. & Ross, D.F. (Eds.) (1987) *Children's eyewitness testimony.* New York: Springer-Verlag

Chomsky, N. (1965) *Aspects of the theory of syntax.* Cambridge, Massachusetts: MIT Press

Christian, J.J., Flyger, V. & Davis, D.E. (1960) Factors in the mass morality of a herd of Sika deer. *Cervus Nippon. Chesapeake Science, 1,* pp 79–95

Cohen, N.J. & Squire, L.R. (1980) Preserved learning and retention of pattern analyzing skills in amnesia: Dissociation of knowing how from knowing that. *Science, 210,* pp 207–210

Cohen, Y.A. (1953) A study of interpersonal relations in a Jamaican community. Unpublished doctoral dissertation, Yale University. In Gleitman, H. (1995) *Psychology,* Fourth Edition. Norton

Cole, M. & Cole, S. (1996) *The Development of Children,* Third Edition. New York: W.H. Freeman and Company

Coren, S. (1996) *Sleep Thieves.* The Free Press

Cornwell, D., & Hobbs, S. (1976) The strange saga of Little Albert. *New Society* (March), pp 602–604

Craik, F. & Lockhart, R. (1972) Levels of processing. *Journal of Verbal Learning and Verbal Behaviour, 11,* pp 671–84

Crocker, J. & Luhtanen, R. (1990) Collective self-esteem and in-group bias. *Journal of Personality and Social Psychology, 58,* pp 60–67

Crook, C. (1994) *Computers and the collaborative experience of learning.* London: Routledge

Curtiss, S. (1977) *Genie: A psychological study of a modern day wild child.* New York: Academic Press

Czeisler, C.A. et al (1982) Rotating shift work schedules that disrupt sleep are improved by applying circadian principles. *Science, Vol. 217,* pp 460–463

Czeisler, C.A., Weitzman, E.D., Moore-Ede, M.C., Zimmerman, J.C. & Knauer, R.S. (1980) Human sleep: Its duration and organisation depend on its circadian phase. *Science, 210,* pp 1264–1267 (9,16)

Darley, J.M. & Batson, C.D. (1973) From Jerusalem to Jericho: A study of situational and dispositional variables in helping behaviour. *Journal of Personality and Social Psychology, 29 (2),* pp 181–188

Darwin, C. (1859/1959) *The origin of species.* New York: Mentor

Darwin, C. (1877) A biographical sketch of an infant. *Mind, 2,* pp 285–294

Dasen, P.R. (1977a) Are cognitive processes universal? A contribution to cross-cultural Piagetian psychology: In N. Warren (Ed.) *Studies in cross-cultural psychology (Vol. 1).* London: Academic Press

Dasen, P.R. (1977b) *Piagetian psychology: Cross-cultural contributions.* New York: Gardner

Dasen, P.R. (1982) Cross-cultural data on operational development: Asymptotic development curves. In T.G. Bever (Ed.) *Regressions in development.* Hillsdale, NJ: Erlbaum

Dasen, P.R. & Heron, A. (1981) Cross-cultural tests of Piaget's theory. In H. Triandis & A. Heron (Eds.) *Handbook of cross-cultural psychology: Vol.4. Developmental psychology.* Boston: Allyn & Bacon

Dasen, P.R., Ngini, L., & Lavallee, M. (1979) Cross-cultural training studies of concrete operations. In L.H. Eckenberger, W.J. Lonner, & Y.H. Poortinga (Eds.). *Cross-cultural contributions to psychology.* Amsterdam: Swets & Zeilinger

Davies, J.H. (1969) *Group performances.* London: Addison-Wesley

Davison, G.C., & Neale, J.M. (1994) *Abnormal Psychology (6th edition).* New York: John Wiley and Sons

Delgado (1969) in Gross, R.D. (1987) *Psychology, the science of mind and behaviour.* London: Arnold

Dement, W.C. & Kleitman, N. (1957) The relation of eye movements during sleep to dream activity: an objective method for the study of dreaming. In R. Gross (Ed.) *Key Studies in Psychology,* Third Edition. London: Hodder & Stoughton

Dement, W.C. & Kleitman, N. (1957) Cyclical variations in EEG during sleep and their relation to eye movements, body motility and dreaming. *Electroencephalography and Clinical Neurophysiology, 9,* pp 673–690

Dement, W.C. & Wolpert, E.A. (1958) The relationship of eye-movements, body motility and external stimuli to dream content. *Journal of experimental psychology, 53,* pp 339–346

Dement, W. (1972) *Some must watch while some must sleep*. San Fransisco: W.H. Freeman

Deschamps, J-C. (1977) Effect of crossing category memberships on quantitative judgements. *European Journal of Social Psychology, 7,* pp 517–521

Desforges, D.M., Lord, C.G., Ramsey, S.L., Mason, J.A., Van Leeuwen, M.D., West, S.C. & Lepper, M.R. (1991) Effects of structured co-operative contact on changing negative attitudes toward stereo-typed social groups. *Journal of Personality and Social Psychology, 60,* pp 531–544

Deutsch, J.A. & Deutsch, D. (1963) Attention: some theoretical considerations. *Psychology Review, 70,* pp 80–90

Deutsch, M. & Collins, M.E. (1951) *Interracial Housing: A psycho-logical evaluation of a social experiment*. Minneapolis, Minnesota: University of Minnesota Press

Diamond, A. (1991) Frontal lobe involvement in cognitive changes during the first year of life. In K. Gibson, M. Konner & A. Patterson (Eds.) *Brain and behavioural development*. Hillsdale, NJ: Erlbaum

Dinges, D.F., Douglas, S., Zaugg, L., Campbell, D., McMann, J., Whitehouse, W., Orne, E., Kapoor, S., Icaza, E., & Orne, M. (1994) Leukocytosis and natural killer cell function parallel neurobehav-ioural fatigue induced by 64 h of sleep deprivation. *Journal of Clinical Investigation, 93,* pp 1930–1939

Dinges, D.F., Douglas, S.D., Hamarman, S., Zaugg, L., & Kapoor, S. (1995) Sleep deprivation and human immune function. *Advances in Neuroimmunology, 5,* pp 97–110

Dodge, K.A., Price, J.M., Coie, J.D. & Christopoulos, C. (1990) On the development of aggressive dyadic relationships in boys' peer groups. *Human Development, 33,* pp 260–270

Dollard, J., Doob, L.W., Miller, N.E., Mowrer, O.H. & Sears, R.R. (1939) *Frustration and aggression*. New Haven, Connecticut: Harvard University Press

Doty, R.M., Peterson, B.E., & Winter, D.G. (1991) Threat and authori-tarianism in the United States, 1978–1987. *Journal of Personality and Social Psychology, 61,* pp 629–640

Doverty, N. (1992) Therapeutic use of play in hospital. *British Journal of Nursing, 1:2,* pp 77–81

Durkin, K. (1995) *Developmental social psychology: from infancy to old age*. Oxford: Blackwell

Eagly, A.H. & Crowley, M. (1986) Gender and helping behaviour: a meta-analytic review of social psychological literature. *Psychological Bulletin, 100,* pp 282–308

Erikson, E.H. (1950) *Childhood and Society*. New York: Norton

Estes, W.K. (1997) Processes of memory loss, recovery and regression. *Psychological Review, 104,* pp 249–256

Evans, C. (1984) *Landscapes of the Night: How and Why We Dream*. New York: Viking

Everson, C.A. (1993) Sustained sleep deprivation impairs host defense. *American Journal of Physiology, 265,* R1148–54

Everson, C.A. (1995) Functional consequences of sustained sleep deprivation in the rat. *Behaviour Brain Research, 69,* pp 43–54

Fisher, S. & Greenberg, R.P. (1977) *The scientific credibility of Freud's theory and therapy*. New York: Basic Books

Flavell, J.H. (1971) Stage-related properties of cognitive development. *Cognitive Psychology, 2,* pp 421–453

Flavell, J.H., Green, F.L., & Flavell, E.R. (1990) Developmental changes in young children's knowledge about the mind. *Cognitive Development, 5,* pp 1–27

Foot, H.C. (1994) *Group and interactive learning*. Computational Mechanics Publications

Foster, R.G. (1993) Photoreceptors and circadian systems. *Current Directions in Psychological Science, 2,* pp 34–39

Foulkes, D. (1985) *Dreaming: A Cognitive Psychological Analysis*. Hillsdale, NJ: Lawrence Erlbaum Associates

French, J.R.P. & Raven, B.H. (1959) The bases of social power. In D. Cartwright (Ed.) *Studies in Social Power*. Ann Arbour, MI: Institute for Social Research, University of Michigan

Freud, S. (1900) The interpretation of dreams. In Strachey, J. (Trans. and Ed.) *The Complete Psychological Works, vols. 4–5*, New York: Norton, 1976

Freud, S. (1905/1953b) Beyond the pleasure principle. In J. Strachey (Ed. and Trans.) *The standard edition of the complete psycho-logical works of Sigmund Freud* (Vol.18). London: Hogarth Press

Freud, S. (1909) Analysis of a phobia in a five-year-old boy. *Pelican Freud Library, Vol. 8,* Case Histories 1 (1977)

Freud, S. (1915a) Instincts and their vicissitudes. Partially reprinted in P. Gay (1989) (Ed.) *The Freudian Reader*. New York: Norton.

Freud, S. (1917) *A general introduction to psychoanalysis*. Translated by Riviere, J. New York: Washington Square Press, 1952

Freud, S. (1920) *Beyond the pleasure principle*. New York: Norton

Freud, S. (1920/1955) Beyond the pleasure principle. In J. Strachey (Ed. and Trans.) *The standard edition of the complete psycho-logical works of Sigmund Freud*. London: Hogarth Press

Freud, S. & Breuer, J. (1895/1966) *Studies in hysteria*. New York: Avon

Frith, U. (1993) Autism. *Scientific American, 268 (6),* pp 78–84

Fromm, E. (1970) *The crisis of psychoanalysis*. Harmondsworth: Penguin

Gaertner, S., Dovidio, J.F., Anastasio, P.A., Bachevan, B.A. & Rust, M.C. (1993) The common in-group identity model: recategori-sation and the reduction of intergroup bias. In W. Stroebe and M. Hewstone (Eds.) *European Review of Social Psychology, (vol.4),* pp 1–26, Chichester: Wiley

Gavey, N. (1992) Technologies and effects of heterosexual coercion. *Feminism and Psychology, 2(3),* pp 325–51 reprinted in S. Wilkinson and C. Kitzinger (Eds.) (1994) *Heterosexuality*, London: Sage

Gay, P. (1988) *Freud, a life for our time.* London: J.M. Dent and Sons Ltd.

Gay, P. (1989) *The Freudian Reader.* New York: Norton

Gilbert, G.M. (1951) Stereotype persistence and change among college students. *Journal of Abnormal and Social Psychology, 46,* pp 245–254

Gillman, R.D. (1968) The dreams of pregnant women and maternal adaptation, *American Journal of Orthopsychiatry, 38,* pp 688–692

Glanzer, M. & Cunitz, A.R. (1966) Two storage mechanisms in free recall. *Journal of Verbal Learning and Verbal Behaviour, 5,* pp 351–360

Godden, D. & Baddeley, A.D. (1975) Context-dependent memory in two natural environments: on land and under water. *British Journal of Psychology, 66,* pp 325–331

Goodman, G.S., Levine, M., Melton, G.B., & Ogden, D.W. (1991) Child witness and the confrontation clause. *Law and Human Behaviour, 15,* pp 13–29

Gordon, N.P. et al (1986) The prevalence and health impact of shiftwork, *American Journal of Public Health,* Vol. 76, pp 1225–1228

Gottesman, I.I. (1991) *Schizophrenia Genesis.* New York: W.H. Freeman

Graves, Z. & Glick, J.A. (1978) The effect of context on mother–child interaction: A progress report. *Quarterly Newsletter of the Laboratory of Comparative Human Cognition, 2,* pp 41–46

Gray, J. & Wedderburn, A. (1960) Grouping strategies with simultaneous stimuli. *Quarterly Journal of Experimental Psychology, 12,* pp 180–184

Gray, J.A. (1975) *Elements of a two-process theory of learning.* London: Academic Press

Gray, J.A. (1987) The ethics and politics of animal experimentation. In H. Beloff and A.M. Colman (Eds.) *Psychology Survey, No. 6.* Leicester: British Psychological Society

Gray, J. A. (1991) On the morality of speciesism. *The Psychologist, 4 (5),* pp . 196–198

Green, D.J. & Gillette, R. (1982) Circadian rhythm of firing rate recorded from single cells in the rat suprachiasmatic brain slice. *Brain Research, 245,* pp 198–200

Green, S. (1994) *Principles of Biopsychology.* Hove: Lawrence Erlbaum Associates

Green, S. (1998) Sleeping. *Psychology Review,* February 1998, pp 23–26

Greenberg, R. et al (1992) A research-based reconsideration of the psychoanalytic theory of dreaming. *Journal of the American Psychoanalytical Association, 40,* pp 531–550

Greenfield, P.M. (1966) On culture and conservation. In J.S. Bruner, R.R. Olver, & P.M. Greenfield (Eds.) *Studies in cognitive growth.* New York: Wiley

Gregory, R.L. (1966) *Eye and Brain.* London: Weidenfeld & Nicolson

Gross, R.D. (1999) *Psychology: The Science of Mind and Behaviour,* Third Edition. London: Hodder & Stoughton

Gusella, J.F., Tanzi, R.E., Anderson, M.A., Hobbs, W., Gibbons, K., Raschtchian, R., Gilliam, T.C., Wallace, M.R., Wexler, N.S. & Conneally, P.M. (1984) DNA markers for nervous system diseases. *Science, 225,* pp 1320–1326

Hall, C.S. (1953) A cognitive theory of dream symbols. *Journal of General Psychology, 48,* pp 169–186

Hall, E.T. (1966) *The hidden dimension.* Gaeden City, NY: Doubleday & Company

Haney, C., Banks, C. & Zimbardo, P. (1973) A study of prisoners and guards in a simulated prison, *Natural Research Reviews, 30(9),* pp 4–17

Harel, L., & Papert, S. (1991) *Constructionism.* Norwood, NJ: Ablex

Harlow, H.F. (1949) Formation of learning sets. *Psychological Review, 56,* pp 51–65

Harris, B. (1997) Repoliticising the History of Psychology. In D. Fox and I. Prilleltensky (Eds.) *Critical psychology: an introduction.* London: Sage

Hartmann, E.L. (1973) *The Functions of Sleep.* New Haven, CT: Yale University Press

Hatfield, E., Cacioppo, J.T., & Rapson, R.L. (1994) *Emotional Contagion.* Cambridge and New York: Cambridge University Press

Hebb, D.O. (1949) *The Organization of Behaviour.* New York: Wiley

Held, R. & Hein, A. (1963) Movement-produced stimulation in the development of visually guided behaviour. *Journal of Comparative and Physiological Psychology, 56,* pp 607–613

Hewstone, M., Islam, M.R. & Judd, C.M. (1993) Models of crossed categorization and intergroup behaviour a replication with penalties. *European Journal of Social Psychology, 64,* pp 779–793

Hirschfeld, L.A. & Gelman, S. (1994) (Eds.) *Mapping the mind: Domain specificity in cognition and culture.* New York: Cambridge University Press

Hobson, J.A. (1989) *Sleep.* New York: Scientific American Library

Hobson, J.A. & McCarley, R.W. (1977) The brain as a dream state generator: An activation-synthesis hypothesis of the dream process. *American Journal of Psychiatry, 134,* pp 1335–1348

Hoffman, H.S., Selekman, W., & Fleshler, M. (1966) Stimulus aspects of aversive control: Long-term effects of suppression procedures. *Journal of the Experimental Analysis of Behaviour, 9,* pp 659–662

Hofling, K.C., Brozman, E., Dalrymple, S., Graves, N. & Pierce, C.M. (1966) An experimental study in the nurse-physician relationship. *Journal of Nervous and Mental Disorders, 143,* pp 171–180

Hopfield, J.J. (1982) Neural networks and physical systems with emergent collective properties. *Proceedings of the National Academy of Sciences of the USA, 79,* pp 2554–2588

Horne, J.A. (1988) *Why we Sleep*. Oxford, England: Oxford University Press

Hovland, C. & Sears, R.R. (1940) Minor studies in aggression: correlation of lynchings with economic indices. *Journal of Psychology, 9,* pp 301–310

Howe, M.J.A. (1980) *The psychology of human learning*. London: Harper & Rowe

Huber-Weidman, H. (1976) *Sleep, Sleep Disturbances and Sleep Deprivation*. Cologne: Kiepenheuser and Witsch

Hunter, I. (1964) *Memory* (revised ed.). Harmondworth, Middlesex: Penguin

Huston, A.C., Donnerstein, E., Fairchild, H., Feshback, N.D., Katz, P.A., Murray, J.P., Rubinstein, E.A., Wilcox, B., & Zukerman, D. (1992) *Big Word, Small Screen: The role of television in American society*. Lincoln, NE: University of Nebraska Press

Hutchins, E. (1983) Understanding Micronesian navigation. In D. Gentner & A. Stevens (Eds.) *Mental models*. Hillsdale, NJ: Erlbaum

Hyde, T.S. & Jenkins, J.J. (1973) Recall for words as a function of semantic, graphic and syntactic orienting tasks. *Journal of Verbal Learning and Behaviour, 12,* pp 471–480

Irwin, M., Mascovich, A., Gillin, J.C., Willoughby, R., Pike, J., & Smith, T.L. (1994) Partial sleep deprivation reduces natural killer cell activity in humans. *Psychosomatic Medicine, 56,* pp 493–498

Irwin, M., McClintick, J., Costlow, C., Fortner, M., White, J., & Gillin, J.C. (1996) Partial night sleep deprivation reduces natural killer and cellular immune responses in humans. *FASEB J, 10,* pp 643–653

Itard, J.M.G. (1801/1982) *The wild boy of Aveyron* (G. Humphrey and M. Humphrey, Trans.). New York: Appleton-Century-Crofts

James, W. (1890) *Principles of psychology*. New York: Holt

James, W. (1892) A plea for psychology as a natural science. *Philosophical Review, 1,* pp 146–153

Jenkins, J.G. & Dallenbach, K.M. (1924) Oblivescence during sleeping and waking. *American Journal of Psychology, 35,* pp 605–612

Jensen, A.R. (1967) The culturally disadvantaged: psychological and educational aspects. *Educational Research, 10,* pp 4–20

Jones, E. (1954) *Hamlet and Oedipus*. New York: Doubleday

Jones, S. (1996) *In the blood: God, genes and destiny*. Hammersmith: Harper Collins

Jung, C.G. *The collected works of C.G.Jung*. H. Read, M. Fordham, G. Adler, W. McGuire (Eds.) (1953) Trans R.F.C. Hull. London: Routledge & Kegan Paul

Kagan, J. (1984) *The nature of the child*. New York: Basic Books

Karlin, R.A., Rosen, L.S. & Epstein, Y.M. (1979) Three into two doesn't go: A follow-up on the effects of overcrowded dormitory rooms. *Personality and Social Psychology Bulletin, 5,* pp 391–395

Karlins, M., Coffman, T.L., & Walters, G. (1969) On the fading of social stereotypes: Studies in three generations of college students, *Journal of Abnormal and Social Psychology, 28,* pp 280–290

Katz, D. & Braly, K. (1933) Racial stereotypes in one hundred college students. *Journal of Abnormal and Social Psychology, 28,* pp 280–290

Kaufman, A.S. & Kaufman, N.L. (1983) *Kaufman Assessment Battery for Children*. Circle Pines, MN: American Guidance Service

Kaye, K. (1982) *The mental and social life of babies*. Chicago: University of Chicago Press

Kelman, H.C. (1958) Compliance, identification and internalisation: Three processes of attitude change. *Journal of Conflict Resolution, 2,* pp 51–60

Kessler, S.(1980) The genetics of schizophrenia: A review. *Schizophrenia Bulletin, 6,* pp 404–416

Kestenberg, J.S. (1976) Regression and reintegration in pregnancy. *Journal of the American Psychoanalytical Association, 24,* pp 213–250

Kilham, W. & Mann. L. (1974) Level of destructive obedience as a function of transmitter and executant roles in the Milgram obedience paradigm. *Journal of Personality and Social Psychology, 29,* pp 696–702

Klahr, D. (1982) Nonmonotone assessment of monotone development: An information processing analysis. In S. Strauss (Ed.) *U-shaped behavioural growth*. New York: Academic Press

Köhler, W. (1925) *The mentality of apes*. New York: Harcourt Brace Jovanovich

Lalonde, R.N. (1992) The dynamics of group differentiation in the face of defeat. *Personality and Social Psychology Bulletin, 18,* pp 336–342

Lashley, K.S. (1950) In search of the engram. *Proceedings from Social Experimental Biology, 4,* pp 454–482. Reprinted in F.A. Beach, D.O.Hebb, C.T. Morgan & H.W. Nissen (Eds.) *The neuropsychology of Lashley*. New York: McGraw Hill

Le Bon, G. (1895) *Psychologie des foules* Paris: Alcan

Leslie, A.M. (1987) Pretence and representation: The origins of 'theory of mind'. *Psychology Review, 94,* pp 412–426

Levinger, G. & Clark, J. (1961) Emotional factors in the forgetting of word associations. *Journal of Abnormal and Social Psychology, 62,* pp 99–105

Levinson, D.J. & Sanford, R.N. (1944) A scale for the measurement of anti-Semitism. *The Journal of Psychology, 17,* pp 339–370

Lewy, A., Ahmed, S., Lathan Jackson, J. & Sack, R. (1992) Melatonin shifts human circadian rhythms according to a phase-response curve. *Chronobiology International, 9,* pp 380–392

Light, P., Buckingham, N. & Robbins, A.H. (1979) The conservation task as an interactional setting. *British Journal of Educational Psychology, 49,* pp 304–310

Linn, M.C. & Hyde, J.S. (1989) Gender, mathematics and science. *Educational Researcher, 18,* pp 17–27

Linn, M.C. & Hyde, J.S. (1991) Cognitive and psychosocial gender difference trends. In R. Lerner, A.C. Petersen, & J. Brooks-Gunn (Eds.) *Encyclopaedia of adolescence.* New York: Garland Publishers

Locke, J. (1690) *An essay concerning human understanding.* Edited by A.D. Woozley. Cleveland: Meridian Books, 1964

Loftus, E.F. & Palmer, J.C. (1974) Reconstruction of automobile destruction: An example of the interaction between language and memory. *Journal of Verbal Learning and Verbal Behaviour, 13,* pp 585–589

Loftus, E.F. & Zanni, G. (1975) Eyewitness testimony: The influence of the wording of a question. *Bulletin of the Psychonomic Society, 5,* pp 86–88

Loomis, A.L., Harvey, E.N. & Hobart, A. (1937) Cerebral states during sleep as studied by human brain potentials. *Journal of Experimental Psychology, 21,* pp 127–144

Lovaas, O.I., Freitas, L., Nelson, K., & Whalen, C. (1967) The establishment of imitation and its use for the development of complex behaviour in schizophrenic children. *Behaviour Research and Therapy, 5,* pp 171–181

Luhtanen, R. & Crocker, J. (1992) A collective self-esteem scale: Self-evaluation of one's social identity. *Personal and Social Psychology Bulletin, 18,* pp 302–318

Malinowski, B. (1927) *Sex and repression in savage society.* New York: Meridian, 1955

Mantell, D.M. (1971) The potential for violence in Germany. *Journal of Social Issues, 27,* pp 101–112

Marks, I.M., Gelder, M., & Bancroft, J. (1970) Sexual deviants two years after electric aversion. *British Journal of Psychiatry, 117,* pp 173–185

Marques, J.M. & Yzerbyt, V.Y. (1988) The black sheep effect: Judgmental extremity toward in-group members in inter- and intra-group situations. *European Journal of Social Psychology, 18,* pp 287–292

Marzillier, J.S., Carroll, D. & Newland, J.R. (1979) Self-report and physiological changes accompanying repeated imagining of a phobic scene. *Behaviour Research and Therapy, 17,* pp 71–77

Masson, J.M. (1984a) Freud and the seduction theory. *Atlantic Monthly,* pp 33–60

Masson, J.M. (1984b) *The assault on truth: Freud's suppression of the seduction theory.* New York: Farrar, Straus and Giroux

Masson, J.M. (1985) *The complete letters of Sigmund Freud to Wilhelm Fliess, 1887–1904.* Cambridge: Harvard University Press

Masson, J.M. (1992) *The assault on truth: Freud and child sexual abuse.* London: Fontana

McAdams, D.P., de St. Aubin, E. & Logan, R.L. (1993) Generativity among young, midlife and older adults. *Psychology and aging, 8,* pp 221–230

McAllister, W.R., McAllister, D.E. & Franchina, J.J. (1965) Dependence of equality judgments upon the temporal interval between stimulus presentations. *Journal of Experimental Psychology, 70,* pp 602–605

McFarland, S.G., Abeyev, V.S. & Abalakina-Papp, M.A. (1992) Authoritarianism in the former Soviet Union. *Journal of Personality and Social Psychology, 63,* pp 1004–1010

McGarrigle, J. & Donaldson, M. (1974) Conservation accidents. *Cognition, 3,* pp 341–350

McGrath, P.A. (1990) *Pain in Children: Nature, Assessment and Treatment.* New York, NY: Guildford Press

McGuire (1995) cited in Schroeder, D.A., Penner, L.A., Dovidio, J.F. & Piliavin, J.A. (1995) *The psychology of helping and altruism: Problems and puzzles.* New York: McGraw-Hill

Meadows, S. (1995) Cognitive development. In P.E. Bryant & A.M. Colman (Eds.) *Developmental psychology.* London: Longman

Meddis, R. (1979) The evolution and function of sleep. In D.A. Oakley and H.C. Plotkin (Eds.) *Brain, behaviour and evolution,* pp 99–125. London: Methuen.

Meeus, W.H.J. & Raaijmakers, Q.A.W. (1986) Administrative obedience: carrying out orders to use psychological-administrative violence. *European Journal of Social Psychology, 16,* pp 311–324

Meijman, T., van der Meer, O., & van Dormolen, M. (1993) The after effects of night work on short-term memory performance. *Ergonomics, 36,* pp 37–42

Meltzoff, A.N. (1995) Understanding the intentions of others: Re-enactment of intended acts by 18 month old children. *Developmental Psychology, 66,* pp 838–850

Mendel, G. (published 1895) in J.W. Kalat (1995) *Biological Psychology*, Fifth Edition. California: Brooks/Cole

Messer, D., Joiner, R., Loveridge, N., Light, P., Littleton, K. (1993) Influences on the effectiveness of peer interaction: Children's level of cognitive development and the relative ability of partners. *Social Development, 2,* pp 279–294

Milgram, S. (1963) Behavioural study of obedience, *Journal of Abnormal and Social Psychology, 67,* pp 371–378

Milgram, S. (1965b) Some conditions of obedience and disobedience to authority. *Human Relations, 18,* pp 57–76

Milgram, S. (1974) *Obedience to Authority an experimental view.* New York: Harper & Row; London: Tavistock

Miller, A.G. (1986) *The obedience experiments: a case study of controversy in social science.* New York: Praeger

Miller, G.A. (1956) The magical number seven, plus or minus two: some limits on our capacity for processing information. *Psychology Review, 63,* pp 81–97

Miller, N., Brewer, M.B., & Edwards, K. (1985) Co-operative inter-action in desegregated settings: a laboratory analogue. *Journal of Social Issues, 41,* pp 63–79

Miller, S.L., & Tallal, P. (1995) A behavioural neuroscience approach to developmental language disorder: Evidence for a rapid temporal processing deficit. In C.D. Cicchetti & D.J. Cohen (Eds.), *Developmental Psychopathology, Vol.2: Risk, disorder, and adaption*. New York: John Wiley & Sons

Mills, W. (1899) The nature of animal intelligence. *Psychological Review, 6*, pp 262–274

Minard, R.D. (1952) Race relations in the Pocohontas coalfield. *Journal of Social Issues, 8*, pp 29–44

Mistry, J. & Rogoff, B. (1994) Remembering in cultural context. In W.J. Lonner & R.S. Malpass (Eds.) *Psychology and Culture*. Boston: Allyn & Bacon

Moldofsky, H. (1995) Sleep and the immune system. *International Journal of Immunopharmacology, 17(8)*, pp 649–654

Moniz, E. (1935) in *Encyclopaedia Britannica*, Fifth Edition, Vol. VIII, p 275

Monk, T.H. & Foulkard, S. (1992) *Making shift work tolerable*. Basingstoke: Taylor & Francis

Mowrer, O.H. (1960) *Learning theory and behaviour*. New York: John Wiley

Muller, D.J., Harris, P.J. & Wattley, L. (1986) *Nursing children: Psychology, research and practice*. London: Harper & Row

Mummendey, A., Simon, B., Dietze, C., Grünert, M., Haeger, G., Kessler, S., Lettgen, S. & Schüferhoff, S. (1992) Categorisation is not enough: Intergroup discrimination in negative outcome allocation. *Journal of Experimental Social Psychology, 28*, pp 125–144

Neisser, U. (1976) *Cognition and Reality*. San Francisco: Freeman

Nelson, K. (1978) Semantic development, and the development of semantic memory. In K.E. Nelson (Ed.) *Children's Language*, Vol 1. New York: Gardner Press

Oginska, H., Pokorski, J. & Oginska, A. (1993) Gender, ageing and shift work intolerance. *Ergonomics, 36*, pp 161–168

Orlansky, H. (1949) Infant care and personality. *Psychological bulletin, 46*, pp 1–48

Oswald, I (1966) *Sleep*. Harmondsworth: Penguin

Oztürk, L., Pelin, Z., Karadeniz, D., Kaynak, H., Cakar, L. & Gözükirmizi (1999) Effects of 48 hours sleep deprivation on human immune profile. *Sleep Research Online*, (2)4, pp 107–111 (http://www/sro.org/1999/ozturk/107/)

Palincsar, A.S. & Brown, A.L. (1984) Reciprocal teaching of comprehension fostering and monitoring activities. *Cognition and Instruction, 1*, pp 117–175

Parkin, A.J. (1993) *Memory: phenomena, experiment and theory*. Oxford: Blackwell

Parkin, A.J., Lewinson, J. & Folkard, S. (1982) The influence of emotion on immediate and delayed retention: Levinger and Clark reconsidered. *British Journal of Psychology, 73, pp* 389–393

Patrick, G.T.W. & Gilbert, J.A. (1898) On the effects of loss of sleep. *The Psychological Review, 3,* pp 469–483

Pavlov, I. P. (1903/1957) *Experimental psychology and other essays*. New York: Philosophical Library

Perkins, C.C. & Weyant, R.G. (1958) The intertrial interval between training and test trials as determiner of the slope of generalisation gradients. *Journal of Comparative and Physiological Psychology, 51*, pp 596–600

Perrin, E.C. & Perrin, J.M. (1983) Clinicians' assessments of children's understanding of illness. *American Journal of Disease in Childhood, 137*, pp 874–878

Perrin, S. & Spencer, C. (1981) Independence or conformity in the Asch experiment as a reflection of cultural and situational factors. *British Journal of Social Psychology, 20*, pp . 205–209

Peskin, J. (1980) Female performance and Inhelder's and Piaget's tests of formal operations. *Genetic Psychology Monographs, 101*, pp 245–256

Peterson, L.R. & Peterson, M.J. (1959) Short term retention of individual items. *Journal of Experimental Psychology, 58*, pp 193–198

Peterson,B.E., Doty, R.M. & Winter, D.G. (1993) Authoritarianism and attitudes toward contemporary social issues. *Personality and Social Psychology Bulletin, 19*, pp 174–184

Piaget, J. (1926) *The language and thought of the child*. New York: Meridian Books

Piaget, J. (1928) *Judgement and reasoning in the child*. London: Routledge & Kegan Paul

Piaget, J. (1932) *The Moral Judgement of the Child*. London: Routledge & Kegan Paul

Piaget, J. (1952b) *The origins of intelligence in children*. New York: International Universities Press

Piaget, J. (1954) *The construction of reality in the child*, New York: Basic Books

Piaget, J. (1973) *The psychology of intelligence*. Totowa, NJ: Littlefield & Adams

Piaget, J. & Inhelder, B. (1956) *The child's conception of space*. London: Routledge & Kegan Paul

Piliavin, J.A., Piliavin, I.M., Loewenton, E.P., McCauley, C. & Hammond, P. (1969) On observers' reproductions of dissonance effects: The right answers for the wrong reasons? *Journal of Personality and Social Psychology, 13*, pp 98–106

Pinker, S. (1994) *The language instinct*. New York, NY: W. Morrow & Company

Plomin, R. & McClearn, G.E. (1993) (Eds.) *Nature, nurture and psychology*. Washington, DC: American Psychological Association

Poole, D.A. & White, L.T. (1993) Two years later: Effects of question repetition and retention interval on the eyewitness testimony of children and adults. *Developmental Psychology, 29*, pp 844–953

Purves, D. & Hadley, R.D. (1985) Changes in the dendritic branching of adult mammalian neurons revealed by repeated imaging in situ. *Nature, 315,* pp 404–406

Ralph, M.R., Foster, R.G., Davis, F.C. & Menaker, M. (1990) Transplanted suprachiasmatic nucleus determines circadian period. *Science, 241,* pp 1225–1227

Rank, S.G. & Jacobson, C.K. (1977) Hospital nurses' compliance with medication overdose orders: a failure to replicate. *Journal of Health and Social Behaviour, 18,* pp 188–193

Raven, M. (1977) *Progressive Matrices.* Windsor: NFER Nelson

Rechtschaffen, A., Gilliland, M., Bergmann, B. & Winter, J. (1983) Physiological correlates of prolonged sleep deprivation in rats. *Science, 221,* pp 182–184

Richards, C.M., Symons, D.K., Green, C.A. & Szuszkiewics, T.A. (1995) The bidirectional relationship between achievement and externalising behaviour problems of students with learning disabilities. *Journal of Learning Disabilities, 1,* pp 8–17

Richards, B. (1998) *The Princess, the Premier and the People*. Eleventh Annual Conference on Psychoanalysis, the Public Sphere. 30–31 January

Riley, J.N. & Walker, D.W. (1978) Morphological alterations in hippocampus after long term alcohol consumption in mice. *Science, 201,* pp 646–648.

Rodin, J. (1976) Density, perceived choice and response to controllable and uncontrollable outcomes. *Journal of Experimental Social Psychology, 12,* pp 564–578

Rogoff, B. (1981) Schooling and the development of cognitive skills. In H.C. Triandis & A. Heron (Eds.) *Handbook of cross cultural psychology (Vol. 4)* Boston: Allyn & Bacon

Rogoff, B. (1990) *Apprenticeship in thinking: cognitive development and social context.* New York: Oxford University Press

Rose, P. & Platzer, H. (1993) Confronting prejudice. *Nursing Times, 89 (31),* pp 52–54

Rosenbaum & deCharms (1960) cited in Gross, R.D. (1999) *Key Studies in Psychology*, Third Edition, London: Hodder & Stoughton

Rosenhan quoted in Milgram, S. (1974) *Obedience to Authority.* New York: Harper Row

Rosenshine, B. & Meister, C. (1994) Reciprocal teaching: A review of the research. *Review of Educational Research, 64,* pp 479–530

Rosenthal, R. & Jacobson, L. (1968) *Pygmalion in the Classroom.* New York: Holt, Reinhart & Winston

Rushforth, H. (1996) Nurses' knowledge of how children view health and illness. *Paediatric Nursing, 8:9,* pp 23–27

Ruttenberg, J., Zea, M.C. & Sigelman, C.K. (1996) Collective identity and intergroup prejudice among Jewish and Arab students in the United States. *Journal of Social Psychology, 136 (2),* pp 209–220

Ryback, R.S. & Lewis, O.F. (1971) Effects of prolonged bed rest on EEG sleep patterns in young, healthy volunteers. *Electroencephalography and Clinical Neurophysiology, 31,* pp 395–399

Rymer, R. (1993) *Genie: a Scientific Tragedy.* New York: Harper Collins

Saegert, S., MacIntosh, B. & West, S. (1975) Two studies of crowding in urban spaces. *Environment and Behaviour, 7,* pp 159–184

Savin, H.B. (1973) Professors and psychological researchers: conflicting values in conflicting roles. *Cognition, 2 (1),* pp 147–149

Saxe, G. (1994) Studying cognitive developments in socialcultural–context: The development of a practice-based approach. *Mind, Culture and Activity, 1,* pp 135–137

Schreiber, F.R. (1973) *Sybil. A Frightening Move.* Harmondsworth: Penguin

Searle, J.R. (1980) Minds, brains and programs. *The Behaviour and Brain Sciences, 3,* pp 417–457

Seligman, M.E.P. (1970) On the generality of laws of learning. *Psychological Review, 77,* pp 406–418

Seligman, M.E.P. (1971) Phobias and preparedness. *Behaviour Therapy, 2,* pp 307–320

Shapiro, C.M., Bortz, R., Mitchell, D., Bartel, P., & Jooste, P. (1981) Slow-wave sleep: A recovery period after exercise. *Science, 2214,* pp 1253–1254.

Sherif, M., Harvey, O.J., White, B.J., Hood, W.R., and Sherif, C.W. (1961) *Intergroup conflict and cooperation: the robber's cave experiment,* Norman, Oklahoma: University of Oklahoma

Siegal, M. (1991) *Knowing children: experiments in conversation and cognition.* Hillsdale, NJ: Erlbaum

Siegel, S. (1977) Morphine tolerance acquisition as an associative process. *Journal of Experimental Psychology: Animal Behaviour Processes, 3:1,* pp 1–13

Siegler, R.S. (1991) *Knowing children: Experiments in conservation and cognition.* Hillsdale, NJ: Erlbaum

Siegler, R.S. (1996) *Emerging minds: The process of changing children's thinking.* New York, NY: Oxford University Press

Siffre, M. (1972) in M. Cardwell, L. Clark & C. Meldrun (1996) *Psychology for A level.* Hammersmith: Collins Educational

Skinner, B.F. (1938) *Behaviour of organisms.* New York: Appleton-Century-Crofts

Skinner, B.F. (1957) *Verbal Behaviour.* New York: Appleton-Century-Crofts

Slobin, D.I. (1975) On the nature of talk to children. In E.H. Lenneberg and E. Lenneberg (Eds.), *Foundation of language development, Vol. 1.* New York: Academic Press

Smith, D.D. & Luckasson, R. (1993) *Introduction to special education.* Boston: Allyn & Bacon

Smith, D.J. & Rutter, M. (1995) *Psychosocial disorders in young people: Time trends and their causes.* Chichester: Wiley

Smith, P.K. & Cowie, H. (1991) *Understanding Children's Development* (2nd Edition). Oxford: Basil Blackwell

Sperling, G. (1960) The information available in brief visual presentation. *Psychological Monographs, 74* (Whole No. 498)

Sperling, G. (1963) A mode for visual memory tasks. *Human Factors, 5,* pp 19–31

Steketee, Turner and Fisher (1980) in Dadds, M.R., Bovbjerg, D.H., Redd, W.H., & Cutmore, T.R.H. (1997) Imagery in Human Classical Conditioning. *Psychological Bulletin, Vol.12, No. 1,* pp 89–103

Stern, W. (1910) Abstracts of lectures on the psychology of testimony and on the study of individuality. *American Journal of Psychology, 21,* pp 273–282

Sulloway, F.J. (1979) *Freud: Biologist of the mind.* New York: Basic Books

Sutherland, P. (1992) *Cognitive development today: Piaget and his critics.* London: Paul Chapman Publishing

Sylva, K. (1994) School influences on children's development. *Journal of Child Psychology and Psychiatry, 35,* pp 135–170

Tajfel, H. (1981) *Human group and social categories.* Cambridge: Cambridge University Press

Tajfel, H., Flament, C., Billig, M.G., & Bundy, R.P. (1971) Social categorisation and intergroup behaviour. *European Journal of Social Psychology, 1,* pp 149–178

Tajfel, H. & Turner, J.C. (1979) An integrative theory of intergroup conflict. In G.W. Austin and S. Worchel (Eds.) *The social psychology of intergroup relations.* Monterey, California: Brooks/Cole

Tajfel, H. & Turner, J. (1986) The Social Identity Theory of intergroup behaviour. In S. Worchel and W.G. Austin (Eds.), *The Social Psychology of Intergroup Relations* (pp 7–24), 2nd edn, Monterey, CA: Brooks/Cole

Tallal, P., Miller, S.L., & Fitch, R.H. (1993) The neurobiological basis of speech: A case for the preeminence of temporal processing. In P. Tallal, A.M. Galaburdn, R.R. Linas, C. von Euler (Eds.) Temporal information processing in the nervous system: Special reference to Dyslexia and Dysphasia. *Annals of the New York Academy of Sciences, 682,* pp 27–47

The Sunday Times, 12 December 1999, News Section, p 3

The Sunday Times, 12 December 1999, p 1

Thomas, D.R. & Lopez, L.J. (1962) The effect of delayed testing on generalisation slope. *Journal of Comparative and Physiological Psychology, 44,* pp 541–544

Thomas, R.M. (1985) *Comparing theories of child development* (2nd edition). Belmont, CA: Wadsworth Publishing Company

Thomas, R.M. (1992) p 295 cited in Cole, M. & Cole, S.R. (1996) *The development of children*, Third Edition. New York: W.H. Freeman & Company

Thompson, K.L. & Varni, J.W. (1986) A developmental cognitive-biobehavioural approach to pediatric pain assessment. *Pain, 25,* pp 283–296

Thorndike, E.L. (1911/1965) *Animal Intelligence* (reprinted). New York: Hafner

Tizzard, B., Joseph, A., Cooperman, O., Tizzard, J. (1972) Environmental effects on language development: A study of young children in long-stay residential nurseries. *Child Development, 43,* pp 92–99

Tolman, E. (1936) Operational behaviourism and current trends in psychology. In E. Tolman (1951/1966) *Behaviour and psychological man.* Berkeley: University of California Press

Tolman, E.C. (1948) Cognitive maps in rats and men. *Psychological Review, 55,* pp 189–208

Tolman, E.C. & Honzik, C.H. (1930) Introduction and removal of reward and maze learning in rats. *University of California Publications in Psychology, 4,* pp 257–275

Tolman, E.C., Ritchie, B.F. & Kalish, D. (1946) Studies in Spatial Learning. 1: Orientation and the short-cut. *Journal of Experimental Psychology, 36,* pp 13–25

Treisman, A.M. (1964) Verbal cues, language and meaning in selective attention. *American Journal of Psychology, 77,* pp 206–219

Tresselt & Mayzner (1960) in F.I.M. Craik and R.S. Lockhart (1972) Levels of processing: a framework for memory research. *Journal of Verbal Learning and Behaviour, 11,* pp 671–684

Triplett, N. (1898) The dynamogenic factors in pacemaking and competition. *Americal Journal of Psychology, 9,* pp 507–533

Tulving, E. (1972) Episodic and semantic memory. In E. Tulving & W. Donaldson (Eds.) *Organization of Memory*, London: Academic Press

Tulving, E. (1974) Cue-dependent forgetting. *American Scientists, 62,* pp 74–82

Tulving, E. (1985) How many memory systems are there? *American Psychologist, 40,* pp 385–398

Tulving, E. & Pearlstone, Z. (1966) Availability versus accessibility of information in memory for words. *Journal of Verbal Learning and Verbal Behaviour, 5,* pp 381–391

Turing, A.M. (1950) Computing machinery and intelligence. *Mind, 59,* pp 433–460

Turner, J,C, (1991) *Social Influence.* Milton Keynes: Open University Press

Unrah, A., McGrath, P., Cunningham, S.J., & Humphreys, P. (1983) Children's drawings of their pain. *Pain, 17,* pp 385–392

Vygotsky, L.S. (1978) *Mind in society.* Cambridge, MA: Harvard University Press

Watson, J.B. (1907) Comparative psychology. *Psychological Bulletin, 4,* pp 288–302

Watson, J.B. & Rayner, R. (1920) Conditioned emotional reactions. *Journal of experimental psychology, 3(1),* pp 1–14

Webb, W.B. (1982) Sleep and biological rhythms. In Webb, W.B. (Ed.) *Biological Rhythms, Sleep and Performance.* Chichester: John Wiley & Sons

Webb, W.B. & Campbell, S. (1983) Relationships in sleep characteristics of identical and fraternal twins. *Archives of General Psychiatry, 40,* pp 1093–1095

Wernicke, C. (1874) p 512 in J.W. Kalat (1995) *Biological Psychology,* Fifth Edition. California: Brooks/Cole

Wersch, J. (1985) *Vygotsky and the social formation of mind.* Cambridge, MA: Harvard University Press

West, J.R., Hodges, C.A. & Black, A.C.Jr. (1981) Prenatal exposure to ethanol alters the organization of hippocampal mossy fibres in rats. *Science, 211,* pp 957–959

Williams, T.M. (Ed.) (1986) *The impact of television: A natural experiment in three communities.* New York: Academic Press

Wimmer, H. & Perner, J. (1983) Beliefs about beliefs: representation and constraining function of wrong beliefs in young children's understanding of deception. *Cognition, 13,* pp 103–128

Winson, J. (1993) The biology and function of rapid eye movement sleep. *Current Opinion in Neurobiology, 3,* pp 243–248.

Wolpe, J. (1958) *Psychotherapy by reciprocal inhibition.* Stanford, California: Stanford University Press

Wolpe, J. & Rachman, S. (1960) Psychoanalytic evidence: a critique based on Freud's case of Little Hans. *Journal of Nervous & Mental Diseases, 131,* pp 135–145

Wood, D.J., Bruner, J.S. & Ross, G. (1976) The role of tutoring in problem solving. *Journal of Child Psychology and Psychiatry, 17,* pp 89–100

Worchel, S., Andreoli, V.A. & Folger, R. (1977) Intergroup co-operation and intergroup attraction: The effect of previous interaction and outcome of combined effort. *Journal of Experimental Social Psychology, 13,* pp 131–140

Wundt, W.M. (1896) *Lectures on human and animal psychology.* New York: Macmillan

Yogev, A., Ben-Yehoshua, N.S. & Alper, Y. (1991) Determinants of readiness for contact with Jewish children among young Arab students in Israel. *Journal of Conflict Resolution, 35,* pp 547–562

Yoos, H.L (1994) Children's illness concepts: old and new paradigms. *Pediatric Nursing, 20:2,* pp 134–145

Zajonc, R.B. (1965) Social facilitation. *Science, 149,* pp 269–274

Zhou, Y. & Riccio, D.C. (1996) Manipulation of components of context: The context shift effect and forgetting of stimulus attributes. *Learning and Motivation, 27,* pp 400–407

Zigler, E. & Child, I.L. (1972) Socialisation. In Lindzey, G. and Aronson, E. (Eds.) *The handbook of social psychology, Vol. 3,* pp 450–489. Reading, Mass: Addison-Wesley

Zimbardo, P.G. (1969) The human choice: individuation, reason, and order versus deindividuation, impulse and chaos. In W.J. Arnold & D. Levine (Eds.) *Nebraska Symposium on Motivation* (Vol. 17, pp . 237–307). Lincoln, NE: University of Nebraska Press

Zimbardo, P.G. (1973) On the ethics of intervention in human psychological research with special reference to the 'Stanford Prison Experiment'. *Cognition, 2,* (2), pp 243–255

Index

Glossary and references sections have not been indexed. However, when authors are mentioned in the text they have been indexed when appropriate. Page references in *italics* indicate figures or tables.

Ablations 185
Ablon, S.L.
  dreams during pregnancy study
    168–71
Accommodation (development) 83
Acetylcholine 198
Achenbach, T.M. & Edelbrock, C. 100
Acoustic coding (of data) 15, 24, 25
Action potential 183
Activation-synthesis model of dreaming
  198
Adaptation 83
Adoption studies 189
Adorno, T.W. et al 51, 53
Age and sleep 194
Agency theory 47
Agentic state 47
Aggression 130, 156, 185
  imitating aggressive models study
    130–5
Agoraphobia 138
'Albert, Little', case study 113, 135–7
Alternative hypotheses 220, 221, *221*
Altruism 38
American Psychological Association
  (APA) 108
Amir, Y. 62
Amnesia 10, 24
Anal stage of development 159, 161–2
Animals *see* Non-human animals
Anna O, case of 145
Anti-Semitism 51, 53, 56
Antrobus, J.S. 198
Anxiety 172
APA (American Psychological
  Association) 108
Applications of research 131, 267
Arab and Jewish groups study 59–61
Aronson, E. et al 55, 62
Arousal 24, 155, 156
Articulatory loop *19*, 20
Asch, S. 43–5
Aschoff, J. & Wever, R. 190
Aserinsky, E. 193, 200
Assimilation 83
Association 113, 119–20
  extinction of 121

spontaneous recovery 121–2
Assumptions 36, 68
Atkinson, R.C & Shiffrin, R.M. 11
Authoritarian personalities 51–3
Authority, struggles against 175
Autism 96–7
  teaching autistic children to speak
    139
  and theory of mind 87–8, 97–8
Autonomic nervous system 155, 182
Autonomy 47, 163
Averages 222–3, 225
Aversion therapy 138
Avis, J. & Harris, P.L. 88
Avoidance learning 126
Axons 183, *183*, 184
Ayllon, J. & Azrin, N.H. 139

Babies, development 83–6
Baby biographies 76–7
Backward conditioning 122
Baddeley, A.D. 22, 139
Baddeley, A.D. & Hitch G. 19
Bahrick, H.P. et al 28
Baillargeon, R. 84
Baka people 88, 101
Bandura, A. 129, 211
Bandura, A., Ross, D. & Ross, S.A.
  imitating aggressive models study
    116, 130–5, 211
Bar charts 223, *223*
Barker, R.G. & Wright H.F. 77
Baron–Cohen, S. 87, 96, 97
  autism and theory of mind study
    97–8
Bartlett, F.C. 30, 31
Batson, C.D. & Burris, C.T. 59
Beaumont, J.G. 202
Behaviour 36, 108, 109
  crowds 63–4
  culture and society and 39
  drugs and 137, 184
  ethical problems in deliberate
    alteration of 139–40
  genetic influences 178
  individuals and groups and 36–9
  influence of nervous system 181

see also Learning approach; Social
  psychology
Behaviour modification 139
Behaviour therapy 137, 140
  aversion therapy 138
  covert sensitisation 138–9
  flooding 138
  implosion therapy 138
  systematic desensitisation 136, 137–8
Behavioural problems, children with
  and classroom peers 98–101
Behaviourism theory xii, 111–13
  and development 71, 72
  operational behaviourism 114–15
  Skinner's 115–16
  see also Learning approach
Beloff, H. 162
Bergman, B.M. et al 202
Berkley group 53
Berkowitz, L. 56
Berry, J.W. et al 91
Bevington, J & Wishart, J.G.
  classroom peers and children with
    behavioural problems study
    98–101
Bias in sampling 214
Bierhoff, H.W. & Klein, R. 38
Biological-maturation framework of
  development 75
Biology xiii, 177
Biopsychology 177
  see also physiological approach
Black box xiv
Blair, Tony 174
Blakemore, C. 10
Bobo doll study 131–5, 211
Bodily rhythms 190
  Circadian rhythms 190–2
  and jetlag 206–7
  and shift work 204–5
  see also Sleep
Body clock 192, 206
Borke, H. 89
Bottom-up processing 3, 4, 6
Bouton, M.E. et al
  context-dependent forgetting study
    26–9

Bowlby, J. 167
BPS (British Psychological Society) 250, 251
Brain xiii, *11*, 183–4, *184*
  compared with computer 4–5
  invasive surgery 185
  non-invasive studies 11, 186–7
  particular areas for particular purposes xiii
Brain cells 183
Brain scanning 11, 186
Brazelton, T.B. 162
Breger, L. et al 162
Breuer, Josef 143–4, 145
British Psychological Society (BPS) 250, 251
Broadbent, D.E. 3, 8–9
Broca, P. xiii, 143
Broca's area (the brain) 143
Brown, J.F. 160
Brown-Peterson technique 15
Bruner, Jerome 67, 75
  and education 95, 103
  and language and thought 70, 94, 95
  theories 93–6
Bryant, P. 98

Calhoun, J.B. 84
Cancer 180
Case, R. 89
Case studies 10, 242–3, *244*
  within cognitive psychology 10
  within cognitive-developmental psychology 76
  within the psychodynamic approach 154
Castration anxiety 160
CAT (computerised axial tomography) scan 186
Cataplexy 207
Catharsis 148
Cells 181, 182, 183
Central executive (memory) 19, *19*
Central Nervous System (CNS) 183–4
Central tendency, measures of 217–18, 222–3, 224–5
Centring 86
Chance factors 118, 226
Charcot, Jean Martin 144
Chemistry xiii
Child abuse 148
Child-centred learning 102
Children and childhood 67–8
  childhood sexuality 147–8, 155
  children as witnesses 33
  in Erikson's Eight Stages of Man 163–5
  ethical standards for research with children 254–5
  feral children 68–9, 74–5

importance of early experiences 146–7, 163
  perception of pain 104–5
  physical development 68
  psychosexual development stages 159–60
  see also Cognitive-developmental psychology
Chinese room analogy 6
Chinese whispers 31
Chomsky, N. 124, 130
Christian, J.J. et al 64
Chromosomes 179
Chunks and chunking 14, 24
Circadian rhythms 191–2
  and jetlag 206
  and shift work 204–5
  see also Sleep
Circannual rhythms 190
Classical conditioning 27, 113–14, 115–16
  and behaviour therapy 137–9
  and the case of Little Hans 168
  compensatory-reaction hypothesis 137
  human examples 122–3
  Little Albert study 135–7
  mechanisms of 119–22
  Pavlov's work and 110–11, 119, 122
  types of 122
Clinical interviews 80, 148–50
Closed questions 236
CNS (central nervous system) 183–4
Coercive power 47
Cognition xii, 2, 67
  importance of cognitive abilities 69
  language and thought 69–71
Cognitive development theory xii
  see also Cognitive-developmental psychology
Cognitive interviews 32–3
Cognitive neuroscience xiii
Cognitive psychology xii, 2, *2*
  contemporary issue
    recovered memories 33–4
  in-depth areas of study
    theories of forgetting 20–4
    theories of memory 11–20
  key application
    eyewitness testimony 29–33
  key assumptions
    computer analogy 4–6
    information-processing approach 2–4
    nativists v. empiricists 6–7
  research methods
    case studies 10
    laboratory experiments 7–9
    scanning techniques 11
  studies within

context-dependent forgetting 26–9
  levels of processing 24–6
Cognitive science xiv–xv
Cognitive-developmental psychology xii, xiv, 67
  contemporary issue
    children's cognitive level and perception of pain 104–5
  in-depth areas of study
    Bruner's theory 93–6
    Piaget's theory 82–92, 96
    Vygotsky's theory 92–3, 96
  key application
    education 101–3
  key assumptions
    focus on development over time 71–5
    importance of cognition and cognitive abilities 67–71
    use of different frameworks 75–6
  research methods
    case studies 76
    clinical interviews 80
    experiments 79–80
    longitudinal studies 81–2
    observations 76–9
  studies in detail
    autistic child and theory of mind 97–8
    influence of classroom peers 99–101
Cohen, N.J. & Squire L.R. 18
Cohort effect 81, 165
Cole, M. & Cole, S. 75, 88
Collaborative learning 93, 99, 103
Collins, 118
Communication 42
Compensatory-reaction hypothesis 137
Competence of researchers 253
Compliance 43
Computer Aided Instruction 102
Computerised axial tomography (CAT) scan 186
Computers xiv, *xiv*, xv
  and cognitive psychology 4–6, *6*
  in schools 102
Concordance rates 187, 188
Concrete operational stage of development (6–12 years) 90–1, 91, 102
  and pain perception 104
Conditioned inhibition 122
Conditioned response (CR) 120, 136
Conditioned stimulus (CS) 119, 120, 122
Conditioning 129
  and memory 26–7, 28–9
  see also Classical conditioning; Operant conditioning
Conditions 222, 231, 233
Conduct of researchers 253

Confederates 45
Confidentiality 10, 253
Conformity 43–5, 45, 49
Confounding variables 228, *230*
Connectionism 109, 110
Conscious mind 108, 109, 146
Consent to studies 252
Conservation 88, 90
    of number 88–9, 89
    of volume 79, 87, 89, 95
Construct validity of research 212
Constructivist framework of
        development 75
Content analysis 244–5, *246*
Context x
Context-change account of forgetting
        26, 27, 28
Context-dependent forgetting 22, 23
    Bouton et al study 26–9
Continuous development 71
Continuous schedules of reinforcement
        125
Control groups 45, 131, 211
Controlled experiments 219
Controls 228, 230, 234
Conversations 246
Coren, S. 204
Cornwell, D. & Hobbs, S. 137
Correlations 187, 189, 235–6
Counterbalancing 231, 232
Countertransference 149, 172
Coursework 259
    assessment objectives 266
    checklist 263–4
    choosing your study 259–60
    evidence for key skills 261–2
    writing up the practical 260–1
Covert observations 240
Covert sensitisation 138–9
CR (conditioned response) 120, 136
Craik, F. & Lockhart, R. 18
    levels of processing and model of
        memory study 24–6
Creationism 257
Crises 163, 165
Critical periods 74, 159
Crocker, J. & Luhtanen, R. 55, 59
Crook, C. 102
Cross-cultural studies 31, 39, 88, 92, 247
    of concrete operations 90–1
Cross-pollination 178
Cross-sectional studies 81, 247
Crowd behaviour 38–9, 63–4
CS (conditioned stimulus) 119, 120, 122
Cue-dependent forgetting 22–3
Cued recall 16–17, 22
Cultural-context framework of
        development 75–6, 103
Culture 36, 75, 111
    and behaviour 39

cross-cultural studies 31, 39, 88,
        90–1, 92, 247
    and development 163
    and memory 31–2
Curtiss, S. 74, 255
Cyclic model of information-processing
        4, *4*
Czeisler, C.A. et al 204

Darley, J.M. & Batson, C.D. 38
Darwin, Charles 68, 77, 108–9, 115,
        146, 257
Dasen, P.R. 90
Data 215, *216*
    access to 255
    personal and questionnaires 236
    qualitative 41–2, 216, 241, 245, *246*
    quantitative 41, 215, 216–18, 222–5,
        226, 241
Data Protection Act (1984) 214, 255
Databases and ethical issues 214
Davies, J.H. 100
Death instinct 155, 156
Debriefing of participants 252–3
Decentration 86–7, 90
Deception by researchers 252
Declarative memory 18
Defence mechanisms 23, 158, 172, 173
Degrees of freedom (df) 228
Deindividuation 38–9
Delayed conditioning 122
Demand characteristics 213, 231, 233,
        237
Dement, W.C. & Kleitman, N. 193
    eye-movement and dream activity
        study 200–1
Dement, W.C. & Wolpert, E.A. 162
Dement, W.C. et al 195
Dendrites 183, *183*
Density and crowding 63–4
Dependent variables (DVs) 80, 114,
        229–30, *230*
Depth of processing (information) 25,
        26
Deschamps, J–C. 62
Descriptive statistics 215, 216–18,
        222–5, *226*
Desforges, D.M. et al 62
Despair 164
Deutsch, J.A. & Deutsch, D. 3
Deutsch, M. & Collins, M.E. 62
Developmental psychology 67
    see also Cognitive-developmental
        psychology
Diamond, A. 86
Diana, Princess 174–5
Diary methods 244, *244*
Dinges, D.F et al 202, 203
Discourse analysis 246, *246*
    within social psychology 41–3

Discourses 42
Discovery learning 103
Discrimination
    in classical conditioning 120–1
    in operant conditioning 127
    prejudice and 51
Displacement (defence mechanism) 158
Displacement (forgetting) 22
Diurnal rhythms 190
Dizygotic (DZ) twins 188
DNA (deoxyribonucleic acid) 179, 180
Dodge, K.A. et al 100
Dollard, J. et al 56
Dominant genes 179
Dopamine 184
Dostoevsky, Fyodor 153
Doubt and shame 163
Doverty, N. 105
Dreams and dreaming
    activation-synthesis model of
        dreaming 198–9
    dream analysis 151–2, 162, 173
    during pregnancy study 168–71
    Freud and 151, 156, 199
        Little Hans case study 166, 167
    REM sleep and dreams study 200–1
    reprogramming theories of dreaming
        199–200
Drives 155, 156
Drugs
    effect of 184
    tolerance and compensatory-reaction
        hypothesis 137
Durkin, K. 93
DVs (dependent variables) 80, 114,
        229–30, *230*
Dynamic 146, 156
Dyslexia 101
DZ (dizygotic) twins 188

Ecological validity of research 9, 212
Ecology, observation of 77
Education 101
    child-centred learning and readiness
        102
    classroom peers and children with
        behavioural problems 98–101
    collaborative learning 93, 103
    computers in schools 102
    discovery learning 103
    learning difficulties 101–2
    reciprocal teaching 93, 103
    scaffolding 92–3, 95–6
    the spiral curriculum 95, 103
    see also Learning approach
EEG (electroencephalogram) 186, 193,
        200
Effect, law of 110
Efforts after meaning 31
Ego 146, 157, 158, *158*, 171, 174

Ego integrity 164
Egocentrism 87, 89, 98
Eichman, Adolf 45
'Eight Stages of Man' (Erikson) 163–5
Electra complex 160
Electroencephalogram (EEG) 186, 193, 200
Electrooculogram (EOG) 186, 193
Elliott, Jane 63
EMG (electromlyogram) 186, 193
Emotional contagion 63
Empiricists 6
Enactive mode 93–4
Endogenous cues 75, 192
Environment and development 114–16
Environmental-learning framework of development 75
EOG (Electrooculogram) 186, 193
Epigenetic principle 163
Episodic memories 18
Equilibration 83
Erikson, Eric 162–3
'Eight Stages of Man' 163–5
Eron, 140
'Eros' (life instincts) 156
Escape learning 126
Estes, W.K. 27
Ethics and ethical issues xi, 250–1
confidentiality 10
databases 214
and deliberate alteration of behaviour 139–40
experiments 231
guidelines 10, 250, 251
and human participants 251–5
and non-human animals 256–9
questionnaires 236, 237
Ethnocentrism 51, 53, 54
Ethnography 242–3
Ethology 77, 118–19
Evaluation 267
Evans, C. 199
Everson, C.A. 202
Evolution 180
Evolutionary theory of sleep 196–7
Examinations
assessment objectives 266
example questions with answers 267–8
example questions chapter by chapter 268–70
key terms 267
tips 267
Exercise, law of 110
Exogenous cues 75, 192
Experimental hypotheses 220, 221, *221*
Experimenter effect 200
Experiments 7, 219–20, *235*
analysis of data 222–5
experimental design types 231–4

hypotheses 220–2, *221*
inferential statistics 225–8, *248*
reliability 212
types of 234–5
use of animals 116–18
validity 212
variables and controls 228–31
within cognitive psychology 8–9
within cognitive-developmental psychology 79–80
within the learning approach 116–18
within social psychology 39–41
Expert power 47
Extinction in classical conditioning 121
Extraneous variables 228, *230*
Eyewitness testimony 32
children as witnesses 33, 34
cognitive interviews 32–3
culture and memory 31–2
reconstructive memory 29–31

Face validity of research 212
False memory syndrome 33, 34, 168
Famous people and identification 173–5
Fatigue effect 231, 232
Feral children 68–9, 74–5
Field experiments 234, *235*
within cognitive-developmental psychology 79–80
within social psychology 39, 40
Fight or flight response 155, 182
Findings 210
Fisher, S. & Greenberg, R.P. 161–2, 199
Fixation 33, 159
Fixed interval schedules of reinforcement 125
Fixed ratio schedules of reinforcement 125
Flavell, J.H. 71–2, 89
Fliess, Wilhelm 148
Flooding therapy 138
Foot, H.C. 103
Forgetting
context-dependent study 26–9
Freud and 23, 150
in long-term memory 22–4
repression and 33
in short-term memory 20–2
see also Memory
Formal operational thought stage of development (12 years+) 90, 91, 92
and perception of pain 104
Foster, R.G. 192
Foulkes, D. 200
Free association 23, 150–1, 156, 173
Free recall 13, 17
French, J.R.P. & Raven, B.H. 47
Freud, Sigmund 34, 143–4, 154–5
and anxiety 172

and childhood 33, 146–7
and childhood sexuality 147–8
and defence mechanisms 158
and dreams 151, 156, 199
evaluation of his theory 157, 161–2
and forgetting 23, 150
and identification 129
and instincts 147, 155–6
Little Hans case study 157, 165–8
model of personality 146, 157, *158*
Oedipus complex 152, 159–60
psychosexual stages of development 159–60
research methods 80, 148, 150, 151, 154, 165
and the unconscious mind 144, 145, 146
use of literature 152–3, 154
Fromm, E. 167
Frustration 160
Frustration-aggression theory 56

Gaertner, S. et al 62
Galvanic skin response (GSR) 23
Gavey, N. 246
Gay, P. 144
Generalisability of studies 215, *216*
Generalisation
in classical conditioning 120
and forgetting 27, 27–8
in operant conditioning 127
in research 215, 258
Generativity 164
Genes 146, 179
discovery of 178–9
Genetics 178
behaviourists and 114
and evolution 180
explaining disease 180
influence on behaviour 178
and physiological research 187–9
use of animals 179–80, 181
'Genie' case study 74–5, 255
Genital stage of development 160
Gestalt school of thought 128
Gilbert, G.M. 50
Gillman, R.D. 168
Glanzer, M. & Cunitz, A.R. 17
Glia cells 182
Godden, D. & Baddeley, A.D. 22
Gordon, N.P. et al 204
Gottesman, I.I. 188
Graphs 224, *224*
Graves, Z. & Glick, J.A. 79
Gray, J & Wedderburn, A. 8
Gray, J.A. 126, 257, 259
Green, D.J. & Gillette, R. 192
Green, S. 257
Greenberg, R. et al 168
Greenfield, P.M. 90

Gregory, R.I. 4
Grief 174
Gross, R.D. 251
Groups
    affecting behaviour 37–9
    classroom peers and children with
        behavioural problems 98–101
    crowd behaviour 63–4
    Jewish & Arab groups study 59–61
    and prejudice 57
    realistic conflict theory 54–5
    reducing prejudice 62–3
    social identity theory 55–6
GSR (Galvanic skin response) 23
Guilt 163
Gusella, J.F. et al 179

H.M., case of 10
Hall, C.S. 162
Hamlet (Shakespearean character) 152,
    153
Handedness 113, 118, 188–9
Haney, C. et al 49, 57–9
'Hans, Little', case study 157, 165–8
Harel, L. & Papert, S. 102
Harlow, H.F. 128
Harris, B. 137
Hartmann, E.L. 197
Hatfield, E. et al 63
Hearing 8–9
Hebb, D.O. 20
Held, R & Hein, A. 8
Helping behaviour 38, 40
Hewstone, M. et al 63
Hibernation theory of sleep 197
Higher order conditioning 120
Hippocampus 10, 13
Histograms 223, *223*
Hobson, J.A. 198
Hoffman, H.S. et al 27
Hofling, K.C. et al 49–50
Holism 128, 182
Homosexuals 138, 139
Horizontal décalage 88
Hormones 181
Horne, J.A. 197
Hovland, C. & Sears, R.R. 56
Howe, M.J.A. 129
Hüber-Weidman, H. 196
Humans
    are they animals? 256–7
    ethical issues when participants 251–5
Hunter, I. 31
Huntington's disease 179
Huston, A.C. et al 140
Hutchins, E. 92
Hyde, T.S. & Jenkins, J.J. 26
Hypnosis 148, 177, 181
Hypothalamus 184, *184*, 192
Hypotheses 7, 220–2, *221*, 227

Hysteria 144, 145

Iconic mode of representation 94
Id 146, 157, 158, *158*, 159, 171
Identification 129, 174
    famous people and 173–4
    see also Modelling
Identity 163, 164
    see also Personality
Illusions, visual ix–x
Imitation 129–30, 141
    imitating aggressive models study
        130–5
Immune system and sleep deprivation
        study 202–4
Implosion therapy 138
In-groups 64
    Jewish & Arab groups study 59–61
    realistic conflict theory 54–5
    social identity theory 55–6
Incidental learning 25
Independent groups experimental design
        233
Independent variables (IVs) 80, 114,
        229–30, *230*, 234
Industry 163–4
Inferential statistics 225–8, *248*
Inferiority 163–4
Information-processing approach 2–4,
        12, *12*, 102
    computer analogy 4–6
    to explain learning difficulties 101–2
    see also Cognitive psychology
Informed consent to studies 252
Infradian rhythms 190
Inherited characteristics 114, 179
    see also Genetics
Initiative 163
'Inner ear' 20
Insight learning 128–9
Instincts 147, 155–6
Institutional racism 51
Instrumental conditioning *see* Operant
        conditioning
Intelligence 178
Inter-observer reliability 78, 213, 241–2
Inter-rater reliability 78, 213, 241–2
Interactionist view of information
        processing 6
Interactions 36, 244, 246
Interference and forgetting 21–2
Internalisation 43
Interneurons 183
Interval data 217, 218, *218*, 222
Interviews 243
    clinical 80, 148–50
    cognitive 32–3
    survey 239–40, *240*
Intimacy 164
Introspection 7, 108, 109, 112

Involuntary behaviour 119, 123
Irwin, M. et al 202, 203
Isolation 158, 164
Itard, Jean-Marc 69
IVs (Independent variables) 80, 114,
        229–30, *230*, 234

James, William 108, 109
Jenkins, J.G. & Dallenbach, K.M. 21
Jetlag 204, 205–7
Jews 45, 51, 53, 56
    Jewish & Arab groups study 59–61
Jigsaw classroom study 55, 62
Jones, E. 152
Jones, S. 180

Kagan, J. 72
Karlin, R.A. et al 64
Katz, D. & Braly, K. 50
Kaufman Assessment Battery 99
Kaye, K. 84
Kessler, S. 189
Kestenberg, J.S. 168
Kitten carousel experiment 8, *8*
Köhler, W. 110, 129

Laboratory experiments 7, 234, *235*
    reliability and validity 213
    to test Freud's ideas 162
    within cognitive psychology 8–9
    within the learning approach 116–18
    within social psychology 39
LAD (language acquisition device) 124
Lalonde, R.N. 55
Lamarck, Jean Baptiste 146
Language 42, 246
    the brain and xiii
    computers and 5
    development 67, 68, 73, 74
    and operant conditioning 124
    and thought development 69–71, 94,
        95
    Vygotsky and 92
    see also Cognitive-developmental
        psychology
Language acquisition device (LAD) 124
Lashley, K.S. 185
Latent content of dreams 151
Latent learning 127, 127–8
Latent stage of development 160
Law of effect 110
Law of exercise 110
Le Bon, G. 63
Leading questions 32, 41
Learning approach xii, 28–9, 108
    contemporary issue
        effect of violence on television
            140–1
    and context-dependent forgetting
            26–7

in-depth areas of study 119
  classical conditioning 119–23
  insight learning 128–9
  latent learning 127–8
  operant conditioning 123–7
  social learning 129–30
  key application
    deliberate alteration of human
      behaviour 137–40
  key assumptions
    importance of the environment
      114–16
    stimulus and response, the
      processes of learning 108–13
  research methods 116
    ethology 118–19
    laboratory experiments 116
    use of non-human animals 116–18
  studies in detail
    conditioned emotional reactions
      135–7
    imitating aggressive models 131–5
Learning difficulties 101–2
Legitimate power 47
Lesions 185
Leslie, A.M. 98
Levels of measurement 216–18, *218*,
  224–5
Levels of processing (LOP) model of
  memory 18–19
  Craik & Lockhart study 24–6
Levels of significance 227
Levinger, G. & Clark, J. 23
Levinson, D.J. & Sanford, R.N. 60
Lewy, A. et al 206
Life instincts 156
Life-span approach 163
Light, P. et al 89
Likert scale 237, *238*
Line graphs 224, *224*
Linear models of information processing
  3–4
Linn, M.C. & Hyde, J.S. 92
Literature, symbols in 152–4
'Little Albert' case study 113, 135–7
'Little Hans' case study 157, 165–8
Loftus, E.F. 32
Long-term memory (LTM) 12, *12*, 15–18,
  24, 25
  forgetting in 22–4
Longitudinal studies 80–2, 247
Loomis, A.L. et al 193
LOP *see* Levels of processing
Lovaas, O.I et al 139
LTM *see* Long-term memory

Magnetic resonance imaging (MRI) 11,
  186
Malinowski, B. 162
Manifest content of dreams 151

Marks, I.M. et al 138
Masson, J.M. 148, 153
Matched pairs experimental design 233
Maturation xii, 75, 82, 83
McAdams, D.P. et al 164
McAllister, W.R. et al 28
McFarland, S.G. et al 53
McGarrigle, J. & Donaldson, M. 89
McGrath, P.A. 104
Meadows, S. 93
Mean average 222–3, 225, *226*
Measurement, levels of 216–18, *218*,
  224–5
Measures of central tendency 217–18,
  222–3, 224–5
Meddis, R. 197
Median 223, 225, *226*
Meijman, T. et al 205
Melatonin 206
Meltzoff, A.N. 89
Memory 11
  cognitive interviews 32–3
  culture and 31–2
  eyewitness testimony 32
  and the hippocampus 10
  levels of processing 18–19
    Craik & Lockhart study 24–6
  multi-store models 11–12, *12*, 24–5,
    25–6
    long-term memory (LTM) 15–18
    the sensory store 12–13
    short-term memory (STM) 13–15
  reconstructive 29–31
  recovered memories 33–4, 168
  trace 25
  use in learning 129
  working memory 19–20, *19*
  see also Forgetting
Mendel, G. 178–9
Mental health and psychoanalysis 171–3
Mental illness 143
Mental operations 86
Metaphysics xiii
Methods *see* Research methods
Milgram, S. 215–16
  obedience study 39, 45–9, 228
Miller, G.A. 14
Miller, N. et al 62
Minard, R.D. 63
Mind
  study of xiii
  theory of 87–8, 89, 97
    autism and 87–8, 97–8
  see also Unconscious mind
Minimal groups 55
Mississippi Burning (film) 38
Mistrust 163
Mnemonics 22
Modality free 19
Modality specific 12

Mode 223, 225, *226*
Modelling 129–30
  imitating aggressive models study
    130–5
  see also Identification
Models (representations) xiii, 12
Modes of representation 93–4, 96
Moldofsky, H. 204
Moniz, E. 185
Monk, T.H. & Folkard, S. 205
Monozygotic (MZ) twins 188
Moral code 157, 174
Motivated forgetting 23–4
Motor neurons 183
Mountain study, Piaget's 73, *74*, 98
Mowrer, O.H. 126
MRI (magnetic resonance imaging) 11,
  186
Muller, D.J. et al 104
Muller-Lyer illusion x–xi, *x*
Multi-store model of memory 11–12,
  12, 25–6
  case against 24–5
  in favour of 24
  and forgetting 20
  long-term memory (LTM) 15–18
  the sensory store 12–13
  short-term memory (STM) 13–15
Multiple personality disorder 24
MZ (monozygotic) twins 188

Narcolepsy 207–8
National Lottery 213
Nativists 6
Natural killer (NK) cells 202, 203, 204
Natural selection 47, 115
Naturalistic observations 76–8, 212,
  240–2, *242*
Naturalistic/natural experiments 40, 234,
  235
  within social psychology 39, 40
Nature/nurture debate 67, 114, 207
  and language development 124
Nazis 45, 51
Necker cube x, *x*
Negative correlations 235
Negative reinforcers 125
Neisser, U. 4
Nelson, K. 33
Neo-Freudians 161
Nervous system 155, 181–2
  and behaviour 181, 184
  central nervous system 183–4
  peripheral nervous system 182–3
Neural networks xiv, 5
Neurons 182–3, *183*, 198
Neuroscience xiii, 177
Neuroses 144, 148, 171–2, 173
Neurotransmitters 183, *183*, 184, 198,
  207

NK (natural killer) cells 202, 203, 204
Nominal data 217, *218*, 222, 225
Non-human animals 109
   crowd behaviour studies and 64
   ethology 77, 118–19
   guidelines for use of 258–9
   should they be used? 256
     case against 258
     case for 257–8
   use in cognitive psychology studies 8,
     27, 28
   use in experiments on learning
     109–10, 116–18
   use in gene studies 179–80, 181
   use in physiological studies 185, 196
Non-participant observations 76, 240
Norms 39
NREM (non-REM) sleep 193, 200, 201
Null hypotheses 220, 221, *221*, 222,
   227
Number, conservation of 88–9, 89
Nurses and children's perception of pain
   104–5
Nurture *see* Nature/nurture debate

Obedience 36, 43
   Hofling et al's study 49–50
   Milgram's study of 39, 45–9
   Zimbardo's study 49, 57–9
Object permanence 84–6
Objectivity 109, 239–40
Observational learning 129–30
   imitating aggressive models study
     130–5
Observations 240–2, *242*, *243*
   in public places 240, 253–4
   validity and reliability 213
   within cognitive-developmental
     psychology 76–9
Obsessive-compulsive disorder (OCD)
   172
Ocean, Humphry 11
Oedipus complex 148, 152, 155,
   159–60, 162, 170
One-tailed tests 227
Ontogeny 71
Open mind, keeping an xi–xii
Open questions 236
Operant conditioning 115–16, 123, 127
   and behaviour modification 139
   and learning language 124
   mechanisms of 124–7
Operational behaviourism 114–15
Operationalisation of concepts 115, 220
Opportunity sampling 214
Oral stage of development 159, 161
Order effects 231, 233
Ordinal data 217, *218*, 222, 225
Orlansky, H. 162
Oswald, I. 197

Outgroups 64
   Jewish & Arab groups study 59–61
   realistic conflict theory 54–5
   social identity theory 55–6
Overt observations 240
Oztürk, L. et al
   sleep deprivation & the immune
     system study 202–4

Pain, children's perception of 104–5
Palincsar, A.S. & Brown, A.L. 103
Paradoxes 27
Parallel processing 4
Parkin, A.J. et al 23, 26
Participant observations 76, 240
Participant variables 228, *230*
Participants 231
   see also Humans; Non-human animals
Patrick, G.T.W. & Gilbert, J.A. 195
Pavlov, I.P. 110–11, 119–20, 122
Peers
   classroom peers and children with
     behavioural problems 98–101
Perception ix, 98
   children's perception of pain 104–5
   kitten carousel experiment into
     perceptual abilities 8, *8*
   perceptual processing 24
   visual illusions x–xi, *x*
Peripheral nervous system (PNS) 182–3
Perkins, C.C. & Weyant R.G. 28
Perrin, S. & Spencer C. 252
Personality 163
   authoritarian and prejudice 51–3
   Freud's model of 146, 157, *158*
Peskin, J. 92
PET (positron emission tomography) scan
   186
Peterson, B.E. et al 53
Phallic stage of development 147,
   159–60
Phenylketonuria (PKU) 179
Philosophy xiii
Phobias 126, 137–8
Phrenologists 177
Phylogeny 71
Physical development 68
Physics xiii
Physiological approach xiii, xiv, 177
   contemporary issue
     narcolepsy 207–8
   in depth area of study
     states of awareness 190–200
   key applications
     jet lag 205–6
     shift work 204–5
   key assumptions 177–8
     genetic influences on behaviour
       178–81
     influence of nervous system on

     behaviour 181–4
   research methods biological 185–7
     genetic studies 187–9
   studies within
     eye movements during sleep and
       dream activity 200–2
     sleep deprivation 202–4
Physiology xiii–xiv, 145, 177
Piaget, Jean xii, 67, 76, 82
   cognitive-developmental theory 82,
     92, 96
     early infancy 83–6
     early childhood 86–90
     middle childhood 90–1
     adolescence 91
     and children's perception of pain
       104
   and constructivist framework 75
   and education 102–3
   and language and thought 70
   research methods 79, 80, 82
   use of own children 76, 77, 81–2
Pie charts 224, *224*
Piliavin, J.A. et al 40
Pilot studies 237
Pinker, S. 75
PKU (phenylketonuria) 179
Pleasure principle 157
Plomin, R. & McClearn, G.E 75
PNS (peripheral nervous system) 181–2
Pointing, act of 92
Positive correlations 235
Positive reinforcers 124–5
Positivism 111
Positron emission tomography (PET) scan
   186
Post-traumatic stress disorder (PTSD) 172
Power, social 47
Practical applications of research 131
Practice effect 231, 232
Pre-frontal lobotomies 185
Precausal reasoning 88
Preconscious 146, 148
Predictive validity of research 161, 212
Pregnancy
   case study of dreams during 168–71
Prejudice 56–7
   and discrimination 51
   frustration-aggression theory 56
   Jewish & Arab groups study 59–61
   and personality variables 51–3
   realistic conflict theory 53–5
   reduction 61–3, *61*
   social identity theory 55–6
Preoperational stage of development
   (2–7 years) 86–90
   and pain perception 104
Preparedness 126
Presumptive consent to studies 255
Primacy effect (memory) 17, *17*–18

Primary acoustic store *19*, 20
Primary circular reactions 83–4
Primary reinforcers 125
Prior consent to studies 255
Prison simulation study 49, 57–9
Proactive inhibition (memory) 21
Problem solving 84, 92, 93
Procedural memory 18
Projection 158
Psychoanalysis 145, 172–3
    aims of 171–2
    disorders treated by 172
    psychoanalysts 149
    and science 157
    see also Psychodynamic approach
Psychodynamic approach 143–4
    contemporary issues 173
        famous people and identification
            173–5
    in-depth areas of study
        Erikson's theory 163–5
        Freud's theory 155–62
    key application
        understanding mental health issues
            171–2
    key assumptions
        importance of early experiences
            146–8
        importance of the unconscious
            mind and motivation 144–6
    research methods
        case studies 154
        clinical interviews 148–9
        dream and symbol analysis 151–4
        free association 150–1
        slips of the tongue 150
    studies in detail
        dreams during pregnancy 168–71
        Little Hans 165–8
Psychology xiii, 108–9, 111
Psychoses 173
Psychosexual stages of development
    159–60
Psychotherapy 145, 172
PTSD (post-traumatic stress disorder)
    172
Punishments 110, 113, 125
Purves, D. & Hadley R.D. 183
Puzzle box experiment 109–10

Qualitative data 41–2, 216, 241, 245,
    246
Quantitative data 41, 215
    experiment data analysis 222–5, *226*
    levels of measurement 216–18
    and observation 241
Quasi experiments 234
Quasi interval data 217, *218*
Quasi random sampling 214
Questionnaires 41, 213, 236–9, *239*, *243*

Questions 237–8
    leading 32, 41
    open and closed 236
Quota sampling 214

Racism
    institutional 51
    see also Prejudice
Ralph, M.R. et al 192
Random sampling 213–14
Randomising 231
Range (statistics) 223, *226*
Rank, S.G. & Jacobson, C.K. 50
Rapid eye movement sleep *see* REM
    sleep
Ratio data 217, 218, *218*
Rationalisation 158
Raven's Standard Progressive Matrices
    99
Reaction formation 64, 158, 159
Realistic conflict theory 53–5, 64
Reality principle 157
Recall 16, 17, 20, 22–3
    see also Forgetting; Memory
Recency effect 17, *17*–18
Receptors 183, *183*
Recessive genes 179
Rechtschaffen, A. et al 196
Reciprocal teaching 93, 103
Recognition 22–3
Reconstructive memory 29–31
Recovered memories 33
Reductionism 128, 182
Referent power 47
Reflexes 83, 119
Rehearsal (memory) 19, 20, 26
Rehearsal loops *12*, 14, 15
Reinforcement xii
    and learning language 124
    schedules of 125–6
    and social learning theory 129
    types of 124–5
Reliability of research 9, 212, *216*,
    241–2
REM (rapid eye movement) sleep 193,
    194, 195, 197–8, 198, 199–200
    and dream activity study 200–1
Repeated measures experimental design
    231, 233
Replication of studies 212
Representative samples 214
Repression (defence mechanism) 23, 24,
    33, 146, 155, 158
Reproduction tasks 94
Reprogramming theories of dreaming
    199–200
Research methods 210, 218
    case studies 242–4, *244*
    content analysis 244–5, *246*
    correlational design 235–6

cross-cultural designs 247
cross-sectional designs 247
diary methods 244, *244*
discourse analysis 246, *246*
experiments 219–35, *235*
interviews 239–40, *240*
issues *216*
    generalisability 215
    qualitative or quantitative data
        215–18
    reliability 212–13
    sampling 213–15
    validity 210–12
longitudinal design 247
observations 240–2, *242*
questionnaires 236–9, *239*
within cognitive psychology 7–11
within cognitive-developmental
    psychology 76–82
within the learning approach 116–19
within the physiological approach
    185–9
within the psychoanalytical approach
    148–54, 165
within social psychology 39–43
    see also Ethics and ethical issues
Resistance 170–1, 173
Response set 237
Responses xii, 67, 109, 114, 119
    voluntary and involuntary 123
    see also Stimulus-response approach
Restoration theory of sleep 197–8
Retina 192
Retroactive inhibition 21
Reversibility 86, 90
Reward power 47
Rewards 113, 124–5, 125, 126
Rhythms, bodily *see* Bodily rhythms
Richards, Barry 173–4
Richards, C.M. et al 100
Right to withdraw from studies 252
Riley, J.N, & Walker, D.W 183
RNA (ribonucleic acid) 179
'Robber's Cave' study 54
Rodin, J. 64
Rogoff, B. 77, 78, 99
Roles 39, 164
Rose, P. & Platzer, H. 51
Rosenbaum & deCharms 132
Rosenshine, B. & Meister, C. 103
Rosenthal, R. & Jacobson, L. 37
Rubin's vase/faces x, *x*
Rushforth, H. 104
Ruttenberg et al 59–61
Ryback, R.S. & Lewis, O.F. 197
Rymer, R. 74, 255

S-R approach *see* Stimulus-Response
    approach
Saegert, S. et al 64

Samples and sampling 213–15, *216*
Saxe, G. 75
Scaffolding 92–3, 95–6
Scanning techniques (brain) 11, 186
Scapegoating 38
Scattergrams 235–6, *236*
Schedules of reinforcement 125–6
Schemata/schemas xiii, 29–30, 83
Schizophrenia 184
    adoption studies 189
    twin studies 186, 188–9
Schreiber, F.R 24
SCN (Suprachiasmatic nucleus) 192
Searle, J.R. 5, 6
Secondary circular reactions 84
Secondary reinforcers 125
Selective attention 3, 13, 20
Self-control 163
Self-esteem and groups 55, 59
Self-fertilisation 178
Self-fulfilling prophecy 37, 178, 242
Self-preservation instinct 155, 156
Self-selected sampling 214–15
Seligman, M.E.P. 126
Semantic differential scales 238–9, *238*
Semantic memories 18
Sensitive periods for learning 74
Sensorimotor stage of development (0–2
        years) 83–6, 94
Sensory buffers 3, *3*
Sensory neurons 183
Sensory store 12–13, 24
Serial position curve 25
Serial reproduction 30–1
Serotonin 184
Sexual abuse 148, 155
Sexual instincts 147, 155, 156
Sexuality 156
    childhood 147–8
Shame and doubt 163
Shaping behaviour 126, 139
Shapiro, C.M. et al 197
Sherif, M. et al 54, 62, 233
Shift work 204–5, 207–8
Short-term memory (STM) 12, *12*,
        13–15, 24, 25
    forgetting in 20–2
Siblings 188
Siegel, S. 137
Siffre, M. 191
Significance, level of 227
Silhol, Robert 153
Simultaneous conditioning 122
Situational variables 228, *230*
Skinner, B.F. 115, 123, 124
Skinner box 118
Sleep 156, 192–3
    age and 194
    evolutionary theory 196–7
    and forgetting 21

and jet lag 206
narcolepsy 207
REM sleep and dreams study 200–1
restoration theory 197–8
and shift work 204, 205
sleep deprivation 195–6
    and the immune system study
        202–4
sleep patterns 193–5, *194*, *195*, 207
    see also Dreams
Sleep apnoea 207
Slips of the tongue 150
Slobin, D.I. 124
SLT see Social learning theory
Smith, D.D. & Luckasson, R. 99
Smith, D.J. & Rutter, M. 99
Snow White (fairy tale) 160
Social cognition xii–xiii, xiv, 36
Social constructionism 111
Social desirability 213, 237
Social facilitation theory 100
Social identity theory 55–6, 64
Social learning theory 116, 129–30
    and effects of TV violence 140–1
    imitating aggressive models study
        130–5
Social power 47
Social psychology xii–xiii, 36
    contemporary issue
        crowd behaviour 63–4
    and hypnosis 177
    in-depth areas of study
        conformity 43–5
        obedience 43, 45–50
        prejudice 50–7
    key application
        prejudice reduction 61–3
    key assumptions
        culture and society affect behaviour
            39
        individuals and groups affect
            behaviour 36–9
    research methods
        discourse analysis 41–3
        experiments 39–41
        surveys 41
    studies within
        group identity and intergroup
            prejudice 59–61
        obedience – prisoners and guards
            57–9
Social representation theory 36
Socialisation 39, 74
    and frustration 56
Society 36, 111, 163, 164
    and behaviour 39
Solso, R. 11
Somatic nervous system 182
Speciesism 257
Speech

learning 124
teaching autistic children 139
    see also Language
Sperling, G. 12
Spinal cord 183, *184*
Spiral curriculum 95, 103
Spontaneous recovery of an association
        121–2
Stage theories of development 71–3, 82,
        105
    Erikson's 'Eight stages of man' 163–5
    Freud's psychosexual theory 159–60
    Piaget's cognitive-developmental
        theory 82–92, 104
Stagnation 164
Standardised instructions 230–1, 236
State-dependent forgetting 22, 23
States of awareness 190
    and bodily rhythms 190–2
    sleep 192–200
Statistics 123
    descriptive 215, 216–18, 222–5, *226*
    inferential 225–8, *248*
Stereotyping xiii, 50–1, 63
    and perception xi
Stimuli xii, 67, 109, 114, 119
    classical conditioning 119
    operant conditioning 124
Stimulus list 16
Stimulus-response (S-R) approach xii, *xii*,
        2, 109–10, 112–13, 119, 129
    see also classical conditioning
STM see Short-term memory
Stooges 43, 45
Stratified sampling 214
Stress 24
Stroop effect 26
Structured interviews 239
Subjectivity 239–40
Sublimation 156
Superego 146, 157, *158*, 159, 171
Superordinate goals 54, 62
Suprachiasmatic nucleus (SCN) 192
Surveys
    interviews 239–40, *240*, *243*
    questionnaires 41, 213, 236–9, *239*,
        243
    within social psychology 41
Survival of the fittest 115, 180, 257
Sutherland, P. 103
Sybil (multiple personality disorder case)
        24
Sylva, K. 101
Symbolic mode of representation 94,
        103
Symbols 174
    dream analysis 151–2, 173
    in literature 152–4
Synaptic gap 183, *183*, 184
Synesthesia 96

Systematic desensitisation 136, 137–8
Systematic sampling 214

Tachistoscope 12
Tajfel, H. 55
Tallal, P. et al 102
Tallying (observation data) 241
Target populations 213
Tchalenko, J. 11
Television, violence on 130–1, 140–1
TEP (token economy programme) 124–5, 139, 139–40
Tertiary circular reactions 84
Thalidomide 185
'Thanatos' (death instinct) 156
Theory 220
Theory of mind 87, 88, 89, 97
    and autism 87–8, 97–8
Thinking *see* Cognition
Thomas, D.R. & Lopez, L.J. 27
Thomas, R.M. 90
Thompson, K.L. & Varni, J.W. 104
Thorndike, E.L. 109–10
Thought *see* Cognition
Time sampling 77–8, 241
Tizzard, B. et al 124
Token economy programme (TEP) 124–5, 139, 139–40
Tolman, E.C. 114–15
Tolman, E.C. & Honziks, C.H. 127
Tolman, E.C. et al xii
Top-down processing 3–4, 6
Trace conditioning 122
Trace decay theory of forgetting 20–1
Transference 149, 170–1, 172
Transposition tasks 94
Treisman, A.M. 3, 20
Tresselt & Mayzner 25

Triangulation 243, *243*
Trigrams 14, 15
Triplett, N. 100
Trobriand Islanders 162
Trust 163
Tulving, E. 18, 22
Tulving, E. & Pearlstone, Z. 16
Turing, A.M. xiv
Twin studies into schizophrenia 188–9
Two-process (factor) theory of learning 126
Two-tailed tests 227
Twycross, Alison 104

Ultradian rhythms 190, 192
Unconditioned response (UCR) 119, 120
Unconditioned stimulus (UCS) 119, 120, 122
Unconscious mind 144, 145–6, 149, 155, 171
    and dreams 156–7
Underachievement 98, 99
Uniforms 38
Unrah, A. et al 105
Unstructured interviews 239
Urges 155, 171

Validity of research 9, 210–12, *216*
Variable interval schedules of reinforcement 125
Variable ratio schedules of reinforcement 125
Variables 80, 187, 228–30, *230*
Victor (Wild Boy of Aveyron) 68–9
Violence
    imitating aggressive models study 130–5
    television 130–1, 140–1

Visuospatial scratchpad *19*, 20
Volume conservation 79, 87, 89, 95
Voluntary behaviours 123
Volunteer sampling 214–15
Vygotsky, Lev S. 67, 75
    and education 93, 103
    and language and thought 70
    theory of 92–3, 96

War of the Ghosts story 30
Watson, J.B. 111–12, 113, 118, 119
Watson, J.B. & Rayner, R.
    Little Albert study 113, 135–7
Wearing, Clive, case of 10
Webb, W.B. 197
Websites, useful 265
Wernicke, C. xiii
Wersch, J. et al 93
West, J.R. et al 183
Williams, T. M. 40
Wimmer, H. & Perner, J. 97
Winson, J. 199
Wishes and urges 155, 171
Witnesses *see* Eyewitness testimony
Wolpe, J. 137, 168
Wood, D.J. et al 93
Worchel, S. et al 62
Working memory model 19–20, *19*

Yogev, A. et al 59
Yoos, H.L. 104

Zajonc, R.B. 100
Zeitgebers 191, 204, 205, 206
Zigler, E. & Child, I.L. 161
Zimbardo's study 49, 57–9
Zone of proximal development (ZPD) 93, 103